USSR

DOCUMENTS

1987

HOW TO ORDER OR SUBSCRIBE

USSR DOCUMENTS (1987–) is an annual publication

Institutions—Send standing order for all volumes as
published for automatic shipping on account. Order
direct from AIP

Individuals and Booksellers—Request pro forma invoice for
subscriptions or for volumes desired.

Separate volumes—Available if not out of print. Prices higher
than the subscription price

Editions—USSR DOCUMENTS appears in limited editions
oriented to subscriptions. Order now to reserve your copy.

Send orders to—Academic International Press, POB 1111
Gulf Breeze FL 32561 USA

USSR DOCUMENTS

1987

THE GORBACHEV REFORMS

Edited by

J.L. BLACK

Academic International Press

1988

This collection has been compiled and edited at the Institute of Soviet and East European Studies, Carleton University, Ottawa, Canada. J.L.Black is Director of the Institute. The "team" of Bianca Pelchat, Karen Ballentine and Ian Martin is made up of graduate students with the Institute. Professor R. Selucky, of Carleton's Political Science Department, who prepared the introduction to Chapter 3, is an Associate of the Institute.

ISEES would like to thank the Graduate Studies and Research Office at Carleton for the financial assistance without which this project could never have been completed in three very hectic months. For subsequent volumes our schedule will be considerably less rushed, as our system of selecting, editing, translating, and organizing will be in place.

Typing and computer entry were undertaken by Margaret Jones, Donna Harper, Cory Peabody, Lydia MacLaren, and Janice Black. Joe Goski, of Keylink Systems, assisted greatly in converting materials from various types of diskettes into a single type for our use.

USSR DOCUMENTS 1987. THE GORBACHEV REFORMS
Copyright © 1988 by Academic International Press

ISBN: 0-87569-105-6

Composition by Iris Knoebl and Barbara Knoelke

Printed in the United States of America

By direct subscription with the publisher.

A list of Academic International Press publications is found at the end of this volume.

ACADEMIC INTERNATIONAL PRESS
Box 1111 Gulf Breeze FL 32561 USA

CONTENTS

CONTENTS

CONTENTS

INTRODUCTION

Until the CPSU Central Committee (CC) Plenum of January 1987 the nature of the Gorbachev phenomenon was still unclear to observers. To some it appeared to be a "wishful thinking" creation of the Western media; to others it appeared as a dramatic signal of real change in a previously immutable Soviet Union.

After that Plenum, and especially Gorbachev's speech on Party cadres, the dust had cleared a bit. Perestroika (restructuring), as an overall policy formulation, could be seen as a clarion call for fundamental change in the practices and behavior in every conceivable dimension of Soviet life. Among the subsequent challenges to CPSU shibboleths, the tenets of which had been carved in stone already in the late 1920s, were the following heresies: multi-candidate elections were proposed; private contracts in agriculture were urged; self-financing schemes and cost accountability were stressed; and limited terms for political office were recommended. By the end of 1987 there had been no questioning of the principles of the CPSU leadership, the inviolability of Marxism-Leninism, or of socialism as the Soviets understand it—but everything else had come under sharp-eyed scrutiny.

The "reforms" themselves were usually deemed to be a return to Leninism. This has been the normal way to rationalize proposals since Stalin simplified Leninism for his own purposes in the 1920s. Khrushchev justified his de-stalinization campaign on the same grounds during the 1950s and early 1960s. But Gorbachev also calls his recommendations "revolutionary". In relation to the Soviet experience, he is certainly right. His bitter criticism of stagnation in the economy, of bureaucratism (formalism), of elitism and corruption both at the center and in the republics; his acknowledgement of rampant moral decay within the government, the Party, and, above all, among Soviet youth; his repeated references to the low productivity of both land and labor, to sterile educational measures, and to political apathy, have been unrestrained.

M.S. Gorbachev was elected General Secretary of the CPSU on 11 March 1985, only hours after the death of his predecessor, Konstantin Chernenko. Even the announcement of his election marked a departure from normal Soviet custom. Gorbachev's picture and short biography were carried on the front page of newspapers, while Chernenko's picture and obituary were relegated to the second page (see, e.g., *Izvestiia*, 12 March 1985). In the past, the deceased leader always had dominated the front pages.

Gorbachev, who had just turned 54, is the fourth person to lead the Party during the 1980s. The rapid transition from Leonid Brezhnev (d. 10 Nov. 82), to Yuri Andropov (d. 9 Feb 84), to Chernenko, and to Gorbachev was a remarkable political sequence for the USSR, where there had been only three leaders since the late 1920s. The period of brief terms as the top office was passed from one tired old man to another did not mean instability at the top so much as it starkly dramatized the degree to which the Soviet system of political leadership had ossified.

The Western media was soon enthralled with Gorbachev's style, and Margaret Thatcher's remark to the effect that she could "do business" with him became a catchword for journalists. Gorbachev helped himself enormously in the public relations game, with which Soviet leaders were supposed to be unfamiliar. The press concentrated on his clothing, his public manner-isms, his worldy wife, and his open and frank approach. Such things as Gorbachev's relative youth, his lack of association with Stalin, and even the fact that he had been too young for combat during the Great Patriotic War, were touted as reasons for great expectations.

The Western media was right for the most part, but perhaps for the wrong reasons. Gorbachev had, in fact, been a member of Komsomol (YCL) when Stalin, as Party leader, was glorified in that organization's songs as the "Lenin of Today." No one who was 10 years old when Germany invaded the USSR in 1941 would have had to be in combat to be permanently influenced by that conflict. Indeed, the "war against fascism" is still so much a part of Soviet daily socialization that its myths are probably more true to most Soviet citizens today than were its realities.

The assumption that Gorbachev was very different from his predecessors may have been overdrawn as well. He embarked on a political career 30 years before he became General Secretary. Shortly after his graduation from the University of Moscow in 1955, with a degree in law, he took up a post as deputy head of agitprop with the Stavropol (about 160 km from his home village of Privolnoe) YCL organization. The next year Gorbachev became First Secretary of that city's YCL Committee. During the 1960s he was Party organizer for the Stavropol Territorial Production Administration, which oversaw kolkhoz and sovkhoz operations. He studied agricultural economics at an agricultural institute, and in 1970 was made First Secretary of the oblast Party Committee. Gorbachev's further political career will be noted later in this collection. Suffice it to say here that he reached the pinnacle only after long and hard *apparat* work, in which he could not have been perceived as a maverick and survived.

The fact that Gorbachev's career was reasonably normal before he reached the Politburo level helps illustrate how desparate the situation must have become to compel Politburo members to support radical restructuring. The greatest catalyst for the changes that characterize the Soviet scene today was the final realization that the economy had failed and that only drastic means would get it back into shape. Technological backwardness compounded Soviet difficulties; so did the "second economy", which flourished alongside graft, corruption, nepotism, and other forms of favoritism in both in both the economic and political spheres— especially in the provinces. Regional imbalances, social stratification, and a widespread spiritual malaise became too obvious to ignore or gloss over with time-worn clichés. Members of the scientific intelligentsia, to whom the government must now turn for "expert" advice, have realized for a long time that the USSR must learn how to take advantage of diverse opinions, individuality, and innovation. Only recently have they been able to express such notions publicly. In order to make their case, however, the advocates of change have had to highlight the failures of socialism. Speaking at Khabarovsk in late July, 1986, Gorbachev abetted this by sharply criticizing those who use dogma to avoid facing up to the real problems facing the USSR.

The CPSU has undergone a reformulation itself, though not entirely because of the advent of Gorbachev. Long overdue new Party Rules and Party Program were approved at the 27th CPSU Congress in March 1986. Gorbachev insisted a few months later that the Party and its cadres—along with "the economy and all other aspects pf society's life"—must change. Restructuring, he said, meant "real revolution" in their way of thinking and behaving (*Pravda* 2 Aug 86).

The General Secretary led the assault on the status quo himself in the time-honored way; that is, he brought in his own people to undertake the task. Ministers and local CPSU Secretaries were replaced in droves during his first few months in office. At the Plenum of the Central Committee which met in April 1985 he promoted Viktor Chebrikov (KGB), Egor Ligachev and Nikolai Ryzhkov, each of whom had been candidate members of Politburo, to full members. Viktor Nikonov, Boris Eltsin and Lev Zaikov were appointed to the Secretariat. Later a few "retirements" were announced (Grigorii Romanov), E. Shevardnadze was moved up to full member of Politburo and then to Foreign Minister, and A.Gromyko was promoted out of the way as "President" of the USSR. Viktor Grishin lost his position as Party head in Moscow to Eltsin; N.Tikhonov lost his post as director of Gosplan to N.Talyzin. These were merely the spectacular tips of the iceberg (See esp. G.Razumovskii in *Partiinaia zhizn*, 12 (1987), 12; and "KPSS v tsifrakh," *ibid.*, 21 (1987), 6-20). The appointment of A.Yakovlev, former ambassador to Canada, and A. Dobrynin, former ambassador to the United States, to the Secretariat in March 1986 was symbolic of Gorbachev's move towards professional and intellectual expertise.

By late1986 the Gorbachev "team" was in place and perestroika was ready to be moved up a pace.

The purpose of this series is to provide scholars, students, and interested individuals with a documentary record in English of the progress of Gorbachev's "reforms" as they take form in the Soviet printed media. Thousands of documents from official statements, new laws, press editorials, and press reports both shape and reflect the momentous events in the USSR today— and bring information about them to the often unsuspecting Soviet public.

We have tried to select a balanced cross-section from the documentation. For reasons of space we have had to limit ourselves mainly to items from the major, all-union press and the authoritative word from government and Party pronouncements. Unfortunately, several important topics have had to be by-passed: religious issues, though touched upon, have not been assigned a feature role in the collection; specific medical, family and social issues—like the increased attention given to AIDS research, prostitution, drug and alcohol abuse, and the role of women—are represented only sparingly; and pieces on the important issue of youth dissaffection are only barely tapped. In foreign policy, pride of place goes here to questions of theory, whereas specific areas of Soviet involvement, for example, in Afghanistan and the arms race, are left to an extensive body of literature in English which already exists on such subjects. The re-writing of Russian/Soviet history is another area of interest which has been set aside to allow for a clear overall exposition of what Gorbachev and his supporters are all about.

All the documents in this collection are complete translations. They have been collated with condensed or partial translations in CDSP and the (often) full translation contained in FBIS, whenever they were available, and with the original Russian source. All introductions and editorial notes, except for R. Selucky's comments on Chapter 3, were prepared by J.L. Black. An attempt has been made to balance subjects by presenting them in documents from each of the four quarters of the year. Although references are made to Russian-language source material throughout the volume, the bibliography is limited to works in English—on the assumption that Russian-language readers are able to turn to the originals.

J.L. Black

Chapter 1

GORBACHEV SPEAKS

The most visible and probably most effective catalyst for reform in the Soviet Union is M.S. Gorbachev himself. During 1987, the General Secretary continued his hectic schedule of speeches, public appearances, and interviews for both domestic and foreign publications. The publication, in both Russian and English, of his book, *Perestroika*, was accompanied by great fanfare in the USSR and abroad. His addresses were published regularly in *Pravda, Izvestiia*, and the republic press, as well as in leading Party organs, like *Kommunist* and *Partiinaia zhizn*. Probably more important, however, were his travels throughout the USSR and highly publicized personal calls for support of his program before a wide variety of audiences.

In 1987 Gorbachev lectured both Soviet and foreign audiences on the "new way of thinking" interminably. He carried the message to Eastern Europe (Prague and Bucharest in April/May). He harangued at length both the 18th Congress of the USSR Trade Unions (February) and the 20th Congress of Komsomol (April). He spoke at length to the World Congress of Women (June); urged workers at the Cosmodrome Baikonur and in Leninsk to be patriotic (May); and gave a long and rather stern lecture to representatives of the domestic mass media and propaganda *aktiv* (July). He sent a lengthy missive to the United Nations in September, and granted extensive interviews to the foreign press—for example, Italy's *L'Unita*, France's *L'Humanité*, and Indonesia's *Merdeka*—and appeared "live" in an interview with Tom Brokaw of the American NBC.

Long speeches made by Gorbachev in the Baltic republics, and at a presentation of a Hero City award to Murmansk also were widely reported in the Soviet press and published in special booklets, in several languages. So too was a keynote address "Party of Revolution—Party of Perestroika" which he gave in Leningrad before an audience of CPSU *aktiv* and veterans of the October Revolution and the first Five Year Plan (see *Partiia revoliutsii—partiia perestroiki*. Moscow: Politizdat, 1987). In this and in all other such addresses, he carefully linked his program of renewal to the early days of Lenin's leadership. On all these occasions he far surpassed his predecessors in performance.

Although Gorbachev has harshly assailed the personality cult which had grown up around Brezhnev, the Soviet and Western media alike have created a cult-like aura around the new Soviet leader himself. In a way very uncharacteristic to Soviet politics, his wife, Raisa has gained prominence in the domestic press. Television has contributed a great deal to the process, for the era of *glasnost* has seen this medium become a vital vehicle in bringing Gorbachev's personal charisma into almost every Soviet home. Some have called it a successful "charm campaign." Gorbachev's distinctive style is crucial to the success of his program, and the fact that he is unusually vigorous and convincing—by any standard—has thrown a completely new variable into the often moribund context of Soviet politics and economics.

The speeches included in this first chapter are those which encompass the entire scope of the *perestroika* campaign. It is worth comparing the tone and the content of major presentations delivered in January with those which he made in October. Other Gorbachev addresses, which have either a specialized audience or a single theme, are included in other, more appropriate chapters.

For references to speeches not included in this collection see his speech to the 18th USSR Trade Union Congress, on 25 February, which was translated for Foreign Broadcast Information Service (FBIS), No.039 (27 Feb 87), R1-R15. Only excerpts appeared in Current Digest of the Soviet Press (CDSP), 39:8(1987),7-9, 13. It was printed originally in both *Pravda* and *Izvestiia* (26 Feb). The addresses delivered in the Baltic republics appeared in *Pravda* and

Izvestiia (22-23 Feb), and were reprinted in a book, *Tverdo idti dorogoi perestroiki i uglubleniia demokratii* (Moscow: Politlit, 1987). Condensed translations are carried in in CDSP, 38:8(1987), 6-7; and full translations are in FBIS, No.037 (25 Feb 87), R5-22; No.038 (26 Feb 87), R21-R27. The very long interview with G.Chiaromonte of *L'Unita* was printed first in *Pravda* (20 May); a translation can be found in FBIS, No.097 (20 May 87), R1-R24. The speeches to Baikonur workers, "To be Patriots of your Homeland...," was in *Pravda* (14 May) and was translated for FBIS, No.94 (14 May); and to the 20th YCL Congress, "Young People are the Creative Force of the Revolutionary Renewal," *Pravda* (17 April). The YCL speech and his welcoming address to the World Congress of Women (23 June) were printed in English as separate Novosti pamphlets.

On Restructuring and the Party's Personnel Policy (27 Jan 87)

Comrades!

To us, members of the Central Committee [CC], the 27th Party Congress assigned a great responsibility—to put into practice a strategic course for the acceleration of the social-economic development of the country. The Politburo recognizes the situation and role of the CC in the current stage of Soviet society.

Because of that, this Plenum will discuss questions which are of vital importance in achieving the successful implementation of the political strategy outlined by the April (1985) CC Plenum, the 27th Congress of the CPSU—the questions of restructuring and the political cadres of the Party.

The April [1985] plenary session and the 27th Party congress opened the way for an objective critical analysis of the current situation in society and adopted decisions of historic importance for the country's future. We have irrevocably begun restructuring and have taken the first steps on this path.

To make an overall political summing-up, one can say confidently that major changes are taking place in the life of Soviet society and positive tendencies are gathering momentum. Before the Plenum meeting, I myself and other Politburo members and CC secretaries had many meetings and conversations with members of the CC, public figures, collective farmers, intellectuals, veterans, and young people. The overall tenor and meaning of their statements was unambiguous: The policy line of renovating our society should be firmly pursued and efforts redoubled in every area.

The CC finds it important that the policy line of the 27th Congress, the practical efforts to fulfill it and reorganization itself have been given broad support by workers, by the entire Soviet people. And that, comrades, is the most important thing to a ruling party.

At the same time, we see that changes for the better are taking place slowly, that the task of restructuring has turned out to be more difficult than it had seemed to us earlier, and that the causes of the problems that have accumulated in society are more deep-rooted than we had thought. The more deeply we go into restructuring work, the clearer its scale and importance become; more and more new unsolved problems inherited from the past are coming to light.

The Politburo's basic assessments of the state of society and its conclusions drawn therefrom have already been reported to the 27th Party Congress and at plenary sessions of the Central Committee. They have been completely confirmed. But today we know more, and therefore it is necessary once more to make a detailed examination of the sources of the current situation and look into the reasons for what happened in the country in the late 1970s and early 1980s.

Such an analysis is necessary to prevent the repetition of mistakes and to implement the Congress's decisions, with which the future of our people and the fate of socialism are linked. This is all the more important because there is still a certain lack of understanding in society, and even in the Party itself, of the complexity of the situation in which the country found itself. Apparently, this can also explain the fact that a number of comrades are asking questions about the measures that the Politburo and the government have taken in the course of restructuring. People frequently ask: Aren't we making too sharp a turn?

We need complete clarity on all vitally important questions, including this one. Only a thorough knowledge of the state of affairs makes it possible to find the right ways to solve complicated problems.

In general, comrades, there is an urgent need to return once again to an analysis of the problems that the Party and Soviet society encountered in the years immediately preceding the April Plenum of the CPSU CC. The experience of the past 18 months has strengthened our resolve to deepen this analysis, to understand the causes of negative processes and to work out measures that will accelerate our progress, provide a guarantee against the recurrence of mistakes, and permit us to move forward, and only forward, demonstrating in practice socialism's inherent capability of constant self-improvement. The Politburo believes that it is precisely on the basis of this approach that we should hold the current Plenum.

I. Restructuring Is an Objective Necessity
Comrades!
Our Plenum is taking place in the year of the 70th anniversary of the Great October Socialist Revolution. Almost 7 decades ago the Leninist party raised over the country the victorious banner of socialist revolution, of struggle for socialism, freedom, equality, social justice and societal progress and against oppression and exploitation, poverty and oppression of nationalities.

For the first time in world history the working man and his interests and needs were made the focal point of state policy. The Soviet Union achieved truly epoch-making success in political, economic, social, cultural and intellectual development as it built socialist society. Under the leadership of the Party, the Soviet people built socialism, won the victory over fascism in the Great Patriotic War, rehabilitated and strengthened the national economy and made their homeland a mighty Power.

Our achievements are enormous and undeniable, and Soviet people are rightfully proud of their successes. They provide a firm foundation for the implementation of current plans and our intentions for the future. But the Party is obliged to see life in its entirety and complexity. No achievements, even the mightiest ones, should obscure contradictions in the development of society or our mistakes and deficiencies.

We have talked about this, and today we must repeat once more: At a certain stage the country began to lose momentum, difficulties and unsolved problems began to pile up, and stagnation and other phenomena alien to socialism appeared. All of this had a serious effect on the economy of the social and spiritual spheres.

Of course, comrades, the country's development did not stop. Tens of millions of Soviet people worked honestly, and many Party organizations and our cadres acted vigorously in the interests of the people. All this restrained the growth of negative processes, but it could not prevent them.

In the economy, and in other spheres as well, the objective need for changes became urgent, but it was not realized in the political and practical activities of the Party and the state.

What was the reason for this complex and contradictory situation?

The principal cause—and the Politburo considers it necessary to say this with total frankness at the plenary session—was that the CPSU CC and the country's leadership, primarily for subjective reasons, were unable to promptly or fully appreciate the need for changes and the danger of the mounting crisis phenomena in society or to work out a clear-cut line aimed at overcoming them and making fuller use of the possibilities inherent in the socialist system.

Conservative inclinations, inertia, a desire to brush aside everything that didn't fit into habitual patterns and an unwillingness to tackle urgent social and economic questions prevailed in both policy-making and practical activity.

Comrades, the executive bodies of the Party and the state bear the responsibility for all this.

The degree of awareness about vital problems and contradictions and social trends and prospects depended in large part on the state and development of theoretical thinking and the existing atmosphere on the theoretical front.

Lenin's dictum to the effect that the value of theory lies in its precise representation of "all those contradictions that occur in life" was often simply ignored. Theoretical notions about socialism in many ways remained on the level of the 1930s and 1940s, when society was tackling entirely different problems. Developing socialism, the dialectics of its motive forces and contradictions, and the actual state of society were not objects of thoroughgoing scientific research.

The causes of this situation go far back into the past and are rooted in that specific historical atmosphere in which, due to certain well-known circumstances, lively discussion and creative thought disappeared from theory and the social sciences and authoritarian assessments and judgments became indisputable truths subject only to commentary.

What took place was a kind of translation into absolutes of the forms of the organization of society that had developed in practice. Moreover, such notions, in point of fact, were equated with the essential characteristics of socialism, regarded as immutable and presented as dogmas leaving no room for objective scientific analysis. The model of socialist production relations became set in stone, and the dialectical interaction between these relations and productive forces was underestimated. The social structure of society was depicted in an oversimplified fashion, as devoid of contradictions and the dynamism of the multifaceted interests of its various strata and groups.

Lenin's theses about socialism were interpreted in an oversimplified way, and frequently their theoretical profundity and significance were emasculated. This also applied to such key problems as public ownership, relations among classes and nationalities, the measure of labor and the measure of consumption, cooperatives, methods of economic management, people's rule and self-management, the struggle against bureaucratic aberrations, the revolutionary-transformational essence of socialist ideology, the principles of instruction and upbringing, and guarantees of the healthy development of the Party and society.

Superficial notions about communism and various kinds of prophecies and abstractions gained a certain currency. This in turn lessened the historical significance of socialism and weakened the influence of socialist ideology.

This attitude toward theory could not help but have a negative effect—and, in fact, it did so—on the social sciences and their role in society. After all, comrades, it's a fact that all kinds of scholastic theorizing, which had nothing to do with anyone's interests and vital problems, were frequently even encouraged in our country, while attempts to make a constructive analysis and to advance new ideas received no support.

The situation on the theoretical front had a negative impact on the resolution of practical questions. Over the decades, outmoded methods were preserved in the practice of economic management and administration, while, conversely, some effective economic forms were groundlessly rejected. At the same time, relations that did not correspond to the actual maturity of society and in a number of instances were at variance with its nature were implanted in production and distribution. Production and incentives were essentially geared to quantitative, extensive development.

Special mention should be made of socialist property. A serious slackening in control over who manages it and how took place. It was frequently eaten away by departmentalism and parochialism and became "no one's," as it were—free of charge, with no real master—and in many instances it came to be used to derive unearned income.

There was an incorrect attitude toward cooperative property, which was portrayed as something "second-rate" and futureless. All this had serious consequences for agrarian and social policy, engendered administrative fiat in relations with collective farms, and led to the elimination of producers's cooperatives. also current were serious errors in views on personal auxiliary farming operations and individual enterprise, misconceptions that also caused considerable economic and social damage.

Serious deformations accumulated in planning. The authority of the plan as the main instrument of economic policy was undermined by subjectivistic approaches, imbalance and instability, a desire to encompass everything, even trivia, and abundant decisions of a branch and regional nature, adopted outside of the plan and often with no consideration for actual possibilities. Frequently plans lacked scientific substantiation, and they were not aimed at forming efficient national-economic proportions, at paying proper attention to the development of the social sphere or at accomplishing many strategic tasks.

The result was that the enormous advantages of the socialist system of economic management, primarily its planned nature, were used inefficiently. In these conditions, irresponsibility spread and various bureaucratic regulations and instructions were invented. Vital work was supplanted by administrative fiat, sham efficiency and paper-shuffling.

Preconceived notions concerning the role of commodity-money relations and the operation of the law of value, and frequently even the outright setting up of these concepts against socialism as something alien, led to voluntaristic approaches in the economy and the underestimation of economic accountability and pay "levelling" and gave rise to subjectivistic elements in price formation, violations in monetary circulation and inattention to questions of the regulation of supply and demand.

Restrictions on the economic-accountability rights of enterprises and associations had especially grave consequences. This undermined the foundations of material incentives, obstructed the achievement of high final results, and led to a lowering of the labor and social activeness of people and a falloff in discipline and order.

In point of fact, a whole system of weakening the economic instruments of power came into being, and a unique mechanism was formed for retarding social and economic development and holding back progressive transformations that make it possible to disclose and utilize the advantages of socialism. The roots of this retardation lay in serious shortcomings in the functioning of the institutions of socialist democracy, in outmoded political and theoretical principles that sometimes did not correspond to reality, and in a conservative mechanism of management.

Comrades, all this had a negative effect on the development of many spheres of the life of society. Take material production. Over the past three Five-Year Plans, the growth rates of national income declined by more than 50%. For most indices, plans had not been fulfilled since the early 1970s. The economy as a whole became unreceptive to innovations and sluggish, the quality of a large part of output no longer met current demands, and disproportions in production became exacerbated.

Attention to the development of machine building fell off. Research and experimental-design work lagged behind the requirements of the national economy and did not meet the goals of the economy's technical reconstruction. Purchases of equipment and many other goods on the capitalist market were excessive and, in many cases, unwarranted.

Negative processes seriously affected the social sphere. An assessment of its state was given at the 27th Party Congress. During the past few Five-Year Plans, the economy's social thrust obviously became weaker, and a sort of deafness to social questions appeared. Today we see what this has led to. While successfully resolving questions of the population's employment and providing fundamental social guarantees, we have at the same time been unable to fully realize the possibilities of socialism in improving living conditions and the food supply, in organizing transportation, medical service and education and in solving a number of other urgent problems.

Violations of the most important principle of socialism—distribution according to work—appeared. the struggle against unearned income was waged indecisively. The policy of providing material and moral incentives for highly productive labor was inconsistent. Large sums of money were paid out in unwarranted bonuses and in various kinds of additional incentives, and reports were padded for the sake of personal gain. A dependent mind-set grew, and a "wage-leveling" mentality began taking root in people's minds. This hit at those toilers who were able and wanted to work better, while at the same time it made life easier for those whose idea of working involves little effort.

Violation of the organic tie between the measure of labor and the measure of consumption not only deforms the attitude toward labor, impeding growth in labor productivity, it also leads to the distortion of the principle of social justice, and this is a matter of great political importance.

The elements of social corrosion that emerged in recent years had a negative effect on society's spiritual temper and imperceptibly sapped the lofty moral values that have always been inherent to our people and in which we take pride—ideological conviction, labor enthusiasm and Soviet patriotism.

The inevitable consequence of this was a falloff in interest in public affairs, manifestations of spiritual emptiness and skepticism, and a decline in the role of moral incentives to labor. The stratum of people, including young people, whose goal in life came down to material well-being and personal gain by any means increased. Their cynical position took on increasingly militant forms, poisoned the minds of those around them, and gave rise to a wave of consumerism. The growth of drunkenness, the spread of drug addiction and the increase in crime became indices of the falloff in social mores.

Instances of a scornful attitude toward laws, hoodwinking, bribetaking and the encourage-ment of servility and glorification had a pernicious effect on the moral atmosphere in society. Genuine concern for people, their living and working conditions and their social well-being was frequently supplanted by political ingratiation—the mass handing out of awards, titles and bonuses. An atmosphere of all-forgivingness took shape, while exactingness, discipline and responsibility declined.

In many cases, serious shortcomings in ideological-political upbringing were covered up by the holding of window-dressing activities and one-shot campaigns and the celebration of numerous anniversaries, at both the central and the local level. The world of day-to-day realities and the world of sham well-being increasingly diverged from each other.

The ideology and mentality of stagnation were also reflected in the state of the sphere of culture, literature and the arts. Criteria for assessing artistic creativity declined. This led to a situation in which, along with works that raised serious social and moral problems and reflected real-life conflicts, there appeared a good many mediocre, faceless works that provided nothing for either the mind or the senses. Soviet society was increasingly penetrated by stereotypes from bourgeois mass culture, imposing banality, primitive tastes and spiritual emptiness.

Here one has to say something about the responsibility of our ideological departments, the editors of magazines of the arts, the executives of the creative unions, literary critics, our writers themselves and workers in the arts for the ideological-artistic thrust of the creative process and for the moral health of the people.

The creative unions' activity did not have enough devotion to principle, exactingness or genuine concern for developing and supporting talented people. Often questions of paramount importance relating to the status and condition of the cultural sphere failed to receive proper attention from the unions' leadership. At the same time, red tape and formalism flourished and an extreme intolerance of criticism appeared. In a number of cases, excessive ambitions began to gain the upper hand over realistic evaluations and self-evaluations.

The situation was aggravated by the fact that a Party approach to artistic creativity was frequently supplanted by unwarranted departmental interference in purely creative processes and by sympathies and antipathies based on personal taste, and methods of ideoligical influence and guidance were supplanted by administrative decisions.

Comrades! The state of the Party itself and of its cadres also had an effect on the social, economic and political situation that developed in the late 1970s and early 1980s. The Party's executive bodies were unable to appraise the danger of the growth of negative tendencies in society and in the behavior of some Communists in time or in a critical way, or to adopt the decisions that life urgently required.

Although Primary Party Organizations had enormous possibilities at their disposal and were operating in virtually all labor collectives, many of them were unable to hold to principled positions. By no means all of them waged a resolute struggle against negative phenomena, an "everything goes" attitude, mutual protection, the weakening of discipline and the spread of drunkenness. A fitting rebuff was not always administered to departmentalism, parochialism, and nationalistic manifestations.

Our Party organizations sometimes were lacking in militancy, exactingness toward Party members and attention to the shaping of Communists' ideological and political qualities. Meanwhile, it is precisely high ideological standards, conscientiousness, readiness to subor-dinate one's personal interests to those of society and selfless service to the people that are the most valuable qualities which are always characteristic of Bolsheviks.

The situation in the Party was also influenced by the fact that in a number of instances Party agencies did not devote the proper attention to strict observance of the Leninist principles and norms of Party life. This was manifested most of all, perhaps, in violations of the collective principle in their work. I mean that there was a weakening of the role of Party meetings and elected agencies, which deprived Communists of the opportunity of actively participating in the discussion of vitally important questions and, in the final analysis, of actually influencing the situation in labor collectives and in society as a whole.

The principle of equality among Communists was frequently violated. Many Party members holding leadership posts were not subject to supervision or criticism, which led to failures in work and serious violations of Party ethics.

We cannot fail to mention the just indignation of working people at the behavior of those executives, invested with trust and authority and called upon to stand guard over the interests of the state and its citizens, who themselves abused their authority, stifled criticism or reaped personal gain, while some of them even became accessories to, or organizers of, criminal actions.

Negative processes connected with the degeneration of cadres and with violations of socialist legality were manifested in extremely ugly forms in Uzbekistan, Moldavia and Turkmenia, a number of provinces of Kazakhstan, Krasnodar Territory and Rostov Province, as well as in Moscow and certain other cities, provinces, territories and republics and in the systems of the Ministry of Foreign Trade and the Ministry of Internal Affairs.

Of course, Party organizations and the Party as a whole waged a struggle against these phenomena, expelling a large number of degenerates from the ranks of the CPSU. Among them were people who had engaged in embezzlement, bribe-taking and report-padding, had violated state and Party discipline or were heavy drinkers.

The overwhelming majority of those who have entered the Party are the best representatives of the working class, the peasantry and the intelligentsia. They have performed and are continuing to perform their Party duty sincerely and selflessly. Even so, it must be admitted that during those years we were unable to erect a solid barrier against dishonest, pushy, self-interested people who sought to derive an advantage from their Party membership cards. To some extent, we deviated from the rule that the main thing is not the quantity of new members but the quality of the Party's ranks. And this had an effect on the Party organizations' fighting efficiency.

Everything I have said, comrades, indicates how serious the situation had become in various spheres of society and how necessary thoroughgoing changes had become. This makes it all the more important to emphasize once again that the Party found in itself the strength and the courage to assess the situation soberly, to recognize the need for cardinal changes in policy, in the economy and in the social and spiritual spheres, and to turn the country onto the path of transformations.

This was the situation, comrades, in which the question of accelerating the country's social and economic development and of restructuring was raised. In essence, what is involved here is a change of direction and measures of a revolutionary nature. We are talking about restructuring and related processes of the thoroughgoing democratization of society, having in mind truly revolutionary and comprehensive transformations in society.

This fundamental change of direction is necessary, since we simply have no other way. We must not retreat, and we have nowhere to retreat to. We must steer the course charted by the April Plenum of the CC and the 27th Congress consistently and unswervingly, go further on and take society to a qualitatively new level of development.

Today there is a need to state once again what we mean by restructuring.

Restructuring means resolutely overcoming the processes of stagnation, scrapping the mechanism of retardation, and creating a reliable and effective mechanism of accelerating the social and economic development of Soviet society. The main idea of our strategy is to combine the achievements of the scientific and technological revolution with a planned economy and to set the entire potential of socialism in motion.

Restructuring means reliance on the vital creativity of the masses, the all-round development of democracy and socialist self-government, the encouragement of initiative and independent activity, the strengthening of discipline and order, and the expansion of openness, criticism and self- criticism in all spheres of the life of society; it means respect, raised on high, for the value and worth of the individual.

Restructuring means steadily enhancing the role of intensive factors in the development of the Soviet economy; restoring and developing Leninist principles of democratic centralism in the management of the national economy, introducing economic methods of management everywhere, renouncing the peremptory issuing of orders and administrative fiat, ensuring the changeover of all elements of the economy to the principles of full economic accountability and to new forms of the organization of labor and production, and encouraging innovation and socialist enterprise in every way.

Restructuring means a decisive turn toward science, a businesslike partnership between science and practice aimed at achieving the highest possible final results, the ability to put any undertaking on a solid scientific footing, and readiness and a fervent desire on the part of scientists to actively support the Party's course aimed at the renewal of society; at the same time, it means concern for the development of science, the growth of its personnel and their active participation in the processes of transformation.

Restructuring means the priority development of the social sphere and the ever fuller satisfaction of Soviet people's requirements for good working, living, recreational, educational and medical-service conditions; it means constant concern for the spiritual wealth and culture of every person and of society as a whole; and it means the ability to combine the solution of large-scale, cardinal problems of the life of society with the resolution of current questions troubling people.

Restructuring means the energetic elimination from society of distortions of socialist morality, and the consistent implementation of the principles of social justice; it means the unity of word and deed and of rights and obligations; and it means the ennoblement of honest, high-quality labor and the overcoming of pay-leveling tendencies and of consumerism.

The ultimate aim of restructuring is clear, I think—a thoroughgoing renewal of all aspects of the country's life, the imparting to socialism of the most up-to-date forms of social organization, and the fullest possible disclosure of the humanistic nature of our system in all its decisive aspects—economic, social, political and moral. This is, comrades, the job we have launched. The reorganization effort is unfolding along the entire front. It is acquiring a new quality not only gaining in scope but also penetrating the deepest fibre of life.

The drive for change has stirred all healthy forces in society to action and given people greater confidence in what they are doing. An objective and self-critical attitude to the state of things, departure from the cut-and-dried, well beaten ways of going about their work, and the search for new, off-beat solutions to problems have become typical of more and more Party committees, mass organizations and worker collectives.

A new moral atmosphere is taking shape in the country. A reassessment of values and their creative reinterpretation is under way, debates have begun over the ways and means of transformations in the economy and in the social and spiritual spheres, and the search for new methods of organizational and ideological work is expanding. Public openness, truthfulness in evaluating phenomena and events, intransigence toward shortcomings and a desire to improve things are becoming increasingly established as actively operating principles of life.

Exactingness, discipline and organization in production are increasing, and there is greater order. The first steps in the restructuring of spiritual life are especially important to us, since if there is no breakthrough in the public consciousness, if there are no changes in people's psychology, thinking and mind-set, success cannot be achieved, comrades.

We have begun a fundamental transformation of the material and technical base, a thoroughgoing reconstruction of the national economy on the basis of scientific and technical progress, and a change in structural and investment policy. Far-reaching target programs have been adopted in the decisive areas of scientific and technological progress. These programs have been taken into account in drawing up the 12th Five Year Plan, which is now being carried out.

Major steps are being taken to improve management. At the beginning of this year, all industrial enterprises and associations were shifted to methods of economic management that have been experimentally verified. A number of branches, enterprises and associations have begun to operate on the basis of full economic accountability and self-financing.

The branches of the economy that are directly involved in satisfying the needs of the population—such as the agro-industrial complex, light industry, trade and the service sphere—have begun to operate on principles that ensure broad independence and increase responsibility. Fundamental changes are being carried out in the management of capital construction. With the aim of stepping up the struggle for high quality in manufactured articles, a system of state product acceptance has been introduced at 1,500 leading enterprises.

The system of foreign economic activity is being restructured. The rights of enterprises and branches with respect to foreign economic ties have been expanded. New forms of cooperation—direct ties between enterprises, joint associations, specialization and production on a cooperative basis with foreign partners—are receiving further development.

With a view to shifting to a comprehensive system of managing the national economy, permanent agencies of the USSR Council of Ministers have been set up to manage groups of related branches. A draft Law on the State Enterprise (Association) has been worked out, and documents dealing with improving the functioning of central economic agencies, ministries and departments in conditions of the new economic mechanism and proposals on organizing new forms of large economic-accountability production structures on the basis of associations and enterprises, as well as on a number of other important questions, are being prepared.

Important measures to improve matters in the social sphere are being carried out. New principles for raising pay in the production branches have been worked out and are being implemented. We have firmly embarked on a course that rejects "wage-leveling" and consistently observes the socialist principle of distribution according to the quantity and quality of work. At the same time, unwarranted restrictions on individual enterprise have been lifted. Favorable conditions for its development are now being created. In the interests of the fuller satisfaction of the population's requirements, the organization of cooperatives in various production and service sectors is being encouraged.

On the basis of an analysis of the situation in housing construction, and taking into account the programmatic goal of providing every family with a separate apartment by the year 2000, additional reserves for stepping up the pace of housing construction and improving its quality have been found. An additional 10% of capital investment for production facilities is being channeled into this endeavor, which will make it possible to increase the volume of housing construction in 1987 by 9.1 million square meters, or almost 8%, in comparison with the figure specified in the Five-Year Plan.

Housing-cooperative and individual construction is expanding. Easy- term credits are being made available for this purpose and the necessary resources are being allocated, and measures are being carried out to develop the do-it-yourself method of housing construction, using enterprises' funds, to build up the production base of the construction industry, and to achieve other goals.

A program has been outlined for the erection and reconstruction of medical institutions, capacities for the production of Soviet-made medicines and medical equipment are being increased, and work is being accelerated to introduce and develop new forms of medical services and to organize medical science. In organic connection with this program, measures are being carried out to improve the population's working and living conditions, to expand preventive health care, to eradicate drunkenness and alcoholism, and to reduce the sickness rate. The wages of medical personnel are being raised.

Thus, comrades, even a brief survey of what has been planned and begun shows how extensive the restructuring work now under way in the country is. The amount of work facing us is enormous but there is no way that it can be avoided. The Party does not have the right to slacken attention to any aspect of the projected changes. All plans must be carried out without fail, to the point and on time.

Needless to say, a number of the measures that we are working out and implementing will not bring a real return at once. But even now the very atmosphere and the new mood in society are changing the attitude toward work and are producing real, practical results.

The results of plan fulfillment for the first year of the Five-Year Plan indicate this. Material national income went up 4.1% as against 3.9% in the Plan and as compared with the annual average of 3.6% in the previous five years. Industrial production grew 4.9%, which is a third more than the average annual increase in the previous five-year period and makes the highest growth rate for the past 9 years.

You know that the 12th Five-Year Plan period is of decisive significance to us in terms of modernizing the country's machine-building sector, updating production assets and speeding up scientific and technological progress. The effort to ensure priority development of the machine-building sector has had to cope with great difficulties but nevertheless it is going on. In the past year the production of industrial robots went up 14%, that of flexible automated production systems 40%. Capital inputs in re-tooling and reconstruction of existing mechanical engineering factories grew 30%. The Politburo will keep constant watch over how the program concerning the machine-building sector is being fulfilled. We hope that machine-builders will cope with the tasks set for them.

Things are looking up also in a number of other industries. The results shown last year in non-ferrous metallurgy, coal mining and the gas industry were not bad and the ground lost in oil production was also being made up. Labor productivity in industry as a whole rose 4.6% as compared with the planned target of of 4.1%. This increase accounted for 96% of the gain in output in 1986. Net production costs dropped noticeably for the first time in many years. The turnover rate of material assets went up, while the stocks of uninstalled plant, including important equipment, were reduced.

Improvements in the agrarian sector are there for all to see. As compared with the average annual harvests in the past five-year period, grain production in 1986 increased by almost 30 million tons, or 17%, potatoes by 9 million tons, or 11%, meat by 1.5 million tons, or 9%, milk 6.5 million tons, or 7%, and [the number of] eggs by almost 6000 million, or 8%.

As you see comrades, agricultural output has begun to grow, something we have not seen in such decisive indices for many years. However, it must be said that the growth in output of such products as vegetables, fruits, sunflower and cotton was either insignificant or zero.

It is also important to note the improvement of the main financial and economic indices in the performance of collective farms and state farms. Labor productivity in the socialized economy increased during the year by 6.9%, the profit rate amounted to 19% and profits went up by 2 billion rubles.

While noting the positive changes in the development of the economy, we must at the same time say that, as a result of extensive losses and unproductive outlays and the nonfulfillment of assignments for expanding trade turnover, the annual plan for the growth of national income used for consumption and accumulation was not fulfilled.

Despite significant increases in comparison with last year [1985], growth in such highly important indices as real income per capita, gross agricultural output, consumer goods production by industry, volume of capital investments, the commissioning of fixed assets and profits for the national economy was lower than plan assignments. No major changes took place in the investment process, and only two-thirds of the facilities included on the state plan's lists went into operation.

Changes in the social sphere have begun, albeit with great difficulty. Following the measures taken to strengthen discipline and combat drunkenness, the number of accidents fell and losses of working time decreased, for the first time since the 1960s. The overall crime rate dropped by nearly 25%, and that for grave crimes fell by 33%. The struggle against violations of legality and order has been tightened up everywhere.

The volume of housing construction grew, making it possible to increase the amount of housing opened for occupancy by 5.21 million sq.m. in comparison with 1985. More kinder-gartens, day-care centers, schools, polyclinics, hospitals and cultural and consumer-service institutions were built.

In short, positive changes have taken place. But the weight of the problems that have accumulated in this important sphere is too great, and we are still too timid in tackling them.

As you know, it was only with great difficulty that untapped potential was found for expanding housing construction and erecting cultural and consumer-service facilities. But, unfortunately, by no means everyone has made proper use of the possibilities that have been made available. Plans for the construction of many of these facilities have gone unfulfilled. The reasons for this lie not only in disorganization on the part of builders but also in insufficient attention on the part of enterprises, ministries, local Soviets and Party committees.

We still have difficulties with respect to trade in food-stuffs and manufactured goods and in the operations of urban transport, municipal services, and public health and cultural institutions. In general, we have not brought about fundamental changes in the development of the social sphere and remain largely at the mercy of old approaches.

In concluding my description of the work that the Party and the entire people are conducting to implement the decisions of the 27th Congress, I would like to say the following. It is very important that we, the members of the CC, take realistic positions, make an objective assessment of what has been done, and view the results obtained not only from the standpoint of the past but, above all, on the basis of the plans we have announced and the promises we have made to the people. This is the only correct Party approach.

We must be clearly aware that we are still in the initial state of restructuring. The main and most complex part of our work lies ahead. We must move forward persistently, step by step and without hesitation, soberly assess what has been done, not be afraid to correct mistakes, and seek out and find new ways and means of accomplishing tasks that arise, making mandatory progress toward our planned goals.

We must firmly learn the lesson of the past—not to allow a gap between decisions and practical work to implement them. We must not take on airs or give way to complacency. I say this once again because we are still running up against this even now. We must act, act and act again— vigorously, boldly, creatively and competently.

This way of putting the question is also dictated by the fact that in many economic, state, Soviet and even Party agencies, and in our labor collectives themselves, by no means everyone is as yet marching in step with life's demands. There are quite a few people who are slow to rid themselves of the burden of the past, who are biding their time and, in some instances, openly obstructing things, impeding the broad development of the people's political, public and labor activeness.

Not everyone has understood that working in the new way means resolutely abandoning old habits and methods. In the final analysis, this depends on the civic stance of each and every person, on a conscientious attitude toward the assigned task and toward one's obligations, for which we are all accountable to the Party, to the country and to our conscience.

Meetings and conversations with working people and Party and economic personnel show that the restructuring is meeting with ardent support. The people are solidly behind the restructuring, as the saying goes. But here is something that draws one's attention. While supporting the new, many people think that restructuring should be carried out somewhere above them or by someone else—by Party, state and economic agencies, in other branches, at related enterprises or in neighboring shops, livestock sections or construction projects. In general, by anyone other than themselves.

No, comrades, while rightly calling for restructuring at all levels, each of us must begin restructuring with himself. Everyone—including workers, collective farmers, members of the intelligentsia—everyone in general, from the labor collective to the CPSU Central Committee and the government—must work in the new way: energetically, creatively and, I'll say it once again, conscientiously. In the immense task of reorganization we, Communists, rely above all on a high degree of awareness and organization, social initiative and the major labor accomplishments of the working class, the leading political force of our society.

While placing a high value on the Party's course aimed at restructuring, the working class and all Soviet people at the same time are expressing concern over the progress of its practical implementation. They are urging the Party not to stop with what has been achieved, to act decisively, to move forward and to steadfastly implement the course that has been set. Comrades, we should draw political conclusions from this.

Since such concern exists in society, apparently our efforts are still insufficient. This means that we are not acting with the proper effectiveness and aggressiveness everywhere and in all things. It means that in a great many places the measures that are being taken and the work that is being conducted still do not correspond to the scope and urgency of the problems that have accumulated, that not everything is proceeding as the times demand. It means, comrades, that the CC has good reason for reflecting and drawing the necessary conclusions.

We understand, of course, that overcoming existing stereotyped ways of thinking and acting is a complex process that is not painless and that takes time and a well-considered approach.

It is perfectly clear that this process cannot proceed autonomously or in isolation from the transformations in political, social, economic and spiritual life.

We must clearly realize that a whole system of measures is needed today. They should include the formulation of theoretical propositions based on today's realities and a thoroughly substantiated vision of the future, a change in public awareness, the consistent development of democratic institutions, the fostering of political standards among the masses, the restructuring of the mechanism of economic management and organizational structures, and, of course, the implementation of an active social policy.

This is the only way in which the retardation mechanism can be removed and the forces of acceleration can obtain the free scope that they need.

I think that today's plenary session of the CC should tell the Party and the people that we face a difficult struggle that requires a high degree of awareness and organization, tenacity and the utmost selflessness from every Communist and every citizen.

Comrades! An analysis of the state in which our society found itself on the eve of the April Plenum of the CC and the experience of restructuring pose a very basic question in a most pointed way. Do we have any guarantees that the process of transformations we have begun will be brought to completion, that past mistakes will not be repeated, and that we will be able to ensure the vigorous development of our society?

The Politburo answers these questions affirmatively: Yes, we do have such guarantees.

They include the single will and joint actions of the Party and the people, united by the experience they have gone through and by an awareness of their responsibility for the present and future of the socialist homeland.

They include the comprehensive development of democracy in the socialist system and the real and increasingly active participation of the people in the resolution of all questions on the country's life; the full restoration of the Leninist principles of openness, public control, criticism and self-criticism; and sincerity in policy, which consists in the unity of word and deed.

Finally, they include the healthy development of the Party itself, its ability to critically analyze its own activity, and its ability to update the forms and methods of its work, to determine— on the basis of revolutionary theory—the prospect for the development of society, and to struggle for the accomplishment of the new tasks that life is posing.

It is precisely the deepening of socialist democratizatiuon, the creative endeavour of Soviet people, the vanguard role of Communists in practical deeds that will ensure both the success and the irreversibility of the revolutionary transformations mapped out by the 27th Congress.

II. To Deepen Socialist Democracy and Develop Self-Government by the People
Comrades!

We now understand better than before the entire depth of **Lenin**'s thought about the vital inner link between socialism and democracy. The entire historical experience of our country has convincingly demonstrated that the socialist system has in practice ensured citizens; political and socio-economic rights, their personal freedoms, and demonstrated the advantages of Soviet democracy and given each person confidence in the future.

But in conditions of reorganization, when the task of intensifying the human factor has become so urgent, we must return once again to **Lenin**'s approach to the question of maximum democratism of the socialist system under which people feel that they are their own masters and creators. "We must be guided by experience, we must allow complete freedom to the creative faculties of the masses," Vladimir **Lenin** said.

Indeed, democracy the essence of which is the power of the man of labor, is the forum for realizing his extensive political and civil rights, his interest in transformations and practical participation in their implementation.

A simple and lucid thought is becoming increasingly entrenched in social consciousness: A base can be put in order only by a person who feels that he owns the house. This truth is correct not only in the worldly sense but also in the socio-political one. This truth must be undeviatingly applied in practice. I repeat, in practice. Otherwise the human factor will be ineffective.

It is only through the consistent development of the democratic forums inherent in socialism, through a broadening of self-government that our achievement in production, science and technology, literature, culture and the arts, in all areas of social life is possible. It is only this way that ensures conscientious discipline. The reorganization itself is possible only through democracy and due to democracy. It is only this way that it is possible to give scope to socialism's most creative force—free labor and free thought in a free country.

The further democratization of Soviet society is becoming an urgent task for the Party. This, strictly speaking, is the essence of the course set by the April [1985] plenary session and the 27th CPSU Congress, aimed at deepening socialist self-government by the people. Needless to say, this does not involve any breakup of our political system. We should use all its possibilities with maximum effectiveness, fill the work of the Party, the Soviets, state agencies, public organizations and labor collectives with profound democratic content, and breathe new life into all the cells of the social organism.

This process is already under way in our country. The life of Party organizations is becoming more vigorous. Criticism and self-criticism are expanding. The mass news media have begun to work more actively. Soviet people have a good feeling for the favorable influence of openness, which is becoming a norm in the life of society.

The congresses of creative unions took part in an atmosphere of devotion to principle and a critical spirit. New public organizations are being created. The All-Union Council of War and Labor Veterans has come into being. The Soviet Culture Fund has been formed. Work is under way on the creation of women's councils. In all of this, there is growing participation by the working people in public affairs and in the administration of the country.

What paths for the further deepening of democracy in Soviet society does the Politburo see?

We will be able to boost effectively people's initiative and creativity if our democratic institutions vigorously and effectively influence the state of things in every work collective, whether it concerns planning, organization of labor, distribution of material and other benefits, or selection and promotion of the most authoritative and competent people to leading positions.

It can confidently be said that the sooner every Soviet citizen feels these changes in his own or her own experience, the more active his or her civic positions and participation in public and state affairs will be.

The development of democracy on the job and the consistent introduction of genuine self-government principles into the work of labor collectives are of paramount importance. The economy is the decisive sphere of the life of society. Tens of millions of people are involved in it every day. That is why the development of democracy on the job is a highly important area of the deepening and expansion of socialist democracy as a whole. This is a lever, which will make it possible to ensure the broad and active participation of the working people in all areas of social life and make it possible to avoid many blunders and miscalculations.

A highly important practical task is to create conditions and introduce forms of organizing production that will enable every working person to feel himself a true proprietor of the enterprise. And this is a lofty and responsible position. It not only gives one broad rights in the real administration of affairs, but also presupposes great responsibility for all that is happening in the work collective.

In the course of socialist construction, diverse forms of the working people's participation in the management of production have been established. The life of labor collectives is unthinkable without Party, trade union, Young Communist League and other public organizations. Recently, the role of workers' meetings and collective contracts has been growing, such new forms of democracy as brigade and shop councils have arisen, and conditions have become ripe for further steps along this path.

Life itself placed on the agenda the need to work out such a fundamental legal act as the Law on the State Enterprise, the draft of which you have been given. The law is called upon to change, in a fundamental way, the conditions and methods of economic management in the economy's basic link, to consolidate the combination of the planning principle and full economic accountability of the activities of enterprises, and to legalize the new forms of self-management brought into existence by the creativity of the masses.

The law contemplates the implementation of one of the most important directives of the Party Congress, namely the line aimed at the effective use of direct democracy. Endowing general meetings and councils of labor collectives, as the draft outlines, with the power to resolve questions connected with production, social and personnel matters will be a major political measure in shifting, to use the words of V.I. **Lenin**, "to real people's self-government."

The consistent implementation of the Law on the State Enterprise, in combination with the complex of measures that are now being carried out in the economic sphere, will, we think, create a new situation in the national economy as a whole, will be an accelerator of the economy's development, and will lead to qualitative improvement in many aspects of the life of society. In view of the enormous significance of this law, the Politburo proposes that its draft be submitted for public discussion. I think that the members of the CC will support this proposal.

Our collective farms and the socialist cooperative system as a whole possess broad and still greatly underutilized opportunities for democratizing the management of the economic and social sphere. The restructuring of the management system in the agro-industrial complex, as well as the decision on the further development of the cooperative system in other branches of the national economy, is creating good prerequisites for making use of these opportunities. In this connection, it would be a good idea, in our view, to hold a new collective farmers' congress to discuss urgent problems of collective farm life, and to make the necessary changes in the Model Charter for the Collective Farm.

The Politburo actively supports the practical steps that are being taken in many republics, territories and provinces to expand other cooperative forms of activity. This will make it possible to more fully satisfy the population's growing requirements for many goods and services, and also to create additional conditions for the development of democracy in the economic sphere and for the better realization of human potential.

Comrades, we must resolutely overcome the vacillations with respect to the cooperative movement that existed in the past and can still be observed today. The cooperative system not only has not exhausted its possibilities, it has great prospects.

Why am I returning to this question and pointedly emphasizing it? Because since the 27th CPSU Congress, despite the decisions adopted by the CC and the government on developing the cooperative system in the sphere of material and technical supply, consumer services, public catering, municipal services, local industry and construction, the matter has not received the proper attention. All sorts of obstacles are being erected in its path, and attachment to administrative-bureaucratic methods of management and rejection of those forms of economic management that do not fit into the traditional notions, even if these forms are vitally necessary, stimulate the working people's initiative and increase their social activeness, are still strong.

Apparently it is difficult for some comrades to understand that democracy is not just a slogan but the essence of restructuring. They must change their views and habits, if they are not to be left outside the mainstream of life. This is our insistent advice to all doubters and laggards.

The question of the election of the managers of enterprises and production facilities, the superintendents of shops, divisions and sections, the heads of livestock sections and teams, brigade leaders and foremen should be singled out. The present stage of restructuring and the transition to new methods of economic management, economic accountability, self-financing and paying one's own way are moving this problem onto a practical plane. This measure is important and necessary, and there is no doubt that it will meet with the working people's approval.

We have begun the wide-ranging changeover of enterprises to full economic accountability, self-financing and paying their own way, and we have introduced a state product acceptance system. This means that the income of an enterprise, all forms of incentives for the members of labor collectives and the scale of the satisfaction of social requirements will depend wholly on the final results of work, on the quantity and quality of output produced and services rendered.

In these conditions, workers and collective farmers are far from indifferent as to who heads their enterprise, shop, section or brigade. Since the collective's well-being depends on the abilities of its leaders, the working people should have real opportunities to influence their selection and monitor their activity.

A certain amount of experience in the open, public selection of managers has accumulated in the country. Thus in Krasnodar Territory, beginning in 1983, more than 8,500 executives have been promoted taking into account the opinion of collectives and Primary Party Organizations. At the same time, over 200 candidates did not receive the working people's support and were turned down. There have been similar experiences in a number of other places as well. People are receiving it well, and it is having a positive effect on the results of work.

In general, comrades, from whatever standpoint we approach this important matter, one conclusion suggests itself: There is an urgent need for change, for democratization of the process of forming the executive personnel of enterprises on the basis of the general application of the elective principle. This, you understand, means a qualitatively new situation, a fundamentally different nature of the working people's participation in the management of production, and a substantial enhancement of the role and responsibility of the collective for the results of its activity.

It is necessary to take all this into account during the practical resolution of the question at hand. But I would like to express one thought right now. We are talking about one-man management. We believe that an elective system not only does not undermine but enhances the prestige of the executive, who feels that he has the support of the people who elected him, and that it increases responsibility for work and mutual exactingness in the collective.

The role of Party and public organizations and economic-management agencies should be comprehended in a new way. A good deal of work will have to be done to instill in all of our cadres a correct understanding of the fact that the expansion of democracy on the job presupposes the organic combination of one-man management and collective leadership, the deepening of democratic centralism and the development of self-government.

The Politburo considers the improvement of the Soviet electoral system to be a fundamental area in the democratization of our life. On instructions from the 27th Congress, appropriate proposals are being worked out on this score.

What needs to be said here? The existing mechanism of the electoral system ensures representation for all strata of the population in the elective bodies of power. The working class, the collective farm peasantry, the intelligentsia, women and men, veterans and young people, and all the country's nations and nationalities are represented in the present Soviets at all levels. The elective bodies reflect the social, occupational and national structure of Soviet society and the diversity of interest of the entire population. In itself, this is an enormous achievement of socialist democracy.

But, like all political, economic and social institutions, the electoral system cannot remain set in concrete, sitting on the sidelines of restructuring and the new processes developing in society.

What is the essence of the proposals and wishes of the working people on these questions that are being received by the CPSU CC, the Presidium of the USSR Supreme Soviet, other central agencies and the mass news media?

On the political level, the matter at hand is deepening democracy in the electoral system and achieving the more effective and more active participation of voters at all stages of preelection and election campaigns.

On a concrete level, most proposals come to suggesting that meetings of voters in labor collectives and at places of residence, as well as at preelectiion conferences, discuss several candidates, as a rule, that elections be held in larger election districts, and that several deputies be elected from each district. Comrades think that this will enable every citizen to express his attitude toward a broader range of candidates and will enable Party and Soviet agencies to get a better knowledge of the population's mood and will.

Responding to these wishes, we should take a new look at the organization of elections themselves and at the practice of nominating and discussing candidates for People's deputy. We must rid the voting procedure of formalism and see to it that the election campaign, as early as this year, tales place in an atmosphere of broader democracy and the interested participation of people in this process.

As far as a legislative act making adjustments to the electoral system is concerned, it would be useful if a draft document were published beforehand for nationwide discussion.

The implementation of these proposals would be the first important step on the path towards the further democratization in the process of the formation and functioning of the bodies of state power. But, obviously, we also need to consider deeper changes and further steps in this direction. Taking into account accumulated experience and new tasks, it is necessary once again to make a very careful investigation of the Leninist legacy on questions of Soviet state construction and to use it in accomplishing the tasks that confront Soviet society today.

It is quite natural that questions of expanding inner-Party democracy be examined within the overall context of the further democratization of Soviet society.

As is known, when the 27th Congress made changes in and additions to the CPSU Statutes, a number of important propositions aimed at strengthening democratic principles in the Party's life were carried out. This work should be continued. It seems expedient to seek advice concerning the improvement of the mechanism of forming Party leadership bodies.

The CC has received many different proposals on this subject. Allow me to report the conclusions that have been drawn on the basis of a generalization of thse proposals.

First of all, about the formation of elective agencies in the Primary Party Organization. The point of most of the proposals on this score is to give full scope to the expression of the will of all Communists without exception during the election of secretaries of Party buros and Party committees and in enhancing their responsibility to those who elect them.

There is also a need to give some thought to changing the procedure for the election of secretaries of district, region, city, provinces and territory Party committees and of Union-Republic Communist Party CCs. Here comrades suggest that secretaries, including first secretaries, could be elected by secret ballot at plenums of the appropriate Party committees. In the process, the members of the Party committee would have the right to enter any number of candidates on the ballot. This measure ought to significantly enhance the responsibility of secretaries to the Party committees that elected them, give them more confidence in their work, and make it possible to more accurately determine the extent of their prestige.

Needless to say, the Party's statutory principle according to which the decisions of higher agencies are binding on all lower-level Party committees, including decisions on personnel matters, should remain immutable.

In the Politburo's opinion, further democratization should extend to the formation of the Party's central leadership as well. I think this is perfectly logical. Apparently it would be logical to democratize elections of leadership bodies in other public organizations as well.

I suggest, comrades, that you will agree with the fact that these measures will strengthen the basis of democratic centralism in the Party life, and will raise the unity and responsibility, the activeness of each Communist, all Party organizations, and the Party as a whole.

Possibly, this will raise the question: but will this not complicate the procedure of the formation of elections to Party organs?

Beginning with the April Plenum of the CC, we have constantly emphasized that the problems that have accumulated in society are connected, to a significant extent, to shortcomings in the activity of the Party itself and in its personnel policy. The Politburo believes that further democratization of the process of forming elective bodies is an important condition for enhancing the Party's vital activity, for infusing fresh forces and for active work by Party organizations, and a guarantee against the repetition of past mistakes.

Elections within the Party are not a pro forma action, and we should approach their preparation in a well-considered manner and in a spirit of lofty responsibility, proceeding from the interests of the Party and society.

The democratization of society poses in a new way the question of control over how Party, Soviet and economic agencies and their personnel work. As far as control "from above" is concerned, here, as you know, appreciable changes have taken place recently. Various "forbidden zones" for criticism and control are receding into the past. At their meetings, the Politburo and the Secretariat of the CC regularly hear reports from Union-Republic Communist Party CCs and territory and province Party committees and examine other fundamental questions of the life of the Party and society in a thorough and comprehensive way. The USSR Council of Ministers and its Presidium have become significantly more exacting with respect to ministries, departments and Union-Republic Councils of Ministers.

Frankly, however, there is still a great deal for the CC's Politburo and Secretariat and the government to do in this area. We still have to return to one and the same question several times and adopt additional measures for its resolution. This was graphically shown, in particular, by a discussion at a recent Politburo meeting of progress in fulfilling the CC and USSR Council of Ministers' resolutions on accelerating the development of machine building. We adopted the necessary decisions, but, as before, they were not carried out completely by the established deadlines. Another reason why this occurs is the fact that many people have still not freed themselves from the burden of old habits toward their duties. Discipline is slack. A great many executives do not follow the principle of unity of words and deeds, and others do more talking than working. We must draw some very serious conclusions from this.

But, despite the great importance of "control from above," in conditions of democratization of society fundamental importance attaches to raising the level and increasing the effectiveness of control "from below," so that every executive and every official constantly feels his responsibility to and dependence on the voters, the labor collectives and the public organizations, on the Party and the people as a whole. The main thing here is to create and strengthen all the tools and forms of real control that come from the working people.

What tools and forms do I have in mind?

First of all, reporting. It is time to unswervingly observe the rule of systematic reporting by all elected and appointed officials to labor collectives and the population. It is necessary that every such report be accompanied by a lively and principled discussion, criticism, self-criticism and businesslike proposals and end with an assessment of the activity of the person doing the reporting.

That will be the implementation in practice of **Lenin**'s behest that the work of elective bodies and executives be open to everyone and be done in sight of the masses. If we achieve such control, there can be no doubt that many causes for complaints and messages to higher organizations will disappear, and most questions raised in them will be solved at local level. In the conditions of extensive democratization, people themselves will put things in order in their work collectives, town, or village.

The Soviets, the trade unions and other public organizations possess enormous possibilities for control. In the Supreme and local Soviets, it is necessary to strengthen democratic principles in the work of sessions, standing committees and deputies and to enhance the effectiveness of regular reporting by officials to the Soviets and the practice of Deputies' inquiries. This approach will further consolidate the prestige of the bodies of people's power with the masses.

While improving control, we must bring order without delay into all kinds of checkups and inspections, which now rain down like an avalanche on enterprises, institutions and organizations, distract people from their duties, and bring an element of nervousness into work. The practical benefit derived from these checkups is meager, as a rule. These are not new questions; they have been spoken of and written about many times. But so far nothing has changed. Evidently the Secretariat of the CC and the Presidium of the USSR Council of Ministers should put these matters into the proper order and consider quality, not quantity, in checkups.

In improving the social atmosphere, it is also necessary to continue to develop openness. It is a powerful lever for improving work in all sectors of our construction and an effective form of control by all the people. Excellent confirmation of this is provided by the experience that has been accumulated since the April Plenum of the CC.

Obviously, the time has come to begin the drafting of legal documents guaranteeing openness. They should ensure maximum openness in the activities of state and public organizations and give working people a real opportunity to express their opinion on any question of the life of society.

Criticism and self-criticism are a tested tool of socialist democracy. It would seem that there are no open objections to that. However, in life we encounter instances indicating that a great many people have not recognized the need to support a critical mind-set in society. Matters sometimes reach the point at which some officials regard even the slightest critical comment as an encroachment on their prestige and defend it by all possible means. More sophisticated officials have appeared, too. They admit the correctness of the criticism and even thank you for it, but they are in no hurry to eliminate the shortcomings, expecting to get away with it all, as they have done in the past.

This attitude towards criticism has nothing to do with our principles and morality. At the present stage, when we are establishing new approaches in social and political life and in the spiritual sphere, the importance of criticism and self-criticism is growing immeasurably. A person's attitude toward criticism is an important criterion of his attitude toward restructuring, toward everything new that is taking place in society.

Here one cannot help saying regretfully that we continue to encounter not only hostility toward criticism but also instances of peresecution for it and the outright suppression of critical statements. Frequently this assumes such dimensions and scope, and takes place in such forms, that the CC has to intervene in order to restore truth and justice and to support honest people who back the interests of the cause. I have already had occasion to speak on this question, but matters are being corrected slowly. Take the articles in the central press for January alone, and you will see that persecution for criticism is anything but a rare phenomenon.

In this regard, the efforts of the mass news media to develop criticism and self-criticism in our society must be supported. Soviet people have duly assessed the merits of the media's position in the struggle for restructuring. The central newspapers and magazines have added more than 14 million new readers, and Central Television's broadcasts on topical subjects garner audiences of many millions. People are attracted by the boldness and depth with which they pose urgent problems concerning the acceleration of the country's social and economic development or affecting various aspects of the life of society. The Part thinks that materials in the mass news media will continue to be distinguished by their depth, objectivity and lofty civic responsibility.

A great deal can also be said about the positive changes that are taking place in republic and local publications. But far from all of them have as yet really joined in the restructuring; they lack devotion to principle and boldness in posing questions and fail to take a critical attitude toward shortcomings. Many Party committees do not always make proper use of the news media—a powerful lever of restructuring—and in some places Party bodies continue to fetter the media's activity.

While continuing to count on principled and constructive criticism of shortcomings and deficiencies, the Party at the same time expects from the mass news media broader coverage of the work experience of labor collectives, Party, Soviet and economic organizations and executives in the conditions of restructuring. We badly need answers to many burning problems restructuring has raised or will raise, I think. We must help everyone to change their ways more quickly in the spirit of the times. As V.I. **Lenin** said, this organizing function of the press should be strengthened from day to day and it should learn in practice to be a collective agitator, propagandist and organizer of the masses.

There should be clarity on yet another issue. We say that Soviet society should have no zones closed to criticism. This is fully applicable to the mass news media also.

Comrades! Genuine democracy does not exist outside the law or above the law. The 27th Party Congress defined the main areas of development of our legislation and of the strengthening of law and order. In the current Five-Year Plan, extensive work will have to be done to prepare and adopt new laws connected with the development of the economy, the social sphere and culture, the socialist self-government of the people, and expanded guarantees of citizens' rights and liberties.

The Politburo has given its support to a proposal for the drafting of new criminal legislation in the near future. The task has been set of making it correspond more fully to the present conditions of the development of Soviet society, protect the interests and rights of citizens more effectively, and lead to the strengthening of discipline in law and order. We must think out and adopt measures to enhance the role and prestige of Soviet courts, strictly observe the independence of judges, decisively strengthen prosecutor's supervision, and improve the work of investigative agencies.

A draft law of the procedure for filing appeals in the court against illegal actions by officials that infringe the rights of citizens has been prepared and will soon be submitted for discussion. Additional steps have been outlined to improve the work of state arbitration and to expand legal propaganda.

When we talk about the democratization of Soviet society—and this is a fundamental question for us—it is appropriate once again to emphasize the main, defining feature of socialist democracy. What I mean is an organic combination of democracy and discipline, independence and responsibility, and the rights and duties of officials and of every citizen.

Socialist democracy has nothing in common with an "everything goes" attitude, irresponsibility or anarchy. genuine democracy serves every person, protecting his political and social rights, and at the same time it serves every collective and society as a whole, upholding their interests.

Democratization of all spheres of life in Soviet society is important first of all because we link with it the further development of working people's initiative and the use of the entire potential of the socialist system. We need democratization in order to move ahead, in order to ensure that legality grows stronger and justice triumphs in society and that a moral atmosphere, in which man can freely live and fruitfully work, is asserted in it.

All our experience teaches us that in a time of great change the Party, in tackling the boldest and most difficult tasks, has invariably turned to Komsomol, to young people, to their enthusiasm and dedication to the cause of socialism, their intransigence toward stagnation, and their commitment to what is progressive. Today, when we talk about the need for democratic changes and about expanding the people's real participation in accomplishing the tasks of restructuring, the question of the position taken by the younger generation assumes enormous political importance.

I would like to repeat once more to the Plenum: We can be proud of our young people, and we pay tribute to their labor—this is both factually true and politically correct.

But the times demand even more energy from everyone. Of course, young people, who have a stake in restructuring, should act more vigorously. Party organizations, their committees and the Komsomol should open prospects for the younger generation and act in such a way that young people in fact become energetic participants in the changes. Preparations for the next Komsomol congress must be approached from these positions.

In work with the Komsomol, we must increase our attention to labor, ideological-political and moral tempering and be quicker and more resolute in getting rid of everything that is unneeded In work with young people, above all an odifying tone and administrative fiat Yes, all of these things exist, and they must be talked about. And whatever the explanation may be—lack of faith in the reasonableness and maturity of the social aspirations and actions of young people, mere overcautiousness, or a desire to mitigate life's difficulties for one's children—we cannot agree with this position.

No, comrades, there is no real way to shape the personality and mold the civic stance of a young person except by including him in a real way in all public affairs. Nothing can make up for a lack of concrete experience. That is why it is important to change the existing situation. What do I have in mind?

Above all, this involves more trust in young people, trust that combines able assistance and freedom in making comradely criticism of mistakes, greater independence in organizing work, studies, everyday life and leisure, and more responsibility for one's own deeds and conduct. It also pre-supposes the right to participate in the management of society at all levels.

An important area of the democratization of public life is the promotion of non-Party comrades to leadership positions. This is a question of principle. One solid guarantee of the health and progress of socialist society is the political and job-related growth of front-ranking workers, peasants, engineers, researchers, physicians, teachers and employees in the service sphere and the constant identification and promotion of talented individuals from among the people.

One sometimes encounters the following viewpoint: The question of promoting non-Party people is out of date, it is said, since there are now more than 19 million people in the CPSU. I think that this is a mistaken opinion. To proceed on this basis means deforming the Party's relationship with the masses, and, frankly, infringing on the constitutional rights of citizens, and by doing so we also restrict our possibilities with respect to personnel. We have had, and have now, a good many wonderful examples of fruitful activity in leadership posts by non-Party comrades. They head plants and factories, collective farms and state farms, construction organizations, research and teaching collectives and engineering services, and they are actively engaged in volunteer work.

The open selection of people for promotion—from among both Communists and non-Party people—would be in keeping with the tasks of democratization and the enlistment of broad masses of the working people in management.

In this respect, there is also the question of promoting women to leadership positions on a broader scale. At present, many women are working, and working successfully, in Party and state posts, in science, public health, education and culture, in light industry, trade and consumer services. Today the country needs to have them become even more actively involved in managing the economy and culture, on both the Union and the republic level. We have the opportunities for this. All we have to do is give women trust and support.

Comrades! There is no fundamental question that we could have resolved in the past or can resolve today without taking into account the fact that we live in a multinational country. There is scarcely any need to prove the importance of socialist principles in the development of national relations. It is socialism that put an end to national oppression and inequality, to every kind of infringement on people's rights because of nationality, and that ensured the economic and spiritual progress of all nations and nationalities. In short, the successes of our Party's nationalities policy are indisputable, and we take rightful pride in them.

But we are obliged to look at the real picture and the prospects for the development of national relations. Today when democracy and self-government are expanding, when the national self-consciousness of all nations and nationalities is growing rapidly and the processes of internationalization are becoming deeper, special importance attaches to the timely and fair resolution of emerging questions on the only possible basis—in the interests of their further convergence and in the interests of all of society.

In this connection, it must be said that the negative phenomena and deformations that we have been combating have also appeared in the sphere of national relations. Now and then, there have been manifestations of parochialism, tendencies to national exclusiveness, feelings of national conceit, and even incidents similar to those that occurred quite recently in Alma-Ata.

The events in Alma-Ata and what preceded them require serious analysis and a principled assessment. We still have to sort all this out carefully. But it is clear even now that what happened should make not only the Communists of Kazakhstan but all Party organizations and their committees face up to the problems of the further development of national relations and of stepping up internationalist upbringing. It is especially important to protect the rising generation from the corrupting influence of nationalism. V.I.**Lenin** taught, "to be able to be an internationalist in deed" and it is our purpose not to interrupt this study.

Our entire experience shows that only consistent, staunch internationalism can success-fully counter nationalist epidemics. Everything that we have accomplished has been accom-plished by working together. If one region produces oil, another provides it with bread. Those who grow cotton receive machines. Each ton of bread, each gram of gold, each ton of cotton, coal and oil, and each machine—from the simplest to the most sophisticated contain a particle of labor of all Soviet people, of the entire country, of our whole multi-national union.

In the spirit of **Lenin**'s demands and in the spirit of the directives of the 27th Congress, we must firmly adhere to a line of seeing to it that all of the country's nations and nationalities are represented in Party, state and economic agencies, including those at the Union level, and that the composition of leadership cadres reflects the country's nationality structure as fully as possible.

Needless to say, we are not talking about the mechanical allocation of places and positions on the basis of nationality—that would mean a vulgarization of the very idea of internationalism. Political, business and moral qualities—that is what determines an official's profile in all instances. We must also not lose sight of the special sensitivity of the national aspects of various problems or of folk traditions in the way of life and in people's psychology and behavior. All of this must be given very careful consideration.

I should say, comrades, that certain leaders' approach to the resolution of questions involving relations between nationalities sometimes lacks the proper responsibility.

From time to time, misunderstandings arise in relations between neighboring districts or provinces of various republics. Sometimes they take the form of disputes that even develop into lawsuits, while officials of Party and Soviet agencies, instead of forestalling or squelching passions, try to avoid fundamental solutions. Political officials must act skillfully in such situations and cool unhealthy emotions.

Our theoretical thinking is greatly in arrears to the actual practice of national relations. What I have in mind is the obviously inadequate study of questions of a nationalities policy corresponding to the present stage of the country's development. After all, it is a fact, comrades, that instead of conducting objective studies of real phenomena in the sphere of national relations and an analysis of actual social, economic and spiritual processes—which in their essence are very complicated and contradictory—some of our social scientists have for a long time preferred to create "panegyrical" tracts that sometimes seemed more like starry-eyed toasts than serious scientific research.

It must be admitted that the mistakes committed in the field of national relations and their manifestations remained in the shadows, and it was not accepted practice to talk about them. This led to the negative consequences that we now have to deal with.

At the 27th Congress, we emphasized the unshakability of our Party's tradition, stemming from V.I. **Lenin**: to show special sensitivity and circumspection in everything that has to do with the development of national relations or affects the interests of every nation and nationality or people's national feelings, and to promptly resolve questions that arise in this sphere.

One of the traditions of Bolshevism is a principled struggle against all manifestations of national narrow-mindedness and conceit, nationalism and chauvinism, parochialism, Zionism and anti-Semitism, in whatever form they take. We must constantly bear in mind that nationalism and proletarian internationalism are two opposing policies, two opposing world views.

Proceeding from these positions, we will be firm and principled. People's national feelings deserve respect, they cannot be ignored, but they also cannot be trifled with. Those who would like to play on nationalistic or chauvinistic prejudices should entertain no illusions on this score and should expect no indulgences.

Principles, comrades, are principles precisely because they are not to be forgone; No doubt, this position—the principled, Leninist position—will be backed by the entire Party, by the entire multi-national Soviet people

III. **Personnel Policy in Conditions of Restructuring**
Comrades!

I think that we all realize full well that success of reorganization depends to a decisive extent on how fast and profound our cadres' perception will be of the need for changes, and how constructive and purposeful their effort will be in implementing the Party's policy. What is necessary today is a personnel policy to match the tasks of reorganization, the need for accelerating social and economic development. In formulating its initial requirements, we ought to take into account both the lessons of the past and the new large-scale tasks life presently poses.

A mighty reserve of highly skilled personnel potential has been created during the years of socialist construction in the country, and the immeasurably higher educational and cultural level attained by workers and peasants and by the entire people is creating favorable conditions for the constant replenishment and renewal of this reserve. Everything that we have accomplished, everything that we have attained is the result of Soviet people's work and is due to our cadres' selfless support.

At the same time, at this plenary session it is also necessary to talk about the mistakes in personnel policy that occurred in recent years and led to major shortcomings in the activity of several elements of the Party, state and economic administrative apparatus and to negative phenomena in society. Many errors could have been avoided if Party agencies had always and consistently conducted a principled and effective personnel policy and had ensured high efficiency in all elements of Party leadership and economic management.

Needless to say, we cannot limit ourselves today to mere recognition of the mistakes that were made. In order to avoid similar errors in the future, we must draw lessons from the past.

What exactly are these lessons?

The first one is the need to promptly resolve urgent personnel questions within the Party CC itself and its Politburo—above all from the viewpoint of ensuring continuity in the leadership and the influx of fresh forces. The violation of this natural process led at a certain stage to a weakening of the work capacity of the Politburo and the Secretariat and, for that matter, of the CPSU CC as a whole and its administrative apparatus, as well as of the government.

In fact, comrades, after the April [1985] plenary session a large part of the Secretariat and a large number of the department heads of the CPSU CC were replaced in a short time, and virtually the entire membership of the Presidium of the USSR Council of Minister was changed. These replacements had to be made, because for a long time there had been no renewal of the membership of the CC or the government and no constant replenishment of them with new personnel, as life demanded. Ultimately, all this had an effect on policy-making and on the Party's practical activity in guiding society.

This cannot and must not be repeated. So that the process of renewal will not be interrupted and continuity not broken, the CPSU CC, the Politburo and Secretariat of the CC, the government and the top echelons of the Party and state leadership should be open to an influx of fresh forces from various spheres of activity. This way of posing the question is fully in keeping with the Leninist understanding of personnel policy and the interests of the Party and the people.

Needless to say, the Party CC has performed an enormous amount of work and is continuing to do so. But the level of this work should never fall, under any circumstances. On the contrary, it should constantly rise and meet the demands made by life, the development of society and the international situation. Any weakening in the activity of the Central Committee is impermissible.

The CPSU CC is called upon to be a model of the implementation of Leninist ideas, principles and methods in work. Our plenary sessions should discuss truly major questions of the life of the Party and the country's domestic and international situation. They should be discussed freely, candidly, with a sense of lofty responsibility, and in an atmosphere of ideological solidarity—but from a broad comparison of viewpoints.

In this connection, I would like to give special mention to the role of the members of the CC and their rights and responsibility. At plenary sessions, it is necessary to ensure the right of every member of the CC to pose questions and to participate in the collective creative discussion of those questions. In the Party—and all the more so at plenary sessions of the CC—there can be no individuals who are beyond criticism, just as there can be none who do not have the right to criticize.

There are many things here that will have to be corrected. Let us say honestly that for several years there were a good many burning problems of concern to the Party and the people that remained off the agendas of plenums. Comrades will recall that more than once plenums of the CC were brief and pro forma. During their entire term on the CC, many members did not have an opportunity to participate in discussions or even to submit a proposal. This atmosphere at plenary sessions of the CC also had an effect on the work style of local Party committees and organizations.

The second lesson from our past experience, comrades, is that we must not underestimate political and theoretical training or the ideological and moral tempering of personnel. Otherwise, the result will be very serious disruptions in the activity of Party committees as bodies of political leadership.

In recent years, these criteria have not always been taken into account in the selection, placement and upbringing of personnel. Frequently an employee's knowledge of the specific features of some branch of production, science, engineering or technology, or his strong will, was the prime consideration. There is no doubt that all this is important, but at the same time one must not lose sight of such leadership qualities as breadth of ideological and theoretical insight, political maturity, moral principles, and the ability to persuade and lead people.

One must admit openly and honestly that the technocratic, "administrative-pressure" style of work did considerable damage to the Party's cause, above all to work with people—that is, the main aspect of the Party's activity. Becoming absorbed in economic work and in a number of instances assuming functions that were not properly theirs, many Party officials slackened their attention to political questions and phenomena of social significance in the sphere of the economy and in social and spiritual life.

Of course, there are objective factors at the basis of this style, too. They are linked with the unresolved state of a number of questions of the management of the national economy and with the lack of an efficient economic mechanism. In this situation, many Party committees, aware of their responsibility and their duty to the people, have been forced to assume the task of solving a considerable number of economic problems. This has been going on for a good many years, has become deeply rooted in the style and methods of work, and has led to a certain deformation in the principles of Party leadership and in the very composition of our personnel.

Large-scale measures to restructure management and the economic mechanisms in the country open up wide opportunities for refining the work of the Party committees and organizations, enhancing Party influence in all spheres of the life of society and practising a political approach to all problems under construction.

I want to emphasize that no one can relieve Party committees of their concerns about and responsibility for the economic situation. As I have already said, what we are talking about is an improvement in the methods of Party leadership that would rule out the usurpation of the functions of economic agencies and petty tutelage over them.

The third lesson we should learn is that, paradoxically, two opposing tendencies coexisted in the personnel policy of recent years. What do I have in mind, comrades?

On the one hand, stagnant phenomena were manifested rather strongly in the personnel corps. Necessary personnel changes and an influx of new people did not take place, sometimes for decades, in the secretariats of a number of Party committees and among officials of Soviet and economic agencies at the local, republic and Union levels.

In mentioning this, I do not want to cast the slightest aspersions on the many hundreds and thousands of outstanding employees, especially at the district and city levels, who have devoted all their energy and knowledge to selfless service to the Party and the people and are continuing to do so. Through their many years of honest work and truly deserved prestige, they have confirmed their right to hold leadership posts. The people highly appreciate the difficult work of the CPSU and their great services and pay tribute to them.

I think that the well-known, and rather well-learned, proposition that personnel stability is necessary in principle needs no proof. But we must not take this proposition to extremes—to the point of absurdity, if you will. We know only too well what this led to and what price is being paid even now for the artificial stability that essentially turned into personnel stagnation.

On the other hand, there has also been another, no less alarming tendency in personnel work, especially at the level of the primary elements of the national economy. I am talking about the heavy turnover, the real musical-chairs process among the executive personnel of industrial enterprises, construction projects, collective farms, state farms and other organizations.

You know how great the role of the highly qualified organizers of production is. The leaders of work collectives—Communists and non-Party people—are the Party's main support in the pursuance of its socio-economic policy. They shoulder a great number of most diverse tasks. In this case I want to ask one question: How could it happen that there was a complete turnover of the heads of labor collectives in many districts and provinces within just a few years?

This can only happen when vital work with personnel and real concern for their political and professional growth and for giving them practical assistance are relegated to the background and replaced by administrative fiat, by hasty and sometimes rash judgments about their activity and capabilities. I think that Party committees should take this very serious reproach as referring to themselves and draw the proper conclusions.

Unfortunately, there are also Party committees and secretaries that cover up blunders, and even failures, in their work with sham exactingness toward personnel and a fake devotion to principle, without thinking about either the essence of the matter or people's fates.

In this connection, I want to mention one other impermissible phenomenon. I mean the intolerance of some executives for independent actions and thinking by subordinates. It frequently happens that, as soon as one employee or another begins to express independent opinions that do not coincide with the opinion of the secretary of the Party committee or the head of the ministry, department, enterprise, institution or organization, these officials try to get rid of that employee as quickly as possible, using any pretexts, sometimes even specious ones. As if this would be better. Better for whom? For the cause? Nothing of the kind! It's always worse for the cause.

In this respect, too, we must all learn from V.I. **Lenin**, who knew how, better than anyone else, to unite people, to organize harmonious work, to support imaginative people, to listen attentively to the opinions of Party comrades and, if need be, patiently make them change their minds. We must learn devotion to principle, exactingness and attentiveness.

The fourth lesson for our personnel work is to increase responsibility for assigned tasks, to enhance discipline, and to create an atmosphere of mutual exactingness. How could it happen, comrades, that many leadership posts—at the district, city, province, republic, and even the Union level—were held for decades by executives who could not cope with their duties, by people who were undependable and undisciplined?

The consequences are well known. For many years a number of branches, including ferrous metallurgy, the coal industry, railroad transport, the machine tool industry, the farm machinery industry, the meat and dairy industry and several others, were headed by executives who did not ensure the accomplishment of their assigned tasks. Everyone seemed to know this—the state of affairs in these branches was frequently criticized at sessions of the USSR Supreme Soviet, at plenary sessions of the Central Committee, and even at Party Congresses. But everything remained the same.

Were not there provinces, republics, cities and districts in which production plans were not fulfilled for many years and social questions were neglected? At the same time, their leaders bore no responsibility for failures in work. They got away with everything.

The same can be said about some executives of enterprises, economic organizations, public health, educational, scientific and cultural institutions and news organs: They have neglected matters for a long time and are not coping with their duties, but on the other hand they know how to expand upon reality, as the saying goes, and have an easy manner. Quite recently, this was sufficient for them to retain their executive armchairs.

It also happens that one executive or another turns out to be in the wrong place and, as they say, doesn't pull his weight. His misfortune is that he has obtained a post and work that are beyond his capacity. How should we act in such cases? It would seem that such mistakes must be admitted and rectified and, without dramatizing them, that the person should be given work that he is able to do.

We should not and cannot be "nice guys" at the expense of the interests of the Party, society and the people. The Party's and the people's interests are above everything else—this is our immutable law. Genuine concern for personnel has nothing in common with complacency and all-forgivingness, philanthropy and ingratiation. We should learn this lesson well, too.

And, finally, there is yet another lesson. It is logical to raise this question at our plenary session: Why have all these accumulated problems in personnel work remained unattended and unsolved for a long time? How could this happen? As you understand, the question is a very serious one.

In the Politburo's opinion, the main factor was the weakness of democratic principles in personnel work. I have already spoken, in a fundamental way, about inner-Party democracy as the principal guarantee of the implementation of the Party's strategic course and the tasks of restructuring. Proposals on such a cardinal question of democratization as the formation of elective bodies in the CPSU have been expressed as well.

Now I would like to single out the question of enhancing the role of all elective bodies. One must frankly admit that, if they had operated vigorously both in the Party and in the state, in the trade unions and other public organizations, many serious deficiencies in personnel work could have been avoided.

Let us look at life with our eyes open, as they say: Excessive growth has taken place in the role of executive agencies, to the detriment of elected agencies. At first glance, everything seems to be proceeding normally. Plenary sessions, [Soviet] sessions and meetings of other elected bodies are held regularly. But their work is often overformalized, and questions of secondary importance or ones that have been decided beforehand are submitted for discussion. As a result, proper control is lacking over the activity of executive agencies and their leaders. It must be said that some comrades have begun to look on elected agencies as a kind of burden that presents only difficulties and obstacles. That's how far things have gone!

The result is a reduced role for deputies to Soviets and members of Party and other collective agencies in the formation of executive committees, in the selection of personnel and in monitoring their activity. Is this not indicated by the nature and style of the relationships between the regular administrative apparatus and the members of elected agencies? Quite often one encounters attempts by apparatus employees to give orders to members of Party committees, other public organizations and deputies to Soviets. In fact, what happens is that democratic mechanisms for the formation and operation of elected agencies are proclaimed but in a great many cases they do not work well, and hence are not effective enough.

That is why, returning once more to what has been said about the development of socialist democracy in the conditions of restructuring, I want to again emphasize the topicality and enormous significance of the proposals that have been formulated on these questions. We must work out and implement measures that will ensure a decisive role for collective, elected agencies. No executive agency, let alone its administrative apparatus, can have the right to usurp the functions of an elected body or dominate it.

The necessary prerequisites—political and legal—should be created for elected agencies to exercise effective control over the executive apparatus, its formation and activity. This will be a reliable guarantee against many mistakes, including mistakes in personnel work.

I think that the plenary session participants understand very well the fundamental importance of this way of posing the question and the urgent need to resolve it.

One of the reasons for the serious deficiencies in personnel policy is the weakening of the role of control agencies, both in the Party and in the sphere of state and public organizations. Many warning signals about abuses and violations in a number of regions and branches of the national economy and in province, territory and republic Party committees escaped their attention. The control agencies' work was often restricted to superficial checkups and pro forma financial audits, the examination of various complaints and minor squabbles. These matters also require attention, of course, but it is impermissible to reduce the agencies' work to them alone, especially now.

The 27th CPSU Congress gave a new thrust to the activity of the control agencies. It is important that all of them, from the district to the central level, justify their lofty purpose and set an example of devotion to principle and fairness.

In general, comrades, we cannot and must not repeat the mistakes of the past. And I don't think anyone will allow us to do so.

These are the main lessons of personnel policy, on which, in the Politburo's opinion, it is necessary to report to the plenary session.

The principal conclusion to be drawn from them is that we must seriously update personnel policy, free it from distortions and omissions, and make it truly up-to-date, more active and purposeful and inextricably linked with the key areas of the struggle for accelerating social and economic development. I repeat that the point at issue is not just perfection of the organization of the work with cadres, but of outlining a personnel policy consistent with the tasks of reorganization. It is not only with such a broad approach that work with the cadres will serve towards carrying out deep-going and revolutionary change.

V.I.**Lenin** taught us to approach the work with personnel above all politically, view it in inseparable connection with the essence of the problems being resolved at the given stage and select personnel "by the new standards, according to the new tasks." What does this mean as applied to the present-day stage in social development?

Today the decisive criterion in personnel policy, a kind of tuning fork for it, is the attitude of personnel toward restructuring and the task of accelerating the country's social and economic development, their attitude not in words but in deeds. Needless to say, we should take into account the fact that the formation and activity of cadres for a long time did not proceed in the best of conditions. Therefore, changes do not come easily. We will have to do painstaking and persistent work to restructure the personnel corps.

We have resolutely embarked on a course aimed at supporting enterprising, thinking and energetic people, who can and want to advance boldly and know how to achieve success. We have many such people. The decisions of the April Plenum and of the 27th Congress have lent them wings and given broad scope for creative activities. Look how the talent has veen revealed again strikingly and powerfully of such economic managerts as Vladimir Pavlovich **Kabaidze** from Ivanova, Boris Ivanovich **Fomin** from Leningrad "Elektrostal" works, Anatoly Alekseevich **Parshin** from the Taganrog "Krasnyi kotelshchik" works, Ivan Vasilevich **Frantsenuk** from the Novolipetsk metallurgical works, the director of the Novocherkasskii clothing factory Raisa Georgieva **Roshchinska**, the director of the Donets mining management, "Socialist Donbass", Iurii Ivanovich **Baranov**, manager of Trust no.18, "Mosoblsel'stroi" Nikolai Il'ich **Travkin**, director of the Belorussian state-farm complex "Mir", Aleksandr Nikolaevich **Duduk**, the famous Kuban brigade leader, Mikhail Ivanovich **Klepnikov**, the state farm chief Vasilii Dmitrievich **Tereshchenko** from Stavropol, Mikhail Grigor'evich **Vagin**, from Gor'kovskii, Iurii Fedorovich **Bugakov** from Novosibirsk province, and many, many others.

Of course, we must resolutely rid ourselves of such methods, if they can be called that, as dressings down, rebukes and reprimands, which are still often employed even now. We are for restructuring, but not for shaking up personnel. We must respect people, comrades, and put more trust in them.

Today everyone has an opportunity to display his capabilities. We should help those who want to work with both advice and comradely exactingness. But as for those who cling to the old ways and remain indifferent to the changes taking place, or those who simply oppose them—they are not going our way, of course.

Thus, the attitude toward restructuring and real actions to implement it are the decisive approach in evaluating personnel. Needless to say, we must take into account other basic qualities as well. Above all, I have in mind implacability toward shortcomings, routine, indifference and passiveness and commitment to everything that is advanced and progressive.

Restructuring requires competence and a high level of professionalism from personnel. Today we cannot get along without up-to-date and all-round training, without thoroughgoing knowledge in questions of production, science, technology, management, economics, the organization of labor, incentives and psychology. In general, we must put the country's intellectual potential into play to the greatest extent possible and substantially increase its creative return.

Good organization and discipline are assuming increasing importance. They are necessary everywhere, but are especially important in conditions of modern production, with the broad application of the latest technologies. In recent years there has been a noticeable increase in the economic growth rates after setting things in order and dealing with carelessness.

Yet this task remains urgent.

Impaired discipline and lowered responsibility have put down too deep roots and are still making themselves felt in a painful way. It was criminal irresponsibility and slackness that were the main causes of such tragic events as the accident at the Chernobyl Atomic Power Station, the sinking of the steamship *Admiral Nakhimov* and a number of air and railway accidents, each of which entailed loss of life.

We must create everywhere an atmosphere that would rule out every possibility of a repetition of such things. Good organization, efficiency and assiduity should become a law for everyone.

Finally, a highly important demand is lofty morality on the part of our personnel, such human traits as honesty, incorruptibility and modesty. We now know, not only from the past but also from current experience, that we will not be able to accomplish the tasks of restructuring without strengthening the moral health of society. It is not happenstance that today we have been having sharp collisions with negative phenomena in the moral sphere. I have in mind the struggle to eradicate drunkenness, embezzlement, bribetaking, abuse of office and favoritism.

Everything that is connected with the moral image of Party members, above all of leaders, is perceived by society in an especially acute way. Our prime task is to restore the pure and honest image of the Communist executive, an image on which a certain shadow has been cast by the crimes of a number of degenerates.

In general conmrades, taking into account the demands of the times we will have to resolutely readjust work with the cadres in all branches of the economy, in all areas of social life, in all echelons of the leadership, both in the centre and in the provinces.

The Politburo understands the essence and main task of today's personnel policy above all as increasing the Party's exactingness toward itself and toward its cadres. Deepening the reorganization of society means rebuilding the work done by the Party and the cadres at all levels—from the CC to primary organizations. This means creatively comprehending and consistently pursuing Lenin's principles and norms of Party life in all sectors.

How is reorganization proceeding in the Party? What example is set by the Party committees, Party leaders and activists?

Today we can say that most Party committees and their leaders have tackled this job with a high degree of responsibility and with sincere desire. Many of them have still not achieved their goals, but with each passing day they are gaining experience and are operating more confidently. These changes are creating reliable prerequisites for accelerating our movement.

All Party personnel are taking the test of restructuring. But they are taking it in different ways. A visible gap has formed between those who are moving ahead resolutely and those who are marking time. The school of restructuring does not come easy to some Party leaders. They can in no way give up the central-control functions that are not proper attributes of Party committees or the desire to resolve questions for everyone—to keep everything in their hands, as the saying goes. But this, as in the past, impedes growth in the responsibility of personnel for their assigned tasks and the development of their initiative and independence.

Instead of developing innovative searches, Party officials frequently react badly to people's initiative and activeness, regarding these traits as all but a natural disaster. But after all, the prime duty of Party committees in the conditions of restructuring is to head the creativity of the masses and help people to eradicate shortcomings as quickly as possible and organize things properly.

At the same time, we must warn comrades against artificially speeding up events and putting the cart before the horse. Restructuring and the acceleration of our movement are based on the objective laws of the development of society. But, as in any social movement, the role of the subjective, personal factor is quite great here. Its influence can be either positive or negative. Therefore, it is extremely important that the process of renewal, which affects human lives in a very sensitive way, be reliably protected against relapses into naked administrative fiat and mechanical approaches to work. Devaluation of the concept of restructuring must not be allowed anywhere, in any element of our social and production system. We must have our eyes open and react immediately when timeserving, personal ambitions and selfish calculations appear under the banner of restructuring, when concrete work on restructuring is supplanted by empty talk and twaddle.

I want to repeat: We will not be able to cope with the tasks of restructuring without the development of democracy, without the broad participation of the working people. Party committees and all personnel must learn to work in conditions of deepening democracy and the growing political and labor activeness of the people.

There have been many occasions when one might become convinced that the process of change tends to have a stronger momentum when the district and city Party committees are more energetic and work in the new manner. This is only understandable. They are the closest to the Primary Party Organizations and work collectives and hence to the frontline of the struggle to speed up the country's social and economic development.

Most of these [district and city Party] committees have taken correct positions and have begun to resolutely and consistently implement the Party's course aimed at restructuring.

At the same time, a study of the state of affairs on the local level, articles in the press and letters from working people to the Party CC indicate that a good many city and district Party committees have personnel who continue to live in the past, to operate in the old way, and, as it were, remain on the sidelines of restructuring. Even if this involved just one city or district Party committee, it still could not be ignored. But in this case we are talking about a widespread phenomenon. Comrades, this should be an object of our concern. In many instances, such a situation in city and district Party committees is explained by the work style and methods of the committees' secretaries and the stance they take.

I think we will be acting correctly if we pay more attention to this highly important level of the Party and help the district and city Party committees to take an active stance in restructuring as quickly as possible. The Primary Party Organizations then will also work still better and lead the work collectives to the set goals. We see how the communists' activity is steadily growing and how inertia and formalism are gradually receding from the work of Party organizations. But there is still a great deal to be done also in this respect. The Primary Party Organizations need efficient aid and support.

An immense responsibility for implementing the strategic course aimed at accelerating social and economic development rests with economic personnel. A changeover is under way in the country from administrative to economic methods of management and to a responsible and creative way of handling affairs. The staff of factories and amalgamations today are being provided with large funds and amounts of materials and equipment to modernize the production facilities and solve social issues. The managers are being granted broad rights not only to make whatever tactical maneuvers are expedient but also to pursue long-term aims within the Five-Year plan period and beyond. In short, a new economic, social and political situation is developing, in which an energetic and competent executive can reveal his abilities well.

Most economic personnel are welcome the important measures undertaken by the Party and the government to reform management and are joining in the practical implementation of these measures in an increasingly active way. We already see a good beginning in the realization of many useful initiatives. The experience of Leningrad and Kharkov in conversting factories to working in shifts is catching on and bringing the first benefits.

In Leningrad itself and Leningrad Province, virtually all leading enterprises have switched to two- or three-shift operations. This has made it possible to increase the number of people employed on the second shift by almost 50,000. Fixed assets are now being used better and updated more quickly. Now their basic funds are being better utilized and more quickly put to work. It seems possible to free up 350,000 sq. m. for active use and up to 120,000 sq. m. less are needed for the new structures. According to preliminary estimates, all this will provide a saving of over 100 million rubles in capital investments, the bulk of which can be channeled into the construction of housing and other social facilities.

The executives and specialists of associations and enterprises that, following the example of the Volga Automotive Plant [in Togliatti] and the Frunze Machine-Building Association in Sumy, shifted to full economic accountability and self-financing at the beginning of the year are displaying considerable creativity.

An interesting experience in mastering the new methods of economic management has been amassed by the Belorussian Railroad and a number of other railroads in the country; this has ensured improvement in the branch's work indices and has raised labor productivity. Labor collectives in a number of provinces of the Ukraine have displayed sharp wits and proprietary enterprise in launchings a wide-ranging movement for resource conservation.The initiative of mine—and foundry—worker teams looking for, and tapping, latent reserves to meet their targets ahead of schedule also deserves to be supported. Labor collectives in Sverdlovsk, Lipetsk and certain other cities are setting a good example in solving housing and other social problems.

In the countryside, the scale of the cultivation of grain and a number of other crops on the basis of the introduction of industrial technologies is expanding. Economic-accountability contract collectives, which are rapidly increasing the production of agricultural products and heightening economic efficiency, are being organized on collective farms and state farms.

All the same, it must be said frankly that the process of the mastering by personnel of up-to-date methods of economic management and approaches to work is proceeding with difficulty, in a contradictory way, and not without painful phenomena and relapses into the old ways. A vivid example of this is the introduction of state product acceptance. Understanding the enormous importance of this measure, many collectives have made good preparations for work in the new conditions. Their work is proceeding, although not without difficulties, labor discipline is growing, and output quality is improving.

But there have also been personnel who bailed out when confronted with high demands. Instead of rolling up their sleeves and tackling the job of improving quality, they began scaring themselves and others with possible complications, conflict situations and even plant shut-downs.

Comrades, I am by no means oversimplifying the situation. But one thing is clear: We Communists and all Soviet people can no longer tolerate a situation in which for years many enterprises turn out products that are hopelessly obsolete, bring serious complaints from consumers, and hold back the country's scientific and technical progress. We have tackled a big task, and we must carry it through to conclusion.

The changeover to economic methods of management and the expansion of the rights of associations and enterprises are creating a new situation for ministries and departments. At the June (1986) plenary session of the CC, we discussed questions of restructuring the style and methods of their work. What has been done since then?

Changes in the work of ministries and departments are taking place, although slowly and not without pain. The branch headquarters are taking a direct part in drafting proposals on switching enterprises to the new conditions of economic management. They are giving more attention to questions of scientific and technical policy, the reconstruction of enterprises and shifting to the output of goods that meet today's demands.

We have strengthened some branches and their subdivisions with capable people. As a rule, energetic specialists who want to run things in the new way and to ensure the introduction of up-to-date work methods have been put in leadership posts. This line must be continued, the activity of the administrative apparatus of ministries and departments must be vigorously improved, and it must be replenished with enterprising and highly skilled personnel.

At the same time, we continue to run into red tape and irresponsibility in the work of ministries and departments to implement the resolutions of the Party and the government. The administrative apparatus is, as it were, a prisoner of old regulations and instructions, operates out of inertia, and refuses to forgo its rights.

Comrades, this is not the first time that we have drawn the attention of executives and personnel of the administrative apparatus of ministries and departments to the need for a fundamental restructuring of their activity. This gives everyone an opportunity to join in work and to master new approaches to the tasks at hand. But we must not allow a ministry or its personnel to be inactive, let alone obstruct restructuring. This warning from the plenary sessions's rostrum is necessary, since what is involved here are the interests of the state and the people and major policy questions. It is appropriate here to recall **Lenin**'s dictum: "The *apparat* exists for policy..., not policy for the apparatus."

Personnel will be placed in new conditions by the restructuring of foreign economic activity, the granting to many ministries and associations of the right to sell on the foreign market, and the granting to all enterprises of the right to enter into direct joint-production ties with partners in the socialist countries. This is something the branch ministries have long sought.

But it must be well understood that success in foreign economic activity is possible only if active use is made of the achievements of science and technology, if personnel receive the appropriate training, if new markets are developed, etc. The main precondition for realizing the opportunities that have been opened up is developing the production of goods of world-level quality.

After the decisions were adopted much time and much effort were spent on various organizational matters, as specifying rights and duties, and the relations between foreign trade organizations and the branch managerial bodies. But the organizational period has already ended.

Now it is necessary to move efforts to the plane of practical deeds, to start vigorously the developments of ties with all foreign partners, first of all in socialist countries.

I have already had the occasion to say that the success of the strategy of acceleration depends first of all on how we are fulfilling the tasks of scientific and technological progress, on how skillfully we are combining the advantages of socialism with all the achievements of the scientific and technological revolution.

Success in the strategy of acceleration depends above all on how we tackle the tasks of scientific and technical progress and how skillfully we combine the advantages of socialism with the achievements of the scientific and technological revolution.

Real achievements here are determined by the state of scientific knowledge, by the advancing of original ideas that can be embodied in fundamentally new machinery and technologies enabling us to make progress in the leading areas of science and engineering. This is the strategic task that restructuring sets for science.

In carrying out this task, everything is important—from the admission of students to higher schools and the quality of specialists' training to the replenishment of the Academy of Sciences with talented scientists, from the work of student scientific societies to the research programs of leading Academy and branch institutes, from the creative atmosphere in scientific collectives to the most effective forms of organizing science and providing it with incentives.

At present, the integration of science with production has taken on special importance. An important role in this matter has been assigned to interbranch scientific and technical complexes. More than 20 of them have already been created. We link great hopes with the activity of these complexes insofar as accelerating the development of new ideas, and especially introducing scientific and technical achievements, are concerned. For this reason, we must show more attention to the work of the interbranch scientific and technical complexes. The Presidium of the USSR Academy of Sciences and the relevant ministries and departments must provide them with everything they need, give them the necessary assistance, and promote effective activity in every way.

Such important questions as the effective coordination of Academy, higher-school and branch science, the integration of the efforts of the natural, technical and social sciences, the comprehensiveness of research, the depth of the level at which fundamental problems are posed and increasing the effectiveness of specific development projects remain crucial and largely unresolved.

I would like to say, addressing our scientists and all scientific personnel on behalf of the plenary session, that if science is to be an active participant in restructuring it must restructure itself in many ways. Life is hurrying us on. He who is not ahead in scientific ideas risks falling behind in everything. That is how the question is posed by our time—a time of the most profound changes in science and technology, changes that are still unknown to mankind.

This obliges Party committees, ministries, departments and economic agencies to face up to the requirements of science, which should constantly feel that it has businesslike support. We know that the Presidium of the USSR Academy of Sciences and its President, Academician G.I. **Marchuk**, have some interesting ideas and proposals on this score. I can assure you that they will find support in the CC and the government.

Prospects for social, economic, scientific, technical and spiritual progress are grounded in large part in the system and quality of education. We have begun the reform of general-education and vocational schools. As you evidently know, the reform is not a simple matter, and therefore it requires unremitting attention along all lines—from strengthening the material and technical base of the schools to the content, forms and methods of the instructional and upbringing process. Decisions have been adopted on restructuring higher and specialized secondary education and on raising the salaries of higher-school personnel, as well as the stipends of [higher- school] students and graduate students. All this will create favorable preconditions for the accelerated development of science and production and the fulfillment of the decisions of the Party Congress. We must carry them out and ensure the fastest possible achievement of high final results.

The system of advanced training and refresher training for specialists will be constructed on a new basis. In today's production conditions, the concrete knowledge, abilities and skills of all personnel should be continuously replenished and improved. The 27th Congress posed the creation of a state system of continuous education as a highly important task that we must accomplish. Only in this way can the competence of personnel be maintained at the level of today's demands, especially in the newer and newest fields of engineering and technology. There is hardly any need to prove how important it is to accelerate the completion of the drafting of proposals on this question.

Finally, a few words about the tasks of the personnel of our planning, financial and other economic agencies. It is now necessary for them to fundamentally restructure their work with an eye to the goals of the economic reform.

The country's economic departments have submitted a good many proposals on the restructuring of management and the economic mechanism. But, frankly speaking, their personnel themselves are slow in restructuring and even, I would say, are lagging behind economic transformations in the sphere of production. But after all, everything taking place there requires substantial changes in the functions of the general economic departments and their local agencies.

The guideline in their work should be the political directives formulated by the 27th Congress. The implementation of the economic reform in the country pursues the goals both of the broad development of independence for the lower levels of the economy and of the further strengthening of the centralized principle in management, with the simultaneous freeing of the center from petty tutelage over branches, associations and enterprises. All personnel, and above all the heads of economic departments, should now act in this vein and give up the old approaches to work.

One more question directly related to the activity of economic- management personnel. The 12th Five-Year Plan directs special attention to the development of the social sphere. This is dictated by the state of affairs in that area. We must more rapidly overcome the gap that has formed between the development levels of the production sphere and the social sphere.

The Party Congress made some serious adjustments in the political directives on these questions, after drawing the conclusion that insufficient attention to the social sphere had become one of the causes of the lag in scientific and technical progress and and in the growth of production efficiency and was impeding the use of available potential.

The fact that for many long years economic managers were not really held accountable for resolving social questions left a serious imprint on their approach to work. This situation must be resolutely corrected. It will be difficult to do so without a firm position by Party committees and without consistent practical steps on the part of the government.

Take a very fresh example. Late last year, the first section of the Astrakhan Gas Complex was commissioned. More than 1.5 billion rubles in capital investments has been put to use there, and an 8,000-strong collective of workers and specialists is at work, but only 3,000 of them have permanent housing. On top of that, a lag in the construction of housing, polyclinics, cafeterias, and other facilities in the social and cultural sphere was incorporated in the plans from the very beginning. Here you have the lamentable result of an incorrect, mistaken approach to social matters at the planning-agency level. The matter must be rectified as quickly as possible. All leading cadres from top to bottom are responsible for conducting a vigorous social policy. Life itself demanded that the interests be given top priority in the activity of leading cadres, while the ability to resolve social questions has become one of the chief criteria of their business and political maturity.

An important role in carrying out the decisions of the 27th Congress belongs to the Soviet, trade union, Komsomol and other public organizations and their personnel. The task of restructuring their activity confronts them in all its magnitude. As a matter of fact, it has already begun.

In what direction should it be continued? This is a question with great political resonance, since it involves some very important institutions of our political system. In carrying out reorganization, one should bear in mind both the current situation and trends in the development of Soviet society in general, of the political system, socialist democracy and the economic mechanism.

I want once again to emphasize the idea that the line aimed at democratization and the creation of a new mechanism of administration and economic management opens up the possibility of achieving the correct combination of political leadership by the Party with an active role for state agencies, trade unions and other public organizations.

We have already adopted basic decisions on improving the activity of the Soviets in present conditions. These decisions will allow the Soviets to prove their worth as genuine bodies of power in their territory. Changes are taking place in the activity of the Soviets, but they cannot satisfy us as yet. We all have a stake in getting the Soviets to begin working properly, in the spirit of the times, as quickly as possible.

Party committees should firmly adopt a line aimed at enhancing the role of the Soviets and not be guilty of unwarranted interference in their affairs, let alone of usurping their functions. It is no less important that the Soviets' executives themselves and the Soviets' administrative apparatus begin to work at full strength and rid themselves of inertia and the habit of constantly looking over their shoulder and waiting for instructions. Democratic principles in the activity of the Soviets and their executive agencies must be strengthened.

At the 27th Congress, we said that there are many questions affecting the fundamental interests of the working people that no one will resolve for the Soviets. This applies to problems of social policy and the improvement of services to the population. However, the Soviets have not fully mastered their new rights and are not making the proper demands on economic managers. This is another reason that last year's plans were not met for many indices of social and cultural construction.

Or take municipal services. How many reproaches with respect to their work are being heard now, especially during subfreezing weather! But after all, this is the direct and vital task of the Soviets. They must fundamentally change their work in improving trade, consumer services, the organization of recreation for the working people and the production of consumer goods, and make broader use of reserves for replenishing food resources.

We are planning important measures in the sphere of public health and public education. They are linked in a very direct way to the activity of the Soviets on various levels. The tasks are mounting, and the Soviets should act more efficiently and more persistently. We have a right to demand this of the personnel who work in the Soviets and in their administrative apparatus. Soviet people expect it of them.

All facets of restructuring affect trade unions. With the increase in the economic independence of enterprises and associations, the trade unions' rights are expanding substantially. At the same time, their responsibility is also increasing significantly in connection with the growth in the powers of labor collectives and the development of self-management. And, of course, no one is relieving the trade unions of their obligations in accomplishing tasks of social policy and defending the working people's interests.

In short, the demands on the personnel of trade union agencies have grown sharply. At present, when the review and election campaign is drawing to an end in trade union organizations and the scheduled congress of the Soviet trade unions is approaching, it is important that the entire complex of topical problems related to reorganization be placed in the focus of attention of the delegates to the congress. Work collectives make up the central link of reorganization. It is there that the trade unions should reveal their potential, should reassess their capabilities and rights and thus increase their contribution to the national cause of socio-economic acceleration.

In launching the struggle for improving the health of society, the Party has proceeded since the very beginning from the premise that this immense work shall be based on the firm foundation of persuasion. Shaping the consciousness of millions of working people in the spirit of restructuring is one of the key directions of ideological activity.

We have succeeded to a certain degree in bringing ideological work closer to life, to the processes taking place in society today. It is largely due to Party organizations, to our propagandists that the ideas of renewal are becoming truly attractive for the masses.

Work on the ideological front is yet to be launched in earnest in many directions, including along the lines of political and economic study, reading of lectures and foreign policy propaganda, atheistic upbringing, and so on.

The CC orients Party organizations toward having the entire Party *aktiv*, all Communists, participate in ideological work. But this in no way removes the tasks of reinforcing ideological sections with highly qualified, trained personnel who have their fingers squarely on the pulse of the times, possess a profound understanding of the essence of the tasks that have been set, and are capable of effectively propagandizing the Party's policy and of persuading and organizing people.

Today's conditions insistently demand that the Party's ideological corps be replenished with people who are thoroughly familiar with economics, jurisprudence, philosophy, sociology, literature and art, who are deeply convinced of the vital necessity of the decisions adopted by the 27th Congress and the course aimed at restructuring.

Comrades! Important new tasks confronting the personnel of Soviet courts, prosecutor's offices, the police and other law-enforcement agencies stem from the need to strengthen socialist legality and law and order in the country.

The CC, attaching great importance to these questions, which are keenly felt by society, recently adopted a special resolution "On the Further Strengthening of Socialist Legality and Law and Order and on Increasing the protection of Citizens' Rights and Legitimate Interests." [For this resolution, see both *Pravda* and *Izvestiia* (30 Nov 86)] It sets important and more difficult tasks for the law-enforcement agencies and their personnel. Party committees and Soviet agencies have been instructed to increase in every way the prestige and devotion to principle of personnel of the courts, the prosecutor's offices, the legal system, the police, the courts of arbitration and the notary's offices, to support volunteer participants in the safeguarding of public order, and to promote the dissemination of legal knowledge.

This Party position commits those who stand guard over the law to do many things. Letters from working people and warning signals from local areas indicate that there are still a good many violations within the law- enforcement agencies themselves and that in some places, as the saying goes, they "fire cannons at sparrows" while leaving grave crimes against the interests of our society and its citizens unsolved.

We are setting the personnel of law-enforcement agencies the task of steadfastly fulfilling the directives of the adopted resolution and persistently learning to work in conditions of expanding democracy and openness, relying on the trust and support of all the people.

A few words about the personnel of the diplomatic corps. At present, a restructuring of the work of the Ministry of Foreign Affairs is under way and a reorganization of the structure of its central apparatus and foreign institutions is being carried out. The leadership is being renewed. This line must be pursued consistently, increasing the efficiency of the diplomatic service and striving to have it correspond fully to the vigorous international activity of the CPSU and the Soviet state.

The state security agencies, which possess ideologically tempered and professionaly trained personnel dedicated to the Party and the people, stand vigilantly on guard over the interests of the homeland. We are certain that the Soviet Chekists [Chekists—security police. The name derives from the Cheka, founded in 1917 to investigate "counter-revolution." Now the term is used for KGB] will continue to promptly uncover and resolutely curb hostile intrigues directed against our country.

Finally, about the tasks of military personnel. Not for a minute is the Party relaxing its efforts to further increase the country's defense capability, and it assigns military personnel a special role in accomplishing this vitally important task. This is what defines their enormous responsibility to the people. The Soviet Armed Forces are also involved in restructuring. They reliably safeguard the peaceful labor of the people and the security of the country, and they are fulfilling their internationalist duty with credit.

The CC firmly counts on Army personnel and the Soviet officer corps in accomplishing the task of strengthening the state's defense capability, and it is certain that, in the present difficult international conditions, Communists and all Army and Navy personnel will act with the greatest responsibility and will increase and improve their skills and the combat readiness of all arms and branches of service. The Soviet people and our Party rely on their Armed Forces. They are doing everything to strengthen them, and they have a right to expect that no aggressive forces will be able to catch us unawares.

Comrades! In conclusion, I would like to talk briefly about the tasks that must be accomplished in the coming year, 1987.

This year, marking the 70th anniversary of the October Revolution, holds special significance for us.

The Soviet people are looking forward to the forthcoming anniversary as they thoroughly reorganize all aspects of public life. The Politburo believes it would be right this year to issue an address to all Party members and all working people in the USSR.

The CC call on Communists, all Soviet people to display a still greater understanding of and a sense of responsibility for what is to be accomplished, for the destiny of the country, for the future image of socialism.

We have achieved much in the decades of socialist construction. But time is putting ever greater demands on us. In the changed conditions Soviet society is passing a test of dynamism, of the ability to climb rapidly the steps of progress. Our economy is passing the test of high efficiency, of receptivity to advanced technologies, of ability to produce first-class output and rival competitors on the world markets.

Our morality, the entire Soviet way of life are being put to a test to check their ability to develop steadily and enrich the values of socialist democracy, social justice and humanism.

Our foreign policy is being put to the test to check its firmness and consistency in the defence of peace, its flexibility and self-control in conditions of the frenzied arms race fueled by imperialism and the international tensions fanned up by it.

In its innermost revolutionary essence, in the Bolshevik audacity of the plans, in its humanistic social purpose, the work being done now is a direct follow-up to the great accomplishmentys started by our Leninist Party in October 1917.

The whole world is today looking at the Soviet people: Will we be able to cope with the task? Will we be able to respond in a worthy manner to the challenge thrown to socialism? We have to give a worthy answer by our deeds, by persevering work. And we cannot put it off.

As you understand very well, comrades, 1987 has been assigned a very important role in the implementation of the Party's strategic course aimed at acceleration. The success of the whole Five-Year Plan, of our very important undertakings and of the fulfillment of long-term plans will depend on how we work. That is why it is so important to focus our attention, from the very first days, on specific matters, on the implementation of outlined decisions. Hence it takes work—painstaking, routine, but extremely important work—on the part of Party committees and organizations, all work collectives on implementing the congress decisions.

We must not only reinforce and develop what was achieved in the first year of the Five-Year Plan in all branches of the economy and in all spheres of life but also go farther and include long-term growth factors in our work on a broader basis. In all these areas, we must without fail achieve appreciable positive changes and make them irreversible.

In orienting personnel toward the accomplishment of current tasks and the unswerving fulfillment of the 12th Five-Year Plan's assignments, we should, as V.I. **Lenin** taught, not lose our perspective but spell out in concrete terms and precisely define the paths of economic and social progress. The preparation of the 13th Five-Year Plan, on the basis of a new system of management making it possible to realize the possibilities and advantages of socialism more fully, will begin in the very near future.

In view of the fact that the radical reform of economic management that has begun affects fundamental questions of the functioning of the socialist economic system and many aspects of political and social life and the style and methods of work, it would be a good idea to examine the entire range of these problems at the next plenary session of the CC.

In view of these growing tasks, we turn to our cadres. What is required of them is organization, efficiency in work and the ability to mobilize to the utmost the creative energies and resources of work collectives. Everyone should learn to be able to react quickly and in a businesslike manner to the arising problems and difficulties which naturally may emerge since new and not easy tasks are being tackled. In essence, all of us have to pass an examination in political maturity in mastering new methods of work and of guidance in all sectors of socialist construction.

In short, the new year has brought forth new and quite responsible tasks in implementing the general guideline of the 27th Party Congress. The Politburo is convinced that the ideas of the congress which have been profoundly understood by all our cadres and which have got hold of their minds and thoughts, will more and more persistently and on an ever larger scale make their way into life. They will determine the pace of our development and guarantee that the country will make fundamentally new advances in the economic, social and cultural spheres.

It is possible to sum up what has been said as follows: We all, and everyone of us should gear up in our work. The mobilizing role of the Party, of all its organizations and of all Communists should manifest itself with particular force in the new atmosphere. It is of importance to continuously keep hold of the pulse of life and to do everything for plans to be implemented.

I would like to seek your advice on the following fundamental question. Perhaps it would be a good idea to convene next year, on the eve of the Party report-and-election campaign, an All-Union Party Conference to examine, from a broad standpoint, progress in the implementation of the resolutions of the 27th CPSU Congress and to sum up the results of the first half of the five- year plan. It would also be proper for this conference to discuss questions of the further democratization of the life of the Party and of society as a whole.

The discussion begun at the conference could be continued at the report- and-election Party meetings and conferences, at which the results of every Party organization's work in restructuring should be rigorously analyzed.

The very fact of the holding of an All-Union Party Conference, in accordance with the CPSU Statutes, would be a serious step in the practical democratization of our Party life and in the development of the Communists' activeness.

Comrades! By formulating the personnel policy in conditions of the reorganization and the acceleration of the country's social and economic development, the Plenum of the CC thereby determines the most important directions of our work for many years to come.

At the Plenum today we constantly turn to Vladimir Il'ich **Lenin**, his thoughts and ideas.

This is not just a tribute of great respect, not only an acknowledgement of **Lenin**'s authority, but it also reflects the pressing desire to revive in modern conditions and revive to the fullest extent possible the spirit of Leninism, to assert in our life the Leninist demands on cadres.

Tirelessly, **Lenin** taught that the success of revolutionary struggle, the success of any cardinal restructuring of society is determined in many ways by the mood set by the Party.

We want to transform our country into a model of a highly developed state, into a society of the most advanced economy, the broadest democracy and the most humane and lofty morality, where the working person will feel himself to be a full-fledged proprietor and can enjoy all the benefits of material and spiritual culture, where his children's future will be secure, and where he will possess everything he needs for a full, meaningful life. We want to force even the skeptics to say: Yes, the Bolsheviks can do anything. Yes, the truth is on their side. Yes, socialism is a system that serves man, his social and economic interests and his spiritual elevation.

Gorbachev,"O perestroike i kadrovoi politike partii," Report to the CPSU CC Plenum. *Pravda* and *Izvestiia* (28 Jan); *Kommunist*, 3 (Feb 87), 5-47; *Partiinaia zhizn*', 4 (Feb 87), 45-54; a translation appeared also in FBIS (28 Jan 87), R2-R48; a condensed translation is in CDSP, 39:4(1987), 8-14, 23-24; 39:5(1987), 8-12; 39:6(1987), 8-14. See also E.Teague, "Gorbachev Discusses Personnel Policy," RFE/RL. RL38/57 (25 Jan 87).

On the Tasks of the Party in the Radical Restructuring of Economic Management (25 Jun 87). Report at the Plenum of the CPSU CC.

Comrades!

We are holding this Plenary Meeting shortly before a most important event in the life of the Party and our entire society. Several months from now the country will celebrate the 70th anniversary of the Great October Socialist Revolution.

The Great October Revolution heralded to the world the birth of a new state of workers and peasants, asserted the humane principles of society's social and economic development, elevated the working man and gave greater scope for the initiative and creativity of the masses.

All this enabled us within a very short period of time in historical terms to turn the country into a mighty industrial power, successfully solve extremely complex social problems, create the great multiethnic alliance of peoples advancing along the road of socialism.

Every generation of Soviet people has made its contribution to the development, strengthening and defence of the gains of the Great October Revolution. We have every reason to be proud of our history and to look to the future with confidence.

At the present stage, guiding themselves by the Leninist teaching and creatively developing it, the Soviet people, the Party are continuing the cause of the Revolution by carrying out the restructuring, by renewing all spheres of society's life.

Today we are to examine one of the cardinal questions of the restructuring. I am referring to a radical reform of the management of the economy, to qualitative changes in the system of the economic mechanism—changes which will open up new possibilities for using the advantages of the socialist system.

Before moving on to this question the Politburo believes it necessary to present to the CC an evaluation of the course of the restructuring effort and of the fulfillment of the 27th CPSU Congress decisions.

I. **Along the Road of the April Plenary Meeting**

Political Results of the Restructuring. Comrades, the period since the April Plenary Meeting is one of the most responsible and politically intensive in the history of our Party and the life of the people. It is characterized by intensive theoretical and practical work, by quest and solution of new problems encountered by Soviet society.

It can be said with confidence that the political situation in the country has substantially changed in these two years. The understanding that the restructuring was necessitated by the mounting contradictions in the development of society is deepening. These contradictions, gradually accumulating and not being solved in time, were actually acquiring pre-crisis forms.

In these complex conditions the Party worked out the course of restructuring. We have started moving forward. The process of renewal is acquiring ever more specific forms, encompassing an ever broader range of problems and spreading to ever new strata of public life.

The restructuring in society is deepening and growing. It is designed first of all to resolve the contradictions forming the main elements of the braking mechanism and thereby to give social development a mighty and irreversible accelerating impulse.

It should be clearly understood that we see the aims of accelerating social and economic development not only in overcoming the lag that has accumulated and the deformations that have appeared in various fields of society's development. Dictated by historic necessity and the altered conditions of an internal and international nature, cardinally altered at that, they are directed at the attainment of a new qualitative state of socialist society.

History has not left us much time to solve this task. The possibilities of socialism, what it gives a person in practice, how socially effective the society is will be judged exactly by the progress of the restructuring drive, by its results.

This, Comrades, determines the scope of the work at hand and the measure of our responsibility.

The changes in society since the January Plenary Meeting show with particular clarity that the country's healthy forces, the working people, firmly declare for restructuring, for acceleration, for the prompt solution of urgent problems and the absolutely definite overcoming of stagnation and conservatism.

Democracy in all walks of life is expanding and deepening. Public organizations are gaining momentum in production management. Public opinion is coming across loud and clear. The media is working more actively for renewal. An offensive is in progress against bureaucratism. Bossy, pressure management is gradually being overcome. Important changes are taking place in the work of cadres as fresh blood is injected.

The democratization experience convincingly shows that we are on the right road. This offers good prospects for perfecting our political system and society as a whole.

The cultural revival can be named among the achievements of restructuring. The public's interest in progress taking place in science, literature, art and the printed and audio-visual media has increased. People want to know more about the country's past, present and future. Public interest in society and state, world outlook, moral and ethical problems has become keener and sharper.

With the reform of the secondary and higher education system, we are making an important modernization. All this is opening up new reserves to further expand and deepen the restructuring.

If we are to speak of a political evaluation of the processes taking place in the economy, I would straightaway mention the changing attitude of people to work and fulfilment of their production duties. In many ways this is determined by the fact that working people are supporting with deeds the policy of renewal, of accelerating social and economic development. That is first.

Secondly, this is connected with the transition of many branches of the economy to new methods of management, to full profit-and-loss accounting and self-financing with a simultaneous development of progressive forms of work organization and notably collective contract.

The new situation has made its impact to a certain measure on economic results, too. On the average, the rates of increment in labour productivity during the past two years have increased to exceed the mean annual figures of the 11th Five-Year Plan period in industry and construction by 30%, in agriculture by 100% and in railway transport by 200%. During 1985-1986 the average rates of increment in industrial production amounted to 4.4% and in agriculture to 3%. The positive trend has also come through in the key capital construction branch which was in a difficult situation. Positive changes are involving difficulty and struggle for other branches of the economy, too.

Additional possibilities have been found for strengthening the material base of the social sphere. Almost 40 billion rubles are being allocated for these aims over and above the sum approved in the Five-Year Plan. This year the rates of increment in capital investments in the social sphere are three times greater than in the national economy as a whole.

You will probably agree, Comrades, that the period after the January Plenary meeting of the CC needs a special analysis and political assessment. What is of primary importance here?

It can be said that a new stage of the restructuring has opened, a stage where concrete tasks are to be tackled in all areas and spheres of society's life.

The January Plenum gave a powerful boost to labor and social activity. It became obvious that no one can stand aside from the restructuring drive—every person must take a position. These past months Soviet people have especially acutely sensed the complexity of the problems that have accumulated and have come to a clearer realization of the need for really cardinal changes and consistent pursuance of the course to renewal. At the same time understanding has deepened in the Party and society that the restructuring is a complex and contradictory process.

The revolutionary transformations in society have brought to the fore the contradiction between the demands for renewal, creativity and constructive initiative on the one hand, and conservatism, inertia and selfish interests on the other. The disbalance between the growing enthusiasm of the masses and a persisting bureaucratic style of work in most diverse fields, that includes attempts to freeze the renewal drive, is just one manifestation of this real contradiction. Prompt and resolute measures are needed in the personnel policy, in the assertion of new approaches and norms of Party, state and public life if we are to overcome this contradiction.

What does the Politburo regard as the most effective means of solving this problem? The answer is clear-cut and definite—extensive development of democracy. Today, and this is again proved by experience, it is the command- and-administer forms of managing society that are braking our movement. Democratic forms alone are capable of giving society mighty acceleration.

The experience of the restructuring and its initial stage calls also for a close look at the actually existing contradiction of interests of various groups of the population, collectives, agencies and organizations. No doubt about it, socialism removes the antagonism of interests. This is a known and correct thesis. But it does not mean in any way that the liquidation of the antagonism of interests is tantamount to unifying or smoothing them over.

Take, for instance, attitudes to restructuring. On the whole there is a general understanding that we cannot live and work in the old way, that we must have renewal and profound transformations. But as soon as this restructuring began drastically to affect actions, penetrate all sections of society and reach the concrete person, there emerged the contradiction between the immediate, narrowly understood, even egoistic interests of separate individuals and groups and the interests of the whole of society, the long-term interests of working people.

We see distinctly the difficulties with which the restructuring is taking place in Party, government and economic bodies. And don't we feel how painfully it is being received in some central agencies? The difficulties of the renewal drive are illustrated by the experience of State acceptance, the anti-drink drive and the order and discipline efforts. This is evidence also by the first steps to introduce profit-and-loss accounting and assert principles linking labor remuneration entirely with end results. All these are real processes, Comrades, contradictions of life. And we must see them and take them into account.

Society cannot take its cue from selfish interests and actions. We must resolutely struggle against them. And here a worthy example is being shown by the working class, by work collectives, especially at those enterprises where State acceptance has been introduced. We know this is no simple matter and it has affected the interests of millions. Yet the working class has clearly determined its position: State acceptance of goods is necessary and it is needed by the whole of society, by the entire people and by every single person.

The working class is boldly marching along the road of renewal. I would say that in all matters the working class is in the vanguard of the restructuring. And this is of decisive importance for its success. Work collectives are eagerly tackling the key issues of social and economic development, spotlighting due and proper fulfilment of contract deliveries. An emulation drive for the 70th anniversary of the Great October Socialist Revolution has taken off. In short, the working class is charging the restructuring drive with high-tension energy.

Against the background of the truly civic stand taken by the working class, the behavior of those who for the sake of their personal advantage are impeding social transformations and standing in the way of the drive for renewal is particularly unseemly. I think the work collectives, the Party and public organizations should display firmness with respect to such people and be implacable to them. Such is the demand of life. And this is how we in the Politburo understand this question.

Under the conditions of the restructuring there arises anew the problem of achieving harmony between public and personal interests. The search for correct ratios between the former and the latter is of tremendous importance, a task of daily practice. The point here is to take into account the entire complex of interests—of the individual, the collective, the classes, nations, peoples, social and professional groups, the complex dialectics of their interrelationships—so as to ensure society's dynamic development.

Interests should also be moulded and directed through the new economic mechanism and through democratic institutes, through policy, ideology and culture. In the long run the purpose of restructuring is to take interests into account, to influence interests and to effect control over them and through them.

Mention should also be made of contradictions in the sphere of labor and distribution relations, which we encountered when beginning the transition to full profit-and-loss accounting, to remuneration according to the end result, to the system of collective and family contracts. What is the problem here? In practice the main principle of socialism, "from each according to his abilities, to each according to his work", was often sacrificed in the name of a simplified concept of equality. These questions are actively discussed today, and not only in the economic but also in the moral and ethical aspects.

It appears to be obvious that equality does not mean egalitarianism. But in practice we often got the latter. The tendency towards levelling off persisted tenaciously. It generated reliance on others, negatively influenced the quality and quantity of work and reduced incentives to increase productivity.

It should be stressed again and again that genuine equality can be ensured only by the entire means at the disposal of socialism.

We take pride in the high degree of social protection given to people in our country. This is what makes socialism what it is, a system of working people and for working people. But work and work alone should be the basis of a person's material and moral standing in socialist society. Every encouragement should be given to creative, highly productive work, to talent, to real contribution to the common cause. And, conversely, passive attitudes, idleness, outdated ways of working and anti-social manifestations should be evaluated accordingly—socially and economically. Precisely here lies the socialist content of social justice.

Comrades, I have dwelt only on a part of the problems in which the contradictory nature of the current phenomena expresses itself. The novelty and scope of the tasks require that constant attention be given to a scientific analysis of the course and socio-economic consequences of the restructuring, to the contradictions in this complex social process. We urgently need a real breakthrough on the theoretical front based on a strict analysis of the entire sum total of the aspects of society's life, a scientific substantiation of the aims and prospects of our movement. We cannot advance successfully by trial and error. This costs society dearly. The art of political leadership requires the ability to identify and effectively solve contradictions, not to gloss them over, not to accumulate them, but to turn them into a source of progress and self-development.

The founders of the Marxist-Leninist teaching have left us inspiring examples of boldness in theory, of deep penetration into the future. The experience of the Paris Commune gave Karl **Marx** the possibility of working out the ways of making the transition from capitalism to communism. Proceeding from the experience of the first years of socialist transformation in Soviet Russia, Vladimir **Lenin** developed and enriched the theory of building socialist society. The task now is to make a profound analysis of the practice of socialist development, the wealth of experience accumulated by us and the fraternal countries taken in its entire diversity. Work in this direction has been started and we already have some important results on which we rely in formulating and pursuing our policy. But the main work is still ahead.

On the whole, Comrades, despite all complexities, difficulties and obstacles, today we have every reason to say at the Plenary Meeting that the restructuring has scored an ideological and moral victory. It is spreading and penetrating deeper.

But as we make such a responsible evacuation we should not allow exaggerations and still less complacency. Actually we are now only riding the first wave of the restructuring. This wave has sent ripples through stagnant waters.

The Party has awakened the activity of the masses. And it is our duty to prevent this upsurge from petering out. We must develop it and give it a chance to manifest itself fully. It is all the more necessary to speak about this since the working people are just as concerned about the destiny of the restructuring as they were at the beginning. People continue to advise, I would say to demand, that we not stop, that we advance further along the road of changes. Recently, in one of the conversations with working people of Leninsk during the trip to Baikonur, I was asked when the restructuring would reach them. I replied that the leaders of the republic and the region were present, could hear our conversation and should think why such a question was being asked and draw appropriate conclusions for themselves.

Or take letters to the CPSU CC, the Presidium of the Supreme Soviet of the USSR and the Council of Ministers of the USSR, to the central newspapers and magazines, radio and television. They are about the same. People write that they are for the restructuring, but that they see no changes around them. The restructuring has not affected the work collectives, the town and villages where they live and work. Many cite facts to prove this. This means that despite tremendous efforts the restructuring drive has in actual fact not reached many localities. This, Comrades, is a very serious symptom. The Politburo cannot ignore the situation. It was discussed many times in the course of preparations for this Plenary Meeting.

What conclusion are we arriving at?

The restructuring was started on the initiative of the Party and is being carried out under its guidance. The Party has roused the country, its ideas have captivated the minds of millions, it has generated tremendous hopes. And if today working people are concerned about the slow pace of transformations this means there are shortcomings in our work.

An alarming tendency has taken shape, Comrades, and it is borne out by facts—a number of Party organizations are out of touch with the dominant moods and lagging behind the dynamic processes now developing in society. Obviously, this question needs to be studied at our Plenary Meeting. Today this is a key point in our work. The way the Party acts will determine how the restructuring drive proceeds.

Two years ago, when we demanded of the leading Party, government and economic cadres that they organize effective work, we often heard in reply: we understand the new tasks, but give us time to assess the situation, and master the new methods and forms of activity, and apply them.

The Politburo responded to this with understanding. We said at the time that everybody was being given both time and a chance to readjust. But, Comrades, there must be no delay. We must not allow restructuring in the Party to lag behind the economic, social and spiritual processes that are taking place. We cannot allow a situation where changes in life and the moods of people would outpace the understanding of these processes in the Party, particularly in its guiding bodies.

Working people are correct when they write that those who wanted to readjust have already done so and have joined the work. But those who have failed to grasp the meaning of the new tasks continue to cling to the old ways and by their inaction actually sabotage the restructuring. That is why the Politburo sets specifically the question of making Communists, the leaders of the Party, government and economic bodies take more responsibility for the state of affairs, for the real solution of glaring problems and for progress in restructuring.

There should be higher demands at all levels. But we must begin with ourselves, with the Politburo, the Secretariat, the Government and Members of the Central Committee.

A tremendous responsibility rests with the Politburo of the CC at this crucial stage in society's development. Of course, it is the prerogative of the CC to evaluate its activity. I want to assure you that in the Politburo there is a deep understanding of responsibility before the

CC, and the Party and people as a whole in tackling the new complex task. Large-scale work has been launched in all areas of the social reform within a short period of time.

I can state that Party and Government leaders are one on the fundamental restructuring issues and home and foreign policy. This unity makes it possible to adopt and confidently implement decisions dictated by the times. I think this is important but especially so at crucial periods of development.

On behalf of the Politburo I must say self-critically that we also see weaknesses in our practical work. There are instances when important decisions on major questions of the country's development are being fulfilled slowly and not in full volume. There has been a principled and frank discussion on this score at the Politburo. Now we have made it a rule at meetings of the Politburo and the Secretariat of the CC to regularly review the implementation of the key decisions adopted after the April 1985 Plenary Meeting of the CC and the 27th CPSU Congress, as a way of controlling their fulfilment.

The Council of Ministers of the USSR has taken an active stand for the restructuring. Yet it must further improve its activities in guiding the economy and attaining the tasks of the social policy. It should consider current business with no less concern than development prospects. The restructuring of the central management bodies has yet to meet the demands of the time.

It is clear to us that the changes which we are introducing are impossible without vigorous work by local Party, government and economic bodies, all leading personnel. A special responsibility rests with them for promoting practical restructuring and the positive features we note today are connected in no small measure with the work of local organizations. But I think you will agree that on the local level the process of restructuring is only beginning to unfold and not everywhere is it proceeding uniformly. There still remain "seats" of inertia and sluggishness. These, too, are realities and we have nor right to fail to see them. Moreover, we have no right to neglect them or leave them without a Party appraisal.

Immediate Tasks of the Present State of Restructuring. Comrades, it is our task to examine critically the state of affairs and objectively analyze the successes and weaknesses of the restructuring effort. What we need is a principled and frank discussion, concrete proposals and constructive ideas.

Let us begin with the development of the national economy. The Politburo drew attention in due time to the complexity and importance of this year's targets. It would have seemed that everyone understood. But serious miscalculations were made already in the very first months of the year leading to malfunction in many sectors of the economy. The Politburo and the Government had to take urgent measures to rectify the situation. And although it is normalizing, considerable losses have been sustained.

What happened at the beginning of the year could have been foreseen and prevented. But this was not done, and primarily responsible are the USSR State Planning Committee (Comrade N.V.**Talyzin**) and the USSR State Committee for Material and Technical Supply (Comrade L.A.**Voronin**).

But miscalculations were made not only by them. The necessary measures were not taken in time by the Ministry of Ferrous Metallurgy (Comrade S.V.**Kolpakov**) and the Ministry of the Chemical Industry (Comrade Y.A.**Bespalov**). The failure by enterprises of these ministries to make contract deliveries made other branches of the national economy falter, notably machine-building.

The Ministry of Engineering for Livestock and Fodder Production (Comrade L.I.**Khitrum**) did not fulfill its five-month plan for equipment supplies to collective farms and state farms. This is due to the substandard organization of work at many enterprises in the industry, and especially inadequate quality of output. The potential created in this industry is not pulling its weight.

Or take the light industry which has been switched over to the new management conditions. The management of the branch, pleading difficulties beyond its control, has declined many orders placed by the trade sector, and curtailed production at a time when there were real possibilities for growth. We had to earnestly make sure that sought-after goods were manufactured instead of producing goods which are not in demand. The attitude of the Ministry of Light Industry and Minister Comrade V.G.**Kluev** is an example of how departmental interests rise above societal requirements and, consequently, above people's interests. There can be no other evaluation of that.

In connection with all that, I would like specially to emphasize the responsibility of central managerial authorities for restructuring. This responsibility should be raised in every way with due account for the new targets.

We have, for example, a program for modernizing machine-building. It is a great cause. Work here has been started on a large scale with an eye to serious end results.

But we should say plainly: we are concerned over the state of affairs in the ministries of machine-tool, heavy and transport engineering, electrical engineering, and machine-building for the light and food industries and households. The state of affairs in instrument-making is still far from fundamental change, although certain efforts are being made in this sector.

The modernization is going slowly in other machine-building ministries, too. We understand, of course, that engineering workers have encountered great complexities and difficulties. It is a question of cardinal restructuring for the entire machine-building sector. But it is hard to understand why many ministers, Party committees and the staff of ministries are acting in this situation as though it were a routine exercise. In the current situation the work of the Bureau for Machine-Building (headed by Comrade I.S.**Silaev**), the State Planning Committee, the State Committee for Material and Technical Supply, and some departments of the CPSU Central Committee obviously lack activity and efficiency. The state of affairs in the engineering sector evidently deserves consideration at the Politburo and the Council of Ministers of the USSR.

Comrades, I have already said that far from all Party and local government bodies have actively joined in the restructuring process. It is marking time in Armenia, for example. The working people of the republic are greatly concerned about the economy there and particularly about ideology and morality. At the same time the leadership of the Communist Party of Armenia and Comrade K.S.**Demirchian**, First Secretary of the Central Committee, feel that the republic is doing quite all right. Moreover, some people even maintain that the restructuring process in Armenia began before the April Plenary Meeting of the CPSU CC. It is hard to judge what they mean.

A totally unjustified tranquility is being shown in the republic. There is no exactingness with regard to personnel, and no effective efforts are being made against bribery, profiteering and protectionism. The CC of the Communist Party of Armenia should profoundly analyze the state of affairs both within the Party organization and in the republic as a whole, consider it from principled positions, and get down to actual rather than verbal restructuring.

Few marked changes for the better have been occurring in the major Gorki Region's Party organization. Many vitally important issues are being tackled there in an unsatisfactory way. The powerful potential of the region is not being utilized duly. The social sphere and the agrarian sector of the economy develop weakly. It may be presumed that the regional Party committee (headed by Comrade Y.N.**Khristoradnov**) and all Party organizations of the region should draw conclusions from the criticism and put things right.

The departments of the CPSU CC are also called upon to act in a new way in the new situation, exerting deeper influence on the state of affairs in the republican, territorial and regional Party organizations, and supervising enactment of the decisions of the CPSU CC.

Comrades, the Party and society have realized that the restructuring is a lasting policy and that Soviet society cannot be led on to new achievements at one fell swoop. But, it turns out, some comrades have understood from this correct and realistic line that the restructuring is not connected with our overall strategic course towards acceleration and that it can be carried out in an unhurried fashion, without particular care, and without going to any trouble. This is a deep misapprehension for at least two reasons.

Firstly, we have already lost years and decades. Secondly, that "beautiful tomorrow" may not happen if everyone does not work today by the sweat of his brow, changing his way of thinking, overcoming inertia, and exploring new approaches. Talk to the effect that "restructuring will wait" is harmful and dangerous. The Politburo puts the question as follows: right now, at the initial stage of the restructuring, in every sector, it is essential for everyone in his own sphere of activity to secure tangible practical results.

Soviet people are aware that many of the goals of the restructuring will take a long time to achieve. But they justly ask the following question: Why are urgent and relatively simple tasks, which would substantially improve working and living conditions and make the moral and spiritual atmosphere healthier, not being tackled today?

The fact that there happens to be no headway in some places and that the positions gained earlier are even being abandoned has not passed unnoticed by our people. Take the work to improve discipline and order. It is a fact that in many places enthusiasm has flagged, and work is being done in an extremely sluggish fashion. Instances of drunkenness have become frequent again. Loafers, spongers, and pilferers—people who live at the expense of others—are feeling at ease again. Comrades, the working people are legitimately concerned over that.

Poor discipline and lack of order are evidenced by periodic major incidents. The causes as a rule turn out to be the same: lack of discipline, negligence, mismanagement, and irresponsibility. Take the violation of Soviet air space by the West German sports plane and its landing in Moscow. This is an unprecedented occurrence from all points of view. It reminds us once again how strong and tenacious the negative trends which were exposed at the April Plenary Meeting of the CC and by the 27th Congress of the Party turned out to be in our society and even in the army. This underscores the need to enhance vigilance, to act even more resolutely, to strengthen discipline, to streamline organization, to enhance responsibility and improve performance, everywhere and at all levels. On behalf of the Politburo and the Defence Council I firmly state the following: There should be no doubt either in the Party or among the people about the ability of the Armed Forces of the USSR to defend the country.

Comrades, when we speak of top-priority tasks and of urgent action, we proceed from the premise that in the first place obvious and widespread shortcomings will be removed and that there will be more order in trade, the service sector, the health care system, and public utilities, i.e. in those sectors of the economy that are directly connected with people's everyday life.

Of course, these matters should be the centre of attention at the government level. But the responsibility of the republic, territorial, regional, district, city and city district authorities for the state of affairs should also be raised. Unfortunately, at times one encounters much talk about the benefits of the restructuring, but little action to meet the simplest of people's needs. Many local officials show the most deep-seated parasitic attitudes. Even in cases where a minimum of effort and attention would be enough, officials keep shifting the burden onto the central authorities, and waiting for assistance from those higher up. Such an attitude is unacceptable. It should be resolutely condemned and done away with. This is where the Party's attention, exactingness, and control are needed but obviously lacking.

At this Plenary Meeting, among top-priority items, I would like to single out the improvement of the supply of our people with food, housing, consumer goods, and services.

We already have both experience and results in this sphere.

Let us take **the food problem**, for instance. The situation here is improving. We have the statistics for the most part. I shall mention only some which characterize changes that have taken place over the past two years. The production of grain increased by 37 million tons as compared with 1984, production of meat (in slaughter weight) went up by one million tons, of milk by 4.3 million tons, and of eggs by 4,200 million.

We can speak of the revitalization of economic life in the countryside. It has become possible due to change in economic conditions, management methods and, above all, the introduction of full cost-accounting, collective- and family-contract systems.

The Politburo maintains that all objective conditions have been created at the present stage for which I would call a kind of spurt to occur in the output of farm products. Possibilities for radical change exist at all collective and state farms.

What should they pay special attention to? To begin with, they should master intensive technologies in the output of farm crops and livestock products, introduce collective- and family-contract systems more widely, and actively solve the social problems of the countryside. This, Comrades, is only one aspect of the matter.

Another aspect consists in resolutely stopping those who continue to intervene in the work of collective and state farms without bearing financial responsibility. At the recent conference at the CPSU CC, the leaders of the collective and state farms requested protection from precisely such illegitimate intervention in the activities of the farms. Our duty is to help the rural workers to call to account those who are unwilling to part with the old methods of work.

Due to change in the procedure for planning the deliveries to the Union- republic stocks, the interest of the republics, territories, regions and districts in boosting the output of farm products has been raised immeasurably. But at the same time their responsibility for the provision of food has grown as well. One should say that this has given a powerful impetus to initiative at the local level. Quite good results are already manifest where the workers promptly and properly understood the meaning of the changes and appreciated the opportunities that had opened up. For example, judging by the results of the first half of the year the Krasnodar Territory successfully coped with the delivery of livestock products to the Union-republic stock. It procured 15,000 tons of meat in excess of that for its own needs. This is more than 35% with respect to the main market stock. In addition, it produced more than 100,000 tons of milk and 65 million eggs.

Or take the Tatar Autonomous Soviet Socialist Republic. Fifteen thousand tons of meat and 59,000 tons of milk have been procured for the local population in addition to the main stock. The situation is similar in the Ivano-Frankovsk, Poltava, Cherkassy, and Chernovtsy regions of the Ukraine. In these four regions, the addition to the meat stock amounted to about 20,000 tons. the regions of Byelorussia produced 25,000 tons of meat and 260,000 tons of milk additionally to improve local supply. The same can be said of the Baltic republics, the Kurgan, Orenburg, Saratov, Ulianovsk and a number of other regions of the Russian Federation.

It is essential in every way to support the desire of organizations at the regional, territorial and republic level to exceed the targets of the Five-Year Plan period by increasing the output of farm products in the public sector and, on that basis, to ensure the delivery of farm products to the state stock without fail, and to improve radically the provision of the local population with them. This is the main direction. The collective and state farms should increase the return on the investments which were channelled into the development of the countryside in recent years.

But all the reserves must be used. It is necessary to return once again to the question of the role of the individual small holding. It is understood in different ways at the local level and there are different attitudes to the utilization of the potential of the small holding.

Here is one example. In the Omsk Region, the production of meat on small holdings has grown from 27,000 to 60,000 tons, or by 120%, over the past decade. There, practically every family living in the countryside raised horned cattle, pigs and poultry. All-round assistance as far as young cattle, feed, and related services are concerned are being rendered to the population. Last year the cooperatives purchased 20,000 tons of meat from the population. The prices of fresh meat at the markets of the region do not exceed 3.5 rubles per kilogram.

But here are examples of a different kind. The Vladimir Region has a big industrial and agrarian potential. Nevertheless only 46 kilograms of meat (in slaughter weight) per capita was produced in the region last year. As a result, a fifth of the meat products sold there is brought from other regions. The situation in the supply of dairy and meat products in such large agricultural regions as Vinnitsa, Kirovograd, Nikolaev, and Yaroslavl is no better.

Local initiative can help quite a lot not only in boosting the output of farm products but also in developing the food industry. Why is 25 to 50% of confectionery brought from other republics to Uzbekistan, Kirgizia, Tadzhikistan, and Turkmenia while they have the richest resources of primary foodstuffs? Local production ensures only 30% of canned fruit and vegetables for the population of Kazakhstan. The rest is brought from elsewhere. Can this be viewed as normal?

Comrades, it is essential to meet the demand for orchard and gardening plots in the next two or three years. It is time to stop alluding to a shortage of land. This is not the case. Land is available. In places where there is really little vacant land, part of the lands belonging to collective and state farms and to enterprises should be allotted. Let us agree finally: it is essential to fully satisfy all the requirements of the working people and to lift unjustified restrictions and to remove obstacles in this manner.

I think houses and small holdings that have remained vacant and untouched for years and sometimes decades in a number of rural areas, particularly in the non-black soil zone, should be put to use more quickly. The number of abandoned houses is now almost 800,000. There is neglected land around them.

People do not understand such an attitude to land and houses. In their applications to the CC and to other organizations they request permission to purchase those houses and to use the land. I believe that it would be right for collective and state farms to lease the abandoned houses with small holdings to city people. And in many cases it will be possible to do that under a contract for the lands to be used for the output of farm products.

The situation with transport, storage and processing of agricultural raw materials also serves as an example of sluggishness in the solution of the food program. It was emphasized at the 27th Congress of the Party that eliminating the losses of agricultural raw materials would make it possible to increase the consumption resources by 20-30% and to save considerable funds. Even a child could handle such arithmetic.

However, in 1986 the State Agro-Industrial Committee, the Ministry of Fisheries, and the Ministry of Baked Products of the USSR did not utilize 450 million rubles of funds allocated for the development of the processing branches.

Just reflect on this fact, Comrades: construction plans for these branches were not fulfilled by a majority of Union and autonomous republics, territories and regions. That is proof of what's wrong with the way we approach this vitally important problem. It appears that produce which we are trying to provide to the population will continue to rot because there is a shortage of both storage and processing facilities. And then losses will be compensated for by importing. Let us stop viewing such things with indifference. The USSR State Agro-Industrial Committee (V.S. **Murakhovskii**) together with local bodies should find out why this is so, and establish basic order where necessary, and most importantly, take a firm course towards the speediest and most fundamental solution to the problem of storage and processing.

I should say that everything that has been said gives reason to think very seriously. The tendency to rely on others in the solution of food issues has become much stronger in recent years. The leaders of many regions took a light attitude to the cause. If there is a shortage of feed, they send telegrams to the CC and the Government. If there is a lack of farm produce, they again send telegrams to the central authorities.

Of course, in no way am I trying to portray everything in one light or to simplify the problem. Many troubles are connected with the general state of affairs in the country, but still the habit of shifting the burden onto others when it comes to solving these issues has infected many of our cadres.

In general, Comrades, the Politburo is of the opinion that we have real opportunities for radically changing the situation with food supply in the next two or three years.

Life provides striking examples which are illustrative of the huge reserves available everywhere. Numerous facts indicate the possibility of a breakthrough both in labour productivity and in the rate of growth of agricultural production. This has been proved by collectives with intensive labour methods established comparatively recently and assigned land and other means of production on a long-term basis. Last year each collective produced 700-800 tons of grain, on average per member. Each workforce made 70,000- 100,000 rubles per person of produce, and in some cases more.

Unfortunately, there are still few such collectives. The family-contract system is insufficiently widespread, although the efficiency of organization and remuneration of labour is high.

Of course, durable machinery, agricultural chemicals, and resilient crop varieties are needed for rapid output increase. But above all we need people infinitely interested in the results of their work and dedicated to it.

We have for long tried to manage the economy based on enthusiasm and, at times, by decree. But we tended to forget about **Lenin**'s precepts that the growth of production can be ensured on the basis of personal interest, material incentives, and with the help of enthusiasm.

It is significant that the **Kozhukhov** brothers from the Bolshevik Collective Farm in Ordynski District, the first members of work collectives using intensive labour methods in Novosibirsk

Region, say they were attracted not only by high wages but, in no lesser degree, independence, realization of their social significance, and pride that they are doing especially useful work.

If a mass movement for highly organized, interested, and intensive labour is added to the high-performance machinery and other resources which our country has available now, the state of affairs will greatly improve. Life shows that in all districts and regions there are people capable of bringing such a fundamental change.

Here are examples. A.A. **Volochenskii**, a member of the CPSU who is a machinery operator at Artyomovskii State Farm in Pytalovo District, Pskov Region, requested the management to assign him a plot of land and calves. Under a contract, 40 hectares of land, including ten hectares of ploughland and twenty hectares of hayland, were allotted to him. A.A. **Volochenskii** repaired a harvester and two tractors which had been written off, and fixed up an abandoned cow shed for the 20 calves.

He is being assisted in his work by his son and daughter, both students, and by his wife, an accountant at the state farm, in their spare time. On the whole, it is planned to produce more than 11 tons of meat within a year. Proceeds will exceed 31,000 rubles. Payment for the young stock provided by the state farm, for fertilizers, seeds, fuel and other resources at intra- farm prices will amount to 23,000 rubles, and wages will be 8,000 rubles.

I think, Comrades, that such an approach can ensure progress for villages in the non-black soil zone. There is so much discarded arable land there.

It was noted even when debating ways of collectivization that large collective farms open up vast opportunities for the application of equipment, fertilizer, and research achievements but that they run the risk of peasants being separated from the land. On the other hand, small farms bind the laborer to the land while offering no opportunities for top-efficient application of science and technology.

Large collective and state farms have been set up and are operating in our country which have a firm material and technology base and skilled personnel. This context makes important efficient use of collective, family contracts; the interests of individual workers should be more clearly linked with collective interests, with care for the land and other means of production.

Does this contradict the principles of socialism? Can this method of work corrupt? No, in fact it was the old practice, when the negligent worker was paid from the budget, which corrupted the farmer.

There are convincing examples of effective work employing the new approach. Party leadership in the Pytalovo District was recently assumed by a young First Secretary, N.N. **Vorobov**. The Communists of the district, assisted by scientists, worked out measures to boost the economy of the farms. The district had a population of 46,000 after the war. Now its population is 17,000. It would seem that there are not enough people to work. The situation was considered and it was decided to employ the collective contract widely. Eight units of collective and state farms of the district have been operating on the basis of the family contract from the start of the year. With the same fodder used, cattle weight gain has doubled in the past five months to 800-1,000 grams a day. Small groups are now employed in nearly 40% of field cropping in the district. The spring sowing took six days as against the usual 15-18 days. District organizations and farm heads are no longer ordering, ticking off, or rigidly monitoring the course of field work; such methods of management are no longer needed.

Here is another example. Candidate Member of the CPSU CC Lidiya **Bryzga** and her husband left the advanced Zhdanov collective farm to join the "Pamiat Ilyicha" collective farm in Brest District of Brest Region, which was a poor performer. She has been heading for two years a contract team of six. The team tend 100 dairy cows and has 50 hectares of pasture land. Lidiya **Bryzga** milks the cows alone. Her husband and daughter prepare fodder and graze the cattle. Milk yields per cow over the two years have increased to 5,580 kilograms from 2,917 kilograms.

There are such examples everywhere. At the Panfilov collective farm in the Uspenka District of Pavlodar Region, a team was formed in 1983 for fattening young cattle stock. A contract was signed between them and the collective farm's board. The team consists of three people: tractor and machine operator 1st class A.Y. **Rudko** leads his daughter and son-in-law. Look at their results in 1986: they catered for 563 calves and achieved a daily weight gain of over a kilogram per calf, with 167,000 rubles worth of produce per team member. The net cost of a centner of meat increment was 95.5 rubles, which compared favorably with the average of 155 rubles on the farm as a whole and 230 rubles in the district. The average monthly wage per team member was 534 rubles. And there is nothing wrong with that because the money is for work, for real products.

Let me ask: has this undermined the collective farm system? No, it hasn't... So this is nothing other than socialism—effective, creative and labour-minded. This happens when people join broadly in the building of socialism: collective work forms make the links of labourer and farm stronger. And people earn a good living by honest work.

A mechanized potato-growing crew at the Zagalskii state farm in the Liuban District of Minsk Region has four people led by I.G. **Sinitskii**, who holds the Order of Labor Glory in three classes. They cultivate 60 hectares of land and have been on a collective contract for two years. Their potato yields per hectare in 1986 stood at 383 centners. The crew achieved the lowest net costs in potato production, 1.5 rubles per centner (as compared with 9 rubles in the republic as a whole), with the lowest labor inputs of 0.54 man-hours per centner of produce (as compared with an average of 2 man- hours in the republic).

The family contract system in vegetable growing has been gaining ground also in Ternopol Region. On the Bohdan Khmelnitskyi, Zolotoi Kolos and Kommunist collective farms in Zaleshchiki District this year a total of 15,000 tons of tomatoes, including 5,000 tons of early-ripening varieties (as compared with 1.5 tons marketed by these farms last year), will be grown on small holdings.

The system is being promoted also in the district centre. Collective farms have allotted vegetable seedlings, hot-house film, fertilizer, pesticides, water pumps and crates to many families. Cultivating early- ripening tomatoes on between 1,500 to 2,000 square metres each, these families gather 7 or 8 kilograms of quality produce per square meter.

In the Kremenets District 600 families have contracted to grow strawberries in their gardens. Agreements have been signed to supply 800 tons of berries. Contracts to grow vegetables, cultivate industrial crops or fatten cattle are reported to have been signed this year in the region by some 25,00 families.

There are many such examples, Comrades. They all demonstrate a possibility for fast growth in agricultural production if we enlist all reserves, all working people and all families in this business and encourage people's initiatives.

And what is happening now? Rural dwellers go to the food store for any produce and have become buyers of food to practically the same extent as urban dwellers. A total of 54% of rural families do not keep cows and 33% do not keep any stock at all.

There are many facts to prove what is still more important: unshackled grassroots initiative and departure from over-organization and from excessive reliance on centralized management make it possible, with the same resources, to achieve a breakthrough in increasing food stocks.

In short, an immense potential has accumulated in agriculture. It should now be actively put to use by combining the possibilities of large-scale publicly-owned farms with the collective and family contract method.

The solution of the **housing problem** is also an urgent matter. As I have already said, the possibility of increasing the rate of housing construction in the country has arisen at the central level. In the twelfth Five-Year Plan period, the volume of housing construction is to be increased by 60 million square metres as compared with the eleventh Five-Year Plan via additional capital investments. In all, more than 15 million families will be provided with apartments in the Five-Year Plan period.

But that is not all. No less resources, and maybe even more, are available to enterprises, collective and state farms, cities, areas and districts, regions, territories, and republics. Many local bodies—and I am pleased to be able to say this—have set about tackling in a businesslike manner the job of providing practically every family with a self-contained apartment or a home of their own by the year 2000, a job given them by the Congress. Quite a number of them are already looking for ways of attaining this goal in a shorter period of time. This is the right attitude and it should be supported in every way.

But, Comrades, it must be said frankly that no fundamental change in housing construction has occurred so far and to a considerable extent this is accounted for not only by a shortage of funds but also by the attitude of many Party, local government and economic bodies and executive personnel. General talk is not always followed up with persistent innovative work, initiative and a search for reserves to accomplish this urgent task.

Quite often one hears that there is a lack of facilities to support the growing housing construction. But this explanation satisfies no one: firstly, if there is a lack of facilities, they should be created; secondly, 20% of the capacity of house-building plants in the country is not being used at all now. These are average data for the country. Enterprises of this kind operate at only 65-70% of their capacity in Azerbaidzhan, Armenia, Kazakhstan, Turkmenia, Uzbekistan, and at 50-65% of their capacity in the Krasnodar and Khabarovsk Territories, Ivanovo, Penza, Rostov, Smolensk, Tashkent, and Tselinograd Regions as well as in Buryat and Kabardino-Balkar Autonomous Republics.

And something else. How can one understand and justify a shortage of housing and building materials in the country while most building-industry enterprises operate in 1.5 shifts a day and shut down on weekends. As a result, up to 50% of calendar time is lost. Why can't they be run continuously? This is precisely what iron and steel workers, chemists, power engineers, and food industry workers do. Engineering workers are switching over to multishift work conditions.

And it is not just the capacity of the house building plants that is being inadequately utilized. Brickyards in the country are operating at only 80 per cent of their capacity at a time when there is a shortage of bricks everywhere. Proper use is not made of them in the Russian Federation, in the Ukraine, and in Kazakhstan. The brickyards operate at only 57-69% of their capacity in the Altain and Krasnoiarsk Territories.

If we are really concerned over the housing problem, can we put up with ministries and departments utilizing only 70-80% of capital investments allocated for increasing the capacity for large-panel housing construction.

I think that today at the Plenary Meeting, we have a right to urge the CCs of the Communist Parties and the Councils of Ministers of the Union Republics, ministries and departments—particularly the Ministries of the Building Materials Industry (headed by Comrade S.D. **Voyenushkin**), the Timber, Pulp-and-Paper and Woodworking Industry (headed by Comrade M.I. **Busygin**)—to resolutely change attitude to housing construction.

Let us, Comrades, think it over and take counsel with the working people. Once we have set about solving this vitally important problem, it should be tackled jointly.

I would even say that the working people will not understand us if we, while developing the restructuring process, do not find real opportunities for accelerating the resolution of the housing problem. The construction of housing is a countrywide task, and it is precisely from that position that it should be approached.

And now, Comrades, about **consumer goods** and **the service sector**, and the situation on the consumer market. Taking into account the importance of the issue, a purpose-oriented state programme has been elaborated. But this in itself is not yet a solution. It is essential to ensure its implementation in practice. Unfortunately, one has to state that the attitude to this very important social task is far from being uniform. Some people really make use of the created prerequisites, they are actively searching for solutions and increasing the production of goods and the provision of services. The example of Belorussia, Lithuania, Estonia, Leningrad, Ulyanovsk and other regions can be cited. Their experience is known in the country.

However, many leaders continue to act according to old simplified schemes, counting mainly on assistance from the centre and on supplies from other regions, rather than relying on their own efforts. I do not want to say, of course, that in this country every region or republic should set up a subsistence economy. But when officials cease to think about utilizing local resources, and count only on those coming from elsewhere, this is nothing but parasitism again. This phenomenon is rather widespread.

I do not think that at the Plenary Meeting it is necessary to go into every detail of the problem, but when one sees what primary consumer goods are being brought from other regions by some republics, territories and regions, one is astounded at how much some of our officials have lost their sense of responsibility for meeting the needs of the people. They bring the simplest of things from afar, including items that could be produced locally without any difficulty. They bring in goods which do not require any allocated resources, new equipment, special production facilities or trained personnel. Comrades, we must bring this unpardonable practice up for popular verdict. The press, radio and television should systematically show how these tasks are handled by economic and local-government bodies. We must let everyone know both those who show a really solicitous attitude to people, and those who are indifferent and lack initiative. People should know everything and have this important work under control.

At the Plenary Meeting of the CC, it must also be said that far from all ministries have turned to manufacture of goods for the people. Eighteen branches, among them the ministries headed by Comrades E.K. **Pervyshin**, P.S. **Pleshakov**, V.M. **Velichko**, A.A. **Ezhevskii**, failed to cope with last year's targets for the manufacture of recreational and household goods.

Some ministries treat the manufacture of consumer goods formally, as a secondary matter. In some places it is viewed only as a burden. The comrades should be aware that they are under a deep misapprehension. The quicker they rid themselves of it the better, both for the business at hand and for themselves.

Up to now we knew we needed more goods of better quality and wider range. But that is not the only thing.

Just look how many facts indicate that the population is poorly supplied even with goods which are in abundance. And if one adds that there is no set order in many trade institutions and enterprises, that service standards are low, that there are many queues because the number of shops is itself insufficient, and that the operating schedules in trade and the services are not always subordinated to the work routine and lifestyle of the population of town and country it becomes understandable why their work evokes criticism so often. These questions should be resolved by local bodies as soon as possible.

The possibilities for replenishing commodity resources through production and procurement by consumers' cooperatives are being poorly utilized in this country. There are many complaints on that score. For the time being this system is operating slowly and much of what could be procured from the population and delivered to the consumer through cooperative organizations is simply lost. We have rendered assistance to Tsentrosoiuz. Its efforts should also be supported by the local authorities.

Comrades, we cannot put up with community and consumer services lagging behind, with the unsatisfactory situation in passenger transport, communications, tourism, physical training and sport. Is it really normal to have such problems when one wishes to have housing and household appliances repaired, or footwear and clothes made both in town and country?

A "shadow economy" ['second economy'] of sorts has emerged in that sphere, and not unexpectedly. Consider the following figure: divisions of the Central Statistical Administration estimate that the population pays about 1.5 billion rubles annually to individuals for services.

We have repeatedly drawn attention to the need for fully meeting the population's requirements for lumber and building materials. Decisions have been passed on that score but both central and local bodies are doing a poor job implementing them.

I believe that the discussion at the Plenary Meeting today of Soviet society's vitally important problems will become a lesson and a stimulus for all officials both in the center and at the local level.

The solution of problems with foodstuffs, housing and goods for the population should be constantly in the field of vision of economic bodies. This fully applies to health care and environmental protection. The situation in these spheres has attracted the attention of the Politburo and the Government in the past two years. Health care and protection of the human habitat are not up to standard. We are taking measures to improve the situation. This is a matter of paramount importance and it demands attention from all and immense practical efforts.

Democratization Is a Decisive Condition of Restructuring. Comrades, a new moral and political atmosphere has been created in our society since the April Plenum of the Party's CC. It is an atmosphere of creativity, quest, realistic appraisal of contemporary actuality and an uncompromising struggle against everything that is holding us back. Therefore the first conclusion that arises from the experience of the past two years is that the atmosphere of openness which has been created in the country and which enables every person to display his civic stance, take an active part in discussing and resolving the vitally important problems of our society, and accelerate processes leading in that direction should not only be preserved and maintained, but also deepened and developed.

Our experience demonstrates that success is achieved where Party, government and economic bodies make full use of the growing political and social activity of the working people. Let me say frankly—we will not be able to cope with the tasks of restructuring if we fail to pursue the policy of democratization firmly and consistently. Let us recall V.I. **Lenin**'s words: "...The more profound the change we wish to bring about, the more we must rouse an interest in and an intelligent attitude towards it, and convince more millions and tens of millions of people that it is necessary." This is how, following Leninist principles, we should act today at this stage of restructuring.

At the same time I must make one more point. Articles appearing in the press, knowledge of the situation at the local level and incoming information demonstrate that the development of openness and democratism is not a smoothly running process and that it is even painful at times. Some comrades have a misconception and fear of democratic changes. This matter is so important that the Plenary Meeting, I believe, will discuss it and take a clear and firm stand on the issue.

As the restructuring is proceeding and the process of democratization of all aspects of the life of our society is running deeper, new realities come into existence and we cannot fail to reckon with them, we simply have no right to fail in that. Our people no longer want decisions related to their interests to be taken without their participation no matter who takes them. Sometimes this gives rise to tense situations. What do they demonstrate? They demonstrate that some local Party, government and economic bodies, a section of our guiding cadres in the centre and at the local level have not yet learnt how to work in conditions of greater democracy. Learning how to do that must not be postponed until some future date, this lesson should be learnt diligently right now. Party Committees and organizations, bodies of state authority should constantly be in touch with public opinion and use it to verify decisions they are about to take plus their actions. Our people stand for democratization both politically and practically.

Mastering new approaches to political work, organizational and ideological activities is not an easy process. Some have difficulties with openness, others find it hard to accept criticism and unfavourable press reports, still others have come to believe that only their own opinion is "infallible". We are encountering all this and not infrequently at that. Let us look at the root of those phenomena. The democratization is not to the liking of those who are afraid of finding themselves subjected to open control on the part of society. They understand perfectly well that they can talk their way out of it when brought to account by their superiors, but the people will hold them responsible in full measure. Democracy is putting everything in order and it is becoming clear who is who and who is capable of doing what.

I must mention certain points that give cause for concern. It is impossible to be fully insured against errors in any major undertaking. They have occurred, occur and will occur. We have now come across situations where someone would like to make use of the atmosphere of openness not in the interests of the restructuring, not in the interests of developing socialism, of working people, but for attaining his own narrow self-serving aims.

Efforts should be made to combat such phenomena and that should be done openly. To live and work in conditions of extended democracy means to have no fear of debates and of the collision of views and positions. All this is natural and essential in the quest for truth, in the effort to resolve the problems that emerge and to accelerate our progress.

But when we say that democracy presupposes spirited, broad and serious discussions and the comparison of differing points of view, it means that attempts at replacing one half-truth with another under the pretext of rectifying it cannot be considered democratic. It is undemocratic when pretending to counter the ambitions of some group and its claims to the ultimate truth, certain people impose on everyone the ambitions of another group, its tastes, predilections and its subjectivist point of view. We are coming across such examples in the media, in the arts and literature, as well as in the scientific community. Party and public organizations are not immune to that phenomenon either.

But on the whole I would like to say that the process of openness, criticism and self-criticism is unfolding in our country on a sound foundation. It is playing a mighty role in rallying together all forces of society on the principles of the restructuring in order to bring about progressive changes in the interests of the people and of socialism.

Comrades, in considering ways for the future democratization of society I would like to touch on the issue of control. Those who took part in a recent meeting at the CPSU CC have said that control is a must, there is no doubt about it, but not the kind we have at present. Abuse of office and crimes discovered in the economic sphere in recent years testify that the existing system of control is inefficient, it has too many elements, it is wasting working hours, diverting a lot of people and funds and, most importantly, it is closely linked with departmental and parochial interests and largely depends on those organizations and officials which it is called upon to control in the first place.

I believe that the Secretariat of the CPSU CC and the Government should deal with the bloated control apparatus and take decisive action to trim it and regulate its activities, to subordinate it to the interests of the state, of the entire people, and of stronger legality.

We should master in full the Leninist principle of socialist control combining broad democratism with Party guidance. We regard people's inspection both as an efficient tool for detecting new issues which demand urgent solution and as one of the most important forms of bringing the masses into the process of self-government, into running the affairs of society and the state.

In the existing conditions we should consider the establishment on the basis of the People's Inspection Committee of a single and integral system of control which would have a wide range of powers throughout the territory of the country, rely on a maximum of openness in its work and discharge its important functions in a comprehensive fashion, proceeding from the point of view of the entire people and in a broad socio-political context.

Comrades, the restructuring under way in our society arouses immense interest in the world. We feel that our problems are understood not only by the working people in the socialist countries, but also by broad sections of the world public and we feel their empathy. The course towards the restructuring has been taken seriously by very different political forces. That course substantially increased the weight, influence and authority of our country; it is convincingly demonstrating the sincerity and peaceful nature of our intentions on the international scene.

Of course, precisely that does not suit quite influential groups in the West, especially in the US. Some members of America's ruling quarters are arguing that glasnost is a challenge to American public diplomacy and that the spirit of the free world, its life today and prospects for its security tomorrow are imperiled by it. They understand that it is difficult to find convincing arguments against the course of our Party towards the restructuring. This is why they are staking mainly on using the process of democratization and openness for suggesting false aims and defective values to us, for sowing doubt among our people concerning the correctness and sincerity of the Party's policy, its course towards the restructuring and improvement of the situation in the country. There is nothing new for us here. That was to be expected and we foresaw that it would be so. Soviet people know well the real worth of such "interest" in our affairs.

We are implementing the policy of restructuring, extending democracy and consolidating the intrinsic values of socialism not for the purpose of pleasing somebody but so that our society can scale new heights—in the process of socio-economic and cultural advancement. And we shall not stray from the road of restructuring.

Comrades, what conclusion can be drawn from the analysis of the current phase of the restructuring?

First of all, we should proceed from the actual political and ideological situation which has taken shape since the April Plenum of the CPSU CC—a complicated and contradictory situation which, nonetheless, is on the whole undoubtedly advantageous for the entire cause of renovation of socialism and the cause of the restructuring. The life of our society is characterized by an increased level of civic activity of all sections of the population and by initiative in raising new questions and overcoming inertia. It is characterized by increased boldness and determination, by the desire of the people to assume responsibility for the affairs of society, for the further extension of democratic principles in the country's life.

This is accompanied by increased confidence that the lofty principles of socialism are inviolable and that they can indeed be implemented today or tomorrow and not some time in the distant future.

Of course, new processes in the ideological and political sphere are not proceeding smoothly and their results vary. A considerable amount of negative attitudes have accumulated in the public consciousness as a reflection of certain phenomena in life itself, and first and foremost, of the gap between words and deeds. There is a certain amount of confusion, misunderstanding and fear of change. We are also witnessing attempts to resist the new ways. It would be unwise not to take note of that. However, it would be far worse, even erroneous, to make an absolute out of the difficulties and shortcomings in our ideological and political development, because that would call into question the restructuring itself and the new favourable political and ideological phenomena it has brought about in the life of socialist society.

We should not fear new problems, new discoveries and new approaches in the ideological and political process. We have enough reason, energy and skill to work Leninist style in conditions of the restructuring, without taking delight in every success along that way, but at the same time without losing heart or becoming panic-stricken when some negative factors make themselves felt. We should learn the difficult and dialectically contradictory art of restructuring.

Comrades, I believe that we should reach agreement at the Plenary Meeting on the following issue. Report-and-election meetings in the primary organizations of the Party will begin in one or two months. It will be appropriate if the meetings of Communists focus on the course of the restructuring, on how Party organizations are functioning and on how all Communists— workers, farmers, intellectuals and our leading cadres are participating in that great undertaking of the entire people. The forthcoming report-and-election meetings in the Party should appraise what has been done and decide what should be done for deepening and accelerating the process of the restructuring.

It is very important that most active supporters of social change, people adhering to principles, aware of the demands of our time, real "engineers" of the restructuring, those who are ready to spare no efforts to make it a success should become leaders of Party organizations at the current stage, a time when large-scale practical work is unfolding.

It will evidently be appropriate to hold Plenary Meetings of the CCs of the Communist Parties of the constituent republics, plenary meetings of Party committees in the territories, regions, areas, cities and districts and to discuss reports of the buros of the corresponding committees about their efforts to direct and supervise the restructuring. Primary organizations should hear reports on the same matter from Party buros and Party committees which are not scheduled for reelection this year in compliance with the Party Rules.

The Politburo regards the forthcoming report-and-election meetings in the CPSU as a most important stage in stepping up the entire activity of the Party in the runup to the All-Union Party Conference. It is proposed to pass a decision during the current Plenary Meeting on the date of the conference. In our Party such conferences were called in between congresses. There was a period before 1941 when this was a regular practice. Many conferences held at crucial stages of history solved problems going far beyond the framework of tactical ones. In some cases they tackled the tasks of a strategic nature, made amendments in the Party Rules and changes in the composition of the central bodies of the Party.

The January Plenary Meeting supported the proposal for calling the Party conference next year in the runup to the report-and-election meetings in the Party organizations.

The Politburo is proposing that *the 19th All-Union Conference of the Communist Party of the Soviet Union be called on June 28, 1988.*

Proceeding from the principled proposals put forward at the January Plenary Meeting and in the course of preparations for the current Plenary Meeting the following questions could be considered at the conference:

1. Progress in implementing the decisions of the 27th CPSU Congress, the main results of the first half of the 12th Five-Year Plan period, and the tasks of the Party organizations in promoting the process of the restructuring.

2. Measures for more democracy in the Party and society,.

It seems that the proposed agenda will make it possible to sum up the political experience accumulated by the Party after the 27th CPSU Congress, appraise our progress along the main avenues of economic and social development, analyze the progress in implementing the radical reform of economic management and the participation of Party and other public organizations, as well as state and economic bodies in the restructuring.

Analysis of how Congress decisions are being realized, evaluation of the political results of work towards the Five-Year Plan targets, and a principled assessment of good and bad points will then make it possible to consider the activities and tasks of each Party organization at report-and- election Party meetings and conferences in an exacting way. This will contribute to more democracy inside the Party, to greater activity by and responsibility of Communists, and to a deeper restructuring process.

II. A Radical Reform of Economic Management. The Major Element of Restructuring

The Necessity and Essence of the Reform. Comrades, today as we discuss radical restructuring of economic management we must keep a realistic picture of the state of our economy as we entered the 1980s. By that time the rate of economic growth had dropped to the level which virtually signified the onset of economic stagnation. We began to concede one position after another, and the gap we knew in production efficiency, output quality and in technology as compared with the most developed countries began to widen.

The economy was developing in an unhealthy manner. There was need of serious changes in structural policy and capital investments so as to impart greater dynamism to the branches on which scientific and technological progress, resource-saving and labor-saving depend. But this was not done. More than that, machine-building was in a neglected state, its production apparatus obsolete and its output more and more behind world standards.

The desire to check declining growth rates by extensive methods brought exorbitant outlays for the fuel and energy branches and hasty commitment of new natural resources to production, their irrational use, an excessive growth of demand for additional labor and an acute shortage therefore in the national economy with a decline in the output-per-asset ratio.

Financial tension grew in the national economy against a background of economic difficulties and declining rates of increment of the national economy.

Let us take the state budget. Outwardly everything looked fine. Spending was covered by revenue, but how was this achieved? Not by increasing the national economy's efficiency but by other means with neither economic nor social justification. In particular, we began to sell extensively oil and other fuel-energy and raw material resources on the world market.

There was a practice of money belonging to enterprises and organizations being groundlessly taken into the budget; this undermined conditions for their normal economic activity.

And, of course, there can be no justification for the increased production and sales of alcoholic drinks. The tax returns on liquor sales grew to 169 billion roubles in the 11th Five-Year Plan period against 67 billion rubles in the 8th Five-Year Plan period.

In short, the country approached the 12th Five-Year Plan period with a serious financial burden. One should add that although the assignments of the past three Five-Year Plans for the growth of production and its efficiency were not fulfilled, spending on wages systematically exceeded the figures set by the plans. This means that a certain part of the money was paid out without any connection with the end results of work.

In these conditions the deficit in the national economy did not diminish. On the contrary, the situation in this respect worsened. In effect, there has been and remains a shortage of everything—metal, fuel, cement, machinery and consumer goods. If we add to this a chronic shortage of manpower, it becomes clear that in such conditions the economy cannot develop normally. The economic incentives for raising quality and efficiency cease to operate and soil is created for growth of prices and a number of other negative processes.

But perhaps the most alarming thing is that we had begun to lag in scientific-technical development. At a time when the Western countries started a large-scale restructuring of their economies with the emphasis on resource saving, the latest science and state-of-the-art technology, scientific-technical progress in our country slowed down. And not because of absence of scientific backing but mostly because the economy was not responsive to innovation. We even used the hard currency earned on the export of oil and other raw material resources mostly for the solution of current tasks and not for modernizing the economy. As the January Plenary Meeting noted, such an economic situation has had an extremely negative effect on living standards and on development of the social sphere. Such, comrades, are the realities.

The Politburo considers it necessary to tell all of this in all frankness once again, with not the last reason for that being that voices are sometimes heard asking: is everything so bad, is there a need to sharpen evaluations, and is a radical restructuring necessary? Maybe, there is the need simply to put pressure from above and to take some other partial measures? I think that if such sentiments prevailed and the current policy were elaborated on the basis of those pronouncements, it would have been extremely hard for the country and for people.

We need in-depth, truly revolutionary transformations to get our economy out of the pre-crisis situation it is in. To this end we have worked out a new economic strategy and set about it. We have changed structural and investment policy, created big purpose-oriented programmes, and set guidelines for research and technology advance. Over the past two years, the first steps have been made in mastering new management methods born of analysis of the situation of the late 1970s and early 1980s. We have undertaken large-scale economic experiments.

But, I would say, the changes achieved in this area are not fundamental or cardinal. The deceleration mechanism has yet to be overcome and replaced with an acceleration mechanism. One has still to compensate for the absence of the latter by extra-economic methods, by administrative pressure.

It has now become a first priority for us to create an integrated, effective and flexible system of economic management.

The task as you understand, is far from easy. The existing management system was established not overnight and it contains numerous strata reflecting the conditions and peculiarities of various periods in the history of our country with all their achievements, contradictions and difficulties.

The foundations for the present system of management were laid down way back in the 1930s. In that difficult period our country, which was far from the most developed economically and which was up against the whole capitalist world, needed to rapidly overcome the technical and economic lag and to bring about quick structural changes in the national economy.

And they were effected in record time. In the years of prewar five-year periods, gross industrial output grew 6.5 times over, and the Soviet Union moved up from fourth to first place in Europe and from fifth to second place in the world. The share of industries manufacturing capital goods increased from 39.5 to 61%. The number of workers in industry trebled over the twelve pre-war years.

To solve these tasks accumulation had to increase sharply in national income. At the beginning of the second five-year period, it exceeded 30% or became twice as great as at the end of the 1920s, and several times greater than in pre-revolutionary Russia. About 60% of the national income was redistributed through the state budget. Huge resources were channeled in a centralized way into the development of heavy industry.

It was precisely for such purposes that a management system based on rigid centralism, over-regimentation of work, and directive assignments and budget appropriations was established. In those special conditions it ensured solution in extra quick time of strategic tasks which had taken capitalist countries decades. The centralized nature of management increased still further during the war years. It was on the whole maintained in the post-war rehabilitation conditions, too.

This nature of management cannot, of course, be explained entirely by objective reasons. There have also been flawed approaches and subjectivist decisions. This should be seen and taken into account in examining present- day problems. But as the years have gone by, the management system has clashed more and more with the conditions and requirements of economic development.

The vigorous scientific and technological revolution, the dramatically increased complexity of the national economy, the need to shift emphasis from extensive to intensive development methods and from quantity to quality, the extended influence of social conditions and the drastically grown significance of the human factor have called for thorough-going change in economic management.

Restructuring economic management has acquired ever greater urgency. It has been debated in scientific and public circles. I can refer you to an article by Academician V.S. **Nemchinov** printed by the journal *Kommunist* in 1964. He wrote way back then, "A primitive understanding of relationships between big and small economic systems can only create an ossified mechanical system in which all management parameters have been set in advance, while the system itself is limited from top to bottom at every given moment and at every given point... Such an economic system limited from top to bottom will brake social and technical progress and sooner or later collapse under the pressure of the real process of economic life."

Over the past few decades there have been repeated attempts to actually change the system of management. They were made in the 1950s, the second half of the 1960s and the late 1970s. But those attempts were not all-out or consistent, only having at best a short-lived effect and not bringing the desired breakthrough. The old economic mechanism, in the meantime, has been stimulating growth less and less and braking more and more.

At this crucial moment when we are close to cardinal solutions, special importance must go to scientific grounding, and theoretical, ideological and political clarity as to the substance and purport of the changes that have begun, and the goals of the management reform. How are we now to proceed? What could we and should we reject? What do we need to strengthen and update? What should be introduced anew?

It is important to stress in this connection that every period in our history has been filled with hard work by the people and marked by major accomplishments. The experience of economic development we have gained is of great value. This experience, for all the achievements, extremes and even mistakes, is a school whose lessons are important both for now and for the future.

The general meaning and thrust of a radical management reform are clear to us. They boil down to this formula: more socialism, more democracy.

It also holds the answer to the question: Doesn't our restructuring drive mean a departure from the foundations of socialism or at least their weakening? No, it doesn't. On the contrary, what we already are doing, planning and proposing should strengthen socialism, remove everything holding back its progress, bring out its immense potential for the people, give play to all advantages of our social system, and lend it the most modern forms.

But what does boosting socialism actually mean? The essence of our revolutionary teaching and all our vast experience demonstrate that socialism should not be seen as an ossified, unchanging system or the practical work to refine it as a means of adjusting complex reality to fit ideas, notions and formulas adopted once and for all.

Views on socialism and its economy are developed and enriched all the time, with account taken of historical experience and objective conditions. We should follow **Lenin**'s example in creatively developing the theory and practice of building socialism, adopt scientific methods and master the art of specific analysis of a specific situation.

The main question in the theory and practice of socialism is how to create on the socialist basis even more powerful stimuli than under capitalism for economic, scientific, technological and social progress and how to best blend planned guidance with the interests of the individual and the work collective. This is the most difficult question that socialist thinking and social practice have been seeking to answer. At this stage of socialism the significance of the question has grown immeasurably.

Many problems need to be tackled in this area. The worker must assume the position of a real master in his work place, collective and in society as a whole: this is how to stimulate higher production efficiency. From the standpoints of theory and practice, the interest of working people as the masters of production comes foremost and represents the most powerful force for expediting social, economic, scientific and technological progress.

What does making the worker a real and active co-proprietor actually mean? It means giving collectives and individual workers broad possibilities to manage public property and increase their accountability for how efficiently it is used. This means ensuring the practical involvement of the broad masses of working people in economic management at every level—from work unit to the entire national economy. This means that the incomes of working people should be geared to performance at their bench and factory and, in the final analysis, to how things are going in the country as a whole, to the end results in general.

More democracy in the economy is indivisibly linked with active use of various forms of cooperative and individual enterprise projects alongside state ownership. We have taken decisions on this score. It should be said, however, that their implementation has drawn varied responses. Quite often, people have talked not about how to use the opportunities opening up more quickly and better, but about how legitimate these forms of economic activities are at this stage of socialism.

Some people even see cooperative and individual labor activities as a revival of private enterprise. I think, Comrades, that both our own experience and the experience of other socialist countries attests to it being useful and necessary to employ these economic forms under socialism skilfully. They help meet people's vital needs ever more fully, crowd out the shadow economy and various forms of abuses and thus facilitate the real process of making social and economic relations healthier.

The problems of correlation between centralized economic planning and independent branch action, and between planning and commodity-money relations deserve to be seriously rethought. We proceed from them being in dialectical unity and complementing each other in an integral economic management system.

In the new economic mechanism the problem is tackled notably through economic norms. Changing over to norm-based methods makes it possible to realize most fully socialism's inherent objective prerequisites of the unity of the interests of society, work collective and individual.

A science-based understanding of socialism implies that the economic system should include commodity-money relations. A well-ordered price and finance-and-credit system whereby the market is won and controlled in accordance with its laws, and enhanced prestige for the rouble help create an effective cost-wise mechanism and strengthen socialism.

Using commodity-money relations in the management system along with the advantages of a plan-based national economy is, of course, more difficult than issuing commands and directives. But that is what our economic executives must do.

Economic emulation and competition is central to activating the motive forces of socialism.

We proceed from the need to step up real competition between factories and organizations, including competition between government-run and cooperative ones, for meeting consumer and national economic requirements better. The winners in this competition should receive tangible economic benefits in reward. This is in line with the principles of socialism and readily understandable.

I should, perhaps, make special mention of the need to introduce competitive principles for the sphere of science and technology too. The point is that one opinion frequently voiced in the past was that the parallel existence of research, development and design organizations amounts to a scattering of forces, duplication of efforts and irrational spending. But experience has convinced us that monopoly for individual organizations is a serious drag on scientific and technological progress and adds up to even heavier losses for society.

I do not want to say at all that we should create parallel structures in every field. But it is a right and worthwhile idea to form different scientific collectives, temporary as well as permanent, to tackle important technological issues. This idea has been earnestly welcomed by engineers, technicians and research workers and is already bearing fruit.

In short, we should renovate our notions about the economic forms of socialism, proceeding from the requirements of Soviet society's development at the present stage, and thereby find scope for an economic overhaul.

Comrades, you have been provided with copies of draft "Basic Provisions for the Radical Restructuring of Economic Management" as prepared by the Politburo and Government.

The aim of restructuring management suggested in the document is to re-orient economic growth from intermediary to final, socially significant results and to public needs, promoting all-round development of the individual, making technology advance fundamental to economic growth, and creating a dependable cost-wise mechanism.

To achieve all this, we must change over from predominantly administrative to mainly economic methods of management at every level, to broad democracy in administration, and to activating the human factor in every way. This changeover involves:

Firstly, a drastic extension in the margins of independence for amalgamations and factories, their conversion to full-scale profit-and-loss accounting and self-financing, increased responsibility for high end results, fulfilment of obligations to clients, a direct linkage of the collective's income level to its work performance, and extensive use of the team contract in labour relations.

Secondly, radically restructuring centralized economic management, raising its qualitative level and focussing it on the main issues that determine the strategy, quality, pace and proportions of development for the national economy as a whole and its optimal balance, while at the same time decisively relieving the centre of interference in the day-to-day activities of subordinate economic bodies;

Thirdly, a cardinal reform in planning, pricing, financing and crediting, transition to wholesale trade in productive goods, and reorganized management over scientific and technological progress, foreign economic activities, labour and social processes;

Fourthly, the creation of new organizational structures to ensure deep specialization and more reliable co-production schemes, the direct involvement of science in production and on this basis a breakthrough to world-standard quality;

Fifthly, going over from an excessively centralized, command system of management to a democratic one, promoting self-administration, creating a mechanism for activating the individual's potential, clearly delimiting the functions and fundamentally changing the style and methods of work of Party, local government and economic bodies.

Starting Point for Restructuring Management. Comrades, we are proceeding to overhaul the economic mechanism starting with the key unit, that is the enterprise/amalgamation. We aim first of all to provide the most favourable economic environment for the latter, to formalize its rights while increasing its accountability, and on this basis to introduce fundamental changes to the activities of all superior economic management bodies.

By setting this order of moves for restructuring, we have taken account of the fact that it is at this level that the principal economic processes take place, it is here that all the goods and services needed by the people are produced and scientific and technological ideas materialize. It is in the work collective that economic and social relations really shape and people's interests—personal, collective and social—intertwine. The social and political climate in our society is in effect determined largely by the situation existing in work collectives.

What is the main drawback of the factory's economic management mechanism today? First, weakness of internal stimuli for self-development. A factory is given production quotas and resources through a system of obligatory indices. Virtually all costs are covered and the marketing of products is effectively guaranteed. Last but not least, workers' incomes are connected poorly with the end result of the work by their collective—contract fulfilment, product quality and profits. The situation is like this: with the present mechanism, manufacturers find it disadvantageous to use cheap source and other materials and unprofitable to improve product quality and apply research innovation.

Under such an economic mechanism, the line between efficient and systematically lagging enterprises is virtually erased. The director-general of the Omskshina amalgamation, Piotr Vasilevich **Buderkin**, raised all these issues rightly at a recent conference at the CPSU CC. The Omsk amalgamation is indeed one of the best in the tire industry. Its products are of high quality and last 50% longer than others'. Over the past 20 years the amalgamation has not failed to honour a contractual delivery commitment. But does the work collective enjoy any benefits for this? In point of fact, it has no advantages, either in the wage growth rate or in the social field, over others.

And can anyone explain the following paradox? Customers pay the same price to the Omsk amalgamation for its tires, whose quality is the best in the country, as to other factories.

Or take an example from the agro-industrial complex. Poultry plants in the Northern Caucasus get a price nearly a quarter less than that paid in other zones of the country for the same product. Yet modern poultry farming based on industrial technology, especially broiler breeding, is conducted in buildings constructed to the same designs and with the same equipment produced at the country's only factory for such machinery. Feed comes from one and the same Ministry of Grain Products.

These are faults in our economic mechanism which, whether we like it or not, is geared to average or even poor work. How can an economy make progress if it offers hot-house conditions for laggards, while hitting front-runners?

We cannot continue in this rut any longer, Comrades. The new economic mechanism should put everything in place. It should provide a powerful lever and incentives for good, enterprising and resourceful work. This is the goal we have declared. It will take time to reach. It is very important to go about selecting the main demands on the new economic mechanism correctly

The main thing we should achieve by adopting the new mechanism is giving broad rights to factories and ensuring real economic independence for them based on full-scale profit-and-loss accounting.

There is a need to do in practice what has already been recognized essential, namely to make sure that the factory, guided by real public requirements, will itself draw up its plan for turning out and marketing products. The plan should be based not on a multitude of detailed targets handed down by superior agencies but on direct commercial orders placed by state organizations, enterprises operating on a self-supporting basis, and trading establishments for a specific quantity of special products of adequate quality.

Factories should be put in such conditions as will prompt economic competition among them to meet consumer demand in the best possible way. The interests of the state will be guaranteed by a system of state commercial orders. But they should offer priority, preferential economic terms, provide for reciprocal accountability of the sides, and be awarded, as a rule, on a competitive basis.

In view of the changed approaches to planning, there has arisen the question of the nature and purpose of target figures. They should help the factory know where it stands in the economic situation. To do this, the target figures should reflect the social need for a particular kind of output, the minimum rate of efficiency and social goals, that is kind of guide the factory to the desired development level. Target figures should not serve as directives and shackle the work collective in drafting its plan and should leave it plenty of room for manoeuvre in choosing decisions and partners when signing economic agreements. Fulfilment of state contracts should be the main criterion for the performance of an enterprise and for rewarding its workers.

The switchover of factories and amalgamations to the pay-your-own-way basis is of fundamental importance. This means that they should cover all their current expenses, including the pay packet, and make investments in modernization and capacity buildup schemes and social amenities for their work collectives at the expense of their own profits. Funding from the state budget will only be preserved for tackling major and important state tasks. Factories at the same time will be granted broad possibilities to draw bank credits on their own responsibility. The work collective should thus bear full economic responsibility for its activities.

A most important role in the new economic management mechanism will belong to stable long-term norms. These will include payments to the state budget for basic assets, land, water and other natural resources, manpower, and interest on credits. These include norms for forming wage funds and meeting social and cultural needs. The prices of manufactured products and the pay rates for services will also be a kind of economic norm. The collective's interests will be blended with national interests through economic methods relying on norms.

The new economic mechanism means fundamental changes in the system of material and equipment supplies to factories—transition from centralized material and equipment supplies to wholesale trade in means of production goods. Factories should be able to buy with money they have earned anything they need for manufacturing, construction and modernization schemes, and social services.

Transition by work collectives to self-management, whereby they decide at their own discretion all production matters at their factories up to, and including the election of top managerial personnel, is becoming a strong stimulus for initiative and independence.

Such are, it seems the main features of the new economic management mechanism for factories and amalgamations. Of course, a number of uncustomary questions might arise during transition to that mechanism. Some have already been raised during the nationwide discussion of the Draft Law on the State Enterprise.

One of these questions is what should be done with those factories which, because of mismanagement, are unable to guarantee payments to the state and a normal level of income for the work collective. I believe various forms of aid can be used here, emanating either from the particular industrial branch or the bank. But if the situation does not improve after such measures, then, proceeding from the priority of society's interests, the question can be raised of reorganizing the enterprise or terminating its activity. Of course, this is an extreme measure. It goes without saying that the state should show concern for providing working people with jobs.

And another question is raised: will not greater independence for enterprises and rejection of the detailed system of mandatory indicators lead to a weakening of the principle of planning and affect the economy's balance?

We believe that these apprehensions are groundless. It is an illusion to think that everything can be foreseen from the centre within the framework of such a huge economy as ours. The activity of the State Planning Committee and other economic agencies to balance the national economy will be backed by economic interests and economic responsibility of enterprises and by a greater role of economic contracts between them. This will make the task of achieving a balance more realistic.

The principal features of the new economic mechanism are reflected in the Draft Law on the State Enterprise (Association). The common view of production personnel, scientists, representatives of central agencies, party and local government cadres and the public is as follows: this is a sound document in line with today's requirements and new tasks. This is a good basis for transition to the new mechanism.

Nationwide discussion revealed a persistent demand: not to give in to habits and notions of inertia, but to move ahead confidently. We must not allow the new law, as frequently happened in the past, to be bogged down in instructions that may make it meaningless and let the restructuring drive drop.

In principle transition to the new methods of economic management has already started. I mean that enterprises and amalgamations of several branches have, as of this year, been working on a full profit-and-loss accounting and self-financing basis. Five-six months are, of course, too brief a period to reveal fully both strong aspects and shortcomings in the new economic mechanism. Especially considering the specific conditions in which this transition is taking place.

The activity of such enterprises is greatly influenced by external factors, above all their "insular situation." This applies both to ties between enterprises and suppliers and consumers adhering to old principles, and to leadership on the part of ministries and central economic bodies operating so far on the basis of old provisions. The transfer of enterprises to principles of full profit-and-loss accounting and self-financing has begun with the Five-Year Plan already in operation and many standards have to be geared to it. Nevertheless, Comrades, this should not stand in our way as we work to introduce new principles of economic management.

Changing Functions of Centralized Economic Management. Comrades, the conditions of full profit-and-loss accounting and self- management of the basic links of the national economy demand that centralized economic management becomes qualitatively new.

The point at issue is a new concept of centralism resting on activity of working people and independence of enterprises, that is, a genuinely democratic centralism as **Lenin** understood it which possesses a far greater potential than centralism thorned by attempts to regulate all and everything.

Firstly, on **national economic planning**. What in the new conditions is the "philosophy" of a national plan? It should define basic priorities and objectives for the country's socio-economic development, trends in structural and investment policy, scientific and technological progress, and targets for scientific, educational and cultural potential and the defence capability.

What is meant in the new conditions is enhancing the role of the task- setting part of planning, above all the concept of the country's long-term socio-economic development for the next 15 years. It should comprise all major programs, balance them and determine ways of attaining strategic goals. A five-year plan defining yearly assignments should be made the basic form of national planning.

To ensure planned proportions and balance in the economy, the ministries and departments as well as the constituent republics will be given target figures. The principal lever to be applied to enterprises will be economic norms and incentives. They should make it profitable to look for ways of meeting social needs most effectively.

And now we must touch upon a question which concerns many. Concern has been expressed that when, in conditions of complete cost-accounting, directive setting of volume targets for amalgamations and enterprises is discarded, there might be a temporary reduction in the rates of growth of production in separate branches, regions, and even the country as a whole.

What can be said on this matter, Comrades? If higher rates of growth through ballooning gross volumes and repeated counting without a real increase of the end results is meant, society gains nothing. It loses.

And we trust that the transition to profit-and-loss accounting, new methods of economic management, broad introduction of a collective contract and other progressive forms of organization and stimulation of work will enhance people's work, tap the resources that have not yet been used, enhance efficiency and thus achieve higher rates of real growth with high quality of products.

It is precisely such a restructuring that is natural and necessary if we are to ensure a new quality of economic growth. And if it affects adversely the indexes of enterprises that operate inefficiently, such a restructuring will play a positive role for the country's national economy as a whole, for development prospect judged by end results, for the degree of meeting social needs.

A radical reform of the pricing system is a most important part of restructuring economic management. Without that, complete transition to the new mechanism is impossible.

Price must play an important stimulating role for improving use of reserves, lowering outlays, improving the quality of products, speeding up scientific and technological progress, and rationalizing the entire system of distribution and consumption. New political and economic approaches corresponding to the contemporary stage of development must be applied.

The available system of pricing has long been geared to cheap natural resources. The existing prices of coal, oil, gas and electricity no longer guarantee self-financing for the fuel and energy sector. They keep up an illusion of cheapness and inexhaustibility of natural resources and promote an orientation for further increased production, consumption and export.

Economically unjustified approaches to pricing have resulted in the emergence and rapid growth of subsidies for production and realization of various kinds of products and services.

The total volume of subsidies from the state budget now exceeds 73 billion rubles a year. On the other hand, an unjustifiably high level of profit for many goods has formed which does not mean efficient production. This is also a fault in pricing.

Those who manufacture goods with prices understated have no incentive to increase output, and those who, because of excessive prices, get surplus profits have no incentive to lower outlays, to enhance effectiveness. In this situation normal economic relations in the national economy are simply impossible.

So we need not to partially improve the system of pricing, but to radically reform pricing with an interconnected restructuring of our entire price system—wholesale, purchase and retail prices, and tariffs.

What is involved is not just the level of prices, but the system for fixing them. Prices for the most important products must certainly be set in a centralized way alongside a state plan and as part of it. At the same time it is expedient in the new mechanism to widen the sphere of contract prices to promote broader rights and economic independence for enterprises.

The reform of wholesale prices must improve the situation in the national economy, boost the effort for higher production efficiency, resource-saving and quality. As to retail prices, the way they are changed, far from eroding living standards, must improve the living conditions of certain categories of the working people, and bring fuller social justice.

One thing must be clear, that because of the importance and complexity of the pricing reform, its preparation must be approached with great responsibility. A vast volume of work has to be carried out within a short period of time, and the necessary forces must be brought into play. It should be borne in mind that, without solving this question, we cannot draft a new-style Five-Year Plan or embark on a comprehensive system of economic management.

In views of the political and social significance of the pricing reform, it must be most broadly discussed countrywide.

The restructuring of the system for material and technical supply in the national economy is closely linked with a reform in pricing. The main vent is transition to wholesale trade in means of production both through direct contacts between suppliers and consumers and through self-sustained wholesale bases. In this case state bodies will ultimately retain the function of regulating and controlling wholesale trade.

Transition to wholesale trade in means of production is not new, but it is only of late that the first real steps have been taken in this area. We must speed up this work and widen its scope so as to complete it in the next few years.

Many weighty reasons, above all transition of enterprises and amalgamations to a profit-and-loss accounting system, necessitate wholesale trade in means of production. I would like to mention another reason: the need to normalize stocks of commodity and material values. These stocks in the key branches of the production sphere have surpassed 300 billion rubles. Considerable volumes of national wealth thus lie idle.

This situation is largely explained by a cumbersome and unwieldy system of material and technical supply which is erratic and prompts enterprises to lay resources in store.

Look what happens to metal. Complaints about its shortage do not abate, while the stockpiles grow. The accumulations of ferrous rolled metal with consumers increased by two million tons in the past six years to reach 9.3 million tons by the beginning of this year. So let us consider: are we short of metal or is it that we cannot use it thriftily? It is certainly not easy to use resources of rolled metal that are piled up in enterprise yards. It might surprise you if I told you that state supply organizations account for only 1.5% of commodity and material stocks, while the rest is scattered throughout the economy.

The following question arose at the conference in the CPSU CC: is wholesale trade possible while resources are in short supply? This argument is invariably advanced whenever the problem of schedules for transfer to wholesale trade is discussed. The conferees said convincingly that it is the very system of resource allotment, of supply that leads to shortages. And this was confirmed by specific examples. The transfer of enterprises to full-scale profit-and-loss accounting will be of decisive importance here. Therefore the sooner we establish direct ties and embark on wholesale trade, the quicker we shall get rid of shortages in supply and of surplus stocks of material values.

And these are not desktop considerations. Take the following fact. Even as collective and state farms have started going over to new profit-and-loss principles, their orders for farm machinery and other resources have decreased considerably. For instance, orders for combines for next year have dropped by approximately 30%. Orders for individual tractor types and other farm machinery, above all the obsolete and non-efficient, are declining. Such is the real situation. So what seems in short supply today might be overproduced tomorrow.

Major problems have piled up **in the field of finances, crediting and money circulation**. A new economic mechanism cannot be created without such problems being resolved too. The main shortcoming in this area now is that financial and crediting resources and monetary funds are divorced from the movement of material values, that the national economy is oversaturated with money. The ruble does not fulfil in full measure its role of an active means of financial control over the economy.

The national finance system has grown largely outdated. It does not stimulate better economic management and often pursues short-term fiscal objectives. Crediting has in a large measure lost its specific role. The limits separating it from gratis financing have become eroded.

By all indications we cannot avoid a radical finance and crediting reform. It must place budgetary relations with enterprises on a basis of norms; block all opportunities for profits before the ultimate realization of goods; and improve the finances of the national economy.

Comrades, not one state in the world of today can regard itself isolated from others in the economic respect. Our country is no exception. The Soviet economy is part of the world's International commercial and financial relations of countries and the latest technological ideas invariably have an impact in one way or another on our own economy.

The measures being taken to improve the management of external economic relations are aimed, specifically, at deepening the Soviet Union's participation in the international division of labour, which is becoming an ever more important factor in the development of the Soviet economy.

On the other hand, not only we and our allies, but all wanting to work with us in new, more favourable conditions will gain from the successful realization of the plans of the restructuring in our country and the modernization of our economy. In other words, the overhaul of the Soviet economy, considering the Soviet Union's significant share in the world economy, will promote broad international cooperation and, hence, better world economic relations.

Important and far-reaching decisions in the sphere of foreign economic policy have been adopted recently. The economic management restructuring provides a vast scope for raising the efficiency of our **external economic ties** and, which is especially important, for enhancing the impact of the external market on the functioning of industries and enterprises, on the quality of their products, on scientific and technological progress.

Of fundamental importance in this connection is increased efficiency in cooperation with socialist countries. The overhaul of the economic mechanism is called upon to create favourable economic, organizational and legal conditions for deep integration of our national economy with the national economies of fraternal countries.

Broad opportunities for this are opened by enterprises getting the right to direct ties with partners in socialist countries. As the recent discussion of this matter in the Politburo showed, this right is not being sufficiently used. One of the reasons is, apparently, the lack of interests of work collectives in terms of profit-and-loss accounting. It is quite apparent that the success of the restructuring largely depends on more effective economic, scientific and technological cooperation with fraternal countries. The Politburo, Secretariat of the CC, and Council of Ministers should keep a watchful eye on development of economic interaction with them.

We must study the experience of our friends closely and profoundly, and apply everything that can be used in the interests of the national economy of the USSR.

In short, Comrades, an important and large-scale reorganization of the activity of the centralized management of the national economy lies ahead. Alongside switching enterprises to a pay-your-own-way basis, this work constitutes a single whole, a radical reform of economic management.

Remodelling Organizational Structures and the Work of Management Bodies. You surely realize, Comrades, that in altering an economic mechanism and adopting new methods of economic management, organizational structures should be revamped.

What can be said in this connection about factories, the **main link in the economy**? Today's enterprises and amalgamations formed in conditions where they had to set up their own blanking shops, tool shops, foundries, maintenance and other sectors, regardless of production costs, a primitive production system and low productivity of labour. Such subsistence economy laid roots within industries, engendering irrational ties and waste of social labour.

Despite all our efforts, the creation of production amalgamations and particularly those with applied research facilities halted, running up against departmental barriers and territorial borders, and a desire of superior authorities to include in amalgamations solely the enterprises of their own ministry, and at times even only of their own department.

What enterprises and amalgamations do we need? There is no one answer here. No set pattern should be used in resolving such an important question. And yet some initial ideas should be mentioned. First of all the composition of enterprises and amalgamations must be in keeping with rational specialization and cooperation, creating conditions for most progressive equipment and technology. It is important to combine in one organization all links of production—from applied research to batch production and technical servicing. And the factor of controllability should definitely be considered. Finally, a monopoly position for amalgamations should be avoided in the manufacture of products.

I believe the switching of enterprises and amalgamations to complete profit-and-loss accounting and self-financing must be combined with granting them the right to launch joint ventures or amalgamations on a basis of share-holding up to and including a complete merger where this is dictated by economic expediency. We are confident that in new conditions the enterprises will be interested in forming all kinds of voluntary amalgamations, involving the creation of new equipment, computing centres for collective use, social and environmental protection facilities, transport junctions, and even schools for training personnel and managers.

But the stand of management bodies should not be passive or conservative. The gate should be thrown wide open to all integration processes.

While 37,000 industrial enterprises covered by the state plan are directly controlled from the centre now, several thousand large sectoral, inter-branch and territorial-branch amalgamations capable of implementing the entire cycle of research—investments—production—marketing—maintenance could be controlled from the centre in future. Alongside them, tens of thousands of medium and small enterprises, including cooperative ones, oriented at servicing large amalgamations and the local market could be under republican and local subordination.

No less important is the question of restructuring **branch management**.

What should be its essence? It should be clear delimitation of the areas for which ministries are responsible and those for which amalgamations and enterprises are. The ministries should really become scientific, technological, planning and economic headquarters of their industries, should account to the country for meeting national economy demands in the products of their industries, be responsible for bringing the technology of production and the quality of goods up to world standards, and vigorously go about improving their sectors structurally and promoting specialization and cooperation, and should work out economic norms, levers and incentives for enterprises in their charge.

The ministries have at their disposal leading research and development organizations and centralized funds which may be used for building new enterprises and supporting work collectives in major modernization and expansion schemes. The vast majority of industrial ministries will be able to actively join in foreign economic activities. Training and retraining of personnel and upgrading their qualifications is an important task of the ministries, and their role will increase immeasurably.

In order to discourage the attempts of the ministries' staff at petty administrative guidance of enterprises, they should be relieved of the functions of operational economic management by eliminating corresponding units and reducing the staff of the ministries and organizations servicing them.

With new functions, the ministries do not need a cumbersome structure and large staff. The question of merging certain ministries might crop up during the implementation of the proposed measures.

A system of management for national economic complexes and groups of interrelated branches is now being set up. The following agencies have been formed and function as permanent agencies under the USSR Council of Ministers: the State Agro-Industrial Committee [Gosagroprom], the State Committee for Construction [Gosstroi], the Bureau for Machine-Building and the Bureau for the Fuel and Power Complex, the Foreign Economic Commission and the Bureau for Social Development.

This system is just being formed. The optimal way of distributing functions between the bodies for running economic complexes, on the one hand, and the USSR State Planning Committee and ministries on the other, has yet to be found.

The policy of turning the permanent government agencies into viable organizations responsible for the development of their particular economic complexes and solving inter-sectoral problems should be consistently pursued. We know from experience that it is precisely at the junction of sectors that major national economic problems arise. It is precisely there that the discrepancies emerge that cause heavy losses. And it is there that vast reserves for improving work are hidden. Strengthening standing government agencies will make it possible to link ministries and departments with them and make management more effective.

In new conditions enhanced demands are made on the quality of work of the **central economic bodies**: the State Planning Committee, the Ministry of Finance, the State Committee for Prices, the State Committee for Material and Technical Supply, the State Committee for Science and Technology, the State Committee for Labor and Social Questions and others. The transition to complete profit-and-loss accounting, radical changes in the activity of ministries, and development of the system of management of national economic complexes cardinally change the functions of these bodies.

As to the USSR State Planning Committee, the stress in its work should shift to determining prospects for development, realizing the fundamental economic and social tasks, and ensuring overall balance in the national economy. The structure of the State Planning Committee as the highest scientific and economic headquarters of the country should be radically transformed in accordance with this. It is important that its general departments, social orientation, science-and technology and regional services be strengthened. All this should be linked in with the functions of the standing agencies of the USSR Council of Ministers.

The question of enhancing the coordinating role of the State Planning Committee with regard to the activity of other central economic agencies is clearly pressing, Comrades.

We have been saying that the new system will be effective only if it succeeds in linking and harmonizing the multiform interests of our society, including the interests of not only enterprises and branches but also the interests of the republics, territories, regions, cities, districts, what we call **area interests**.

It should be borne in mind that unless local possibilities and initiative are tapped in a radical reform, the cause might be seriously affected for the worse.

It would not be amiss to recall, Comrades, that many ideas behind the important experiments and the contemporary management philosophy originated at local level and were realized by local bodies. The team contract in agriculture and construction, in industrial production, new forms of area management of the economy, progressive undertakings in railway transport, in the sphere of public service, in trade, and transition to self-financing and many other things emerged on the initiative of work collectives with vigorous support from local Party, government and economic agencies.

A number of decisions on enhancing the role of republican agencies and local Soviets have been adopted of late. They have met with approval. And yet the question of area management has not been given due attention and has not been solved so far. Cardinal measures are required.

Our experience indicates that the activity of territorial agencies should be concentrated above all on the problem of a comprehensive development of a region, on the most rational use of local manpower, natural, productive and economic resources. Definite steps have already been taken in this direction. I mean establishment of agencies to manage the agro-industrial complex, construction, and production of consumer goods and services.

Area agencies can do a lot to set up inter-branch production facilities, to ensure a better use of unique equipment, secondary resources, and shape the production infrastructure. There is broad scope for their activity in these areas.

The social sphere is certainly a most important sphere for area management, and notably the Soviets. I have two remarks to make in this connection. The first concerns the protection of interests of the social sphere in large cities. We, Comrades, should arrest the escalation of construction of production facilities in such cities to the detriment of their social development.

Why shouldn't we consider and implement a system under which ministries and departments will be permitted to build production facilities only if they simultaneously allocate funds to area agencies so as to develop the social sphere on a basis of justifiable norms. I think such an approach would help put urban development in order.

The second remark is about the role of territorial agencies in organizing cooperative and individual labour activity. There exist now practically all the necessary decisions at the state level on this score. Many working people would like to form cooperatives for resolving some or other tasks connected with meeting the requirements of people. There are a lot of people wishing to be engaged in individual labor activity. It seems that there is everything for developing this important process. Nevertheless, it proceeds with difficulty and very slowly. There is one reason behind this: the lack of initiative in local government bodies, inattention to this matter and at times the unwillingness to tackle it, [along with] various bureaucratic obstacles. But it is a direct duty of the local government bodies to deal with the matter and they must be fully responsible for this.

Thus, no matter what aspect of our economy is taken, the need for bolstering the role of territorial bodies, above all the Soviets, is felt everywhere. Organizational measures seem to be indispensable, too. We believe it is expedient to set up production and economic boards at the executive committees of Soviets at regional and territorial levels to draw up plans for regional development and coordinate all economic activities on a given territory.

All in all, Comrades, we need such a system of management that would suit new principles of the economic activity, the essence of economic methods. The competence and responsibility of government agencies at all levels and in all spheres should be clearly delimitated in that system and the best conditions for the functioning of the main link—enterprise and amalgamation—should be created.

Social Aspects of Restructuring Management. Comrades, man with his real interests and motives is central to our economic policy and economic practice.

We must realize that the time when the management consisted of orders, bans and appeals, has gone. It is now clear to everybody that such methods can no longer be employed for they are simply ineffective. To create a powerful system of motives and stimuli encouraging all workers to fully reveal their capability, work fruitfully, use production resources most effectively—such is the requirement of the times.

Everything is extremely important in this: the organization of work and forms of incentive, the system of employment, the situation in the consumer market, the state of social and cultural services. Each of these areas should be considered from the viewpoint of activating the human factor.

The question of the need of a qualitatively new approach to the organization of work is posed acutely. The current practices, as a rule, have long become outdated. We need such labor organization that would correspond to the present-day requirements of the scientific and technological progress, would encompass the best national and world experience and, what is particularly important, would suit the new conditions of economic management and principles of self-government.

After a series of certain experiments it has become clear to us all that the new economic mechanism is best suited by the team contract and other effective forms of labor organization and incentives. It is only on that basis that full profit-and-loss accounting is possible and it can be applied to every collective and work place.

The system of pay and labor incentives must be arranged in a new way. The law on the enterprise guarantees enterprises the right to raise the wage rate and establish extra payments. The incentive possibilities are dramatically expanding. But it is particularly important that actual pay of every worker be closely linked to his personal contribution to the end result, and that no limit be set. There is only one criterion of justice: whether or not it is honestly earned.

Intensification of social production and creation of a corresponding economic mechanism encourage us to appraise in a new way effective employment in our society.

The number of work places grew rapidly at the previous stages, in conditions of predominantly extensive production development. Filling vacancies was the main problem then. The situation is radically changing now. The scale on which the excessive workforce will be trimmed will increase considerably with the speedup of scientific and technological progress. The new economic mechanism will give incentives for this. The need in labor resources for public services, culture, education, health service and recreation facilities will increase at the same time.

Such a rearrangement of the workforce requires close attention and well-considered organizational measures. We must ensure social guarantees for employment of the working people, for their constitutional right to work. The socialist system has such opportunities.

The rights of state agencies for labour and social issues must be expanded in the new situation, and their responsibility must be enhanced.

I have mentioned that a large gap has formed in recent years between monetary incomes and solvent demand of the population, on the one hand, and available commodities, on the other. In 1971-1985 the volume of money in circulation grew 3.1 times while consumer goods production only doubled. We must consistently and firmly pursue the line, within the economic management reform, of making production of consumer goods fit people's demands. Work merely to stock warehouses is not only wasteful. It is absurd whichever way you look at it. Better close down such production. I think this question merits the closest attention.

And the point of the matter is not only that the solvent demand of the population be met with available supply. Thought must apparently be given to drawing fuller the funds of the population into the solution of a number of other tasks. Many people would like to acquire housing with personal funds through cooperative and individual housing construction. There has been no real advance in this. Quite the contrary, the share of cooperative housing construction has been declining markedly until recently. This is certainly not right.

Considerable funds could be borrowed from the population for setting up leisure and tourist amenities, and for building paid sports facilities on the local level. The population could invest funds on definite terms into the cooperatives that are being set up now in public services and other areas.

And here we approach another matter. To overcome deformation of demand, we must double or treble the development rate of the entire sphere of paid services, introduce additional stimuli there, and provide more resources. Estimates indicate that by taking this road we can assure an annual increase of services at the rate of 15-20%.

All this and many other things would make it possible to soon improve the situation in the market of goods and services and to strengthen money circulation. Let those responsible for this, in the centre and at the local level, ponder the issue.

The passivity of those managers who are not using the new opportunities to attain social targets is particularly intolerable today. The old habit of approaching social problems from the leftover principle, and the existing sponger psychology are still manifest in this area. and both things should be eradicated once and for all. It is work collectives, and they only, that are to solve their social problems. And work collectives, cities and districts, regions and republics must act energetically, rationally, and enterprisingly, as befits a proprietor.

Restructuring of Management Should be Efficiently Organized with Party and Political Backing. Comrades, a radical reform of the economic management is not a single act, but a process which will take a certain time to complete. And there must be no delays about this, for that might be the main danger. Too much time has been wasted. In any case we must usher in the 13th Five-Year Plan period with a new economic mechanism, though the adjustment could be continued later.

The Politburo deems it unacceptable for a lack of reliable organizational backing, and tardiness and lack of coordination of action to lead, as in the past, to delays and incomplete reform.

In this connection it is proposed that the Plenary Meeting endorse the "Guidelines for the Radical Restructuring of Economic Management," a document which contains both fundamental and concrete directives for establishing a new system of economic management. It is also proposed that it should become a Party directive for the entire subsequent work in this area.

What is the organizational intent of the planned economic management restructuring?

Its starting point will be the adoption by the USSR Supreme Soviet of the Law of the USSR on the State Enterprise (Association). A whole package of specific measures on major matters of the management restructuring is proposed for adoption by the end of this year so as to bring centralized management into accord with the law on the enterprise.

From the year 1988, the new principles will be applied to the operation of enterprises and amalgamations manufacturing about two-thirds of the entire industrial output, including all machine-building, metallurgy, the main part of enterprises of the fuel-and-energy branches, as well as of the chemical, timber, light, food, fishing industries and all types of transport. The transition to new conditions of economic management must be completed in 1989.

The restructuring of the most important economic management functions will be effected parallel with this before the end of the Five-Year Plan period: planning, pricing, finance and crediting, material and technical supply. Stable economic norms of long-time action for the 13th five-year period will be set.

A new Five-Year Plan is to be worked out in a new way, on the basis of the system of economic management introduced. First of all broad independence in concluding agreements on the basis of economic norms and orders of consumers must be provided for enterprises. All work should be organized in such a way as to ensure that the Five-Year Plan is adopted before the beginning of the five-year period itself.

Comrades, the organizational aspect of the changes planned should include a vast programme of legislative activity with the legal mechanism of the economic reform formalized.

The approach is simple: there must be no lack of clarity in the question of legality or illegality of some or other actions in the sphere of economic management. The principle that all not banned by law is permitted should be applied more broadly.

All norm-setting act contradicting the Law on the Enterprise should apparently be annulled after the adoption of the law, and the issuance of norms by departments should be placed within a strict juridical framework.

A system should also be created for promptly informing work collectives of laws and decrees of the government. People should know the laws which regulate their life and activity.

The role of legal control by the procurator's office over the observance of laws by all organizations and officials is increasing vastly in this connection. The role of State Arbitration in the regulation of economic activity should be seriously enhanced.

I would like to emphasize particularly the need for maximum openness in the entire process of working out and making decisions on social and economic life, for regular and widely covered accountability of representatives of the economic bodies. Publications of drafts and decrees, and broad information about proposals on questions discussed must become a rule. This is the subject of a new Law on nationwide discussion of the most important questions of state life, a draft of which will be submitted to the upcoming session of the USSR Supreme Soviet.

There is a major acute problem of radically restructuring our statistics. A sharp turn towards qualitative indices, broader information on regional and social development, and various selective surveys are needed. No serious socio-economic analysis and, consequently, competent approach to problems is possible without this. We must also broaden the margins for publishing materials on economic and social statistics.

Comrades, it is now especially necessary to increase Party influence in all aspects of our work, to achieve skillful guidance of social processes and work out new creative approaches. From the CC to the Primary Party Organization, our main task in switching the economy to the new system of management is to ensure the normal functioning of the national economy. This is important precisely because during the transition period we will have to solve simultaneously a number of major and complex tasks in economic development, carry out the structural reorganization of the national economy, implement measures to accelerate scientific and technological progress, a radical reform of management and deepen its democratic principles.

One should also remember that in the period of time necessary for comprehensive resolution of these matters, the new and old methods of management will be used concurrently. This brings forth problems, unusual in character and complexity, which the Party organization must tackle. The latter must be in the vanguard of all the changes that are being carried out.

The ongoing reform affects essentially all tiers of our economic edifice. The large-scale, diverse work which is carried out at all levels of the national economy to reconstruct the economic mechanism, must receive constant and unflagging attention from Party organizations and committees. They have to impart a political, national meaning to the effort to restructure economic management.

The role and responsibility of Party organizations at enterprises and amalgamations are particularly great. They are undergoing a test of political maturity and capacity for action. Their Party position and practical work will largely determine the transition to new methods of economic management and the implementation of principles of self-government in work collectives.

We are sure that all Party organizations, and all Communists and personnel will take up the outstanding economic problems with redoubled energy, fully mindful that the restructuring of our economy is the decisive, major condition for advancement towards increasing the well-being of the Soviet people and towards all-round progress of our socialist homeland.

Comrades, such are the ideas and principles underlying the planned restructuring of the system for managing our economy—the most thorough-going and sweeping reform of its kind over the years of building socialism. We are duty-bound to knuckle down to effecting it with a feeling of tremendous political responsibility to the people and to the future of the country.

The main purpose of the reform is to provide further stimuli and impulses to economic growth and lay a solid material foundation for Soviet society's accelerated social and cultural progress.

The restructuring drive under way across the land is directly continuing the cause of the October Revolution and consistently realizing the ideals inscribed on the banner of our revolution whose 70th anniversary we shall celebrate this year.

The restructuring drive is our response to the historic challenge of the times. Our Party and our people will respond to it in the same manner as when accomplishing the greatest social revolution, building socialism and winning a historic victory of global significance in the Great Patriotic War.

It has always been this way when we were facing the tasks of a historical choice. It will be the case this time too.

"O zadachakh partii po korennoi perestroike upravlenniia ekonomiki," *Kommunist*, 10 (1987), 5–46; *Partiinaia zhizn'*, 13 (1987), 4–41; *Pravda* and *Izvestiia* (26 June). Condensed translations can be found in CDSP, 39:26 (1987), 3–17 and FBIS, No. 125 (30 Jun 87), R1–R22.

Speech in Murmansk (1 Oct 87)
Dear Comrades!
I have come to you to familiarize myself with the life of the Soviet Polar Region, to get first-hand information about your work and concerns and, first and foremost, to fulfil the honorary mission entrusted to me by the CPSU CC and the Presidium of the USSR Supreme Soviet and present the Hero City of Murmansk the high award of the Homeland.

Murmansk's glorious history is a bright mirror reflection of the destiny of our country. Soviet power was proclaimed here on the second day after the armed uprising in Petrograd. Today, recalling those days, we admire the heroism and selflessness displayed by working people in the Far North during those legendary days and years.

Throughout the hardships of the Civil War when the very existence of the Soviet Republic was at stake, Murmansk's workers together with revolutionary soldiers and seamen bravely fought against the interventionists and White Guards. They prevented the transformation of the Kola Peninsula from falling into a staging area for an offensive on Red Petrograd.

Large-scale construction in keeping with the plans for industrialization was begun in the first five-year plan periods.

The Great Patriotic War was a stern test for city dwellers as it was for all Soviet people. The defence of the Soviet Polar Region lasted 40 months. The plans of the German fascist command to seize Murmansk failed. The city not only held out, it paralyzed the enemy's strike forces and steadfastly defended the state border.

Communists and Komsomol members were the first to take up arms. The troops of the Karelian front (which included the "Polar division", set up in Murmansk) played a decisive role in defeating the alpine regiments of the fascists on the Bolshaia Zapadnaia Litsa River. The marines and guerrilla units carried out devastating raids behind the enemy lines. Men, fighting at the front, were replaced at their machines by women and teenagers. Murmansk fishermen caught fish under enemy fire.

Murmansk during the war was a major centre of cooperation of the countries of the anti-Hitler coalition. And Murmansk again saw men in American and British uniforms, but in a quite different capacity, not what they had been twenty years before—this time they were allies. We have not forgotten, nor shall we ever forget how allied convoys with weapons and equipment for the Soviet Army broke their way through the Hitlerite blockade to reach Murmansk. The courage of Soviet, British and American sailors who made this operation possible remains a vivid symbol of cooperation between our peoples in the period of the Second World War.

The memory of those events sears us with the burning truth of selfless heroism. The great courage of Soviet troops and workers on the home front was especially manifest here on the Kola Peninsula, in the rigorous conditions of the Far North. Their profound feeling of civic responsibility for the future of the socialist land gave the Murmansk people the strength to surpass the limits of human endurance. These patriots will never be forgotten. What was the Valley of Death will remain in popular memory forever as a Valley of Glory.

The heroic defenders of Murmansk had absorbed the fortitude and gallantry as well as the wisdom of many generations of northerners, starting from the ancient Russian Pomors. Let us recall, for example, that it was here at Murmansk, in the arduous fishing trade, that a great son of Russia, a scientist of genius and an ardent patriot, Mikhail Vasilevich **Lomonosov**, spent his youth. It is to these parts, to the Kola Peninsula, that [Emelian] **Pugachev**'s men were sent to external exile. This was the place that the families of many political exiles, revolutionaries, chose to take refuge during the years of the tsarist autocracy.

The October Revolution opened a new chapter in the history of this region and created favorable conditions for the tapping of its natural wealth. Inspired by the ideas of social progress, the people enthusiastically embarked on sweeping changes in order to advance along the path of socialism.

Murmansk today is among the biggest ports in the USSR. It has become a base for Arctic development, pioneering a northern sea route, exploring the Kola Peninsula and surrounding seas and exploiting their riches. New cities have sprung up in the region. A number of major scientific centres and industrial enterprises such as the Severonikel combine and the Apatit amalgamation have been built. It is here that the Red-Bannered Northern Fleet carries out its duties. It is here that our nuclear-powered ice-breakers have their main base. Murmansk fishermen are making a considerable contribution to the country's food resources.

The military and industrial contributions of the people of the region and the city have won them high awards. Murmansk is a city with a heroic past and a radiant future, a city of fine revolutionary traditions and labor accomplishments which are continued today. It was, is and we are sure, will remain the nation's dependable outpost in the Arctic.

Permit me, dear Comrades, to fulfil the mission entrusted to me and to present to Murmansk the Order of Lenin and the Gold Star medal.

Comrades,

On behalf of the CPSU CC, the Presidium of the USSR Supreme Soviet and the Council of Ministers of the USSR I heartfully congratulate you, participants in this solemn meeting, all inhabitants of the city and region, the soldiers of the local garrison, the sailors of the Northern Fleet with the high well-deserved award and the conferring of the honorable title "Hero City" on the city of Murmansk.

We convey our cordial gratitude and appreciation to the participants in the Great Patriotic War—those who fought at the front, to the partisans and workers of the rear. I wish you good health and creative forces, glorious veterans of war and labour.

It is a great honor to be a citizen of and to live in a Hero City. It means, I think, first of all, to be keenly aware of one's responsibility for the state of affairs not only in this city, but also in the country as a whole, to be a citizen in the loftiest sense of the word, and set an example of steadfast patriotism, real service to the interests of the people and fidelity to the cause of socialism.

To live and work in a Hero City means not only to develop production. It means to build not only high-rises, but also social relations of a new kind. It means fighting shortcomings, breaking inertia, and initiating everything new and progressive that is associated today with restructuring, renewal, democratization and openness.

To be an inhabitant of a Hero City, in short, means to enhance its honor and glory everywhere and in all respects, the honor and glory of every factory and organization, of every work collective.

And you have people on whom you can rely. In the national economy of the Murmansk Region there are quite a few collectives noted for their ability to work. There are hundreds of real past masters in their jobs who show the highest responsibility in their work and put their hearts into it, who actively draw on all that is new in the life of the country.

Among those whose labor is especially productive and who are noted for their social activity are:

—head of a building team, USSR State Prize winner Semon Konstantinovich **Shitov**;

—depot engine drive, Honorable Railwayman Boris Vasilevich **Kozlov**;

—worker of the Murmansk fish-packing plant and deputy of the RSFSR Supreme Soviet Melguzova Antonina **Alekseevna**;

—Hero of Socialist labour, Merited Doctor of the RSFSR Piotr Andreevich **Baiandin**;

—Merited School Teacher of the RSFSR Zinaida Ivanovna **Dmitrieva**; delegates to the 27th Congress, Murmansk shipyard pipelayer Iuri Grigorevich **Baskakov** and fishing fleet captain Nikolai Ivanovich **Gutskalov** and many many others. I heartfully congratulate you, Comrades, with your success, I congratulate all front-rank workers, innovators and restless, daring and exploring people.

I have had a lot of meetings and conversations with working people recently. They were businesslike and open. The talk was about restructuring, its successes and difficulties, about problems and ways to resolve these problems, and about work which is directed towards the future.

It was very important for me, for the Political Buro of the CC to be reminded again and again that Soviet people realize the necessity and urgency of the changes that have been started. The spirit of renewal is manifested ever more clearly in the life of your city and this is the main thing now.

Our meeting is held not long before a great national day, the anniversary of the October Socialist Revolution.

The path we have traversed over these seven decades has been far from smooth. It was a truly heroic path. The Soviet people have proved equal to resolving the huge tasks of restructuring society on new socialist principles.

The creation of a mighty power, our common home, in which scores of nations and peoples live and work shoulder to shoulder, is the crowning result of the work and struggle of all generations of Soviet people.

We take pride in the achievements of our Revolution. It is not for nothing that it is called Great. But this very greatness obliges us to see the problems that have accumulated in society and to see the new demands of present-day life.

It is precisely the lofty responsibility of the Party for the destiny of the people, for the destiny of socialism, that suggested the need to speed up the country's social and economic development.

We now have to do many things all at once, to make up for the opportunities lost over the past decade. But we have to do this. We cannot avoid this work. No one will do it for us.

Revolutionary construction, the implementation of the great ideals and goals of the October Revolution now continues at a qualitatively new stage, in cardinally changed internal and external conditions.

What can be said about the restructuring now taking place in society?

First of all, there have undoubtedly been positive changes not only as regards awareness of its tasks and problems, but also concerning practical approaches, concrete actions and their results.

We are now more fully and deeply aware of many things in our life than we were in the days of the 1985 April Plenary Meeting of the CPSU CC and even the 27th Congress.

The fundamental directions of the work to be done in the political, economic and social areas have been determined in the just over two years that have passed since the April Plenary Meeting. The road to changes has thus been fully opened.

We now realize more clearly that in order to implement our plans and intentions, we all have to put in much work, to rebuild by joint efforts many things in our society.

We are not satisfied with the housing situation, the quantity and quality of goods and services, the functioning of the social sphere, the activity of state and economic organizations, and so on. These issues received priority attention here as well, during meetings on Murmansk land. But all this is connected with our work and with our attitude to it. So it turns out that we must ourselves change if the situation in society is to be changed the way we want. We know now that the restructuring affects everyone of us without exception and that it involves certain difficulties.

We were saying quite recently that we need a new policy—new decisions and bold approaches. We have such a policy now. There are new ideas and intentions implemented in concrete solutions today in every area of life. A new moral atmosphere without which profound transformations cannot be embarked on is thus emerging.

We all study now. We are learning great lessons from life.

We are learning lessons of truthfulness and openness.

We are learning lessons of responsibility and discipline.

We are learning lessons of wider democracy.

We are learning lessons of internationalism and patriotism.

The first results of the restructuring are most felt in the political climate of our society. It can now be said that the new way of thinking and conduct is emerging step by step in conflicts of opinion and sometimes in heated debates. I would say the social well-being of man is improving. This I feel with particular keenness on Murmansk land.

And one of the most noble tasks of the restructuring is precisely that of elevating working people, enhancing their prestige and dignity and expanding their capabilities and talents. This is the lofty aim and meaning of socialism.

The working people have seen for themselves how potent openness, criticism of shortcomings, and the drive for more democracy are as vehicles for renovation and restructuring. They expect restructuring to produce changes in the conditions of their life.

With this aim in view the CPSU CC and the government, well aware of the fact that the implementation of the restructuring program will take some time and require immense effort, are seeing to it that issues of vital importance for the people are dealt with promptly in the course of the restructuring process.

At the June Plenary Meeting of the CPSU Central Committee we brought **to the fore such tasks, as the provision of the population with foodstuffs, housing and consumer goods.**

What has been done at the initial stage of the implementation of the social programme drafted by the Party?

In the past two years the cash incomes of the population have increased by approximately 16 billion rubles in annual average terms. The salaries of physicians and teachers and grants of students at secondary specialized and higher educational establishments have gone up. Pensions to certain categories of working people have been increased.

In the sphere of foodstuffs—during the same period the annual average meat output increased by almost two million tons, milk output- by 8.5 million tons, and egg output—by seven billion eggs. More grain, sugar beet and some other crops are being harvested. Changes for the better in foodstuff consumption are taking place on that basis. They are more substantial in those regions and republics where collective and state farms are operating better and where the possibilities of personal small holdings are used skillfully. Now the following principle operates: each republic, territory and region have an assignment for a five-year plan on the supply of products to the union and republican fund. And all the rest is kept to meet local needs. This is why everything produced in excess of the assigned plan will be kept for local consumption. This is stimulating not only every collective and state farm, and every work collective: every district and region is interested in it.

The scale of housing construction has increased. Last year 6.87 million sq.m. of housing more than in 1985 were built through the use of all sources of funding. In January-August 1987 the state alone put into service new houses with an area of 6.7 million sq.m. more than in the corresponding period of last year.

Investments in the construction of schools and pre-school child-care centres, clubs and cultural centres, hospitals, outpatient clinics and sports structures were substantially increased.

The situation regarding **the output of consumer goods** is also beginning to change, albeit slowly and with difficulty. The range of services offered to the population is expanding. All sectors of the national economy are increasing their contributions to the output of consumer goods and services. Let us get it straight: this process proceeds with great difficulties. Far from all have understood so far that no one can stay aloof from the problems involved in the accomplishment of this immensely important state task.

Last year the overall turnover of goods grew by nearly eight billion rubles, while sales of alcoholic beverages dropped by 10.7 billion rubles. This means that we coped with the task of setting off the loss of a substantial portion of "drunken" incomes. However, for the time being we do not meet to the full the growing consumer demand of the population. In the eight months of the current year, despite diminished proceeds from alcohol sales as against the previous years, goods turnover grew by 5.8 billion rubles compared with the corresponding period of last year.

So, there are some positive changes. But when the consumer market situation is evaluated as a whole it must be frankly admitted: we are still very far from a radical change in that sphere. Our efforts must not be slackened either in the centre or on the periphery. On the contrary, they should be intensified. This especially applies to quality and variety.

Soviet people ardently support the state course towards **improving the health of the people**. A document of great social and humanistic significance—the Guidelines for the Development of Health Services in the Country—was published for a nationwide discussion. This is a very major national program. Huge resources will be channelled into its realization.

Let me put it straight: we are ready to invest in health care, as in the educational sphere, the maximum possible share of that which we produce over and above plans. Even today additional financial resources to the sum of 5.6 billion rubles were found and devoted to the urgent needs of health care for the remaining three years of the Five-Year Plan period.

In a word, Comrades, our long-term and short-term plans in the social sphere are important. **Our approach is clear**—more concern for the people, more concern for their work and life. But these plans are directly linked with the acceleration of economic development, with the better work of every enterprise, collective and state farm, construction site, research establishment, laboratory, design bureau and so forth. And this means that **for us the economy is the main area of restructuring**.

We have lately boosted performance in industry, in the agrarian sector and in capital construction. However, alongside certain changes for the better there are setbacks, notably in machine building, the chemical and light industries. We are concerned about that. The situation in machine building where deep-running modernization is in progress is a source of special concern. And we must surmount existing difficulties by all available means and ensure the success of the undertaking.

Thus, changes do take place in our economy. But there had been no breakthrough so far. It would be unreasonable to believe that these ambitious goals can be attained in some two or three years, that during this period a dramatic change can take place in the fulfilment of those truly revolutionary tasks. We must do much in order to bring it about. There should be no illusions here, for it is a matter of restructuring the building, not merely repainting the walls. The main work lies ahead.

This question is often asked: what should be done? Let me say this: **At the first stage we had to clarify the situation in the economy**, in its individual sectors and regions and determine where to start from, to make the necessary structural changes, alter the policy of capital investment, and establish priorities. And, of course, we had to decide how we should run economic affairs, what forms of administration and what mechanism of management we needed, what new approaches we should take, and what incentives we should provide in order to encourage the initiative of working people, including production workers, scientists and designers.

We completed this work in the main and adopted relevant documents. They were endorsed by the June Plenary Meeting of the Party's CC. The chief among these is the Law on the State Enterprise.

The next stage has set in now. Every decision taken should now be implemented so that practical deeds follow our decisions. And, mind you, in strict compliance with what we have decided.

This effort, Comrades, should be started—if it has not been done yet—**by setting things in good order, by strengthening discipline and organization** in all production collectives, enhancing the responsibility of everyone for conscientiously fulfilling his immediate obligations. This is the starting point from which all of us should travel—doing one's job conscientiously. A simple answer for all of us, for everyone, no matter what post one holds, no matter what is one's employment position in our society.

In the past, society paid dearly for its failure to solve the problems of order and organization. This is all the more impermissible now.

Young workers at the Severonikel plant were right when they said that discipline has become rather loose among all of us in general. And this is why things should be set in good order everywhere both at the top and in the republics, regions, districts and in work collectives. Everywhere, Comrades. This is very important now when we are effecting a radical reform of our economy, when work should be done in a new fashion, when initiative, self- reliance and a high sense of responsibility are needed for accomplishing scientific, technological and organizational tasks, for putting new methods of management to work.

Hence, the first and very important task of all work collectives—decisively to set things in good order, ensure good organization, stronger discipline and the greater initiative of the working people. Our senior officials and Party organizations should be pace-setters in their respect.

Until now many of them used to nod at those at the top: let them straighten things out first. By the way, many Party bodies and managers used to refer very widely to those on high to justify their own idleness and passivity, especially when working people literally assailed them, demanding that they make real steps towards restructuring, changing the state of affairs and solving problems that have piled up in each work collective, in one or another town or region. The decisions adopted cut the ground from under such officials. The near future will clarify many things and show who is worth what. It is important to work now. All political directives are here, decisions have been adopted and tasks set. Everyone should act.

In a word, those who are still 'in the trenches' marking time should rise without delay and go into the offensive against shortcomings, neglect and lagging.

Today we particularly count on initiative and vigour, on working people's principled attitude—this is how we put the question. And it is by this that economic bodies should be guided, as well as our leading personnel and Party organizations. **Everything is the concern of working people**. It is their country, it is their system, it is their society. They are masters. Party organizations, cadres serve the people, the entire Party serves the people. Not the other way round. In production, members of work collectives should feel and behave as real masters. Any attempts—no matter from what quarter—to hinder the exercise of this right or the manifestation of the working people's initiative should be resolutely stopped.

Everything that is being done to improve the state of affairs, to remove all that impedes advance and the introduction of new methods of management, innovations and achievements of scientific and technological progress—is not only legitimate but vitally needed by our society.

The meaning of the decisions of the January and June Plenary Meetings of the CPSU CC is to draw all working people into a real process of introducing order and organization at enterprises and in running the production and social affairs there. This is the main intent also of the Law on the State Enterprise.

That is why, Comrades, I want to say the following: do not wait any longer for instructions from above. You know the political directives. The relevant legal documents have been adopted. Now it is necessary to act, release grassroots initiative. Officials and Party organizations should do everything for this process to develop faster and gain momentum.

In this connection I have pleasant impressions of my visit to Murmansk Region and conversations with people. The people's initiative and their desire to be real masters make themselves felt already. As V.N. **Ptitsyn**, First Secretary of the Regional Committee, noted, in appraising today's situation in the region in general, it should be stressed outright that working people are pressing the managers and the Party organizations hard. They mean good, they want intensification.

If some people in economic, government or Party organizations are scared of that, it is only because they are not used to it. This is how things should be under socialism. Time will pass and you yourselves will look for ways to draw the collective's attention to any question, to resolve any question with its participation. This is the principal means. If a real alliance of leading personnel, Party organizations and work collectives is formed as a result, it will be a decisive force. Technology is a good thing. But if there is no such alliance, nothing will be achieved. People are the chief protagonists. Democracy and new methods of economic management are the chief means to set this force in motion. This is the conclusion the January and June Plenary Meetings of the CPSU CC arrived at.

I would like to dwell particularly on the following. **It is very important now to look very closely into everything that concerns the Law on the Enterprise, self-supporting and collective contract, which we call the new economic mechanism**. This, Comrades, is not at all simple. I recall 1986 when we were preparing for the first stage of introducing the state quality control system. Some took this seriously, other presumptuously. The first coped with their task well from the beginning of this year, though not without difficulties, while the latter found themselves in a flutter. So much so that some of them cannot get rid of it to this day. Comrades, there is nowhere to retreat.

We had a conversation in the port today. Dockers told us: we were given loaders but they do not work. Why? The quality is bad. That is one example. Here are others: someone bought a TV set, several days or hours later it was out of order. A tractor was supplied to a collective farm or a combine harvester to a village, but it takes another month to put them to working order. Can we depart from quality requirements, from the state quality control system, Comrades? Why then do we spend our working hours, strength, raw materials and energy on producing a no-good product. I don't want to deride everything. A lot of good things are being done in the country. Take defences, for instance. We are not inferior in anything here. So, we can work. quality control inspectors in defences sphere work in a way that makes everybody sweat: workers, designers, engineers and managers. This is the way the state quality control system should operate. Then we will have the technology and commodities we want. If that is not done, why do we need money, what to buy with it? We should think hard.

Why then do we go to work every morning? For what? All of us, our entire society should ponder over this situation. We cannot forego state quality control. I have already spoken about this on behalf of the CC many times and expressed profound gratitude to the working class for its understanding, class understanding of the fact that we cannot retreat from the line towards improving quality. The working class rendered us immense support in this respect. But some managers imply got lost.

We ought to thoroughly study the experience with state quality control and operation of our enterprises in these conditions and draw proper conclusions so as not to find ourselves in a difficult situation when, on 1 January 1988, 60% of our economy start operating on cost-accounting, self-financing and self-repayment principles. This is more far- reaching than state quality control. As in the case of state quality control, we cannot give up cost-accounting, self-financing and self-repayment.

We cannot retreat from what we have started. We began a war on drunkenness—we cannot retreat, although many are discontented. We hear about remarks made on account of the government by people queueing up to buy this poison. That we know. Locally, some find it hard to withstand this pressure. We foresaw that too but the biggest mass of people are all for sobriety. If we waver the frontline of our restructuring will collapse.

Once self-financing is introduced, the situation at enterprises will change, the entire economy will move forward, and end results will be favourable. Thus, Comrades, new opportunities will present themselves for solving the entire complex of social problems. Tons of oil and ore, and cubic metres of gas are not an end in themselves, cubic metres of timber, tons of pig iron and steel and so forth are not the final result. We need all in order to have a bigger national income which we would use to improve all aspects of our society's and our people's life. By the way, we have many tons now. But we spend 50 to 100% more energy and material resources per unit of national income than other developed countries. So it turns out that our national income could be 50 to 100% bigger with the same resources, provided this is done properly, on the basis of new technologies, on the basis of scientific and technological progress. Think how vast these possibilities are, how wasteful our wealth has made us. I've already said and I repeat and shall repeat myself because that's how it is. We are swimming in resources. It is shameful how we treat them. We already feel what it may come to. Perhaps this sort of talk is not for an occasion such as this. But that's Leninist style.

Speaking of self-financing, work under this system will be rewarded and encouraged properly. This should also be kept in mind. In simple words, without using categories and terms of political economy, this reduces to one thing—encouragement for good performance and a befitting evaluation for a shoddy one.

I do not go into the economic substance of cost accounting intentionally . But since all this makes incomes of the working people and, hence, their status and well-being, dependent on the final results, one burning issue comes to light. What I want to say is that when an enterprise is self- financing, the working people and work collectives are all extremely interested in having at the head of teams, production sections, shops, technical services and enterprises as a whole, competent, modern, able people to whom they can entrust their fate and on whom they can depend. This means that preparation for work in conditions of cost-accounting includes the discussion and solution of personnel problems. Everything should be done in such a way as is demanded by the times and as the working people believe it should be done—democratically.

Industrial headquarters and national economic bodies must assist enterprises during this difficult transitional stage. This is the most important task for them now. These two days, while in Murmansk, I heard with concern many complaints about ministries, primarily, because they are slow in conveying new economic quotas to enterprises. But, without them, one cannot start preparation for and the transfer to self-supporting.

I want to stress once again that we must prepare to work under the new system in all seriousness and understand that this concerns millions of people, that this concerns the most important and decisive sphere of our society—the economy.

The experience which we have accumulated in the past more than two years in all branches using the new methods of management, new approaches, new forms of organizing production, experience which was gained in the course of the nationwide discussion of the Law on the State Enterprise convinces us that we are on the correct path. Despite the initial difficulties this is a very promising endeavor for all of us, Comrades, for our society, for socialism. And we must solve all problems arising at this stage with a feeling of great responsibility.

Not everything will be achieve at once. Probably there will be miscalculations and some mistakes are possible. We must treat all this calmly, democratically, openly, without panic and demagogy, and seriously. For everything that has been planned is meant to accelerate the country's socio-economic development, to improve the life of working people. This should be clearly understood. For in the long run every increment in the economy will raise the people's living standard and make itself felt first of all in the social sphere. All these questions are now being widely discussed in the mass media—the press, radio and television. This is a normal process. It helps us to understand things better and to act consciously, confidently and effectively.

The question of wholesale, purchase and retail prices is now being discussed along with many other problems of restructuring. Many people here ask me: "How will this problem be handled?" I would like to say that this is an important element in the new economic mechanism and it is impossible to fulfil the task of switching to new methods of management without getting to the bottom of the matter of prices, both wholesale, purchase and retail prices. The conversations in Murmansk and Monchegorsk, and information reaching the CPSU CC and the government show that the discussion of prices has given rise to certain apprehensions among working people, indeed the entire population of the country. This is understandable.

These apprehensions boil down to the following: is the present leadership planning to solve all economic problems by lowering the people's living standards? I have already spoken on this matter both at the Congress and the Plenary Meetings of the CC. I want to say once again that we have to deal with the matter of prices just as other matters of the new economic mechanism.

First, this should be done with the aim of accelerating our economy's development, increasing the output of necessary products and commodities in the country, raising the national income and improving the well-being of working people. This is the aim.

Second. We will act in the same manner as at the early stage of the restructuring, after the April Plenary Meeting of the CC, i.e. we will act openly. We will discuss, countrywide, all the main questions of our society's life. And, of course, the question of prices, which concerns the entire society, and every family. When it is ripe it will surely be submitted to the working people for discussion. Everything must be clear and there should be no anxiety.

Do you know the situation with prices? I will cite several examples. The price that the state pays to the collective and state farms for their farm produce, particularly livestock products, is 50 or 100% higher than their retail price. For this reason last year's meat and milk subsidies amounted to 57 billion rubles. Many people do not know this, they are not aware of the situation.

Hence the lack of a proper attitude towards foodstuffs. You know it yourselves. You can see children using a loaf of bread as a football. Tremendous amounts of foodstuffs are wasted. There are examples of a different sort. Lady's boots cost 120-130 rubles, and 62 kg of meat, which is today's average per capita quota of meat, costs about the same. In other words, the value of meat consumed by a person annually is equal to that of a pair of boots. This is the present situation. This is why no one thinks carefully about foodstuffs.

However, the main thing is that families with larger incomes consume more meat and milk and, consequently, benefit more from the subsidies. This is another problem we are facing.

We are now thinking how best to approach this question. I should like to quote some figures showing the paradox of the situation in this country. Take food products of equal caloric value. If we take the price of bread in the Soviet Union for one unit, its price in the USA will be 5.5, in Britain 3.6, France 4.1, West Germany 4.9, and Hungary 1.5. Those figures are for wheat bread. The situation is the same with meat, milk and so on.

The problem does exist, and it must be solved. But first it is necessary to find the approach to it that would not spoil the living standards of the population.

I ask you: are we thinking in the right direction?

[**Voices**: yes, of course].

As these problems raise their heads, I would like to say once again that you must not get the impression that the leadership is planning some "secrets of the court of Madrid." No, it is nothing of the sort. This is not our way of solving economic problems at the expense of the living standards of the working people. As I have stated already, all the economic tasks will be accomplished if we all work better.

Another point I would like to mention at our meeting. **Comrades, we must pursue a steady policy of economizing**. We must save labor, we must save resources and we must save money. Here many things are wrong. I confirm this with a very important example. Since over a period of many decades the emphasis in managing the economy and in fact the whole of society was on centralization, command and injunction, the governmental and managerial apparatus, as well as the apparatus of public and, to some extent, Party organizations have swelled too much.

Some 18 million people are now employed in our sphere of administration, 2.5 million of them are in the apparatus of administrative and law enforcement bodies and some 15 million in the managing bodies of associations, enterprises and organizations. All this amounts to 15% of the country's manpower resources, with one manager for every 6-7 employees.

Now as we are advancing along the road of extensive democratization, development of initiative and responsibility of work collectives, of increasing their independence, and as we are introducing methods of management by economic encouragement rather than injunction, it is only natural that we should give serious thought to ways of simplifying the bloated administrative apparatus. Earlier, when any problem arose in the sphere of economy or in society in general, it was immediately suggested that an organization be set up for attending to it, as though it could help. But it did not.

We shall tackle this problem with a sense of responsibility and in a well-considered manner, showing concern for every person, his future and the future of his family. In each case we should decide everything in a socialist manner. There is much work in this country, and work will be found for everyone, a lot of work.

On the managerial staff we can economize a great deal. Right now we spend more than 40 billion rubles a year on this apparatus (I have mentioned its size), while our national income has only increased in recent years by some 20 billion rubles.

The CPSU CC and the government decided to put scientific institutions on a pay-your-own-way system. This is being done to increase returns from the research potential accumulated in the country as well as to make another saving. These measures are more than vital, they are just.

Yesterday, Comrade **Ermakov**, Director of the Severonikel plant, said: now that we have adopted a cost-accounting system, we shall pay science for the real effect it has given us. Until now, because the state paid for it, we signed a treaty irrespective of what science gave us. Today we cannot do it. It is our money, we should follow the cost-accounting and self-financing principles. Therefore, the employees of research institutions should also think how to bring more honey into our socialist hive. Let those who fail to bring profit disband themselves. This is also democratic. For socialism means payment for the results of work done. And if there are no results, there should be no pay. By the way, in keeping with a decision passed by the Council of Ministers we have already closed two branch institutes which produced nothing essential for the economy over the last years. A decision has now been taken to switch science to the self-supporting basis. This is in the interests of society and the research works themselves. Frankly speaking, talented research workers insist that real work, real contribution should be paid for. The principle of socialism: from each according to his abilities, to each according to his work should be strictly observed.

We shall continue to take decisions and adopt measures that make everyone employed in the economy more thrifty and cost-conscious. This is the purpose of the planning and management reform and one of the goals of the restructuring. We should also appeal to the conscience of everyone to combat mismanagement mercilessly. There still remains a lot of it to be cleared up in every sector of the national economy and, indeed, in every collective and at every work-place. Think of all the losses incurred in harvesting and the storage of farm produce, in wood-felling and construction. All of you sitting here can apparently cite without a moment's hesitation scores of examples proving that mismanagement is widespread. It is our enemy. We still are impermissibly wasteful and extravagant. We should realize this and change absolutely everything in the country for the better.

When we learn to be thrifty and achieve proper economic order in the way things are done where we work, the economy will benefit tremendously. It will no longer be needed to build dozens of new enterprises costing billions of rubles, and the results of the restructuring will be more tangible. Remember that waste has a most adverse effect on morality. Ending waste will make the moral climate in which we live, work and rest, still healthier.

It ought to be stressed, Comrades, that having implemented radical economic reform, our society will enter the decisive phase of its restructuring. Talking yesterday with managers from the mining complex in the Murmansk Region I said: the Political Buro believes that the restructuring process has reached a crucial stage. The success of this tremendous historic undertaking depends on competent political and economic leadership and the working people's high sense of responsibility. These are the two main factors. Let us act together, with such an understanding of our crucial situation.

If something goes wrong and produces an unexpected, unforeseen or undesirable effect anywhere, it is not reason enough to be disappointed or give up further effort.

This is reason for something else, for posing the question the Marxist, socialist and scientific way: what has prevented the plans from being realized? Why do apathy, inertia and wait-and-see attitudes still persist? after finding the causes, decisive action should be taken to remedy the situation.

It will, of course, take a long time to overcome the consequences of stagnation. We have in a way got accustomed to it. Our psychology had adapted to its conditions, requirements and manifestations. Egalitarian tendencies and parasitic attitudes have become widespread. I would even say that psychologically stagnation suited many. Some people are still nostalgic for that time. This must be seen and understood. This is reality and we should act with due account of it.

Knowing this does not mean putting up with it and letting things slide. For us seeing and understanding is only a first step, an indispensable prerequisite for changing the situation. It is only by introducing economic and social measures and by raising general political and cultural standards that we shall be able to cope with all our problems, and that in an atmosphere of openness. This will tell most appreciably on the people's morality and their civic stand. Oblomovshchina and socialism go different ways—this we should clearly and firmly say to ourselves.

On the whole, the restructuring is gaining both speed and scope and taking firmer hold. It is our common task to make this drive consistent and ensure it the required speed. I would like to repeat once more: everything that we have planned can only be accomplished by our own effort. There will and can be no miracle. It is only with our own hands that we can improve our life, something we are vitally interested in. This is what we have to say.

Comrades, it is through the prism of the common effort, the restructuring tasks as a whole that you should look at the situation in your region, too. I have already spoken of your contribution. We highly appreciate it. But all the same I have criticisms to make concerning your work.

First of all, let me say this. You live in the Far North. The composition of the population here is quite specific, the tasks are specific, and the conditions in which they are handled are specific. Many of the city residents work at sea, thousands of miles away from home. Extra concern should be shown for these people, social and cultural services should be available to them.

Looking at the issue from this standpoint, I would like to call attention to the low rates of housing construction which has made housing an acute problem, especially for fishermen. The situation has now changed somewhat. However, the calculations made by regional organi- zations on the basis of data supplied by work collectives show that these rates do not measure up to the task of solving the housing problem by the year 2000. The situation must be changed and the rates stepped up.

There are some problems with child-care centers, schools, medical, cultural and sports facilities.

It pained us to hear the grievances expressed by workers yesterday. The capacity of the Severonikel plant has doubled over the past 6-7 years, but neither heads of the enterprise, nor heads of the industry have shown enough concern, party approach or conscience, while handling these immense tasks, to take care of the people coping with these production assignments. Once again, the approach to the social sphere rested on the take-what-remains principle. Whatever does remain. As a result, Vladimir N. **Ermakov** and I, and other comrades, were embarrassed to hear yesterday such complaints as: there is nowhere to leave children, there is a shortage of pre-school centers. This is outrageous and shortsighted. It is utter irresponsibility.

Of course, Comrades, these are no easy tasks which I mention. Resolute measures are needed, the capacities of pre-fabricated house-building should be better used. The region should get down to developing building material production. It has unique opportunities for that, rarely found elsewhere. They could have everything here. But cement is brought into the Murmansk Region. Building materials are in short supply. The output of the Kildin brickworks, built in 1936, is falling due to dilapidated fixed assets.

Does it not indicate how local regional organization treat these matters and show the ministries' attitude to the solution of questions concerning social restructuring in the region? And yet enterprises of our major ministries are operating here in the North. Can they not see to it that normal conditions be created for the inhabitants of the harsh region? We will be recommending that all these questions be considered in their entirety. But I ought to say that the Regional Party Committee and the Regional Executive Committee should also act more resolutely. No pains, no gains.

In per capita consumer goods production, you are 36% below the average for the Russian Federation. I understand that the economic structure here is rather special—you produce raw materials. But it is possible to produce cement out of local raw materials and supply it to the national economy as a consumer commodity for retail trade, for the development of individual construction, for gardeners. Can the question be solved? It can. But it isn't being solved. By the way, there is a surplus workforce emerging now in the Murmansk Region. It must be employed. Can women not be engaged in production? Especially women from the families of servicemen. They are, as a rule, educated people. Is it not possible to get in touch with such centres as Leningrad and Riga and organize here branches of radio-engineering and electronics? This would add to the potential.

The Minister of Shipbuilding, I.S. **Belousov**, is present here. The ministry manufactures for itself a large quantity of automatic devices and instruments. Could this not be produced here? But no, Igor Sergeevich says: in Murmansk, not only must wages be paid, but there must also be wage differentials. Is it right to talk like that?

One-quarter of the industrial enterprises of the region and of Murmansk itself has not as yet been involved in the manufacture of consumer goods. This won't do, Comrades.

The population is having problems with repairing flats, domestic appliances and tailoring. Cooperatives are keeping a very low profile.

Take your neighbours, the Arkhangelsk Region. Two-three times less fruit, vegetables and potatoes are marketed through cooperatives in the Murmansk Region than in the Arkhangelsk Region. This means that passive, inert people are heading the cooperatives. I must praise as a real accomplishment the increase in the local production of broilers, pork and milk in recent years. This is good. Ways and reserves should be sought to develop that further and reduce the importation of produce. This would be more reliable, more profitable and stable. It is far from clear why there should be only 18 hectares of greenhouses in the region. There is one principle: one square metre per capita. There are 1,100,000 people living in your region. So, there should be 100 hectares of greenhouses. Greenhouses are assembled from pre-fabricated units. The State Agro-Industrial Committee can assemble as many units as are ordered. We assemble them in many countries. The capacities are great. Everything has been mastered here. The majority of Northern and Siberian cities have long since solved the problem of vegetable supplies from greenhouses.

In the specific conditions of the North, it is an important task to preserve and use everything that is brought in. Look, in 1986, you lost during storage and wrote off as livestock fodder 40,000 tons of potatoes and other vegetables and fruit. This, Comrades, amounts to 22% of the volume marketed. I understand that this might depend on quality as well, but, probably, on storage too. Is it not possible to have dependable facilities so as to solve this problem once and for all in large towns and cities? Where are the regional and city organizations looking? It means that their approach is based on the take-what-remains principle, too.

What concerns us are the unfavourable tendencies observed in the development of the fishing industry, your major economic sector. The set targets are not being met. There are a lot of problems here: vessels standing idle in part for longer than necessary and shortcomings in processing. Today we heard some interesting ideas and proposals on that score. It's good that they were corroborated by concrete findings by amalgamations producing equipment for fish processing. I believe that we should help the region tackle that problem. But fishermen themselves should give the matter some thought, too. They should act more decisively at the local level, and Party organizations should keep these questions in the focus of attention. I believe that the Ministry of Fisheries and the Minister, Comrade [N.I.]**Kotliar**, who is present now, will also take measures.

The problem of the comprehensive utilization of resources and natural riches of the Kola Peninsula has acquired great importance now. I'm speaking first of all of apatite-nepheline ores. Many approaches have been found here. Researchers have made concrete suggestions. It requires huge investments. I heard figures of three and more billion rubles mentioned. But I think that yesterday's talk will benefit both the centre and all those who are associated with that problem. In the coming days the Ministry, the State Planning Committee, the government, and the comrades here will think these problems over. We shall consider these matters at a Politbureau Meeting. The interests of the entire country are involved and they must be thoroughly considered.

Comrades, I would like to express the hope that the working people of Murmansk and the Murmansk Region will persistently tackle the tasks facing the region and the country. And I believe that you have sufficient skill both to tackle the most difficult tasks and to uphold the Party line. You don't have to borrow patriotism from any one. I wish you every success.

Comrades, millions of people throughout the world are watching the restructuring process in our country with immense interest. Our bold embarking on large-scale constructive work and revolutionary change demanding consolidation of all the country's efforts is convincing evidence of our confidence that peace can be preserved, that mankind does have a future.

Indeed, the international situation is still complicated. The dangers to which we have no right to turn a blind eye remain. There has been some change, however, or, at least, change is starting. Certainly, judging the situation only from the speeches made by top Western leaders, including their 'program' statements, everything would seem to be as it was before: the same anti-Soviet attacks, the same demands that we show our commitment to peace by renouncing our order and principles, the same confrontational language: "totalitarianism", "communist expansion", and so on.

Within a few days, however, these speeches are often forgotten, and, at any rate, the theses contained in them do not figure during businesslike political negotiations and contacts. This is a very interesting point, an interesting phenomenon. It confirms that we are dealing with yesterday's rhetoric, while real-life processes have been set in motion. This means that something is indeed changing. One of the elements of the change is that it is now difficult to convince people that our foreign policy, our initiatives, our nuclear-free world programme are mere 'propaganda'.

A new, democratic philosophy of international relations, of world politics is breaking through. The new mode of thinking with its humane, universal criteria and values is penetrating diverse strata. Its strength lies in the fact that it accords with people's common sense. Considering that world public opinion and the peoples of the world are very concerned about the situation in the world, our policy is an invitation to dialogue, to a search, to a better world, to normalization of international relations. This is why despite all attempts to besmirch and belittle our foreign policy initiatives, they are making their way in the world, because they are consonant with the moods of the broad masses of working people and realistically-minded political circles in the West.

Favorable tendencies are gaining ground in international relations as well. The substantive and frank East-West dialogue, far from proving fruitless for both sides, has become a distinguishing feature of contemporary world politics. Just recently the entire world welcomed the accord reached at the talks in Washington to promptly complete drafting an agreement on medium- and shorter-range missiles to be later signed at the top level. Thus we are close to a major breakthrough in the field of actual nuclear disarmament. If it happens, it will be the first such breakthrough to be achieved in the post-war years. So far, the arms race has proceeded either unimpeded or with some limitations, but no concrete move has as yet been made towards disarmament, towards eliminating nuclear weapons.

The road to the mutual Soviet-American decision was hard. Reykjavik was a crucial event along that road. Life has confirmed the correctness of our assessment of the meeting in the Icelandic capital. Contrary to panic vacillation of all sorts, sceptical declarations and propagandistic talk about the 'failure', developments have started moving along the road paved by Reykjavik. They have borne out the correctness of the assessment we made, as you remember, just 40 minutes after the dramatic end of the meeting.

Reykjavik indeed became a turning point in world history, it showed a possibility of improving the international situation. A different situation has developed, and no one could act after Reykjavik as if nothing had happened. It was for us an event that confirmed the correctness of our course, the need for and constructiveness of new political thinking.

Full use of the potential created in Reykjavik has yet to be made. Glimmers of hope have emerged, however not only in the field of medium- and shorter- range missiles. Things have started moving in the field of banning nuclear testing. Full-scale talks on these problems will soon be held. It is obvious that our moratorium was not in vain. This was not an easy step for us either. It engendered and intensified worldwide demands for an end to the tests.

I can't undertake to predict the course of events. By no means everything depends on us. There is no doubt that the first results achieved in Washington recently and the forthcoming meeting with the President of the United States may cause a kind of peaceful "chain reaction" in the field of strategic offensive arms and non-launching of weapons in outer space as well as in many other issues which insistently call for international dialogue.

So, there are signs of an improvement in the international situation but, I repeat, there are also disquieting factors that threaten to aggravate sharply the world situation.

It would be irresponsible on our part to underestimate the forces of resistance to change. Those are influential and very aggressive forces blinded by hatred for everything progressive. They exist in various quarters of the Western world, but the largest concentration of them is observed among those who cater directly for the military-industrial complex, both ideologically and politically, and who live off it.

Here is a recent and fine example. A series of hearings on the subject "**Gorbachev's Economic Reforms**" began at the Joint Economic Committee of the US Congress on 10 September, with Senators and Congressmen participating. The hearings are both open and closed-door ones. Speakers include representatives of the Administration and Sovietologists from the Central Intelligence Agency, the US Defence Department and from various scientific centres. In general, it is quite normal and even good that in America officials of such a level should want to gain a thorough understanding of what is taking place in the Soviet Union and what our restructuring means for the rest of the world and for the United States itself.

Various views are being expressed, including diametrically opposed ones. There is a good deal that is sensible and objective in them. Some can be debated in earnest and it would not be bad, I would say, to pay attention to some of the things in them. The committee members also heard an opinion that the United States "should welcome the restructuring" because it will reduce a risk of a nuclear clash.

But different kinds of recommendation are also being made at these hearings to the Administration and to Congress. Here is one such, almost word for word: if the Soviet Union attains the targets planned by the 27th Congress of the CPSU, that will, first of all, raise its prestige in the international arena and heighten the CPSU authority in the country and abroad and..., thereby, increase the threat to US national security. Who would ever have thought of such a conclusion? Moreover, success of the restructuring may weaken the political and economic unity of Western Europe, for the USSR will reach its market. The USSR will exert greater political influence on the developing countries, since Soviet military and other aid to them may be increased, and some of them will want to adopt the model of the Soviet economy if it proves competitive vis-a-vis the US economy.

And still further: the restructuring is dangerous because it will strengthen the Soviet Union's positions in international financial and economic organizations. Those analysts see a particular threat in the Soviet Union's increased influence in the world arena due to its initiatives in the field of arms control and the prospect of signing a treaty on medium-range missiles.

Just listen to the conclusion they drew as a result: **the failure** of the socio-economic policy being pursued by the Soviet Union under the leadership of the CPSU and the Soviet government **would accord** with US national interests.

In order to "facilitate" such a failure the following is recommended: to speed up the programmes of costly ABM systems under SDI and draw the USSR into the arms race in order to hinder its restructuring; to allocate still more funds for the development of expensive high-accuracy weapons and space- based military systems; for the same purpose to increase the amount of military and other aid to groups and regimes which are actively fighting against the governments of the countries supported by the Soviet Union; to hinder the establishment of economic and trade contacts by the USSR with other countries and international organizations; fully to rule out the possibility of the transfer of advanced technology to the USSR and other socialist countries, and to tighten control over the activities of COCOM [COCOM is Coordinating Committee for NATO] its member countries.

Such are the views expressed overtly and cynically. We cannot but take into account such a stance. The more so as assurances of peace intentions, which we often hear from USA officials are immediately accompanied, at one go, so to speak, by the lauding of 'power politics' and by arguments very similar to those being used by the authors of the recommendations which I just mentioned.

Militarist and anti-Soviet forces are clearly concerned lest the interest among the people and political quarters of the West in what is happening in the Soviet Union today and the growing understanding of its foreign policy erase the artificially created 'image of the enemy', an image which they have been exploiting unabashedly for years. Well, it's their business after all. But we shall firmly follow the road of restructuring and new thinking.

Comrades, speaking in Murmansk, the capital of the Soviet Polar Region, it is appropriate to examine the idea of cooperation between all people also from the standpoint of the situation in the northern part of this planet. In our opinion, there are several weighty reasons for this.

The Arctic is not only the Arctic Ocean, but also the northern tips of three continents: Europe, Asia and America. It is the place where the Euroasian, North American and Asian Pacific regions meet, where the frontiers come close to one another and the interests of states belonging to mutually opposed military blocs and non-aligned ones cross.

The North is also a problem of security of the Soviet Union's northern frontiers. We have had some historical experience which cost us dearly. The people of Murmansk remember well the years 1918-1919 and 1941-1945.

The wars fought during this century were severe trials for the countries of Northern Europe. It seems to us they have drawn some serious conclusions for themselves. And this is probably why the public climate in those countries is more receptive to the new political thinking.

It is significant that the historic Conference on Security and Cooperation in Europe was held in one of the northern capitals—Helsinki. It is significant that another major step in the development of that process—the first ever accord on confidence-building measures—was achieved in another northern capital—Stockholm. Reykjavik has become a symbol of hope that nuclear weapons are not an external evil and that mankind is not doomed to live under that sword of Damocles.

Major initiatives in the sphere of international security and disarmament are associated with the names of famous political figures of Northern Europe. One is Urho **Kekkonen**. Another is Olof **Palme**, whose death at the hand of a vile assassin shocked Soviet people. Then there is Kalevi **Sorsa**, who has headed the Socialist International Advisory Council for many years now. And we applaud the activities of the authoritative World Commission on Environment and Development headed by Prime Minister Gro Harlem **Brundtland** of Norway.

The Soviet Union duly appreciates the fact that Denmark and Norway, while being members of NATO, unilaterally refused to station foreign military bases and deploy nuclear weapons on their territory in peacetime. This stance, if consistently adhered to, is important for lessening tensions in Europe.

However, this is only part of the picture.

The community and interrelationship of the interests of our entire world is felt in the northern part of the globe, in the Arctic, perhaps more than anywhere else. For the Arctic and the North Atlantic are not just the 'weather kitchen', the point where cyclones and anticyclones are born to influence the climate of Europe, the USA and Canada, and even in South Asia and Africa. One can feel here freezing breath of the 'Arctic strategy' of the Pentagon. An immense potential of nuclear destruction concentrated aboard submarines and surface ships affects the political climate of the entire world and can be detonated by an accidental political-military conflict in any other region of the world.

The militarization of this part of the world is assuming threatening dimensions. One cannot but feel concern over the fact that NATO, anticipating an agreement on medium- and shorter-range missiles being reached, is preparing to train military personnel in the use of sea- and air-based cruise missiles from the North Atlantic. This would mean an additional threat to us and to all the countries of Northern Europe.

A new radar station, one of the Star Wars elements, has been made operational in Greenland in violation of the ABM Treaty. US cruise missiles are being tested in the north of Canada. The Canadian government has recently developed a vast programme for a build-up of forces in the Arctic. The USA and NATO military activity in areas adjoining the Soviet Polar Region is being stepped up. The level of NATO's military presence in Norway and Denmark is being built up.

Therefore, while in Murmansk, and standing on the threshold of the Arctic and the North Atlantic, I would like to invite, first of all, the countries of the region to a discussion on the burning security issues.

How do we visualize this? It is possible to take simultaneously the roads of bilateral and multilateral cooperation. I have had the opportunity to speak on the subject of "our common European home" on more than one occasion. The potential of contemporary civilization could permit us to make the Arctic habitable for the benefit of the national economies and other human interests of the near-Arctic states, for Europe and the entire international community. To achieve this, security problems that have accumulated in the area should be resolved above all.

The Soviet Union is **in favor of a radical lowering of the level of military confrontation** in the region. Let the North of the globe, the Arctic, become a zone of peace. Let the North Pole be a pole of peace. We suggest that all interested states start talks on the limitation and scaling down of military activity in the North as a whole, in both the Eastern and Western Hemispheres.

What, specifically, do we mean?

Firstly, a nuclear-free zone in Northern Europe. If such a decision were adopted, the Soviet Union, as has already been declared, would be prepared to act as a guarantor. It would depend on the participating countries how to formalize this guarantee: by multilateral or bilateral agreements, governmental statements or in some other way.

The Soviet Union simultaneously reaffirms it readiness to discuss with each of the interested states, or with a group of states, all the problems related to the creation of a nuclear-free zone, including possible measures applicable to the Soviet territory. We could go so far as to remove submarines equipped with ballistic missiles from the Soviet Baltic Fleet.

As it is known, the Soviet Union earlier unilaterally dismantled launchers of medium-range missiles in the Kola Peninsula and the greater part of launchers of such missiles on the remaining territory of the Leningrad and Baltic military areas. A considerable number of shorter-range missiles was removed from those districts. The holding of military exercises was restricted in areas close to the borders of Scandinavian countries. Additional opportunities for military detente in the region will open up after the conclusion of the agreement on "global double zero".

Secondly, we welcome the initiative of Finland's President Mauno **Koivisto** on **restricting naval activity** in the seas washing the shores of Northern Europe. For its part, the Soviet Union proposes consultations between the Warsaw Treaty Organization and NATO on restricting military activity and scaling down naval and airforce activities in the Baltic, Northern, Norwegian and Greenland Seas, and on the extension of confidence- building measures to these areas.

These measures could include arrangements on the limitation of rivalry in anti-submarine weapons, on the notification of large naval and airforce exercises, and on inviting observers from all countries participating in the European process to large naval and airforce exercises. This could be an initial step in the extension of confidence-building measures to the entire Arctic and to the northern areas of both hemispheres.

At the same time we propose considering the question of banning naval activity in mutually agreed-upon zones of international straits and in intensive shipping lanes in general. A meeting of representatives of interested states could be held for this purpose, for instance, in Leningrad.

The following thought suggests itself in connection with the idea of a nuclear-free zone. At present the Northern countries, that is Iceland, Denmark, Norway, Sweden and Finland have no nuclear weapons. We are aware of their concern over the fact that we have a testing range for nuclear explosions on Novaia Zemlia.

We are thinking how to solve this problem, which is a difficult one for us because so much money has been invested in the testing range. But, frankly speaking, the problem could be solved once and for all if the United States agreed to stop nuclear tests or, as a beginning, to reduce their number and yield to a minimum.

Thirdly, the Soviet Union attaches much importance to **peaceful cooperation in developing the resources of the North, the Arctic**. Here an exchange of experience and knowledge is extremely important. Through joint efforts it could be possible to work out an overall concept of rational development of northern areas. We propose, for instance, reaching agreement on drafting an integral energy programme for the north of Europe. According to existing data, the reserves there of such energy sources as oil and gas are truly boundless. But their extraction entails immense difficulties and the need to create unique technical installations capable of withstanding the Polar elements. It would be more reasonable to pool efforts in this endeavour, which would cut both material and other outlays. We have an interest in inviting, for instance, Canada and Norway to form mixed firms and enterprises for developing oil and gas deposits on the shelf of our northern seas. We are prepared for relevant talks with other states as well.

We are also prepared for cooperation in utilizing the resources of the Kola Peninsula, and in implementing other major projects in various forms, including joint enterprises.

Fourthly, the scientific exploration of the Arctic is of immense importance for the whole of mankind. We have a wealth of experience here and are prepared to share it. In turn, we are interested in the studies conducted in other sub-Arctic and northern countries. We already have a programme of scientific exchanges with Canada.

We propose holding in 1988 a conference of sub-Arctic states on coordinating research in the Arctic. The conference could consider the possibility of setting up a joint Arctic Research Council. Should the partners agree, Murmansk could host the conference.

Questions bearing on the interests of the indigenous population of the North, the study of its ethnic distinctions and the development of cultural ties between northern peoples require special attention.

Fifthly, we attach special importance to **the cooperation of the northern countries in environmental protection.** The urgency of this is obvious. It would be well to extend joint measures for protecting the marine environment of the Baltic, now being carried out by a commission of seven maritime states, to the entire oceanic and sea surface of the globe's North.

The Soviet Union proposes drawing up jointly an integrated comprehensive plan for protecting the natural environment of the North. The North European countries could set an example to others by reaching an agreement on establishing a system to monitor the state of the natural environment and radiation safety in the region. We must hurry to protect the nature of the tundra, forest tundra, and the northern forest areas.

Sixthly, the shortest sea route from Europe to the Far East and the Pacific Ocean passes through the Arctic. I think that depending on progress in the normalization of international relations **we could open the North Sea Route to foreign ships**, with ourselves providing the services of ice- breakers.

Such are our proposals. Such is the concrete meaning of Soviet foreign policy with regard to the North. Such are our intentions and plans for the future. Of course, safeguarding security and developing cooperation in the North is an international matter and by no means depends on us alone. We are ready to discuss any counter proposals and ideas. The main thing is to conduct affairs so that the climate here is determined by the warm Gulfstream of the European process and not by the Polar chill of accumulated suspicions and prejudices.

What everybody can be absolutely certain of is the Soviet Union's profound and certain interest in preventing the North of the planet, its Polar and sub-Polar regions and all Northern countries from ever again becoming an arena of war, and in forming there a genuine zone of peace and fruitful cooperation.

This is how, Comrades, we approach internal and international issues, how we understand the connection between the former and the latter. In both, our policy has proved its viability and constructive spirit. We are convinced that there is no other way to security and social progress but creative labour in the name of happiness and freedom of man inside the country and the development of equal cooperation between states on the world scene.

We are legitimately proud of the fact that our country has always stood at the sources of socialist practice and new thinking. In the last 70 years the world has changed beyond recognition—materially, spiritually and politically. The impact made by the Great October Revolution on the social and ideological progress of mankind is the greatest contribution to contemporary and future civilization. It is within our powers and in our interests to multiply this contribution by the practical results of restructuring.

May I wish you, your families and all working people of the region success in all your efforts to transform our country, in studies and life and to congratulate you once again on the 70th anniversary of the Great October Revolution which you are celebrating in your Hero City.

"Rech' v Murmanske," *Pravda* and *Izvestiia* (2 Oct); a translation is also in FBIS, No.191 (2 Oct 87), R27-R42; a condensed translation is in CDSP, 39:40(1987), 1-8. The speech was delivered at the ceremonial Meeting on the Occasion of the Presentation of the Order of Lenin and the Gold Star Medal to the City of Murmansk.

October and Perestroika. The Revolution Continues (2 Nov 87)
Dear Comrades
Esteemed foreign guests,
It is seventy years since the unforgettable days of October 1917, those legendary days that started the count of the new epoch of social progress, of the real history of mankind. The October Revolution is truly humanity's finest hour, its radiant dawn. The October Revolution is a revolution of the people and for the people, for every individual, for his emancipation and development.

Seventy years is nothing compared to world civilization's ascent through the centuries, but in terms of the scale of achievements history has known no other period like the one our country has experienced since the victory of the October Revolution. There is no greater honor than to be pioneers, devoting one's strength, energy, knowledge, and ability to the triumph of the October Revolution's ideals and goals!

The jubilee is an occasion for pride. Pride in what has been achieved. Severe trials fell to our lot. And we withstood them honorably. We did not simply withstand them, but wrested the country out of its state of dislocation and backwardness, turned it into a mighty power, transformed life and changed man's inner world beyond recognition.

In the cruelest battles of the 20th century we safeguarded the right to our own way of life, and defended our future. We have legitimate grounds for pride in the fact that our Revolution, our labor and struggle continue to exercise a most profound influence on all aspects of world development—politics and the economy, the social sphere, and the consciousness of our contemporaries.

The jubilee is an occasion for remembrance. To remember those millions of people who have each contributed to our common socialist gains. To remember those who smelted steel, grew crops, taught children, developed science and technology, and attained the summits of art. And in sad memory of those who fell in battle defending the country, and enabled our society to advance at the price of their lives. In unfading recollection of what we have lived through, of the path we have travelled, because it was all this that created the present day.

The jubilee is an occasion for reflection. On how difficult and complicated our affairs and destinies were at times. There were not only heroic feats but tragedies, not only great victories but bitter failures as well. We reflect on the seventy years of intense constructive endeavour from the positions of the people ready to mobilise all their strength and socialism's enormous potential for the revolutionary transformation of life.

The jubilee is also a glance into the future. Our achievements are imposing, substantial and significant. They are a lasting foundation, the basis for new attainments and for society's further development. It is in advancing socialism and in developing the ideas and practices of Leninism and the October Revolution that we see the substance of our present-day affairs and concerns, our prime task and moral duty. and that necessitates serious and thorough analysis of the historical significance of the October Revolution, of everything that has been done in these seventy post-October years.

I. **The October Road: Road of Trailblazers**
Comrades, our road as trailblazers has been long and difficult. No brief analysis can encompass it. There was a burden of the material and amoral heritage left over by the old world, World War I, the Civil War, and the intervention. There was the novelty of change and the related hopes of people, the rate and scale of the invasion of the new and unusual, sometimes leaving us no time to look around and think. There were subjective factors, which played a special part in the periods of revolutionary storms. There were notions of the future, often simplistic and straightforward, and full of the maximalism of revolutionary times. And there were also the pure, ardent strivings of the fighters for a new life to accomplish things as quickly, and as fairly as possible.

The past—its heroism and drama—cannot fail to thrill our contemporaries. We have one history, and it is irreversible. Whatever emotions it may evoke, it is our history, and we cherish it. Today we turn to those October days that shook the world. We look for and find in them both a dependable spiritual support, and instructive lessons. We see once again that the socialist option of the October Revolution has been correct.

The objective logic of mankind's historical progress has led up to that frontier. For all the contradictions and the many possible ways of civilization's progressive development, the October Revolution was a natural result of the development of the ideas and the many centuries of the working people's struggle for freedom and peace, for social justice, and against class, national, and spiritual oppression.

The year 1917 showed that the choice between socialism and capitalism is the main social alternative of our epoch, that in the 20th Century there can be no progress without advance to socialism, a higher form of social organisation. This fundamental conclusion is no less relevant today than when it was first drawn by **Lenin**. Such is the logic of society's progressive development.

The Revolution in Russia has become, as it were, the summit of the aspirations for liberation, the living embodiment of the dreams of the world's finest minds—from the great humanists of the past to the proletarian revolutionaries of the 19th and 20th Centuries. The year 1917 absorbed the energy of the people's struggle for self-sustained development and independence, of the progressive national movements, and the peasant uprisings and wars against serfdom abounding in our history. It embodied the spiritual search of the 18th-century enlighteners, the heroes and martyrs of the Decembrist movement, and the ardent champions of revolutionary democracy, and the moral dedication of the prominent figures in our culture.

Crucial for the future of our country was the time when at the dawn of the 20th century Vladimir Il'ich **Lenin** put himself at the head of a close- knit group of like-minded people and set out to organise a proletarian party of a new type in Russia. it was this great Party of **Lenin** that roused the nation, its best and most devoted forces, for an assault on the old world.

The cornerstone in the success of the October Revolution was laid by the First Russian Revolution of 1905-1907. This includes the bitter lessons of the Ninth of January, the desperate heroism of people fighting on the Moscow barricades in December, the exploit of thousands of known and unknown freedom fighters, and the birth of the first workers' Soviets, the prototypes of Soviet power.

The victory of the October Revolution was also rooted in the gains of the February 1917 Revolution, the first victorious people's revolution in the imperialist epoch. After the February victory the Revolution went forward with incredible speed. its leading characters were the workers and peasants wearing soldiers' greatcoats. The spring of 1917 showed all the might of the people's movement. At the same time, there surfaced its limitations, the contradictions in the revolutionary consciousness at that stage, the power of historical inertia, with the result that for a time the exploiter classes departing from the scene took advantage of the fruits of the people's victory.

The February Revolution provided the October Revolution with its main weapon—power organised in the revived Soviets. The February Revolution had been the first experience of real democracy, of political education of the masses through an experience acquired in the intricate conditions of dual power. The February Revolution was unique in that it provided an opportunity for power to be taken over peacefully by the working people—something which, regrettably, did not finally come about owing to historical circumstances. The February Revolution was a major historical landmark on the road to the October Revolution.

In the complicated intertwining and confrontation of the class forces that were involved in the February Revolution, **Lenin**, with the insight of genius, saw opportunities for the victory of a socialist revolution. His April Theses were a scientific foresight and a model of a revolutionary action programme in those historical conditions. **Lenin** made clear not only the logic of the bourgeois-democratic revolution growing over into a socialist revolution, but also the form of that process—through the Soviets, through their Bolshevisation, the essence of which was to help the people, the masses, to understand the purpose of their own struggle, and to carry out the revolution consciously in their own interests. The road from the February to the October Revolution was a time of swift social change, a time of a rapid growth of the political awareness of the masses, of a consolidation of the revolutionary forces and their vanguard, the Party of **Lenin**.

At that time, between February and October, **Lenin** and his comrades-in- arms demonstrated the art of political guidance with extraordinary force, supplying a good lesson in the living dialectics of revolutionary thought and action. The Party leadership showed its ability for collective creative search, getting rid of stereotypes and slogans that had only yesterday, in a different situation seemed incontestable and the only possibility. One may say that the very course of **Lenin**'s thought, the entire activity of the Bolsheviks, marked by swift change of form and method, flexibility, unusual tactical solutions, and by political audacity—all this was a vivid example of anti-dogmatic, truly dialectical, and therefore new, way of thinking. That and only that is how real Marxist-Leninists think and act—especially at times of change, at critical turning points, when the future of the revolution and peace, socialism and progress, is at stake.

Let us go back to April 1917: to many, both friends and foes, **Lenin**'s program of going over to a socialist revolution seemed a utopia, something next to unbridled fantasy. But life has shown that only such a program could and did become the political foundation for the further development of the revolution and, in fact, the basis for social salvation, for averting national catastrophe.

Let us recall the July days of 1917. It was a painful moment when the Party was compelled to give up the slogan of passing power to the Soviets. But there was no other choice, because the Soviets had, for a while, fallen into the hands of Socialist-Revolutionaries and Mensheviks, and were helpless before the counter-revolution. And how sensitive Lenin was to the pulse of the Revolution, how brilliantly he determined the beginning of a new revival of the Soviets, which, in the process of struggle, were acquiring a truly popular essence, which enabled them to become the organs of a victorious armed uprising, and then also the political form of worker-peasant government.

All these are not simply pages in the chronicle of the Great Revolution. This is also a constant reminder to us, those who are living today, of the lofty duty of Communists always to be in the vanguard of events, to be able to take bold decisions, to assume full responsibility for the present and future.

The October Revolution was a powerful surge of millions of people which combined the vital interests of the working class, the everlasting aspirations of the peasantry, the thirst for peace of soldiers and sailors, and the unconquerable striving of the peoples of multinational Russia for freedom and enlightenment. The Bolshevik Party managed to find the main point in that intricate conglomerate of diverse interests, to combine the different tendencies and aspirations, and to concentrate them on solving the Revolution's main issue, that of power. And in its very first decrees, those on peace and on land, the state of the dictatorship of the proletariat responded to the needs of the time, and expressed the vital interests of the working class and, indeed, the absolute majority of the people.

Today, it is essential that we remember one more important, fundamental lesson of those October days. Highly relevant in our time is Lenin's reply to the question posed by life, by revolutionary activity—the question about the relationship of the theoretical "model" of the road to socialism and the actual practices of socialist construction. Marxism-Leninism is a creative doctrine, not a set of ready-made guidelines and doctrinaire prescriptions. Foreign to all sorts of dogmatism, the Marxist-Leninist doctrine ensures vigorous interaction between innovative theoretical thought and practice, the very course of the revolutionary struggle. The October Revolution is a most instructive example thereof.

It will be recalled that many leaders of the working-class movement of those days, even prominent ones, did not see the October Socialist Revolution as an objective development: they held that it went against the "rules", that it was contrary to the prevailing theoretical views. As they saw it, capitalism in Russia had not created all the requisite material and cultural preconditions for socialism by October 1917. It is instructive and useful, I think, to recall what Lenin replied to these critics of our Revolution. "You say that civilization is necessary for the building of socialism," he retorted. "Very good. But why could we not first create such prerequisites of civilization in our country as the expulsion of the landowners and the Russian capitalists, and then start moving towards socialism?"

Those who treated Marxism dogmatically and pedantically cannot understand its central point: its revolutionary dialectic. This latter is characteristic of all of **Lenin**'s post-revolutionary activity. It helped accomplish the political and moral exploit of the Brest [Litovsk] Peace literally on the edge between the possible and impossible, saving thousands upon thousands of lives and securing the very survival of the socialist Motherland.

One more example. Like **Marx** and **Engels**, **Lenin** was convinced that the armed defence of the Revolution would be provided by a people's militia. But the concrete conditions prompted a different solution. The Civil War and the intervention from outside, imposed on the people, called for a new approach. A worker-peasant Red Army was formed by **Lenin**'s decree. It was an army of a new type which covered itself with eternal glory in the Civil War and in repulsing the foreign intervention.

Those years brought severe trials for the newly-established Soviet government. It had to settle the elementary and crucial question of whether socialism would or would not be. The

Party mobilised the people to defend the socialist Motherland, the gains of the October Revolution. Hungry, ill-clad and unshod, the poorly armed Red Army crushed a well-trained and well-armed counter-revolutionary army which was being generously supplied by imperialists of East and West. The fiery dividing line of the Civil War ran right across the country, across every family, wreaking havoc with the habitual way of life, with the psychology and fate of people. The will of the nation, the striving of millions towards a new life, won out in this deadly clash. The country did everything it could to help the newly-established army; it lived and acted by **Lenin**'s slogan: "Everything for victory".

We will never forget the exploit of those legendary heroes—gallant sailors and cavalrymen, men and commanders of the young Red Army, and the Red partisans. They had safeguarded the Revolution; everlasting glory is their due!

The decision to launch a new economic policy, which substantially widened the notions of socialism and the ways of building it, was imbued with profound revolutionary dialectics.

Or take the following issue: as you know, **Lenin** criticised the limitations of "cooperative socialism". Yet in the specific conditions that arose after the October Revolution, when power was won by the people, **Lenin** had second thoughts on this score. In his article, *On Cooperation*, he put forward the idea of socialism being a society of "civilised cooperators".

Such was the power and audacity of Marxist dialectics, which expressed the essence of the revolutionary doctrine and which **Lenin** had so brilliantly mastered. He held that in building the new world, we shall have again and again "to improve the work, redo it, start from the beginning".

Yes, we have had to improve and re-do things again and again, endure long and hard struggle, and go through historical processes of a crucial, revolutionary nature. And they have in many ways changed the circumstances and conditions of our advance. They have also changed us—they have seasoned us, enriched us with experience and knowledge, and given us still greater faith in the success of the Revolution.

Assessing the path we have travelled from the point of view of world history, one sees again and again that we have accomplished in a short time what took others centuries to accomplish.

The socialist revolution occurred in a country with a medium-level development of capitalism, a highly concentrated industry, a predominantly peasant population, and deep-going survivals of feudalism and even of earlier social systems. Russia gave the world truly great achievements in science and culture, even though three-quarters of its population could neither read nor write. The country was ravaged to the extreme by imperialist World War I and an incompetent government.

There were no models to go by in the building of a new life and a tireless search for constructive solutions was required. To the Communist Party the aim was clear: revolution and the socialist path, Soviet government. And **Lenin** led the Party along that path.

Out of the complex material of multistructured Russia, the principles and standards of the future socialist system crystallised, and so did unprecedented forms of organizing society. What in the beginning were purely theoretical notions about the forms of government by the people, about the ways and limits of socialising property, about the organisation of socialist production, the initiation of a new, comradely discipline, and about the place and role of the individual in the new society, were clarified and filled with a real and tangible content.

The main purpose of the October Revolution was to build a new life. And this building did not cease for a single day. Even a short respite was used to continue building and to look for ways leading to the socialist future.

The early 1920s were highlighted by a spectacular surge of popular initiative and creativity. Those years were a truly revolutionary laboratory of social innovation, of a search for the optimal forms of the alliance between the working class and the working peasantry, and of the shaping of a mechanism for meeting all of the working people's interests.

The Party switched over from organizing production and consumption by methods of War Communism, which had been necessary due to war and dislocation, to more flexible, economically justified, "regular" instruments of influencing social realities. The measures of the New Economic Policy [NEP] were directed towards building the material foundations of socialism.

These days we turn ever more often to **Lenin**'s last works, to his ideas of the new economic policy, and seek to extract from this experience everything valuable and needed today. Certainly, it would be a mistake to equate the NEP with what we are doing today at a fundamentally new level of development. Today, the country does not have those individual peasants with whom the shaping of an alliance determined the most vital aims of the economic policy of the 1920s.

But the NEP also had a more distant target. The task was set of building a new society "not directly relying on enthusiasm," as **Lenin** wrote, "but aided by the enthusiasm engendered by the great revolution, and on the basis of personal interest, personal incentive and business principles.... That is what experience, the objective course of the development of the revolution, has taught us."

Speaking of the creative potential of the new economic policy, we should evidently refer once more to the wealth of political and methodological ideas underlying the food tax. We are of course interested not in its forms of those days that had been meant to secure a bond between workers and peasants, but in the potentialities of the idea of the food tax in releasing the creative energy of the masses, enhancing the initiative of the individual, and removing the bureaucratic obstacles that limited the operation of the basic principle of socialism: "From each according to his ability, to each according to his work."

The socialist construction that was started under **Lenin**'s leadership brought about many fundamentally new elements.

Methods of planned economy were worked out and applied for the first time in world history. The General Plan for the Electrification of Russia was indeed a discovery, a whole line of advance in the world's economic thinking and practice. It was not only an imposing electrification plan, but also a project, as conceived by Lenin, of a "harmonious coordination" of agriculture, industry and transport, or, in modern-day terms, a comprehensive programme for the distribution and development of the country's productive forces. **Lenin** called it the second programme of the Party, "a plan of work aimed at restoring our entire economy and raising it to the level of up-to- date technical development".

A new culture was taking shape, absorbing both past experience and the multicolored wealth, daring, and originality of talents, of striking personalities whom the Revolution had aroused and inspired to serve the people. Of everlasting significance for us, not only for its results but also for its experience and method, is the initial, Leninist stage of forming the multinational Soviet state.

When thinking of the time when "NEP Russia will become socialist Russia", **Lenin** could not, and never meant to, draw the picture of the future society in every detail. But the ways and means of advancing to socialism through the building of a machine industry, through a broad-scale establishment of cooperatives, through the enlistment of the working masses to a man in running the state, through organizing the work of the state apparatus on the principle of "better fewer, but better" and through the cultural development of the entire mass of the people, through the consolidation of the federation of free nations "without lies or bayonets"— this and this alone was to shape the face of the country as it attained a fundamentally new level of social order.

In **Lenin**'s last works, which were extraordinarily rich intellectually and emotionally, there emerged a system of views and the very concept of socialist construction in our country. This is an immense theoretical asset for the Party.,

Lenin's premature death was a terrible shock for the whole Party and the Soviet people. The grief was immeasurable, the loss irreparable. This was clear to everyone. Undertakings of colossal historical importance lay ahead. Without **Lenin**, relying on his doctrine and his behests, the Party leadership was to find the optimal solutions that could consolidate the gains of the Revolution and lead the country to socialism in the concrete conditions of the Soviet Russia of that time.

History set the new system a rigid ultimatum: either it would in the shortest possible time build its own social, economic and technical basis and survive, giving the world the first example of a just society, or fade out and remain in the memory of time at best as a heroic but unsuccessful social experiment. Vital and crucial significance, in the full sense of the word, was attached to the question of securing a swift rate of socialist change.

The period after **Lenin**, that is, the 1920s and the 1930s, occupied a special place in the history of the Soviet state. Radical social changes were carried out in about fifteen years. An incredible lot happened in that period—both from the point of view of search for optimal variants of socialist construction, and from the point of view of what was really achieved in building the foundations of the new society. Those were years of hard work to the limits of human endurance, of sharp and multifarious struggle. Industrialisation, collectivisation, the cultural revolution, the strengthening of the multinational state, the consolidation of the Soviet Union's international positions, new forms of managing the economy and all social affairs—all this occurred in that period. And all of it had far- reaching consequences.

For decades, we have been returning to that time again and again. This is natural. Because that was when the world's first socialist society had its beginnings, when it was being built. It was an exploit on a historical scale and of historic significance. Admiration for the exploits of our fathers and grandfathers, and the assessments of our real achievements will live forever, as will the exploits and achievements themselves. And if, at times, we scrutinise our history with a critical eye, we do so only because we want to have a better and fuller idea of the ways that lead to the future.

It is essential to assess the past with a sense of historical responsibility and on the basis of the historical truth. This must be done, firstly, because of the tremendous importance of those years for the future of our country, the future of socialism. Secondly, because those years are in the centre of the everlasting discussions both in our country and abroad, where, along with a search for the truth, attempts are often being made to discredit socialism as a new social system, as a realistic alternative to capitalism. Lastly, we need truthful assessments of this and all the other periods of our history—especially now with the restructuring in full swing. We need them not to settle political scores or, as they say, to let off steam, but to pay due credit to all the heroic things in the past, and to draw lessons from mistakes and miscalculations.

And so, about the 1920s and the 1930s after **Lenin**. Although the Party and society had **Lenin**'s conception of building socialism and Lenin's works of the post-revolution period to go by, the search for the way was not at all simple; it was marked by keen ideological struggle and political discussions. In their centre were the basic problems of society's development, and above all the question of whether socialism could be built in our country. Theoretical thought and practice were searching for the directions and forms in which to carry out socio-economic transformations, and for the ways to accomplish them on socialist principles in the concrete historical conditions the Soviet Union was in.

Practical constructive work that called for a great sense of responsibility was on the agenda. Above all, the country squarely faced the question of industrialisation and economic reconstruction without which the building of socialism and the strengthening of the defence capability were unthinkable. This followed from **Lenin**'s explicit directions, from his theoretical heritage. The question of socialist changes in the countryside, too, arose on the same plane and also according to Lenin's behests.

Thus, what was involved was large-scale and crucial matters, problems, and objectives. And though, I repeat, the Party had **Lenin**'s guidelines on these issues, sharp debates started over them.

It is evidently worthwhile to say that before and after the Revolution, in the first few years of socialist construction, far from all Party leaders shared **Lenin**'s views on some of the most important problems. Besides, **Lenin**'s recommendations could not encompass all the concrete issues concerning the building of the new society. Analyzing the ideological disputes of those times, we should bear in mind that carrying out gigantic revolutionary transformations in a country such as Russia was then, was in itself a most difficult task. Historically, the country was on the march, its development was being sharply accelerated, and all aspects of social life were changing rapidly and profoundly.

Reflecting the whole range of the interests of classes, social groups and strata, the needs and objectives of the times, the historical traditions and the pressure of urgent tasks, and also the conditions of the hostile capitalist encirclement, the ideological struggle was indissolubly intertwined with events and processes in the economy and politics, and in all spheres of life.

In brief, it was extremely difficult to get one's bearings and find the only correct course in that intricate and stormy situation. To a considerable extent, too, the character of the ideological struggle was complicated by personal rivalries in the Party leadership. The old differences that had existed in Lenin's lifetime, also made themselves felt in the new situation, and this in a very acute form. **Lenin**, as we know, had warned against this danger. In his *Letter to the Congress* he had stressed that "it is not a detail, or it is a detail which can assume decisive importance". And that was largely what had happened.

Their petty-bourgeois nature took the upper hand in the case of some respectable leaders. They took a factional stance. This agitated the Party organisations, distracted them from vital affairs, and interfered in their work. The leaders in question continued to provoke a split even after the vast majority of the Party saw that their views were contrary to **Lenin**'s ideas and plans, and that their proposals were erroneous and could push the country off the correct course.

This applies first of all to Leon **Trotskii**, who had, after **Lenin**'s death, displayed excessive pretensions to top leadership in the Party, thus fully confirming **Lenin**'s opinion of him as an excessively self-assured politician who always vacillated and cheated. **Trotskii** and the Trotskiiites negated the possibility of building socialism in conditions of capitalist encirclement. In foreign policy they put their stakes on the export of the revolution, and in home policy on the tightening of the screws on the peasants, on the city exploiting the countryside, and on administrative and military methods in running society. Trotskiiism was a political trend whose ideologists took cover behind leftist pseudo-revolutionary rhetoric, and who in effect assumed a defeatist posture. This was actually an attack on Leninism all down the line. The matter practically concerned the future of socialism in our country, the fate of the Revolution.

In these circumstances, it was essential to disprove Trotskiiism before the whole people, and expose its anti-socialist essence. The situation was complicated by the fact that the Trotskiiites were acting in common with the "new opposition" headed by Grigori **Zinoviev** and Lev **Kamenev**. Being aware that they constituted a minority, the opposition leaders had again and again saddled the Party with discussions, counting on a split in its ranks. But in the final analysis, the Party spoke out for the line of the Central Committee and against the opposition, which was soon ideologically and organisationally crushed.

In short, the Party's leading nucleus headed by Joseph **Stalin** had safeguarded Leninism in an ideological struggle. It defined the strategy and tactics in the initial stage of socialist construction, with its political course being approved by most members of the Party and most working people. An important part in defeating Trotskiiism ideologically was played by Nikolai **Bukharin**, Felix **Dzerzhinskii**, Sergei **Kirov**, Grigorii **Ordjonikidze**, Jan **Rudzutak**, and others.

At the very end of the 1920s a sharp struggle started over the ways of putting the peasantry on the socialist road. In substance, it revealed the different attitude of the majority in the Political Bureau and of the **Bukharin** group on how to apply the principles of the new economic policy at the new stage in the development of Soviet society.

The concrete conditions of that time—both at home and internationally—necessitated a considerable increase in the rate of socialist construction. **Bukharin** and his followers had, in their calculations and theoretical propositions, underrated the practical significance of the time factor in building socialism in the 1930s. In many ways, their posture was based on dogmatic thinking and a non-dialectical assessment of the concrete situation. **Bukharin** himself and his followers soon admitted their mistakes.

In this connection, it is appropriate to recall **Lenin**'s opinion of **Bukharin**. "**Bukharin**," he said, "is not only a most valuable and major theorist of the Party; he is also rightly considered the favourite of the whole Party, but his theoretical views can be classified as fully Marxist only with great reserve, for there is something scholastic about him (he has never made a study of dialectics, and, I think, never fully understood it)." The facts again confirmed that **Lenin** had been right.

Thus, the political discussions of that time reflected a complex process in the Party's development, marked by acute struggle over crucial problems of socialist construction. In that struggle, which had to be endured, the concept of industrialization and collectivization took shape.

Under the leadership of the Party, of its CC, a heavy industry, including engineering, a defence industry and a chemical industry abreast of the times, were built in a brief period practically from scratch, and the General Electrification Plan was completed. These achievements were symbolised by the Magnitogorsk steelmaking plant, the Kuznetsk coalfields, the Dnieper hydropower station, the Ural heavy engineering works, the Khibiny plant, the motor works in Moscow and Gorky, aircraft plants, the Stalingrad, Cheliabinsk and Kharkov tractor works, the Rostov agricultural machinery works, the city of Komosomolsk-on-Amur, the Turksib railway, the Grand Ferghnana canal, and many other great building projects of our early five-year plans. Dozens of research institutes and a broad network of higher educational establishments were founded in those days.

The Party charted a previously unknown method of industrialization: to begin building a heavy industry at once, without reliance on external sources of finance, and without waiting years for capital to accumulate through the expansion of light industry. This was the only possible way in those conditions, though it was incredibly difficult for the country and the people. It was an innovative step in which the revolutionary enthusiasm of the masses was taken into account as a component of economic growth. Industrialization raised the country to a fundamentally new level in one jump. By the end of the 1930s the Soviet Union had moved to first place in Europe and second place in the world for industrial output, becoming a truly great industrial power. This was a labor exploit of epoch-making significance, and exploit of liberated labor, an exploit of the Bolshevik Party.

And looking at history with a sober eye, considering the aggregate of internal and international realities, one cannot help asking whether a course other than that the Party chose could have been taken in those conditions. If we wish to be faithful to history and the truth of life, there can be only one answer: no other course could have been taken. In those conditions, with the threat of imperialist aggression building up visibly, the Party was increasingly convinced that it was essential not to just cover but literally race across the distance from the sledgehammer and wooden plough to an advanced industry in the shortest possible time, for without this the cause of the Revolution would be inevitably destroyed.

The viability of the Party's plans, understood and accepted by the masses, and of the slogans and objectives embodying the revolutionary spirit of the October Revolution, found expression in the astonishing enthusiasm shown by millions of Soviet people who joined in building the country's industry. In most difficult conditions, in the absence of mechanization, on semi-starvation rations, people performed miracles. They were inspired by the fact that they had a hand in a great historical cause. Though they were not sufficiently literate, their class instinct told them that they were participating in a momentous and unprecedented undertaking.

It is our duty and the duty of those who follow us to remember this exploit of our fathers and grandfathers. Everyone must know that their labor and their selfless dedication were not in vain. They coped with everything that fell to their lot, and made a great contribution to the consolidation of the gains of the October Revolution, to laying the foundations of the strength that enabled them to save the Motherland from a deadly peril, to save socialism for the future, for all of us, comrades. Hallowed be their memory!

At the same time, the period under review also saw some losses. They wore in a sense connected with the successes I have just referred to. Some had begun to believe in the universal effectiveness of rigid centralisation, in that methods of command were the shortest and best way of resolving any and all problems. This had an effect on the attitude towards people, towards their conditions of life.

A system of administrative command in Party and government leadership emerged in the country, and bureaucratism gained strength, even though **Lenin** had warned about its danger. And a corresponding structure of administration and methods of planning began to take shape. In industry—given its scale at the time, when literally all the main components of the industrial edifice were conspicuous—such methods, such a system of administration generally produced results. However, an equally rigid centralization-and-command system was impermissible in tackling the problems of refashioning rural life.

It must be said frankly: at the new stage there was a deficit of the Leninist considerate attitude to the interests of the working peasantry. Most important of all, there was an underestimation of the fact that the peasantry as a class had changed radically in the years since the Revolution. The principal figure now was the middle peasant. He had asserted himself as a farmer working the land he had received from the Revolution and he had, over a whole decade, become convinced that Soviet government was his kind of government. He had become a staunch and dependable ally of the working class—an ally on a new basis, an ally who was becoming convinced from his own experience that his life was increasingly taking a turn for the better.

And if there had been more consideration for objective economic laws and if more attention had been given to the social processes taking place in the countryside, if in general the attitude of this vast mass of the working peasantry, most of whom had taken part in the Revolution and had defended it from the White Guards and the forces of intervention, had been politically more judicious, if there had been a consistent line to promote the alliance with the middle peasant against the kulak, then there would not have been all those excesses that occurred in carrying out collectivization .

Today it is clear: in a tremendous undertaking, which affected the fate of the majority of the country's population, there was a departure from **Lenin**'s policy towards the peasantry. This most important and very complex social process, in which a great deal depended on local conditions, was directed mostly by administrative methods. A conviction had arisen that all problems could be solved in a stroke, overnight. Whole regions and parts of the country began to compete: which of them would achieve complete collectivization more quickly. Arbitrarily percentage targets were issued from above. Flagrant violations of the principles of collectivization occurred everywhere. Nor were excesses avoided in the struggle against the kulaks. The basically correct policy of fighting the kulaks was often interpreted so broadly that it swept in a considerable part of the middle peasantry too. Such is the reality of history.

But, comrades, if we assess the significance of collectivization as a whole in consolidating socialism in the countryside, it was in the final analysis a transformation of fundamental importance. Collectivization implied a radical change in the entire mode of life of the preponderant part of the country's population to a socialist footing. It created the social base for modernising the agrarian sector and regearing it along the lines of advanced farming techniques; it made possible a considerable rise in the productivity of labour, and it released a substantial share of manpower needed for other spheres of socialist construction. All this had historical effects.

To understand the situation of those years it must be borne in mind that the administrative-command system, which had begun to take shape in the process of industrialization and which had received a fresh impetus during collectivization , had told on the whole socio-political life of the country. Once established in the economy, it had spread to its superstructure, restricting the development of the democratic potential of socialism and holding back the progress of socialist democracy.

But the aforesaid does not give a full picture of how complex that period was. What had happened? The time of ideological-political tests of the utmost gravity to the Party was actually over. Millions of people had joined enthusiastically in the work of bringing about socialist transformations. The first successes were becoming apparent. Yet at that time methods dictated by the period of struggle against the hostile resistance of the exploiter classes were being mechanically transferred to the period of peaceful socialist construction, when conditions had changed cardinally. An atmosphere of intolerance, hostility, and suspicion was created in the country. As time went on, this political practice gained in scale, and was backed up by the erroneous "theory" of an aggravation of the class struggle in the course of socialist construction.

All this had a dire effect on the country's socio-political development and produced grim consequences. Quite obviously, it was the absence of a proper level of democratization in Soviet society that made possible the personality cult, the violations of legality, the wanton repressive measures of the thirties. Putting things bluntly—those were real crimes stemming from an abuse of power. Many thousands of people inside and outside the Party were subjected to wholesale repression. Such, comrades, is the bitter truth. Serious damage was done to the cause of socialism and to the authority of the Party. And we must state this bluntly. This is necessary to assert **Lenin**'s ideal of socialism once and for all.

There is now much discussion about the role of **Stalin** in our history. His was an extremely contradictory personality. To remain faithful to historical truth we must see both **Stalin**'s incontestable contribution to the struggle for socialism, to the defence of its gains, and the gross political errors, and the abuses committed by him and by those around him, for which our people paid a heavy price and which had grave consequences for the life of our society. It is sometimes said that **Stalin** did not know about instances of lawlessness. Documents at our disposal show that this is not so. The guilt of **Stalin** and his immediate entourage before the Party and the people for the wholesale repressive measures and acts of lawlessness is enormous and unforgivable. This is a lesson for all generations.

Contrary to the assertions of our ideological opponents, the personality cult was certainly not inevitable. It was alien to the nature of socialism, represented a departure from its fundamental principles, and, therefore, has no justification. At its 20th and 22nd Congresses the Party severely condemned the **Stalin** cult itself and its consequences. We now know that the political accusations and repressive measures against a number of Party leaders and statesmen, against many Communists and non-Party people, against scientists and cultural personalities were a result of deliberate falsification.

Many of the accusations were later, especially after the 20th Party Congress, withdrawn. Thousands of innocent victims were completely exonerated.

But the process of restoring justice was not carried through and was actually suspended in the middle of the sixties. Now, in line with a decision taken by the October 1987 Plenary Meeting of the CC, we are having to return to this. The Political Buro of the CC has set up a commission for comprehensively examining new and already known facts and documents pertaining to these matters. Appropriate decisions will be taken on the basis of the commission's findings.

All this will also be reflected in a treatise on the history of the Communist Party of the Soviet Union, which will be prepared by a special commission of the CC. This is something we have to do, the more so since there are still attempts to turn away from painful matters in our history, to hush them up, to make believe that nothing special happened. We cannot agree to this. This would be disregard for the historical truth, disrespect for the memory of those who were innocent victims of lawless and arbitrary actions. Another reason why we cannot agree to this is that a truthful analysis must help us solve today's problems of democratization , legality, openness, overcoming bureaucracy, in short, the vital problems of perestroika. That is why here too we have to be quite clear, concise, and consistent.

An honest understanding of our enormous achievements as well as of past misfortunes, their full and correct political evaluation, will provide real moral guidelines for the future.

In drawing up a general balance-sheet of the period of the twenties and thirties after **Lenin**, we can say that we have covered a difficult road, replete with contradictions and complexities, but a truly heroic one. Neither gross errors, nor departures from the principles of socialism could divert our people, our country from the road it embarked upon by the choice it made in 1917. The momentum of the October Revolution was too great! The ideas of socialism that had gripped the masses were too strong! The people felt themselves involved in a great effort and began enjoying the fruits of their work. Their patriotism acquired a new, socialist meaning.

And all this was brought out forcefully in the grim trials of the Great Patriotic War of 1941-1945.

In the West there is now much talk about the situation on the eve of the war. Truths are being laced with half-truths. This is being done especially zealously by those who are displeased with the results of World War II—its political, territorial, and social results, by those who are bent on changing these results. That is why they are eager to present the historical truth upside down, to confuse the cause-and-effect relationships, and to falsify the chronology of events. In this context they are resorting to any lies in order to saddle the Soviet Union with the blame for World War II, the road to which was allegedly cleared by the Ribbentrop-Molotov non-aggression pact [23 Aug 39]. This matter deserves greater consideration.

Actually, it was by no means on 1 September 1939, that World War II became a tragic reality. Japan's seizure of Northeast China (the "Manchurian incident" of 1931-1932), Italy's attack on Ethiopia (in 1935) and on Albania (in the spring of 1939), the German-Italian intervention against republican Spain (1936-1939), and Japan's armed invasion of North and then Central China (in the summer of 1937)—these were the initial conflagrations of World War II.

It is a different matter that in those days the West still pretended that this did not concern it or did not concern it enough to come to the defence of the victims of aggression. Hatred of socialism, long-term designs, and class selfishness prevented a sober assessment of the real dangers. Moreover, fascism was persistently being offered the mission of a strike force in an anti-communist crusade. Following Ethiopia and China, Austria and Czechoslovakia were flung into the furnace of "appeasement", the sword hung over Poland, over all the Baltic and Danube states, and propaganda was being conducted openly in favour of turning the Ukraine into a wheatfield and livestock farm of the "Third Reich". Ultimately, the main thrusts of aggression were being channelled against the Soviet Union, and since the scheming to divide up our country had begun long before the war, it is not hard to see how limited our options were.

It is said that the decision taken by the Soviet Union in concluding a non-aggression pact with Germany was not the best one. This may be so, if in one's reasoning one is guided not by harsh reality, but by abstract conjectures torn out of their time frame. In these circumstances, too, the issue was roughly the same as it had been at the time of the Brest peace: was our country to be or not to be independent, was socialism on Earth to be or not to be.

The USSR made great efforts to build up a system of collective security and to avert a global slaughter. But the Soviet initiatives met with no response among the Western politicians and political intriguers, who were coolly scheming how best to involve socialism in the flames of war and bring about its head-on collision with fascism.

Outcasts already by virtue of our socialist birth, we could under no circumstances be right from the imperialist point of view. As I said, the Western ruling circles, in an attempt to blot out their own sins, are trying to convince people that the Nazi attack on Poland and thereby the start of World War II was triggered by the Soviet-German non-aggression pact of 23 August 1939. As if there had been no Munich Agreement with **Hitler** signed by Britain and France back in 1938 with the active connivance of the USA, no Anschluss of Austria, no crucifixion of the Spanish Republic, no Nazi occupation of Czechoslovakia and Klaipeda, and no conclusion of non- aggression pacts with Germany by London and Paris in 1938. By the way, such a pact was also concluded by pre-war Poland. All this, as you see, fitted neatly into the structure of imperialist policy, was and is considered to be in the nature of things.

It is known from documents that the date of Germany's attack on Poland ("not later than September 1") was fixed as early as April 3, 1939, that is, long before the Soviet-German pact. In London, Paris, and Washington it was known in minute detail how the preparations for the Polish campaign were really proceeding, just as it was known that the only barrier capable of stopping the Hitlerites could be the conclusion of an Anglo-Franco-Soviet military alliance not later than August 1939. These plans were also known to the leadership of our country, and that was why it sought to convince Britain and France of the need for collective measures. It also urged the Polish Government of the time to cooperate in curbing aggression.

But the Western powers had different designs: to beckon the USSR with the promise of an alliance and thereby to prevent the conclusion of the non- aggression pact we had been offered, to deprive us of the chance to make better preparations for the inevitable attack by **Hitler** Germany on the USSR. Nor can we forget that in August 1939 the Soviet Union faced a very real threat of war on two fronts: in the west with Germany and in the east with Japan, which had started a costly conflict on the Khalkhin-Gol.

But life and death, scorning myths, went into their real orbits. A new chapter was beginning in contemporary history, a most grim and complex one. At that stage, however, we managed to stave off the collision with the enemy, an enemy who had left himself and his opponent but one choice: to triumph or to perish.

The aggression to which we were subjected was a merciless test of the viability of the socialist system, of the strength of the multinational Soviet state, of the patriotic spirit of Soviet men and women. We withstood this test by fire and sword, comrades!

We withstood it because for our people this war became a Great Patriotic War, for in a struggle with such an enemy as German fascism the issue was one of life or death, was one of being free or of being enslaved.

We withstood it because this became for us a war of the entire people. Everyone rallied to the defence of the country: young and old, men and women, all the nations and nationalities of our great country. The generation born of the October Revolution and brought up by the socialist system likewise entered their first battle. Unprecedented staunchness and heroism on the battlefield, a courageous struggle by the partisans and underground resistance behind the enemy lines, and tireless work in the rear almost round the clock... That's what the war was for us.

Soviet men and women fought and worked to defend their country, the socialist system, the ideas and cause of the October Revolution. When this calamity came to our common home, the Soviet people did not flinch, did not falter—either under the blows of the initial setbacks and defeats, or under the weight of the millions of deaths, the torment and the suffering. From the first day of the war they had implicit faith in the coming Victory. In their soldiers' greatcoats and workers' overalls they did everything that was at the limit and beyond the limit of human endurance to hasten that long-awaited day. And when, on the 1418th day of the war, Victory did come, the entire delivered world heaved a sigh of relief, paying tribute to the victorious, heroic, and hard-working Soviet people, to their gallant Army, which had fought its way over thousands of kilometers, each of which had cost many lives and no end of blood and sweat.

The Great Patriotic War brought out to the full the talent of outstanding military leaders who had emerged from the midst of the people—Georgi **Zhukov**, Konstantin **Rokossovskii**, Alexander **Vasilevskii**, Ivan **Konev**, and other distinguished marshals, generals, and officers—those who commanded fronts and armies, corps, divisions, and regiments, companies and platoons. A factor in the achievement of Victory was the tremendous political will, purposefulness and persistence, ability to organise and discipline people displayed in the war years by Joseph **Stalin**. But the brunt of the war was borne by the ordinary Soviet soldier—a great toiler of the people's own flesh and blood, valiant and devoted to his country. Every honor and eternal glory to him!

Millions of veterans of the Great Patriotic War are in our ranks today too, taking a vigorous part in our revolutionary restructuring, in the renewal of society. Our filial thanks to them!

The moving spirit behind all our efforts on the battlefield and at work was our Leninist Party. At the front, in the trenches Communists were the first to rise to the attack, their example inspiring others; in the rear they were the last to leave their workbenches, the fields and livestock farms. Soviet men and women, as never before, sensed that the Communist Party was their party and that the Communists were showing in practice what it meant to be the people's vanguard at a time when the flames of war were raging and when the issue was one of life or death.

It may be said with confidence: the years of the Great Patriotic War are one of the most glorious and heroic pages in the history of the Party, pages inscribed by the courage and valor, by the supreme dedication and self-sacrifice of millions of Communists. The war showed that the Soviet people, the Party, socialism, and the October Revolution are inseparable and that nothing on earth can shatter this unity.

Socialism did not just stand fast and did not simply achieve victory. It emerged from this most terrible and destructive of wars stronger morally and politically, having enhanced its authority and influence throughout the world.

When the war ended, our ill-wishers predicted an economic decline in our country and its dropping out of world politics for a long time; they considered that it would take us half a century, if not more, to cope with the aftermath of the war. But within an extremely short period of time the Soviet people had rebuilt the war-ravaged towns and villages, and raised from their ruins factories and mills, collective and state farms, schools and colleges, and cultural institutions.

And once again this was a manifestation of the great strength of the socialist state: the will of the Party motivated by an understanding of the supreme interests of the Land of the October Revolution; the staunchness and proletarian wisdom of the workers, who had shouldered the main burden of the peaceful transformation of the country's industrial might and of repairing the ravages of war; and the self-sacrifice, patience, and patriotism of the farmers, who gave up everything they had to feed the ruined country. It was also a manifestation of the friendship of the peoples, of their mutual assistance, of their readiness—working together as brothers— to help those who had suffered particularly, to promote the recovery of those areas of our common Motherland that had been steamrollered especially mercilessly by the war.

It was the heroism of everyday work in those difficult post-war years that was the source of our achievements, of the economic, scientific and technical progress, of the harnessing of atomic energy, of the launching of the first spaceships, and of the growth of the people's economic and cultural standards.

But during this very same time—a time of new exploits by the people in the name of socialism—a contradiction between what our society had become and the old methods of leadership was making itself felt ever more appreciably. Abuses of power and violations of socialist legality continued. The "Leningrad case" and the "Doctor's Plot" were fabricated. In short, there was a deficit of genuine respect for the people. People were devotedly working, studying, seeking new knowledge, accepting difficulties and shortages, but sensing that alarm and hope were building up in society. And all this gripped the public's consciousness soon after Stalin's death.

In the middle of the fifties, especially after the 20th Congress of the Communist Party, a wind of change swept the country, the people's spirits rose, they took heart, became bolder and more confident. It required no small courage of the Party and its leadership headed by Nikita **Khrushchev** to criticise the personality cult and its consequences, and to reestablish socialist legality. The old stereotypes in domestic and foreign policy began to crumble. Attempts were made to break down the command-bureaucratic methods of administration established in the thirties and the forties, to make socialism more dynamic, to emphasise humanitarian ideals and values, and to revive the creative spirit of Leninism in theory and practice.

The desire to change the priorities of economic development, to bring into play incentives related to a personal interest in work results keynoted the decisions of the September 1953 and July 1955 Plenary Meetings of the Party CC. More attention began to be devoted to the development of agriculture, housing, the light industry, the sphere of consumption, and to everything related to satisfying human needs.

In short, there were changes for the better—in Soviet society and in international relations. However, no small number of subjectivist errors were committed, and they handicapped socialism's advance to a new stage, moreover doing much to discredit progressive initiatives. The fact is that fundamentally new problems of domestic and foreign policy and of Party development were often being solved by voluntaristic methods, with the aid of the old political and economic mechanism. But the failures of the reforms undertaken in that period were mainly due to the fact that they were not backed up by a broad development of democratization processes.

At the October 1964 Plenary Meeting of the Party CC there was a change of the leadership of the Party and the country, and decisions were taken to overcome voluntaristic tendencies and distortions in domestic and foreign policies. The Party sought to achieve a certain stabilisation in policy, and to give it realistic features and thoroughness.

The March and September 1965 Plenary Meetings of the Party CC formulated new approaches to economic management. An economic reform and big programmes for developing new areas and promoting the productive forces were worked out and began to be put into effect. In the first few years this changed the situation in the country for the better. The economic and scientific potential was increasing, the defence capacity was being strengthened, and the standard of living was rising. Many foreign policy moves enhanced the international prestige of our state. Strategic parity with the USA was achieved.

The country had at its disposal extensive resources for further accelerating its development. But to utilise these resources and put them to work, cardinal new changes were needed in society and, of course, the corresponding political will. There was a shortage of both. And even much of what had been decided remained on paper, was left suspended in midair. The pace of our development was substantially retarded.

At the April 1985 Plenary Meeting of its CC and at its 27th Congress the Party frankly identified the causes of the situation that had arisen, laid bare the mechanism retarding our development, and gave it a fundamental assessment.

It was stated that in the latter years of the life and activities of Leonid **Brezhnev** the search for ways of further advancement had been largely hampered by an addiction to habitual formulas and schemes which did not reflect the new realities. The gap between word and deed had widened. Negative processes in the economy were gathering momentum and had, in effect, created a pre-crisis situation. Many aberrations had arisen in the social, spiritual and moral spheres, and they were distorting and deforming the principles of socialist justice, undermining the people's faith in it, and giving rise to social alienation and immorality in various forms. The growing discrepancy between the lofty principles of socialism and the everyday realities of life was becoming intolerable.

The healthy forces in the Party and in society as a whole were becoming more and more acutely aware of the pressing need to overcome negative phenomena, to reverse the course of events, to secure an acceleration of the country's socio-economic development, and to bring about a moral purification and renewal of socialism.

It was in response to this extremely acute social need that the April 1985 Plenary Meeting of the CC put forward the concept and strategy of accelerating the country's socio-economic development, and the course aimed at a renewal of socialism. These were given more elaborate theoretical and political formulation in the decisions of the 27th Party Congress and subsequent plenary meetings of the CC, and assumed their final shape in the general policy of a revolutionary reorganization of all the aspects of socialist society's life.

The idea of restructuring rests upon our seventy-year history, on the sound foundation of the basically new social edifice erected in the Soviet Union; it combines continuity and innovation, the historical experience of Bolshevism and what socialism is today. It is up to us to continue and carry forward the cause of the pioneers of the Revolution and of socialism. And we are certain to achieve this by our work, by making creative use of the experience of the generations that blazed the October trail before us and for us!

Comrades, we are following a revolutionary road, and this road is not for the weak and faint-hearted; this is a road for the strong and the brave. And that is what the Soviet people have always been—in the years of the greatest social transformations, in the years of ordeals of war, and in the years of peaceful constructive work. It is the people who shape their history, their destiny—never simple, but inimitable and invaluable, just as human life itself is. And this is one hundred times more true when we speak about the history of socialism, about continuing the cause of the Great Revolution.

The working class was and still is the cementing force and vanguard of the people. Even at the dawn of the revolutionary movement it followed **Lenin**'s admonition: "Fight for freedom, without **even for a minute** abandoning the idea of socialism, without ceasing to work for its realisation, to prepare the forces and the organisation for the achievement of socialism." It was the working class, in alliance with all the working people, that carried out the Great October Revolution, that built socialism, and safeguarded it in bitter clashes with the enemy, It endured, suffered, and withstood everything! Today, too, it stands in the vanguard of developing socialism, of the revolutionary perestroika. Glory to it and great honor!

Our Leninist Party emerged and developed as a militant and active vanguard of the working class. It was from the working class that it gained its mighty confidence, firmness, discipline, and tenacity in the struggle for the ideals of socialism, its profound and humane understanding of life. Now, too, as a party of all the people, it has retained these finest features of that militant and constructive class. Today, as well as at every stage of socialism's history!

It is the principal definitive message of our history that all these seventy years our people have lived and worked under the Party's leadership in the name of socialism, in the name of a better and more just life. This is the destiny of a creative, constructive people!

II. Socialism in Development and Restructuring

Comrades, we have been led to the conclusion about the necessity for restructuring by pressing needs brooking no delay. But the more deeply we examined our problems and probed their meaning, the clearer it became that perestroika also has a broader socio-political and historical context.

Perestroika implies not only eliminating the stagnation and conservatism of the preceding period and correcting the mistakes committed, but also overcoming historically limited, outdated features of social organisation and work methods. It implies imparting to socialism the most contemporary forms, corresponding to the conditions and needs of the scientific and technological revolution, and to the intellectual progress of Soviet society. This is a relatively lengthy process of the revolutionary renewal of society, a process that has its own logic and stages.

Lenin saw the historic mission of socialism in the need to prepare by many years of effort for the transition to communism. The leader of the Revolution spoke highly of the ability of **Marx** and **Engels** "to analyze the transitional forms with the utmost thoroughness in order to establish, in accordance with the concrete historical peculiarities of each particular case, **from what and to what** the given transitional form is passing". In short, our teachers warned us repeatedly that the path of building the new society is a long series of transitions.

We have every reason to view perestroika as a definite historical stage in the forward movement of our society. And in reply to **Lenin**'s question "from what and to what" we are passing, it must be said quite definitely: we have to impart to socialism a new quality or, as they say, a second wind, and this requires a profound renewal of all aspects of society's life, both material and spiritual, and the development of the humanitarian character of our system to the fullest possible extent.

The purpose of restructuring is the full theoretical and practical reestablishment of **Lenin**'s conception of socialism, in which indisputable priority belongs to the working man with his ideals and interests, to humanitarian values in the economy, in social and political relations, and in culture.

Our hope of achieving revolutionary purification and renewal requires tapping the enormous social potentialities of socialism by invigorating the individual, the human factor. As a result of restructuring socialism can and must make full use of its potentialities as a truly humanitarian system serving and elevating man. This is a society for people, for the flourishing of their creative work, wellbeing, health, physical and spiritual development, a society where man feels he is the full-fledged master and is indeed that.

Two key problems of the development of society determine the fate of restructuring. These are the democratization of all social life and a radical economic reform.

Restructuring, continuing as it does what the October Revolution began, has moved the task of deepening and developing socialist democracy to the forefront. The democratization of society is at the core of perestroika, and on its progress depends the success of perestroika itself and—one can say without exaggeration—the future of socialism in general. This is the surest guarantee of changes, both political and economic, ruling out any movement backward.

The changes taking place in the country today constitute what is probably the biggest step in developing socialist democracy since the October Revolution.

In reorganizing our economic and political system, it is our duty to create, first of all, a dependable and flexible mechanism for the genuine involvement of all the people in deciding state and public matters. Secondly, people must be taught in practice to live in the conditions of deepening democracy, to extend and consolidate human rights, to instill a contemporary political culture among the masses. In other words, to teach and to learn from each other about democracy.

As we mark the 70th anniversary of our Revolution and ponder over the future, we have to take a closer look at how the process of the democratization of society is proceeding and what stands in its way. The difficulties and contradictions arising are considerable and at times unexpected; there is no avoiding a conflict between the new and advanced and the old and outdated. There is some uncertainty and hesitancy.

In the early days following the October Revolution **Lenin** pointed out that the workers and peasants were still "timid", still not resolute enough, not yet accustomed to the idea that it was for them to take over all the levers of administration. "But the Revolution of October 1917 is strong, viable and invincible," he wrote, "because it **awakens** these qualities, breaks down the old impediments, removes the worn-out shackles, and leads the working people on to the road of the **independent** creation of a new life."

Today, too, we see how difficult people find it to adapt to the new situation, to the possibility and necessity of living and solving all problems democratically. Many are still "timid", act irresolutely, fear responsibility, and are still in the grip of obsolete rules and instructions. The task is to cultivate in people a taste for independence and responsibility in their approach to production and social matters of any scale, to develop self-government as government of the people, exercised by the people themselves and in the interests of the people.

The development of self-government will proceed above all through the Soviets, which must, in accordance with the Party's plans, completely live up to their role as the authorised and the decision-making bodies. Lately, the rights and possibilities of the Soviets at all levels have been substantially extended. This process will continue. Consequently the Soviets will gain in strength and Soviet democracy will be deepened.

We have begun improving the electoral system. The elections held in June this year convinced us that the new approach is correct and fruitful. They showed the people's increased political activity, their interest in getting their really best representatives elected to the Soviets, although this time too there were instances of formalism and unnecessary regimentation.

Restructuring and the development of democracy makes it possible to fully use the energy, potentialities, and power of the trade unions, the Young Communist League, and other public organisations, including those that have arisen in recent years, such as the All-Union Council of Veterans of War and Labor, the women's councils, the Cultural Foundation of the USSR, and V.I. Lenin Soviet Children's Fund. It is important that their everyday activities be connected with the solution of vital problems and reflect the interests of broad sections of the people.

Much that is new and encouraging has appeared in the work collectives and in neighbourhood activity. Broad opportunities are opening up for lofty initiatives, for solving all pressing problems promptly and without red tape.

The new processes taking place in the country also call for new approaches to the problems of general, political and legal culture, and to, I would say, the use of socialist democracy. It is the deficiencies in these areas that are largely responsible for such evils as bureaucracy, power abuses, kowtowing, and the waste and irresponsibility. The proper use of socialist democracy rejects methods of commands or "pressure", organisational vagueness, and the substitution of empty talk for deeds. All these are alien to socialism. It is also beyond doubt that the broader and deeper democracy is, the more attention must be given to socialist legality and law and order, the more we need organisation and conscientious discipline.

Democracy must not be confined to the political sphere. It must permeate all spheres of human relations. We proceed from the premise that socialism is a society of growing diversity in people's opinions, relationships, and activities. Every person has his own social experience, his own level of knowledge and education, his own perception of what is occurring. Hence, the tremendous variety of views, convictions, and assessments, which, naturally, require careful consideration and comparison. We are for a diversity of public opinion, a richness of spiritual life. We need not fear openly raising and solving difficult problems of social development, openly criticising and arguing. It is under such conditions that the truth is born and that correct decisions take shape. Socialist democracy must fully serve socialism, the interests of the working people.

The purpose of the radical economic reform now under way in the country is to assure, over the next two or three years, a transition from a predominantly centralized command system of management to a democratic system based mainly on economic methods and on an optimal combination of centralism and self-management. This implies a radical expansion of the independence of enterprises and associations, their transition to the principles of self-accounting and self-financing, and the endowing of work collectives with all the powers necessary for this.

The economic reform is no longer just plans and intentions, still less abstract theoretical discourses. It is becoming a part of life. Today a considerable number of enterprises and associations in industry, construction, transport, and agriculture are working on the principles of self-financing and self-supporting. From the beginning of next year enterprises producing 60% of our industrial output will be operating on this basis. The Law on the State Enterprise (Association) will have become effective.

All this is already having an effect on practical economic activity. Work collectives are showing a growing interest in the financial and economic results of their performance. They are beginning to keep track of inputs and outputs in a serious way, to save in things big and small, and to find the most effective ways of dealing with problems as they arise. Today we must once again firmly say: the Party will not tolerate any departure from the adopted principles of the economic reform implementation. All the scheduled changes must and will be carried out in full.

The economic reform and restructuring as a whole forcefully bring the individual to the forefront. Social justice requires that we give more attention to the specific abilities of each person, and reward morally and materially those who work better and more, those who set others a good example.

True talents and outstanding personalities are society's invaluable assets; they must be recognized, and all the necessary conditions must be created for their work and life. We want the dignity, knowledge, work, and ability of everyone to be respected everywhere. So that an honest, hard- working, creative person will know that his work will be properly appreciated, that he will always be given the chance to prove that he is right and will find support, while an idler, a moneygrubber, a bureaucrat, and a boor will be rebuffed and unmasked. The favourable changes that are taking place in our country—and they are receiving extensive coverage in the mass media—have the vigorous support of the people.

A sloppy attitude towards work is today particularly intolerable. The person who is armed with up-to-date knowledge and machinery produces more and more, and his work becomes increasingly dependent on the activities of the thousands of other participants in social production. In these circumstances the negligence of even a single worker, engineer, or scientist can have extremely grave consequences and is fraught with enormous losses for society.

I would like to emphasise the growing importance of intellectual work, of the interaction of science, technology, and society, of the humanitarian, moral and ethical aspects of science, and scientific and technical progress. We want that all the achievements of science and technology to be put at the service of man, and that they do not upset the environmental balance. We are drawing harsh lessons from such a tragic event as the Chernobyl nuclear power plant accident. We advocate an end to the use of science for military purposes. Today, engineers, scientists, physicians, educators, writers and those working in the arts must enhance their sense of social responsibility, their professional competence and make their creative achievements more worthwhile.

In restoring the principle of material incentives to its rightful place and in paying more attention to the collective forms of these incentives, we should not allow an underrating of socio-cultural, moral or psychological incentives. They are of exceptional importance for the normal development of the relations of collectivism and comradeship and the socialist way of life and for the firm establishment of our Soviet values in the thoughts and actions of our people.

Comrades, we have every right to say that the nationalities question has been solved in our country. The revolution paved the way for the equality of our nations not only in a legal but also in socio-economic terms, having done a great deal to level up the economic, social and cultural development of all our republics, regions and peoples. One of the greatest gains of the October Revolution is the friendship of the Soviet peoples. It is, indeed, a unique phenomenon in world history. And for us, it is one of the chief buttresses of the strength and stability of the Soviet state.

Today, as we honor the outstanding achievements of the Leninist nationalities policy, the peoples of our country express their profound respect and gratitude to the great Russian people for its selflessness, its genuine internationalism and invaluable contribution to the creation, development and consolidation of the socialist Union of free and equal republics, to the economic, social, and cultural progress of all the peoples of the Soviet Union.

So, comrades, let us cherish our great common asset—the friendship of the peoples of the USSR. And let us, therefore, never forget that we are living in a multinational state, where all social, economic, cultural, and juridical decisions inevitably have a direct and immediate bearing on the nationalities question. Let us act as **Lenin** would, and build up the potential of every nation, everyone of the Soviet peoples, to the maximum.

National relations in our country are a vital issue in our life. We must be extremely considerate and tactful in all things that concern the national interests and national sentiments of people; we must ensure the most active participation of members of all nations and nationalities in fulfilling the diverse tasks of our multinational society. We intend to make a more indepth analyzis and to discuss these issues in the nearest future with an eye to what restructuring, democratization and the new stage in its development are introducing in the life of the country.

The friendship and cooperation of the peoples of the USSR is sacred to us. This has always been the case and will continue to be so. It is consonant with the spirit of Leninism, with the traditions of the October Revolution and with the vital interests of all nations and nationalities in our country.

Comrades, Soviet society's passage to a radically new quality, its breakthrough into the future is only possible along a broad front, which includes the intellectual sphere of socialist society—science and education, literature and art—and the social and moral values of the Soviet people. Spiritual culture not only makes society's life more beautiful, it also performs functions essential to its existence and embodies its intellectual and cultural potential. It could be described as an agent strengthening the social fabric, as a catalyst of its dynamic development.

We should keep raising the prestige of socialist culture. Scholars, scientists, inventors, writers, journalists, artists, actors and teachers—all those who work in various sphere of culture and education—must be advocates of restructuring. The Party counts on our intelligentsia's vigorous civic and social involvement.

The Soviet people are now an enlightened people, something the great educators of the past could only dream about. But here, too, we cannot afford to be complacent. Our accomplishments should not allow us to close our eyes to the enormous scope and seriousness of the tasks we must tackle today. We see that the educational system has in many respects fallen short of today's requirement. The quality of education in schools, colleges and universities and of the training of workers and specialists does not fully meet the needs of the day.

We must surge ahead and bring about radical changes in this sphere too. That is the way the Party approaches the reform of secondary education and vocational training, the reorganization in higher education. The CPSU CC has decided to examine topical issues of education at one of its plenary meetings.

Such, comrades, are the strategic tasks we are to accomplish in the course of revolutionary restructuring covering all aspects of the life of socialist society.

Thirty months have elapsed since the April Plenary Meeting of the CPSU CC. What are our achievements? What stage have we reached? I believe that raising those questions is both pertinent and essential at this jubilee session.

The general conclusion made on this score at the plenary meeting the CPSU CC has just held is that we are at a turning point. By and large, we have passed through the first stage of our restructuring effort. A concept of restructuring has been worked out on the basis of an indepth analyzis of the situation and of the outlook for the country's development. A fresh political, moral and psychological atmosphere has been created in our country. The Party has succeeded in making people more concerned about public affairs, in promoting their initiative, in making them more exacting, more critical and self-critical, in enhancing openness, and in paving the way for tangible changes in people's thinking and attitudes.

Support for restructuring and the demand that it make steady progress are the main features of the position taken by a majority of the Soviet people at the current stage. Industrial workers, collective farmers and the intelligentsia show understanding of the need to enhance discipline, efficiency and the quality of labor. A vigorous search for new forms of labor organization and remuneration is under way at factories, construction sites, collective and state farms, and research establishments. People are making greater demands on themselves, on executives and experts, and they are combating mismanagement and irresponsibility. We greatly appreciate this civic stand of our people, and see it as an obvious and weighty expression of support for the course towards restructuring taken by the Party.

There is a reason to speak of certain positive shifts that have occurred on the practical plane, first and foremost in the socio-economic sphere. Output growth rates have increased. Changes of a qualitative nature are in the offing in the economy, major scientific and technological programs are under way, and our engineering industry is being modernized. The development of agriculture, particularly of animal husbandry, is showing increased stability.

You all know, comrades, how unfavorable the weather was in most regions of our country this year. Nevertheless, we succeeded in harvesting more than 210 million tons of grain. This was the result of strenuous efforts by the people and by the Party which encouraged them to work in a new way.

The improvements that have begun in the economy have made it possible to initiate important measures in the social sphere. The scale of housing construction has increased noticeably, and the service sector is expanding. The incomes of working people are growing. The salaries of teachers and medical personnel have been raised. Major programs are being implemented in education and health care.

Still, all that is only a beginning. Today we can say that we are entering a new stage of restructuring, the stage at which all our policies, all our decisions are taking the shape of practical action, being translated into reality. This calls for a great effort on the part of our people—the working class, the farmers, the intelligentsia, and all our cadres. From now on, our ideas, plans, attitudes and methods of work will have to pass the test of practical application.

One can now feel a growing pressure in everything. But that is the vibrant pressure of creative, vigorous effort, of political and intellectual activity. There is a mobilizing quality to this pressure, comrades, and it makes you feel good.

I would like to stress that viewed from this angle, the next two or perhaps three years will be particularly complicated, decisive and, in a sense, critical. The principal reason is that we will have to simultaneously tackle large-scale tasks in the economy, in the social sphere, in the reorganization of government and public administration, in ideology and in culture.

In the economic sphere, we must effect far-reaching structural changes, achieve a breakthrough in accelerating scientific and technological progress, largely reorganize the economic mechanism, and thus take a decisive step in switching the economy top the track of intensive development.

The difficulty of the forthcoming period also lies in the fact that the transformations will come to affect the interests of ever greater masses of people, social groups and strata, and of all cadres. We are confident that widespread support of restructuring by the people and a profound understanding of the need for the changes, for the vigorous and unflagging pursuit of restructuring despite the difficulties arising in its course will continue to shape the situation in our country.

But it would be a mistake to take no notice of a certain increase in the resistance of the conservative forces that see restructuring simply as a threat to their selfish interests and objectives. This resistance can be felt not only at management level but also in work collectives. Nor can one really doubt that the conservative forces will seize upon any difficulty in a bid to discredit restructuring and provoke dissatisfaction among the working people. Even now there are those who prefer to keep count of the slipups instead of getting down to combating shortcomings and looking for new solutions. Naturally, these people never say that they oppose restructuring. Rather, they would have us believe that they are fighting against its negative side- effects, that they are guardians of the ideological principles that supposedly might be eroded by the increasing activity of the masses.

But, comrades, isn't it time to stop trying to scare us with all sorts of slipups? Of course negative side-effects are inevitable in any undertaking, particularly if it is novel. But the consequences of marking time, of stagnation and indifference have a much greater impact and cost a lot more than the side-effects that arise temporarily in the course of a creative effort to establish new forms of society's life.

We should learn to spot, expose and neutralize the maneuvers of the opponents of restructuring—those who act to impede our advance and trip us up, who gloat over our difficulties and setbacks, who try to drag us back into the past. Nor should we succumb to the pressure of the overly zealous and impatient—those who refuse to accept the objective logic of restructuring, who voice their disappointment with what they regard as a slow rate of change, who claim that this change does not yield the necessary results fast enough. It should be clear that one cannot leap over essential stages and try to accomplish everything at one go.

Restructuring carries on the revolutionary cause, and today it is absolutely essential to master the skill of exercizing revolutionary self- restraint. The self-restraint does not mean that we should sit back or drift with the current. It implies an ability to assess the situation realistically, not to back down before difficulties, not to panic, not to lose one's head over either success or failure—an ability to work strenuously and purposefully every day and every hour, to find and apply in everything the best possible solutions dictated by life itself.

Hence the need for confident, unswerving and purposeful efforts to implement what we have mapped out, to attain the objectives and accomplish the tasks that have been set. Our approach should consist in identifying and analyzing contradictions, grasping their nature and, on this basis, devising a system of political, economic, social, organizational and ideological measures. That is the only approach.

Comrades, the success of restructuring depends above all on the energy and commitment of the Party and of every Communist, on the force of their example. At this juncture of historic responsibility, at this time of socio- economic transformations, the Communist Party has boldly launched a resolute struggle for society's renewal and taken on the most difficult part of the task. We can say with confidence that the great cause of the October Revolution, the cause of revolutionary restructuring, is in firm hands. The Communists will discharge their duty with a high sense of responsibility before our people and our age.

The priority task today is to radically improve the activities of Party organizations, of Party bodies and cadres. We must bring about a breakthrough in the work of every Party organization; every Party committee and every Communist should step up their efforts. Things have started moving and decisively at that wherever this has been done, wherever Party leaders and Communists have aroused the initiative and enterprise of the masses, wherever they have boldly taken the path of democratisation and openness, of cost- effective management and the collective contract, wherever the door has been opened to new forms of labor organization and incentives, of meeting human needs. But we can see that some cities, districts and regions, and even some republics have not yet got down to restructuring in earnest. That is a direct result of political and organizational inertia and lack of initiative displayed by Party committees and their leaders. This also should be seen. This is also our realities.

A turn for the better is a special responsibility that now rests with the Primary Party Organizations. They are in fact at the heart of restructuring. It is the initiative of the Primary Party Organizations on which the progress of the transformations, the skill in mobilizing and inspiring people, and the ability to achieve tangible improvements depend above all. To sum up, comrades, restructuring will not succeed without a drastic invigoration of the activities of all Party organizations. And so we must have a more businesslike and a more democratic discipline. Then we will be able to put restructuring into high gear and impart a new impetus to socialism in its development.

III. **The October Revolution and Today's World**

Comrades, without the Great Revolution in Russia, the world would not be what it is today. Before that turning point in world history, the "right" of the strong and the rich, as well as annexationist wars, were a customary and standard feature of international relations. The Soviet government, which promulgated the famous Decree of Peace as its first legal act, rose against this state of affairs and introduced into international practice something that used to be excluded from 'big politics'—the people's common sense and the interests of the working masses.

During the few years when **Lenin** directed Soviet foreign policy, he not only worked out its underlying principles but also showed how they should be applied in a most unusual and abruptly changing situation. Indeed, contrary to initial expectations, the rupture of the "weakest link" in the chain of the capitalist system was not the "last, decisive battle" but the beginning of a long and complex process.

It was a major achievement of the founder of the Soviet state that he discerned in time the actual prospects the victory in the Civil War opened before the new Russia. He realized that the country had secured not merely a "breathing-space" but something much more important— "a new period, in which we have won the right to our fundamental international existence in the network of capitalist states". In a resolute step, **Lenin** suggested a policy of learning and mastering the art of long-term "existence side by side" with them. Countering leftist extremism, he argued that it was possible for countries with different social systems to coexist peacefully.

It took only 18 to 24 months in the wake of the Civil War to end the international political isolation of the state of workers and peasants. Treaties were concluded with neighbouring countries and then, at Rapallo, with Germany. Britain, France, Italy, Sweden and other capitalist countries extended diplomatic recognition to the Soviet Republic. The first steps were taken to build equitable relations with Oriental countries—China, Turkey, Iran and Afghanistan.

These were not simply the first victories of **Lenin**'s foreign policy and diplomacy. They were a breakthrough into a fundamentally new quality of international affairs. The main trend of our foreign policy was established. We have every right to describe it as a Leninist policy of peace, mutually beneficial international cooperation and friendship among nations.

Naturally, not all our subsequent foreign policy efforts were successful. We have had our share of setbacks. We did not make full use of all the opportunities that opened before us both before and after World War II. We failed to translate the enormous moral prestige with which the Soviet Union emerged from the war into effective efforts to consolidate the peaceloving, democratic forces and to stop those who orchestrated the Cold War. We did not always respond adequately to imperialist provocations.

It is true that some things could have been tackled better and that we could have been more efficient. Nevertheless, we can say on this memorable occasion that the fundamental line of our policy has remained in concert with the basic course worked out and charted by **Lenin**—consonant with the very nature of socialism, with its principled commitment to peace.

This was overwhelmingly instrumental in averting the outbreak of a nuclear war and in preventing imperialism from winning the Cold War. Together with our allies, we defeated the imperialist strategy of "rolling back socialism". Imperialism had to curb its claims to world domination. The results of our peace-loving policy were what we could draw on at the new stage to devise fresh approaches in the spirit of the new thinking.

Naturally, there have been changes in the **Lenin**'s concept of peaceful coexistence. At first it was needed above all to create a modicum of external conditions for the construction of a new society in the country of the socialist revolution. Continuing the class-based policy of the victorious proletariat, peaceful coexistence subsequently became a condition for the survival of the entire human race, especially in the nuclear age.

The April 1985 Plenary Meeting of the CPSU CC was a landmark in the development of Leninist thought along this line too. The new concept of foreign policy was presented in detail at the 27th Congress. As you know, this concept proceeds from the idea that for all the profound contradictions of the contemporary world, for all the radical differences among the countries that comprise it, it is interrelated, interdependent and integral.

The reasons for this include the internationalization of the world's economic ties, the comprehensive scope of the scientific and technological revolution, the essentially novel role played by the mass media, the state of the Earth's resources, the common environmental danger, and the crying social problems of the developing world which affect us all. The main reason, however, is the problem of human survival. This problem is now with us because the development of nuclear weapons and the threatening prospect of their use have called into question the very existence of the human race.

That was how **Lenin**'s idea about the priority of the interests of social development acquired a new meaning and a new importance.

Since the April Plenary meeting we have made our vision of progress towards a safe world and durable peace sufficiently clear to everyone. Our intentions and our will are recorded in the decisions taken by the highest political forum of the Party—the 27th Congress—as well as in the new edition of the CPSU Program, in the program for nuclear disarmament set forth in the Statement of January 15, 1986, in the Delhi Declaration, in other documents, and in official statements by the Soviet Union's leaders.

Acting jointly with the other countries of the socialist community, we have submitted several important initiatives to the United Nations, including a project for devising a comprehensive system of international peace and security. The Warsaw Treaty states have addressed NATO and all European countries with a proposal on reducing armed forces and armaments to a level of reasonable sufficiency. We have suggested comparing the two alliances' military doctrines in order to make them exclusively defensive. We have put forward a concrete plan for the prohibition and elimination of chemical weapons and are working vigorously in this direction. We have advanced proposals on devising effective methods for the verification of arms reductions, including on-site inspection.

We have come out resolutely for strengthening the prestige of the United Nations, for the full and effective use of the powers conferred upon it and its agencies by the international community. We are doing our best to enable the United Nations, a universal mechanism, to competently discuss and ensure a collective search for a balance of interests of all countries, and to discharge its peacemaking functions effectively.

The most important thing is that our concept and our firm dedication to peace are reflected in practical action, in all our international moves, and in the very style of our foreign policy and diplomacy which are permeated with a commitment to dialogue—a frank and honest dialogue conducted with due regard for mutual concerns and for the advances of world science, without attempting to outmanoeuvre or deceive anyone. And so, now that more than two years have elapsed, we can say with confidence that the new political thinking is not merely another declaration or appeal but a philosophy of action and, if you will, a philosophy of a way of life. In its development, it is keeping pace with objective processes under way in our world, and it is in fact already working.

The October 1986 meeting in Reykjavik ranks among the events which have occurred since the new stage in international affairs began, which deserve to be mentioned on this occasion and which will go down in history. The Reykjavik meeting gave a practical boost to the new thinking, enabled it to gain ground in diverse social and political quarters, and made international political contacts more fruitful.

The new thinking with its regard for universal human values and emphasis on common sense and openness, is forging ahead on the international scene, destroying the stereotypes of anti-Sovietism and dispelling distrust of our initiatives and actions.

It is true that, gauged against the scope of the tasks mankind will have to tackle to ensure its survival, very little has so far been accomplished. But a beginning has been made, and the first signs of change are in evidence. This is borne out, among other things, by the understanding we have reached with the United States on concluding in the near future an agreement on medium- and shorter-range missiles.

The conclusion of this agreement is very important in itself: it will, for the first time, eliminate a whole class of nuclear weapons, be the first tangible step along the path of scrapping nuclear arsenals, and will show that it is in fact possible to advance in this direction without prejudice to anyone's interests.

That is obviously a major success of the new way of thinking, a result of our readiness to search for mutually acceptable solutions while strictly safeguarding the principle of equal security.

However, the question concerning the agreement was largely settled back in Reykjavik, at my second meeting with the USA President.

In this critical period the world expects the third and fourth Soviet-US summits to produce more than merely an official acknowledgement of the decisions agreed upon a year ago, and more than merely a continuation of the discussion. The growing danger that weapons may be perfected to a point where they will become uncontrollable is urging us to waste no time.

That is why we will work unremittingly at these meetings for a palpable breakthrough, for concrete results in reducing strategic offensive armaments and barring weapons from outer space—the key to removing the nuclear threat.

What, then, are the reasons for our optimism, for regarding comprehensive security really attainable? This deserves to be discussed here in detail.

At this new turning point in world history as we are celebrating the 70th anniversary of our Revolution which could not have won without theoretical preparation, we are examining the theoretical aspects of the prospects of advancement toward durable peace. The new way of thinking has helped us to generally prove that a comprehensive system of international security in the context of disarmament is needed and possible. Now we must prove that the attainment of this goal is necessary and feasible. We must identify the laws governing the interaction of the forces which, through rivalry, contradictions and conflicting interests, can produce the desired effect. In this connection we should begin by posing some tough questions—of course, tackling them from Leninist positions and using Leninist methodology.

The first question concerns the nature of imperialism. We know that it is the major source of the war threat. It goes without saying that external factors cannot change the nature of a social system. But, given the current stage of the world's development and the new level of its interdependence and integration, it is possible to influence that nature and block its more dangerous manifestations? In other words, can one be sure that the laws operating in the integral world, in which universal human values have top priority, will restrict the scope of the destructive effects produced by the operation of the egocentric laws which benefit only the ruling classes and are basic to the capitalist system?

The second question is connected with the first one: can capitalism get rid of militarism and function and develop in the economic sphere without it? Is it not a delusion on our part to invite the West to draw up and compare conversion programs for switching economies over to civilian production?

The third question: can the capitalist system do without neocolonialism which is currently one of the factors essential to its survival? In other words, can this system function without the inequitable trade with the Third World which is fraught with unforeseeable consequences?

Another related question: how realistic is our hope that the awareness of the terrible threat the world is facing—and we know that this awareness is making its way even into the higher echelons of the Western ruling elite—will become a part of practical policies? After all, however forceful the arguments of common sense, however well-developed the sense of responsibility, however powerful the instinct of self-preservation, there are still things which must not be underrated and which are determined by economic and, consequently, class-based interest.

In other words, the question is whether capitalism can adapt itself to the conditions of a nuclear-weapon-free world, to the conditions of a new and equitable economic order, to the conditions in which the intellectual and moral values of the two world systems will be compared honestly. These are far from idle questions. The course history will take in the next decades will depend on the way they are answered.

But even posing these questions is enough to grasp the gravity of the task that lies ahead. We will see them answered in due time. Meanwhile, the viability of the program for a nuclear-free and safe world will not only depend on its flawless scientific substantiation but will also be tested by the course of events—something that is influenced by a wide variety of factors, many of them new.

It is in fact already being tested. Here, too, we are loyal to the Leninist tradition, to the very essence of Leninism—an organic blend of theory and practice, an approach to theory as a tool of practice and to practice as a mechanism verifying the viability of theory. This is how we are acting, introducing a new way of thinking into our foreign policy activities, adjusting it and defining it more clearly using the political experience gained in practice.

To sum up, what are we counting on when we know that a safe world will have to be built jointly with capitalist countries?

The postwar period has witnessed an indepth modification of the contradictions that used to determine the principal trends in the world's economy and politics. I refer above all to the trends that inevitably led to wars, to world wars between capitalist countries themselves.

Today the situation is different. It is not only the lessons of the past war but also the fear of sapping its own strength in the face of socialism, by now a world system, that have prevented capitalism from allowing its internal contradictions to go to extremes. These contradictions began to began to evolve into a technological race and were dampened with the help of neocolonialism. A kind of new "peaceful" repartitioning of the world was started, in line with the rule **Lenin** identified—"according to capital", the bigger share going to whoever was strongest and wealthiest at the moment. Some countries began to "ease" tensions in their economies by rechannelling resources into the military-industrial complex on the pretext of a "Soviet threat". The changes occurring within the technological and organizational infrastructure of the capitalist economy also helped to clear up contradictions and to balance different interests.

But that is not all there is to it. Since an alliance between a socialist country and capitalist states proved possible in the past, when the threat of fascism arose, does this not suggest a lesson for the present, for today's world which faces the threat of nuclear catastrophe and the need to ensure safe nuclear power production and overcome the danger to the environment? These are all perfectly real and acute problems. Grasping them is not enough: practical solutions must also be found.

The next point. Can a capitalist economy develop without militarization? This brings to mind the "economic miracle" in Japan, West Germany and Italy—although it is true that when the "miracle" came to an end, they switched back to militarism again. But here one should examine the degree to which this switch was rooted in the essential laws governing the operation of contemporary monopoly capital and the role played by extraneous factors—the "contagious example" of the USA military-industrial complex, the Cold War and its spirit, considerations of prestige, the need to have one's own "mailed fist" to be able to talk to one's competitors in a commonly understood language, and the desire to back one's economic invasion of the Third World with power politics. Whatever the actual reasons, there was a period when the modern capitalist economy developed rapidly in several countries whose military spending was minimal. The relevant historical experience is available.

This issue can also be considered from a different angle—the other way round. Ever since the war, the USA economy has been oriented toward and dependent on militarism which at first seemed even to stimulate it. But then this senseless and socially useless squandering of resources led to an astronomical national debt and to other problems and maladies. In the first analyzis it has turned out that supermilitarization increasingly aggravates the domestic situation and upsets the economies of other countries. The recent panic on the New York Stock Exchange and on other stock exchanges around the world—a panic without precedent in almost 60 years—is a grave symptom and a grave warning.

The third point: the inequitable, exploitative relations with the developing countries. For all the fantastic innovations in the development of "alternative" (man-made) resources, developed capitalism has been made and will be unable to do without these countries' natural resources. That is an objective fact.

The calls for severing the historically shaped world economic ties are dangerous and offer no solution. But the neocolonialist methods of using the resources of others, the arbitrary practices of the transnational corporations, the bondage of debt, debts that are nearing the trillion-dollar mark and obviously cannot be repaid, also lead to an impasse. All this gives rise to acute problems within the capitalist countries themselves too. The various speculations on this score are essentially aimed at making the Third World a kind of scapegoat and blaming it for the numerous difficulties—including the declining living standards—in the major capitalist countries.

Attempts are made time and again to "rally the nation together" on a chauvinistic basis, to lure the working people into a "partnership" in the exploitation of other countries, while making the masses accept the policy of new capitalist modernization. However, none of these or similar stratagems can do away with the problem itself. They can only mitigate it temporarily. Inequitable trade remains a fact that will eventually culminate in an explosion. It appears that Western leaders are beginning to understand that this outcome is a distinct possibility, but so far they have been merely trying to resort to various palliatives.

Indeed, the novelty of the international and political processes of our time has not yet been fully grasped and assimilated. Yet,this will have to be done because the ongoing processes have the force of an objective law: there will either be a disaster or a joint quest for a new economic order which takes into account the interests of all on an equal basis. We see the way to establishing such an order in the implementation of the "disarmament-for-development" concept.

Thus, when looking for an answer to our third question, too, we see that the situation does not seem to defy resolution. In this area as well contradictions can be modified. But this necessitates understanding reality and mapping out practical actions in the spirit of a new thinking. And this, in turn, will facilitate the advance toward a more secure world. In a nutshell, here as well we are facing a historic choice dictated by the laws of our largely interconnected and integral world.

There is another important, even decisive, fact. Socialism is a component part of this world. Having begun its history 70 years ago and then grown into a world system, it has in fact determined the character of the 20th Century. Today it is entering a new stage in its development, demonstrating, once again, its inherent potentialities.

Think, for instance, of the vast potential for peaceful coexistence inherent in just the Soviet Union's restructuring. By making it possible for us to attain the world level in all major economic indicators, restructuring will enable our vast and wealthy country to become involved in the world division of labor and resources in a way never known before. Its great scientific, technological and production potential will become a far more substantial component of world economic relations. This will decisively broaden and strengthen the material base of the all-embracing system of peace and international security. And that, by the way, is another highly important aspect of restructuring, the place it is assigned in contemporary civilization.

The class struggle and other manifestations of social contradictions will influence the objective processes favoring peace.

The advanced forces of the working-class movement are looking for ways to enhance its political awareness. They have to carry on their activities in a highly complicated, new and changing situation. The issues involved in safeguarding the economic rights and interests of the masses, and indeed those related to the struggle for democracy, including democracy in production, have acquired a new meaning. For instance, workers are sometimes offered a "partnership", but it is a partnership under which the sanctum of business is inaccessible to them and free election of the managerial personnel is out of the question.

The Western world abounds in "theories" claiming that the working class is disappearing, that it has become completely absorbed by the "middle class", that it has changed socially, and so on and so forth. True, the changes undergone by the working class are substantial and far-reaching. But it is in vain that its class adversary is seeking consolation in this and trying to disorient and confuse the working-class movement. The working class, a numerically predominant force today within its new social boundaries, has the potential to play a decisive role, especially at abrupt turning points in history.

The motives for that may be different. One of the most probable ones is the insane militarization of the economy. The transition to a new phase of the technological revolution on militarizt grounds may serve as a powerful catalyst, especially as it paves the way to war, thus affecting all sections of the population and taking mass protests beyond the confines of economic demands. Therefore, here, too, the ruling class, the masters of monopoly capital, will have to make a choice. It is our belief, and it is confirmed by science, that at the present level of technology and organization of production, the reconversion and demilitarization of the economy are feasible. This would be tantamount to opting for peace.

The same concerns the consequences of the crisis in relations between the developed and the developing world. If things come to the verge of an explosion and it proves no longer possible to enjoy the benefits of exploiting the Third World, the question of the unacceptable and inadmissible character of a system unable to exist without this may acquire a political dimension and become very acute. In general, in this sense, too, capitalism is facing a limited choice—either to let things reach the breaking point or to heed the laws of the interconnected and integral world, one that calls for a balance of interests on an equal basis. The situation, as we see it, makes this not only necessary, but possible too. All the more so since forces in the Third World are acting along the same lines.

The decline of the national liberation movement is a common phrase. However, what is apparently happening is that one concept is being replaced by another and the novelty of the situation is being ignored. As far as the impulse for liberation is concerned, the one that was present at the stage of the struggle for political independence, it is certainly waning. And this is only natural. As for the impulse essential to the new, current stage of the Third World's development, it is only just beginning to be formed. One has to be aware of this and refrain from yielding to pessimism.

The factors that make up the impulse are varied and heterogeneous. Among them is a powerful economic process which sometimes takes on paradoxical forms. For instance, certain countries, while retaining some features of backwardness, are reaching the level of a great power in the world economy and politics. There is also an increase in political vigour in the process of the formation of nations and the strengthening of genuine nation-states, among which an important place is held by countries with revolutionary regimes. There is also the wrath bred by the dramatic polarisation of poverty and wealth, and the contrast between possibilities and realities.

An urge for national identity and independence makes itself increasingly felt in the organizations reflecting the processes of inter-state consolidation among the developing countries. To a greater or lesser extent this is characteristic of all the organizations, and their number is not small—the Organization of African Unity, the League of Arab States, the ASEAN, the Organization of American States, the Latin American Economic System, the South Pacific Forum, the South Asian Association for Regional Cooperation, the Organization of the Islamic Conference and, especially, the Non-Aligned Movement.

They represent a wide spectrum of conflicting interests, needs, aspirations, ideologies, claims, and prejudices typical of precisely this stage. Although they have already turned into a noticeable factor in world politics, none of them has yet fully revealed its potentialities. But their potentialities are colossal, and it is even hard to predict what they will yield in the next 50 years.

One thing is clear: this is a world of its own, seeking organizational forms for effective and equitable participation in solving problems common to the whole of humankind. It represents two and a half billion people. One can envision the gigantic strides it will make not only in exerting its influence on world politics, but also in playing an original role in shaping the world economy of the future.

For all their might, it is not the transnationals that will determine the Third World's development; it is more likely that they will be forced to adjust to the independent choice that has been or will be made by the peoples. The peoples and the organizations representing them are vitally interested in the new world economic order.

There is another important point to be made. In the last few decades, development within the capitalist world itself has given rise to new forms of social contradictions and movements. These include movements to remove the nuclear threat, protect the environment, eliminate racial discrimination, rule out policies dividing society into the privileged and the underprivileged, prevent the disaster threatening industrial areas that have fallen victim to present-day capitalist modernization. These movements involve millions of people and are inspired and led by prominent figures in science and culture, people enjoying national and international prestige.

Social democratic, socialist and labor parties and mass organizations similar to or connected with them are continuously playing an important role in the political processes in a number of countries, and in some countries they are increasing their influence.

Thus, according to all economic, political and social indications everywhere in today's world the thesis **Lenin** regarded as one of the most profound in Marxism is being vindicated: as the soundness of a historical action increases, the masses involved in this action will grow in number as well. And this is always an unmistakable sign and the most powerful factor of social progress and, consequently, of peace.

Indeed, the grandeur and novelty of our time is determined by the peoples' increasingly obvious and open presence in the foreground of history. Their present positions are such that they must be heeded immediately rather than in the long run. The new truth thereby brought into sharp focus is that the constant need to make a choice is becoming increasingly characteristic of historical advancement on the threshold of the 21st Century. And the right choice depends on the extent to which the interests and aspirations of millions, of hundreds of millions of people are heeded.

Hence the politicians' responsibility. For policy an only be effective if the novelty of the time is taken into account—today the human factor figures on the political plane not as a remote and more or less spontaneous side effect of the life, activity and intentions of the masses. It directly invades world affairs. Unless this is realised, in other words, unless a new thinking, one based on current realities and the peoples' will, is adopted, politics turn into an unpredictable improvisation posing a risk both to one's own country and to other nations. Such politics have no lasting support.

Such are the reasons for our optimistic view of the future, of the prospects of creating an all-embracing system of international security.

This is the logic behind our stand on defence issues, too. As long as there is a danger of war and as long as the drive for social revanche remains the core of Western strategies and militarist programs, we shall continue to do everything necessary to maintain our defence capability at a level ruling out imperialism's military superiority over socialism.

Comrades, during these jubilee days, we duly commend the accomplishments of the world communist movement. The October Revolution, which has retained to this day its international momentum, is the source of the movement's viability. The world communist movement grows and develops upon the soil of each of the countries concerned, but there is something that the image of a Communist has in common, no matter what his nationality is, no matter what country he works in. It is loyalty to the idea of the best, communist society, loyalty to the working people—above all the working class, and the struggle for their vital interests, for peace and democracy.

I feel this anniversary is the right occasion to mention the Third, Communist International. The truth about it has yet to be restored in full, and its authentic and complete history has yet to be written. For all the drawbacks and errors in its activities and for all the bitterness the recollection of certain chapters in its history may evoke, the Communist International is part of our movement's great past. Born of the October Revolution, the movement has become not only a school of internationalism and revolutionary brotherhood. It has made internationalism an effective instrument furthering the interests of the working people and promoting the social progress of big and small nations. It has produced a whole galaxy of true knights of the 20th Century, men of honor and responsibility, of lofty aspirations and unflinching courage, who took the sufferings of the millions of oppressed all over the world as their own, who heard their pleas and roused them to struggle.

Communists were the first to sound the alarm about the danger of fascism and the first to rise against it; they were also its first victims. They were the first—coming from all over the world—to engage in armed struggle against fascism in Spain. They were the first to raise the banner of Resistance in the name of the freedom and national dignity of their peoples. It was Communists, above all Soviet Communists, who made a decisive contribution to the crushing defeat of fascism in World War II.

And later, and today too, Communists have been fighting in the front ranks against reaction and obscurantism of every hue with the same irreconcilability and courage. They are people of legendary heroism and dedication. There are hundreds of thousands of them, organised and united by a single will, iron discipline, and commitment to their ideals.

The time of the Communist International, the Cominform, even the time of binding international conferences is over. But the world communist movement lives on. All parties are completely and irreversibly independent. We declared that as early as the 20th Congress. True, the old habits were not discarded at once. But today this has become an unalterable reality. In this sense, too, the 27th Congress of the CPSU was a final and irrevocable turning point. I think this has been actually proved by our relations with fraternal parties in the course of restructuring.

The world communist movement is at a turning point, just as is world progress itself and its motive forces. The communist parties are looking for their new place in the context of the profound changes unfolding as we are about to enter a new century. Their international movement is undergoing a renewal and is united by respect for the principles of confidence, equality, and sincere solidarity that have also been renewed. The movement is open to dialogue, cooperation, interaction and alliance with all other revolutionary, democratic and progressive forces.

The CPSU has no doubts about the future of the communist movement as one that offers an alternative to capitalism and involves the most valiant and consistent fighters for peace, for their countries' independence and progress, for friendship among all the peoples on Earth.

Comrades, the emergence of the world socialist system is the most important landmark in world history since the October Revolution. It is 40 years since socialism became the common destiny of many nations and a most important factor in contemporary civilization.

Our Party and the Soviet people highly appreciate the opportunity to cooperate with our friends who, just like us, have also assumed responsibility on a state level for socialism and its advancement for several decades now. All the socialist states have accumulated a great deal of interesting and useful experience in solving social, economic and ideological tasks and in building a new life.

The socialist system, the quests and experience it has tested in practice are of importance to the whole of mankind. It has offered to the world its own answers to the main questions of human existence, and confirmed its humanitarian and collectivist values centered on the working man. The socialist system instills in him a sense of dignity, a feeling of being master of his own country; it gives him social protection and confidence in the future. It secures for him broad access to knowledge and culture, and creates conditions for putting the individual's abilities and gifts to good use.

We all take pride in what has been achieved by the peoples in socialist countries, especially because their achievements are an outcome of many years of fruitful cooperation, a result of family and personal ties, and of the joint work and study of tens of thousands of people.

The heights reached enable us to have a clearer view of many things. Life has corrected our notions of the laws and rates of transition to socialism, our understanding of the role of socialism on the world scale. It would never occur to us to claim that all the progressive changes in the world are due to socialism alone. But the way mankind's vital problems have been posed, the way solutions to them are being sought prove that there is an inseparable link between world process and socialism as an international force. This link is especially evident in the struggle to avert nuclear catastrophe and in that balance of world forces which enables various peoples to more successfully uphold the socio-political choice they have made.

The accumulated experience ensures a better possibility of building relations between socialist countries on the following universally recognized principles:

—unconditional and full equality;

—the ruling party's responsibility for the state of affairs in the country; its patriotic service to the people;

—concern for the common cause of socialism;

—respect for one another; a serious attitude to what has been achieved and tested by one's friends; voluntary and diverse cooperation;

—a strict observance of the principles of peaceful coexistence by all. This is what the practice of socialist internationalism rests on.

Today the socialist world appears before us in all its national and social variety. This is good and useful. We have become convinced that unity does not mean identity and uniformity. We have also become convinced that there is no "model" of socialism to be emulated by everyone, nor can there be any.

The totality and quality of actual successes scored in restructuring society for the sake of the working people is the criterion of socialism's development at each stage and in each country.

We are aware of the damage that can be done to relations between socialist countries by a weakening of internationalist principles, by a departure from the principle of mutual benefit and mutual assistance, by a neglect of the common interests of socialism on the international scene.

We are pleased to state that of late our relations with all socialist states have become more dynamic and are improving. And cooperation in the framework of the Warsaw Treaty and CMEA certainly has become more fruitful and businesslike, which, however, does not set their member-countries in any essential way apart from other socialist countries.

The 27th Congress clearly defined the CPSU's position: that which ensures the combination of mutual interests with the interests of socialism as a whole is of decisive importance in politics and all other areas of our interaction with every socialist country. The strengthening of friendship and utmost development of cooperation with socialist countries is the top- priority goal of the Soviet Union's foreign policy. Welcoming today the delegations from socialist countries, we convey our greetings through them to the peoples of socialist countries.

Dear comrades,

Esteemed foreign guests,

In all our thoughts and deeds we have been inspired by the invigorating force of communist ideas. Inscribed on the banner of the Revolution, they inspired millions of people to struggle and labor, people who held these ideas sacred and regarded them as the purpose and meaning of their life.

The people's labor and struggle, their unabated perseverance in striving for their freely chosen goal, their joys and sufferings have become embodied in the reality of today's socialism advancing along the road of revolutionary restructuring. In this lies the force of the October Revolution, a revolution that continues.

For 70 years now the Soviet people have been led by their well-tried vanguard, the Leninist Party. The Party and revolution, the Party and the October Revolution are inseparable!

The victory of the socialist revolution would have been impossible without a party equipped with the Marxist-Leninist theory. Without the Party that learned to build a new society, there would be no socialism and there would not be our great country. Nor would we have a base for the present renewal of all aspects of society and for the country's accelerated socio-economic development. It is the imperative of the day that under the new conditions, too, the Party should take the lead in revolutionary renewal, enhancing, perseveringly and consistently, the effectiveness of its policy and promoting democratization in all areas and at all levels of public life.

That the Party's role should grow is natural. But words and formal rituals have little to do with it. The Party's role is determined by the depth and honesty of analysis and assessment, by the well thought-out policies and resolute action, by the ability to correlate the particular and the general, the personal and the social, the present and the long-term. It is determined by the heightened responsibility of all Party organizations and of each Communist for the state of affairs in society.

Our Party has a membership of some 20 million, which equals one-tenth of the country's adult population. It is an enormous force. However, the potential of the Party's influence, the Party's impact on restructuring has not yet been fully brought into play. The preparation for and holding of the 19th All-Union Party Conference should give a powerful impetus to improving the complicated and intricate work along these lines.

Today, the fate of the great cause of the revolution, of the great Leninist cause is in our hands. We are again blazing the trail. And this imposes special responsibility on the Party, on all of us. To put it in **Lenin**'s phrase, "The time of revolution is a time of action, of action from both above and below." This is the tradition that has been carried on by the party of a new type since its inception. This is also a demand made of the vanguard of Soviet society at the present stage in socialism's development which is both highly complicated and inspiringly novel.

Comrades, in 1917 humanity crossed the threshold and embarked on its true history. However, the past 70 years, the economic upheavals and social cataclysms that generated fascism and World War II, as well as the Cold War, the arms race, the threat of thermonuclear catastrophe and global crises have shown that the past still has a considerable part of humanity in its grip. And yet, we are justified in regarding the time we are living in, the juncture between the 20th and the 21st Century, as unique in terms of the profound social changes and the global scope of the tasks that face the peoples of the world.

We can see today that humanity is not really doomed to always live the way it did before October 1917. Socialism has evolved into a powerful, growing and developing reality. It is the October Revolution and socialism that show humankind the road to the future and identify the new values of truly human relations:

—collectivism instead of egoism;

—freedom and equality instead of exploitation and oppression;

—genuine power of the people instead of the tyranny of the few;

—the growing role of reason and humanism instead of the spontaneous and cruel play of social forces;

—humankind's unity and peace instead of discord, strife and war.

The present generation, and not only that in our country, is responsible for the fate of civilization and life on Earth. It is this generation that will determine, in the long run, whether the beginning of a new millennium in world history will be the latter's tragic epilogue or whether it will signal an inspiring prologue to the future.

Slightly more than thirteen years are left before the beginning of the 21st Century. In the year 2017 the Soviet people and the whole of progressive humanity will mark the centenary of the Great October Revolution.

What is the world going to be like when it reaches our Revolution's centenary? What is socialism going to be like? What degree of maturity will have been attained by the world community of states and peoples? Let us not indulge in guessing. But let us remember that the foundations for the future are being laid today. It is our duty to preserve our inimitable civilization and life on Earth, to help reason win over nuclear insanity, and to create all the necessary conditions for the free and all-round development of the individual and the whole of humanity.

We are aware that there is a possibility of infinite progress. We realize that it is not easy to ensure it. But this does not frighten us. On the contrary, this inspires us, giving a lofty and humane purpose to our life and injecting it with a profound meaning.

In October 1917 we parted with the old world, rejecting it once and for all. We are moving towards a new world, the world of communism. We shall never turn off that road!

"Oktiabr' i perestroika: revoliutsiia prodolzhaetsia," *Pravda* and *Izvestiia* (3 Nov); *Kommunist*, 17 (Nov 87), 3-40, *Partiinaia zhizn'*, 22 (1987), 3-34; condensed translations are available in FBIS, No.212 (3 Nov 87), R38-R61, and CDSP, 39:44(1987), 1-10; 39:45(1987), 12-16. This report, perhaps the most important by Gorbachev during 1987, was delivered in the Kremlin Palace of Congresses, to the CPSU CC Jubilee meeting, the USSR Supreme Soviet, and the RSFSR Supreme Soviet, to mark the 70th anniversary of the Great October Revolution.

See also E.Teague, "Gorbachev Opens Seventieth Anniversary Celebration," RFE/RL. RL432/87 (2 Nov 87).

Chapter 2

POLITBURO WEEKLY COMMUNIQUES

Although it is barely mentioned in the CPSU Rules (See *Rules* of the CPSU (1986), Art. 38), the Politburo of the Central Committee of the Communist Party of the Soviet Union (CPSU CC) is the Party's most powerful organ. Its chairman, M.S.Gorbachev, the General Secretary elected by the CC, is therefore the country's most powerful individual. The Politburo normally meets on Thursday afternoons, so that its brief communiqués often appear in *Pravda* on Fridays. These reports are important because of the overall messages they carry about priorities. The Politburo's authority is supreme, for it establishes all the guidelines for economic, military, cultural, domestic, and foreign policy in the USSR.

There are differences of opinion within the Politburo, but the body speaks publicly in one voice. All full members have the right to vote on Politburo, but there is an "inner circle" which tends to dominate. Those members who also have positions on the CC Secretariat have clear priority in political influence.

The year 1987 saw several dramatic changes in the Politburo make-up. With the removal of D.A. Kunaev in the January Plenum, ostensibly "in connection with his retirement on pension" (*Pravda*, 29 Jan), but in reality for his long-time connection with Brezhnev and for corruption, and G.A. Aliev's resignation in October because of the "state of his health" (TASS, 21 Oct), the body became more Russian than ever before. Only V.V.Shcherbitsky, a Ukrainian, N.N. Slyunkov, a Belorussian elected in June 1987, and E.A. Shevardnadze, a Georgian, were non-Russians among the 13 full members left at the year's end. The last-named was the only non-Slav. All seven of 1987's Candidate members were Russian. There were still no women on Politburo in 1987. A.P.Biryukova, who was elected to the Secretariat in March 1986, remains the closest female to that exalted position since E.A. Furtseva served between 1957 and 1961.

One Candidate member lost his post on Politburo during 1987. S.L.Sokolov, USSR Defence Minister since December 1984 and Marshall of the Soviet Union, was forced to resign in May (*Pravda*, 31 May) because a small private airplane flown by a citizen of the Federal Republic of Germany was able to "violate" the Soviet border and land beside Red Square in Moscow without having had his flight "cut short." In November, B.N.Eltsin was fired as First Secretary of the Moscow City Party, "for major shortcomings" (*Pravda*, 12 Nov), but he still held his place as Candidate member of Politburo at the end of 1987. On the "Eltsin" affair, see the essay by T.R.Colton (1988).

At the June Plenum three new full members were elected to Politburo, bringing its membership to fourteen. One of them, A.N. Yakovlev, had been appointed as Candidate only in January. His function on the Secretariat as Chief of Propaganda and his strong support of Gorbachev in the cultural sphere, made him a competitor to Egor Ligachev, who had been the chief ideologist of the CPSU. Viktor Nikonov, who is in charge of agriculture in the Secretariat, was another Gorbachev appointee to Full membership. Nikolai Slyunkov, the third appointee, apparently is closer politically to "Premier" Nikolai Ryzhkov than he is to Gorbachev. As the economic administrator in the CC Secretariat, Slyunkov is a key figure in Gorbachev's program of perestroika. The appointment of these three CC Secretaries to the rank of Full member of Politburo appeared to strengthen Gorbachev's position. One might add that by the end of 1987, 10 of the Central Committee secretaries, not counting Gorbachev himself, had been appointed to that important post since his election as General Secretary.

POLITBURO MEMBERSHIP 1987

Full Members

M.S.Gorbachev, Russian, born in 1931. Elected in 1980, General Secretary since 11 March 1985. Chairman, State Council of Defense; member Presidium, Supreme Soviet.

G.A.Aliev, Azeri, born in 1923. Elected 1982. First Deputy Chairman, Council of Ministers. Major General. *Resigned* from Politburo on "health grounds", 21 October, and from the government on the 23rd.

V.M.Chebrikov, Russian, born 1923. Elected 1985. Chairman KGB. Army General.

A.A.Gromyko. Russian, born 1909. Elected 1973. Chairman, Presidium, Supreme Soviet ("President").

D.A. Kunaev. Azeri, born 1912. Elected 1971. First Secretary Kazakh Central Committee. Member, Soviet of Union, Supreme Soviet. *Replaced* "in connection with his retirement," 28 January 1987.

E.K. Ligachev. Russian, born 1920. Elected 1985. Secretariat (Ideology, Cadres). Member Supreme Soviet; Chairman, Commission of Foreign Affairs, Soviet of the Union.

V.P.Nikonov. Russian, born 1929. Elected 26 June 1987. Secretariat (Agriculture, Forestry). Member Supreme Soviet. Deputy Chief, Agroindustrial Complexes.

N.I.Ryzhkov. Russian, born 1929. Elected 1985. Chairman, USSR Council of Ministers ("premier").

V.V. Shcherbitsky. Ukrainian, born in 1918. Elected 1971. First Secretary, Ukrainian Central Committee. Member Presidium, USSR Supreme Soviet.

E.A.Shevardnadze. Georgian, born in 1928. Elected 1985. USSR Minister of Foreign Affairs since 1985.

N.N.Slyunkov. Belorussian, born in 1929. Elected 26 June 1987; had been Candidate since 1986. Secretariat (Economic Administration). Member, Presidium USSR Supreme Soviet.

M.S.Solomentsev. Russian, born in 1913. Elected 1983. Chairman, CPSU Control Commission.

V.I.Vorotnikov. Russian, born in 1926. Elected 1986. Chairman, RSFSR Council of Ministers. USSR Ambassador to Cuba, 1979-82.

A.N.Yakovlev. Russian, born in 1923. Elected 26 June 1987; had been Candidate since January 1987. Secretariat (Propaganda, Culture). Commission of Foreign Affairs, Council of Nationalities, Supreme Soviet. Academician. USSR ambassador to Canada, 1973-83.

L.N.Zaikov. Russian, born in 1923. Elected 1986. Secretariat (Military-Industrial). First Secretary of Moscow Gorkom CPSU, 12 November 1987 (replacing Eltsin).

Candidate Members

P.N.Demichev. Russian, born 1918. Elected 1964. 1st Deputy Chairman of Presidium, USSR Supreme Soviet.

V.I.Dolgikh. Russian, born in 1924. Elected 1982. Secretariat (Heavy Industry, Power). USSR Minister of Culture, 1974-86.

B.N.El'tsin. Russian, born 1931. Elected 1986. First Secretary Moscow Gorkom CPSU (*fired* 11 November 1987); Member of Presidium, USSR Supreme Soviet.

S.L.Sokolov. Russian, born in 1911. Elected 1985. Minister of Defense ("Retired" as Minister, 28 May 1987 because of FRG airplane landing on Red Square). Marshall of the USSR. **Resigned** from Politburo in June.

Y.F.Solov'ev. Russian, born in 1925. Elected 1986. First Secretary, Leningrad Obkom CPSU. Member Presidium USSR Supreme Soviet.

N.V.Talyzin. Russian, born in 1929. Elected 1985.First Deputy Chairman, Council of Ministers. Chairman Gosplan.

D.T.Yazov. Russian, born in 1923. Elected 26 June 1987. Replaced Sokolov as Minister of Defence in May.

6 JANUARY At a session held on 6 January the Politburo of the CPSU CC discussed proposals having to do with the implementation of the restructuring of higher and specialized secondary education which has been developed according to the guidelines set by the 27th CPSU Congress.

The documents under discussion outline measures to greatly improve the quality of training and the use in the national economy of specialists with higher education. In this regard, plans call for a radical restructuring of the educational-upbringing process and a shift to training broadly qualified specialists, based on a mastery of basic scientific knowledge and job skills and active cooperation with appropriate enterprises, associations and organizations. There are plans to create a new organizational-economic mechanism of cooperation between the higher school and branches of the national economy so as to provide both specialized training and advanced training of personnel in accordance with contracts. Part of the cost of such training (is) to be borne by branches of material production.

It was emphasized that improving the selection and placement of science-teaching and science personnel is a crucial condition for increasing the effectiveness of training and upbringing for future specialists. This means that restructuring graduate studies is an important stage in post-graduate education. Doctoral programs will be established at major higher schools and scientific institutions. Plans call for the introduction of a new process for the certification of science-teaching personnel and for the creation of more favorable conditions for the recruitment of prominent economic specialists and leading scholars for teaching positions in higher schools.

Ways of enhancing the role that higher-school research plays in accelerating scientific and technical progress and improving the quality of the training given to specialists who are mastering new technology were determined. Plans call for assuring that basic research at high schools, and especially universities, get priority. (They also call) for tripling or quadrupling the volume of experimental design and experimental work and on this basis, expanding the scale of scientific research and shortening the time required to put the results into practice.

Measures are being drawn up to further improve the material and everyday living conditions of higher-school staff, graduate students and undergraduate students.

After approving the bulk of the documents having to do with the restructuring of higher schools' work, the Politburo ordered the appropriate organizations to continue working on them. Their goal is further improvement in the planning of training for specialists, an increase in the quality and quality of equipment allocated to higher-school research, and for the participation of ministries, departments, associations and enterprises in this important work.

The Politburo discussed and approved a program of steps for the fulfillmnent of resolutions passed at a working meeting of the leaders of Communist and Workers' Parties of the CMEA member-states that was held in Moscow.

After discussing the results of talks between Comrade N. I. **Ryzhkov** and G. **Lazar**, Chairman of the Council of Ministers of the Hungarian People's Republic, the Politburo noted the increased effectiveness of Soviet-Hungarian cooperation and its modernization on the basis of intensified specialization. It also noted that the wider use of new, advanced forms of production and scientific and technical cooperation should help successfully resolve the problems of accelerating the social-economic development of the Soviet Union and the Hungarian People's Republic.

The session of the Politburo of the CPSU CC discussed certain other questions related to economic construction and ideological work, as well as foreign-policy work aimed at easing international tension and developing equal cooperation and mutually advantageous relations with all countries.

Pravda (7 Jan 87); full translations can be found in CDSP, 39:1 (1987), 17-18, and FBIS, No. 004 (7 Jan 87), R3-5. No further Russian language titles will be indicated in this section, since all appeared in *Pravda* under the heading, "V Politburo TsK KPSS." Politburo reports also are carried in most other Party papers, in *Izvestiia*, and in major weeklies, such as *Ekonomicheskaia gazeta*.

22 JANUARY At its January 22 session, the Politburo of the CPSU CC, in its supervisory role, reviewed the question of progress in fulfilling the CPSU CC and USSR Council of Ministers' resolutions on accelerating the development of machinery manufacturing.

As the meeting noted, the measures the Party and government have adopted have resulted in a situation in which the development of the machinery-manufacturing branches as a whole is progressing in a dynamic manner and has been accompanied by substantial changes in production and management. Last year, plan targets for increased production and labor productivity were overfulfilled. Reconstruction of production is being undertaken at a greater pace; capacities are being used with greater effectiveness, and deliveries to the national economy of computer equipment instruments, modern machine tools, press machinery, and other equipment have also increased. The shift of ministries and many enterprises to operation under the conditions of full financial autonomy is expanding.

At the same time, the Politburo drew attention to the fact that the restructuring in the machinery-manufacturing complex as a whole is not being carried out at the pace that the times require. The development and production of new machines and instruments is proceeding slowly. No radical breakthrough has been achieved in sticking to delivery discipline. Funds allocated for the construction, reconstruction and retooling of enterprises are not being fully expended. Emphasizing that the pace of reconstruction of the entire economy depends to a great degree on a rapid upturn in machinery manufacturing, the Politburo instructed the appropriate Party and state agencies to concentrate their efforts on the elimination of existing shortcomings and the unconditional fulfillment of the plan assignments which are aimed at accelerating the development of the machinery-manufacturing complex's technical level and the quality of output.

A resolution was adopted on measures to further improve the operation of state arbitration agencies and to strengthen their role in providing legality and contractual discipline for the economy. The resolution provides for a restructuring of the work of these agencies, an increase in their powers and a growth in their ability to bring influence to bear in protecting the interests of enterprise and organization as the transition to full economic accountability and self-financing takes place. The Communist Party CCs of the republics and the territory, province and city Party committees were instructed to intensify Party guidance of the operation of state arbitration agencies, to improve work having to do with selecting personnel for these agencies, by placing them and doing upbringing work with them. And they must raise the standards by which contractual discipline at all levels of our economic mechanism is enforced.

The CPSU CC, the USSR Council of Ministers and the All-Union Central Council of Trade Unions have adopted a resolution for further improving services to the elderly and handicapped. The resolution calls for expanding the construction of homes for war and labor veterans, fitting them with modern equipment, furniture and furnishings, and improving medical, cultural, consumer and other forms of social services to this category of citizens. The attention of Party, Soviet, economic and trade-union organizations was drawn to the need to firmly eliminate existing deficiencies and to greatly improve the operation of social-security institutions.

The fact was noted that the USSR Council of Ministers will in the near future draw up and adopt measures to radically improve the material security of orphaned children and children no longer under their parents' care who are being raised in children's homes, boarding schools and infants' homes, as well as to strengthen the physical facilities and equipment of these institutions.

After reviewing the draft charter for secondary general-education schools that is being drawn up in accordance with the decisions of the 27th CPSU Congress and the Basic Guidelines for Public-Education Reform, the Politburo found it expedient to submit that highly important document to a broad cross-section of teachers and parents for discussion and to have it reviewed at Union-republic teachers' conferences, as well as at the All-Union Teachers' Congress that is to be convened this summer.

After discussing the results of Comrade N. I. **Ryzhkov's** visit to the Republic of Finland, the Politburo noted that this visit, and the talks which took place with President **Koivisto** and Prime Minister **Sorsa**, expressed the conviction that the agreements signed during the visit will promote a further expansion and improvement of mutually benefical trade, economic, scientific and technical cooperation between the USSR and Finland. They will widen that cooperation and strengthen it with new forms.

The Politburo approved the results of Comrades E. A. **Shevardnadze** and A.F. **Dobrynin**'s working visit to the Democratic Republic of Afghanistan and their meetings and talks with Afghan leaders. The talks, which were held in the spirit of the Moscow talks between Comrades M. S. **Gorbachev** and **Najib**, reaffirmed the two countries' desire to pursue a firm and consistent policy of further strengthening friendly good-neighborly relations between them. Noting the successful implementation of plans for Soviet-Afghan cooperation, the Politburo expressed support for the policy of national reconciliation in Afghanistan that the People's Democratic Party of Afghanistan has proclaimed, and for the decisions adopted by the extraordinary plenary session of the PDPA Central Committee and the session of the DRA Revolutionary Council. It took special note of the importance of the Afghan leadership's call for a cease-fire and of the significance of this step for restoring peace on Afghan soil. The Politburo emphasized again that the DRA government's desire for an early political settlement of the situation in and around Afghanistan serves the fundamental interests of all the countries of the region and serves to ensure peace and security in Southwest Asia and the Near East.

The meeting of the Politburo of the CPSU CC also examined certain other questions of domestic policy and Party construction, as well as of cooperation with fraternal Communist and Workers' Parties in the struggle for peace and social progress.

Pravda (23 Jan 87); a translation can be found in FBIS, No. 015 (23 Jan 87), R1-R2; and a condensed version in CDSP, 39:4 (1987), 28.

29 JANUARY At a session held on January 29, the Politburo of the CPSU's CC discussed priority questions on organizing the implementation of the decisions made by the January plenary session of the CPSU CC on restructuring and personnel policy. The Secretariat and the departments of the CPSU CC were charged with drafting appropriate measures, thoroughly studying the proposals and observations made by the Plenum participants, and initiating practical work to accelerate restructuring and the qualitative improvement of work with cadres in accordance with the decisions of the Plenum of the CPSU CC.

The Politburo supported the All-Union Central Council of Trade Unions' proposals that the draft Charter of USSR Trade Unions, with changes and additions arising from documents of the 27th Party Congress, be submitted for broad discussion. The proposed changes are aimed at the further development of trade union democracy, the strengthening of organization and discipline, and the development of the labor and political activity of trade union members in accomplishing the tasks of acceleration and restructuring.

The results of the All-Union Socialist Competition for 1986 were summarized and discussed. It was emphasized that in summing up these results particular attention should be devoted to the implementation of plan commitments and contractual pledges for delivery, production plans for consumer goods, state procurement of agricultural crops, economic assignments, and improving the quality of output. The implementation of plans for the construction of housing, hospitals, schools, and children's preschool institutions should be a compulsory priority.

A report given by Comrades A.N. **Yakovlev**, A.F. **Dobrynin**, and V.A. **Medvedev** on the results of the meeting of secretaries of the Central Committee of fraternal parties of socialist countries on international and ideological questions that was held 22-23 January in Warsaw were heard and approved. It stressed the importance of the concrete measures the session outlined to improve cooperation on foreign policy and ideology, and to strengthen their interaction on the basis of the principles set forth at a working meeting of the leaders of fraternal parties of the CMEA member-states in Moscow. The appropriate departments and organizations have been ordered to carry out the necessary measures to implement the agreements that were reached.

Pravda (30 Jan 87); a translation can be found in FBIS, No. 020 (30 Jan 87), R19 and a condensed version is in CDSP, 39:5 (1987), 20.

5 FEBRUARY At a meeting that took place on 5 February, the Politburo of the CPSU CC discussed and approved measures that the government has drafted on the basis of decisions of the 27th Party Congress and the January Plenum of the CPSU CC, for the purpose of creating cooperatives in the area of consumer-goods production, consumer services and food supply.

As was noted at the meeting, those cooperatives are called upon to help meet the public's demand for food-service products and for consumer services and goods more completely, thereby supplementing the existing system of state enterprises and organizations in those areas. Foillowing the model charters, the cooperatives will work on a self-supporting and self-financing basis and will carry full responsibility for the results of their business activities. Plans call for recruiting participants in the cooperatives from among pensioners and other citizens who are not engaged in social production, and also from university and secondary-school students. Local Party and Soviet agencies have been ordered to provide all possible help in the formation of cooperatives and (to encourage) the success of their work.

The question of improving conditions for the activities of creative unions was examined at the Politburo meeting. It was stressed that the further advancement of Soviet literature and art and the enhancement of their role in the spiritual life of society will present creative unions with vitally important tasks in creating works of all types and genres that will be important from an ideological and artistic point of view. Taking this into account, the CPSU CC and USSR Council of Ministers have adopted a resolution outlining measures for further stimulating the work of the writers', filmmakers', composers', theater workers', and artists' unions, strengthening their physical facilities, and improving publishing and the publicizing of literature and the arts.

A resolution of the CPSU CC, the USSR Council of Ministers, the All-Union Council of Trade Unions and the All-Union Young Communist League Central Committee has been adopted concerning the further advancement of creative technical work by amateurs. This resolution calls for the organization of creative technical clubs at enterprises, organizations, Palaces and Houses of Culture and other institutions of city and district Soviet executive committees, and for providing these clubs with equipment, tools and materials. Appropriate ministries and departments have been ordered to establish a procedure for financing the clubs, giving them material and technical support, and rewarding those who produce the best results. Measures are outlined for publicizing amateur creative work more intensively and for holding regular shows, competitions and exhibitions devoted to new developments. Chief machinery ministries have been appointed to be responsible for developing such creative work for principle types of machinery. Coordination of this work has been assigned to the USSR State Committee on Inventions and Discoveries.

The Politburo discussed the results of the work of the CPSU CC's Party Control Committee in 1986. It was noted that the Party Control Committee stepped up its supervision of the implementaion of the decisions of the 27th Party Congress and the CC on crucial questions of socioeconomic development, strengthening Party and state discipline, confirming Leninist norms of Party life and combatting negative phenomena. While approving the work of the Party Control Committee, the Politburo emphasized that the most important task of Party Control agencies is to (make) effective checks on the implementation of Party decisions and to improve their own supervisory work . Strict supervision of the work of the cadres must be established in all sectors of Party life and state, economic and public affairs. Tasks of fundamental importance include intensifying the struggle against inertia, bureaucratic rigidity and other phenomena that are alien to socialism, and making every executive and each Communist strictly responsible for observing the requirements of the CPSU Program and Statutes and the standards of communist morality.

The Politburo of the CPSU CC discussed a number of other questions of organizational work in carrying out the decisions of the January Plenum of the CPSU CC, as well as questions of Party and state development and of foreign-policy work aimed at ensuring peace and the security of peoples.

Pravda (6 Feb 87); full translations can be found in FBIS, 3, no. 025 (6 Feb 87), R1-R2; and in CDSP, 39:6 (1987), 21.

12 FEBRUARY At a regular meeting on 12 February, the Politburo of the CPSU CC discussed the performance of the country's economy in January 1987. It was noted that the fuel and power complex and a number of other branches and areas of industrial production continued to develop successfully according to plan assignments. In agriculture, more milk and meat was purchased than in January of the year before. However, industry as a whole failed to meet the January plan. Production of many types of industrial output in physical units failed to reach the planned level. The volume of capital construction declined.

As it was pointed out in the discussion, the failure to fulfill the plan resulted mainly from failures in organizational and economic work and from the unsatisfactory preparation of a number of branches and regions of the country to meet the increased demands on the economic performance of associations and enterprises , as well as from difficulties in rail transport, construction and other areas of the economy, attributable to the harsh winter.

The Politburo ordered that Party, Soviet and economic agencies adopt exhaustive measures to make up the lost production and to meet the pace of the annual plan in the shortest possible time. The Politburo expressed its confidence that Communists and all Soviet people will mobilize their will and their potential energies to fulfill the plan within the confines of 1987.

The session adopted a resolution of the CPSU CC, the USSR Council of Ministers and the All-Union Central Council of Trade Unions on shifting associations, enterprises and organizations in industry and other branches of the economy to multiple-shift operations. The resolution is to be implemented in 1987-88. The production facilities that are made available as a result are to be utilized to retool shops and sections, to increase the production of highly important types of output (above all, consumer goods) and to resolve employees' social questions. Funds saved in the construction of new industrial facilities are to be allocated to the construction of housing and the improvement of employees' working and living conditions. In regards to the switch to multiple-shift operations, plans call for quickening efforts to restructure the operation of organizations and institutions in the service sphere and their social and culture branches. The Politburo stressed that the transition to multiple-shift operations is to be carried out concurrently with the resolution of these social issues.

In order to give workers, foremen and other specialists a greater interest in working the evening and night shifts, a number of additional moral and material incentives, privileges and benefits are to be introduced for them. In connection with the implementation of these measures, the attention of Party, Soviet, economic, trade-union, and Young Communist League agencies was called to the need to make a more thorough study of all questions having to do with the switch to multiple-shift operations, to speed up organizational and mass political work in labor collectives and to further raise standards for the selection and placement of personnel.

On hearing a report by Comrade A.A.**Gromyko** on the work of the USSR Supreme Soviet in 1986, the Politburo stressed the importance of further improving the work of the commissions of the two houses and of the Deputies to the USSR Supreme Soviet, and of drafting and adopting legislative acts aimed at democratizing public life, expanding openness, strengthening socialist legality and ensuring that working people participate actively in resolving all issues of state and public life.

The Politburo approved a resolution of the CPSU CC and the USSR Council of Ministers on steps to help the Georgian Republic relieve the effect of the natural disaster in that republic.

Reviewing issues related to preparations for regular elections to local Soviets and of people's judges and people's assessors of district (city) people's courts, the Politburo observed that the upcoming election campaign is expected to play an important role in improving the performance of local Soviet and law-enforcement agencies. (These agencies are expected to) further develop socialist democracy, and to enhance Soviet people's labor and political activism in the struggle to accelerate social and economic development and to successfully fulfill the 1987 plan and the Five-Year Plan as a whole. In accordance with the decision of the January (1987) Plenum of the CPSU CC, it was deemed expedient to make certain changes in election practices.

The Politburo approved the results of Comrade M.S.**Gorbachev**'s meeting with A.S.**al-Beedh**, General Secretary of the Yemen Socialist Party Central Committee, and of the Soviet leaders' talks with the party and government delegation of the People's Democratic Republic of Yemen. The appropriate ministries and departments were ordered to provide for the further development of cooperation with Democratic Yemen along party and state lines.

The meeting of the Politburo of the CPSU CC heard a report by Comrade E.A.**Shevardnadze** on the results of his visit to the German Democratic Republic and the Czechoslovak Socialist Republic. It also discussed certain other questions of domestic and foreign policy.

Pravda (13 Feb 87); a condensed translation can be found in CDSP, 39:4 (1987), 18-19.

27 FEBRUARY The Politburo of the CPSU CC discussed and approved a report by Comrade M.S.**Gorbachev** on the results of his trip to the Latvian and Estonian Republics and of his meetings and discussions with Party *aktiv* and working people. The exchange of views which took place in the labor collectives, primary Party organizations, and the conversations with workers, kolkhoz workers, engineering and technical workers, representatives of the creative intelligentsia, and students on topical questions connected with the restructuring, are of great significance for the implementation of the decisions of the January 1987 Plenum of the CPSU CC, and for the fuller use of the material and technical, cultural and spiritual potential created in those republics. In restructuring, directives based in principle on matters of economic and socialist democracy and of the role and place of Party bodies at the raion level, in particular, ought to be applied in practice in the activities of all Party organizations and labor collectives. Taking into account the ideas expressed by M.S.**Gorbachev**, the need was stressed for the adoption by the Party, state and economic organizations, of measures to activate the work to fulfill the decisions of the 27th CPSU Congress, and to mobilize Communists and all working people in the implementation of plan targets for 1987. Corresponding state and economc bodies have been instructed to review matters concerned with the renewed fixed productive assets industry, with increasing the output and raising the quality of consumer goods, with the development of the social sphere, and with improving material and technical supply to enterprises of the Latvian and Estonian SSSRs and to adopt the necessary measures.

The Politburo discussed preparations for the 70th anniversary of the Great October Socialist Revolution. A resolution of the CPSU CC on this matter states that the 70th anniversary of the October Revolution is a great public holiday for the Soviet people and a review of the historic achievements of socialism. At the same time, it is also a milestone— a high look out from which to evaluate of the results and lessons of the road traversed, of the changes taking place in the world and of the new tasks facing Soviet society in the present, extremely important stage of its development.

Political, organizational and ideological measures were delineated to assure that preparations for the anniversary actively stimulate an upsurge in the labor and political activism of Communists, non-Party people, young people and all the country's working people. Emphasis was put on the importance of disclosing the organic link between the accomplishments of the October Revolution and today's essentially revolutionary transformation of all dimensions of life in Soviet society. Particular attention was drawn to the need to conduct propaganda from the position of truth and realism, to frankly disclose deficiencies, and to recruit the working people in a decisive struggle to eliminate them and in persistent efforts to improve socialism and to achieve the CPSU's program objectives. An appeal from the CPSU CC to the Soviet people in connection with the 70th anniversary of the Great October Socialist Revolution was approved. The appeal will be published in the press.

A resolution of the CPSU CC and the USSR Council of Ministers on measures to improve the operation of collective farm markets was adopted. The resolution calls for greatly improving their physical facilities and for increasing the amounts of farm output shipped to and sold by them. (It also called) for implementing several other measures aimed at improving the public's supply (of food) and having an effective economic impact on lowering market prices. It was decided to transfer collective-farm markets from the jurisdiction of the USSR Ministry of Trade and the Union-Republic Ministries of Housing and Municipal Services to the jurisdiction of consumers' cooperative organizations. Councils of Ministers and local Soviet executive committees from the Union and Autonomous Republics, in conjunction with consumers' cooperative organizations, are ordered to take full responsibility for supervising collective-farm markets, ensuring the necessary conditions for their operation, and developing their physical facilities and equipment.

The Politburo of the CPSU CC also discussed several other issues of the CPSU's and Soviet state's domestic and foreign policy affairs.

Pravda (27 Feb 87). This Politburo report and Gorbachev's several speeches made in Latvia and Estonia were reprinted in *Tverdo idti dorogoi perestroiki i uglubleniia demokratii* (Moscow: Politlit, 1987), 77-78. A full translation of the Politburo report also can be found in FBIS, No. 41 (2 Mar 87), R1-R2; and a condensed text is in CDSP, 39:9 (1987), 21.

5 MARCH At a session on 5 March, the Politburo of the CPSU CC considered the question of additional measures to speed up progress in the mechanization of agriculture. A CPSU CC and USSR Council of Ministers' resolution on this question calls the attention of the relevant ministries and departments to the serious lag in the implementation of the program for mechanizing agricultural production. (It sets out) additional measures for dramatically speeding up the development of designs, increasing the output of new agricultural equipment, and improving its quality.

The resolution provides for a further increase in farm-machinery production capacity, improved labor organization, increased use of shift work, improved facilities for design and research organizations, and the application of advanced materials and components. It enlists enterprises of the USSR Agro-Industrial Committee in the production of specialized agricultural equipment for regional use. Party and state bodies have been instructed to speed up organizational and political work to assure the timely and unconditional fulfillment of the assigned tasks regarding fitting out the country's Agro-Industrial Complex in the most complete way with modern and reliable equipment.

Following the directives of the 27th Party Congress, the Politburo approved recommendations for certification procedures for high level staff employees of Soviet agencies and public bodies. Such certification is to become an important way of collectively evaluating the work of cadres, giving them an incentive to upgrade their qualifications, and increasing their responsibility for their assigned work and for staff work standards. It is to be conducted in a business-like manner in an atmosphere of adherence to principle and objectivity, of wide openness and strict observance of the laws. The certification commissions provided for by the model regulation on certification determine whether officials pass the requirements for the positions they hold. (They) give an evaluation of (the officials') political work and moral qualities, and make the necessary recommendations to the governing bodies.

The meeting approved government proposals for shifting the USSR State Committee for Foreign Tourism to full economic accountability, foreign-exchange self-sufficiency, and self-financing. Specific organizational and economic measures are planned to ensure efficient work by the USSR State Committee for Foreign Tourism, to more fully satisfy demands from foreign and Soviet citizens' for tourist services, and to eliminate existing deficiencies in this area. The implementation of these measures will make it possible to improve the quality of foreign tourism and to raise it to the level of present-day requirements.

The Politburo heard M.S.**Gorbachev**'s report on his meetings with A.**Fanfani**, President of the Senate of the Italian Republic, and G.**Andreotti**, Italian Minister of Foreign Affairs. It was noted that the meaningful exchange of opinions on matters of European and international security is very important for revitalizing the East-West political dialogue and for the search for ways of improving the international atmosphere.

The session reviewed the results of talks between the Soviet leadership and S.**Hermannsson**, Prime Minister of Iceland, who is in the Soviet Union on an official visit. It noted the proximity of the two sides' opinions on questions of bolstering international security and stability and curbing the arms race, and on the need for joint actions by large and small states in the cause of maintaining peace.

The Politburo approved the results of M.S.Gorbachev's conversation with A.**Fava**, General Secretary of the Argentine Communist Party. The unity of views held by the CPSU and the Argentine Communist Party on questions of the world situation today, which were discussed, were noted with satisfaction. There was an affirmation of their readiness to promote the comprehension and solution of the problems facing the international Communist and workers' movement. (They also agreed) to continue the quest that is in the spirit of the times for a means of communication and cooperation between fraternal parties, based on equal rights and interaction between communist and other forces in the struggle for a nuclear-free world and for the survival of mankind. Emphasis was laid upon the mutual striving by the CPSU and the Argentine Communist Party to continue developing the traditional comradely relations linking the two parties.

After hearing N.N.**Slyunkov**'s report on the CPSU's delegation's trip to Portugal, the Politburo noted with satisfaction the unity of views between the CPSU and the Portuguese Communist Party on fundamental questions of the struggle for peace, democracy and social progress. The CPSU's unflagging solidarity with the PCP's attempt to defend the democratic gains of the Portuguese people was affirmed.

The session of the Politburo of the CPSU CC also discussed certain other questions of economic construction and of ideological and Party organizational work, as well as questions concerning the development of cooperation with foreign countries.

Pravda (6 Mar 87); a translation can be found in FBIS, No. 44 (6 Mar 87), R1; a condensed translation is in CDSP, 39:10 (1987), 20.

19 MARCH At its 19 March session, the Politburo of the CPSU CC discussed basic guidelines for restructuring the system for organizing people's political and economic education. Noting the tremendous importance of strengthening Marxist-Leninist theoretical training, tempering cadres in ideological and moral matters and instilling in them the new type of political and economic thinking, the Politburo outlined serious deficiencies and accumulated negative phenomena in political instruction and mass economic education.

Fundamental guidelines for restructuring the existing education system were approved. Plans call for making major changes in its organizational structure and for bringing the content, forms and methods of study into line with the tasks of accelerating the country's social and economic growth, activating the human factor and democratizing all spheres of public life. It is essential to ensure that Communists and non-Party people fully master the decisions of the 27th Party Congress, the CPSU Program, key questions of the Party's innovative policy, present-day achievements of managerial science, and the new management methods. There are plans for improving the quality of curricula and textbooks, expanding the production of educational equipment, greatly intensifying the training for propagandists and upgrading the role of Marxist-Leninist universities and political-education centers and facilities. It was deemed appropriate to combine economic and vocational instruction in an organic fashion.

The Politburo emphasized that restructuring the political and economic education of working people requires a fundamental improvement of Party supervision of this most important area of ideological work. The draft Basic Guidelines for Restructuring the System for Working People's Political and Economic Education will be printed in the press for widescale discussion.

A report was heard from A.N.**Yakovlev** on the results of the official visit to Spain of the delegation of the foreign affairs committee of the USSR Supreme Soviet's two houses. It was noted that Soviet-Spanish relations in various areas are growing in a spirit of mutual understanding on important international problems and on a mutually beneficial basis of cooperation in the economic, scientific, technical and cultural spheres. It was noted with satisfaction that the Soviet-Spanish political dialogue, which in recent years has become an influential force in European and world politics, is taking on an increased importance in connection with the accelerated attempts by European countries to achieve concrete agreements on questions of reducing nuclear weapons, reducing the level of military confrontation in Europe, and establishing an atmosphere of trust and cooperation there.

The session of the Politburo of the CPSU CC also discussed certain other questions of Party organizational work and of state organization and development, as well as matters of relations with foreign countries.

Pravda (21 Mar 87); full translations can be found in both FBIS, No. 44 (24 Mar 87), R1; and CDSP, 39:12 (1987), 14-15.

26 MARCH At its 26 March meeting, the Politburo of the CPSU CC discussed measures for assuring fulfillment of the 12th Five-Year Plan's allocations for the development of physical facilities and equipment in the social and cultural sphere.

There still has been no fundamental change in this sphere. Assignments for the construction of hospitals, children's preschool institutions, clubs and vocational technical schools have not been met.

The Politburo gave a critical assessment of shortcomings in the resolution of problems affecting the working people's vitally important interests and the mistakes made in this area by Union-Republic Party Central Committee and Councils of Ministers, and by ministries and departments.

In order to ensure that Five-Year Plan allocations for the commissioning of social and cultural facilities are fulfilled without fail, a series of measures has been delineated for implementing a program of social and cultural construction in 1988-1990. The Politburo set the task of overcoming the present lag and clarified assignments for the commissioning of about 630 million square metres of housing, as opposed to the 595 million stipulated in the five-year plan.

The Union Republic Councils of Ministers recommended that these social and cultural objectives should be supported in accordance with the necessary and strict adherence to the existing norms for ongoing construction; [and also] to facilitate a broader application of the present Two-Year construction goals; to direct no less than an additional 10% of capital investment toward new housing construction; to strengthen new construction organizations, and to increase the rigor of investigations into the execution of standing directives.

It was stressed that implementation of the program outlined for accelerating the development of physical facilities and equipment in the social sphere should be a matter of paramount political importance for all Party, state and public organizations. The fulfillment of the established plans for the contruction of housing and of cultural and consumer- service facilities is to be constantly monitored, and there is to be greater openness in the work being done to implement them.

The Politburo of the CC also discussed the question of improving research for the development of the country's agro-industrial complex. It noted that research is seriously lagging behind real-life demands and practical needs and that our existing scientific potential is not being fully utilized. [The Politburo] stressed the need for stimulating and perfecting the work of our scientific community, construction engineers, technologists, and specialists by improving their skills by means of training and upgrading programs.

The Politburo deemed it expedient to draw up and implement measures for the development of research facilities and equipment, as well as to increase salaries and work incentives for scientific personnel, designers, technologists and specialists and to fundamentally improve their training and refresher training.

The session discussed a report by E.A.**Shevardnadze** on the results of his visits to the Socialist republic of Vietnam, the Lao People's Democratic Republic of Kampuchea, Australia, Indonesia and Thailand and a report by A.P. **Biryukova** [Appointed to the Secretariat of the CPSU CC in March, 1986, which makes her the highest ranking female in Soviet politics] on a CPSU delegation's trip to Vietnam.

The Politburo also discussed certain other questions concerning the implementation of the decisions of the 27th Party Congress in the sphere of domestic and foreign policy.

Pravda (27 Mar 87); partial translations can be found in FBIS, No. 44 (27 Mar 87), R1; and in CDSP, 39:13 (1987), 19-20.

2 APRIL In a session held on 2 April, the Politburo of the CPSU CC discussed the progress being made in the work of implementing the program of liquidation of the results of the accident at Chernobyl Atomic Power Station. It was noted that the first two generating units are operating smoothly and that the deactivation of other facilities and towns in the contaminated areas is continuing. The construction of housing and social and consumer-service facilities for those evacuated is under way on a broad scale. Note was taken of the fact that the appropriate ministries and departments are taking additional measures to step up the pace of the work, speed the construction of the city of Slavutich and ensure the dependable protection of water resources during spring flooding.

The Politburo discussed the question of taking steps to fundamentally improve the country's statistics. It noted the importance of this work in the current restructuring of management and the economic mechanism. Principle directives on methods of further developing statistics were issued and also to raise the level of the analysis of the economic and social development process and of scientific and technical progress. Attention was drawn to the need for increasing the accuracy and the openness of statistical information, the rationalization of reports and ensuring their absolute reliability. In the realization of these objectives, the continued improvement of statistical agencies' physical plant and equipment and the improved training of skilled economists and statisticians were seen to be of the greatest importance.

The Politburo of the CPSU CC examined the problem of ensuring the protection and efficient use of Lake Baikal's natural resources. It gave a principled evaluation of the unsatisfactory fulfillment of regulations which exist on this matter. In order to make a definitive decision on the problem, the CPSU CC and the USSR Council of Ministers' resolution on protecting Baikal's natural resources was adopted. The heads of the interested ministries and departments, local Party and Soviet agencies, scientists, specialists, writers and other representatives of society participated in the preparation of this document. It outlines a complex of organizational, scientific, economic and technical measures that make it possible to radically improve the ecological situation of the basin of Lake Baikal.

Directives have been given for the reclassification of the Baikal Pulp-and-Paper Combine and the implementation at other enterprises located in this area of large-scale measures to prevent the pollution of Baikal and of the air in the zone. It was decided to widen the network of tourist centers there and, at the same time, the establishment of conditions for organizing tourism and public recreation that guarantee the preservation of the landscape and the plant and animal life.

The Politburo considered the progress made in the preparation of a draft USSR law on the procedure for appealing to the courts for relief from officials' illegal actions that violate citizens' rights. After the draft is discussed in the Permanent Commissions of the Chambers of the USSR Supreme Soviet, it will be submitted for consideration by the USSR Supreme Soviet in accordance with established procedure. It was stressed that the passing of the law will serve to further develop democracy, strengthen legality and raise the accountability of officials.

On discussing the results of the meetings in Moscow of the Committee of Foreign Ministers of the members of the Warsaw Treaty Organization, the Politburo supported the collectively prepared steps for eliminating the nuclear threat, banning chemical weapons, advancing the Budapest initiative for the reduction of armed forces and conventional weapons in Europe and developing the general-European process, and also strengthening the cooperation between the allied states in foreign policy.

The Politburo heard a report by M.S.**Gorbachev**, N.I.**Ryzhkov**, and E.A. **Shevardnadze** on the results of talks with Great Britain's Prime Minister, M. **Thatcher**.

The important significance [of the talks] for bilateral relations and the international sphere was noted. In the new conditions which now exist in Europe and in the world, the dialogue with a major Western Power and a permanent member of the UN Security Council was continued. It allowed for the open expression of views on relations between states with different social systems, on regional conflicts and other important problems, and—especially—on their perspectives about disarmament. Their resulted a deepening awareness of the positions and clarification of each other's intentions.

Agreements were signed on specific problems of bilateral relations. The hope was expressed that M. **Thatcher**'s visit would be followed by active bilateral economic and cultural connections.

The conversations showed that both sides recognize the importance of solving the problem of medium-range missiles, even though Great Britain continues to impose stipulations on any approach to an agreement. They express their willingness to eliminate chemical weapons, take action to reduce military confrontation in Europe—from the Atlantic to the Urals—enrich the Helsinki process, and to advocate a settlement of regional conflicts by political means.

In the cardinal questions of world development, there remain principal differences. The decisive disagreement of the Soviet leadership with the position that the conduct of international affairs and national security is only possible by relying on nuclear arms, even though this position encourages the spread of such weapons and risks a general catastrophe, was made clear.

The Politburo is convinced of the necessity of continuing and deepening the political dialogue with Great Britain and other Western states in the spirit of new thinking, with the aim of overcoming the present distrust and improving the international climate.

A report was heard from M.S.**Solomentsev**, about the results of a trip by a delegation of the CPSU CC Party Control Commission to the People's Republic of Bulgaria. It was noted that during the visit there took place useful meetings and contacts which brought valuable experiences to the activities of the control organs of the CPSU and the Bulgarian Communist Party.

It examined A.I.**Lukianov**'s [Appointed to CPSU CC Secretariat in January 1987] report on a CPSU delegation's visit to Denmark at the invitation of Denmark's Social Democratic Party and of G.P.**Razumovskii**'s report on a CPSU delegation's participation in the work of the 26th Austrian Communist Party Congress.

At the Politburo meeting there was also discussed certain other questions concerning state construction and personnel policy, and also the growth of cooperation with liberated countries and the struggle for peace and social progress.

Pravda (3 Apr); *Partiinaia zhizn'*, 8 (Apr), 3-4; a translation can be found in FBIS, No. 64 (3 Apr 87), R1-R2; a condensed text is in CDSP, 39:14 (1987), 16-17.

16 APRIL At its regular meeting, the Politburo of the CPSU CC approved the slogans of the CPSU CC for International Working People's Solidarity Day, 1 May.

At the session, the Politburo discussed the results of the growth of the economy during the first quarter and the tasks in organizing the fulfillment of the Plan for 1987. It was noted that total industrial production for the first three months of the year increased by 2.5% in comparison with the same period for last year. In March, industry reached an average daily rate that corresponded to the level of the annual allocation. The quarterly plan was over fulfilled by the branches of the fuel and energy complex. More dwellings were built than was planned. Agricultural production increased by 8.7%.

At the same time, plans were not fulfilled by the machine-building and the chemical and timber complexes, or the construction ministries, or rail transport. The decline in volume of production in light industry was not solved, and trade turnover assignments were not met. The Politburo has set before the ministries, the Party, local Soviets and economic bodies the task of taking all necessary measures to create conditions for stable and efficient work by the enterprises. [These conditions will enable enterprises] to implement the measures laid down to make up the lag which has developed.

Attention was paid to raising the technical standard and quality of output produced [by enterprises] and to absolutely fulfill plan targets and deliveries according to contracts. It was pointed out that, in dealing with these tasks, fuller use should be made of the opportunities being opened up by new methods of economic management. All enterprises, associations and organizations are obliged to take steps to improve their financial positions.

The importance of daily attention to the resolution of social problems, to improve shopping facilities, and to satisfying the needs of the population for goods and services was stressed.

Measures to provide for the country's requirements for vegetable oil were approved. It was deemed useful to provide collective and state farms with incentives for increasing their production of oil-bearing seeds through the introduction of intensive farming methods. Strengthening physical facilities and equipment of the oil and lard industry was also supported.

Proposals worked out by the government to introduce changes in the tax laws in connection with the implementation, starting in May 1987, of the USSR Law on Individual Enterprise were approved. A procedure is being established for taxation of this activity that will give citizens a greater interest in developing cooperative forms in the areas of consumer-goods production, consumer services, and food service and in acquiring additional income in accordance with their labor expenditures.

The Politburo noted that, in some republics and provinces, efforts to enlist working people broadly in individual enterprise and cooperative activity are progressing slowly. Local agencies are advised to eliminate bureaucratic obstacles in this area and to create normal conditions and a normal environment for such activity.

After discussing the state of affairs in environmental protection in the Lake Ladoga basin, the Politburo noted that a number of USSR ministries and departments and local Soviet and economic agencies have relaxed their attention to the implementation of environmental protection measures, [and that they] are violating established deadlines for the construction of new treatment facilities, and are using the existing ones inefficiently. This has resulted in a deterioration in the ecological situation in the Lake Ladoga basin and has been the cause for working people's proper complaints to the central agencies.

Plans call for a deep analysis of the ecological system of the Lake Ladoga basin, the preparation of a scientifically proven long-range forecast, and the determination of further measures to resurrect a proper ecological environment in that area. The pulp plant on the lakeshore will be transformed so that it will manufacture non-polluting products. Party bodies and state agencies are ordered to to examine the question of the personal responsibility of executives guilty of failure to meet their assignments in the construction of environmental-protection facilities and of unsatisfactory utilization of operating treatment facilities.

The appropriate agencies have been directed to prepare a long-range, comprehensive program for solving the country's ecological problems.

A resolution of the CPSU CC and the USSR Council of Ministers was adopted on creating, based on the physical facilities and staff of the N.E.Bauman Higher Technical School, an institution of higher learning of a new type that will train highly-qualified specialists in research-and-instruction complexes, with students participating actively in research and experimental design work. It is envisioned that a modern stock of materials and equipment will be created for the new institution of higher learning, and that instructional and laboratory buildings, as well as production and housing structures, will be built.

The results of the official visit by M.S.**Gorbachev**, General Secretary of the CPSU CC, to the Czechoslovak Republic, which took place from 9-11 April of this year, were also discussed. The Politburo approved the work done by M.S.**Gorbachev** in the course of his visit, as well as the results of his talks and negotiations with G.**Husak** and other Czechoslovak leaders.

It was noted that the visit opened a new page in the history of Soviet-Czechoslovak relations. From the meeting issued a renewed commitment to the union and solidarity of both Soviet and Czechoslovak communists, the peoples of both countries, and their mutual determination to support the whole structure of cooperation between the USSR and Czechoslovakia at a new and more elevated level.

The agreements reached in Prague will create genuine opportunities for more profound economic, scientific and technical cooperation, and extensive contacts among people.

The Politburo of the CPSU CC noted with satisfaction the solidarity of the CSR, the CSR leadership, and the working people of Czechoslovakia with the CPSU's policy of restructuring, democratization, and acceleration of social and economic development—a solidarity that was strikingly demonstrated during the visit.

It was noted that M.S.**Gorbachev**'s delineation at the Prague meeting of the internationalist principles by which the CPSU intends to be guided in its relationships with fraternal parties prompted a broad favourable response. The conviction was expressed that new successes in the development and improvement of the socialist system of international relations and division of labor will be achieved on this basis.

It was emphasized that a new Soviet initiative on the question of liquidation of short and medium range missiles in Europe, and other problems of disarmament open a path toward lessening the intensity of military confrontation in Europe, and that [this initiative] fully corresponds to the interests of all European countries.

The Politburo discussed reports by M.S.**Gorbachev**, N.I.**Ryzhkov**, and E.A.**Shevardnadze** on their discussions with USA Secretary of State, G. **Shultz**. It was emphasized that whether a solution can be found to the major questions of disarmament, especially in regards to medium- and short-range missiles, and whether the atmosphere in Soviet-American relations and in international affairs can be changed for the better, will depend on the conclusions drawn by the USA administration from what the Soviet leadership proposes to and informs G. **Shultz** of during the course of the talks.

The Soviet leadership is prepared to work together to settle these questions in an atmosphere of active dialogue and a search for mutual understanding that characterized the talks in Moscow with G.**Shultz**, and the exchange of information between M.S.**Gorbachev**, A.A.**Gromyko**, Ye.K.**Ligachev**, A.F.**Dobrynin**, and a delegation from the USA Congress headed by Speaker of the House, J.**Wright**.

The Politburo examined and approved the results of the official friendly visit by V.M.**Chebrikov** to the Republic of Cuba and his friendly meetings with F.**Castro** and other Cuban leaders.

The Politburo of the CPSU CC heard N.V.**Talyzin**'s report on the trip of a Soviet Party and state delegation to the People's Republic of Mozambique to participate in the celebration to mark the tenth anniversary of the Treaty of Friendship and Cooperation between the USSR and the PRM, and also examined other questions of domestic and foreign policy.

Pravda (18 Apr 87); a translation can be found in FBIS, No. 076 (21 Apr 87), R1-R2; a condensed text is in CDSP, 39:16 (1987), 20-21.

23 APRIL At its session on the 23 April, the Politburo of the CPSU CC, in keeping with the instruction of the 27th Party Congress, examined a range of questions having to do with the restructuring of the finance and credit mechanism and the price-formation system in order to create the conditions for a change to economic methods of management and for implementing the provisions contained in the Draft Law on State Enterprise (Association).

In the course of the discussion it was stressed that the new method for financing, extending credit, and pricing should contribute in all possible ways to accelerating the country's social and economic growth, applying the achievements of scientific and technical progress, speeding up the intensification of production and conserving resources, and should guarantee the amalgamation of state, collective and individual interests and the undiminished implementation of the Party's policy of improving the welfare of Soviet citizens.

An improvement in this labor should contribute to further economic effectiveness and to the implementation of the principles of full economic accountability, self-financing and self-support for associations and enterprises. It is foreseen that the relation between enterprises and the state budget will be altered basically and placed on a normal footing, and that they will be freed from petty overseeing and detailed regulations from financial agencies. It was stressed that it is necessary to improve financial and economic work at all management levels and to increase the accountability of ministries and departments for financial conditions and the results of management in their branches.

Plans call for upgrading the role and responsibility of banks in carrying through the Party's economy strategy, and for increasing their influence on the national economy. Steps are planned that will turn credit into an effective economic means under the new economic circumstances, to maintain strict adherence to the basic principles of granting credit, to strengthen payment discipline, and to prevent the application of credit as a means to cover losses and mismanagement. Methods have been found to improve the structure of the banking system further, to make credit institutions economically accountable, and to upgrade their style and methods of work.

The Politburo of the CPSU CC studied and approved the results of M.S.**Gorbachev**'s talks with W.**Jaruzelski**, First Secretary of the Polish United Workers' Party Central Committee and Chairman of the State Council of the Polish People's Republic, during his friendly visit to the USSR.

The Declaration of the Soviet-Polish Cooperation in the Area of Ideology, Science and Culture that was signed during the talks significantly advances the entire range of cooperation between the two countries in this important area of social life. Deep restructuring in the USSR and the policy of socialist renewal being carried out in the PPR create favourable prerequisites for vigorous interaction and exchanges of experience between the public organizations, creative unions, scientific institutions, and ministries and departments of the fraternal countries, and for broad contacts among their working people.

The agreements reached during the visit on the questions of a further intensification of economic cooperation and direct ties between Soviet and Polish enterprises were approved. Satisfaction with the unity of approach to cardinal issues of international policy, disarmament, and the strengthening of peace and security in Europe, and throughout the world, was expressed. The Politburo gave specific instructions regarding the implementation of the main provisions of the Declaration and the development of other lines of Soviet-Polish cooperation.

A report was heard from M.S.**Gorbachev** on his talks with Mengistu Haile **Mariam**, General Secretary of the Ethiopean Workers' Party Central Committee and Chairman of the Provisional Military Administrative Council of Socialist Ethiopia, who was in the USSR on a friendly visit. The Politburo noted with satisfaction the common approaches that the USSR and Ethiopia take to key problems of the modern era, and their mutual desire to continue developing and deepening cooperation between our countries.

At the session, the Politburo of the CPSU CC examined P.N.**Demichev**'s report on a Soviet government delegation's visit to the Republic of Iraq, and also discussed certain other questions having to do with fulfilling the resolutions of the 27th Party Congress and the January Plenum of the CPSU CC.

Pravda (24 Apr 87); FBIS, No. 080 (27 Apr 87), R1-R2; a condensed translation can be found in CDSP, 39:17 (1987), 15.

30 APRIL At a meeting held on 30 April, the Politburo of the CPSU CC examined the results of the All-Union Communist Subbotnik [A Subbotnik, or volunteer workday, is a term taken from the Russian word for Saturday, and refers to labor given to the state freely during one's holidays or overtime.] dedicated to the 117th anniversary of the birthday of V.I.Lenin. The Communist Subbotnik, in which 159 million people participated, was marked by a clear demonstration of the level of the political and labor activity of the Soviet people, and their creative strengths which were directed towards the bringing to fruition the resolutions of the 27th Party Congress and the January (1987) Plenum of the CPSU CC for the anniversary celebration of the 70th anniversary of Great October Revolution. The CPSU CC, the Council of Ministers of the USSR, the VTsSPS [Presidum of the Supreme Soviet], and the TsK VLKSM [Central Committee of Komsomol] undertook to decide the means by which the earnings of the Subbotnik, based on the wishes of those who worked, will be applied towards the reconstruction and technical upgrading of medical institutions.

The Politburo examined the government's propositions about the basic directives for restructuring the state system for planning the economic and social growth of the country, and the system of material-technical supply with the aim of bringing them into line with new requirements, which have been a consequence of the transfer to economic methods of directing the national economy.

In the course of the discusssion, it was emphasized that the planned management of the economy as a unified national-economic complex is an important achievement and benefit of socialism, and is the main instrument for the realization of the economic policies of the Party. The new system of planning, by drawing upon economic methods, must strengthen the influence of the plan on the accelerated development of the national economy, increase its effectiveness, assure the democratization of management, the broadening of the economic independence of enterprises (associations), and strengthen their responsibility on the basis of new draft Law on the State Enterprises (Associations). [They will also] provide labor collectives with a broader initiative in the achievement of high final results. It is intended that openness will be expanded and wide public discussion of major economic, scientific-technical and ecological problems will be introduced.

It was decided to change the forms and methods of planning in a fundamental manner. They will be put on a normative basis and on a system of government regulations, [thereby] freeing the ministries and enterprises from petty supervision and detailed regulation of the work of the enterprises.

Measures were outlined for fulfilling the forms and methods of organizing the material-technical supply for the national economy. These measures are directed at the creation of a mobile all-state system with wholesale trade and a direct connection between consumers and producers, designed to assist in an effective utilization of resources, [and] a more balanced and reliable material-technical supply.

In response to the new tasks, it was stipulated that the complete structure of Gosplan SSSR and Gossnab SSSR [Gosplan is USSR State Planning Committee; Gossnab is USSR State Material and Technical Supply Committee.] would be examined to strengthen the cooperation between them and also to coordinate their activities with those of the permanent bodies of the USSR Council of Ministers and of ministries and departments.

The question of increasing the role of the USSR State Committee for Science and Technology in the management of the country's science-technical progress was discussed. Attention was drawn to the necessity for a fuller use of the accumulated scientific and technical potential, to strengthen the integration of science and production, and to ensure the close connection between the academic, official and higher-school science. Measures were discussed for improving the Committee's work, for stepping up the forecasting and analytical work in determining ways for the development of science and technology, for the re-working of an economic mechanism for the management of science-technical progress. and for switching research and project-construction [design] institutes and organizations to full economic accountability and self-financing. The importance of questions about the realization of the Comprehensive Program for the scientific-technical progress of CMEA member-countries to the year 2000, was emphasized.

The Politburo approved the results of the visit by M.S.**Gorbachev** and other Soviet leaders with H. **Assad**, General Secretary of the Arab Socialist Renaissance Pary, and President of the Syrian Arab Republic. The conversations, which took place in an atmosphere of trust and mutual understanding, emphasized the unchanged course of the leaders of both countries towards multi-sided Soviet-Syrian cooperation, [and] disclosed new and beneficial perspectives for the continued development of friendly relations between the Soviet Union and Syria on the basis of the Charter of 1980. They noted with satisfaction their common opinions on a broad circle of international problems, among them the Near East. Particularly important was the mutual recognition of the need to arrange an international conference in order to overcome by logic the tensions and conflicts which are forced on the peoples and countries of the Near East by the imperialist circles and their allies, and to achieve a change in inter-bloc conflicts.

The Politburo approved the results of talks held by M.S.**Gorbachev** and N.I.**Ryzhkov** with G.**Atanasov**, Chairman of the Council of Ministers of the People's Republic of Bulgaria, who came to the USSR for an official friendly visit. Positively evaluating the work that has been done to establish direct relations and to create joint Soviet-Bulgarian enterprises and associations, the Politburo of the CPSU CC gave concrete instructions for increasing the dynamism and effectiveness of the integration process between the USSR and Bulgaria.

The results of M.S.**Gorbachev**'s meeting with R. **Urbany**, Chairman of the Luxemburg Communist Party, were discussed. The meeting confirmed the importance of friendly relations between communist parties of different countries and of their mutual understanding on the basis of adherence to common ideals for the resolution of their national aims and success in the struggle for the reconstruction of international relations in the interest of peace and security of all peoples.

The results of a working visit of Ye.K.**Ligachev** to the Hungarian People's Republic were discussed. It was noted that the talks with Hungarian leaders and meetings with party and economy *aktiv* helped to illustrate new possibilities for deepening economic and scientific-technical integration, strengthening ideological cooperation, improving inter-party connections, and activating joint study of accumulated experiences which can assist in moving forward Soviet-Hungarian cooperation.

The meeting of the Politburo of the CPSU CC also discussed several other questions of domestic and foreign policies.

Pravda (1 May 87); *Partiinaia zhizn'*, 10 (May 87), 5-6. A translation also can be found in FBIS, No. 040 (1 May 87), R1-R3; a condensed version is in CDSP, 39:18 (1987), 16-17.

7 MAY At its regular meeting, the Politburo of the CPSU CC discussed the question of letters received in the CPSU CC from working people, and measures for the implementation of the suggestions contained in them in the course of practical work to fulfill the decisions of the 27th Party Congress and the January (1987) Plenum of the CPSU CC.

It was noted with satisfaction that in their letters communists and non-Party people unanimously support the Party's course of restructuring in all spheres of public life, the improving of economic relations, and the growth of democracy, openness, criticism and self-criticism. In many of the letters, there were expressed ideas on the theoretical and practical questions of restructuring. Positive examples were cited of work under the new conditions, and concrete suggestions were made to improve matters. At the same time, there were a number of letters in which existing shortcomings were reported, [as were] facts about violations of discipline and order, the repression of criticism and opposition to the conduct of the reforms.

The CPSU CC highly values the support of the working people for the Party course of restructuring, and considers their strong political and labor activity as an important guarantee of the irreversible character of the changes, and of the multi-sided progress of Soviet society. Departments of the CPSU CC, ministries and departments, local Party, Soviet and economic organs are ordered to pay greater attention to the practical realization of proposals from working people and have been informed of the necessity to fully utilize these proposals in the process of preparation for the upcoming Plenum of the CPSU CC.

The Politburo discussed the speed of the fulfillment of the Comprehensive Program for the Development of Consumer Goods and the Service Sphere for the years 1986-2000. It was noted that in several areas the resolutions from the CPSU CC and USSR Council of Ministers for the fulfillment of this program are not being carried out satisfactorily.

Party and government organs have been ordered to undertake measures to eliminate these defects. The executives of ministries who have been responsible for the failure to upgrade consumer goods have been warned about their personal responsibility for assuring the planned levels of output of these goods. The attention of boards and Party committees was turned to the necessity of raising the responsibility of cadres for the radical improvement of the quality and variety of goods, for an acceleration in the tempo of their renewal, and for the expansion of the production of articles which meet with world standards.

It has been recommended that the growth of paid services at all branches of enterprises, regardless of their basic function, be accelerated, giving special attention to services for the repair and construction of housing, the servicing of motor vehicles, tourism and excursions, physical culture and sport. Instructions were given also to activate individual enterprises and to create cooperatives for the production of consumer goods and consumer services.

The task to reconstruct the work of the trade unions on the basis of the new economic mechanism was decided upon, to increase their influence on industry in order to raise output, to improve the variety and quality of goods, to more fully utilize existing potential for the unfailing fulfillment of the plan for retail trade and for substantially improving the public diet.

Attention was drawn to the increased role and responsibilities of local Party and Soviet agencies for ensuring consumer goods and services, and for balancing profits and expenditures. Directives were issued for the re-examination of priorites in the plan for the development of consumer goods and services, to assure the implementation of the goals of the 12th Five-Year Plan, the Comprehensive Programs and the resolutions connected to them from the Party and state.

The meeting examined the question of the further improvement of the work with young people in connection with the results of the 20th Congress of the VLKSM [Komsomol]. The Politburo regards the Congress highly as an imprtant political event not only for the Komsomol, but for Soviet society at large. The Congress convincingly demonstrated the full support of young men and women for the policy of the CPSU to accelerate the social and economic development of the country, to more energetically draw the younger generation into the general work of restructuring, and to prepare it for concrete participation in the normalization of social life on the basis of socialist democracy. It was noted with satisfaction that the Komsomol again showed a deep devotion to the ideals of the Party, and maintained its high purpose of being their strongest proponent and hope for the future.

The attention of Party and Komsomol organizations was called to the necessity for further raising the contribution of the Komsomol to the struggle for the revolutionary renewal of all sides of our lives, to the fundamental reconstruction of the economy, to scientific-technical progress, and to the inculcation in young people of the means to interpret and to evaluate social phenomena from class Marxist-Leninist positions. It was decided that all Party, Soviet, state and social organizations should raise questions of the work, political ideology, morality, military-patriotic and international education of youth in the course of their special and everday discussions.

As a way of controlling earlier decisions, efforts towards the development of direct connections between enterprises and associations, and towards the creation of joint enterprises, international associations and organization of the Soviet Union with the member-countries of CMEA were discussed. It was decided that the inculcation of new forms of cooperation have great significance for the broadening of the scale and level of dynamism of the economic and scientific-technical cooperation with the socialist countries on the way to a general development of specialization and coperation in production.

Measures were presented for the activization of efforts to adjust the mechanism for cooperation by means of new integrational forms, above all in questions of planning, pricing and material-technical guarantees. The importance of training and raising of the qualifications of cadres of specialists, and for strengthening Party influence in assuring the effectiveness of foreign economic activity was emphasized.

The Politburo approved the results of the meeting of M.S.**Gorbachev** with G.**Marchais**, the General Secretary of the French Communist Party. The meeting marked an important stage in the development of cooperation between the CPSU and the FCP, and expressed new approaches by both parties in the struggle for peace, democracy and socialism. Mutual interests between the CPSU and the FCP and the development of cooperation between the USSR and France were outlined as an important stage in European and world politics. Soviet and French communists, in spite of any obstacles, will continue to sponsor normal, mutually beneficial relations between their two countries and to foster mutual understanding and friendships between the Soviet and French people.

The Politburo approved the results of conversations and visits of M.S.**Gorbachev** and E.A.**Shevarnadze** with the Mexican Foreign Minister B.**Sepulveda**, which strengthened the mutual understanding with this large country of the Western hemisphere in questions of international security, disarmament and development, and the normalization of centers for conflict. [They] also outlined new possibilities for mutually beneficial and multi-sided bilateral cooperation.

At the session the Politburo of the CPSU CC also discussed several other questions of foreign and domestic policy.

Pravda (9 May 87); *Partiinaia zhizn'*, 10 (May 87), 3-4; a translation also can be found in FBIS, No. 090 (11 May 87), R1-R3; a condensed translation is in CDSP, 39:19 (1987), 17-18. No date for the actual session was given in the Soviet reports, but we have assigned it to 7 May because the meetings normally take place on Thursdays.

14 MAY At its meeting of 14 May, the Politburo of the CPSU CC discussed questions connected to the preparation of the report and other documents for the forthcoming Plenum of the CPSU CC on the radical restructing of the management of the national economy.

The Politburo considered the results of the national discussion of the Draft USSR Law on State Enterprises (Association). As it was noted at the session, the project has evoked deep interest and approval from the Soviet people. Special support has been given to such parts of the draft as the transfer to full economic accountability and self-financing, the increased autonomy and responsibility of enterprises, and the implementation of authentic socialist self-management.

The numerous proposals and observations expressed by working people help the concretization of the provisions of the draft law which are connected with the role of labor collectives in social production and with the elections of economic leaders. The Politburo emphasized that the adoption of this important legislative act will set a solid foundation for a future unified system of economic management. It was recognized as expedient that the Draft Law, after reworking in light of the remarks and observations by the working people, be discussed at the next Plenum of the CPSU CC and presented for consideration by the USSR Supreme Soviet.

In accordance with the directives of the 27th CPSU Congress, (the Politburo) examined proposals about the guidelines for the restructuring of the system for managing labor and social development in an organic connection with the shift to the new economc methods and expanded democracy. It was deemed necessary to enhance the effectiveness of the management of social development at all levels, with the intention of broadening the rights and possibilities of labor collectives in the solution of social questions on the basis of provisions in the Draft USSR Law on the State Enterprises (Association). Measures were outlined to improve the efficiency of labor and to increase the incentive role of labor wages, to upgrade the effectiveness of social measures which are aimed at the improvement of living conditions for the Soviet people.

It was pointed out that in accordance with the new tasks, the role and responsibilities of Goskomtrud [Goskomtrud is State Committee for Labor and Social Questions.] for carrying out an active state policy in the field of labor, wages, pension guarantees and social development, will be increased.

The results of M.S.**Gorbachev**'s meeting with T.**Zhivkov'** [General Secretary of the Bulgarian CP] were discussed and approved. The Politburo noted that cooperation of the two fraternal parties and countries continued to develop successfully. It maintained their resolution to actively cooperate in the aim of lessening the nuclear threat, to work for disarmament and the creation of an encompassing system for international security. Questions on the further development of economic and other ties between the Soviet Union and Bulgaria were discussed.

The Politburo of the CPSU CC discussed the results of conversations and talks of A.A.**Gromyko** and E.A. **Shevardnadze** with the Minister of Foreign Affairs of Thailand, S.**Savetsila**, and also discussed certain other questions on which appropriate decisions were undertaken.

Pravda (15 May 87); *Partiinaia zhizn'*, 11 (Jun 87), 5; a condensed translation may be found in CDSP, 39:20 (1987), 21.

21 MAY At its regular session, the Politburo of the CPSU CC discussed measures to improve the USSR Council of Ministers' work in conditions of the struggle for the acceleration of the social and economic growth of the country. It was noted that in light of the decisions of the April (1985) Plenum of the CPSU CC and the 27th Party Congress, the state has taken major economic and organizational measures to develop the economy in a steady, dynamic manner and to put an end to signs of stagnation. Simultaneously, an efficient means of managing the national economy has not been completed. For this purpose, the necessary steps have been delineated to improve the management of complexes of connected industries and the methods by which they work, and to improve the work of central economic ministries and departments and the Councils of Ministers in the Union republics. Propositions designed to make the forms and methods by which the *apparat* of the USSR Council of Ministers operate more effective were approved.

After examining the direction of the restructuring of the activities of the ministries and departments in the area of material production, the Politburo approved measures to eliminate current negative phenomena and deficiencies in the manner by which ministries and departments are organized and function, and to change the role and tasks of ministries and departments in the new economic circumstances as determined by the Draft USSR Law on the State Enterprise (Association). Tasks were set forth for restructuring the organizational arrangements used in the management of production and for restructuring the style and methods of *apparat* work in the ministries and departments.

Questions about the improvement of Republic managing bodies were considered. It was emphasized that the proposed measures are meant to widen the rights of Councils of Ministers of the republics and autonomous republics, and of the executive committees for territorial and provincial Soviets of people's deputies. (The measures will) increase their responsibility for the comprehensive development of the area's economy, and for the creation of conditions for the acceleration of economic and social development of the regions in the context of a unified national economic complex, and for the satisfaction of the people's various needs. It was recognized as necessary, in light of the expanding economic independence of enterprises, to specify the functions of republic and local organs of government.

The question of creating a center in Ulyanovsk for the application of microelectronics and automation in machine building, on which to expand fundamental and applied research, and to develop the production of (such technology) during the current Five-Year Plan and subsequently, was studied.

While discussing the progress made in fulfilling the CPSU CC's resolutions against drunkenness and alcoholism, the Politburo noted that great efforts are being made in the central area and at local levels to support a sober way of living and to promote a feeling of dislike towards drinking. This encourages the improvement of the moral atmosphere in society, and strengthens labor discipline and law and order. At the same time, this work is not being undertaken with persistence, aggressiveness and consistency in a number of places, and (progress in this matter) has deteriorated in those areas recently. Concern was expressed about the fact that home brewing recently has spread into some regions with the indulgence of local officials.

The CPSU CC indicated that it is necessary to increase efforts to implement the CPSU CC resolutions intended to eliminate drunkenness and alcoholism, to give them new impulse, and to make them more efficient and systematic. (The resolutions) are intended to assure the proper combination of upbringing, economic, medical and legal measures, and improved efforts to develop a movement for a sober way of life. A number of concrete measures to fundamentally improve anti-alcohol propaganda, to organize leisure time for people, to improve their health, to develop physical facilities and to enhance the efficiency of the work done by addiction treatment centers, were outlined. Attention was turned to the expansion of the production of consumer goods and for implementing the plan for trade turnover.

The Politburo approved the results of talks of M.S.**Gorbachev** with Nguyen Van **Linh**, General Secretary of the Vietnamese Communist Party Central Committee, who was in the Soviet Union for an official friendly visit. Special attention was given in the course of their conversation to the process of restructuring and the renewal of different aspects of life, which is underway in both the Soviet Union and in Vietnam in response to decisions made by the 27th Congress of the CPSU and the 6th Congress of the VCP. Significance was attached to the achievement of an understanding about measures to raise the effectiveness of Soviet-Vietnamese cooperation, shifting it to new progressive forms. The full unity of views of the CPSU and VCP on questions of bilateral relations and international affairs was noted with satisfaction. It was emphasized that the Soviet Union will continue to be closely related to the VCP in firmly supporting peace, stability and goodwill in the Asia-Pacific region.

The results of conversations and talks of M.S.**Gorbachev**, N.I.**Ryzhkov**, and E.A.**Shevardnadze** with the Premier of France, J.**Chirac**, were discussed. It was noted that that the current condition of Franco-Soviet relations is not in keeping with the needs and possibilities of both countries, neither from the point of view of their mutual interests, nor from the point of view of their role in European and world affairs. Emphasizing the need to continue and deepen Soviet-French political dialogue, the hope was expressed that France will take a constructive approach to ensure international security by reducing nuclear competition, limiting all types of weaponry, and cutting armed forces, above all in Europe. Instructions were issued jointly with the French side to undertake measures for the implementation of the ideas expressed in the course of the conversations for the arrangement for active bilateral relations.

A report was heard from M.S.**Solomentsev** about a CPSU delegation's participation in the work of the 12th Greek Communist Party Congress, and on his talks with the Greek Prime Minister, A. **Papandreou**. It was noted that the visit of the delegation to Greece assisted in the further growth of friendship and cooperation between the Soviet and Greek peoples.

At the meeting of the Politburo of the CPSU CC information from P.N.**Demichev** on his trip to the People's Republic of Bulgaria was heard, as was V.I. **Dolgikh**'s report of his trip to the Korean People's Democratic republic. Each had headed a delegation from the USSR Supreme Soviet.

Information from V.A.**Medvedev** on the participation of a CPSU delegation to the 8th Congress of the West Berlin Socialist Unity Party was also heard.

A report from G.P.**Razumovskii** on the results of a meeting of secretaries of Central Committees of communist and workers' parties, which met in Bucharest during 12-13 May to study questions of party-organizational work, was discussed and the CPSU delegations' activity there was approved.

The session of the Politburo of the CPSU CC also discussed several other questions about domestic and foreign policy.

Pravda (23 May 87); *Partiinaia zhizn'*, 11 (Jun 87), 3-4, a translation can also be found in FBIS, 101 (27 May 87), R1-R3, and a condensed translation is in CDSP, 39:21 (1987), 22-23. No date was given for the actual meeting in the Soviet reports; the 21st was a Thursday, the day when the regular meeting usually takes place.

30 MAY At a meeting held on 30 May 1987, the Politburo of the CPSU CC discussed a report from the USSR Ministry of Defense about the circumstances in connection with the violation of the Soviet Union's airspace by an airplane flown by M **Rust**, a citizen of the FRG [Federal Republic of Germany].

During the discussion of this matter, it was established that the airplane, which belongs to a Hamburg flying club, had been discovered by anti-aircraft defense radar when it approached the USSR state border. Soviet fighter planes circled the West German plane twice.

At the same time, the Politburo noted that the command of the Anti-aircraft Defense Forces displayed impermissible carelessness and indecision in failing to cut short the intruder-plane's flight without resorting to combat means. This incident indicates serious deficiencies in arranging combat readiness in regard to the protection of the country's airspace, a lack of proper vigilance and discipline, and major shortcomings in troop leadership on the part of the USSR Ministry of Defense.

For reasons of negligence and lack of organization in cutting short the violation and a lack of proper supervision over the work of the Anti-aircraft Defence Forces, the Politburo found it necessary to relieve Comrade A.I.**Koldunov** of his duties as Commander-in-Chief of the Antiaircraft Defense Forces. A decision on improving the leadership of the USSR Ministry of Defense was adopted.

The Politburo of the CPSU CC again stressed the basic importance of the task of raising the level of the Armed Forces' combat readiness and discipline, of skillfully managing troops, and making sure of their constant ability to cut short any violation of the sovereignty of the Soviet state.

The fact that the USSR Procurator's Office is conducting an investigation of all the circumstances relating to the violation of USSR airspace, and of the actions of officials in the matter, as well as the matter of the legal responsibility of the citizen of the Federal Republic of Germany, was pointed out.

Pravda (31 May 87); *Izvestiia* (1 Jun 87); a full translation of the *Pravda* piece can be found in CDSP, 39:22 (1987), 1. On the same pages of *Pravda* and *Izvestiia* (and many other papers in the USSR), it was announced that Marshall S.L. Sokolov had been relieved of his duties as Minister of Defense "in connection with his retirement on pension."

4 JUNE At its session which met on 4 June, the Politburo of the CPSU CC discussed the results of the regular meeting of the Political Consultative Committee [PCC] of the member countries of the Warsaw Treaty Organization, which met in Berlin on 28-29 May.

The Politburo approved the work which was conducted at the meeting by a Soviet delegation led by M.S.**Gorbachev**. The Warsaw Treaty Organization's highly valued and supported document on military doctrine, which clearly reflects the defensive character of socialism's military strategy, serves for the development of a dialogue between the WTO and NATO and for the strengthening of trust in Europe.

In Berlin there again emerged a unity of the fraternal countries in their attitude towards international events and in tasks which they wish to resolve jointly. Noting the positive changes in the atmosphere of international relations, in many ways from the initiatives taken by socialist states, the Politburo stated that the West unjustifiably delays their answers to these initiatives, which are directed at decisions which would free European people of problems, among which the most important is the necessity to liquidate medium and strategic nuclear missiles in Europe, to limit the risk of surprise attack.

The great significance of the measures outlined at the PCC for the improvement of the mechanism for foreign-trade cooperation, shared information, consultations and other forms of cooperation between the members of WTO were stressed.

The agreements obtained in M.S.**Gorbachev**'s talks with E.**Honecker** on 28 May in Berlin were approved.

The results of the official friendly 25-27 May visit that the General Secretary of the CPSU CC, M.S.**Gorbachev**, made to the Socialist Republic of Romania, were studied, (as were) the results of his conversations with N. **Ceaucescu**, General Secretary of the Romanian Communist Party and the President of the SRR. The visit reflected the feelings of friendship and fraternal solidarity that unite our parties and peoples, and enable us to determine ways of further developing the entire complex of Soviet-Romanian relations and cooperation — in the political, economic, cultural, scientific and other fields, and to demonstrate the conviction of the two fraternal countries to actively cooperate in the struggle for the consolidation of peace and security of peoples.

At the meeting, the Politburo examined a range of questions connected with the raising of the technical level of the development of atomic [nuclear] energy and for assuring its safety.

Tasks were set for the creation of a new generation of highly dependable and economical reactor plants and nuclear stations, raising the quality and resource potential of nuclear power station equipment, ensuring their safety from fire. Measures were assigned for the fundamental improvement of design and survey work, standardizing designs for nuclear stations, improving their construction, their supply of materials and equipment, and ensuring the delivery of proper equipment by means of the development of a construction industrial base. Corresponding measures were mapped out for existing nuclear stations and for those under construction.

The Politburo approved recommendations drawn up by the government for strengthening the material-technical base of industrial rail transport in the 12th Five-Year Plan. Measures were outlined for the introduction of an automatic system for managing shipments and for strengthening the cooperation between the transport sections of the ministries and departments with the railroads. The creation of new types of locomotives, freight cars, and track machinery are envisioned, as are the reduction of manual labor, the construction of unloading complexes, rolling stock repair facilities, and the increase of spare parts facilities.

A resolution on measures to improve the role of the Procurator's supervision of the strengthening of socialist legality and legal procedure was adopted. Noting that the USSR Procurator's Office [On the Procurator General of the USSR, see Articles 164-168 of the Constitution (Fundamental Law) of the USSR, 1977.] holds a very important place in the system of government agencies that are called upon to strengthen legality and legal procedure, the Politburo said that in recent years the level of supervision over the observance of the laws in the economic sphere has declined. Law enforcement agencies have not always ensured the necessary defence of the rights and interests of citizens and the strict observation of legal norms.

The Politburo stressed the need to radically restructure the work of the Procurator's Office, and to decisively improve the style, forms and methods of its activity, so that the Procurators can stand guard firmly over Soviet laws, state interests and the rights of the working people. (They must also) act in a principled and decisive manner, and actively lead the struggle against crime and other illegalities. In its work the Procurator's Office must operate in conditions of openness, drawing upon the public at large, unremittently fighting against instances of callous attitudes towards the fate of people, phenomena of bureaucratism and departmentalism, cases of suppression of criticism, and all those things which impede restructuring and the moral regeneration of society.

The agencies of the Procurator's Office were advised to concentrate their basic attention on actively supervising the way in which officials from ministries and departments, enterprises and organizations, other responsible people, and all citizens fulfill their duties in observing the laws and to immediately disclose and stop all violations of legality. In connection with this, it was deemed necessary to invest the Procurator's agencies with additional powers.

The Politburo heard a report from A.F.**Dobrynin** about a visit to India and his conversations with Prime Minister R.**Gandhi** and other Indian leaders. It confirmed the intention to consistently bring to life the Soviet-Indian agreements achieved in the course of M.S.**Gorbachev**'s visit to India in November 1986, and to develop and strengthen the traditional ties of friendship and cooperation between the USSR and India for the good of the peoples of both countries, and in the interest of peace and international security.

At the meeting, the Politburo of the CPSU CC also examined certain other questions of domestic and foreign policy.

Pravda (5 Jun 1987); *Partiinaia zhizn'*, 12 (Jun 1987), 3-4; a full translation can be found in ΓDIS 108, (5 Jun 87), R1-R2; a condensed translation is in CDSP, 39:23 (1987), 18.

11 JUNE At its meeting of 11 June, the Politburo of the CPSU CC studied the question of transfer of associations, enterprises, and national-economic organizations to full economic accountability and self-financing. The resolution on this question adopted by the CPSU CC and the USSR Council of Ministers calls for a switch to be accomplished in stages over the course of 1988-1989. In this resolution it is stipulated that a differentiated approach that takes into account the specific uniqueness of various branches of the economy is to be provided. It was noted that the transfer to full economic accountability and self-financing is creating the necessary conditions for implementing in practice the stipulations of the USSR Law on State Enterprise (Associations).

The implementation of the above-mentioned measures is a very important step towards the realization of the resolutions of the 27th Party Congress on the restructuring of the management of the national economy, the strengthening of democratic principles in the activity of labor collectives, the widening of autonomy and responsibility of enterprises for production and social development, the stimulating of socialist initiative, and raising the effectiveness of production and the quality of products.

Party, state, economic and public organizations and aktiv are ordered to strengthen, by organization and political work, the inculcation in the activities of the associations, enterprises and organizations of the principles of full economic accountability and self-financing, and to regard such work as the most important of their tasks.

The Politburo studied the question of the work of the Kazakh Republic Party orgaization in the matter of internationalist and patriotic education of the working people. It was noted that the Kazakh SSR, with the many-sided and unselfish assistance of all the fraternal peoples of the country had achieved significant success in economic, social, and cultural development. Relations of equality, trust, and mutual respect exist among the multi-national peoples of the Republic. Nevertheless, the republic's previous leadership allowed distortions to occur in fulfilling the nationality policy, in applying the principles of social justice, and in deciding party personnel matters. Party Committees had reduced their work on the international and patriotic education of working people considerably.

The Politburo stated that the deviations from the norms of Party life and the violations of the Leninist principles of nationality policy which had taken place in Kazakhstan were intolerable. (The Politburo) demanded that the republic's Party Committees undertake the most decisive measures to eliminate the insufficiencies. Any phenomena of chauvinism and nationalism, national localism and self-conceit must be regarded as an encroachment against our greatest victory—the fraternal friendship of peoples and the international unity of Soviet society.

It was stressed that internationalism in practice should be demonstrated mainly in the broadening of Kazakhstan's contribution to the country's overall economic complex, in an increased return on the research and production potential that has been established in the republic, in an active contribution to the fulfillment of the entire country's tasks, and in improving the living conditions of the working people of the republic. Special attention was given over to the questions of enlarging the national working class contingent, particularly in the leading branches of industry. It was pointed out that favoritism, and the selection of personnel on the basis of nepotism, tribe, community, or friendship must be eliminated, and that proper representation in management agencies, in the Party and Soviet apparat, and in public organizations must be open to all the peoples and nationalities in the republic. The inculcation of strong internationalist convictions and patriotic sentiments must become the main thrust of organizational and political work among the masses. The Union-Republic Communist Party CC and the Party Committees of both territory and province have been ordered to make a thorough study of the level of this type of work in light of the guidelines of the 27th Party Congress and the January (1987) Plenum of the CPSU CC.

The question of ascertaining in a final form the conditions of the All-Union Socialist Competition for the 12th Five-Year Plan was studied. With the aim of increasing the effectiveness of socialist competition, it was decided that from here on it was necessary to concentrate [the competition] directly upon labor collectives and as much as possible to direct the competition towards achieving a high quality of product, assuring conservation of resources, meeting delivery schedules strictly on the basis of contracts, applying the achievements of science, technology, and progressive experience, and on accelerating the construction of housing, social and cultural facilities. It is intended that the conditions of the competition be made clear, so as to make it more concrete and to take into better account specific local conditions.

The meeting of the Politburo of the CPSU CC also discussed certain other matters of domestic and foreign policy.

Pravda (12 Jun 87); a condensed translation is in CDSP, 39:24 (1987), 23-24.

1 JULY At a meeting which took place on 1 July, the Politburo of the CPSU CC discussed the question of top-priority measures in connection with the organization of the implementation of the decisions of the June (1987) Plenum of the CPSU CC on the tasks of the Party in the radical restructuring of the management of the economy. The Secretariat and the departments of the CPSU CC were ordered to examine the concrete proposals and criticisms expressed by the participants of the Plenum, and also from working people in letters, on the questions of restructuring economic management; and to bring proposals for implementing them to the Politburo. The USSR Council of Ministers was ordered to determine the order and means of realizing an integrated system of management, to assure constant control over the implementation of the USSR Law on the State Enterprise (Association). The necessity for Party organizations to undertake purposeful organizational and political work in order to fulfill the decisions of the Plenum, and the preparation for the 19th All-Union Conference of the CPSU, was pointed out.

The Politburo examined measures to assure the steady work of the national economy during the Winter period, 1987/88. In adopting decisions on these questions, the CPSU CC and the USSR Council of Ministers decided upon the principle measure with which to assure the more complete satisfaction of the peoples' needs in the Winter for fuel oil, electrical and heating energy. Special attention of the ministries and departments of the republic and autonomous-republic Councils of Ministers was drawn to the decrees from the Soviet of Peoples' Deputies in relation to diverse and qualitative preparations for Winter living and other objects of social importance, to assure that both the population and municipalities are served with high-quality fuels.

The Politburo approved the results of conversations between M.S.**Gorbachev** and J.**Batmunkh**. It was noted with satisfaction that Soviet-Mongolian cooperation has become all the more multi-sided and dynamic, in order to assist each other in decisions on the real social-economic tasks for both countries, and for the fulfillment of plans to strengthen peace and security in Asia. In light of the agreements reached during the talks, Soviet organizations were ordered to coordinate with the Mongolian side concrete measures to strengthen cooperation in the fields of industry and agriculture and to deepen bilateral ties in ideology, science, and culture.

The results of M.S.**Gorbachev's** meeting with the leader of the Republic of Zimbabwe and the Chairman of the non-Aligned movement, R.**Mugabe**, were approved. It was noted that equal and mutually beneficial cooperation between the USSR and Zimbabwe is developing on a rising plane and has good prospects. It was emphasized that the Soviet Union considers the movement of non-alignment to be an important positive factor in international politics, and will unfailingly support this position in its foreign policy activity.

Approving the conversations of M.S. **Gorbachev** with the General Secretary of the UN, J.**Perez de Cuellar**, the Politburo noted the increasing role that the United Nations Organization has taken in achieving a balance in the various interests of all states—large and small, and in achieving a peaceful society without which it would not be possible to gain stability in international relations.

Information on the results of N.I.**Ryzhkov**'s talks with a party and government delegation from the GDR [German Democratic Republic] was studied. It was emphasized that further raising of the level and quality of economic and scientific-technical cooperation between the USSR and the GDR on the basis of continued introduction of progressive methods, is very important. The appropriate Soviet departments and organizations were given concrete instructions in this regard.

The results of an official friendly visits of E.A.**Shevardnadze** to the PRB [People's Republic of Bulgaria], the HPR [Hungarian People's Republic], and the SFRY [Socialist Federal Republic of Yugoslavia] were discussed. The great significance [of the visits] for dynamic cooperation of the socialist countries in international affairs was noted.

The session of the Politburo of the CPSU CC also discussed certain other questions of domestic and foreign policy.

Pravda, (2 Jul 87); *Partiinaia zhizn'*, 14 (Jul 87), 3-4; a full translation can be found in FBIS 127 (2 Jul 87), R1-R2; a condensed version is in CDSP, 39:26 (1987), 20-21.

16 JULY At its regular meeting, the Politburo of the CPSU CC discussed the organizational, political and economic measures connected to the practical fulfillment of the decisions of the June (1987) Plenum of the CPSU CC. (The Politburo) affirmed organizational and propagandistic measures adopted in order to fulfill the decisions of the Plenum. Ways and means for acting upon the proposals offered by participants in the Plenum of the CPSU CC were determined. (The Politburo) approved the work of the USSR Council of Ministers for an integrated plan to coordinate the practical restructuring of the management of the economy.

During the discussion of these questions at the meeting, the Politburo stressed that the key to the solution of the set tasks lay with the assurance of actual participation of a wide mass of the people in the management of the economy and, in that regard, each working person is to support the economy in his work place, in the collectives and in society at large. In this connection, attention was called to the need for strict application and practice of the provisions in the Law on the State Enterprise (Association).

Documents having to do with the improved management of the economy, and determining the guidelines for restructuring in the fields of planning, material-technical supply, pricing, finance-credit mechanism, and other spheres of activity, were approved. (The documents) had been completed in light of the decisions of the CPSU CC Plenum and the USSR Supreme Soviet meeting.

The question of further expanding the state product acceptance system was discussed. The decree on this question adopted by the CPSU CC and the USSR Council of Ministers noted that the introduction of a state product acceptance system raises the level of product quality. It improves labor organization and improves technological discipline. The measures undertaken have the active support of the working class and all the working people of the country.

Additionally, it was recognized as necessary to introduce, beginning 1 January 1988, the state product acceptance system to a series of enterprises which produces goods that are most important to the national economy, as well as consumer goods. [It will be introduced also] to enterprises in the processing divisions of the agro-industrial complex and in construction, and to enterprises which supply materials and components for goods covered by state acceptance. In certain republics, territory, and provincial spheres, plans call for expanding the state product acceptance to new housing, children's pre-school facilities, and other social and cultural facilities.

The Politburo of the CPSU CC examined the question of strengthening the material-technical base for research in high-energy physics and the program for its development to the year 2000. It outlined plans for the construction at the country's leading centers of unique accelerator complexes and a series of other experimental units, and for the reconstruction, widening, and building of experimental and production facilities. The USSR Academy of Sciences, the USSR State Committee for Science and Technology, in cooperation with the appropriate ministries and departments were ordered to undertake measures for the wide development of fundamental and applied work in this field of science.

The question of radically improving education, instruction and material support for orphans and children who are left without parental support was studied. Measures were determined for improving the education-upbringing process, improving medical services, and for the further development and strengthening of the material-technical base of infant-care centers, children's homes, and boarding schools. The task of carrying out a decisive solution to the question of upbringing for children and adolescents was assigned to Party, trade union and Komsomol organizations, Soviet and economic organs, labor collectives at base and sponsoring enterprises, and to the public at large. The necessity for considering this work a most important Party, state and public concern was pointed out. The public recommendation for the creation of a V.I.Lenin Soviet Children's Fund—an All-Union mass organization in which the efforts of citizens, labor collectives, public organizations and creative unions are combined in order to develop in all possible ways the Leninist traditions of a caring and concerned attitude towards children, was supported.

The Politburo discussed the results of talks and negotiations by M.S.**Gorbachev** and A.A.**Gromyko** with FRG President R.**von Weizsaecker**, and those by E.A.**Shevardnadze** and A.N.**Yakovlev** with FRG Vice-Chancellor and Minister of Foreign Affairs, H.-D.**Genscher**, which took place during the official visit of the FRG President in the Soviet Union.

The talks and meetings with government officials of the FRG in Moscow were useful. They made it possible to compare the positions of our countries in international affairs, to focus attention on the questions of terminating the arms race and disarmament, of fundamentally improving the situation in Central Europe, and of the necessity for a fresh approach to solving contemporary problems.

The most important issue is to free the European continent from medium and strategic missiles. In this connection, the hope was again expressed that the government of the FRG will not impede the process and will undertake corresponding steps to facilitate the achievement of agreements reached on this question at Geneva.

It was noted that, in spite of political and ideological contradictions and different military-strategic orientations, the USSR and FRG can be partners. The Soviet side maintained its readiness, for the development of stability, not to undermine the political relations with the FRG which is a significant West European partner under these conditions. The FRG demonstrated an analogous readiness not to change these relations.

A number of conditions exist to make possible cooperation between the USSR and the FRG for the creation of a common European home based on the recognition of and respect for realities in Europe, and on a strict observance and fulfillment of the Moscow Agreement. By means of the combined efforts of both countries, the USSR and the FRG can open a new, productive page in their relations. This is in the interests of the peoples of both countries, as well as of the entire continent.

The results of the visit of N.I.**Ryzhkov** to Austria was studied, as were the results of his negotiations with the Chancellor of the Austrian Republic, F. **Vranitzky**, and other officials. It was noted that this visit continued the tradition of fruitful Soviet-Austrian relations, and showed a mutual interest in expanding cooperation between the two countries in the political and economic fields, and in the area of cultural and humanitarian relations.

The Politburo heard a report from A.F.**Dobrynin** on the results of a consultative meeting of communist and revolutionary-democratic parties, entitled, "For Peace, Security, and Good-Neighbor Cooperation in the Asia-Pacific Region," which met in Ulan Bator, 7-9 July, and approved the activity of the CPSU at that meeting. (The Politburo) noted the great significance of the desire expressed by the fraternal parties participating in the meeting to make multi-lateral contacts more regular and varied, in order to together seek ways of strengthening peace, eliminating tensions, and improving the political climate in Asia and the Pacific Basin—matters of vital interest to the peoples of this huge and most populated region of the planet.

A report from G.P.**Razumovskii** [appointed to Secretariat of CPSU CC in March 1986] on the result of the visit to the Chinese People's Republic by a delegation from the Legislative Proposals Committee of the USSR Supreme Soviet was heard. It was noted with satisfaction that the meetings and talks that were held during the visit with the leadership of the appropriate committee of the National People's Congress and with other Chinese officials, and the exchange of information on the work of supreme organs of government took place in a comradely setting. They were interesting and useful. A positive evaluation was given to plans for a further widening of parliamentary ties between the USSR and PRC, and also for contacts at the level of local agencies of government.

The session of the Politburo of the CPSU CC also examined certain other questions of domestic and foreign policy.

Pravda (18 Jul 87); *Partiinaia zhizn'*, 15 (Aug 87), 3-4, a full translation can be found in FBIS 138 (20 Jul 87), R1, and a condensed version in CDSP, 39:29 (1987), 19-20. Although no date was given for the meeting in the Soviet reports, the 16th is included here because it is Thursday.

23 JULY At its meeting of 23 July, the Politburo of the CPSU CC approved a list of basic question for study in the Politburo and CPSU Central Committee in the second half of this year, revised in accordance with the directives of the June (1987) Plenum of the CPSU CC.

The question of urgent measures to implement the demands of the June Plenum for a more complete resolution of the tasks of the Food Program (was discussed). In this regard, the need to raise the interest and to develop the initiative of collective farms, state farms, and the population in increasing production and the sale of farm goods was emphasized. (The Politburo) outlined the task of activating the work of food producing branches of industry, other enterprises of the agro-industrial complex, organizations of consumer cooperatives, and auxiliary farming enterprises; and to eliminate those obstacles which have held back the growth of food production. In order to fulfill these tasks, independent local agencies are assigned a special role to effectively stimulate the moral and material interests of the labor collectives and of all farmers.

To increase personal auxiliary farming's contribution to solving the food supply problem, it was recommended that the norms for keeping cattle and revising the maximum size of personal plots be re-examined. Provisions were made to better supply individual auxiliary farming operations with feed and fodder, young cattle and poultry, and small machinery; and to give them greater assistance in selling their products. It was pointed out that requests from citizens for the allocation of orchard plots and vegetable gardens are to be granted as soon as possible.

The Long-Term State Program for Comprehensive Development of the Productive Forces of the Far Eastern Economic region, the Buryat Autonomous Republic, and Chita Province for the Period up to the Year 2000, which was prepared in connection with the decisions of the 27th CPSU Congress, was approved.

The program foresees a higher rate of growth for the Far East and Transbaikalia than in the rest of the country in housing, cultural-service facilities, industrial production, and growth of export potential. (It also foresees) strengthening the region's food supply base. The program stipulates measures for the rational use of natural resources and environmental protection. It has in sight the creation in the Far East of a highly efficient national economic complex which will become a part of the system of national and international division of labor.

The USSR central economic organs, ministries and departments of the USSR, the RSFSR Council of Ministers, and local Party, Soviet and economic agencies of the far East and Transbaikalia are ordered to study the aims of the program at the very least as a fundamentally formed state law, and in all ways to encourage every possibility for it to be successful.

The Politburo discussed the results of the talks that M.S.**Gorbachev** and N.I.**Ryzhkov** had with K.**Groesz**, member of the Politburo of the Hungarian Socialist Workers Party and Chairman of the Council of Ministers of the HPR. It was noticed that now, when both countries are about to decide upon important economic problems, there arises the greatest possibility of cooperating. The Soviet Union and Hungary have much to offer each other on a path of deepening economic and scientific-technical cooperation, the creation of joint ventures, and on exchange of experiences. Instructions were given to the appropriate agencies to deal with the concrete questions set out during the course of the visit.

The Politburo approved the results of M.S.**Gorbachev**'s talks with **Najib**, General secretary of the CC of the People's Democratic Party of Afghanistan, in the course of which firm support for the course set out by the PDPA for national reconciliation in the country was expressed. The implementation of steps in the interests of rapid normalization of the situation in Afghanistan was discussed. It was stressed that the Soviet Union firmly insists that Afghanistan will be an independent, sovereign, and non-aligned state.

(The Politburo) examined and approved the results of a trip by V.P.**Nikonov** to Poland and A.P.**Biryukova**'s trip to Bulgaria, and discussed certain other questions of domestic and foreign policy.

Pravda (24 Jul 87); *Partiinaia zhizn'*, 15 (Aug 87), 5-6; a full translation can be found in FBIS no. 143 (17 Jul 87), R6-7; a condensed version is in CDSP, 39:30 (1987), 19.

6 AUGUST At a session held on 6 August, the Politburo of the CPSU CC discussed the draft Basic Guidelines for the Development of Public Health Protection, and the Restructuring of the USSR's Public Health Care System During the 12th Five-Year Plan to the Year 2000, as well as top-priority measures for improving the country's health-care system in 1988-1990 which were outlined in accordance with the resolutions of the 27th CPSU Congress. The documents determine ways of fundamentally improving the work of health-care agencies and institutions, research institutes and medical schools. [They also] make more efficient use of the personnel of health services and their material and technical potential; and greatly improve the quality of medical assistance to the public. Large-scale measures have been determined to strengthen the preventative aspect of health care, improve the environment, and improve the living and working conditions of the Soviet people. [Steps also have been taken to] involve them in regular physical exercise, to step up the battle against drunkenness and alcoholism, and to improve the structure of their diet.

Plans call for a major increase in capital investment for the construction of hospitals and polyclinics, as well as in the money allocated for equipping them. Health-care institutions are raising their norms for expenditure on food and medicine. Other plans call for the full satisfaction of demands for Soviet-made drugs and for substantial increases in the production of medical equipment.

These plans necessitate the restructuring of the system of managing, planning, and financing health care and medicine, developing medical research and treatment organizations, inter-branch scientific-technical complexes, and experimental enterprises at research institutions. (They) also give executives more independence in using labor, materials, and financial resources.

It has been decided that the draft Basic Guidelines for the Development of Public Health Protection and the Restructuring of the Public Health Care System will be published in the press for nation-wide discussion.

The Politburo supported proposals put forward by the All-Union Central Council of Trade Unions, the Soviet Women's Committee, and by ministries and departments, for expanding benefits to pregnant working women and mothers with small children, and for introducing to this end a number of additions to existing labor laws. In particular, the plans call for the establishment, for these types of women workers, a part-time workday or week, at their choice, lowering output and service quotas for pregnant women and assuring that they are shifted to other, less laborous working conditions.

A proposal to transform the USSR Central Statistical Administration in the Union-Republic USSR Statistics Committee was approved. It was noted that the implementation of a policy of restructuring and the radical reform of economic management require qualitatively new standards of performance by statistical organs. They have been assigned the task of providing more up-to-date information, assuring its reliability, openning up access to it, and more carefully analyzing the processes of the country's economic and social development.

The Politburo approved the results of M.S.**Gorbachev**'s meeting with Malaysian Prime Minister Mahathir **Mohamad**, and of the talks between V.S.**Murakhovskii**, First Vice-Chairman of the USSR Council of Ministers, and the head of the Malaysian government. It was noted that the exchange of views and the accords which were reached contributed to the strengthening of mutual understanding and cooperation. The readiness of the Soviet Union to develop relations with ASEAN and its member states was confirmed.

The results of M.S.**Gorbachev**'s talk with J.**Chissano**, Chairman of the Frelimo Party and President of the People's Republic of Mozambique, and the results of the Soviet-Mozambique talks, were approved. The invariable solidarity of the Soviet Union with Mozambique and the principled line aiming at developing comprehensive cooperation with that country were stressed.

The session of the Politburo of the CPSU CC discussed certain other questions related to the country's socio-economic growth and the Party and state's activities in the area of foreign policy.

Pravda (7 Aug 87); a full translation can be found in FBIS no. 152 (7 Aug 87), R1-R2; a condensed version is in CDSP, 39:32 (1987), 20.

13 AUGUST At a session held on 13 August, the Politburo of the CPSU CC discussed the question of the accelerated development of priority concerns in the area of chemical science and technology. It was noted that chemistry plays a vast role in the scientific-technical progress of the country. Its achievements are at the root of mechanical engineering, medicine, and in many branches of the production of consumer goods. (The Politburo) set the task of satisfying the economy's requirements for modern, high-quality chemical products and materials on the basis of the all-round development of scientific research and the elaboration and introduction of advanced technological processes and facilities.

In the resolution adopted by the CPSU CC and USSR Council of Ministers on this question, important guidelines for pure and applied chemical research were determined. Their implementation will assure a substantial increase in the effectiveness in that field of science and in the work of industry, and the putting into practice fundamentally new [and] highly economical products. It is envisioned that a new generation of structural and composite materials, and other chemical products with significantly superior properties to those now in existence, will be created.

It is intended to widely use the achieved results to expand the role of chemistry in the economy, to improve public health care, to raise the safety level of chemical processes, and to reduce their harmful effects on the environment. The plans call for new forms of organized science and for the introduction of its results, and for a higher level of training for chemical specialists.

The Politburo supported a proposal for the publication of a basic 10-volume work, the *Great Patriotic War of the Soviet People* It is to be prepared by the Ministry of Defense, the USSR Academy of Sciences, and the CPSU CC's Institute of Marxism-Leninism.

Additional measures directed at preventing the outbreak of AIDS in the country, and the deepening of international cooperation in the struggle against this disease, were approved.

After examining the results of E.A.**Shevardnadze**'s trip to Geneva, the Politburo gave a positive evaluation of its results. It stressed the importance of the high priority the Geneva Conference gave to disarmament, and the turning of (the Conference) into an ongoing universal organ in the system of negotiations for disarmament. The Politburo especially noted the need to achieve a real agreement on the liquidation of two classes of nuclear weapons possessed by the USSR and the USA—medium-range and operational-tactical missiles, and the destruction of all nuclear warheads, including those used on West German Pershing-1As.

At the meeting of the Politburo of the CPSU CC, certain other questions of Party and state life were discussed.

Pravda (14 Aug 87); *Partiinaia zhizn'*, 17 (Sep 87), 3; translation in FBIS, no. 158 (17 Aug 87), R1; a condensed translation is in CDSP, 39:33 (1987), 14-15.

20 AUGUST At a meeting held on 20 August, the Politburo discussed the question of improving work in the USSR Council of Ministers and the restructuring of its apparat.

Concrete proposals which the goverment has drawn up were approved. They make up a part of a complex program for radically restructuring management of the economy, (a program) created in accordance with the resolutions of the 27th Party Congress and the June (1987) Plenum of the CPSU CC. It was stipulated that the level of activity of all organs of the USSR Council of Ministers be significantly raised, and to direct that activity towards the implementation of effective measures for accelerating the national economy and more fully satisfying the needs of the people. The adopted decision sets the tasks of substantially improving the work of the government apparat in accordance with the current requirements of the Party, and determines its new structure. The number of people working for the apparat is to be reduced.

The Politburo examined the question of the further development of Soviet architecture and city planning. In the resolution adopted by the CPSU CC and the USSR Council of Ministers, measures were set out to raise the level of architecture, to improve the planning and development of cities and villages, to improve the economic mechanism, and to strengthen the incentives for quality products. The great importance of architecture and city planning in the moral and aesthetic upbringing of Soviet people was noted.

With the aim of improving the organizational structure of the management of architecture and city planning, it was deemed expedient to create a unified system of Union-Republic agencies of management and to reorganize the State Committee for Civil Construction and Architecture under Gosstroi USSR [Gosstroi USSR is State Committee for Construction Affairs.](Gosgrazhdanstroi) into the State Committee for Architecture and City Planning under Gosstroi USSR (Goskomarkhitektura).

A proposal of the USSR Council of Ministers and the VTsSPS [All-Union Central Council of Trade Unions] about the introduction of optional annuities to provide increased pensions for workers, office employees, and collective farmers, was approved. Such annuities will be a major social measure by the state for improving the living conditions of veterans of labor. The source of the supplemental pension will be an annuity fund to be formed from personal contributions by the persons holding annuities and from the USSR state budget.

At the meeting questions connected with the Soviet delegation's participation in the upcoming 42nd Session of the UN General Assembly were discussed.

The Politburo of the CPSU CC also discussed certain other questions of social-economic construction, and the development of ties with foreign countries, and adopted appropriate decisions about them.

Pravda (21 Aug 87); *Partiinaia zhizn'*, 17 (Sep 87), 3. Full translations can be found in FBIS, no. 162 (21 Aug 87), R1 and CDSP 39:34 (1987), 20-21.

3 SEPTEMBER At its 3 September session, the Politburo of the CPSU CC examined the results of the draft, "Basic Guidelines for Restructuring the System of Political and Economic Instruction for the Working People", which was discussed in Party, Komsomol and trade union organizations, in ministries and departments, and in the mass media. It was noted that the document everywhere received full support and approval as a concrete program of action on one of the most important categories of ideological work. In the course of the discussion, the creators of the draft received and studied a large number of comments, notes, and recommendations, which were submitted by local Party committees.

In the resolution adopted, the CPSU CC ordered the Party, economic management, trade union and Komsomol agencies to work out and to implement measures for the restructuring of political and economic training for the working people and to achieve a radical rise in the quality and results of the studies. The necessity to spread economic teaching throughout the country in the present school year was mentioned, as was the mission to assure the inculcation among the Soviet people of the new economic thinking, of training working people in methods of economic management, habits of work in conditions of full self-financing, and the democratization and self-management of industrial life.

The Politburo of the CC adopted a resolution entitled, "On Urgent Measures to Accelerate the Solving of the Food Problem in Accordance with the Directives of the June (1987) Plenum of the CPSU CC." It was noticed that the CC of the Party considers it a most important and crucial political task to achieve in short order a significant increase in tho production of food by everywhere activating all sources for fulfilling it. Accelerated growth of collective and state-farm production is a sound basis for resolving the food problem of the country. The achievement of this aim can be served by a fuller realization of the potential by the auxiliary farming of enterprises and individuals and by collective cultivation and vegetable gardening. For the creation of favourable conditions for this development of agriculture, the CPSU CC and the USSR Council of Ministers has adopted special resolutions, which will be published.

In accordance with the directives of the June (1987) Plenum of the CPSU CC on restructuring the operation of the ministries and departments in the sphere of material production in the new economic conditions, (the Politburo) adopted a resolution on the transformation of the Union-Republic Ministries of Geology, Coal Industry, and of Ferrous Metallurgy, into All-Union Ministries.

The results of admissions into the Party during the first half of this year were discussed. As it was pointed out while this question was discussed, Party Committees and Primary Party Organizations as a whole have strengthened their requirements for admission, have improved their selection of CPSU cadres from workers, collective farmers, and members of the intelligentsia who gave a good account of themselves in the conditions of restructuring. Greater attention is being paid to enhancing the vanguard role of Party members and candidate members. However, not everyone has drawn practical conclusions from the directives of the 27th Party Congress on strengthening the Party ranks. Artificial growth rates are still allowed, as is an unscrupulousness in the admission of new members, and formalism in work with young Communists.

Party Committees and Primary Party Organizations were ordered to make a deep analysis of the circumstances of this work and to assure undeviating observance of the requirements about the strict individual criteria for recruitment of CPSU members, on the basis of wide openness, and in light of the opinions of labor collectives and public organizations.

The results of the All-Union Socialist Competition for Successfully Wintering Cattle and for Increasing the Production and Procurement of Animal Husbandry Products, were examined. In the period from October 1986 to June 1987, a growth in the output of basic animal husbandry products was achieved. Procurements of milk increased by 5%, milk and eggs were up by 4%, above all as a result of intensive factors, the rational use of feed, the mastering of economic accountability, collective and family contracts, and other progressive forms of organizing labor and by the stimulation of work.

The CPSU CC, USSR Council of Ministers, the All-Union Central Council of Trade Unions, and Komsomol awarded many Honorary Certificates to collective farms, state farms, mixed farms and other enterprises, organizations and associations, and also to a series of rural regions in Autonomous Republics, territories, and provinces, and five Union Republics: the RSFSR, Belorussian SSR, Lithuanian SSR, Latvian SSR, and the Kirgiz SSR.

The session of the Politburo of the CPSU CC discussed certain other questions of the country's domestic life and its foreign policy.

Pravda (4 Sep 87); *Partiinaia zhizn'*, 18 (Sep 87), 3-4, a condensed translation can be found in CDSP, 39:36 (1987), 16-17.

10 SEPTEMBER At a meeting held on 10 September, the Politburo of the CPSU CC examined the question of speeding up completion of the harvest and of preparing collective and state farms, and other enterprises of the agro-industrial complex for winter. It was pointed out in the course of the discussion that a solution to the food question is determined to a great degree by the results of the current agriculture year.

The harvest is being carried out in difficult weather conditions. However, many Party Committees and Soviet and economic organs are not in all cases assessing the seriousness of the situation properly, and are not taking the most thorough measures to complete the full range of Autumn field work and to prepare cattle for wintering. In several autonomous republics, territories and provinces, the harvesting of grains, potatoes and other late crops is going ahead at a reduced pace. Farms have been slow in replenishing state supplies, providing the population with fruits, vegetables and potatoes, and meeting the feed and fodder requirements of cooperative owned cattle with their own production. The preparation of cattle for winter and the construction of granaries and processing enterprises are not going ahead satisfactorily.

Insofar as completing the autumn field work and making preparations for winter are concerned, the resolution that the Politburo adopted views the existing situation as extremely strained. The decision stresses that it is required of all Party, local Soviet and economic bodies, industrial construction, transportation and other enterprises and organizations to adopt urgent and exhaustive measures that will ensure that the situation improves in the shortest possible time.

The session discussed the matter of setting up cooperatives to produce confectionary and baked goods, so as to sponsor better satisfaction of demand for varied and high-quality products of those types. It called for the setting up of cooperatives as soon as possible under the affiliation of directorates of the executive committees of the local Soviets, enterprises and organizations of the confectionary and baking industry, trade and public catering, and within the system of the Central Union of Consumer's Cooperatives, which have been instructed to render them all-round assistance. The principles of economic independence, self-recouping and self-financing have been assumed as the basis for the activity of the cooperatives.

The Politburo discussed the question of increasing the quality of public health care and of improving the operation of public health facilties in Moscow. A resolution of the CPSU CC and the USSR Council of Ministers on this question sets tasks to the year 1995 for the construction and organization of out-patient facilities, polyclinics, and hospitals; and for the establishment of treatment and diagnostic centers, specialized diagnostic centers, and health care facilities for mothers and children. Plans call for accelerating the introduction of new methods of preventing, diagnosing and treating diseases, for enhancing the efficiency of state sanitary supervision, and for upgrading the physical facilities and equipment of the sanitation and epidemiological service. The resolution also delineates several steps for the improvement of social and living conditions for employees of treatment and preventative facilities in the capital city.

The Politburo examined a report from a government commission that investigated the causes of a train crash that took place in August 1987 at the Southeastern Railway's Kamenskaia Station. The investigation showed that the collision was a result of a criminally negligent attitude on the part of several railroad officials toward the performance of their prescribed duties. The specific cause was the departure of a freight train with a partly disconnected braking system, which led to the electric locomotive's crash into a passenger train. The catastrophe caused a great many deaths. The Politburo expressed profound condolences to the victims' relatives and to the nearest and dearest. They have been granted the necessary state assistance.

The USSR Procuracy has since instituted criminal proceedings. A.S.**Goliusov**, the chief of the Southeastern Railway, has been dismissed from his post. S.S.**Barbarich**, Chief of the Railway Cars Chief Directorate of the Ministry of Railways has been relieved from his position and has had Party proceedings instituted against him. S.I.**Solovöv**, USSR Deputy Minister of Railways and Chief Inspector of Traffic Safety, and P.I.**Kelperis**, Chief of the Locomotive Chief Directorate, were strictly punished within the Party.

The Politburo discussed the results of a conference of secretaries of the Communist Party and Workers' Party CCs of the members of CMEA, which met in Sofia to discuss economic matters, and approved the CPSU delegation's work at the conference. The work at the conference helped speed efforts to create specific measures to restructure the mechanism of socialist economic integration and the operation of the CMEA, measures that were set out at the working session held by the leaders of the CMEA fraternal Parties in Moscow, November l986. Attention was drawn, at the conference, to the usefulness of an exchange of views on issues of Party supervision of the economy and foreign policy.

The Politburo of the CPSU CC adopted resolutions at the session on a number of other issues concerning the Party's and state's economic, social and foreign policies

Pravda (11 Sep 87); a translation can be found in FBIS, no. 176 (11 Sep 87), pp. 28-29; a condensed version is in CDSP, 30:37 (1987), 19-20.

17 SEPTEMBER At a meeting held on 17 September, the Politburo of the CPSU CC examined and basically approved a draft statute on the state production association. The statute stipulates that, in the creation of this largest organization structure at the primary level of the national economy, which operates on full economic accountability and self-financing, can include enterprises, associations, and organizations of one or several branches. The state production association can be all-union or regional. Its component enterprises may preserve their autonomy and be guided in their activity by the USSR Law on the State Enterprises (Association). The management of the state production association will function on a democratic basis by a council of directors and a general director elected by it. The enterprises, associations and organizations included in this structure compose a council of directors of workers' collectives.

The session discussed and approved measures to further improve the direction of branches of the country's wood-chemical complex. A resolution was adopted to form, as a permanent agency of the government, a Bureau of the USSR Council of Ministers for the Wood-Chemical Complex. Its most important tasks will be to widen the scope of the chemistry use in the national economy, and to fully satisfy the requirements of the country in progressive types of chemical, petrochemical, pulp-and-paper, wood processing, medical and microbiological products.

In accordance with the directives of the June (1987) Plenum of the Party CC, (the Politburo) examined and basically adopted a resolution of the CPSU CC and the USSR Council of Ministers, "On the Transfer of Scientific Organizations over to Full Economic Accountability and Self-Financing." As the resolution emphasizes, research, project design, industrial design and engineering organizations must be guided in their activity by the provisions of the USSR Law on the State Enterprise (Association).

It is planned to switch away from financing scientific organizations by ministries and departments, to direct financing of research and development by clients, who will contract for the work directly and pay for the work after it has been completed.

USSR ministries and departments and the Councils of Ministers of Union Republics are ordered to switch their scientific organizations over to the new conditions of work, within the schedule set for the transfer of associations and enterprises of the branches of the national economy over to full economic accountability and self-financing, and also with due regard to the specifics of academic and general school research.

Additional measures for the improvement of foreign economic activity under the new economic conditions were outlined, as were measures aimed at assuring that ministries, departments, Union Republics, associations, enterprises, state farms and collective farms speed up their work with organizations of socialist, developing and capitalist countries. Proposals for significantly widening the right of organizations to make independent decisions in the field of foreign economic cooperation were endorsed.

The Politburo of the CPSU CC approved the results of work by the Soviet Party-state delegation, led by L.N.**Zaikov**, which participated in the celebration to mark the proclamation of the People's Democratic Republic of Ethiopia. It was emphasized that the formation of the PDRE and the transition to constitutional forms of government and people's rule are a historical event in the life of the people of Ethiopia, and mark a new stage in the development of the Ethiopean revolution.

It was noted with satisfaction that talks with the General Secretary of the CC of the Ethiopean Workers' Party, President Mengistu **Haile**, and other Ethiopean leaders, which took place in an atmosphere of comradely mutual understanding, confirmed their mutual positions on the key problems of the contemporary world, and that both hope to develop and strengthen the relationship of friendship and cooperation between our countries.

The Politburo of the CPSU CC also discussed certain other questions of economic and social development of Soviet society and the foreign policy activity of the Soviet state.

Pravda (18 Sep 87); *Partiinaia zhizn'*, 19 (Oct 87), 3-4; a full translation also can be found in CDSP, 39:39 (1987), 26-27.

24 SEPTEMBER At its meeting on 24 September, the Politburo of the CPSU CC examined and approved a resolution of the USSR Council of Ministers, "On the Comprehensive Reconstruction and Development of Moscow's Historic Center in the Period until the Year 2000." In it, the basic concepts for the development of the center of the capital are reflected, and concrete measures for realizing them are outlined. An important place is allocated to the reconstruction and restoration of historical and cultural monuments, the expansion of museums and exhibition halls, the construction of trade and public eating enterprises, facilities for health care, and the development of transportation links and engineering communications.

It was especially emphasized that the planned measures have a great social and political importance. They must be implemented on a high engineering and architectural level, on the basis of serious scientific-historical research and in conditions of wide openness, with an active participation by the public, both in the country at large and in the capital, in the discussion of the projects.

The Politburo of the CC discussed and approved measures for improving the organization of the sale of goods produced by cooperatives and by citizens who are engaged in individual labor activities. To this end, it permitted the creation of trade cooperatives, and with the agreement of executives of local Soviet people's deputies permitted the openning of small stores, stalls and kiosks. It was deemed expedient to enlist for the sale of such goods the state trade commission's stores and consumer's cooperatives. It was decided also to form for this purpose a series of special stores under the USSR Ministry of Trade [Mintorg] and the USSR Central Union of Consumer's Cooperatives [Tsentrosoiuz], and permission was granted to rent small individual stores for cooperative or family contract operations.

In order to further develop and raise the level of scientific research in the field of traumatology and orthopedics, and significantly to improve medical aid for the public, a decision was adopted about the organization of an All-Union Kurgan Research Center for, "Restorative Traumatology and Orthopedics." The decision of the CPSU CC and the USSR Council of Ministers on this question envisions the creation of the above-mentioned center on the basis of the Kurgan Scientific Research Institute for Experimental and Clinical Orthopedics and Traumatology. Plans call for setting up a network of affiliates to this Center in the Moscow Province, Leningrad, Vladivostok, Volgograd, Kazan, Krasnodar, Krasnoiarsk, Omsk, Sverdlovsk, and Ufa.

The tasks have been determined for constructing and putting into operation complexes for treatment and rehabilitation, laboratory buildings, clinics, and social, cultural and consumer amenities. Measures were outlined which aimed at widely spreading into medical practice the experiences of the collective headed by Professor G.A. **Ilizarov** as regards the development and utilization of new and effective methods for treating patients.

(The Politburo) examined the question of serious shortcomings in the performance of the Azerbaidzhan Institute of National Economy. The upper school runs the training of specialist on a low level, and there have been discovered extremely flagrant violations of the established admissions regulations. Its material-technical base has been found to be in a state of neglect. An unsatisfactory moral and psychological atmosphere permeates the collective. The Politburo agreed with the recommendation of USSR Council of Ministers on the liquidation of the Azerbaidzhan Institute of National Economy. In order to satisfy the requirements of the Azerbaidzhan SSR national economy for economic cadres, a decision was adopted to create in Baku an affiliate of the Leningrad Finance and Economics Institute. The USSR Ministry of Higher and Secondary Specialized Education [Minvuz] has been instructed that it should raise the personal responsibility of VUZ leaders for the standards of specialist training, of educational and scientific research work, for high quality teaching cadres, and for the condition of the material base. It was recommended that a regular certification of the country's higher educational establishments should be carried out.

The Politburo of the CPSU CC also discussed certain other questions of domestic and foreign policy and adopted appropriate decisions on them.

Pravda (25 Sep 87); *Partiinaia zhizn'*, 19 (Oct 87), 5-6; FBIS, 3, no. 186 (25 Sep 87), 43-44; a condensed translation is in CDSP, 39:39 (1987), 21.

9 OCTOBER At its meeting on 8 October, the Politburo of the CPSU CC approved the Slogans of the CPSU CC for the 70th Anniversary of the Great October Socialist Revolution. The text of the Slogans will be published in the press. The Politburo of the CC heard a report from the General Secretary of the CPSU CC, M.S.**Gorbachev**, on his trip to Murmansk Province and approved the results of the work which he undertook there. Instructions were given to the central economic departments, ministries and the VTsSPS [All-Union Central Council of Trade Unions] to study the questions raised by working people, Party and economic *aktiv* during meetings and talks, and to bring appropriate proposals for study by the Politburo of the CPSU CC.

The Politburo discussed drafts of the State Plan for the Economic and Social Development of the USSR and of the USSR State Budget for 1988. The First Secretaries of the CCs of the Communist Parties of the Union Republics took part in the disccussions of the draft Plan. During the discussion, it was noted that the draft Plan and Budget intended to solve the strategic path set by the 27th Party Congress for the acceleration of development in Soviet society, by means of guidelines set by the January and June (1987) Plenums of the CC for the radical restructuring of economic management.

The draft Plan is formed on the basis of assignments for the 12th Five-Year Plan and is aimed at further improvement of the quality of economic growth, accelerating the increase in production potential, and raising the efficiency of its use. (The Plan calls for) outstripping the growth of machine building, improving the structure of social production, and balancing the branches [of the economy]. It intensifies the line on rational use of material and labor resources, proceeding from the assumption that resource preservation is, in essence, the only source for satisfying the growing needs of the national economy. An important place in the draft Plan is assigned to the implementation of the Comprehensive Program for the Scientific-Technical Progress of the CMEA Member Countries.

The draft is aimed at the implementation of a strong social policy and stipulates higher targets for the production of consumer goods and the development of services, in comparison to those set in the Five-Year Plan. [It also stipulates] an increase in capital investments to expand housing construction, to strengthen the material base in the social-cultural sphere, and also to increase budget assignations for measures, carried out in a centralized fashion, to raise the standard of living for the people.

The draft State Budget for 1988 intends to fulfill the need to improve the efficiency of the economy, and to concentrate financial resources on the key parts of social and economic development. A special role is assigned to strengthening the economic regime.

The Politburo approved basically the draft Plan and Budget for 1988 and deemed it expedient to submit them for study at the upcoming session of the USSR Supreme Soviet.

After the draft Plan for 1988 was discussed, it was made clear that much of its success will depend upon the results of work in the current year. The task to surmount the matter of lags in a series of branches, and to assure the unconditional achievement of tasks set for the 4th quarter of 1987, was laid before the ministries and departments. Party, Soviet, economic, trade union, and Komsomol agencies were given orders to widely expand their organizational and mass-political work, for the successful fulfillment of the tasks of the Plan and to undertake by means of labor collectives the socialist obligation to prepare the national economy for winter.

At the meeting, the Politburo emphasized the special significance of the Plan for 1988 for the strengthening of the incremental development of the national economy, reliable work of all its branches, and decisively to put into practice radical reforms of the management of the national economy. At the beginning of the new year, with the introduction of the Law on the State Enterprise (Association), 60 percent of all industrial production will be released to enterprises and associations, which will operate on the principle of economic accountability and self-financing. In this regard, the Politburo turned its attention to the need for a multiple and qualitative preparation of the ministries and departments, associations, enetrprises, labor collectives, for work under the new conditions. It is very important that every enterprise and association set up its production program and conclude contracts for consumer goods. (These programs), which should evolve from national economic interests and established economic norms, will take steps to radically raise the level of economic work and fully utilize their potentials and resources.

Measures for organizing the implementation of the CPSU CC and USSR Council of Ministers resolution of 17 July 1987, "On Improving the Work of Republic Administrative Bodies," were discussed and approved. They determined the principle rule for the development of a general scheme of managing the economies of the Union Republics, territories, and provinces. In that regard, the necessity to assure a qualitative change in administrative units and to reduce the numbers and cut the costs of management apparat, while at the same time raising the effectiveness of its work, was stressed. It has been deemed expedient to bring the organizational structure of government into full accordance with the increased role of the Union Republics, local Soviets of People's Deputies, and with the new economic methods of management.

The Politburo of the CPSU CC heard a report about the trip by Comrade V.I.**Dolgikh** to the Mongolian People's republic, and ordered the executives of the appropriate USSR ministries and departments to examine concrete questions of the further growth and improvement of Soviet-Mongolian cooperation.

The Politburo of the CPSU CC discussed certain other questions of foreign and domestic policy, and made appropriate decisions on them.

Pravda (9 Oct 87); *Partiinaia zhizn'*, 20 (Oct 87), 3-4; a condensed translation can be found in CDSP, 39:41 (1987), 26-27.

15 OCTOBER At its session of 15 October, the Politburo of the CPSU CC approved the measures formulated by the USSR Council of Ministers and the Estonian Republic Council of Ministers on the transfer of the Estonian Republic State Agro-Industrial Committee's enterprises and organizations to full economic accountability and self-financing.

(The Politburo) has requested agricultural, processing, and other enterprises and organizations to expand independence in the sphere of planning; (it) has granted to collective farms and state farms further rights in selling their products; it has introduced wholesale trade in material and technical resources; and it has implemented other measures with the purpose of giving employees greater incentives to raise production and make it more efficient.

Recommendations for more restrictions on the construction (expansion, reconstruction) of industrial production facilities, and administrative and public buildings in Moscow were studied. It was deemed expedient to concentrate the efforts of construction organizations on erecting facilities which are directly related with speeding up scientific and technical progress, serving the public, and developing still more the capital city's municipal services and the physical facilities of cultural institutions. A number of earlier decisions on the construction of such facilities is permitted only where it is necessary to repair their equipment or for creating normal working conditions after the number of positions and workers has been cut down.

The Politburo approved the results of talks that M.S.**Gorbachev**, A.A.**Gromyko**, and N.I.**Ryzhkov** had with the President of the Republic of Finland, M.**Koivisto**. The talks showed that, on both the Soviet and Finnish sides, there is a strong resolve to continue the consistent advance along the road of good neighbourliness and trust, equitable partnership, and a respectful attitude towards each other's distinctiveness. The 1948 Treaty of Friendship, Cooperation, and Mutual Assistance continues to be a firm foundation for the development of relations between the Soviet Union and Finland.

A report by E.A.**Shevardnadze** on the results of his talks in Washington with USA President, R.**Reagan**, and Secretary of State G.**Shultz**, was heard. (The Politburo also heard **Shevardnadze**'s report on) discussions with statesmen from several countries during the current session of the UN General Assembly, and on his official visits to Brazil, Argentina, and Uruguay, as well as a working visit to Cuba.

The Politburo noted the importance that a successful completion of work on the pact to eliminate Soviet and US medium and short-range missiles has for the development of an agreement in principle on this matter, which was obtained during the talks in Washington. The work done by the Soviet delegation, led by E.A.**Shevardnadze**, to strengthen international peace and security at the 42nd Session of the UN General Assembly, was approved. (The Politburo) emphasized that the talks in Cuba confirmed the unanimity of opinions on key problems of the present day, and the mutal desire to improve Soviet-Cuban cooperation in all ways. It noted the importance of further improving the relations of the USSR with Brazil, Argentina, Uruguay, and other Latin American countries in the interests of the peoples of our countries, and in the development of a complex for international security and equal cooperation.

The Politburo approved the results of Ye.K.**Ligachev**'s meeting with A.S.**al-Biedh**, General Secretary of the Yemen Socialist Party CC. It maintained the unfailing desire of both sides to strengthen friendly cooperation between the CPSU and the Yemen Socialist Party, and between the Soviet Union and the People's Democratic Republic of Yemen.

On hearing the report by A.F.**Dobrynin** of his trip to the FRG, the Politburo emphasized the importance of continued general development of state relations between the USSR and the FRG, from the point of view of the interests of both countries, and of progress towards building a peaceful "European home." It confirmed the CPSU's desire to continue accelerating its ties and cooperation with the Social Democratic Party of Germany and with other Social Democratic and socialist parties on defeating the threat of nuclear war and in solving other world problems.

The session of the Politburo of the CPSU CC examined certain other questions of the development of the Soviet economy, and also of the foreign policy activity of our Party and state.

Pravda (16 Oct 87); a translation can be found in FBIS, no. 200 (16 Oct 87), 48-49; a condensed one is in CDSP, 39:42 (1987), 20-21.

12 NOVEMBER At its regular meeting, which met on 12 November, the Politburo examined the results of measures passed in connection with the 70th anniversary of the Great October Socialist Revolution. In the resolution adopted in this regard it was noted that the fact that the jubilee celebration will be one of the greatest political events, is clearly demonstrated by the intense enthusiasm of our Soviet peoples, their solidarity around the Communist Party, their powerful support for the policy of acceleration, restructuring, and renewal of all spheres of our social life.

The celebration of the 70th anniversary of the Great October Socialist Revolution confirmed the great international authority of the CPSU and the Soviet state, which everwhere evoked the interest of world society in the ideas and nature of the course underway in the USSR of restructuring, and the leading role of our contry in the struggle for peace and social progress.

It was emphasized that M.S.**Gorbachev**'s report, "October and Restructuring: The Revolution Continues," at the ceremony meeting has fundamentally important significance for all of the Party's activities and for the life of Soviet society.

In the report, from the position of revolutionary dialectics and creative thinking based on the deep implications of historical experience, he made an exhaustive examination of the basic problems of internal and world development. He spoke of the political power and moral strength of the Party, decisively rejected complex theoretical dogma and stereotypes, and stimulated a creative search for new ways to develop pure and applied science. The report contained a constructive program for the fulfillment of the general line of the CPSU on restructuring, and to ensure peace on earth.

The Politburo stated that Party, Soviet, and economic organs, trade unions, and Komsomol organizations must center their attention on the key problems which will determine the fate of restructuring—the democratization of public life and radical economic reform. The necessity to decisively end the political and organizational sluggishness, and the lack of initiative on the part of a large number of Party committees and their leaders. For this purpose, one should fully utilize the preparations for the 19th All-Union Party Congress.

The celebration of the Great October Revolution demonstrated the effectiveness of the CPSU course to develop relations among world socialist parties, and cooperation with them on basic principles, strengthened by the work accomplished at the meeting of the leaders of fraternal parties from the CMEA countries in Moscow, November 1986.

The Politburo noted the exceptional significance of the Meeting of Representatives of the Parties and Movements Participating in the Celebration of the 70th Anniversary of Great October. In the spirit of the principled line drawn up by the 27th Congress, (the Politburo) confirmed the CPSU's desire to develop relations with Communists and workers, revolutionary-democratic, socialist, social-democratic, and labor parties, and mass democratic organizations and movements. Reflecting important changes in the world situation, in public opinion, and in progressive political tendencies, the meeting marked the beginning of a broad dialogue among international leftist forces and the establishment of contacts between them with the main aim of eliminating the threat of war and solving other cardinal problems of mankind.

The Politburo approved the results of meetings and talks of Soviet leaders with a number of leaders of parties and governments, who came to Moscow for the purpose of the Great October jubilee. It was generally understood that, in the spirit of new thinking, the most important problems of world politics are the questions of deepening bilateral relations, achieving agreement on general aims for the solution of international situations, and reaching concrete forms of cooperation in such relations.

The session of the Politburo of the CPSU CC examined and approved the general plan for the development of the city of Leningrad and Leningrad Province in the period up to 2005. It noted that for the first time the plan provided for a complex development of the city and the province, and for building economic and social planning into the urban planners' designs. The prospectus for the development of the largest region of the country must be carried out on the basis full coordination of its highly developed scientific-technical and industrial potential, the development of its social sphere and its cultural structure, and on its own base for food supply.

The general plan calls for a rational location on the town territory of facilities connected with peoples' work, daily lives, and leisure time, and for the improvement of architecture and urban planning on the basis of the careful preservation of historical traditions and the restoration and reconstruction of unique historical and artistic monuments in the city of Leningrad and its suburbs.

The Politburo examined and approved the results of Soviet-American talks that were held in Moscow in October and then continued in Washington. It was emphasized that the cardinal new proposals in the area of nuclear of nuclear disarmament that were proposed by M.S.**Gorbachev** in his talk with USA Secretary of State, and developed in the message that was sent by the General Secretary of the CPSU CC and handed to the President of the USA, R. **Reagan** by E.A.**Shevardnadze,** create the needed objective preconditions for the upcoming substantive and constructive dialogue on a high level.

The Soviet leadership intends to take actions so that the signing of the first treaty in history on the liquidation of an entire class of nuclear weapons is accompanied by the achievement of tangible results based on the platform formulated at Reykjavik, in the field of a deep reduction of strategic offensive weapons in conditions of strict observance of the ABM Treaty. (The ABM Treaty) is of basic significance for stability and also the strengthening of the basis for equalizing and developing the growth of Soviet-American relations.

Approving the results of the regular meeting of the Committee of Foreign Minister of the Warsaw Treaty members, in Prague, 28-29 October, the Politburo noted with satisfaction that the position of the USSR during the talks with the USA on nuclear and space weapons enjoyed the solid support of its allies. It stated that the allied states have confirmed their resolve to attempt to formulate a comprehensive system of international peace and security, and they support efforts to assure the security of all states on an equal basis and in all spheres of international relations.

Information on the visit of a USSR Supreme Soviet delegation to the USA, led by V.P.**Nikonov,** was discussed. The importance of expanding trade and economic ties in the agro-industrial complex between Soviet organizations and enterprises and USA companies, was studied.

The session of the Politburo of the CPSU CC also discussed certain other questions of the domestic and foreign policy of our country.

Pravda (13 Nov 87); a condensed translation can be found in CDSP, 39:46 (1987), 23-24.

26 NOVEMBER At its meeting on 26 November, the Politburo of the CPSU CC discussed and generally approved proposals by the government for restructuring the system for improving the qualifications and the higher training of management personnel and specialists in the national economy in connection with current economic reform, new methods, and the acceleration of scientific-technical progress. A single state system for upgrading the qualifications of personnel will be placed on a new footing, and a change to ongoing from periodic training of management personnel and specialists in all branches is called for during the period of the 12th Five-Year Plan. Differentiated forms and methods of advanced training are being set out. The results of the improvement in qualifications will be considered when personnel are certified.

The further development of the network of educational institutions is called for, [as are] the creation of interbranch institutes for improving qualifications, and the establishment of special departments and divisions at higher schools and technicums. Measures were outlined to upgrade the organization and methods of managing the work being done by educational institutions within the system for improving qualifications and the advanced training of personnel; and to strengthen their material base.

The Politburo of the CC studied the question of transferring agricultural, industrial, and other enterprises and organizations under the USSR State Agro-Industrial Committee to full economic accountability and self-financing in 1988-1989. A series of measures have been outlined to increase the effectiveness with which the agro-industrial complex sphere of the economy operates. They are intended to assure a better balance in the development of all its branches, the deeper integration of agriculture and the processing industry, the improvement of economic methods of production and an increase in economic efficiency. Party committees have been instructed to step up their organizational and political work to accelerate the economic reform of the agroindustrial complex to genuinely involve the broad masses of the working people in carrying out, and—in order to stimulate the activity of labor collectives— to make fuller use of financial autonomy, of team and family contracts and other progressive forms of organizing and providing work incentives.

The Politburo approved the results of M.S.**Gorbachev**'s conversation and A.A.**Gromyko**'s talks with M.**Soares**, President of the Portuguese Republic, which were an important event in the relationship between the Soviet Union and present day Portugal. The meetings and talks that took place gave fresh impetus to the development of Soviet-Portuguese relations and contacts in various fields, and to the deepening of mutual understanding between the two countries over fundamental national issues. Stress was laid on the importance of expanding the political dialogue between the Soviet Union and Portugal, aimed at helping to lead the world out of a state of confrontation and onto a road of cooperation in improving the situation in Europe, at lowering the level of military confrontation, and at strengthening the climate of détente and trust.

The Politburo discussed and approved the results of the official friendly visit to India by N.I.**Ryzhkov**, who took part in the opening ceremony of a Festival of the Soviet Union in that country., During conversations with R.**Gandhi**, Indian Prime Minister, the two sides expressed mutual satisfaction with the high level of the development of Soviet-Indian relations, and their hope for continued expansion and improvement of cooperation between the two countries in the interests of strengthening peace and international security based on the New Delhi Declaration of the principles of a nuclear-free and nonviolent world. They agreed on the need to continue to strengthen and expand trade and economic connections and to improve and deepen cooperation of new types, such as cooperation and specialization of production, the creation of joint enterprises, and the establishment of direct links between Soviet and Indian organizations and enterprises. It was noted that the Festival of the Soviet Union in India and the Festival of India in the USSR had helped to broaden contacts between the people of the two countries and to promote mutual spiritual enrichment.

The Politburo approved the results of E.A.**Shevardnadze**'s talks with US Secretary of State G.**Shultz** on 23-24 November in Geneva, when the provisions of the Soviet-American treaty on on the elimination of medium and short range missiles were agreed upon. Thus, the treaty will be ready for signatures at the upcoming meeting between M.S.**Gorbachev**, general Secretary of the CPSU CC, and President R.**Reagan**. One of the most important accords reached at Reykjavik between the top leaders of the USSR and the USA has therefore reached fruition, and an important step has been taken along the road to a nuclear-free world.

It was noted with satisfaction that the negotiations in Geneva made the reaching of mutual understanding on several issues for the agenda of the upcoming talks in Washington possible. The work done at the Geneva meeting was deemed useful and necessary. The session of the Politburo of the CPSU CC considered certain other questions of our country's foreign policy and economic development.

Pravda (27 Nov 87); FBIS, no. 228 (1987), 54; a condensed version can be found in CDSP, 39:48 (1987), 16-17.

17 DECEMBER At its meeting on 17 December, the Politburo of the CPSU CC discussed the results of the Soviet-American summit in Washington. The Politburo approved fully the work done by M.S.**Gorbachev** during his official visit to the US.

Signing the Treaty on the Elimination of Medium and Short Range Missiles between the USSR and the US is an important milestone in international development. A practical start has been made in constructing a world without nuclear weapons. This Treaty is historic insofar as it deals for the first time with the real destruction of two classes of nuclear weapons of the USSR and the United States. The most stringent verification measures envisioned by the Treaty reliably assure the monitoring of its implementation by both sides. The Soviet-US Treaty corresponds to the interest of all peoples and increases the level of security on a global scale.

Determined and concentrated efforts made it possible to achieve great progress on the problem of fundamentally reducing strategic offensive weapons while assuring the observance of the ABM Treaty. This question continues to be a main issue in Soviet-American relations. The USSR acts on the premise that there is a realistic hope of achieving the task of preparing a corresponding agreement to be signed in Moscow when the US President undertakes the reciprocal visit to the USSR during the first half of 1988.

During the talks, the mutual intent to facilitate the development of bilateral Soviet-USA relations, and to establish a frank and constructive dialogue on humanitarian problems was expressed. Despite the confirmation of serious differences in discussing the situation in a number of regions in the world, the Soviet side held a consistent course in a quest for new approaches in the settlement of conflict situations, while firmly defending the right of all peoples to choose their own path of development without external influence.

The Politburo approved the results of a meeting of the leaders of the Warsaw Treaty states in Berlin, 11 December 1987. The meeting represented a new step in the development of political cooperation among the fraternal countries. It was noted with satisfaction that the participants in the meeting completely supported the accords reached in Washington, and highly evaluated their significance for strengthening the security of socialist countries and the world community as a whole. The Politburo stressed the importance of continuing close contacts with the socialist countries for the duration of the Soviet-USA disarmament talks, and of active interaction on topical problems of strengthening peace, security and good neighborly cooperation in Europe and in other areas of world politics.

At its meeting, the Politburo discussed proposals on the necessity for a thorough technical modernization of the USSR's railroads. The accelerated development of the economy necessitates an accompanying development of rail transport—especially the delivery of advanced categories of rolling stock, other machinery and equipment, and means of automation in order to fully provide for the shipping requirements of the national economy and of the public.

The USSR State Planning Committee, the USSR Ministry of Railroads, the USSR Council of Ministers Bureau on Machine-Building, the USSR State Committee for Science and Technology, the USSR Academy of Sciences, the USSR State Construction Committee, and the USSR State Supply Committee, with the participation of other appropriate ministries and departments of the USSR, were ordered to develop, by 1989, a state program for radical modernization of railroad trunk lines during the period 1991-2000.

At its meeting the Politburo summarized the first results of work to speed up the recommendations, made by M.S.**Gorbachev** in his speech at Murmansk, on fundamentally reducing military confrontation and for transforming the northern regions of the earth into a zone of peace and beneficial collaboration. It was noted that the Murmansk initiatives were met with interest from all nations bordering the Arctic, but to date the USA reaction and the reaction of the NATO leadership to the proposals on limiting military activity in the region have not been constructive. The session of the Politburo approved measures to further speed up work to move the Murmansk proposals to a practical level of dialogue with both the interested states and societal forces in the northern countries.

The Politburo approved the results of a trip of a CPSU delegation, led by Ye.K.**Ligachev**, to attend in the 26th French Communist Party Congress. The Congress prepared a policy for strengthening the positions of French Communists in their selfless struggle on behalf of the working people, and for peace and socialism. The wide unity of opinions of the CPSU and the FCP on the basic problems of the present day was noted with satisfaction, and the CPSU's willingness to continue to promote the development of comradely relations that have traditionally prevailed between Soviet and French Communists was reaffirmed.

The frank and businesslike atmosphere of the discussions in Paris with officials and politicians of the French government emphasizes the urgency of continuing the Soviet-French dialogue. Under current conditions, the development of mutually beneficial cooperation between the USSR and France, and the constructive participation of France in joint attempts for disarmament and building European security, takes on great importance.

The meeting heard a report from L.N.**Zaikov** on the meeting of first secretaries of socialist capital-city party committees, which was held in Warsaw. It was noted that in conditions where the socialist countries have entered a period of revolutionary renewal of all aspects of life—a period of deep and creative quests and reforms—it is very important to study combined experiences and utilize them, and to further develop and deepen cooperation among the fraternal countries' labor collectives and their Party, trade union, youth and other public organizations.

The Politburo approved the results of discussions by M.S.**Gorbachev** and A.A.**Gromyko** with K.**Kuanda**, President of the Republic of Zambia. Importance was placed on expanding friendly Soviet-Zambian relations and of further strengthening the Soviet Union's contacts with the frontline states and national liberation movements of Southern Africa.

The Politburo approved the results of discussions by M.S.**Gorbachev** and talks by N.I.**Ryzhkov** and E.A.**Shevardnadze** with Australian Prime Minister, R. **Hawke**. The importance was noted of deepening Soviet-Australian political dialogue with the aim of strengthening peace and security in the Asian and Pacific region and throughout the world; and of further expanding mutually beneficial cooperation between the two countries in various spheres.

The session of the Politburo of the CPSU CC also discussed certain other current questions of the foreign policy of the CPSU and of the economic and social development of Soviet society.

Pravda (18 Dec 87); a translation can be found in FBIS, no. 243 (18 Dec 87), 30-31; a condensed translation is in DCSP, 39:51 (1987), 20.

24 DECEMBER At a regular session on 24 December, the Politburo of the CPSU CC discussed proposals for changes in USSR and Union-Republic labor law in connection with the restructuring of the economic management. These changes are expected to bring labor law into conformity with the Law on the State Enterprise (Association), which is soon going to be in effect, and with other resolutions adopted recently by the USSR Government. There are plans for greatly expanding the authority of labor collectives in resolving labor questions, giving trade unions a more active role, strengthening the guarantees of the rights of working people, and creating the needed conditions for further enforcing labor discipline, and providing incentives for responsible and highly productive labor.

The recommendations on these issues were approved and will be presented to the Presidium of the USSR Supreme Soviet and the highest bodies of state power in the Union Republics.

Proposals of the USSR State Agro-Industrial Committee and the All-Union Collective Farm Council on the wisdom of making additions and amendments to the model collective farm charter were approved. There are plans to publish a draft of the model charter in the press for widescale discussion. It will then be submitted to the Fourth All-Union Collective Farm Congress for review in accordance with established procedures.

At the session, the Politburo approved measures presented by the Presidium of the USSR Academy of Sciences and the Presidium of the V.I.Lenin All-Union Academy of Agricultural Sciences, and reviewed by the USSR Council of Ministers, which wasintended to improve the use of water resources and the supply of water to the national economy and to the population. The proper planning and administrative agencies were advised to take these proposals into consideration while preparing draft plans for economic and social development in the 13th Five-Year Plan, and in subsequent Plans. (They are also advised) to assure that annual plans for the current Five-Year Plan provide specific measures to ensure the economical use of water resources, taking into consideration the implementation of the new economic mechanism.

The Politburo described activities to take place in connection with the forthcoming celebration of the 70th anniversary of the Soviet Army and Navy.

The Politburo discussed the question of restructuring the activities of the USSR Chanber of Commerce and Industry, and upgrading its role in the system of the economic, scientific, technical, and commercial ties of the USSR with foreign countries. It was emphasized that in the context of a basic reform of foreign economic connections, the USSR Chamber of Commerce and Industry should cooperate closely with USSR ministries and departments and maintain widescale contacts with associations that encourage commercial cooperation, and with other interested organizations and firms in the Soviet Union and abroad.

The Politburo expressed approval of the results of the meeting of M.S.**Gorbachev**, and the negotiations of A.A.**Gromyko**, with King **Husseln** of Jordan, and with the meetings held between N.I.**Ryzhkov**, E.A.**Shevarnadze**, and D.I.**Yazov** and representatives of the Jordan leadership. It was noted that as a result of these meetings and talks, relations between the Soviet Union and Jordan have received further development in the spirit of mutual trust and cooperation. The importance of further deepening cooperation with Jordan and other Arab countries in the interests of consolidating peace, removing the obstacles to regional conflicts, and finding just solutions, acceptable to all interested parties, of the Near East problem, the acuteness of which is felt with particular force today, was stressed.

The Politburo also adopted decisions on certain other issues of the country's social and economic development, and the foreign activity of the CPSU.

Pravda (25 Dec 87); a translation can also be found in FBIS, no. 248 (28 Dec 87), 48-49; and a condensed version is in CDSP, 39:52 (1987), 25-25.

Chapter 3

NEW LAWS

The legal documents published in this chapter deal with various aspects of perestroika. The official Soviet translation of *perestroika* is "restructuring," which implies a more radical change than the literal translation "reconstruction." Western observers have accepted "restructuring" as the proper translation. Some of the laws are focused on the most fundamental problems of economic reforms; others change, or amend, laws or decrees about social conditions, violations of administrative law, traveling abroad and/or emigration by Soviet citizens. These represent but a cross-section of laws issued in the USSR during 1987.

In the USSR, law is a political instrument which determines rules or norms of behavior by citizens, enterprizes, state and social agencies. Law traditionally has been subordinated to politics. If a law is ambiguous, then it has most likely been purposely left open to different interpretations by ruling political bodies. Ambiguity in a law may be the consequence of several circumstances; for example, ambiguity in the Law on the State Enterprise reflects differences in views held by various groups in Party/state ruling agencies. In other cases, lawmakers formulate provisions for a law vaguely enough that it may be applied differently in each case.

The law most instrumental to economic reforms is the Law on the State Enterprise (Association). It defines the enterprise (association of enterprises) as the basic unit of the Soviet national economy, determines its duties and obligations, its structure, rights and management, its planning, production and social activities, distribution of its income, and so on. The Law is written in the language of a programatic/political document whose main objective is not only to facilitate perestroika, but also to satisfy competing interests of various factions of the ruling elite. The authors of this legal document tried to reconcile contradictory, perhaps even mutually exclusive priorities of both supporters and opponents of the economic reform. As a result, the Law is a compromise acceptable to both factions. The compromise, however, detracts from the conduciveness of the Law to successful reform; for example, it demands that the enterprise harmonize centralized command planning based on the principle of democratic centralism with its right to make economic decisions and to conduct its business independently of the state planning agencies. Another inconsistency in the Law lies in the assertion that enterprises must accept quotas, prices, normatives, state orders, and still be fully responsible for all their liabilities—whereas various state agencies, which can still give commands to their subordinated economic units, are not responsible for their liabilities. The provision of the Law that "consumer needs be paramount for the enterprises" will be difficult to apply to enterprises which remain subject to command planning.

Some organization principles for state enterprises set by the Law are mutually exclusive; for instance, the enterprise is subject to *edinonachalie* (one-man management) and, at the same time, to self-management by labor collectives. Moreover, one of the most important duties of the management-technological policy-is uniformly decided upon and executed by the superior ministry, while selection, training and appointments of personnel is a joint responsibility of the enterprise's management and Party organization.

Such inconsistencies of the Law stem from the fact that the present stage of economic reform is characterized by surviving principles of the old economic system and, at the same time, by many new principles typical of the desired new system. If perestroika is to proceed smoothly, reformers' interpretation of the Law must prevail over the interpretation maintained by perestroika's opponents. If the two factions block each other, however, the entire economic reform may be compromised.

Another legal document, "On Questions Having to do with the Creation, on USSR Territory..." is ambiguous for different reasons. The Soviet government wants to attract foreign capital for joint ventures first of all in those branches which are most important for economic modernization. That is why the law-makers left the paragraphs dealing with taxation and with usage of natural resources open to arbitrary decisions by Soviet authorities. As a result, there is no guarantee that joint enterprises will get equal treatment. If they are created in a preferred branch, they may pay no taxes at all. If they are created in a branch which is low on the Soviet list of priorities, they may pay the full tax rate. Similarly, arbitray decision may be made about which joint venture will have inexpensive access to mines, water and forests, and which will not.

The remaining documents carried in this chapter are supportive of the basic objectives of perestroika and, with one or two qualifications, are true to the spirit of the reforms. The decree on "Certification of Officials ...", for example, confuses elected and appointed officials. While appointed officials may be legitimately subject to such certification, the process is scarcely proper for elected officials who are *de facto* certified by those who elect them. The "Law on Nationwide Discussion ..." adds nothing new to Soviet practices. There was a nationwide discussion on Stalin's constitution, as well as on Brezhnev's constitution and his education reform project. If the new law were to bring about something typical of the spirit of perestroika, it should have stated that results of nationwide discussions are binding on decision-makers and lawmakers, that is, on the leaders of the Soviet Union.

The extent to which 1987 law making demonstrates the state of flux now current in Soviet society can be demonstrated by their variety. A law was passed in August making the transmission of AIDS a criminal offence [*Izvestiia*, 26 Aug]; in September another law decreed the expansion of benefits for working pregnant women and women with small children [*Vedomosti Verkhovnogo Soveta SSSR*, No.36 (9 Sept 87), Item 586]; and the RSFSR passed sweeping legislation against prostitution [*Vedomosti Verkhovnogo Soveta RSFSR*, No.23 (1493), (4 Jun 87), Item 800]. More important, perhaps, was a resolution accepted in the CPSU CC in June which included a series of resolutions designed to "raise the supervisory role of the Procurator's office in strengthening socialist legality and law and order." [*Pravda* (12 June)]

Many legal documents published in this chapter have two things in common. In the first place, if for different reasons, they are ambiguous and open to arbitray application by the authorities. And in the second place, the rights of citizens/enterprises do not empower their bearers to make claims which the state is obliged to satisfy.

Radislav Selucky

On Question Having to Do with the Creation on USSR Territory, and the Activities of Joint Enterprises, International Associations and Organizations with the Participation of Soviet and Foreign Organizations, Firms, and Management Bodies (14 Jan 87)

The Presidium of the Supreme Soviet of the USSR decrees:

1. That the Joint Enterprises established on the territory of the USSR, with the participation of Soviet and foreign organizations, firms and management bodies pay taxes on profits in amounts and ways determined by the USSR Council of Ministers. The tax will be based on receipts and accounts of the union budget.

The Joint Enterprises will be free from payment of taxes on profits during the first two years of their activity.

The USSR Ministry of Finance has the right to lower the tax, or fully free the individual taxpayer from taxes.

2. That the penalty for an amount of taxes not paid on schedule will be based on the regulations established for foreign persons, Provision for Penalties on Unpaid Taxes and Taxes Paid Late, set in a Law of the Presidium of the USSR Supreme Soviet in 26 January 1981.

3. That, if not otherwise stipulated by contract between the USSR and corresponding foreign state, a portion of the profits due to the foreign participant in the joint enterprise is subject to tax in an amount defined by the USSR Council of Ministers.

4. That the land, its mines, water, and forests, may be conceded to joint enterprises either for paid or unpaid usage.

5. That disputes between joint enterprises, international institutions and organizations with Soviet state, cooperative and other public organizations, their disputes among themselves, as well as disputes between participants of joint enterprises, international institutions or organizations on questions concerning their activity is subject to consideration in the courts of the USSR, either by agreement of the parties in a court of arbitration, or in situations stipulated by the Soviet legal system—in the organs of state arbitration.

In connection with Article 9 of the Soviet Law of 30 November 1979, "Concerning State Arbitration in the USSR" (*Vedomosti Verkhovnogo Soveta SSSR*, No. 49, [1979], p. 844), after the words "and by organizations" insert the words "by joint enterprises, international institutions, and organizations of the USSR and other member-countries of CMEA."

Chairman of the Presidium of
the USSR Supreme Soviet
A. **Gromyko**
Secretary of the Presidium of
the USSR Supreme Soviet
T. **Menteshashvili**
Moscow. The Kremlin 13 January 1987
No. 6362-XI

"O voprosakh, sviazannykh s sozdaniem na territorii SSSR i deiatel'nost'iu sovmestnykh predpriatii, mezhdunarodnykh ob'edinenii i organizatsii s uchastiem sovetskikh i inostrannykh organizatsii firm i organov upravleniia," *Vedomosti Verkhovnogo Soveta SSSR*, No. 2 (2388), 14 Jan 87, p. 35.

On the Introduction of Certification for Officials of the Staffs in Soviet and Public Bodies (25 Mar 87)

In accordance with the decision of the 27th CPSU Congress and the January plenary session of the CPSU, in the interests of improving the operation of Soviet and public bodies and improving personnel work, certification will be instituted for officials of such bodies.

All persons holding responsible staff positions in such bodies will be subject to certification, to be conducted after every election to said bodies. Certification of executive officials elected to such bodies will be conducted before the expiration of said bodies' terms of office.

Certification commissions will determine officials' fitness for the jobs they hold, evaluate their political, professional and moral qualifications, and make recommendations to the appropriate higher authority.

Within two months from the day of certification, the higher authority will examine the recommendations of the commissions and, in strict accordance with the law, will decide on incentive pay for achievement, changes in pay, transfer to other work, or firing, and will direct the attention of the parties being certified to shortcomings in their work.

Certification should help to eradicate departmentalism and parochialism, irresponsibility, bureaucracy and red tape; it should foster devotion to principle, self-discipline, organization, competence and professionalism, a sense of the new, initiative, intolerance toward shortcomings, the ability to evaluate self-critically and to take responsibility, and sensitivity toward the opinions of others.

"O vvedenii attestatsii otvetstvennykh rabotnikov apparata sovetskikh i obshchestvennykh organov," *Vedomosti Verkhovnogo Soveta SSSR*, No. 12 (2398), 25 Mar 87. Item 153, pp. 147-149. Abstracts in translation can be found in CDSP, 39:15 (1987), 18.

Law of the USSR on the State Enterprise (Association) (1 Jul 87)*

In accordance with the USSR Constitution, this law determines the economic and legal basis of the economic activity of socialist state enterprises (associations), strengthens state (public) ownership of the means of production in industry, construction, the agro-industrial complex and other branches, and expands opportunities for the participation of labor collectives in the efficient use of this property, in the management of enterprises and associations and in handling state and public affairs. The law deepens the principle of centralization in the accomplishment of highly important tasks of the development of the national economy as a single whole, provides for the strengthening of economic methods of management, the [broad] use of full economic accountability and self-financing, the expansion of democratic principles and the development of self-management, and defines the relationship between enterprises (associations) and bodies of state power and management.

* Bracketed materials were contained in the original draft, and removed from the final text.

I. THE ENTERPRISE (ASSOCIATION) IS THE BASIC UNIT OF THE NATIONAL ECONOMY

Art.1.The State Enterprise (Association) and Its Tasks

1. State enterprises (associations), along with cooperative enterprises, are the basic unit of the single national-economic complex. Enterprises (associations) play a principal role in the development of the country's economic potential and in the achievement of the supreme goal of social production under socialism—the fullest possible satisfaction of people's growing material and spiritual requirements.

The law defines the principles of the organization and activity and the legal status of state enterprises and associations (hereinafter referred to as enterprises, except in instances that deal with the special features of associations).

2. At the state enterprise, the labor collective, using public property as its proprietor, creates and augments the people's wealth and ensures the combination of the interests of society, the collective and each worker. The enterprise is the socialist commodity producer; it produces and sells output, performs work and provides services in accordance with the plan and contracts on the basis of full economic accountability, self-financing and self- management and the combination of centralized management and the independence of the enterprise.

The enterprise carries out its activity in industry, agriculture, construction, transportation, communications, science and scientific services, trade, material and technical supply, the service sphere and other branches of the national economy. Regardless of its particular speciality, the enterprise carries out the production of consumer goods and provides paid services to the population. It may conduct several types of activity (agro- industrial, industrial-and-trade, industrial-and-construction, research-and- production and others) simultaneously.

The enterprise is a juristic person, it enjoys the rights and performs the duties connected with its activity, and it possesses a specific part of public property and has its own balance sheet.

3. The enterprise's chief task is satisfying in every way the social requirements of the national economy and of citizens for its output (work, services), which should have high consumer properties and be of high quality, and doing so with the smallest possible outlays, as well as increasing its contribution to the acceleration of the country's social and economic development and, on this basis, ensuring growth in the well-being of its collective and of its members.

The consumer's demands are binding on the enterprise and their complete and timely satisfaction is the supreme meaning and norm of the activity of every labor collective.

To carry out its chief task, the enterprise ensures:

—the development and increased efficiency of production, its all-round intensification, the acceleration of scientific and technical progress, growth in labor productivity, resource conservation and an increase in profits (income) [based on the accelerated utilization of scientific and technical achievements, growth in labor productivity and resource conservation];

—the social development of the collective, the formation of an up-to-date material base for the social sphere, the creation of favorable possibilities for highly productive labor, the consistent implementation of the principle of distribution according to labor, social justice, and the protection and improvement of the human environment;

—the self-management of the labor collective, which creates for each worker a deep personal interest in the thrifty utilization of public property and his organic participation in the affairs of the collective and the state.

Art.2. Principles of the Enterprise's Activity

1. The enterprise's activity is built on the basis of the state plan of economic and social development as a highly important instrument of implementing the economic policy of the Communist Party and the Soviet state. Guided by [In accordance with] control figures, state orders, long-term scientifically substantiated economic normatives and ceilings, as well as consumers' orders, the enterprise independently works out and confirms its own plans and concludes contracts.

2. The enterprise operates on the principles of full economic accountability and self-financing. The production and social activity of the enterprise and payment for labor are carried out using money earned by the labor collective. The enterprise recovers its material outlays through receipts obtained from the sale of output (work, services). Profit or income is the generalizing index of the enterprise's economic activity. The enterprise must use part of the profit (income) to fulfill commitments to the budget, to banks and to the higher-level agency. The other part is left completely at its disposal and, together with money for the payment of labor, forms the collective's economic-accountability income and is the source of the enterprise's vital activity.

3. The enterprise's activity in conditions of full economic accountability and self-financing is carried out in accordance with the principle of socialist self-management. The labor collective, as the full- fledged master of the enterprise, independently resolves all questions of production and social development. Achievements and losses in the enterprise's work have a direct effect on the level of the collective's economic-accountability income and on the well-being of each worker.

4. Enterprises operate in conditions [The role] of economic competition among themselves [enterprises, as], a highly important form of socialist competition, for the fullest possible satisfaction of consumer demand for efficient, high-quality and competitive output (work, services) with the smallest possible outlays [is growing]. The enterprise, which ensures the production and sale of the best output (work, services) with the smallest possible costs, obtains a large economic-accountability income and an advantage in its production and social development and in pay for its employees.

The state uses planning and [broadly] employs competitive designing and production, financial and credit levers and prices for the all-round development of economic competition among enterprises, while restricting their monopoly position as producers of a certain type of output (work, services).

5. The enterprise operates on the basis of socialist legality. In conditions of full economic accountability and self-financing, it is endowed with extensive rights the observance of which is guaranteed by the state. In the interests of carrying out the tasks and exercizing the powers established by this law, the enterprise has the right at its own initiative, [for carrying out its activity and can] to make all decisions [on all production and social questions] if they are not at variance with existing legislation.

The enterprise bears complete responsibility for the observance of the interests of the state and the rights of citizens, the safekeeping and augmentation of socialist property, the fulfillment of commitments that it has made and ensuring a level of profitability necessary for work in conditions of full economic accountability and self-financing [loss-free work], and it strengthens state, production and labor discipline.

The enterprise's activity must not disrupt the normal working conditions of other enterprises and organizations or worsen the living conditions of citizens.

6. The state is not responsible for the commitments made by the enterprise. The enterprise is not responsible for the commitments of the state, nor for those of other enterprises, organizations and institutions.

Art.3. The Collective's Economic Accountability Income, Its Distribution and Use

1. The collective's economic-accountability income is the source of the enterprise's production and social development and of payment for labor, it is at the enterprise's disposal, it is used independently, and it is not subject to withdrawal.

With the authorization of the higher-level agency, the enterprise may use the following forms of economic accountability:

—based on the normative distribution of profits. Settlements are made with the budget and the higher-level agency, and interest on credits is paid, out of profits. The residual profit formed after these settlements is at the disposal of the labor collective. Based on normatives, the following funds are formed from the residual profit: the fund for the development of production, science and technology; the fund for social development; and the material incentive fund or other similar funds. The wage fund may be formed on the basis of the net output normative or another measure of output. In this case, the collective's economic-accountability income is formed out of the wage fund and the residual profit;

—based on the normative distribution of income obtained after the recovery of material outlays out of receipts. Settlements are made with the budget and the higher-level agency, and interest on credits is paid, out of income, after which the collective's economic-accountability income is formed. The single pay fund is formed as the remainder of the collective's economic-accountability income after the formation from it of the following funds: the fund for the development of production, science and technology; and the fund for social development or other similar funds, determined on the basis of normatives applied to the economic-accountability income.

A financial reserve and a foreign-currency payments fund may be formed at the enterprise.

(From the economic-accountability income and on the basis of normatives, the wage fund is formed, as well as the following economic incentive funds: the fund for the development of production, science and technology; the fund for social development; and the material incentive and financial reserve or other similar funds. A foreign-currency payments fund is also formed at the enterprise.)

2. The enterprise uses the wage fund to pay employees according to their labor contribution [in accordance with base wage rates and salary scales, as well as premium and incremental pay].

The material incentive fund is expended for the payment of bonuses, monetary rewards and other forms of incentives [other needs of the labor collective] and for material assistance.

The enterprise may, instead of a wage fund and a material incentive fund, form a pay fund, which serves as the sole source of all payments to workers for the results of their labor.

3. The enterprise uses the fund for the development of production, science and technology for the financing of research and experimental-design projects, for the renewal and expansion of fixed assets on an up-to-date technical basis, for increasing the enterprises working capital, and also for other purposes of production development.

The enterprise independently uses [the sum total of] depreciation allowances, channeling them, according to the established normative, into the fund for the development of production, science and technology or into another similar fund. [It carries out all types of repair work using money it has earned.]

4. The labor collective uses the fund for social development for housing construction, the all-round strengthening of the material and technical base of the social and cultural sphere, the maintenance of its facilities, the implementation of health-improvement and mass-cultural measures, and the satisfaction of other social requirements. [The enterprise has the right, with the consent of the labor collective, to channel part of the money in the material incentive fund into these purposes.]

5. The enterprise has the right, with the consent of the labor collective, to channel part of the money in the material incentive fund (the pay fund) into the fund for social development and to channel part of the money in the fund for the development of production, science and technology into housing construction, within the limits established by legislation.

6. The enterprise forms, out of the unit cost of output (work, services) and according to a normative, a repair fund, the money in which is used to carry out all types of repairs on fixed assets.

Art.4. The Enterprise's Material and Technical Base and Monies

1. The enterprise's material and technical base and monies—i.e., its [the] property [under its management]—consists of fixed assets and working capital, as well as other physical assets and financial resources. The enterprise exercizes the rights of possession, use and administration of this property.

The enterprise must constantly ensure the reproduction of the material and technical base on a progressive basis and make efficient use of production capacities and fixed assets.

2. With a view to achieving a full return from its production potential, the enterprise establishes a two-shift—and, for one-of-a-kind or expensive equipment or when production conditions make it necessary—a three- or four- shift schedule of operation. The employment of a different schedule of operation by an enterprise requires the permission of the higher-level agency and the consent of the local Soviet and the appropriate trade union agency.

3. The enterprise's working capital is completely at its disposal and is not subject to withdrawal. A shortage in an enterprise's working capital is covered using the collective's economic-accountability income, and the enterprise replenishes its working capital out of its own resources. The enterprise must ensure the safekeeping, rational utilization and accelerated turnover of working capital.

4. The enterprise has the right:

—to transfer to other enterprises and organizations and to sell, exchange, rent, make available free of charge for temporary use or loan [unused] buildings, structures, equipment, means of transportation, implements, raw materials and other physical assets, as well as to write them off the books if they wear out or become obsolete;

—to transfer material and monetary resources, including money from the material incentive fund, with the consent of the labor collective, to other enterprises and organizations that perform work or services for the enterprise.

Receipts from the sale of unused property and rent payments (if the rental of property is not the enterprise's basic activity) in the indicated instances are channeled into the fund for the development of production, science and technology, while losses resulting from transfers to other enterprises and organizations, as well as from the sale and writing off of property, are covered by the enterprise using the appropriate economic incentive funds of the enterprise.

II. MANAGEMENT OF THE ENTERPRISE (ASSOCIATION) AND SELF-MANAGEMENT OF THE LABOR COLLECTIVE

Art.5. The Structure of the Association and the Enterprise

1. In accordance with the goals and tasks of economic activity and the special features of the structure and organization of management, various types of associations and independent enterprises operate in the branches of the national economy. The basic types of associations are production and research-and-production associations. The associations, regardless of the territorial location of its structural units and the independent enterprises that are parts of it, functions as a single production-and-economic complex and ensures the organic combination of the interests of the development of branches and territories. It carries out its activity on the basis of a single plan and balance sheet.

The enterprise and the association organize factory-based service for their output and factory-outlet trade and create, where needed, the appropriate subdivision for this.

2. The production association is created for the production of certain types of output (work, services) on the basis of the more efficient use of scientific and technical potential, developed specific-article specialization, and production cooperation and combination. It consists of structural units that carry out industrial, construction, transportation, trade and other activities. Research, design and technological organizations and other structural units may also be parts of the association.

3. The research-and-production association is created for the development and production, in the shortest possible time, of highly efficient sets of machinery, equipment, instruments, technological processes and materials that determine scientific and technical progress in the relevant areas of great national-economic importance. It is created on the basis of research (design, technological) organizations or enterprises (production associations) that possess a developed design and experimental base, and it functions as a single research-and-production complex.

4. The enterprise consists of subdivisions that operate on the principles of internal economic accountability or a collective contract: production facilities, shops, divisions, sectors, livestock sections, brigades, teams, bureaus, laboratories, and other.

Part of the material incentive fund and the fund for social development, the amount depending on the results of the activity of the enterprise's subdivisions, may be allocated, according to a procedure established by the enterprise, to those subdivisions [operating on the principles of internal economic accountability or a collective contract].

5. In the association, its structural units operate on the basis of economic-accountability principles and in accordance with the provisions concerning these principles as confirmed by the association, and these units consist of subdivisions. A structural unit may have a separate balance sheet and bank account.

The association allocates the necessary fixed assets and working capital to the structural unit and determines procedures for carrying out relations within the association and resolving disputes among structural units, as well as the responsibility for nonfulfillment of their commitments.

The structural unit, within the bounds of the rights granted to it by legislation and the association, is in charge of the property allocated to it and concludes economic contracts with other organizations on behalf of the association.

The association may grant the structural unit the right to conclude economic contracts on behalf of the structural unit and to bear responsibility for the property allocated to it under such contracts. When the property allocated is insufficient, the association bears responsibility for the structural unit's commitments.

The structural unit forms the material incentive fund and the fund for social development according to the procedure established by the association and depending on the results of its activity. The money in these funds may not be withdrawn by the association without the consent of the structural unit's labor collective. The association has the right to put part of the fund for the development of production, science and technology, as well as of other funds, at the disposal of the structural unit.

6. The composition of the association is established by the higher-level agency, the structure of the structural units that are part of the association is established by the association, and the structure of the enterprise and its subdivisions is established by the enterprise.

The management of the association is carried out, as a rule, by the executive and the management of the head structural unit (head enterprise) of the association and is organized, in the main, according to a two-level system with direct subordination to the ministry, state committee or department.

Independent enterprises that enjoy rights in accordance with this law may be a part of the association. The association directs such enterprises, performing [performs] the function of a higher-level agency with respect to them, and has the right to centralize, fully or partially, the performance of their individual production & economic functions. In doing so, enterprises' resources that are necessary for performing the indicated functions may be centralized, with the enterprises' consent.

7. To effect a further rise in the level of production concentration, enterprises, associations or organizations may be included in the makeup of major organizational structures—state production associations. Enterprises, associations and organizations that are parts of such associations retain their economic independence and operate in accordance with this law.

Art.6. Management of the Enterprise

1. The management of the enterprise is carried out on the basis of the principle of democratic centralism and the combination of centralized management and the socialist self-management of the labor collective. Socialist self-management is realized in conditions of broad openness through the participation of the entire collective and its public organizations in working out highly important decisions and monitoring their fulfillment, the election of executives, and one-man management in the administration of the enterprise. The pooling of the working people's efforts and the development of their initiative for achieving high work results, the instilling of good organization and discipline in personnel and an increase in their political consciousness are ensured on the basis of self-management.

The enterprise's Party organization, as the political nucleus of the collective, operates within the framework of the USSR Constitution, directs the work of the entire collective, its self-management agencies and the trade union, Young Communist League and other public organizations, and monitors the activities of the management.

Social and economic decisions affecting the enterprise's activity are worked out and adopted by the executive with the participation of the labor collective, with Party organizations, as well as trade union, YCL and other public organizations, operating in the collective in accordance with their charters and legislation.

2. The enterprise carries out the election of executives (as a rule, on a competitive basis), which ensures an improvement in the qualitative composition of leadership cadres and the strengthening of their responsibility for the results of their activity. The elective principle applies to the heads of enterprises, structural units of associations, production facilities, shops, divisions, sectors, livestock sections and teams, as well as top foremen and brigade leaders. [Social and economic decisions affecting the enterprise's activity are worked out and adopted by the executive with the participation of the labor collective, with public organizations operating in the collective in accordance with their charters and legislation.]

3. The executive of an enterprise or a structural unit of an association expresses the interests of the state and the labor collective. He is elected by a general meeting (conference) of the labor collective by secret or open ballot (at the discretion of the meeting or conference) for a term of five years and is confirmed by the higher-level agency. If the candidate elected by the labor collective is not confirmed by the higher-level agency, a new election is held. In doing so, the higher-level agency must explain to the labor collective its reasons for refusing to confirm the results of the election.

The executive of an enterprise or a structural unit of an association may be [is] relieved of his duties by the higher-level agency on the basis of a decision of the general meeting (conference) of the labor collective or, by authorization of the collective, by the council of the labor collective.

The executive of a head structural unit (head enterprise) elected by the labor collective is confirmed by the higher-level agency as the executive of the association. If the management of an association is exercized by an isolated apparatus, the association's executive is elected at a conference of representatives of the labor collectives of its structural units and enterprises. The executive of an association [He] is relieved of his duties ahead of schedule according to the same procedure.

The executives of subdivisions—production facilities, shops, divisions, sectors, livestock sections and teams—as well as foremen and brigade leaders, are elected by the appropriate collectives, by secret or open ballot [according to the same procedure], for a term of up to five [two or three] years and are confirmed by the enterprise's executive. The aforementioned executive may be [are] relieved of their duties ahead of time by the enterprise's executive, on the basis of a decision by the collective of the appropriate subdivision.

The executives of enterprises, the structural units of associations and subdivisions, as well as foremen and brigade leaders, who are relieved of their duties before the expiration of their terms may be reelected or assigned to other work according to a procedure established by legislation with respect to persons removed from elective office.

Deputy executives and executives of the legal and bookkeeping services and the quality-control services of enterprises are appointed to their posts and removed from them by the executive, according to established procedure.

4. One-man management in the system of the enterprise's self-management is carried out by the executive of the enterprise and by the executives of the structural units of associations and subdivisions (one-man management expresses the will of the labor collective and the interests of the state. It is ensured by the executive—the general director, director or manager. The executive is endowed with special rights with regard to the organization of the enterprise's activity, is responsible to the labor collective and the state for the results of that activity, and ensures compliance with legislation. He directs the work of the management and performs the necessary economic operations).

The executive (general director, director, manager) of the enterprise directs all the enterprise's activity and organizes its work. He is responsible to the state and the labor collective for the results of the enterprise's work.

The executive of an enterprise acts on behalf of the enterprise without authorization, represents the enterprise before other enterprises, institutions and organizations, disposes of the enterprise's property, concludes contracts, issues authorizations, and opens settlement and other bank accounts for the enterprise.

Within the bounds of the enterprise's jurisdiction, its executive issues orders and instructions that are binding for all employees of the enterprise. The decisions of executives of structural units and subdivisions and of foremen and brigade leaders are binding for all employees subordinate to them.

[The management of an association is exercized by the executive and management of the head structural unit (head enterprise) of the association and is organized, as a rule, according to a two-level system with direct subordination to the ministry, state committee or department].

5. The general meeting (conference) is the basic form of exercizing the labor collective's authority.

The general meeting (conference) of the labor collective:

—elects the executive of the enterprise and the council of the labor collective and hears reports of their activity [in exercizing the labor collective's authority];

—examines and confirms [draft] plans for the social and economic development of the enterprise and determines ways of increasing labor productivity and profit (income), improving production efficiency and output quality, preserving and augmenting public property, and strengthening the material and technical base of production as the foundation of the collective's vital activity;

—approves the collective contract and authorizes the trade union committee to sign it with the enterprise's management on behalf of the labor collective; makes socialist pledges; approves factory labor regulations submitted by the management and the trade union committee; and

—examines other very important questions of the enterprise's activity.

6. A meeting (conference) of the enterprise's labor collective is convened by the council of the labor collective as needed, but at least twice a year. Questions are submitted for examination by the meeting (conference) at the initiative of the council of the labor collective, the management, Party, trade union, YCL and other public organizations, People's Control agencies and individual members of the collective, as well as of the higher- level agency.

Art.7. The Council of the Enterprise's Labor Collective

1. In the period between meetings (conferences), the council of the labor collective of the enterprise (the structural unit of the association) exercizes the powers of the labor collective. The council concentrates primary attention in developing the working people's initiative and increasing each employee's contribution to the common cause, and it carries out measures to achieve high final results of the enterprise's activity and to obtain economic- accountability income for the collective.

The council of the labor collective:

—monitors the fulfillment of the decisions of general meetings (conferences) of the labor collective and the implementation of critical comments and proposals by workers and office employees, and provides the labor collective with information on their fulfillment;

—hears reports from the management on progress in the fulfillment of plans and contractual commitments and on the results of production-and- economic activity, and maps out measures to facilitate more efficient work by the enterprise and the observance of the principle of social justice [and adopts counterplans];

—in conjunction with the elected agencies of Party, trade union and YCL organizations, confirms the conditions of socialist competition and sums up its results;

—handles [examines] questions of improving the management and organizational structure of the enterprise, seeing to it that employees' pay corresponds to their personal contribution, and effecting the just distribution of social benefits;

—adopts decisions on the use of the fund for the development of production, science and technology, the material incentive fund and the fund for social development, on channeling money into the construction of residential buildings, children's institutions and public dining facilities and on the improvement of working conditions and job safety and of medical, consumer and cultural services to workers and office employees, and handles other questions of the social development of the collective;

—handles [examines] questions of the training and advanced training [and placement] of cadres, the observance of factory labor regulations and [the state of] state, labor and production discipline at the enterprise, and maps out measures to strengthen it;

—monitors the granting of benefits and privileges to innovators, front- ranking production workers and war and labor veterans using money in the material incentive fund and the fund for social development;

—hears reports from representatives of the collectives of subdivisions, submits proposals concerning the use of moral and material incentives for labor successes, and examines questions of granting state awards;

—handles questions of electing the councils of collectives of production facilities, shops, divisions, sectors and other subdivisions, and determines their rights within the bounds of the powers of the council of the labor collective of the enterprise (structural unit of the association);

—handles other questions of production and social development, if they do not fall within the jurisdiction of the meeting (conference) of the labor collective.

The council of the labor collective works in close contact with the management and with Party, trade union, YCL and other public organizations.

2. Decisions of the council of the labor collective that are adopted within the bounds of its authority and in accordance with legislation are binding for management and [all] the members of the labor collective.

3. The council of the labor collective is elected by a general meeting (conference) of the collective of the enterprise (structural unit of the association) by secret or open ballot for a term of two or three years. Workers, brigade leaders, foremen, specialists and representatives of management and of Party, trade union, YCL and other public organizations may be elected to the council. The council's size is determined by a general meeting (conference) of the labor collective. Management representatives must not exceed one-fourth of the total membership of the council of the labor collective. In regularly scheduled elections, at least one-third of the council's members, as a rule, are newly elected.

The council of the labor collective elects a chairman, vice-chairmen and a secretary of the council from among its members. Council sessions are held as needed, but at least once a quarter. The members of the labor collective's council perform their duties on a voluntary basis.

A member of the council of a labor collective may not be dismissed or subjected to any other disciplinary penalty without the consent of the council of the labor collective.

A member of the council who has not justified the collective's trust may be removed from the council by decision of a general meeting (conference) of the labor collective.

The enterprise's management creates the necessary conditions for the effective activity of the council of the labor collective.

[4. Decisions on questions of social development, the organization of labor and wages are adopted by the council of the labor collective and the enterprise's management, in conjunction with the trade union committee and the YCL organization, within the bounds stipulated by legislation.]

Art.8. The Enterprise's Personnel

1. Work in the selection, placement and upbringing of personnel at the enterprise is conducted by the management and the Party organization, with the active participation of the council of the labor collective and trade union, YCL and other public organizations.

The enterprise forms a stable labor collective that is capable of achieving high final results in conditions of full economic accountability and self-financing and on the basis of self-management. It sees to it that personnel correspond to the growing demands of present-day production; it develops in employees businesslike efficiency and responsibility for the accomplishment of the enterprise's tasks, instills the best labor traditions and a spirit of pride in their collective in personnel, and increases their stake in attaining the highest possible labor productivity; and it strives to ensure that each employee values his job.

2. The enterprise displays constant concern for the steady growth of the vocational skills and continual rise in the political, general-education and cultural level of its personnel, and for the transfer of employees with an eye to their skills and the interests of production. For this purpose, the enterprise conducts the training and retraining of personnel, organically combining vocational and economic studies, ensures growth in the skills of employees directly on the job and in educational institutions, reinforces the physical plant of educational facilities, organizes training combines, courses and centers and schools for the study of advanced labor methods, and develops mentorship.

The enterprise creates the necessary conditions for combining instruction with work and grants the benefits stipulated by existing legislation. With their consent, employees may be sent by enterprises for instruction in specialized secondary and higher educational institutions, as well as to graduate school, with the payment of a stipend. The enterprise makes payments, in established amounts, for the training of specialists for the enterprise in higher educational institutions and for the advanced training of employees.

The enterprise provides assistance to educational institutions in training young people for work and in molding their vocational interests.

3. The enterprise's leadership cadres should possess lofty business, political and moral qualities, socialist enterprise and devotion to principle, and should be able to create a united collective and to ensure the combination of the interests of the labor collective with the public interest. Today's executive needs lofty professionalism and knowledge of the fundamentals of management science and economic thinking, qualities that make it possible to see long-term prospects and to manage efficiently.

The enterprise creates a reserve of leadership cadres and conducts constant work with them.

4. With a view to improving the selection, placement and upbringing of personnel, improving their business skills and the quality and efficiency of their work and ensuring closer ties between wages and the results of labor, the enterprise is to conduct the certification of executive personnel and specialists [ensuring that personnel correspond to growing demands, the certification of executives, specialists and office employees is conducted at the enterprise].

On the basis of the certification results, the executive of the enterprise makes a decision on [promoting or demoting employees,] raising or lowering employees in trade title and skill category, raising or lowering their salaries, establishing, changing or abolishing salary increments, and promoting them or relieving them of their duties. If subdivision executives who have been elected by collectives are, on the basis of certification results, deemed unfit to hold their posts, they may be relieved of their duties on the basis of a decision by the collective of the relevant subdivision.

Art.9. The Enterprise's Relations With the Higher-Level Agency and the Local Soviet

1. Relations between the enterprise and the higher-level agency (ministry, state committee, department or other higher-level agency) are built on the basis of planned management and observance of the principles of full economic accountability, self-financing and self-management at the enterprise.

All bodies of state power and administration are to facilitate in every way the development of economic independence, initiative and socialist enterprise on the part of enterprises and their labor collectives.

Management of the enterprise is carried out primarily by economic methods on the basis of control figures, state orders, long-term economic normatives and ceilings. The list of control figures, economic normatives and ceilings established for the enterprise is confirmed by the USSR Council of Ministers. The higher-level agency does not have the right to transmit to the enterprise control figures, economic normatives and ceilings over and above the confirmed list. The composition of state orders is confirmed by the USSR State Planning Committee and USSR ministries (departments). For enterprises under the jurisdiction of republic ministries and departments, as well as for consumer goods and paid services (except for state orders of the USSR State Planning Committee and USSR ministries and departments), the composition of state orders is confirmed by the Union-Republic Council of Ministers. The basic planning data established for the enterprise are to be strictly coordinated.

The enterprise is guided by the demands of the uniform technical policy conducted in the branch by the ministry or department, and it obtains assistance from the ministry or department in the training and retraining of personnel and in the implementation of foreign economic ties.

In all its activity, the higher-level agency must ensure conditions for efficient work by the enterprise, strictly observe the enterprise's rights, further their complete implementation, [and] not interfere in the enterprise's day-to-day economic activity, and also provide information on its activity to the enterprise's labor collective.

The higher-level agency counteracts the monopoly tendencies of individual enterprises, to this end carrying out measures to overcome the overstating of unit cost and prices, stagnation in the technical development of production, and artificial restrictions on the production and marketing of output enjoying consumer demand.

[The adjustment of economic normatives, as well as the transmission to enterprises of indices not stipulated by legislation, is forbidden. Established indices are to be strictly coordinated.]

2. The enterprise, on the basis of an established normative, transfers to the higher agency part of its profit (income) for the creation of centralized funds and reserves. The higher-level agency may use these funds and reserves to allocate money to the enterprise for the implementation of measures necessary for the development of the branch.

3. [The enterprise is guided by the demands of the uniform technical policy conducted in the branch by the ministry or department, and it obtains assistance from the ministry or department in the training and retraining of personnel and in the implementation of foreign economic ties.]

The higher-level agency must monitor the enterprise's activity, its observance of legislation, and the safekeeping of socialist property. A comprehensive audit of the production and financial-and-economic activity of the enterprise is conducted by the higher-level agency not more often than once a year, with the involvement of interested organizations.

The ministry, department or other higher-level agency may transmit instructions to the enterprise only in accordance with its jurisdiction as established by legislation. If a ministry, department or other higher-level agency issues an act not in accordance with its jurisdiction or that violates legislative requirements, the enterprise has the right to appeal to a state court of arbitration to have the act in question declared invalid, in full or in part.

Losses inflicted on an enterprise as a result of the fulfillment of a higher-level agency's instructions that violate the rights of the enterprise, as well losses that are in consequence of the improper exercise of the higher-level agency's duties with respect to the enterprise, are subject to compensation by [the] agency [that issued these instructions]. Disputes over the question of compensation for losses are settled by a state court or arbitration.

4. In accordance with legislation, the enterprise actively participates in work conducted by the Soviet to ensure the comprehensive social and economic development of the area in question and the best possible satisfaction of the population's requirements, and also in the formation of the local budget according to established normatives.

The enterprise interacts with the Soviet in its work to find and put into operation reserves for accelerating the development of production and improving its efficiency. Part of the money saved by the enterprise through the implementation of measures organized by the Soviets to use reserves for production growth and resource savings is transferred to the Union-Republic (in republics not divided into provinces) and Autonomous-Republic Councils of Ministers and local Soviet executive committees to be used for the economic and social development of the respective areas.

The enterprise clears technical and economic feasibility studies and technical and economic estimates for the construction of facilities and lists of authorized construction projects, with respect to established indices, with the appropriate Union-Republic (in republics not divided into provinces) and Autonomous-Republic Councils of Ministers and local Soviet executive committees.

The local Soviets facilitate the efficient activity of enterprises in their areas and adopt [with a view to the work of enterprises maintaining two or three shifts] measures for the creation of operating schedules favorable to these enterprises' employees for trade, public-catering, consumer-service, public health and cultural organizations and municipal transportation, as well as convenient operating schedules for children's institutions.

5. The enterprise performs work or services not envisaged by the plan but stipulated in assignments from a higher-level agency or the Soviet's decisions on the basis of economic contracts, with outlays reimbursed by the enterprises and organizations for which the work or services are performed (with the exception of outlays on eliminating the consequences of natural disasters and accidents).

III. THE ENTERPRISE'S PRODUCTION AND SOCIAL ACTIVITY

Art.10. Planning

1. The planning of the enterprise's activity is carried out in accordance with the principle of democratic centralism on a scientific [the] basis, with [of] the broad participation of the labor collective in the making and discussion of plans. It proceeds from the need to satisfy consumers' growing [requirements and] demand for high-quality output (work, services) with the smallest possible outlays and to ensure growth in the collective's economic-accountability income as the main source of the self-financing of its production and social development and of pay.

2. Proceeding from the long-term tasks of the branch and taking into account plans for the comprehensive development of the area [On the basis of initial indices determined by the draft Basic Guidelines for the Economic and Social Development of the USSR for the five-year plan and the long-term future], the enterprise works out the prospects [proposals] for its production and social development. It provides for measures for expanding production and raising its technical level, updating output and improving its quality in accordance with the requirements of the domestic and world markets, making the fullest possible use of scientific and technical achievements, and actively participating in nationwide, branch and scientific-technical programs and joint programs with CMEA member-countries.

3. The principal form of the planning and organization of the enterprise's activity is the five-year plan of economic and social development (with breakdowns [assignments broken down] by year). The enterprise works out and confirms the five-year plan independently [on the basis of control figures, long-term economic normatives and state orders, as well as orders placed by consumers for output (work, services) and ceilings on centrally distributed material resources]. It uses initial planning data as the basis for forming the five-year plan: control figures, state orders, long-term economic normatives and ceilings, as well as direct orders from consumers and material-and-technical supply agencies for output (work, services). [During the drafting of the five-year plan, the enterprise provides for the complete utilization of production capacities, employs progressive and scientifically substantiated norms for labor outlays and the consumption of raw and other materials, power and fuel, makes substitutions for materials and articles in short supply, draws secondary resources into economic turnover on a broad basis, and strives to reduce production costs and increase profits.]

In doing so, the enterprise proceeds from the fact that:

—control figures reflect social requirements for the output produced by the enterprise and minimal levels of production efficiency. They are not directive in nature, they should not fetter the labor collective in drafting the plan, and they should leave it broad scope to choose solutions and partners when concluding economic contracts. Control figures include an index of output (work, services) in value terms (adjusted) for the conclusion of contracts, profit (income), foreign-currency receipts, the most important general indices of scientific and technical progress, and indices for the development of the social sphere. During the period that the new economic mechanism is being mastered and the changeover to full economic accountability, unsubsidized operations and self-financing is being completed, control figures may also include indices of labor productivity and the materials-intensiveness of output;

—state orders guarantee the satisfaction of top-priority social requirements and are issued to enterprises for the commissioning of production capacities and facilities in the social sphere using state centralized capital investments, as well as for the delivery of certain types of output that are necessary above all for the accomplishment of nationwide social tasks, the fulfillment of scientific and technical programs, the strengthening of defense capability and ensuring the country's economic independence, and for deliveries of agricultural output. State orders are issued to the enterprise by the higher-level agency and may be placed on a competitive basis; they must be included in the plan. When state orders are issued, provision should be made for the mutual responsibility of the two parties—the executor and the client;

—long-term economic normatives are stable throughout the five-year plan and ensure close coordination between state interests and the economic- accountability interests of the enterprise and the material interest of employees. Economic normatives determine relations with the budget, the formation of the wage fund, economic incentive funds and other aspects of the economic activity of the enterprise, and are established with a view to special regional features;

—ceilings establish the maximum size of state centralized capital investments for the development of interbranch production facilities, new construction and the accomplishment of especially important tasks in accordance with a list of enterprises and facilities included in the state plan, of amounts of construction-and-installation and contract work, and of centrally allocated material resources to provide for the requirements of production and construction.

[To ensure that the indices stipulated by control figures are met, the enterprise draws up production plans and concludes economic contracts for the delivery of output (work, services) based on state orders, as well as on the product mix planned independently in accordance with direct orders from consumers. The enterprise accepts state orders for mandatory execution.]

4. The enterprise works out and confirms its annual plans independently, proceeding from its five-year plan [confirmed economic normatives, state orders] and concluded economic contracts [and demand for output (work, services)]. In doing so, the enterprise plans output (work, services) and other indices of economic and social development, putting the five-year plan's assignments into concrete form; with the appropriate organizations and enterprises, it resolves questions of the provision of material and technical resources and of contract construction-and-installation work. During the drafting of plans, the ministry, department or other higher-level agency, in conjunction with the enterprises, ensures the comprehensive coordination of their proposals. [The enterprise concludes delivery contracts, seeing to it that they correspond fully to the plan, state orders and direct orders of consumers.]

Contracts for the production and delivery of consumer goods are concluded as a result of the free sale of articles at wholesale fairs, which are the basis for planning the product mix, improving the quality of goods and raising the indices that determine the production and social development of the enterprise.

[When demand exists and additional production reserves and resources have been identified, the enterprise adopts, at the labor collective's initiative, a counterplan exceeding the indices stipulated in the five-year plan.]

5. During the drafting of the Five-Year Plan, the enterprise provides for the complete utilization of production capacities, employs progressive and scientifically substantiated norms for labor outlays and the consumption of raw and other materials, power and fuel, makes substitutions for materials and articles in short supply, draws secondary resources into economic turnover on a broad basis, and strives to reduce production costs and increase profits. [The list of indices, economic normatives and ceilings established for the enterprise in five-year and annual plans is determined by the USSR Council of Ministers. The higher-level agency does not have the right to transmit to the enterprise plan indices, normatives and ceilings that do not conform to this list. The economic normatives established for the enterprise are stable and are not subject to revision.]

The enterprise must strictly observe plan discipline and completely fulfill [strive for the unconditional fulfillment of] plans and contractual commitments.

6. The enterprise of Union (Republic) subordination must clear its draft [Five-Year and annual] plans with the appropriate Union-Republic (in republics not divided into provinces) or Autonomous-Republic Council of Ministers and with the local Soviet executive committee on questions of the development of the social sphere, services to the population, the production

of consumer goods, construction, number of employees, the utilization of labor resources, environmental protection, and land, water and forest use [and other indices established by legislation]. Measures to implement the voters' mandates are taken into consideration in the enterprise's draft plans.

Art.11.Scientific and Technical Progress and Improving Quality

1. The enterprise's activity in the field of scientific and technical progress should be geared to the continuous rise in the technical level and organization of production, the improvement of technological processes, turning out products of the highest quality that are competitive on the world market, the timely updating of output and the fullest possible satisfaction of consumers' needs and demands. The enterprise develops the production of specialized technological equipment. Scientific and technical development projects are carried out by the enterprise, using its own forces and research and design organizations whose services it enlists.

The quality of output (work, services) is decisive in the public assessment of the results of each labor collective's activity. Concern for the reputation of their enterprise should be a subject of professional and patriotic pride for workers, engineers, designers and executives.

2. The large-scale, comprehensive and timely employment of achievements of science and technology and the production of efficient and high-quality output are a highly important means of increasing the enterprise's profit (income) and ensuring the self-financing of its production and social development. The enterprise sells output the parameters of which meet or exceed the highest world achievements at higher prices. For the production of obsolete articles and poor-quality output, the enterprise gives discounts from wholesale prices and incurs material responsibility and inescapable losses in the collective's economic-accountability income, wages and social benefits.

3. The enterprise must ensure the strict observance of technological discipline, standards and technical specifications and reliability, trouble- free operation and operational safety for the equipment it produces. It monitors the quality of output (work, services), strengthens its own quality- control services, provides assistance to the work of the state product acceptance system, and organizes warranty and post-warranty repairs, as well as factory-based service for the equipment it produces.

4. For the purpose of accelerating scientific and technical development projects and raising the level of the integration of research and production, the production association and the enterprise:

—ensure the top-priority development of their own research and experimental facilities; may create scientific-technical and design subdivisions and strengthen them with cadres of research personnel and specialists;

—set up stable and direct ties with research, design and technological organizations;

—conclude [economic] contracts, on the basis of economic accountability, for the performance of research and development projects by scientific institutions, higher educational institutions, the organizations of scientific and technical societies, inventors and rationalizers and other enterprises, regardless of their departmental subordination.

5. The research-and-production association must take a leading position in the creation and wide-scale introduction in production of highly efficient equipment, technological processes and new-generation materials. It is responsible for the scientific and technical level of the output (work, services) produced in the national economy on the basis of its specialty.

Research, design and technological organizations must ensure a high level of research and development work and the implementation in this work of long-range demands for the quality of output (work, services), develop output on the highest world level and progressive basic technologies and fundamentally new ones, and actively promote their broad application in the national economy. The indicated organizations bear material responsibility for transmitting to production development projects that do not meet the highest world level in terms of basic indices, and when this is the case their executives and development personnel are subject to disciplinary liability and may incur losses in wages and material incentives.

6. Enterprises, production and research-and-production associations and research organizations are to make wide use of various forms of scientific and technical competition in their

activity and are to create an atmosphere of creativity in labor collectives. With a view to selecting the most efficient solutions to scientific and technical problems and developing the initiative of scientists, specialists and workers, contests and parallel design projects are conducted, and temporary scientific collectives are created. The development of the most important national-economic output is carried out, as a rule, on a competitive basis. Enterprises, associations and organizations that have achieved successes as a result of scientific and technical competition and that have won contests receive priority in material and moral incentives and increase their profits (income).

Interbranch scientific and technical complexes unite the efforts of enterprises and carry out the coordination of the research, experimental- design and technological work that they perform in the main areas of scientific and technical progress, as well as work relating to the manufacture of experimental models and bringing them to series production.

7. The enterprise must strive [strives] to involve all members of the labor collective in the accomplishment of tasks of accelerating scientific and technical progress, improving output quality and raising the level of production organization and standards, and it encourages the working people's scientific and technical creativity in every way. The enterprise organizes work relating to invention and rationalization at the enterprise and exchanges of experience and conducts reviews; it creates quality groups and employs other forms of the working people's creative participation in improving quality; and it ensures the safekeeping of technological, patent and license information.

Art.12. Technical Reequipment and Reconstruction

1. The enterprise must make efficient use of production potential, increase the shift index of equipment operation, carry out the continuous updating of equipment on an advanced technical and technological basis, and strive for all-out growth in labor productivity. It draws up a program for the uninterrupted modernization of its material and technical base and concentrates efforts and resources on the technical reequipment and reconstruction of production on the basis of progressive designs.

2. The enterprise carries out technical reequipment, reconstruction and expansion using the fund for the development of production, science and technology and other analogous funds, as well as bank credits, and, as a top priority, makes provision for the necessary resources and contract work.

Centralized financing is allocated to the enterprise for conducting large-scale measures for the reconstruction and expansion of existing production facilities, as well as for the construction of social facilities, in special cases. The list of appropriate enterprises and [production and social] facilities is confirmed in the state plan.

3. The enterprise has the right:

—to work out, using its own forces or on a contractual basis, design-and- estimate documentation for carrying out work related to the technical reequipment, reconstruction and expansion of existing production facilities, as well as for the construction of nonproduction facilities;

—to confirm [(within the established limits of estimated cost)] design- and-estimate documentation and lists of authorized construction projects for production and nonproduction facilities the construction of which is carried out using the economic-accountability income of the enterprise's collective and bank credits;

—to confirm production schedules for construction-and-installation work, coordinating them with contractors;

—to refuse to accept obsolete designs from developers of design documentation.

4. The enterprise carries out the technical reequipment, reconstruction and expansion of existing production facilities by efficiently combining the do-it-yourself and contract methods of construction. It ensures the observance of normative construction schedules, norms for putting production capacities into operation, and the rate of return on investments.

For the performance of construction-and-installation work by the contract method, the enterprise concludes a contract for the entire period of construction.

The contracting enterprise, in conjunction with the client and subcontracting organizations, ensures the commissioning of facilities under construction by the established deadlines and is responsible for their quality.

Art.13. The Social Development of the Labor Collective

1. The implementation of an active social policy as a powerful means of increasing production efficiency, developing the labor and public-political activeness of the enterprise's employees, instilling collectivism in them and establishing a socialist way of life should be [is] a very important area of the enterprise's activity. The enterprise must show concern for improving working and living conditions and for satisfying the interests and needs of its employees, their families, and war and labor veterans.

The enterprise's labor collective and each of its employees earns the money for social development through their highly productive labor. Possibilities for satisfying the collective's requirements for social benefits are determined by the final results of the enterprise's work and the collective's economic-accountability income. Questions of social development are resolved by [with the direct participation of all members of the] labor collective.

The enterprise carries on its social activity in close cooperation with the local Soviet.

2. The enterprise must assign paramount importance to activating the human factor, improving working conditions, increasing the creative content of work, and gradually transforming labor into a prime necessity. To this end, the enterprise:

—strives for a sharp reduction, and in the long run the elimination, of heavy physical, monotonous and low-skill labor;

—employs technological production processes that are safe for workers and the population and meet the requirements of sanitary norms and safety measures, and ensures the prevention of accidents and the elimination of on- the-job injuries;

—introduces automation and mechanization on a broad scale, and improves the organization of workplaces and the [scientific] organization of labor;

—creates more favorable conditions for working women;

—provides comprehensive assistance to young people in improving their vocational training and raising their general education and cultural level.

3. In order to create favorable social conditions for employees directly on the job, the enterprise:

—organizes public catering, provides hot meals for all employees, uses—when necessary—money in the fund for social development to lower the cost of meals in its cafeterias and snack bars, and actively develops its own auxiliary farming operations;

—improves medical services to employees, strives to reduce the incidence of disease while ensuring a comprehensive approach to preventive-medicine and medical-treatment activity, provides premises to public health institutions free of charge, and expands and strengthens treatment and preventive-medicine facilities;

—actively develops diversified paid services, striving for the fullest possible satisfaction of employees' needs, and facilitates the efficient use of their free time.

4. With a view to the accelerated development of the material base of the social sphere and the creation of conditions for healthy everyday life and recreation for employees and their families, the enterprise:

—channels the bulk of the money in the fund for social development into the construction of residential buildings, children's institutions and other social facilities;

—strives to provide the family of each employee with its own apartment or individual home as quickly as possible, carries out the construction and operation of, and timely repairs on, the residential buildings belonging to it using its fund for social development and bank credits, organizes cooperative construction, provides employees with all possible assistance in individual housing construction, and issues loans for this purpose;

—develops a network of kindergartens, day-care centers, Young Pioneer camps and other children's institutions;

—carries out the construction of, repairs on and the operation of sanatoriums and rehabilitation centers, boardinghouses, houses of culture, tourist and athletic facilities, and other recreational facilities;

—develops in every way physical culture, sports and the amateur creative activities of employees and members of their families;

—promotes the development of collective orchard and vegetable growing;

—carries out the distribution of housing, accommodations in vacation homes and sanatoriums, orchard and garden plots, and other social benefits.

The enterprise's management and trade union committee, with the consent of the council of the labor collective, are [The enterprise is] authorized to allocate housing out of turn to certain highly skilled specialists and other employees in view of their labor contribution. The enterprise may [and to] provide material incentives to employees of medical, children's, cultural-enlightenment and athletic institutions, public-catering organizations and organizations that provide services to the labor collective but are not parts of it.

5. The enterprise's labor collective promotes the strengthening of the family and creates favorable conditions for women that allow them to successfully combine motherhood with participation in labor and public activity. Questions involving women's working and living conditions are to be resolved with the active participation of the women's council.

6. Labor collectives show constant concern for war and labor veterans, pensioners, disabled persons and children, surround them with attention, provide them with the necessary assistance, create conditions for enlisting able-bodied pensioners and disabled persons in work that they are able to do, involve them in the public life of the collective, and make available to them the possibilities that the enterprise has for medical and other services, recreation and leisure-time activities. The enterprise takes part in the construction of homes for the elderly and the disabled, exercises sponsorship of these homes, as well as of children's homes, boarding schools and infants' homes, and provides them with material and financial assistance.

7. The enterprise actively promotes the efficient work of schools, [and other] educational and medical-treatment institutions [and the involvement of pupils in socially useful labor. It], and it may finance, using its own money, appropriate measures [the repair, outfitting and construction of general-education schools, vocational-technical schools and other educational institutions, create school and interschool workshops, production-training combines and shops, and assign specialists as foremen to instruct pupils. Premises, equipment, instruments, tools and materials may be made available or transferred free of charge by the enterprise to schools, other educational institutions and children's institutions].

The enterprise that is assigned to a general-education school or vocational-technical school as its base enterprise organizes the labor training of the school's pupils and creates the necessary conditions for this.

Art.14. Labor and Wages

1. At the enterprise, the USSR citizen realizes his constitutional right to work and to be paid in accordance with the results of his work and its quantity and quality.

It is the duty of every employee to work honestly and conscientiously, to increase labor productivity, to improve output quality, to take care of and augment public property, and to observe labor discipline.

The enterprise must make effective use of the labor of employees and, on this basis, strive to improve the collective's well-being and to successfully accomplish tasks of its production and social development. It should, along with material incentives, make extensive use of diverse forms of moral incentives to employees for high achievements in work.

The wages of each employee are determined by the final results of work and by the employee's personal labor contribution and are not limited to a maximum amount.

2. For the fullest possible utilization of labor potential and the creation of conditions for the highly productive activity of every employee, the enterprise:

—establishes technically [scientifically] substantiated labor norms and revises them in step with the improvement of the organization of labor and production and the implementation of technical measures [of the organizational-technical conditions of production];

—strives for the performance of growing amounts of work with a relatively smaller number of personnel;

—conducts the certification and rationalization of workplaces, determines the necessary number of them, and abolishes superfluous workplaces;

—establishes forms of the organization of employees' labor [and of categories of work], sets wage scales, assigns workers to wage categories and specialists to salary categories, and organizes the introduction of advanced methods of labor;

—establishes a schedule of working time and rest time [operations], clearing it with the local Soviet, introduces flexible schedules, authorizes short workdays and short workweeks, organizes homework, and also determines the length of additional vacation time, in accordance with legislation.

The enterprise provides, on the basis of openness, an objective assessment of the employee's personal labor contribution to the results of economic activity, encourages conscientious labor, creates [and must create] an atmosphere of intolerance toward violators of discipline and shoddy workmen, and employs [employ] strict material, disciplinary and public sanctions against them.

3. With a view to increasing the efficiency of labor, strengthening the collective interest in and responsibility for the results of work, and molding in employees a proprietary attitude toward the use of means of production, the enterprise:

—uses brigade economic accountability and the brigade contract as the basic collective forms of the organization of labor and of incentives for it. When necessary, engineering and technical personnel and other specialists are included in the brigade.

—converts sections, shops and other subdivisions to the contract form. The work of these subdivisions is organized on the basis of a contract between the collective and the management, with the necessary property assigned to the subdivision in question and pay based on long-term normatives;

—when necessary, employs the family contract.

4. The enterprise forms, according to the established normative, a wage fund (pay fund) based on the final results of work. It must ensure, in accordance with confirmed normatives, priority growth for labor productivity in comparison with growth in average wages.

[The higher-level agency confirms for the enterprise a wage-fund normative for executive, engineering, technical and office employees.] Within the limits of the wage fund, determined according to the [given] normative, the enterprise, taking into account the specific nature of the production facility and the tasks confronting it, independently establishes the wage fund for certain categories of employees—designers, technologists, research personnel—and for employees of quality-control services [as well as a wage- fund normative for employees of quality-control services and a wage-fund normative for engineering, technical and office employees]. The enterprise must ensure a relative reduction in the number of managerial personnel and in the percentage of money channeled into its maintenance [percentage of money channeled into the maintenance of managerial personnel].

The enterprise determines the total number of employees and their composition by occupation and skill, and it confirms the staffing.

5. The enterprise must use pay as a highly important means of stimulating growth in labor productivity, accelerating scientific and technical progress, improving output quality, [and] increasing production efficiency and strengthening discipline. It ensures the introduction of new base wage rates and salary scales, using money earned by the labor collective.

The enterprise has the right:

—to determine forms and systems of employees' pay, while preventing wage- leveling;

—to determine jobs for which remuneration is paid according to higher wage rates, and also to provide additional benefits to workers and office employees in light of specific working conditions;

—to introduce premium pay for combining occupations (positions), expanding service zones or increasing the amount of work performed, including for positions and occupations regarded as different categories of employees, without restrictions on the amounts of this premium pay, [and to establish premium and incremental pay] using and within the limits of savings in the wage fund that are formed on the basis of the base wage rates (salaries) of released employees;

—to establish, using savings in the wage fund, pay increments for each category of employee: for workers, for occupational skill; for executives, specialists and office employees, for high achievements in work and the on- schedule performance of especially important jobs;

—to establish salaries for subdivision executives, specialists and office employees without keeping to the average salaries according to the table of organization and without taking the relationships among their numbers into account;

—to determine specific areas for using the material incentive fund;

—to work out and confirm procedures for paying bonuses to workers, executives, designers, technologists and office employees of structural units and subdivisions;

—to ensure preference in providing labor incentives for designers, technologists and other employees [specialists] who are directly involved in the development and introduction in production of the latest equipment and technologies, inventions and rationalization proposals.

6. Improvements in the organization of labor and in pay, measures for the social development of the labor collective and the distribution of social benefits, and monitoring of the correct application of established systems of pay and of settling accounts with the working people are carried out at the enterprise in conjunction with or with the consent of [with the participation of the trade union committee.

Art.15. Material and Technical Supply

1. The material and technical supply of the enterprise is carried out proceeding from the need for its efficient and smooth operation and the economical use of material resources, while keeping the necessary level of resource stocks as low as possible [according to a confirmed normative].

In accordance with its plans of economic and social development, the enterprise determines requirements for resources and acquires them [through the system of ceilings (central allocations) or] by way of wholesale trade or through a centralized procedure. [In step with the expansion of production and the satisfaction of demand for production and technical output, as well as an increase in the influence of full economic accountability and self- financing on the reduction of material production costs, wholesale trade is to be expanded and is to become the basic form of material and technical supply to the enterprise.]

By way of wholesale trade, the enterprise acquires outside the system of ceilings (central allocations) material resources in accordance with its orders, on the basis of contracts concluded with enterprises and other agencies of material and technical supply or with manufacturers of output.

Certain material resources subject to the system of ceilings (central allocations) are allocated to the enterprise by centralized procedure. The enterprise independently determines, on the basis of contracts with suppliers, the product mix of and the delivery schedules for these resources.

On the basis of direct ties, an enterprise carries out its own material and technical supply independently for output sold on the basis of direct ceiling-free orders, as well as for centrally distributed output.

Wholesale trade is to be expanded and is to become the basic form of material and technical supply to the enterprise.

2. The enterprise bears economic responsibility for the fulfillment of its commitments under delivery contracts. The agencies of material and technical supply must satisfy in good time the valid requirements of enterprises for material resources. Territorial agencies of material and technical supply play a basic role in organizing the reliable supply of material resources to the enterprise and effective monitoring of deliveries [bear economic responsibility for the complete satisfaction of enterprises' orders]. They bear economic responsibility for output deliveries in instances in which they play the role of supplier. The material and technical supply of construction done by the do-it-yourself method is carried out, regardless of the sources of financing, by territorial agencies of material and technical supply, on the basis of statements of requirement from enterprises.

The enterprise has the right to conclude contracts with agencies of material and technical supply for the organization of comprehensive supply, preliminary preparations for the industrial consumption of delivered materials, the rental of technical devices, the provision of information, and the performance of other services.

3. The consumer-enterprise has a preferential right to the maintenance of existing direct, long-term economic ties with manufacturers and the expansion of such ties, and it selects the form of delivery: directly by the manufacturer or through a supply-and-marketing enterprise.

Agencies of material and technical supply are forbidden to arbitrarily revise existing direct, long-term ties with enterprises.

4. When the enterprise [regularly] receives deliveries of output that deviates, in terms of quality, from existing state standards, technical specifications or concluded contracts, and also when the enterprise is given poor-quality design and technical documentation, it has the right to unilaterally annul a contract with a supplier or developer and to demand reimbursement for losses suffered as a result of the contract's annulment.

At the request of the enterprise, the agency of material and technical supply or the higher-level agency assigns another supplier to it.

5. The shipper-enterprise is responsible for the presentation of freight, demurrage and the underloading of means of conveyance, and the transport enterprise is responsible for disruptions in making means of transportation available for the delivery or shipment of output stipulated by the plan and contracts and for the on-schedule delivery of freight and its safekeeping, according to a procedure established by legislation [in the amount of any damage caused]. Enterprises that supply water, electricity, heat and gas and other energy-supply organizations bear economic responsibility to consumer-enterprises for the observance of established ceilings and supply schedules.

Art.16. The Sale of Output, Work and Services

1. The enterprise sells its output, performs work and provides services in accordance with economic contracts with the consumers, trade enterprises and enterprises of material and technical supply or through its own network for the sale of output, the performance of work and the provision of services. It is to completely fulfill commitments stemming from contracts in terms of quantity, product mix (assortment), schedules, quality of output (work, services) and other conditions. The fulfillment of orders and contracts serves as a major criterion for evaluating the activity of enterprises and providing material incentives to labor collectives. The enterprise must study demand and engage in advertising. Payment by the consumer for output (work, services) delivered in accordance with the terms of contracts is the final stage of the enterprise's production-and-marketing activity and an inalienable condition for the implementation of full economic accountability and self-financing.

2. On condition that contractual commitments have been fulfilled, the enterprise has the right to use [above-plan] output for its own needs, sell it to other enterprises, organizations and the population or exchange it with other enterprises, as well as output that consumers and agencies of material and technical supply that have concluded delivery contracts have rejected (with the exception of certain types of output determined by legislation).

3. When contractual commitments are not observed, the enterprise bears economic [property] liability and reimburses losses to the consumer, according to established procedure. The payment of fines and penalties for the violation of contractual terms, as well as reimbursement for losses inflicted, does not free the enterprise from fulfilling its commitments to deliver output, carry out work or provide services.

4. The purchaser-enterprise must pay on time for output (work, services) supplied to it in accordance with a contract using its own money and, in certain cases, using bank credits. It is responsible for making payments according to established schedules, and it pays a fine for late payments.

When the enterprise does not have its own funds to settle accounts for output (work, services) and lacks the right to obtain credit, the higher- level agency allocates money to it [payment will be made by the higher agency] using **appropriate** centralized funds and reserves, on condition that the money is to be repaid. [When there is a shortage of money, the higher-level agency uses bank credits.]

Art.17. Finances and Prices

1. The enterprise's financial activity should be directed toward the creation of financial resources for the production and social development of the enterprise and toward ensuring growth in profits (income) through increasing labor productivity, reducing unit cost, enhancing the quality of output (work, services) and improving the use of production assets.

2. The enterprise carries out financial activity in accordance with Five-Year and annual financial plans. It is responsible for the on-schedule fulfillment of its commitments to the budget, banks, the higher-level agency, suppliers, contractors and other organizations. The enterprise must strive for high efficiency in the use of the financial resources remaining at its disposal.

3. The enterprise must take part in the formation of the revenues of the USSR State Budget, the money in which is channeled into the implementation of major economic and social undertakings, the strengthening of the country's defense capability and other requirements of the state.

The enterprise's financial relations with the state budget are built on the basis of long-term economic normatives. The enterprise pays a charge to the budget for the resources at its disposal, contributes part of its profit (income) [according to a normative], and also makes other payments stipulated by legislation, including payments to the local budget, according to established normatives.

Normatives for the distribution of profit (income) between the enterprise and the [state] budget should provide for the state's equally intensive [equal] requirements for the use by enterprises of production assets and labor and natural resources [and may be established in the form of differentiated scales of payments, tax rates and other normatives].

Charges for production assets are paid, as a rule, on the basis of a norm that is the same for all enterprises. Charges for labor resources reimburse the state's expenditures on training the work force and providing social, cultural, municipal and consumer services to employees and members of their families. Through charges for natural resources (land, water, commercial minerals), a differential rent that stems from differences in the natural productivity of these resources is withdrawn.

Along with payments to the budget for resources, taxes are levied on the profits (income) of enterprises remaining after payments for resources and the payment of interest on credits.

The withdrawal and redistribution of the profits (income) and other financial resources of the enterprise over and above the established normatives, norms and rates, as well as in instances not stipulated by legislation, are prohibited.

4. The enterprise must work without showing a loss. In the case of temporary planned-loss operations, the enterprise is financed by the higher-level agency using centralized assets and reserves within the limits of the subsidy established in the Five-Year Plan, with progressive reductions. It must work out measures to strengthen its financial position, to eliminate the unprofitable production of output (work, services) within an established time period, and to ensure operation at a profit.

5. The enterprise makes reimbursement for losses inflicted on other organizations and the state [by the irrational use of resources] and pays fines, penalties and other [economic] sanctions established by legislation using the collective's economic-accountability income. Sums of money obtained by the enterprise as reimbursement for losses and [economic] sanctions are channeled into increasing the collective's economic-accountability income.

6. The enterprise exercises its rights and duties in the field of price formation in accordance with the basic principles of the state administration and regulation of prices. Prices should reflect socially necessary outlays on the production and sale of output, its consumer properties, quality and effective demands. They [prices] are used as an active means of influencing growth in production efficiency, improvement in output quality and reduction in the unit cost of output (work, services). The enterprise must ensure the economic validity of prices and of plans for prices or calculations for them, priority growth for national-economic effect in comparison with outlays, and a relative reduction in output prices for consumers [and the observance of ceiling prices].

7. The enterprise sells its output (work, services) based on prices (rates) that are centrally established, as well as under arrangements with consumers or independently.

8. The enterprise is responsible for the strict observance of price discipline and must prevent the overstating of prices. Profits obtained in an unwarranted manner by the enterprise as a result of violations of state price discipline or nonobservance of standards and technical specifications are subject to withdrawal into the budget (using the collective's economic-accountability income) and are excluded from reporting data on plan fulfillment.

An enterprise that overstates prices and obtains unwarranted profits makes an additional payment into the budget, using the collective's economic- accountability income, in the form of a fine in the amount of the illegally obtained profits. When the producer overstates prices for output (work, services), the consumer has the right to annul the contract that has been concluded for its delivery.

9. Enterprises must be guided by centrally established prices (rates) for output (work, services), as well as by prices (rates) confirmed by ministries and departments.

The enterprise has the right, with the concurrence of the client, to apply markups (discounts) to centrally established wholesale prices for the fulfillment of additional requirements with respect to changes in the consumer properties of output and the making up of complete sets of articles.

10. With a view to expanding independence in economic activity, giving fuller consideration to the individual needs of consumers and providing incentives for the production of high-quality output [and new equipment], the enterprise has the right to apply prices based on arrangements with consumers (contract prices) for production-and-technical output manufactured to fill one-time and individual orders, new output or output that is in production for the first time and new nonfood consumer goods, as well as certain types of foodstuffs sold under agreement with trade organizations, for a period of up to two years on the basis of the established list, for the final output of research and design organizations, for agricultural output purchased from the population by state farms and other state agricultural enterprises, for output purchased and sold by cooperative organizations [consumer goods, scientific and technical development and agricultural output sold to consumers' cooperative organizations and purchased from the population by state farms and other state agricultural enterprises], and for other types of output (work, services) stipulated by legislation.

State price-formation agencies determine the procedure for establishing contract prices and monitor their application.

11. The enterprise independently confirms prices (rates) for production- and-technical output, consumer goods and services to which centrally confirmed prices are not applied, as well as for output (services) that is for its own consumption or is sold in its own trade network.

State farms and other state agricultural enterprises have the right to independently establish prices for [the industrial output they produce, for] part of the planned and all of the above-plan agricultural output that is sold through their own trade networks and on collective farm markets [and also for output sold within the agro-industrial combine, and to establish rates for services].

As full economic accountability, self-financing, wholesale trade and direct economic ties develop, the application of contract and independently confirmed prices will expand.

Art.18. Credit and Settlement

1. In conditions of full economic accountability and self-financing, the enterprise [actively] uses bank credits for [purposes of] production and social purposes [development], on condition that the principles of credit operations are strictly observed: The credit is provided, it is directed to a specific purpose, it is granted for a specific time, it is to be repaid, and it is in fact repaid.

[Short-term and long-term bank credits may be provided to the enterprise.] Short-term credits are issued by the bank to the enterprise for purposes of current activity on the basis of broad-category objects of credit operations. Long-term credits are granted for purposes of production and social development [the development of production on terms specifying the recovery of outlays, as well as for the construction of residential buildings and other social facilities], with subsequent repayment of the credit using money in the fund for the development of production, science and technology and the fund for social development (or other similar funds).

The enterprise resolves all questions associated with credit operations in the credit institutions at the place where it has its current account or account for financing capital investments.

The enterprise is responsible for the effective use of credits. Sanctions are applied against enterprises that violate the terms of credit operations. When there is a systematic failure to meet schedules for the repayment of loans, the enterprise loses the right to obtain new credits; in certain instances, it may use credits guaranteed by the higher-level agency.

2. The enterprise must settle accounts with respect to its commitments on time. The enterprise pays fines and penalties for late settlements. The enterprise makes all settlements, including payments into the budget and the payment of wages, in the calendar order in which settlement documents are received (when payment dates arrive).

Banks pay the enterprise interest for the use of temporarily free money in its fund for the development of production, science and technology, as well as in the fund for social development.

3. Banks may declare an enterprise that systematically violates payments discipline insolvent, and they report this fact to the basic suppliers of goods and materials and to the higher-level agency. The bank determines the order of priority with regard to payments on such an enterprise's commitments. Creditor-enterprises may stop delivering output to, performing work for and providing services to an enterprise that has been declared insolvent. The enterprise and its higher-level agency must take steps to eliminate mismanagement and strengthen settlements discipline.

The bank writes off compulsorily exacted fines and penalties and other sanctions to the enterprise's current account. The enterprise is reimbursed by the guilty party for illegally written off sums [fines and penalties] in amounts greater than those wrongfully exacted. Disputes over such restitutions are examined by arbitration agencies and courts.

Art.19. Foreign Economic Activity.

1. The enterprise's foreign economic activity is an important component of all the enterprise's work. It is carried out, as a rule, on the basis of foreign-currency unsubsidized operations and self-financing; its result is an organic part of the results of the enterprise's economic activity and directly affects the formation of the economic incentive fund and the foreign-currency payments fund.

The enterprise ensures the delivery of output for export as a top priority.

2. Cooperation with enterprises in the socialist countries, the broadening and deepening of socialist economic integration and the development of effective cooperative arrangements are of priority importance in the enterprise's foreign economic activity.

In relations with enterprises and organizations of the CMEA member- countries, the enterprise:

—establishes direct ties, resolves questions of production and scientific-technical cooperation, including the determination of the economic terms of cooperation, including contract prices, and concludes economic contracts;

—reaches agreement on the product mix and the volume of export-import deliveries of output based on cooperative arrangements and on the provision of services, and carries out transfers of material resources and the appropriate technical documentation;

—conducts research, design and experimental work, creates joint collectives of scientists and specialists for this purpose, exchanges scientific and technical documentation under mutually agreed-upon conditions, and provides assistance in the training of personnel;

—participates in the activity of joint enterprises, international associations and organizations that are created on the basis of the USSR's international treaties.

3. The enterprise puts into effect economic ties with firms in the capitalist and developing countries according to the principles of mutual advantage and equality. Cooperative production and scientific-technical arrangements on a long-term and balanced basis, as well as the creation of joint enterprises and production facilities, are the basic forms of the development

of such ties. The procedures for the creation of joint enterprises and production facilities on USSR territory and for their activity are determined in accordance with Soviet legislation.

4. The right to directly carry out export-import operations (including markets in capitalist and developing countries) and to create an economic- accountability foreign trade firm for this purpose may be granted to an enterprise that provides substantial deliveries of output (work, services) for export.

Enterprises that do not have the right to independently enter the foreign market participate in determining the best terms for the export of their output (work, [and] services) through the foreign trade associations of their own or other ministries and departments.

5. With a view to strengthening economic accountability, increasing economic interest and responsibility, and to expanding independence in carrying out export-import operations, the enterprise:

—engages in cooperation with foreign partners on the basis of economic contracts;

—creates a foreign-currency payments fund, formed on the basis of stable, long-term normatives from money received through the sale of finished output (work, [and] services) for export, as well as all foreign-currency receipts from operations involving cooperative deliveries and the sale of licenses;

—may obtain a bank credit in foreign currency for the creation and development of export production facilities, on condition that the credit is repaid using foreign-currency receipts from the export of output;

—bears economic responsibility for the effectiveness of foreign economic ties and the rational use of foreign-currency resources in the interests of developing production and raising its technical level;

—pays compensation for losses from the nonfulfillment of assignments for the export of goods or of contractual commitments using its foreign-currency resources;

—pays all fines and other sanctions in foreign currency to the foreign purchaser using the foreign-currency payments fund, if the violation of commitments was its fault.

6. With a view to the technical reequipment and reconstruction of production and the performance of research, experimental-design and other work, the enterprise carries out imports of output using and within the limits of the foreign-currency payments fund or borrowed money. It also has the right to acquire in the CMEA member-countries, for the needs of its labor collectives, medical equipment and cultural, consumer, sporting and other goods that are not included in the state allocation plans.

Money in the enterprise's foreign-currency payments fund is not subject to withdrawal and may accumulate for use in subsequent years.

7. The enterprise may acquire in the USSR Foreign Economic [Trade] Bank, on credit terms, transferable rubles and national currencies of countries of the socialist commonwealth in order to conduct scientific and technical work and to develop efficient production facilities related to cooperative arrangements.

Art.20. Nature Use and Environmental Protection

1. The enterprise must, in the interests of present and future generations of Soviet people, ensure the efficient use and reproduction of natural resources, make solicitous use of them in accordance with the purposes for which they are made available to it, protect the environment from pollution and other harmful influences, and carry out the organization of production on the basis of waste-free technologies as the main guideline for preserving the environment.

The enterprise ensures the comprehensive use of commercial minerals and other natural resources; it is to make rational use of agricultural land and conduct the recultivation of land and other measures to protect the environment.

The environmental-protection measures carried out by the enterprise should fully offset the negative influence of production on the environment.

In designs for the expansion, reconstruction and technical reequipment of production, the enterprise provides for environmental-protection structures and installations; it builds them and sets up their efficient and uninterrupted operation.

2. The enterprise makes established payments for the use of natural resources as part of national property, and it carries out environmental- protection measures using its own money and credits. In certain instances, such measures are financed through centralized sources.

3. In its work with respect to environmental protection and the use of natural resources, the enterprise is under the control of the local Soviet and other agencies that exercise state monitoring in the field of environmental protection and the use of natural resources.

The enterprise reimburses damages caused by environmental pollution and the irrational use of natural resources, and it bears material responsibility for the nonobservance of legislation on environmental protection. Enterprise activities that flagrantly violate the established regulations for nature use may be suspended until the violations are eliminated.

Art.21. The Enterprise's Joint Production and Social Activity

1. In order to make more efficient use of production potential, expand the production of goods and services, jointly solve scientific and technical problems and develop the infrastructure, the enterprise, on its own initiative or at the suggestion of local Soviets or other organizations, develops cooperation primarily with enterprises located in the given territory. They may pool their efforts to accomplish interbranch, branch and regional tasks. With this in view, the enterprise has the right:

—to jointly perform work related to the reconstruction and technical reequipment of production, the acceleration of scientific and technical progress, the improvement of output quality, the development of consumer- goods production, and the provision of services to the population;

—to create, according to established procedure, interbranch production facilities, time-sharing computer centers, and research, design, repair, construction, trade and other joint enterprises and associations;

—to carry out the construction and operation of facilities of the production infrastructure, auxiliary agricultural operations, environmental- protection structures, residential buildings, and other production, social, cultural, municipal and consumer-service facilities;

—according to established procedure, to amalgamate with other enterprises, up to and including complete merger, if this is dictated by the interests of cooperation and technological ties and the efficient obtaining of final output;

—to organize the training of specialists, and to create (in conjunction with educational institutions) production-training enterprises.

In order to carry out the aforementioned and other joint activities, enterprises conclude contracts that provide for the pooling of financial, labor and material resources on a pro rata basis, as well as for the resolution of questions relating to the organization and activities of joint enterprises and associations.

Higher-level agencies and local Soviet executive committees take steps to develop joint activities by enterprises and help them in the fullest possible exercise of the rights they have been granted in this field.

2. The enterprise may participate in the activity of interbranch and interfarm territorial-production associations created by Union-Republic (in republics not divided into provinces) and Autonomous-Republic Councils of Ministers and local Soviet executive committees.

3. Cooperatives may be created under the auspices of the enterprise, according to established procedures. The enterprise provides assistance to these cooperatives, as well as to citizens who engage in individual enterprise under contracts with the enterprise.

Art.22. Record-Keeping, Reporting and Monitoring

1. In order to exert an active influence on all economic activity and analyze the ways, forms and methods of developing production, and with a view to ensuring efficient management and preventing opportunities for the emergence of certain disproportions in the fulfillment of plan assignments, the enterprise keeps records of the results of work, monitors the course of production, and keeps current-operations, bookkeeping and statistical records.

The enterprise is to:

—use advanced forms and methods of record-keeping and information processing based on the broad application of up-to-date computing equipment;

—compile reporting documents and present them to the appropriate agencies by established deadlines, and ensure the authenticity of reports and balance sheets;

—strictly monitor the rational and economic use of material, labor and financial resources, wage a resolute struggle against mismanagement and wastefulness, take steps to prevent such phenomena, and report embezzlement and flagrant violations of legislation to internal-affairs agencies or agencies of the prosecutor's office;

—enhance the role and responsibility of the legal, [and] bookkeeping and other functional services for the observance of legality and contract and financial discipline and for output quality.

Executives of enterprises, [and] structural units and subdivisions and other guilty parties bear personal responsibility for instances of report- padding, hoodwinking and other distortions of state reporting and are subject to disciplinary, material or criminal liability. All instances of report- padding and hoodwinking are discussed in the labor collective.

The forms of the enterprise's reporting documents and the places and times at which they are to be submitted are determined according to established procedure. Requests for and the submission of any other reporting documents are prohibited.

2. Audits and inspections of the enterprise's activity may be conducted by, along with higher-level agencies, financial, banking and other administrative agencies in accordance with the functions of monitoring the enterprise's activity that are assigned to them by legislation. An audit or an inspection may be conducted at the request of law-enforcement agencies or People's Control Committees.

All types of audits and inspections should promote the increased efficiency of economic management and should not disrupt the normal pace of the enterprise's work. The results of audits and inspections are reported to the labor collective.

3. A People's Control Committee (group, post) is elected at the enterprise; the enterprise's management must provide it with every possible assistance in its work, examine its proposals and recommendations, and take the necessary steps to eliminate shortcomings that are disclosed.

Art.23. The Creation of the Enterprise and Termination of Its Activity

1. Enterprises are created according to the procedure established by the USSR Council of Ministers.

The reorganization (merger, annexation, division, detachment, transformation) of enterprises and the termination of their activity are [is] effected, according to established procedure, by decision of the agency that is empowered to create the enterprise in question.

The enterprise's activity may be terminated:

—if there is no need for its further operation and it cannot be reorganized, or for other reasons stipulated by legislation;

—when an enterprise has operated at a loss for a long time and is insolvent, when there is no demand for its output, and in the event that measures taken by the enterprise and the higher-level agency to ensure the profitability of operations [in conditions of full economic accountability and self-financing] have brought no results.

2. When an enterprise is reorganized or liquidated, the higher-level agency guarantees the rights of the dismissed employees as established by the USSR Constitution and legislation. Employees receive personal warnings of the date of dismissal no later than two months before the reorganization or liquidation of the enterprise. They retain their average wages and uninterrupted work records during the job-placement period, but for no more than three months.

The agency that has made the decision to reorganize or liquidate the enterprise and the local Soviet provide every possible assistance in the job placement of the dismissed employees. Citizens' claims and suits against the enterprise that is being liquidated may be brought against the higher-level agency.

Employees for whom jobs cannot be found in accordance with their occupations, specialties or skills are hired for new jobs on condition that they complete retraining within the time period stipulated when the labor contract was concluded.

3. The enterprise has a charter setting the goals of its activity, which is confirmed by the higher-level agency. As of the day that the charter is confirmed, the enterprise becomes a juristic person and enjoys the rights and performs the duties associated with its activity.

The enterprise has a seal bearing its name and a depiction of the USSR State Emblem or the Union-Republic emblem (depending on the enterprise's subordination).

Art.24. On Guarantees of the Observance of the Rights of Enterprises (Associations)
Agencies of state power and administration are responsible for the observance of the provisions of the USSR Law on State Enterprise (Association), given the adoption of normative documents pertaining to the practical implementation of this law, and they build their relations with enterprises and associations in strict accordance with the aforementioned law.

Art.25. Special Features of the Application of This Law
Special features of the application of this law in certain types of enterprise are determined by the USSR Council of Ministers.

A. **Gromyko**
Chairman of the Presidium
USSR Supreme Soviet
T. **Menteshashvaili**
Secretary of the Presidium
The Kremlin, Moscow, June 30, 1987

Law of the USSR on the Nationwide Discussion of Important Questions of State Life
(1 Jul 87)
The further deepening of socialist democracy and the development of the people's self-government presupposes the expansion, for every citizen of the USSR, of real possibilities of exercising his or her constitutional right to participation in the management of state and public affairs and in the discussion of draft laws and decisions of national and local significance, as well as of major questions of public life submitted for discussion by public organizations in accordance with their statutory tasks.

This law is designed to facilitate the development of citizens' participation in working out decisions on important questions of state and public life on the basis of broad openness and the comparison and consideration of various opinions and proposals of the working people.

I. GENERAL PROVISIONS

Art. 1. Nationwide Discussion of the Most Important Questions of State Life
In accordance with the USSR Constitution, the most important questions of state life are to be submitted for nationwide discussion.

Draft laws and other highly important questions of state life are submitted for nationwide discussion by the USSR Supreme Soviet or the Presidium of the USSR Supreme Soviet.

Art. 2. Discussion of Important Questions of the State Life of the Union Republics
In a Union Republic, draft laws and other important questions of the state life of the Union Republic may be submitted for public discussion.

Draft laws and other important questions are submitted for public discussion by the Union-Republic Supreme Soviet or the Presidium of the Union-Republic Supreme Soviet.

Art. 3. Discussion of Important Questions of the State Life of Autonomous Republics
In an Autonomous Republic, draft laws and other important questions of the state life of the Autonomous Republic may be submitted for public discussion.

Draft laws and other important questions are submitted for public discussion by the Autonomous-Republic Supreme Soviet or the Presidium of the Autonomous-Republic Supreme Soviet.

Art. 4. Discussion of Questions of Local Significance by the Population
Decisions on important questions of local significance that affect the interests of the population residing in the area in question are adopted by the Soviets of People's Deputies and their executive committees after preliminary discussion of these questions by the population.

Questions of local significance are submitted for discussion by the population by the Soviets of People's Deputies or their executive committees.

Art. 5. USSR, Union-Republic and Autonomous-Republic Legislation on the Discussion of Important Questions of State Life

The procedures for nationwide discussion of the most important questions of state life are defined by this law.

The procedures for public discussion of important questions of the state life of the Union and Autonomous Republics, as well as for the discussion of the population of questions of local significance, are defined by Union- and Autonomous-Republic laws based on this law.

Art. 6. The Participation of USSR Citizens in Discussions

USSR citizens are guaranteed free participation in the discussion of important questions of state and public life.

In the discussion of questions of all-Union, republic and local significance, USSR citizens have the right to participate directly, as well as through public organizations, labor collectives, meetings at places of residence, voluntary initiative agencies, meetings of servicemen in military units, and the mass news media.

Any direct or indirect restrictions on the rights of USSR citizens to participate in discussions on the basis of parentage, social or property status, race or nationality, sex, education, language, attitude toward religion, time of residence in a given locality or kind and nature of occupation are prohibited.

Art. 7. Participation by Public Organizations and Labor Collectives in the Preparation and Holding of Discussions

Organizations of the Communist Party of the Soviet Union, trade unions, the All-Union Lenin Young Communist League, cooperatives, women's and war and labor veterans' organizations and other public organizations and labor collectives participate in the preparation and holding of discussions of important questions of state and public life.

Art. 8. Ensuring the Holding of Discussions

The holding of discussions of important questions of all-Union, republic and local significance is ensured by the Soviets of People's Deputies.

Art. 9. Openness in the Holding of Discussions

Discussions are held on the basis of broad openness. Draft laws and other important questions of state life submitted for discussion are published in the press, publicized on television and radio, and brought to the attention of the population by other means.

The mass news media give comprehensive coverage to the progress of discussions, publish proposals and critical comments made by citizens, state agencies, public organizations and labor collectives, as well as surveys of proposals and critical comments that have been received, and inform the public of the results of discussions.

Art. 10. Expenditures Related to Discussions

Expenditures related to the discussion of draft laws and other important questions of state life, as well as to the discussion by the population of draft decisions of local Soviets of Peoples' Deputies and their executive committees, are paid by the state.

Art. 11. Liability for Violating the Legislation on Discussions

Officials of state and public agencies who commit violations of this law, as well as individuals who hinder USSR citizens in the free exercise of their right to participate in discussion, incur liability as established by law.

II. PROCEDURES FOR NATIONWIDE DISCUSSION

Art. 12. Submitting Questions for Nationwide on Discussion

Draft laws and decisions affecting the basic areas of the country's political, economic and social development and the exercise of the Soviet citizen's constitutional rights, liberties and duties, as well as other highly important questions of state life coming within the jurisdiction of the USSR, are submitted for nationwide discussion.

Draft laws and other questions are submitted for nationwide discussion by a decision of the USSR Supreme Soviet or the Presidium of the USSR Supreme Soviet, adopted at their initiative or on a proposal by a Union Republic. Recommendations on the advisability of submitting a draft law or other question for nationwide discussion may be made by standing committees of the Council of the Union or the Council of Nationalities, the USSR Council of Ministers, all-Union agencies of public organizations or other agencies and individuals who, in accordance with the law, submit a draft law or other question to the USSR Supreme Soviet or its Presidium.

Draft laws and materials on other questions are published in the newspaper *Izvestiia*, other central newspapers, in the republic press and, when necessary, in the local press no later than 10 days after the decision is adopted to submit them for nationwide discussion. They may also be published in specialized periodicals.

At the same time that a question is submitted for nationwide discussion, the USSR Supreme Soviet or its Presidium establishes the time schedule and the procedures for organizing work to examine proposals and critical comments received during the nationwide discussion, and it entrusts the implementation of this work to the appropriate standing committees of the USSR Supreme Soviet's Council of the Union and Council of Nationalities or sets up a special commission for this purpose.

Art. 13. Organizing the Discussion of Draft Laws and Other Questions. Summarizing Proposals and Critical Comments

Union, Republic and local Soviet and other state agencies and executives of enterprises, institutions and organizations, in conjunction with public organizations, ensure the broad discussion of draft laws and other questions and create the necessary conditions for this.

Citizens may send proposals and critical comments on draft laws and other questions submitted for nationwide discussion directly to the Presidium of the USSR Supreme Soviet or to the Presidiums of Union- or Autonomous- Republic Supreme Soviets, local Soviet executive committees or other state and public agencies.

Draft laws and other questions submitted for nationwide discussion may be discussed at sessions of Soviets of Peoples' Deputies or at meetings of their agencies and Deputies' groups, at meetings of public organizations, labor collectives and citizens at their places of residence, by voluntary initiative agencies, at meetings of servicemen in military units, in the press and on television and radio.

Proposals and critical comments received during a nationwide discussion are summarized, as appropriate, by the Presidiums of Union- and Autonomous- Republic Supreme Soviets, executive committees of local Soviets of People's Deputies, other state and public agencies, and the mass news media. In order to summarize proposals and critical comments that have been received, the indicated agencies may form commissions and working groups. Proposals and critical comments, in generalized form, are sent to the Presidium of the USSR Supreme Soviet.

Art. 14. Summing Up the Results of Nationwide Discussions

Proposals and critical comments received by the Presidium of the USSR Supreme Soviet from citizens, labor collectives and state and public agencies concerning a draft law or other question are examined and taken into consideration during the final work on the draft by the appropriate standing committees of the chambers of the USSR Supreme Soviet or by the special commission or agency that has submitted a question to the USSR Supreme Soviet or its Presidium. For the preliminary examination of proposals and critical comments, they may form preparatory commissions and working groups made up of People's Deputies, appropriate specialists, scientific and cultural figures and representatives of state and public agencies and scientific institutions.

The mass news media provide regular information to the population about proposals and critical comments that have been received and about progress in examining them, and organize the explanation of the provisions of a draft law or other question.

The results of the nationwide discussion of a draft law or other question are examined, as appropriate, by the USSR Supreme Soviet or the Presidium of the USSR Supreme Soviet, and the population is informed of the examination.

Proposals and critical comments not related to the subject of a draft law or other question that is under discussion are directed through the proper channels to the appropriate state and public agencies, which examine them according to established procedure.

III. DISCUSSION BY THE POPULATION OF IMPORTANT QUESTIONS OF LOCAL SIGNIFI-CANCE

Art. 15. Submitting Draft Decisions and Other Questions for Discussion by the Population

Draft decisions of local Soviets of People's Deputies and their executive committees concerning plans for comprehensive economic and social development and the budget, the ensuring of socialist legality, the safeguarding of law and order and the rights of citizens, the work of enterprises, institutions and organizations involving service to the population and other important questions of state, economic, social and cultural construction at the local level are submitted for discussion by the population.

Draft decisions of local Soviets and their executive committees and other important questions are submitted for discussion by the population by the local Soviet or its executive committee at their initiative and also on the basis of proposals by the standing committees of Soviets, Deputies' groups and Deputies, agencies of public organizations, labor collectives, meetings of citizens at their places of residence, and other agencies and organizations stipulated by Union- and autonomous-republic legislation.

Draft decisions of local Soviets and their executive committees are published in the local press or brought to the attention of the population by other means.

Art. 16. The Examination of Questions Submitted for Discussion by the Population

Questions submitted for discussion by the population may be given preliminary examination at sessions of lower-level Soviets of People's Deputies, at meetings of their executive and administrative agencies, standing committees and Deputies' groups, at meetings of public organizations and labor collectives, at citizens' meetings at places of residence and at meetings of voluntary initiative agencies, and they are discussed in the local press and on television and on radio.

Proposals and critical comments from agencies, organizations and citizens are sent to the executive committee of the appropriate Soviet and are taken into consideration during final work on draft decisions, as well as in practical activity. Proposals and critical comments that because of their content fall into the jurisdiction of higher-level state agencies are sent to them for examination.

The results of a discussion are reported by the executive committee at a session of the Soviet of People's Deputies and are brought to the attention of the population.

A. Gromyko
Chairman of the Presidium
USSR Supreme Soviet
T. Menteshashvili
Secretary of the Presidium

"Zakon SSSR. 'O vsenarodnom obsuzhdenii vazhnykh voprosov gosudarstvennoi zhizni'," *Pravda* and *Izvestiia* (1 Jul); full translations also can be found in FBIS (1 Jul 87) R38 and CDSP, 39:28 (1987), 13-14. On this and the following law on appealing the actions of officials, see another Soviet perspective in L. Sobolev, *Fighting Bureaucracy, an Internal Enemy. Perestroika. What's New in Legislation*. Moscow: Novosti, 1987.

Law of the USSR on Procedures for Appealing to the Courts Unlawful Actions by Officials that Infringe Upon the Rights of Citizens (3 Jul 87)

USSR citizens possess the full range of social, economic, political and personal rights and liberties proclaimed in and guaranteed by the USSR Constitution and Soviet laws. Respect for the individual and safeguarding the rights and liberties of citizens are the duty of all state agencies, public organizations and officials.

USSR and Union-republic legislation stipulates the right of citizens to appeal to the courts for protection of their personal, property, family, labor, housing and other rights and liberties.

This law defines the procedures for appealing to the courts unlawful actions by officials that infringe the rights of citizens.

Art.1 The Right to Take Complaints to Court

A citizen has the right to take a complaint to court if he believes that an official's actions have infringed his rights.

Actions carried out individually by officials on their own account or on behalf of the agency they represent can be appealed to the courts.

Art.2 Actions by Officials That Are Subject to Judicial Appeal

Actions by officials, committed in violation of the law or exceeding their authority, that infringe the rights of citizens are actions as a result of which:

—a citizen is illegally deprived of the opportunity to fully or partially exercise a right granted to him by a law or other normative act; or some duty is illegally placed on a citizen.

Art.3 The Limits of the Effect of This Law

Actions by officials with respect to which criminal-procedure and civil-procedure legislation or legislation on procedures for examining labor disputes, on discoveries, inventions and rationalization proposals, on administrative-law violations, on individual enterprise and other USSR and Union-republic legislation provide for different appeal procedures, as well as actions related to ensuring the country's defense capability and state security, cannot be appealed to the courts in accordance with this law.

Art.4 Submitting Complaints

A complaint may be submitted to a court only after the citizen has taken his complaint against an official's action to the appropriate higher-level official or agency.

A complaint against an official's action may be submitted to a court by a citizen or by his representative, as well as by, at the citizen's request, a properly authorized representative of a public organization or labor collective.

A complaint against an official's action is submitted to the district (city) people's court having jurisdiction in the place of work of the official whose actions are the subject of the complaint.

Art.5 Time Periods for Taking Complaints to the Courts

A complaint may be submitted to a court within one month of the day on which a citizen receives a refusal to satisfy his complaint from an appropriate higher-level official or agency or of the day on which the time period established by law for examining the complaint expires.

If someone fails to submit a complaint within the established time period and has a valid reason for not having done so, the time period may be reinstated by a court.

A ruling by a judge refusing to accept a complaint may be appealed to a higher-level court within 10 days after the ruling of refusal is made.

Art.6 The Examination of Complaints

The court examines a complaint and the court's decision is executed in accordance with the rules of civil procedure, with the exceptions and amendments established by this law and other USSR and Union-republic legislative acts.

A complaint is examined by a court within a 10-day period; in open session, as a rule; and with the participation of the citizen who submitted the complaint and the official whose actions are the subject of the complaint.

If the citizen or the official whose actions are the subject of the complaint cannot appear in court and has a valid reason for not doing so, the case can be heard with the participation of a representative of the citizen who submitted the complaint or a representative of the official.

Failure to appear at a court hearing without valid reason on the part of the citizen who submitted the complaint or of the official whose actions are the subject of the complaint or of their representatives is not an obstacle to the examination of the complaint; however, the court may deem an appearance of the citizen who submitted the complaint or of the official whose actions are the subject of the complaint to be mandatory.

Representatives of public organizations and labor collectives, as well as officials of the appropriate higher-level agencies or their representatives, may participate in the court hearing.

The court must study the materials presented by the appropriate higher-level officials or agencies that have deemed the official's actions that are the subject of the complaint to be legal, and it also may hear explanations from other persons and study relevant documents and other evidence.

Art.7 Court Decisions on Complaints

The court renders a decision based on the results of its examination of the complaint.

If the court deems the official's actions that are the subject of the complaint to be unlawful, it renders a decision that the complaint is valid and that the official in question must remove the violation of the citizen's rights.

If the court establishes that the actions that are the subject of the complaint were taken in accordance with the law and were within the bounds of the official's powers and that the citizen's rights were not infringed, the court renders a decision refusing to satisfy the complaint.

The court's decision on the complaint is forwarded to the official whose actions were the subject of the complaint or to the appropriate higher-level agency or official for removal of the violations of the law or other normative acts.

The court and the citizen are notified of the measures taken to execute the court's decision on the complaint no later than one month from the time the court's decision was handed down. If the decision has not been executed, the court takes the measures stipulated by existing legislation.

Art.8 The Court's Supplementary Rulings

If, during its examination of a complaint, a court comes to the conclusion that the established procedure for examining citizens' proposals, requests and complaints was violated, or that red tape, suppression of criticism and persecution for criticism, or other violations of legality, occurred, the court issues a supplementary ruling and sends it to the appropriate higher-level official or agency. The indicated official or agency must report to the court within one month on the measures it has taken with respect to the supplementary ruling.

If, during its examination of a complaint, a court discovers indications of a crime in the actions of an official or other person, it reports this to the prosecutor or institutes criminal proceedings.

Art.9 Protesting Court Decisions

A court's decision on a complaint is not subject to appeal, but it can be protested by way of prosecutor's supervision.

The lodging of a protest suspends the execution of the decision.

Art.10 The Liability of Citizens for Submitting Complaints to the Courts for Slanderous Purposes

The submission by a citizen of a complaint to a court for slanderous purposes entails liability in accordance with existing legislation.

Art.11 Exemption from State Fees

Citizens' complaints against officials' actions that are submitted to courts are not subject to a state fee.

Art.12 The Assessment of Costs Related to the Examination of Complaints

Costs related to the examination of a complaint may be charged by the court to the citizen, if the court renders a decision refusing to satisfy his complaint, or to the official, if it is established that his actions were illegal.

A. **Gromyko**
Chairman of the Presidium
USSR Supreme Soviet
T. **Menteshashvili**
Secretary of the Presidium
The Kremlin, Moscow, June 30, 1987

"Zakon SSSR. 'O poriadke obzhalovaniia v sud nepravomernykh deistvii dolzhnostnykh lits, ushchemliai-ushchikh prava grazhdan'," *Pravda* and *Izvestiia* (2 Jul); full translations also can be found in FBIS (2 Jul), R7, and CDSP, 39:29 (1987), 12-13.

Regulations for Travel to Socialist Countries (30 Jul 87)

In order to give immediate consideration to matters concerned with the implementation of bilateral and multilateral cooperation with socialist countries, the rules for travel by Soviet citizens to socialist countries have been simplified, and cooperation with those countries is being improved in the sphere of local ties.

Under the new rules, USSR and Union- and Autonomous-Republic ministries and departments, the central and republic agencies of public organizations, and executives of enterprises and associations, of scientific, cultural, educational and public-health institutions, of institutions of higher learning and secondary schools, and of the news media and creative unions, and also Party, Soviet, trade union, Komsomol and other public organizations that have ties with foreign partners in the countries of socialism will, on their own authority, send delegations and individual members to all the socialist countries for a period of up to one year. Trips by members of the CPSU are to be cleared with the Party committee. those by members of the Komsomol—with the Komsomol committee, and those by members of trade union—with the trade union committee.

Executives of associations, enterprises, institutions and organizations involved in cooperative ventures with partners in the socialist countries are permitted to travel on short official trips to those countries with the verbal approval of top officials of the appropriate ministries, departments or other central institutions.

Plans or quotas for inter-party, parliamentary (Union-republic level), economic, scientific and technical, ideological, cultural and sports ties, or for cooperation in the sphere of public organizations and tourist exchanges, are justification for travel to socialist countries. Agreements and contracts concluded between enterprises and organizations of the USSR and their partners in socialist countries are also valid reasons for such travel.

Now, local Party bodies will autonomously settle issues of cooperation in the area of local friendly ties and will also, where necessary, establish official contacts with partners outside the framework of existing ties.

The State Foreign Economic Commission of the USSR Council of Ministers has been advised to take up questions having to do with arranging for direct barter between friendly regions of the USSR and fraternal countries.

The new regulations provide that, when necessary for production purposes, Soviet specialists who have been sent to one of the socialist countries may travel to other socialist countries with the permission of the executive of the Soviet agencies that sent them in the first place.

Union-Republic Ministries of Foreign Affairs, Autonomous-Republic Ministries of Internal Affairs, and internal affairs administrations of territory, province and city Soviet executive committees will, on the basis of declarations from executives of ministries, departments, associations, enterprises, institutions and organizations located in their territory, issue official-business passports to people being sent on business to the socialist countries.

Travel documents for tourists travelling to socialist countries are to be issued in the same manner as that stipulated for travel by Soviet delegations and individual executives.

It is intended that the responsibility for arranging, and for the results of, official travel to the socialist countries be borne by executives of associations, enterprises, institutions and organizations, and by secretaries of Party organizations, chairmen of trade-union organizations, and secretaries of Komsomol organizations.

"Novyi poriadok vyezda v sotsstrany," *Pravda* (30 Jul); a full text can also be found in CDSP, 39:30 (1987), 17-18.

On the State Plan for Economic and Social Development of the USSR in 1988 (21 Oct 87)

The Supreme Soviet of the Union of Soviet Socialist Republics resolves

Art.1 To ratify the State Plan for the Economic and Social Development of the USSR in 1988 as submitted by the USSR Council of Ministers, taking into consideration the amendments proposed by the Planning and Budget Committees, the Industry Committees, the Power Engineering Committees, the Transportation and Communications Committees, the Construction and Building Materials Committees, the Agro-Industrial Complex Committees, the Science and Technology Committees, the Consumer Goods and Services Committees, the Housing and Municipal Services Committees, the Foreign Affairs Committees, the Public Health and Social Security Committees, the Public Education and Culture Committees, the Committees on Questions of Women's Working and Living Conditions and the Protection of Mother and Child, the Youth Affairs Committees and the Committees on Environmental Protection and the Rational Utilization of Natural Resources of the Council of the Union and the Council of Nationalities.

Art.2 To establish the following basic indices for the State Plan for the Economic and Social Development of the USSR in 1988:

	percent increase over 1987 plan		percent increase over 1987 plan
National income produced	4.3	Profits from the economic activity state enterprises (associations) and organizations	7.9
Real income per capita	2.7		
Public consumption funds	6.5		
Labor productivity:		Retail trade turnover of state and cooperative trade—total	2.6
in industry	4.5		
in construction	4.	Sales volume of paid services to the population	11.9
in rail transport	7.5	Capital investment in the national economy from all sources of financing	3.6

In carrying out the strong social policy worked out by the 27th CPSU Congress, to ensure the centralized implementation of measures to raise the people's living standard:

—to continue the process of a phased increase in the public health and social security personnel;

—to begin the introduction of new salaries and wage rates for personnel in the cultural branches;

—to introduce regional wage differentials for workers and office employees for whom they have not yet been established in the northern districts of Kirov Province and in nonproduction branches in the northern and eastern regions of the Kazakh Republic.

—to increase the norms for spending money on the feeding of patients and the acquisition of medicines and bedding in public health institutions;

—to introduce the free dispensing of medications for the outpatient treatment of children up to three years of age and of persons suffering from bronchial asthma, as well as the cut-rate dispensing of medications, with patients paying 50% of the cost, to persons who are Group I or Group II invalids as a result of job-related mutilations or occupational or general illnesses;

—to increase, for children's homes and boarding schools of all types, the norms for spending money on the acquisition of housekeeping equipment and on the provision of amenities.

To channel 1.4 billion rubles from the USSR State Budget into the implementation of centralized measures begun in 1987, as well as new measures, to improve the people's living standard.

To continue the repayment of state internal loans.

On the basis of the broad use of the opportunities created by the new conditions of economic management, to carry out a further increase in the base wage and salary rates of personnel
in the production branches of the national economy, using money earned by enterprises.

To ensure the priority allocation of money and resources to solving the housing problem
and improving the health of Soviet people, raising their educational and cultural level and
satisfying their spiritual requirements.

With a view to developing the material and technical base of the social sphere, to
commission in 1988, through all sources of financing, residential buildings with a total floor
space of 128.9 million square meters, preschool institutions with room for 966,000 children,
children's homes accommodating 9,100 youngsters, general-education schools with room for
1,668,500 pupils, boarding schools for orphans and children left without parental care with
space for 4,000 youngsters, hospitals with 77,800 beds, and outpatient polyclinics able to
handle 197,900 visits per shift.

Art. 3 Guided by the directives of the January and June (1987) plenums of the CPSU CC,
the Basic Provisions for the Fundamental Restructuring of Economic Management that were
confirmed by the June plenum, the decisions of the seventh session of the 11th USSR Supreme
Soviet and the USSR Law on the State Enterprise (Association), the USSR Council of Ministers,
the Union-Republic Council of Ministers and USSR ministries, state committees and departments are to ensure, during the implementation of the State Plan for the Economic and Social
Development of the USSR in 1988, the unswerving fulfillment of the Party's economic strategy,
the intensification and increased efficiency of social production, and the consistent, step-by-
step creation of an integral, efficient and flexible system of economic management, based
above all on the principles of full economic accountability, unsubsidized operations and self-
financing and the strengthening of democratic principles in the activity of labor collectives and
of their responsibility for the achievement of high final results in production and social
development.

To ensure constant monitoring over the fulfillment of the USSR Law on the State Enterprise
(Association) and strict observance of the rights granted to enterprises. To strengthen in every
way democratic principles in managing the processes of the economic and social development
of society. To create real prerequisites for the realization of the personal stake of all working
people in improving the efficiency of production, and to actively introduce the collective contract
and other progressive forms of the organization of labor and incentives. To develop economic
rivalry between enterprises as a new form of socialist competition.

To concentrate the efforts of labor collectives on accomplishing the tasks of accelerating
scientific and technical progress, ensuring the integration of science and production, and introducing into the national economy equipment and technologies that meet present-day demands
for the development of society. To actively pursue a line aimed at resource conservation and
the all-out economizing of raw and other materials, fuel, power, agricultural output and all
natural resources.

Art. 4 The Soviets, guided by the directives of the 27th CPSU Congress and the June (1987)
plenum of the CPSU CC with respect to the restructuring of territorial administration in the new
conditions of economic management, are to improve the efficiency of the management of
development in their areas. To make wider use of the rights they have been granted for the
comprehensive accomplishment of economic, social and environmental-protection tasks, for
bringing into play all reserves for accelerating social and economic development, for expanding
the construction of housing and social and cultural facilities and, taking public demand into
account, for expanding the production of manufactured consumer goods and food and the
volume of paid services provided by enterprises and organizations located in areas under their
jurisdiction. To promote in every way the development of cooperative forms and citizens'
individual enterprise.

Art. 5 To instruct the USSR Council of Ministers to examine the proposals and comments set
forth in the conclusions of the Planning and Budget Committees and other standing committees
of the Council of the Union and the Council of Nationalities on the State Plan for the Economic

and Social Development of the USSR in 1988, as well as the proposal and comments made by Deputies at the meetings of the chambers of the USSR Supreme Soviet, and to adopt the appropriate decisions.

A. **Gromyko**
Chairman of the Presidium
USSR Supreme Soviet
T. **Menteshashvili**
Secretary of the Presidium
The Kremlin, Moscow, Oct 20, 1987

"Zakon SSSR. 'O gosudarstvennom plane ekonomicheskogo i sotsial'nogo razvitiia SSSR na 1988 god'," *Pravda* and *Izvestiia* (21 Oct); a full translation can be found in FBIS (21 Oct 87), 46-47; and CDSP, 39:47 (1987), 15-16.

Chapter 4

PERESTROIKA

Perestroika—restructuring—is what the Gorbachev "reforms" are all about. Gorbachev describes the term himself in his 1987 book (which has the subtitle "New Thinking for our Country and the World") as a means by which "the potential of socialism" can be better utilized. On the other hand, many Western observers see perestroika as a desparate gamble with which to repair a crisis in socialism. The reality lies somewhere in between, as the following materials suggest.

The documents contained in the following several sections have been chosen to represent the multi-faceted nature of restructuring in the Soviet Union. The perestroika process began with attempts to find means for the acceleration (*uskorenie*) of the national economic and social progress. By the end of 1987 a widely-disseminated textbook on the mechanism of acceleration was already in its second edition (*Strategiia uskoreniia. Uchebnoe posobie* (Moscow: Politlit, 1987), 288 pp.). The Gorbachev agenda—first outlined to the CPSU CC Plenum of 11 March 1985 when he called for "the acceleration of the social-economic development of the country," (*Pravda* 12 Mar 87)—was in full swing.

The CPSU also is in the throes of renewal, signals for which include old-style exhortations about dedication alongside calls for inner-Party debate, secret ballots, and limited terms of office. Glasnost has brought to public forums issues which traditionally were deemed to be CPSU monopolies; among them, nationality issues, cultural/historical taboos, and economic planning. "Democratization" also implies a greater role of the masses in what has always been regarded as Party affairs; for example, trade union elections, enterprise and collective farm management. There are further plans for juridical reform, a reorganization of mental and health care services, and a drastic reexamination of the school system. All these trends are both shaped by and are reflected in perestroika.

At the year's end, a "new stage" of perestroika was summarized in a CPSU CC report as "democratization of the entire social life and a radical economic reform." Gorbachev emphasized in that report that the role of the CPSU was important during the first stage of perestroika, but that it had been only on an "impromptu" basis. Now, he said, the Party should provide long-term planning; its members should show the way in deeds rather than merely direct the process. The long report ended with the admonition: "In short, comrades, concrete deeds come to the fore now. The emphasis in our activity is shifted toward constructive work for organizational, ideological, political, and moral assurance of the tasks of the second, decisive stage of perestroika" (*Pravda*, 21 Nov 87).

For general reading on perestroika, aside from items in the Bibliography (below), see the works of Abel G.Aganbegyan, an Armenian economist from the Novosibirsk SSR Academy whom Gorbachev brought to Moscow to bring dynamism into state planning; and Tatyana Zaslavskaia, president of the Soviet Sociological Association. Both have appeared in English in *Moscow News* (See, e.g., "The Restructuring is for Us," No.9 [1 Mar 87]), and both have been interviewed by the Western media. See also Russian language pieces in *Pravda* (16 Feb), *Sovetskaia Rossiia* (24 Mar), and *Literaturnaia gazeta* (18 Feb). For a sweeping overview, see T.McNeill, "Gorbachev's First Three Years in Power. Reform and Its Prospects," RFE/RL. RL75/88 (29 Feb 88).

THE PARTY

In his January 1987 speech on restructuring and the Party's personnel (cadre) policy Gorbachev urged CPSU cadres to take the initiative and justify their claim to be at the vanguard of Soviet society. Party activists were told to lead the way towards the fruition of perestroika by means of action—not speeches. Editorials in *Pravda* were very criticial of CPSU members who violated "moral and legal norms," suppressed criticism, and called useless meetings (e.g., *Pravda* 3,5,6,7,12 Jan). The Party was told regularly to take special care in helping to select enterprise managers and collective farm directors who understood both the new economic methods and the demands that were being placed on them (e.g., *Pravda* 22 Jan; 14 Feb; 7 Mar).

Gorbachev made dramatic changes himself in the all important personnel of the CC *apparat*. By the end of 1987 he had changed 19 of the 24 CC heads of departments and more than half of the first deputies of the departments of the CPSU CC. Furthermore, CC voting membership was reduced from 319 to 307, and candidate membership was increased from 151 to 170, with nearly 70 percent of the candidates being newly elected. Thus the changeover in the CC echoed the dramatic changes in the Politburo which have been mentioned in Chapter 2. On this, see, A.Rahr, "The Apparatus of the CC of the CPSU," RFE/RL, RL136/87 (10 Apr 1987); Dawn Mann, "The Organizational Party Work Department," *ibid*, RL 402/87 (15 Oct 1987); Rahr, "Turnover in the Central Party Apparatus." *ibid*, RL 256/87 (9 Jul 1987); and Rolf H.W.Theen, "The Reorganization of the Central Committee Apparatus under Gorbachev." Unpublished paper. Canadian Association of Slavists (8 July 1988). The following documents give a clear indication of the continued importance to Gorbachev of the message he delivered to the Party in January, and of the variety of ways in which the CPSU hoped to fulfill his requirements.

George Smirnov. **Questions of Theory. The Revolutionary Essence of Reorganization** (13 Mar 87).

Turning points occur in history when new major problems are becoming urgent, when there is a special need to understand them not only for political leaders but also for the broad masses. Karl **Marx** had in mind precisely such moments when he said that ideas became a material force as soon as they took hold of the masses. Today one of the most popular and widespread concepts is "a new mode of thinking." These words reflect the turning point of our time, the need for speeding up socio-economic progress, to strive to attain a qualitatively new level of the socialist development of current society.

The most difficult aspect of the current situation is, perhaps, to realize the dramatic question: how could it happen that having carried out the greatest revolution which has drastically changed the course of developments in the country and the world, having created a vast economic, scientific, technical and intellectual potential and having experienced the glory of momentous accomplishments, we have today to engage in criticism and self-criticism in such a decisive form? Why does the way Soviet people lived and worked until now no longer suit them?

To answer these questions we must reveal the essence of concrete socio-economic and political phenomena, relations between people and the motives behind their behavior.

At the January (1987) Plenum of the CPSU CC a principled step was taken in analyzing the historic period that preceded the April (1985) Plenum of the CC. It was bluntly pointed out that the CPSU CC and the country's leadership, owing above all to subjective reasons, failed to assess in good time and fully the need for changes, the danger of growing crisis phenomena in our society and to work out an efficient policy to overcome them and to fully utilize the possibilities inherent in the socialist system.

As if spellbound we looked at the centralized forms and methods of management and planning which took shape in the 1930s and were partly improved later, accepting them at every step as the only correct ones and the fullest expression of the essential descriptions of the socialist system.

It may be recalled that the need for a proper correlation of centralism and local initiative were a matter of permanent concern for **Lenin**. Alas, this concern was not given due attention. We lost a great deal by withdrawing hundreds of thousands of work collectives, millions of specialists and workers from resourceful economic activity, having deprived the enterprises of their cost-accounting rights. The attempts to somehow change the economic machinery proved rather weak and inconsistent and, therefore, produced no results.

It was even more complicated with the implementation of the principle: "From each according to his ability, to each according to his work." It is generally known that the policy of bringing the standard of wages closer was proclaimed. The idea in itself is fair. But in the process of its implementation we actually reduced the level of remuneration of skilled labor, especially that of engineers, physicians and teachers. Wage levelling tendencies led to a drop of material interest in productive and high-quality labor. A host of negative consequences was engendered by prejudice against the role of commodity-money relations and the functioning of the law of value.

Finally, embezzlement, bribery, profiteering, the practice of receiving unearned incomes became deep-rooted on a rather large scale in an atmosphere of complacency and all-permisssiveness because of weaker control over the measure of labor and consumption. And this gave rise to relapses of the petty-bourgeois way of life and the petty-bourgeois mentality.

These materialized components of the braking mechanism of the soci-economic development are not inherent, as objective necessity, in the socialist economic system. The roots of this braking, as it was stressed at the January Plenum of the CC, lie in the serious shortcomings of the operation of socialist democracy, in obsolete political and theoretical maxims.

One should think that it would be more correct to say that such a policy of the former leadership had also a political motive. The point is that the measures carried out by the Party leadership after the October (1964) Plenum of the CC [It was at this Plenum of the CPSU CC that Nikita **Khrushchev** was formally relieved of his position as First Secretary of the CPSU and member of Politburo, and replaced by **Brezhnev**.] were actually directed against the democratization of the Party and state machinery, carried out until then, although not as a system and purposefully. For example, some standards of democracy, introduced into the Party Rules, have been revised. Gravitation towards stable, earlier checked, above all centralized, forms of management emerged. There was a fear of searches, a reluctance to change the existing state of affairs and so on.

This is, in short, the social nature of the braking mechanism which formed in Soviet society and influenced the origin of stagnation phenomena in its development. Speaking philosophically, the gnosiological roots lay in absolutizing centralism, and social roots in the lack of faith in the creative abilities of the people and in a watchful attitude towards democratic methods.

As to its social nature and political orientation, socialist democracy is the highest achievement in history. But from the viewpoint of the maturity of its institutions, its forms and methods, serious shortcomings arose, which paralyze people's activity and the Party's creative forces. Formalism during election campaigns, underestimation of openness, shortcomings in control, especially "from below" and so on proved to be the main cause of unresponsive masses and miscalculations in management, poor effectiveness of the decisions taken, irresoluteness and sluggishness in carrying out the policy taking shape.

Disposing of vast opportunities and operating practically in all collectives, many Primary Party Organizations failed to hold out on principled positions. Far from all of them fought resolutely against negative phenomena, all permissiveness, mutual guarantees, weaker discipline, the spreading of drunkenness and alcoholism. A rebuff was not always given to narrow departmental outlook and parochialism, and to manifestations of nationalism. All these negative processes could not but tell on the people's mood and morality. Such values of socialist society as ideological conviction, labor enthusiasm and Soviet patriotism were depreciated. It gave rise to callousness and scepticism. A section of people appeared among the youth as well, for whom profit became the main motive of life.

The questions begs itself: how could the dominating influence of socialist ideology, standards and principles of socialist mentality be preserved with such an outbreak of negative phenomena? The thing is that socialist traditions and ideas were inherent and deep-rooted in the people and the Party and, therefore, negative manifestations did not undermine the foundations of socialist mentality and socialist values. At the same time, the institutions of socialist democracy in the established form were not able to oppose negative phenomena effectively .

The question of stimulating broad masses of workers to run state affairs was not put at one time as a practical task, was not tied up with the solution of urgent economic, social and other problems. Meanwhile, as we know very well, **Lenin** could not think of socialism without it. He repeatedly spoke of the need for the *general* participation of the working people in running public affairs, and in that period regarded the lack of knowledge and the low socio-political and cultural level of the working people as an obstacle to solving this task, since an illiterate person is out of politics.

At present the society's need for the general participation of the masses in running social affairs is becoming increasingly vital. There is an economic basis to underpin this process. The transition of enterprises to new conditions of economic management, introduction of self-repayment and self-financing increases the responsibility of the working people, collectives and their heads for the results of management by many times. Under these conditions a work collective must be vested with rights and finances to run the economy independently. Not only the fulfilment of state plans, but also the material well-being of the collectives, and the satisfaction of people's cultural and everyday needs. depends on the abilities of a leader, his competence and initiative. Naturally, the democratic way of choosing leaders will substantially influence their conduct, the effectiveness of their activity, the level of organizational and political work among the personnel.

In the new situation the aggregate owner—the people—are becoming through the work collective the actual masters of public property, they are receiving real rights and opportunities to dispose of this property in the interests of society and the work collective at each concrete sector. A fundamentally new economic, social and political atmosphere is being created, in which relations between those who lead and those who are led are being built on profoundly democratic principles.

The outlined measures on expanding the social base of Soviet democracy will function on the same principles. To achieve this openness, criticism and self-criticism must be not just a moral or even a political but also a juridical standard, and must be supported by appropriate legislation. A major contribution to this will be made by the adoption of the Law on State Enterprise (Association), the provision of its staff with extensive rights and the institution of councils of enterprises.

Why are we talking about the revolutionary essence of what is taking place, about the revolutionary character of the transformation carried out? Actually, a revolution means qualitative changes in established social relations. Why can't we confine ourselves to a comparatively harmless and customary term—reform? Isn't it actually a reform we are talking about, using the words "revolution" and "revolutionary" rather as an image, as some metaphor to emphasize the seriousness of what is taking place, to emphasize the determination of our intentions?

The delicacy of this problem is that what is meant here is not a socio-political revolution when the foundations of economic relations of the old system are destroyed and a fundamentally new political government, expressing the interests of overthrowing classes, is established. The situation is different here. The point is not to destroy public ownership of the means of production, but to strengthen and utilize it more effectively. The point is not to renounce the basic principles of socialism: "From each according to his ability, to each according to his work," but to use it with greater consistency in the interests of social justice. The point is not to break up the state machinery but to further strengthen the socialist state of all people, deepen socialist democracy and develop people's socialist self-management.

A comparison with collectivism and cultural revolution suggests itself. What are the difference between the current revolutionary transformations and collectivization and cultural revolution?

Firstly, in society today there are no antagonistic classes, the elimination of which and the destruction of whose ideology would constitute the essential feature of a revolution.

Secondly, the measures carried out today are all-embracing and must affect all spheres of life.

Thirdly, the current reorganizations are being put into effect on socialist foundations and are aimed at strengthening these foundations, at developing them in every way, finishing and improving the edifice of socialism, at turning Soviet society into a really mature socialism.

Insomuch as the process of reorganization has intensified, it affects the interests of practically all people, which is quite natural: some are inspired by it, others are bewildered and the third category of people who simply do not like it. The latter includes shirkers and those who have got used to running the sector entrusted to them as their own domain, and outright embezzlers of public funds. Among the opponents of reorganization there are also honest people who are under the spell of old ideas. They proceed from the principle that nothing has to be changed because it is not known whether things will be better. Obviously, long educational and political work will be needed to successfully carry out the set policy. However, it can be said that the people as a whole have actively backed reorganization and are increasingly doing so.

The driving force of reorganization is the working class which is faithful to revolutionary traditions. The nature of the working class and of the transformations it accomplishes in the course of the socialist revolution presupposes the presence of the strongest critical element. Let's recall the well-known assessment of the proletarian revolution given by **Marx** in his work *The Eighteenth Brumaire of Louis Bonaparte*. These revolutions, he wrote, "criticize themselves constantly ...come back to the apparently accomplished in order to begin it afresh, deride with unmerciful thoroughness the inadequacies, weaknesses, and paltrinesses of their first attempts ...."

From this one can draw the following important conclusion: the need for critical approach to the work done, the need for remaking and putting finishing touches to what has been accomplished are the natural features of the revolutionary processes now taking place, and the building of a new society.

Now let's try to briefly formulate the summarized importance of the measures being carried out and the processes taking place in the Soviet Union. This constitutes a radical and profound, resting upon the labor and social activity of the masses, overcoming of phenomena alien to socialism, conservative ways of thinking, forms and methods of work. This means the establishment of new, progressive forms in the organization of social relations that meet Leninist ideas about socialism as a society based on the principles of collectivization, social justice and democracy. Finally, this is an accelerated movement of society and a break in its gradual development. All this put together will signify a leap from one level of society to another of higher quality, a leap prepared, on the one hand, by the historic achievements of socialism and, on the other, by urgent needs for eliminating negative phenomena, tendencies and obsolete forms of social life. Such are the basic signs of the continuing and deepening socialist revolution, such is the revolutionary essence of the reconstruction in Soviet society.

The reconstruction unfolding now is only the beginning of more significant and deeper changes which must make available the vast potentialities of socialism, give full play to their development and, thereby, prove that genuine progress of humankind is possible only through the socialist reconstruction of society.

Smirnov, "Voprosy teorii. Revoliutsionnaia sut' obnovleniia," *Pravda* (13 Mar 87). Smirnov is a Corresponding Member of the USSR Academy of Sciences. A translated version appeared in *Moscow News*, No. 14 (5 Apr 87), 1a-1c.

Restructure the Training of Party Cadres (4 Apr 87)

On 3 April a conference was held at the CPSU CC at which questions of the training and retraining of Party, Soviet and ideological cadres were discussed in the light of the decisions of the 27th CPSU Congress and the CPSU CC January (1987) Plenum. The conference was attended by secretaries of union republic Communist Party control committees, party kraikoms and obkoms, leaders of Party higher education establishment and courses, heads of faculty, journalists, and representatives of a number of ministries and departments.

Opening the conference, L.N.**Zaikov**. member of Politburo and secretary of the CPSU CC, said: "Two months have passed since the CPSU CC January Plenum, which was a major political event and a special landmark in the path of renewing all aspects of the life of the Party and the people. Basic cadre policy guidelines in conformity with the current stage of restructuring were elaborated.

The Party CC constantly keeps sight of restructuring progress. The reports received from the local level are a clear indication of the people's unanimous support for the course of the CC April and January Plenums and the decisions of the 27th CPSU Congress. This applies to the improvements of the economy and social life, to the Party's struggle to solve social questions and to our country's international initiatives. People see great positive changes in the reinforcement of social justice and approve of them in every way. The cadre policy is fully supported and the process of electing leaders has begun with vigor. In short, life is becoming more businesslike and the struggle against window dressing and ostentation is intensifying. This is pleasing.

In political and practical terms a most important task is to clearly understand the essence of restructuring and to determine its pace. There must be no slackening or complacency, vacillation, or loss of momentum and energy in implementing restructuring. The restructuring of work to train and retrain Party, Soviet, and ideological cadres is part and parcel of the process of restructuring Soviet society. It is part of the whole, and all the characteristics of the transformation taking place in the country apply to it.

Proceeding from the aims of the 27th Congress and the January Plenum, the Party CC deemed it necessary to convene this conference to review progress in implementing the CPSU CC resolution, "On Improving the Party-Political Education of Leading Cadres in Light of the Decisions of the 27th CPSU Congress."

Since the publication of this document, a number of measures to restructure the work of Party education establishments have been implemented. Naturally, in the course of their implementation questions are arising that need to be clarified and call for an exchange of views in order to gain a more profound understanding of the transformations that are being carried out. There are major problems too whose solution will require substantial collective efforts."

As M.S.**Gorbachev** emphasized in his report to the CPSU CC January Plenum, it is necessary to proceed on the basis that all Party cadres are undergoing the test of restructuring but not all of those pass it with equal success. Work on the ideological front has still to be truly developed in many spheres, including political and economic education and the staffing of various sectors with highly qualified and trained cadres.

We all need to step up our work, develop criticism and self-criticism, resolutely eliminate everything that is slowing us down, strive for the fulfillment of socioeconomic development plans, unite the masses around the revolutionary cause of the all-round renewal of the life of the Party and all society, and vigorously establish the atmosphere of the 27th CPSU Congress.

CPSU CC Secretary G.F.**Razumovskii** delivered the report at the conference.

The following took part in the debate: G.G.**Bartoshevich**, secretary of the Belorussian Communist Party CC; R.G.**Yanovskii**, rector of the CPSU CC Academy of Social Sciences; V.N.**Konovalov**, secretary of the Azerbaidzhan Communist Party CC; I.P.**Grushchenko**. director of the Ukrainian Communist Party CC Higher Party School; N.P.**Silkova**, secretary of the Krasnoiarsk CPSU Kraikom; V.I.**Lukin**, secretary of the Leningrad Higher Party School Party committee; F.V.**Dogonkin**, Chief of the Uzbek Communist Party CC Party Organizational Work Department; A.V.**Rodnikov**, head of the Penza CPSU Obkom courses; G.V.**Aleshin**, secretary of the Estonian Communist Party CC; V.N.**Shostakovskii**, rector of the Moscow Higher Party School; Iu.I.**Tarasov**, head of the Leningrad Higher Party School Department of Party and Soviet Building; G.P. **Razzhigaiev**, head of the Saratov CPSU Obkom Organizational Party Work Department; Iu.A.**Lukin**, head of the CPSU CC Academy of Social Sciences Department of Socialist Cultures; and F.I.**Potashev**, head of the Rostov Higher Party School Department of the History of the CPSU.

The main task is to transform party higher educational establishments into one of the main channels for building up a cadre reserve for all components of the Party *apparat*. It is planned within the next 10-15 years to create conditions enabling most Party officials, beginning with full-time Party organizational secretaries, to obtain higher Party political education and to radically increase the scale of the activity of Party higher educational establishments. The student contingent will increasingly be made up of young Party *apparat* workers, mainly Party gorkom and raikom instructors and full-time Party organization secretaries, among whom only 6 and 10 percent, respectively, have higher Party political education now. At the same time, the task of training cadres at other levels must also be resolved more swiftly. In 1986, for example, 410 more Party gorkom and raikom secretaries than 2 years ago were enrolled at Party VUZ's. The conference deemed this approach correct.

Experience has shown that the existing form and period of study at higher Party schools based on higher education make it possible to acquire the amount of fundamental knowledge required for present-day ideological and political training of cadres. The view was expressed that the training of cadres with secondary education at higher Party schools needs to be expanded and deepened. These schools must ensure in practice that students obtain a full higher Party political education and expand the training of leading cadres from among leading workers and collective farm members.

It was stressed at the conference that openness, electivity, control from below, certification, and other democratic forms and methods should be extended to the education sphere and the entire cadre training process. The CC assists the process of horizontal transfers of personnel and meets requests for the placement of personnel in responsible posts by way of promotion from other regions. Party higher educational establishments are also beginning to operate on this principle. Enrollments on an interregional basis have sharply increased. This will help the solution of international tasks in cadre policy and accords with the progressive trends in forming the reserve.

The report and speeches devoted much attention to improving the quality of cadre training on the basis of extensive and systematic studies of the experience of the Party, Soviet, and ideological organizations and labor collectives. Party higher educational establishments have multifaceted contacts with local organizations, there is a tradition of studying their experience, and new ways and forms of disseminating this experience are being sought. However, there are also substantial shortcomings. Above all, there are delays in the study and generalization of new experience. Therefore it is deemed expedient in the organization of these matters to rely on long-term joint programs of Party educational establishments on the one hand and Communist party control committees and Party kraikoms and obkoms on the other. The Academy's Institute for the Study and Generalization of the Experience of Party, Soviet, and Ideological Work will play the role of a scientific and methodological center. Higher Party School laboratories are being improved. The capability for the automated processing of sociological information and holding of mass opinion polls is being created. Regular traineeships of teachers, students, and postgraduates in Party committees are being introduced.

Study courses for cadres were exhaustively discussed at the conference. In view of the dynamism of our development, the CC deemed it necessary to introduce 2-3 week mass refresher courses for officials to be held twice within each 5-year period. Courses at higher Party schools have been transformed into qualification enhancement departments. It is planned to substantially develop courses at Party committees for their base and regular staff. Specific proposals for training the grass-roots *aktiv* were introduced. The qualification enhancement system must constantly draw on the most valuable experience and the most progressive ideas, it must organize discussions with a view to their formal approval and the deepening of knowledge, and it must provide a platform for the best specialists and Party and state officials.

A complex of measures to improve and raise to the requisite level the content of leading cadre training was examined in particular. This is the central, the key task of Party higher educational establishments and, above all, the rectorates, Party organizations, and professorial and teaching staff.

The April Plenum and the 27th CPSU Congress opened a new stage in the theoretical interpretation of reality. Social Sciences are returning to the ground of precise studies of the past and the present. The social process of restructuring has engendered a situation in which many questions can no longer be studied from old positions. This calls for a certain reassessment of values and the theoretical and methodical elaboration of whole spheres of training. A number of fundamental propositions was put forward in the report and the speeches of Party higher educational establishment leaders and heads of these establishments' faculties.

It is above all a question of the need to observe the unity principle in studies of the component parts of the theory of Marxism-Leninism and the CPSU's historical experience. This principle has stood the test of time and of the practical building of socialism. The systematic study of the theory of Marxism-Leninism, coupled with the in-depth elucidation of new problems, provides the basis for the further enhancement of the standard of cadres' theoretical training. It was emphasized that the time has come to move on from teaching the rudiments in the sphere of philosophy to teaching leading cadres to draw scientific and philosophical generalizations from reality. Party cadres must be well-versed in questions of methodology, they must be aware of this most important function of Marxist-Leninist philosophy in respect of the specific methodologies of individual sciences.

It is necessary to overcome the stagnation in the political and economic training of leading cadres. It is necessary to focus special attention on the in-depth study of the processes underway in the economic mechanism and on mastering modern methods of analysis. Totally new tasks are arising in the interpretation of the processes that are increasingly prevalent in international economic cooperation.

It is important to ensure that students master the wealth of new assessments in the struggle for peace and disarmament, in the deployment of the main political forces of the present time and their role in the social process, and in the specifics of the ideological struggle between the two social systems.

The study of the questions of Party and Soviet building provides the basis for the trend toward professionalism. Party building specialists have made a considerable effort in recent years to invest this discipline with scientific rigor in the definition of the subject matter and the identification of the laws governing the Party's development. However, as the speakers noted, Party officials are dissatisfied with the content of the course on Party building.

The dialectical approach of program and textbook authors, scientists, and teachers to the process of the development of the Party is still wanting. Program and textbook compilers frequently forget that in real life all objective observations become subjectivized and are embodied in the activity of Party collectives and individual Communists. This means that the most interesting and important aspect from the viewpoint of cadre training is forgotten—namely, showing and revealing the transition from objectivity to the subjective factor and the identification of the role and tasks of the latter in the restructuring of Party leadership. All too frequently it is the middle link of the chain—economic fact, political conclusion, forms of Party solution of the question—which drops out. Hence the application of old forms to new conditions, administration by injunction, excessive paper work, and other manifestations of formalism. This is why it is important through a model outline of economic theory in the truest sense of the word and through the teaching of modern methods of economic analysis to lead students to political generalizations, thus providing them with a reliable platform for the assessment of various forms of Party work, elimination of the obsolete, and promotion and development of the new.

The determining factor in the professionalism of a Party worker is his ability personally to engage in the ideological education of the working people, his predisposition for ideological work. This predisposition must be molded as a part of the course of study on Party building without infringing upon its integrity. The decision to introduce a Party discipline—Party and Soviet building—for graduates from Party higher educational establishments was greeted with approval.

A special characteristic of the present time is the unusually close connection between the ideological, political, cultural, and moral aspects of the education of leading cadres. Party higher educational establishments can and must play an important role in the struggle for the pure and bright image of the Party member. The inclusion in Party VUZ syllabuses of a new subject—the bases of socialist culture—has met with great interest.

Party VUZ's activity in the organization of scientific work was assessed critically. It was noted that the scientific collectives of the Academy [of Social Sciences] and higher Party schools display the same deficiencies in the development of social sciences research as pointed out in CPSU CC decisions with reference to a number of scientific establishments of the USSR Academy of Sciences and the journal *Kommunist*, and at the conference of heads of social science faculties at the country's VUZ's. They have been invested with special responsibility for the organization of research into the laws governing the development of the Party, its leading role, and the socialist political system.

The cardinal issues are the cadres of Party VUZ's. It is they who determine the quality of the training of those who will be entrusted with ensuring the progress of restructuring and acceleration. However, at present, both in the Academy and in party schools there are teachers who cannot cope with the demands of the times, who are unable to introduce a breath of truly fresh air into the content of their lectures and lessons, to enhance their exactingness towards students, and to restructure their methods of instruction. The proportion of old people among the teaching staff is increasing. There are not enough doctors of sciences and professors among the teachers. Experienced teachers are not doing enough to train their scientific successors. Yet in view of the sharp increase in the volume of cadre training and the review of the training and teaching load quotas, the number of teachers is to be increased substantially, by 100-150 percent.

Speakers noted that the role of Party organizations at Party VUZ's is to be enhanced substantially. Party Committees, the buros of shop organizations, and Pary groups exert little influence on the organization of training, methodological, scientific research, ideological and educational work, and the quality of student training. Their activity is not a genuine school for training leading cadres. The decisions they adopt are not specific enough, and the results they produce are poor. Attention was drawn to the fact that Party organizations must create truly comradely relations in teaching and student collectives based on a healthy moral and political climate.

The conference participants were unanimous in the view that the whole system of training and retraining of cadres must become an effective Party instrument in the education of leading workers of a new type capable of managing the restructuring successfully and achieving real results in the acceleration of the country's socioeconomic development.

Taking part in the conference were the heads of CPSU CC Departments V.A.**Grigor'ev** and Yu.A.**Skliarov** [Propaganda]; N.E.**Kruchina** [Administration of Affairs], CPSU CC Administration of Affairs; A.D.**Lizichev**, chief of the Soviet Army and Navy Main Political Directorate, and senior officials of the CPSU CC.

"Perestroit' podgotovku kadrov partii," *Pravda* (4 Apr); *Izvestiia* (5 Apr); a translation is also in FBIS, No. 070 (13 Apr 87), R1-R5; a condensed version is in CDSP, 39:14 (1987), 10-12. See also G. Razumovskii, "Sovershenstvovat' podgotovku i perepodgotovku rukovodiashchikh kadrov partii," *Kommunist*, 9 (1987), 3-13.

Energetically Carrying Out Restructuring (13 Nov 87)

The Moscow Party Gorkom Plenum took place in a spirit of Party frankness, principles and free exchange of opinions. It diuscussed the resolution of the CPSU CC October(1987) Plenum on Comrade B.N.Eltsin.

M.S.**Gorbachev**, General Secretary of the CPSU CC, addressed the Plenum on this question. He gave a briefing on the Party CC plenum held on 21 October this year, at which questions connected with the 70th anniversary of the Great October Socialist Revolution and certain current tasks of restructuring were submitted for examination.

The CC Politburo, M.S. **Gorbachev** said, saw it as necessary to demonstrate the historic significance of October and make a detailed analysis of everything accomplished in the 7 decades since October. It was important to reveal in all its fullness the difficult, pioneering path of the Soviet people and the Leninist party, to relate it to our present-day concerns and deeds, and to give an all-around interpretation of the lessons of the past. It was incumbent on us to study carefully the complex events of past years, since otherwise there can be no honest and truthful policy, there can be no successful progress.

In approaching the jubilee the Politburo deemed it necessary once again to evaluate the course of the restructuring and some of the results of the revolutionary transformations for which the party CC April (1985) plenum laid the foundations, and to analyze work in implementing the course of the 27th Party congress. It was planned to examine how the key problems of society's development are being tackled, problems on which the fate of the restructuring depends crucially. This means, first and foremost, the democratization of public life and radical economic reform.

The main propositions of the report devoted to the 70th anniversary of October were unanimously approved by the CC plenum.

There was also full support from the CC members for the Politburo's ideas on the nature and significance of the present moment, the course and pace of the restructuring, and its next tasks. It was stressed that in the main the first, initial stage of the restructuring has been completed—the stage of elaborating the party's new course and creating its ideological, theoretical, and organizational platform. The main thing now is the practical implementation of the program that has been elaborated. From this viewpoint, it was said at the Party CC plenum, the next 2-3 years will be decisive and in this sense critical. Basically this will be a test of the ability of the party, its CC, all Party, Soviet, and economic cadres, and also the labor collectives to ensure the successful implementation of the decisions elaborated on radical questions of the restructuring.

The CC plenum drew attention to the fact that in this difficult period we must simultaneously resolve a range of interconnected tasks covering the economy, the social and spiritual spheres, and the development of all that concerns the democratization of Soviet society.

The work load will indeed increase, and the Party, the cadres, and all the labor collectives must be ready for this. This stage must proceed successfully in order to uncover extensive new opportunities for accelerating the restructuring, first and foremost in the economic sphere, and thus to ensure reliable preconditions for the resolution of major socio-economic tasks and for society's transition to a fundamentally new condition. I wish to emphasize once again that the CC members were united on all these questions.

A dissonant note was struck by the statement made at the plenum by Comrade B.N. **Eltsin**. He said that he has no observations to make on the report and that he supports it fully, but would like to touch on a number of questions that have come to his notice in his time on the Politburo. It should be said, M.S. **Gorbachev** went on, that as a whole Comrade **Eltsin**'s speech was politically immature and extremely confused and contradictory. The speech did not contain a single constructive proposal and was based not on analysis and facts, but on distortions, and in essence, as the CC members assessed it, it was demagogic in its content and nature.

Comrade **Eltsin** basically tried to call into question the Party's work on restructuring since the CC April plenum and the 27th CPSU Congress and the nature of the current changes, and went so far as to say that the restructuring effectively does nothing for people.

In Comrade **Eltsin**'s opinion, the CC plenum's aim of implementing the tasks of the new stage of the restructuring in the next 2-3 years is erroneous and disorients the party and the masses. Here he displayed complete theoretical and political helplessness in analyzing the course of the restructuring, and proved incapable of understanding that in this enormous job of renewing Soviet society, the Party and all the working people have to resolve both long-term and medium-term tasks and achieve a marked improvement in the next few years in satisfying the people's urgent needs. All his arguments basically amonted to pompous talk. In particular, in his opinion, the party leadership lacks "revolutionary vigor" in implementing the restructuring.

There was a particularly sharp reaction among CC members to Comrade **Eltsin**'s attempts to represent in a distorted light the work and the atmosphere in the CC Politburo, first and foremost on questions concerning the principles of collegiality.

Naturally, M.S. **Gorbachev** stressed, in itself the fact of a CC member's speaking out at a plenum with criticisms of the Politburo, the Secretariat, and individual comrades should not be seen as anything out of the ordinary. It is normal. In this respect our position is unequivocal: In the Party there should be no zones closed to criticism or workers protected from it. We will continue to develop criticism and self-criticism at all levels.

In this case, what happened was something entirely different. At a crucial political moment, when the CC's attention was focused on fundamental questions of the theory and practice of our development, Comrade **Eltsin** tried to lead the plenum's work in a different direction, declaring his own special position on a number of questions.

In view of the nature of Comrade **Eltsin's** statement at the plenum, it was decided to conduct an exchange of opinions. Twenty-six CC members took part in the discussion.

I must say, M.S. **Gorbachev** went on, that Comrade **Eltsin**'s speech aroused perplexity and indignation among the CC members. The plenum displayed complete unanimity in assessing this speech, deeming it to be politically erroneous. Not one of those who spoke supported Comrade **Eltsin**. The main question formulated by the CC members was this: Can Comrade **Eltsin** really see nothing positive in the country's life since the CC April plenum?

The plenum participants said that a new atmosphere has been created in our society, and is continuing to improve. Activeness is springing up among the people, the party is emerging from a state of prolonged stagnation, and processes of democratization and glasnost are in progress. All this is of decisive significance for the country's fate. In 2 and 1/2 years the theory and policy of restructuring have been elaborated. In every respect this has been an exceptionally fruitful time in the life of the party and the whole of society.

But we were not only engaged in formulating the political and socioeconomic strategy of restructuring. Major national programs have been elaborated and are being introduced on the development of machine building and computer equipment and on increasing the production of consumer goods. The practice of state acceptance has widened, which is having a positive effect on the quality of goods. A major event was the adoption of the Law on the State Enterprise (Association).

The new methods of economic management and the new economic mechanism create real conditions for increasing the efficiency of social production.

For all the difficulties, opportunities have been found for resolving certain urgent social questions. Of course, there are still difficulties with food, but there has been an increase in the production of agricultural produce. In the first 2 years of the 5-Year Plan the pace of housing construction increased, and additional capital investments were switched over to this area. In 1987 housing commissioning will be 15 percent up on 1985. Wages for medical personnel and teachers, student grants, and also pensions are increasing, and reforms are being implemented in higher and secondary education. An additional 6 billion rubles has been allocated to the urgent needs of the health service. And these are only some of the measures in the social sphere.

The Politburo sees the main task now as shifting the center of gravity to monitoring the fulfillment of adopted decisions, to carrying out organizational work, and to stepping up demand. Not a single party organization—including the Moscow party organization—should remain beyond control.

M.S. **Gorbachev** then dwelt on the question of the pace of restructuring. The CC June (1987) plenum concluded that the country is entering a new stage of restructuring during which we will have to overcome considerable difficulties. To that end we must step up our efforts in all directions of work. And the progress of restructuring in the time ahead will largely depend on how skillful and vigorous our actions are during this period.

Pondering on what happened with Comrade **Eltsin**, M.S. **Gorbachev** continued, one cannot help remembering **Lenin's** warnings about the high responsibility of leaders and the accuracy of their political positions. Vladimir **Ilych** once said that there is an objective logic of struggle, which "inevitably leads even the best people—if they insist on the incorrect position they have adopted—to a position which to all intents and purposes is indistinguishable from unprincipled demagoguery."

That is indeed the case in life, when mistakes spring from personal ambitions and the desire to stand out, and if things do not go as they should and the prople in question have to be corrected, they start to dig in their heels and give free rein to their own ambition. Then mistakes occur, are exacerbated, and may turn into an unacceptable position.

I think that we are dealing with just such a situation here. Comrade **Eltsin** placed his personal ambitions above the interests of the party. Incidentally, he had these manifestations pointed out to him by the Politburo, and he promised to draw the necessary lessons. But, as we can see, these promises were not worth very much. In the overall opinion of CC members, the irresponsible and immoral actions of Comrade **Eltsin** were damaging the thing we need most just now—the pooling of all forces and the mobilization of all potential in order to resolve the major tasks of restructuring.

At the end of his plenum speech Comrade **Eltsin** stated that his work in the CC Politburo was not working out for various reasons-"lack of experience and, perhaps, lack of support." He posed the question of being released from his duties as candidate member of the CC Politburo.

Certain explanations are needed here, M.S. **Gorbachev** continued, starting with the fact that I knew about Comrade **Eltsin's** intention to resign before the CC plenum. While on vacation, I received a letter from him containing a request to resolve the question of his continuing both in the Politburo and in the post of first secretary of Moscow party gorkom. After returning from vacation I talked with Comrade **Eltsin** and we agreed that it was not the time to discuss the question and that we would meet and discuss everything after the October holidays. Nonetheless, Comrade **Eltsin**, violating party and purely human ethics, decided to raise the issue directly at the plenum, bypassing the Politburo.

As for the motive which Comrade **Eltsin** puts forward as the reason for his resignation— lack of support fromt he CC Secretariat—it should be said bluntly that this statement is quite absurd and does not correspond with reality.

M.S. **Gorbachev** went on to note that the CPSU CC sees the Moscow Party organization as a reliable bulwark in the implementation of the party's general line. It is from this position that the Politburo approaches all questions concerning the activity of the city party organization and the interests of the capital's working people. These are examined in the most attentive way by the Politburo and government.

The members of the Moscow Party gorkom know that immediately after the city party conference the CC Politburo adopted a resolution supporting the city Party organization's efforts in instilling order in the city, eradicating negative phenomena, and solving urgent problems in the economy, the social sphere, and other areas. Corresponding instructions were then issued to central and republic organs.

The CPSU CC examined and approved the concept of the comprehensive socioeconomic development of Moscow City in the period through the year 2000. It was deemed necessary to draw up in 1987-1988 a plan for the development of Moscow and Moscow Oblast as a single economic complex for the period through 2010.

The question of the comprehensive reconstruction of Moscow's historic city center in the period through the year 2000 was also examined. A USSR Council of Ministers resolution was adopted on this question. Questions linked with the formation of a public cultural center on a site adjoining Red Square were resolved separately.

The CC Politburo supported Moscow CPSU Gorkom's proposal regarding the elimination of the existing disproportions in the city infrastructure by Moscow's 850th anniversary. There are plans for a considerable expansion in the scale of the construction of housing and trade, public health, education, and municipal services projects, for the removal from Moscow of certain production units that do not conform with zoning regulations and are harmful, and for relieving city construction organizations from performing work outside the Moscow zone. The question of ensuring that the union republics and construction organizations from the CMEA countries take part in the construction and reconstruction of major projects in the capital is being studied.

Large-scale measures to improve the quality of medical aid to the population and improve the work of the capital's public health institutions, to improve supplies of fruit and vegetable produce and potatoes to the population, and to supply water have been formulated.

The city is being given substantial assistance in resolving one of the most acute problems -improving transport servies. Measures to develop the Moscow subway and the Moscow railroad terminal have been formulated. The government is examining questions connected with developing city road passenger transportation in Moscow in 1988-1990.

Measures are being studied to strengthen the material and technical base and build up the capacities of construction organizations, develop the food and baked goods industry, and radically improve trade and public catering. It is planned to substantially strengthen the material and scientific and technical base of a number of educational and scientific establishments.

That is by no means a complete list of the questions relating to Moscow that have already been resolved or are currently being examined. We have acted in this way so far, and we shall continue to act in this way.

The question naturally arises: Why has this happened? What are the reasons for such behavior by Comrade **Eltsin**? The Politburo carefully analyzed this question and concluded that the reasons lie primarily in his understanding of restructuring and the methods by which it should be carried out.

His critical approach toward shortcomings and his resolute statements about rapidly overcoming the accumulated problems and getting rid of negative phenomena in the capital's life met with definite understanding and support from working people. And it must bluntly be said that this made it possible initially to achieve certain changes for the better. But it is clear that, no matter how important and crucial work to analyze past activity, criticize shortcomings, and formulate decisions may be, the most important thing is what ensures the success of work—it is constant painstaking activity by all party organizations, all cadres, and all labor collectives. But the Moscow CPSU Gorkom leadership lacked this understanding and ability to conduct matters. Under the influence of Comrade **Eltsin**, the Gorkom Buro attempted to achieve the necessary changes at one fell swoop, via pressure, hectoring, and blatant administration by decree. These, as is well known, are methods from the old arsenal and could not provide stable long-/term successes.

Moreover, after initially going in for sweeping statements and promises—something that was to a considerable extent fueled by his immoderate vanity and desire to be always in the public eye—Comrade **Eltsin** neglected and slackened his leadership of the city party organization and work with cadres.

Seeing that things had begun to grind to a halt and that the situation in the capital was not improving and in some respects had even deteriorated, Comrade **Eltsin** tried to shift the responsibility for his own mjor shortcomings in work onto others—primarily onto leadings cadres. The party gorkom, on Comrade **Eltsin**'s initiative and with his most active participation, essentially in the second phase began the cadre shakeup that he had previously been told was impermissible. At one Politburo session before the January CC plenum he was warned that if what lay behind his talk of a shakeup was his practical intention regarding the Moscow city party organization, he would not receive support. At the time Comrade **Eltsin** reacted to this correctly. He said literally this: "I am a young man in in the Politburo. I have been taught a lesson today. I needed it. It has not come too late. And I will find the strength to draw the right conclusion."

However, he did not draw the proper conclusion. All this had a serious impact on the activity of all city orgainzations and on the general situation in party organizations and, as he himself admitted, led to a decline in the labor and political activeness of Communists and working people.

In general, comrades, Comrade **Eltsin**'s style and methods, which are characterized by pseudorevolutionary phrases and pseudodetermination, proved inadequate. As life has shown, all he was capable of was mouthing appeals and slogans, but when the time came to reinforce the words by concrete deeds what was shown was impotence, fuss, and panic. By all accounts he also sensed a decline in support from Moscow's Communists.

The CPSU CC adopted the following resolution:

1. To recognize Comrade B.N. **Eltsin**'s speech at the CC October (1987) Plenum as politically erroneous.

2. To instruct the CPSU CC Politburo and the Moscow party gorkom to examine the question of Comrade B.N. **Eltsin**'s request to be released from his duties as first secretary of the Moscow CPSU Gorkom in the light of the exchange of opinions which took place at the CPSU CC Plenum.

In accordance with the plenum's instructions, the CC Politburo examined this question and after comprehensively considering the situation which has taken shape it reached a conclusion on the need to strengthen the Moscow CPSU Gorkom's leadership.

Next to speak was Moscow CPSU Gorkom member F.F. **Kozyrev-Dal**. When I was appointed chairman of the Moscow Agroprom, he said, I sincerely believed the words and promises of Comrade **Eltsin**, secretary of the Moscow Party gorkom, about supporting this work, but just 10 months later I felt compelled to begin a personal letter to Comrade **Eltsin** with these words: "Because of a lack of any prospect of being received by you, I feel bound and consider it my duty as a Communist to write you a letter."

Yes, comrades, I did receive a reply to my request for a meeting on questions of the Moscow Agroprom's work although not from Comrade **Eltsin** in person but via his assistant, who said that my prospects of a meeting with Comrade **Eltsin** were nil.

Nor was I received even after my letter had been read, even though the letter showed in detail the entire mechanism acting as a brake on the activity of the Moscow Agroprom. The letter made a direct statement about the negative role of Comrade **Nizovtseva**, Party gorkom secretary, and the lack of support for all promising areas of the Agrprom's work from the party gorkom.

Perhaps this is a coincidence? No, comrades, this is a system. A system of combatting the sober, correct, and truthful position which **Eltsin** like to speak about so much from the public platform.

It was only later that I realized that Comrade **Eltsin** was not interested in projects yielding a real return. He needed instant, showy measures which created an effect even if not backed up by his own efforts. He needed prestige at any price. He did not want to consider the sober analysis of the objective situation and the trends of its development. I can only qualify that as political adventurism. Other negative phenomena snowballed. There was an intensification of the administrative and burocratic style of leadersip on the part of the gorkom and its secretaries. Comrade **Eltsin** usurped the leadership of the city Party organization, elements of Bonapartism began to be displayed, and cadre policy was utterly corrupted. The only actions taken were destructive. Comrade **Eltsin** came to believe in his own impunity and set himself apart from the rest by singlehandedly settling people's fates and being accountable neither to them nor to the CPSU CC.

In the light of what has been said, I cannot regard Comrade **Eltsin**'s conduct at the CC plenum as either a coincidence or a mistake. It was far from being a mistake but a calculated and well-timed stab in the back for the party CC and its Politburo; one aimed at reaping ambitious political dividends. Comrade **Eltsin**'s act was one of frank adventurism. A betrayal of the cause of restructuring and the cohesion of our party ranks—that is how I assess Comrade **Eltsin**'s activity and his stance at the CPSU CC plenum. On the basis of this assessment I propose that he be relieved of his duties as first secretary of the Moscow Party Gorkom.

What happened is to a certain extent on our consciences, too, Moscow Gorispolkom Secretary Yu.A. **Prokofev** said, because we saw Comrade **Eltsin**'s mistakes but did not stop him in time. Here in this hall there are a good few people to whom we whispered that this was wrong, it was a mistake. But we lacked the courage to speak out at the Party gorkom plenum, clearly we did not have complete faith in glasnost or restructuring.

When addressing the 27th party congress, Comrade **Eltsin** said that he had not taken this stance before because he lacked the courage and political maturity. You have the courage, but you lacked political maturity then and still do today. Why is that? It is due to your character.

There are people who set themselves on a pedestal by their actions, and there are people who build themselves a pedestal by denigrating those who stand alongside them. This is the difference between the position of a true Communist and that of Boris Nikolaevich **Eltsin**. A state of struggle is characteristic of you all the time. You wallow in struggle, pressure, and aggression all the time, you are constantly exposing someone, then you can parade on your charger in front of ordinary people. And whatever failures may occur, you nevertheless look good because you struggled, you issued warnings, you fired people. But when it comes to Comrade **Eltsin**'s political competence, I witnessed his meeting with the "Pamiat" society. You know what this society represents. Comrade **Eltsin** invited them to the Moscow City Soviet and spoke to them. He surrendered one position after another. And to whom? To hysterical women and reactionaries!

And what eulogies of you personally were tolerated in *Moskovskaia Pravda*—you were splendid and bold and sensitive. This is simply self-propaganda.

Moscow Communists trusted you but you did not understand this. Instead of relying on gorkom members and on the aktiv and rallying people around you, you began to dismiss cadres. What have you achieved, who are your supporters now?

Only one conclusion can be drawn: On political grounds we cannot have such a Party gorkom secretary. Such a man must not be involved in political work at all.

L.I. **Matveev**, USSR Ministry of Foreign Affairs administrator of affairs, characterized Comrade **Eltsin**'s conduct as political adventurism, a treacherous stab in the back for the party whose place, time, and goal were calculated. First, the time—the eve of the 70th anniversary of October, when the whole world was watching us; the place—the supreme forum, the party CC forum; and the aim—to set the Moscow city Party organization against the party CC and split the Politburo.

I move the following proposal. First, that the party CC's decision be fully supported. Second, that Comrade **Eltsin** be relieved of his duties as first secretary of the Moscow CPSU Gorkom for displaying political adventurism and political immaturity, for his attempt to split the party ranks and to set the Moscow city party organization against the party CC, and for violating Leninist principles of cadre work.

V.A. **Zharov**, deputy chairman of the Moscow Gorispolkom, supported the assessment of Comrade **Eltsin**'s speech at the CC plenum as a blow against the party leadership, the Moscow Party organization, and its authority, and a blow coming moreover at a period of most complex, most difficult work. It is a gamble on a split. Tomorrow we will probably hear political speculation abroad and from our own people about a crisis in restructuring and we will see people trying to make Boris Nikolaevich **Eltsin** into a Jesus **Christ** figure who has suffered for his terribly revolutionary commitment to social renewal and democracy.

The members of the Moscow CPSU Gorkom, unlike Comrade, assess the situation soberly and correctly, everyone realizes that we are merely beginning the work, everyone realizes that in the interval since the congress the party CC and the government have been able to create a mechanism of restructuring and that this mechanism has begun to work.

Most important decisions have been adopted and the CC and the government are doing a great deal to develop Moscow, but it must be admitted, we must all clearly realize this, that this is sometimes being done at the expense of other regions.

It would seem most convenient for us members of the Moscow Party gorkom to use the following argument: Like you, we did not approve of Comrade **Eltsin's** speech at the CC plenum, we did not hear it, it doesn't concern us, we are only voting and making an assessment today. All the same, let us ponder the fact that we are also to blame for Comrade **Eltsin's** speech and greatly to blame. Our blame lies in the fact that Comrade **Eltsin** gradually worked up to this speech and was making ultra left-wing and overly radical statements from the outset of his activity.

We all justified these by saying that routine must be shattered and that cadre replacements were really necessary. But then cadre replacements became sporting competitions that were reported to us: At one *aktiv* 30 percent of the first secretaries were replaced, at another 50 percent and at another approximately 80 percent went.

We all failed to draw the main conclusion for ourselves: that it was time in conditions of restructuring to use our right to criticize at the party gorkom plenum also and not only behind the scenes. We must all draw this conclusion.

Two years ago, A.I. **Zemskov**, first secretary of the Voroshilovskii CPSU Raikom, pointed out in his speech, the party CC recommended Boris Nikolaevich to us. I think even now that the recommendation was correct, that changes were overdue at that time in Moscow, and that a great deal has changed over these 2 years. However, I support those who said here that alarm signals linked with the first secretary's work style began to emerge increasingly clearly as time passed.

All of us here are unanimous that Comrade **Eltsin's** position does not reflect the position of the Moscow Party gorkom. Not only because the form of its expression was not discussed but because it also essentially does not accord with our aspirations. We do not think of ourselves in isolation from the work of the party CC.

I believe that this act of misconduct—there is no other word for it—is no accident but stems from Comrade **Eltsin's** work style. The personal nature of his decisions, his isolation from the party *aktiv*, from the Party gorkom members, and from the raikom secretaries—this is the prism through which his activity must be examined. It is disgraceful when for 2 years not a single raikom first secretary, to my knowledge, was able to telephone the gorkom secretary direct. For 2 years we wanted to speak to the gorkom first secretary. Comrade **Eltsin** cut himself off not only from party raikom secretaries. But how did formalism flourish? It was important to criticize, but it was no longer important who was criticized or for what—people were criticized or dismissed for a reason or for no reason. We remember this from examples involving the Kievskii party raykom and the city people's control committee. And I, too, have felt all this in my own personal experience.

Lack of glasnost in work with the reserve, haste in work with cadres—it was a real merry-go-round, this is the only word for it. And when it all went around for the second and the third time, it turned into a bad joke.

We Party gorkom members do not have and cannot have a line that differs from the CC's. We need coherence and cohesion.

I support the party CC's decision and assessments and believe that Boris Nikolaevich cannot be first secretary of Moscow Party gorkom.

Academician V.S. **Semenikhin**, general designer at a scientific research institute, emphasized that restructuring has become the conviction of scientists and workers and that the course taken by the party at the April plenum has inspired both ordinary people and leaders. I have been on the party for many years, and I had a talk with Boris Nikolaevich right at the start, when he arrived. I wanted somehow to put him in the picture and convince him that the Moscow party organization had very stong, proven cadres who, it is true, had stagnated. It seemed to me at first that he had the correct attitude.

Do you remember how our first plenum went? Some 30 people spoke, with animation and without any constraints. But what happened next? We restructured nothing in the work of the Party gorkom. Regulated plenums, preplanned speeches, the cadre merry-go-round. After 8 months I secured an audience with him and said that the gorkom members were just going through the motions and that no one discussed any questions with us before submitting them to a plenum. We were called together once a quarter. I, for example, did not once in 2 years attend the gorkom buro on any question. Incidentally, I was not too shy to say so to certain gorkom buro members. Hence the natural outcome.

After my conversation with Comrade **Eltsin** I asked three times to speak at a plenum as a Party gorkom member. The last time Boris **Nikolaevich** pointed to the clock: There was no time. And the speeches which were made had been planned in advance. Of course that is not democratization of our party life, it is not restructuring. In this sense we have lost time.

I fully subscribe to the decision which the CPSU CC has made with regard to Comrade **Eltsin**. He has gone astray and displayed political immaturity, and he must not lead the Moscow Party organization.

I.M. **Golovkov**, first secretary of Kirovskii CPSU Raikom, pointed out in his speech that Comrade **Eltsin** is an experienced, vigorous, strong-willed, hardworking leader. People followed him, although, at the same time, the speaker recalled, there was concern about the peremptory nature of his judgments, his disregard for the principles of continuity, his inablility to value people, his lack of proper tact and respect for cadres, and his inadequate patience and tolerance. All that harmed the cause to a considerable degree and caused consternation among the aktiv. No references to extreme situations can justify unfairness toward people or the relishing of mistakes and blunders on the part of comrades in the Party.

Quite frankly, it is difficult now to speak with people and answer their questions. Boris **Nikolaevich**'s actions should be regarded as a bodycheck to the cause of restructuring, a bodycheck to all Muscovites. This has always been and is a forbidden method. It shames the capital's reputation. I believed you, Boris Nikolaevich, but it is inadmissible for a politician of your rank to behave like that, and I believe that you have simply lost the right to head the capital's party organization.

I must also reproach the CPSU CC. Meetings are held in many parts of the country between secretaries of the CPSU C and working people and the party *aktiv*, and it is hard to overestimate their importance. You watch televison and think to yourself: Why does this sort of thing not happen here? Why does Moscow seem to have been overlooked in the last 2 years?

Today's plenum, I am sure, will be a good lesson for us all. Above all, it is a hard lesson that responsibility and principledness must distinuguish our actions every hour of every day. It is also an object lesson in internal party democracy which the CPSU CC has taught us today. And it is a lesson of belief in the success of our entire restructuring.

Comrade **Eltsin** forgot that he was not representing himself in the CPSU CC but the more than 1 million Communists here in the capital, A.N. **Nikolaev**, first secretary of the Baumanskii CPSU Raikom, said. To cast even a shadow of doubt that Muscovites might take a different position to that of the CC is blasphemous. It is an enormous party crime, if you like, it cannot be described otherewlse. I have thought long and hard about whether this is pure chance, but I am sure that it is not. This act reflects Comrade **Eltsin**'s character and mode of action.

The revolutionary nature of restructuring throws a very clear light on who is who. Who is the real leader of restructuring, who is a political fighter, and who is trying to solve his ambitious problems and achieve his ambitious aims on the wave of restructuring. Comrade **Eltsin** very quickly acquired the domineering tendencies against which he fulminated at the party congress. This was a gap between words and real deeds. He soon came to believe in his own infallibity and cut himself off from the party *aktiv*. A total of 250 party raikom plenums were held during this crucial period, and Boris Nikolaevich attended only 2 of them. Yet these plenums were held to resolve key problems of restructuring at raion level.

It may be said that Boris Nikolaevich visited dozens of enterprises and organizations in the city. Yes, these meetings did take place but they were purely excursions. They were limited to producing an ostentatious effect and were no more than walks through shops, laboratories, and so forth.

Instead of analysis, what became firmly established in the Party gorkom was a practice of compiling dossiers whereby people zealously produced negative information for Comrade **Eltsin**'s file, after which this information was poured forth in long, scathing speeches at gorkom plenums, which only served to demoralize the party *aktiv* and induce a sense of confusion, loss of confidence, and uncertainty. This was accompanied by a cadre merry-go-round. We have lost many dedicated, experienced people—some of them irrevocably—and this lies on the conscience of Comrade **Eltsin**. In general what began to be welcomed in our organization was a style whereby criticism had to border on abuse and self-criticism had to amount to self-annihilation.

Twenty-six Moscow programs loudly brought to Muscovites' attention by their authors have proved to be unbalanced, ill-considered, and a public relations exercise.

Today I cannot overemphasize the responsibility of members of the Moscow CPSU Gorkom Buro and gorkom secretaries for the situation that has taken shape. They worked alongside **Eltsin** but lost their own identity and began to actively relay Comrade **Eltsin**'s exaggerated, excited perception of reality. I believe that we do not have the right to accept Comrade **Eltsin**'s resignation but we do have the right to refuse to put our trust in him.

I would like to say, I.N. **Koniukhova**, first secretary of the Zheleznogorozhnii Party raikom, began, that the decision of the Party CC is absolutely correct.

Boris Nikolaevich forgot that it is necessary to think about people. And, especially, that one should rely on one's comrades-in-arms. V.I. **Lenin** taught us that a Communist leader must prove his right to leadership by this alone and that he must find more and more helpers. But Comrade **Eltsin** did not find them and did not even try to find them. And when people tried to help him he did not listen. On the other hand, the Party Gorkom Buro and the gorkom secretaries clearly did little to counteract this style. At the first meeting, when Comrade **Eltsin** became secretary of the gorkom, he said: Your voices were hard to hear, you must speak up. So we did, but he still did not hear us.

There is no one in our country who does not love Moscow. But you, Boris Nikolaevich, unfortunately love neither Moscow nor Muscovites. You very often just flirt with people.

An unsuitable style has developed in the Party gorkom. We must learn our lesson from this and combat this style. Comrade **Eltsin does** not have the right to lead the Moscow city Party organization.

Two years ago, V.A. **Zheltov**, first secretary of the Krasnogvardeyskii Party raikom recalled, when the CPSU CC recommended Communist B.N. **Eltsin** to us, it was in view of his best characteristics—his initiative, creativeness, and will. It must be said frankly that Comrade **Eltsin** abused the trust of the CC. Tremendous damage has been caused to the prestige of a large Party organization.

The statement made by Comrade **Eltsin** has in fact played into the hands of our opponents. They are citing it and brandishing it like a banner. This is the worst testimonial a Communist could wish for.

Clearly a sore point has come to the fore here, the problem of domination. A situation where people act according to the slogan, "I came, I saw, I conquered," is untenable. This slogan is not for us.

Now about cadres. Frankly speaking, many people in the Party *aktiv* remember not only the hard-line style, but also what might be described as a brutal approach to drafting character references when the focus is on the worst aspects. For whom are these references intended? For Party comrades? It is necessary to stress a person's best qualities, to help him to prove himself.

Many of B.N. **Eltsin**'s professional qualities deserve respect, R.V. **Zhukova**, first secretary of the Zhdanovskii CPSU Raikom noted. However, there is one very negative trait, it is distrust of one's colleagues. This distrust, this suspiciousness grew into a political approach.

It is a great pity that the Party gorkom buro proved incapable of countering the negative traits in the character of its leader when it should have stood up to him, when it should have assessed the leader's actions more critically and helped him to overcome the negative traits in his character.

Unfortunately, the Party gorkom organizational department proved unequal to this task. Many assessments of the activities of Party raikom first secretaries were drawn up on the basis of anonymous letters.

The tenor of the assessments of people's work was always negative and this gave rise to distrust and a colossal vaccum in cadres. We must draw conclusions from this sad political lesson in the life of the city Party organization and we will not fail to do so.

It is now very important for the Party gorkom to change its style of work, to ensure more trust while maintaining high exactingness and respect for Party cadre workers and members of the Party gorkom. It is necessary for the Party *aktiv* to be more mature and principled and to critically assess the results of its work.

I must admit, V.V. **Skitev**, chief of the Moscow CPSU Gorkom Party Organizational Work Department, then said, that working as chief of the department with Boris Nikolaevich was, frankly speaking, torture. The rank table always prevailed over you in demands for numerous unjustified replacements of all kinds of leaders.

We tried to resist this. We managed to save some of our comrades, to transfer them elsewhere. However, some of them we lost. Furthermore, Comrade **Eltsin** engaged in political manipulation when he declared that allegedly the CC had raised the question of punishing two first secretaries and expelling them from the Party.

We had to report questions pertaining to work with the cadre reserve to the CPSU CC Department virtually secretly since Comrade **Eltsin**'s interest in the cadre reserve during the 2 years dried up completely. Artificially, without approval, mainly for the sake of self-advertisement, a new Party raikom structure was being set up.

I do not want to sidestep responsibility for what has happened. But working was very difficult. The organizational department was essentially transformed into an administration for serving the 'diplomatic corps.' It was downgraded to the compilation of papers for all kind of statements and endlesss speeches. As a result the department lost contact with primary organizations and Party raikoms. The Party gorkom buro also lost contact. I can say that at the latest plenum it was planned on Comrade **Eltsin**'s intiative to expel a number of workers from the gorkom buro despite the fact that they worked harder that other members of the buro.

There was much window dressing. Recall the mass campaign under the slogan City Day into which we sank an enormous amount of Party time, money, and effort while neglecting the report and election campaign which dealt with the key issue of how Communists were implementing restructuring. Or another example. The department prepared a whole series of proposals pertaining to the restructuring of the work of Primary Party Organizations which were based on Party raikom proposals. However, these too were discarded as unnecessary.

Two years ago, A.M. **Larionov**, chief of the Moscow City Main Administration for Vocational and Technical Education, said, the first steps taken by Comrade **Eltsin** inspired hope and optimism. But a number of questions gradually arose. The principles and criteria that guided Boris Nikolaevich in his choice of cadres are still unclear to me. He replaced 22 raikom secretaries and sometimes simply settled scores with comrades. You woro rocallod from loave a week early and told that there would be a discussion about raion problems. But instead of this you would be made to run the gauntlet of quite unexpected accusations, leaving you bewildered. We have, by the way, just heard from Comrade V.V. **Skitev**, but he, after all, was personally engaged in this. He was perhaps forced to do so, I don't know, but he did not have the guts to object.

Clearly the role of every member of the Party gorkom buro must be assessed personally. After all, comrades couuld surely have gone to the Party CC, which is just down the road.

I would like to talk particularly about the comprehensive targeted programs. Very many of them have been adopted, but they have been produced one after the other, without thorough preparation or any coordination. They are devoid of any economic basis. No help at all is given in implementing them. Such a style, in my opinion, is plain and simple demagoguery.

We appreciate our involvement in everything that happened in our city Party organization, Moscow CPSU Gorkom Secretary A.A. **Nizovtseva** observed. I would like to talk about Boris Nikolaevich's actual speech at the Party CC plenum. I took part in the work of the plenum and witnessed the speech. It had no support and was unanimously condemned by all members of the Party CC. Everyone voted in favor of recognizing Comrade **Eltsin's** speech as politically erroneous.

The speech has undoubtedly done serious harm to our Party organization; I would go so far as to say that it has undermined its authority. Only unity on our part, the unity which is being displayed today in the speeches by the participants in our plenum, can rectify matters in this situation, and the question of whether Boris Nikolaevich can be first secretary of the Party gorkom is no longer an issue for anyone.

A few words about how this could have happened. We who have worked alongside Boris Nikolaevich, the secretaries and buro members, as distinct from many others, met with him frequently. It would be wrong and dishonest if I said that we ever heard him wrongly formulate any political tasks. But nevertheless we probably did lack the necessary critical view of Boris Nikolaevich's work. We in fact deluded ourselves, we in fact overestimated, perhaps, both his experience and knowledge.

Now, having heard my comrades' speeches, I am convinced once again of how great the demands placed on members of the buro and secretaries of the Party gorkom are and that we have much to change in our work style.

Yu.S. **Karabasov**, secretary of the Moscow CPSU Gorkom, said, among other things: I must also talk primarily about the Party gorkom buro. I attended the plenum as a candidate member of the Party CC. The question of our reponsibility for Boris Nikolaevich **Eltsin's** speech already arose then, on that day, when we had to face the participants in the Party CC plenum.

How do I understand Boris Nikolaevich's speech? It was confused, irresponsible, and unconvincing, he presented his ideas in a general way without adducing any evidence. His statement about resignation was, if you wish, for show, an attempt at blackmail, a sign of political immaturity. There is no other assessment possible.

Today, Boris Nikolaevich, I must say that we were sincere and honest in our attitude toward you and followed you enthusiastically. But much now has to be reassessed. The situation in the buro seemed to us to be characterized by the necessary collegiality and critical spirit, and there was the opportunity for exchange of opinions. But, by all accounts, Boris Nikolaevich, it was, to a considerable extent, a game to you. Because when the crunch came, when the principle of collectiveness should have operated, you did not need the buro anymore.

I am certain that we will emerge from this situation with dignity, the unity of the plenum and the Party gorkom guaranteeing this, in my view, and I think the Muscovites will support us, I also think that we must assure the CC repeatedly today that it can rely on us.

Professor V.A. **Protapopov** of the Economics Faculty of the Moscow State University named for M.V. Lomonosov, pointed out that he has worked as secretary of the Leninskii Party raikom for 11 years and been awarded a certificate for good work by the Party gorkom. He therefore has the moral right to say whatever he thinks about what has happened without having to look over his shoulder. He was convinced that Comrade **Eltsin's** speech at the CC should be described as demagoguery. That is the most accurate term.

The cadre merry-go-round which has occurred in our organization is absurd and does not benefit restructuring. Many people have gotten the idea that the most important thing in restructuring is to change people around. The more changes you make, the sooner you will be told that you are restructuring. The impression given is that you are satisfied when you have used methods of this kind to remove people who maybe wanted sincerely to work. Everything was smashed into fragments, but when it came to creation, this is where you faltered, Boris Nikolaevich. This kind of political error committed by a first secretary and candidate member of the Politburo can only be assessed as they have been assessed by the Party CC and are being assessed by us today. A person who is a repository of these errors cannot lead a Party organization like the Moscow Party organization.

Mikhail Sergeyevich, comrade Politburo members, we have always been, are, and will remain the Party's assistants.

Today, when almost 2 years have elapsed since Comrade B.N. **Eltsin's** election, Per-vomaiskii Party raikom First Secretary V.A. **Vasilev** said, I am increasingly convinced that many of the promises he gave, which were constantly couched in loud phrases, were not only backed up with concrete action but in many respects worsened the situation. The concepts of the unquestionability of authority and infallibility of leaders were verbally condemned, but what was asserted in practice was an authoritarian work style, which is manifestly intolerable in a Party organization, pariticularly in deciding cadre questions.

What might figuratively be called a "behind closed doors" method of work emerged. There was a loss of confidence. Innumerable commissions would turn up at the most critical moment. They would dig around, drag things out, and accumulate quantities of background material of a kind which would denigrate the work of the Party organization, primary Party organizations, the Party raikom, and other raion organizations. They we would be branded with the merciless label of 'subtle stage-managing of affairs,' as *Moskovskaia Pravda* wrote. No, we did not engage in subtle stage-managing of affairs. We were simply leaned on.

The promises and calls to reduce paper work and separate Party and economic work were not backed up in practice. In practice we were simply castigated for economic failings. I have brought with me a telegram on government notepaper which we received at the Party raikom last September. We all received such telegrams. I quote:

"To the first secretary of the Party raikom:

"I ask you to personally take charge of work to impose order in the organization of trading in fruit and vegetable produce in the raion. Throughout September there must be daily monitoring of the fulfillment of the approved minimum product range and of the work of each trading outlet in observing the rules of trade." I think this needs no comment.

Virtually every speech by Comrade **Eltsin** involved a negative assessment of any area of the capital's development. Here, as a rule, a whole collection of statistics was cited which was used for public manipulation denigrating matters in Moscow.

Self-aggradizement, an authoritarian work style, and an unwillingness to heed Party comrades' views is what led, in my view, to Comrade **Eltsin's** provocative conduct at the Party CC plenum.

V.S. **Sablin**, chief of the Glavmosdorupravlenie [Main Highways Administration], wholly and fully supported M.S. **Gorbachev's** speech and subscribed to the assessment of Comrade **Eltsin's** politically immature speech at the Party CC plenum. Comrade **Sablin** noted that Boris Nikolaevich **Eltsin** has many attractive characteristics. But one characteristic, which is a determining characteristic for a Party worker-work with cadres-does not stand up to criticism. It is simply intolerable

A.A. **Logunov,** rector of the Moscow State University named for M.V. Lomonosov, stressed that the Party's assessment of Comrade **Eltsin's** speech at the CPSU CC plenum is unequivocal. His speech gave powerful encouragement to every kind of speculation.

I have been a direct participant in CPSU CC Politburo and Secretariat discussions on certain questions-relating to the development of science, higher education, and the higher education system. On every occasion these have been democratic and comprehensive discussions in, I would say, a really comradely and businesslike atmosphere. Everybody speaks equally, and it is attempted to accumulate everything of value and take everything useful into account. How can it be said that it is impossible to freely express your opinion in the CC and CC Secretariat?

Now to restructuring. It is like oxygen for our society. We were steadily sliding toward the abyss. This slide has now been stopped. Of course, this is not a simple process. It is very important to support everything valuable in good time and channel it in the right direction. This concerns cadres too. As many of them should be replaced as are needed for the interests of work. Only on the basis of the interests of work and not in order to look as though we have restructured ourselves in a major way.

Ingrained fear of speaking the Party truth was the ground on which the atmosphere that gave rise to Boris Nikolaevich's speech was created in the Party gorkom. This style must be revamped without fail.

Today, whether buro members or not, N.Ye. **Koslova**, first secretary of Sverdlovskiy Party raikom said, we find it very hard and difficult to speak because you recognize your responsibility and because it is a question of the city of Moscow and its Party organization—a key organization for the Party CC.

I would like to say that very many of us, including me, are becoming bold in retrospect. The atmosphere in the Party gorkom buro was not easy-and I ask you to believe this, it was not easy-and recently it had become clearly troubled. This could be seen in Boris Niko-laevich's behavior. He was very nervous. But we did not dare ask him what had happened.

In sharing and understanding my personal guilt, Mikhail Sergeevich, I would also like to mention today that the Moscow organization is a large organization and the fact that not everything was going smoothly here could have been seen not only by each member of the Party gorkom buro but by Party CC workers, who had not visited the Party gorkom buro at all recently. I do not recall anyone from the Party CC at sector chief level paying us a visit.

It is very difficult, we are very ashamed. And the demands which will clearly be made have my full backing, but we must act in such a way that tomorrow there will be a growing assurance in working Moscow that we going the right way.

A.S. **Yeliseev**, rector of the N.E. Bauman Moscow Higher Technical College, said: In my opinion, after what we have heard we can probably agree that Boris Nikolaevich **Eltsin** made a blatant political mistake, after which he could no longer remain secretary and leader of the Moscow Party organization or remain in the Politburo or leading Party organs. The mistake was too great.

I believe that what has happened should be a great lesson for us all. Are we not making similar mistakes, are there not grains of the authoritarian style of leadership in us, do we always know how to consult with our comrades?

Incidentlally, as a gorkom member, I would not fully dissociate myself from his guilt. I take part in the work of Party gorkom plenums and have never heard speeches like today's, even half as sharp, even one-third as sharp. There is a point at which we start to lose our prin-cipledness. Let us pluck up courage to speak out in good time, and then we will avoid such mistakes.

All this is the result of a protracted disregard of the norms of Party life.

I would like to assure the Party CC and Politburo that the Moscow city Party organization is strong and will draw the correct conclusions from what has happened.

The Party gorkom buro, Yu.A. **Beliakov**, second secretary of the Moscow CPSU Gorkom, said, wholly supports and shares the assessment which the CPSU CC plenum made of Comrade **Eltsin's** speech. This was our firm position from the very beginning. This assessment was made today in Mikhail Sergeevich **Gorbachev's** speech.

On behalf of the Moscow CPSU Gorkom Buro I must state that we wholly support the CC and Politburo on questions of domestic and foreign policy and in restructuring.

Comrade **Eltsin's** plenum speech was completely unexpected for us, and we assessed it as immature and intemperate and assess it as a blow against the city Party organization. The Moscow Party organization has never had and will never have any differences with the general line and practical actions of the Party CC.

The statement about Boris Nikolaevich's resignation is an attempt to introduce precisely such differences. That is how we assess the affair. The negative consequences of Comrade **Eltsin's** speeches are hard to overestimate. By his speech and resignation demand, Comrade **Eltsin** gave rise to doubts about restructuring and the changes taking place in the country.

This blow was struck on the eve of the 70th anniversary of October, at a critical moment in restructuring. The blow was against all the matters in which Boris Nikolaevich himself was taking the most active part. He was working hard, selflessly, and creatively, and his work was having a marked influence on the ciry Party organization's work. So the blow was all the more painful for us and its consequences were all the graver. The name of the Moscow Gorkom first secretary is now being utilized by dubious elements that are trying to turn Moscow against the CPSU CC.

A Party leader, especially one at such a level, must visualize all the consequences of his actions and bear full responsibility for them.

Very serious criticism of the Party Gorkom Buro has been voiced today. We fully accept it, it is fair, although bitter.

The Party Gorkom Buro does not shirk responsibility for what happened, we were clearly not exacting and demanding enough with the first secretary.

The requisite critical view of Boris Nikolaevich's work was lacking. A special responsibility for this lies with the Party gorkom secretaries. We are clearly aware of this today. So we are paying all too high a price for our errors.

The opinion of the Party Gorkom Buro is unanimous. Comrade **Eltsin** can no longer be leader of the Moscow city Party organization.

I want to assure the CC and the Politburo that the restructuring process in Moscow does not end with Comrade **Eltsin**'s speech and this error. The process continues. Much work lies ahead. Allow me on behalf of the members of the gorkom to assure you that the Moscow city Party organization and all Moscow's working people will work hard to implement the tasks set by the CC. And we will cope with them.

Comrades!-V.V. **Vinogradov**, first secretary of Sovetskii CPSU Raikom, said to the plenum participants. I cannot include myself among the ranks of the aggrieved. I am one of the few raikom secretaries who have been working for a long time in the city Party organization; according to the statistics, few of us remain.

Comrade **Eltsin** has positive qualities. This was the reason why he became secretary of the Party obkom in Sverdlovsk and secretary of the gorkom in Moscow. But that is not the point at issue today. The point at issue today is that by his actions he has caused very great damage and harm to both the Party and the Moscow city Party organization and showed himself in the worst possible light at the CC Plenum.

I think that it is not altogether correct to say today, as the gorkom secretaries are doing, that this was surprising and perplexing. I think that that is not altogether so. The explosion had been brewing, and the foundation of it is Comrade **Eltsin**'s ambitiousness, his harshness, not firmness, and his inability to listen to people.

He criticized the CC for lacking democratism, yet he was given the opportunity to speak at the CC Plenum. Thus an atmosphere was created there in which even the absolutely demagogic statements that he came out with could be made. But could we speak out openly? On many questions we remained silent and squeezed our lips together so hard it actually hurt.

What methods were used? They turned the whole raion upside down to dig the dirt on **Vinogradov**, yet I have spent 17 years in elective Party and soviet work. I was elected by a plenum.

My patience ran out, and I went to Comrade **Beliakov**, second secretary of the Party gorkom, and frankly said: Either dismiss me, or stop what you're doing. They stopped. They even apparently praised the raion at the last plenum.

Boris Nikolaevich was out of touch with us, and he was not alongside us in the ranks. He hovered somewhere above us. He was not very concerned with ensuring that we link arms and resolve a great cause in a single formation.

Even today I simply cannot understand how Boris Nikolaevich, when he drove over to the raion for a report and election meeting in a shop organization, managed to ensure that I could not attend. Comrade **Skitev** has never been able to explain to me why I did not attend.

Of course, Boris Nikolaevich won Muscovites over with his dynamism and drive, he drove around a great deal and had a lot of contact with people. But it seems to me that on these trips he was more concerned about his personal authority than that of the gorkom. And why this contempt for raikom first secretaies? Almost everyone carries some brand. Pardon the harsh words, but we very often had to wash ourselves clean of the assessments that were made of us Party raikom first secretaries. Even precinct inspectors were given the right to shadow us, what was said about us was: See if those sons of bitches are getting up to anything. Boris Nikolaevich, a person of your rank cannot say things like that merely for the sake of playing up to an audience.

In conclusion I should like to say that I feel very deeply about Comrade **Eltsin's** action. It is a grave blow, it is a stern lesson to us, to everyone. But today I should like to assure the

Party CC, the Politburo, and the Party leaders present here that if at a hard and difficult time we have held out then, having straightened ourselves up, in unity and monolithic formation, we can do a very great deal and will unfailingly do it.

In his speech B.N. **Eltsin** said: I think there is no need to provide an evaluation of myself here inasmuch as my action was simply unpredictable. Today, at the CC Plenum, at the Politburo, at the gorkom buro, and at this plenum, I have heard a great deal I never heard before in my life. Perhaps that was to some degree the reason for what happened.

I merely want here to give a firm assurance and to say, Mikhail Sergeevich, to you and the Politburo members and CC secretaries present here, to the Party gorkom members, and to all those who are at the gorkom plenum today, first that I give my sincere Party word that of course I had no ulterior motive [umysly] and there was no political orientation in my action.

Second: I agree today with the criticism which has been voiced. Comrade Eliseev was probably right in saying that if it had come earlier it would have been of benefit.

I must say that I believe in, that I have absolutely firm Party confidence in, the Party's general line and the decisions of the 27th congress. I have absolute confidence in restructuring and in the fact that however hard its path may be it will nonetheless triumph. It is another matter, and here we have indeed sometimes had different nuances in our evaluations of it, that it is proceeding differently for different regions and even for different organizations. But, of course, I believe in restructuring and there can be no doubts here. I am stating this absolutely honestly to you Communists after working together in the Party organization for 2 years. And any action of mine which contradicts this statment of mine should of couse lead to expulsion from the Party.

At the beginning of last year I was recommended by the Politburo and was elected Party gorkom first secretary at a plenum here and a buro was formed. And it must be said that the buro worked very fruitfully. A Moscow gorispolkom was formed, and basically I have in mind the chairman and his deputies who, of course, and many people noted this, began to engage in specific work. But from approximately the beginning of this year I started to notice that things were going badly for me. You remember that at the Party gorkom plenum we said that if things are going badly for him every leader must always say so honestly, go and say honestly to his higher-ranking Party organ: Things are going badly for me. But here, of course, there was also a tactical error. Obviously this was connected with overwork and so forth. But for me, and I cannot speak for the entire buro, things did indeed start to go badly in my work. Today this has perhaps been expressed most clearly in the fact that it was easier to give promises and to elaborate comprehensive programs than it was to implement them. That is the first point. Second, it was in that period, that is recently, that one of my chief personal features started to operate-that is my ambition, which has been mentioned today. I tried to combat it but, unfortunately, not successfully.

The main thing for me now as a Communist of the Moscow organization is, of course, what to do, what decision to take to minimize the damage to the Moscow organization. Of course, it is damage, and damage has been inflected, and it will be difficult for the new gorkom first secretary, for the buro, and for the Party gorkom to ensure that this wound which has been inflicted, this damage which has been caused, and not just to the Moscow organization, to ensure that work is done to heal it as rapidly as possible. [sentence as published]

I cannot agree that I do not love Moscow. other factors were at work but no, I had time to fall in love with Moscow and I tried to do everything womehow to eliminate the shortcomings which existed before.

It was particularly hard for me today to hear very specific criticism from those Party comrades with whom I have worked for 2 years and I would say that I can deny none of it.

Not because I need to beat my breast, since you realize that, as a Communist, I have lost the political face of a leader. I bear a great burden of guilt before the Moscow Party organization, a very great burden of guilt before the Party gorkom, before you, of course, before the buro, and, of course, I bear a very great burden of guilt personally before Mikhail Sergeevich **Gorbachev**, whose prestige is so high in our organization, in our country, and throughout the world.

As a Communist I am sure that the Moscow organization is united with the Party CC and that it has marched and will march ver confidently behind the Party CC.

M.S. **Gorbachev** then delivered the concluding speech at the plenum.

An important question, he said, was submitted for discussion at today's plenum. The content and atmosphere of the discussion once again showed the maturity and great political potential of the Moscow City Party organization and its Party committee. A frank, Party-/minded discussion took place, in a spirit of high exactingness and responsibility. Correct decisions were elaborated and adopted.

The CC Politburo and I, as general secretary, are firmly convinced that the Moscow City Party organization is our buttress, and a reliable buttress.

And the Muscovites, as has been the case at every stage of socialist building, are setting an example of intensive work today, now that the revolutionary renewal of society is under way.

You may be confident, M.S. **Gorbachev** went on, that Moscow's concerns are the CC's paramount concerns. As has already been noted, the CC has adopted a number of major decisions aimed at developing the city's economy, social sphere, and cutlure. our common concern now is to put all our plans into practice, to ensure that the Muscovites can sense the changes, and to resolve concrete problems step by step and rectify matters with regard to housing, transport, and trade.

We have submitted a proposal that a separate resolution be adopted on the development of the health care system in Moscow, so as to ensure that Moscow issues are not swamped in the general schemes and appropriations.

If you take social questions, which have become acute in Moscow-we are talking about housing, health care, transport, schools, theaters, museums-there is only one solution: Tor create a powerful, modern construction base appropriate to the scale of Moscow and the Muscovites' needs.

In a word, the Moscow City Party organization must substantially step up the work in every avenue.

I think there should be a different atmosphere both in the Party gorkom and in the city, so that people work with more initiative, not from fear, as the saying goes, but from conscience. Staunch work and persistent efforts are needed. Moscow's potential is such that if it suffers hitches, it affects the whole country, but if it operates to full capacity, the whole country feels that too, and weightily. Therefore I wish the Party organization greater efficiency, greater practicality, and greater exactingness and initiative. A worker with initiative will always find a solution as to how to act and how to lead people after him.

Today's plenum is another hard, but instructive lesson. And hard lessons are not assimilated eeasily or by everyone. When you hear some people talk, they are solidly behind the restructuring, they will draw conclusions, they assure you of their devotion to advanced ideas. But when you listen to them, there is such a fusty smell of stagnation in their statements and assurances that you can hardly stand it. Today we need deeds, not assurances, actions, not promises.

Today's lesson must not be forgotten. It is a lesson for the CPSU CC too. I am not going to embark on self-justification now and recount in detail what was done to prevent the errors in the work of the gorkom leadership that we have discussed today. I personally am upset by what has happened. After all, I had conversations with Boris Nikolaevich **Eltsin.** Searching, frank, one-on-one conversations.

I must say, Boris Nikolaevich, your ambitions hampered you, hampered you greatly. On the eve of the January plenum and at the CC plenum itself we tried firmly to set you right. There was another discussion on the eve of the June plenum.

I wish to support the comrades who spoke of the positive aspects of B.N. **Eltsin's** work. But all the same, politically he was not up to it, it proved beyond his power to head a Party organization like the Moscow City organization.

At the CC January (1987) plenum, when we analyzed the reasons for the stagnation, the reasons why, at a certain stage in the past, the CC Politburo and Secretariat were not up to the job, and what must be done to prevent a repetition of this, we were united in our conclusions. There must everywhere be an atmosphere of true Party-mindedness, criticism and self-criticism, and collegiality. No complacency. Open, comradely Party discussion is the best atmosphere, the only one in which fruitful ideas can be formulated and the correctness of policy be checked. Collectiveness and collegiality are a tremendous force.

At the CC October (1987) Plenum, when all the comrades had spoken and assessed Comrade **Eltsin's** speech as politically erroneous, I asked if there were any other proposals. Comrade V.A. **Zatvornitskii** have really cut me to the quick.

We are the Party of the working class, of the entire people. We bear responsibility for our every decision, for every practical step. The working class has achieved restructuring through suffering and is solidly behind the changes, the renewal, and the moral improvement of society.

Our enemies call us utopians and predict that we will fail. They say so because they fear our restructuring. Prior to the January plenum they declared that this was just another campaign. A new team of the country's managers has come in, it is criticizing the old team and settling scores, and this means nothing will get done. When the January plenum had been held, and the June plenum had been held, they panicked. Everthing is being done now to sow doubts among the working class and lack of faith among the working people and to compromise restructuring.

Let them speak! It is their usual ploy to say spiteful things against us.

Ours is a difficult path, but we have gone uphill and are now standing not on quicksand but on solid ground, and therefore we will stand our ground! We have such tremendous potential that we can resolve everything that has been planned. Our policy is a realistic policy. I am confident that Muscovites will make the contribution on which the country, the CC, and the government are counting, and we will support you.

"Energichno vesti perestroiku," *Pravda* (13 Nov); *Izvestiia* (14 Nov); a translation also is in FBIS, No. 219 (13 Nov 87), 59-73; a condensed version is in CDSP, 39:45 (1987), 1-4,28; 39:46 (1987), 7-12, 28. On the Eltsin Case, see especially Timothy R. Colton, "Moscow Politics and the Eltsin Affair," *The Harriman Institute Forum*, 1:6 (Jun 88), 8 p.

ECONOMICS AND TRADE

Abel Aganbegyan, **Difficult Steps Towards Restructuring** (8 Jan 87)·

Q We are going to talk mainly about the new economic strategy and restructuring, but let us begin with another question first: What has necessitated this revolutionary change? Why the sudden need?

A Why "restructure"? Because the old economic structure, the old economic policy, the old management system, the old development patterns, that is, everything that determines the economy's advance, did not correspond with the new conditions and new requirements. The growth rates of the national income, usually the most reliable indicator of economic development, the bank of wealth from which society obtains funds for both consumption and accumulation, have dropped by 150 percent in the past fifteen years. The consequences are very grave, indeed. We should have halted the negative tendency and worked out "acceleration" much earlier; yet we continued in our set ways, automatically applying old methods, without regard for the new conditions that had already begun to emerge.

Q What are these "new conditions"?

A Major changes have taken place in international markets. Equally significant changes have been taking place internally: we have experienced a halt to the growth of all production resources—labor , raw material, investments and assets. We had previously developed by drawing more and more resources into our production. We cannot continue this way any longer. We must begin to meet the challenge presented by the scientific and technical revolution which has entered a new stage. Man's place in the economy has also changed radically, but we have held on too long to the so-called residual principle of distribution—allocating funds from the national budget into the social sphere only after ensuring an increase in production.

In the 1970s and early 1980s there was a marked fall in production and labor productivity growth rates and progress in science and technology also slowed down.

It became clear that it was not enough to make minor adjustments in the running of the economy: new, radical measures—"restructuring"—were necessary. This was finally formulated by the April 1985 Plenary Meeting of the Party CC .

The 27th Congress of the CPSU called for a resolute departure from the old methods of drawing in more resources and for the formulation of policies which would lead to an acceleration of our social and economic development necessary to start shifting the stagnation.

Q Could you tell us more? What is envisaged in the 12th Five Year Plan period (1986-1990) and beyond, towards 2000?

A First of all, we need to improve the 3 percent annual increase in the national income—first to 4 percent , and by the 1990s to 5 percent. At the same time this must be achieved by reducing the requirement of resources and by improving substantially the economic efficiency: in other words, labor productivity must increase, raw material, fuel, etc., must not be wasted and the return on assets ratio must increase significantly. Unlike in previous years, in the present Five Year Plan period two-thirds of economic growth must result from the greater emphasis on more efficient utilization of resources, rising to three-quarters in the 1990s.

Q Would I be correct in drawing a parallel with the 1920s when our country carried out restructuring based on the State Electrification Plan, which meant essentially that the most modern technology—electricity—was key to the success of development of the economy? Is new technology of the present day as decisive in the present restructuring?

A Unfortunately, it is not quite as simple as that. Acceleration of progress in science and technology is not the only precondition for improving our economic development. There must be a far-reaching re-organization of the entire system of production, of the management system and of the social sphere. All this should be regarded as a package, as a unity, as a single organism in which not one body can exist independently of the other.

Scientific and technical progress may and will act as a "locomotive" in developing the economy by making production more efficient. Unfortunately, the past few years did not bring any major breakthrough in science and technology. We have just carried out improvements. A radical change is necessary in this area, too. Today, we would expect the emergence of revolutionary technologies capable of raising labor productivity several times over; we would expect generations of fundamentally new machines or equipment systems capable of running the entire complex of production. This is the aim of the new investment policy, this is the core of the reconstruction of our economy's entire material and technological base. During the current five-year plan period, the overall rate of replacement of obsolete equipment will be doubled.

Q Why is engineering and not, say, electronics, being given priority?

A Well, for one thing, the development of all areas of production depend primarily on engineering, which is used here in the broadest sense and includes electronics and instrument-making. Engineering is a priority precisely because new technologies and new inventions can only be tested through engineering. Our scientists are criticized—perhaps justly, perhaps not—for the extremely slow rate at which their inventions are being introduced. But more often than not it is the fault of engineering. Taking this into account, investment in engineering is to rise by 80 per cent in the present Five Year Plan period. Engineering is to receive unprecedented funds for development—63 billion rubles over the next five years, and these funds must be used wisely. This means in effect that by 1990 almost 60 percent of the technical base in engineering is to be renewed. This will facilitate a good increase in the level of our engineering output, yet it will by no means resolve the problem completely. Studies have shown that 71 percent of serial engineering output does not correspond to modern requirements. In machine-tool construction and instrument-making 86 percent and 83 percent of output respectively are below world standards. Our country suffers serious losses which can no longer be sustained. It is necessary to stop certain lines of production altogether and to replace them by better, more modern ones. Whilst only 3.1 percent of all engineering products were modernized in 1985, we are now aiming for this figure to be 13 percent.

The production of machinery is set a very high target: by 1990, 80-90 percent of all products must measure up favorably to the highest standards in the world. By replacing old equipment, productivity must rise one and a half times, reliability twice. The consumption of metal per unit of product is to be reduced by 12 -18 percent Many reconstruction plans have to be redrawn with this target in mind.

Q There are plenty of examples showing that the reorganization in engineering is not going smoothly. Could you name a large old-fashioned plant whose reconstruction is going well and could serve as an example?

A There are many such examples. Personnel changes at the top brought many new young directors who have set about the job with energy and zeal, boldly breaking down not only the ramshackle workshops but also longstanding practices. The establishment of direct links with similar enterprises in the socialist countries will be combined with the best technological and scientific experience of our country.

We could mention one example—the Gorky Car Factory. It would be difficult to find a more complex enterprise with such old machinery, some of it pre-war, producing outdated cars. The plant goes back to the 1930s, when much of the labor was manual. So they started to reconstruct this giant. It was given a relatively small amount of hard currency—much less than the new Volga Car Factory. The plant management had to decide how best to make use of it. The option was to purchase automated lines abroad which would produce modern automobiles. That's what is usually done. Or, one could consider spending a part of the foreign currency on creating own automated production with specially developed equipment. Then some of the money could be spent on the development of new models and new machines and on quality control. There may be some left for the purchase of the best foreign cars in order to see for oneself what the world standards are.

GCF chose the latter as the best strategic alternative. They have started producing machinery and parts themselves. For example, they obtained permission to use some Ivanovo plant designs which allowed the setting up of automated lines for various processes, including casting. So the old factory suddenly developed a truly modern casting process and greatly improved working conditions. By the end of the present Five Year Plan period this old car factory will begin to use new techniques and new equipment in the mass production of a totally new diesel-engine truck. To come back to the target figures, the new product will be 50 percent more economical than the old one, 70 percent more efficient and twice as reliable. Every 10,000 of the new type trucks will save the national economy 65 million rubles. Moreover, there is now a production basis strong enough to allow for further improvements.

Q There is currently a lot of talk about the need for radical reform of the entire management system. Why is restructuring in this area not proceeding as quickly as one would wish? What is hampering progress?

A The essence of radical reform consists above all in a shift from bureaucratically administrative methods to true economic management. The interrelationship between the supply, financing and prices needs a fundamental shakeup. We must move away from a direct centralized allocation of capital goods to an apparatus of wholesale buying and selling. This cannot be done at once for the simple reason, which may sound somewhat contradictory, that enterprises have too much money at their disposal. As soon as they were allowed to buy what they pleased, the old fashioned "acquisitive instinct" they have developed would come into play, and they would increase stocks out of all proportion.

This is not mere speculation. A large-scale experiment has already shown that as soon as enterprises are given the go-ahead to make special purchases, they buy equipment and material "for the rainy day". The value of stocks in all enterprises in our economy exceeds 460 billion rubles! This is not far off the total figure for national income. Moreover, the stocks are growing twice as fast as production. Stock of material resources was acquired largely through credit; there were years when production increased by 3-4 percent and credit by 10-15 percent. As a result, there is an enormous amount of spare money, not geared to the real requirements of production. For this reason alone, the introduction of wholesale trade is necessary and it must go hand in hand with the reform of finance and credit, as stated in the Political Report to the 27th Congress of the CPSU.

We also need to devise a special mechanism which would prevent the growth of excess stocks, otherwise wholesale trade will not function.

Another vital question is that of the pricing policy. The new economic mechanism must discourage waste; it must encourage economy and efficiency; the churning out of more of the same old goods must give way to goods of better quality and better design. The system as it is encourages waste and it must not be tolerated any longer.

All parts of the economic "trinity"—supply, financing and prices—must undergo a change. Improving one without the others would not help. Experience has shown that a price reform alone takes at least two years of preparation. Yet without it there can be no advance to new economic managemen

Q But neither can we sit idly by...?

A Certainly not. A lot of individual regulations and procedures can be removed without waiting for fundamental restructuring. Some of the changes can only be achieved in waves, as it were. In industry, the first wave of restructuring is to introduce incentives as to encourage fulfilment of contractual obligations to the greatest extent possible. Annual planning of wage funds allocated to individual enterprises is abandoned for establishing long-term economic indices. Individual enterprises exercise their right to plan their labor requirement and to set wages.

These are not radical measures but they are in tune with restructuring and have already yielded some positive results. Contractual deliveries have improved, labor productivity has increased somewhat already and there are first signs of saving in the cost of production In 1986, 44 percent of industrial enterprises were working under this experiment. The remainder will adopt similar measures in 1987. That is good but not enough. We have to go further.

Q And now for the second major wave of restructuring which began in 1987. It entails transition to a complete self-financing system, such as exercised already by the VCF and the Sumy Engineering Enterprise.

A Self-financing is, of course, a more far-reaching measure. It moves away from the old-time disposal of budget and incentive funds. Profit in self- financing becomes the main economic indicator and a fixed percentage of profit (long-term indicator) is all important to management decisions. Investment must be made to stimulate production, and enterprises are being given a great deal of freedom in fund application. Their relationship with higher financial bodies and ministries is becoming more meaningful. Very pleasing results can be gained if this system is applied properly, as was the case of VCF and of the Sumy Engineering Enterprise. For example, after one year of the new experiment at the Sumy Engineering Enterprise, output increased 14 percent and profit 32 percent. This enabled the corporation to carry out reconstruction, to improve the quality of production and working conditions.

In 1987, self-financing is fully practiced in five sectors of the economy, in a number of large enterprises, in the USSR Merchant Marine Industry, and in some parts of trade. If this system proves its worth (and it is very likely that it will), it will predominate as early as in 1988. We believe that self-financing will bring more tangible progress in raising labor productivity, production efficiency and the quality of products. Yet, I am sorry to say, that even this is not enough!

We need to look to a third—the most important—wave of restructuring. The third wave will be characterised by a radical expansion of individual enterprise's independence. This wave requires careful preparation. It will gain momentum only if the pricing system and the financial and credit mechanisms are also changed, when the transition to wholesale trade and trading between enterprises is completed. Then it will be possible to reduce drastically the number of old-type plan indicators, including those on the centrally planned list of products. It will be possible to do away with the present form of annual planning altogether and make the Five Year Plans a true target. There will be a supply and demand system, developing contractual relations not only horizontally (between enterprises) but also vertically. We will then be truly "managing" our economy.

Q But you will agree that if enterprises are to be given these rights they will have to be taken away from someone, say, from the ministries? Experience shows that they do not want to give up their sinecure. What is to be done? How can one 'placate' those who have been used to calling the tune?

A. That is indeed a problem, and a very difficult one at that. Some estimates put the number of legally binding instructions at about 200,000. Needless to say, many of them must be outdated. And it is not altogether clear which of them are in strict accordance with the law and which are not, and this puts the manager with initiative in a very difficult situation. Many control bodies have stepped up their activity under the pretext of restructuring and it is very easy to find "culprits", which is why many managers are simply afraid to exercise their independence, seeing that it has only brought their neighbors to grief.

Perhaps the solution lies in the following: first, we need a law which clearly stipulates the rights and duties of the enterprises. The Political Bureau of the CC of the CPSU is considering such a bill.

As to all the administrative organizations of our "super-structure", they should operate under clear regulations, defining their terms of reference which would not be enforceable by law. Then, if they do anything unjust towards an enterprise, the whole law-enforcement system would come to the management's defence.

This problem is also linked with the redistribution of rights—away from the sectoral ministerial bodies towards enterprises themselves. It is interesting that once such a redistribution of rights is under way, it immediately becomes clear that whole chunks of the sectoral apparatus may be dispensed with. For example, many engineering ministries have dismantled central administrative bodies responsible for a group of enterprises with substantial staff reductions. The ministries are supposed to shed detailed supervision, but, unfortunately, they are still too often holding onto day-to-day management though it would be much more effective if they were to hand this over to lower levels of management. The ministries could then be transformed into truly specialist headquarters of their sector—a stipulation of the 27th Congress of the CPSU. Major reform has not yet penetrated the national economy and there is still too much scope for using old methods of management.

Q In other words, the lower and the top managements are for restructuring, but the "middle link" is, as it were, resisting it?

A Why "as it were"? They *are* resisting it. It is like this. A person is learning to swim. Even if no one interferes, it is still not a simple matter. Our economic system, too, needs to find how to swim in the sea of different approaches and to learn how to use the new levers and the new incentives. That is difficult in itself, for we have no experience in this direction. But it is even more difficult if someone grabs the swimmer by the hands and feet and tries to push his head under water. Brakes of this kind complicate the restructuring process, especially as every manager has the alternative of standing still on the bank and waiting to see whether his bolder colleague, attempting to start reforms, will swim or sink.

Q But there must be something which makes the offer of independence attractive?

A There is. without waiting for the entire strategy to gain momentum, the Party and government have been seeking consistently, step by step, to expand the independence and responsibility of individual enterprises.

I'll cite two examples. First: cooperation with foreign enterprises was made easier in the summer of 1986. Seventy enterprises under the jurisdiction of different ministries were given the right to enter independently the world market, including the capitalist one.

Second: in October 1986, the CPSU CC gave official approval to the collective management of the Construction Enterprise No. 18 whose director is Nikolai **Travkin**. This enterprise is managed by a council which has worker representatives. Each individual's contribution affects the results. The wage funds and bonuses are the concern of all. The principle of collective contracts is not limited to work teams but is beginning to be espoused by workshops and, in some cases, by entire enterprises. It is cited as an example which could be applied on a much wider scale. It not only highlights the direct connection between work and pay but also allows for a democratic participation of the workforce.

Q I know a little about Enterprise No. 18, where what we call the "human factor" is key in the new management strategy. Can you enlarge on this?

A Indeed, one might think that as a result of the scientific and technical revolution, it is science and technology which are the principal moving force in development. One might very well ask where the human element comes in. Yes, science and technology and its application to the various technological processes is a key aspect. But one must also consider the other aspect: the most advanced findings can be applied only through highly educated and qualified personnel, both individually and as a collective. This is why we attach so much importance to education and training.

There is an old saying that if you give a man a fish he will be well fed once, but if you teach him how to fish he will be well fed for life. It is more important to teach than to provide.

The changes under way in our country are aimed to benefit the people, to make our people's life more pleasant, more beautiful. The notion of 'acceleration' entails an orientation towards people's needs, towards tackling the many pressing social problems. The 12th Five Year Plan stipulates the doubling of the growth rate of foodstuffs and of services and a 50 percent increase in the growth rates of consumer goods in general. There is to be a substantial increase in the building of houses and apartments, of children's institutions, of schools, hospitals, polyclinics, and of cultural amenities. A radical program for the improvement in health care is being drafted. Retirement pensions will be increased. Manual labor, especially arduous labor, will be reduced to a minimum and the working conditions generally will be improved. The economists are finally paying attention to the importance of the protection of the environment.

Work should be enjoyed by people; tedious work should be made easier through mechanization and automation. Moreover, we must try to evoke the feeling in people that they are the masters. This can be achieved only through greater independence of enterprises and through extended rights of the collective.

If we could only "burst the dam" of creativity and initiative, tap the potential of each individual. Remember how much our country once benefitted from the popularity of gliding and radio enthusiasts. Computerization is the order of the day. Worldwide experience shows that many important inventions have been made by individuals or small groups. It happened to be two young fellows in a garage and not a mighty electronics corporation which put together the first personal computer. We must remove all obstacles in the way of our inventors. Currently, a new law facilitating inventions is being drafted.

Of course, we must not forget material incentives. Those who work better should receive higher rewards. We should not look down on earning extra money by honest means after regular work. The new law on self-employment has been passed, lifting many restrictions. The opportunities are still wanting. Why do some socialist countries have research cooperatives and special banks which finance inventions, yet we do not? I believe one should take a look at this area, too. The acceleration of our country's economic development and the new orientation towards people's needs are one and the same continuous process.

A. Aganbegyan, "Neprost'ye shagi perestroiki," *Nedelia* No. 1 (8 Jan). Interviewer was Boris Konovalov. Aganbegyan, an economist and academician, was director of the institute of Industrial Production of the Siberian Branch (Novosibirsk) of the USSR Academy of Sciences. He is founder and editor of the magazine EKO (Economics and Organization of Industrial Production), and a chief adviser to Gorbachev and the Politburo.

G. Popov, **Problems and Opinions. Restructuring in the Economy** (20 and 21 Jan 87)

I

As was noted in the New Year's address to the Soviet people, we have been able to move ahead in practically every sector of the economy. But the forces of stagnation are still making themselves felt, restructuring is going slowly, old approaches are holding us back, and inertia is strong. What form should the real levers of acceleration take? To answer that question, one must take a closer look at the factors that M.S.**Gorbachev** identified as putting a brake on our progress.

It is still too early to don placards reading "We have restructured." And in a general sense, one must not oversimplify the task of true restructuring. What's more, restructuring is made more difficult by the fact that there is still little knowledge about concrete ways of implementing the strategic line laid down by the 27th CPSU Congress. We know what the problems are, but what's not yet entirely clear is how to resolve them in practical terms.

Apart from such objective reasons, there are subjective ones as well. They are subjective, but in no sense accidental, since they are rooted in the previous system of predominantly administrative management.

Naturally, few people openly urge that administrative methods be retained. But covert attachment to such methods, hidden behind concern for the planning principle and for centralism, is still quite widespread. In practice, this means an attachment to oversight. The argument runs approximately as follows: Every employee and every enterprise and institution has only to completely meet his or its responsibilities, whether they be a matter of official instructions or of obligations to clients, and everything will be as it should in the economy. Therefore, the argument goes, we need to increase and toughen the punishments for violations of any sort.

The more far-sighted champions of retaining administrative levers feel that the problem is a broader one. It lies not in the violations themselves but in those who commit them—in the executives. Therefore, we need to resolutely get rid of employees who do not measure up.

But, one wonders, how is the line to be drawn between those who measure up and those who do not? One district Party committee secretary, when reproached for poor performance, objected: "But the people here feel that I'm doing a good job. Convene a plenary session and ask them." He was confident of his support. But it wasn't worth much, if one considers that over a protracted period of time the secretary in question had been building the Party committee in such a way that he would be very "comfortable" with it in plenary session. In a situation of that sort, an appeal to democracy smacks more of a travesty of democracy and serves as a cover for the same sort of administrative rule.

There are attempts to use command-type methods, but in a modernized form that is in keeping with the spirit of the times. In this connection, let me hazard a few remarks about placing excessive hopes in the state product acceptance system. The benefits of the system are obvious. At the same time, one should recall that for many years a multitude of oversight bodies—economic, state, Party and public—fought substandard output but were simply unable to eradicate it. There's good reason for that. All administrative methods of oversight presuppose the existence of ideal employees—employees who are not self-serving and who cannot be bought -to do the overseeing. But why should the state product acceptance system succeed in finding the kind of employees that other agencies were unable to find? The new inspectors, like everyone else, will have to "get ahold of" tickets in order to make a business trip on schedule, "nab" a hotel room, get their kids into a Young Pioneer camp, obtain housing, and so on. Inevitably, the inspectors will gradually become exactly like the people around them. This, of course, will undercut their ability to combat violations and will erode the working people's faith in their objectivity. But without the support of the masses, punitive measures won't help much.

Of course from a breakdown in discipline, and poor leadership in the directing of the economy follows huge losses, not to mention the appearance of embezzlers and those who "feed in the trough.". It is necessary to struggle against all of these factors. But will only punitive measures suffice?

One of my acquaintances was named to an executive position in a ministry. In his previous job at a factory, he had fought for many years for a new type of economic accountability. But within a few months of joining the staff of the ministry, he began saying that enterprises could not be given broad powers. Strange as it may seem, this metamorphosis occurred because of his conscientiousness. At the factory, the desire to do a good job in accomplishing the enterprise's tasks made him fight to expand its independence, while at the ministry, his conscientious efforts to ensure across-the-board fulfillment of plan assignments for the branch as a whole made him an opponent of true economic accountability.

As we see, the matter is not simply one of people but of the management mechanism as well. In my opinion, even if all existing instructions, norms and laws were fully observed, true acceleration could scarcely be achieved. Administrative methods can achieve quite a lot, but their powers are limited. They are particularly poor at fighting for scientific and technical progress, managing brainpower, and boldly jettisoning old ideas and methods that are no longer effective.

Administrative methods and oversight procedures are generally preferred by executives who do not have a solid command of their business and who are capable only of formally matching results against norms. Thus, for them restructuring means conducting intensive checkups. That gives causes a kind of nonstop pursuit of remiss executives. The most dangerous tactic is to punish any and all divergence from the rules, whether committed for the good of the common cause or for personal advantage. The result is to teach executives to fear experimentation, to take a passive stand, and to change nothing. That is why I believe we must bank primarily on economic methods. What is happening in that area?

One of the brigades at a major Leningrad plant switched to contractual work. In a few months' time it fulfilled its annual plan assignment and found itself without materials, orders, or even money to pay it wages. After all, the plant didn't get any additional resources, and the other shops still had no need for the brigade's finished output. In a word, acceleration in one area yields few results without a change in the principles of economic accountability, planning and supply throughout the entire production system.

Or take the well-known decision of the USSR State Committee on Labor and Social Questions on the matter of pay rates and salaries. It spells out in detail, for both types of remuneration, whose rates can be increased for what and by how much. The plant is supposed to earn the money for these purposes itself. The intention is good. In adopting innovations, however, one must keep in mind not only their pluses but also the cases where they will not work, and act in such a way as to avoid hitches. It's not all that important for an employee to know what part of his 250 rubles in pay is wages and what part is bonus. He's going to get his 250 rubles regardless. That's yet another variant of a rather typical approach: It appears that economic levers are being improved, but in fact they are being complicated by a mass of purely administrative limitations and barriers.

But the USSR State Committee on Labor and Social Questions has yet to solve the main problem—making pay a reflection of end results. The lion's share of any enterprise's wage fund is still formed on the basis of the gross-output indicator, regardless of labor-intensiveness and quality of output. Enterprises are still very limited in their ability to provide incentives for improving the yield from labor.

Finally, let us look at the most progressive method—self-support and self-financing. Some people are already inclined to see this as the full economic accountability that is mentioned in the documents of the 27th Party Congress. Let us look at what things self-support currently applies to. Does it apply to direct orders from customers? To the enterprise's own initiatives? Hardly. Self-support applies to directive-type plan assignments handed down from above and based, moreover, on prices that do not reflect customer demand. Prices have remained unchanged—cost-plus in substance and administratively imposed in form. In summary, self-support does exist, and that is a plus, but it is incomplete because it does not put the entire responsibility for work results squarely on the enterprise's employees. Many of them go right on striving for an understated plan at all costs, because even where self-support exists, the wage fund is not linked to end results the way it should be.

Although an enterprise can now earn its own money for expansion and modernization of production it is still allowed to purchase goods with only a small part of that money, as was the case after 1965, when the fund for the development of production was created. To spend the rest of the money, the enterprise still has to write statements of requirement, submit them for approval, and get them included in the plan. Self-financing applies only to the scientific and technical progress that gets approved by the ministry.

There is no doubting the fact that the economic accountability of the large-scale experiment is more thoroughgoing than in the past. There is even less doubt that economic accountability in the context of self-support and self-financing is more thoroughgoing than was the original version. But the principal shortcomings of the earlier procedure have yet to be overcome. And therefore announcing "full economic accountability as of 1 Jan 1987" is more than anything a reflection of our old habit of issuing rousing reports. After all, many enterprises operate at a loss and are not ready for a transition to self-support and full economic accountability.

Thus, many of the present innovations have yet to reach the threshold that marks the beginning of a real transition from predominantly administrative management methods to predominantly economic ones. As a result, though these recent months have indeed been a factor in acceleration, they have not fully engaged the principal levers of effectiveness because they are incomplete and lack comprehensiveness. What exactly prevents the transition to a bold economic system capable of sustaining an extended period of growth? This will be addressed in the concluding half of this article.

II

Perestroika moves slowly because, as was outlined in the first part of the author's article yesterday, still great expectations rest with administrative leadership methods, but the economis matters are changed only simply. Why does this happen? And how do we find a solution?

Behind the attempts to retain administrative-management methods and the timidity in applying economic methods there are real people. Employees of various economic bodies who stand to lose their jobs as a result of restructuring are a principal retarding factor. They are joined by employees in the administrative apparatus of ministries and departments whose positions and roles are closely tied to the shortcomings in the existing management system— to shortages of goods and housing and to the distribution of those items, for example.

Restructuring is also being retarded by employees and agencies whose jobs and existence are not threatened, but whose status and role are being changed. In connection with the transition to economic methods, they are to go from their administrative-command roles to operating on the basis of material incentives for their subordinates. And that is no simple matter. When I issue commands I'm always right, and my subordinates are obligated to carry out my orders. They are not free to question my competence. But if I manage through an appeal to people's interests and if, moreover, my subordinates have the right to discuss an order that is detrimental to their interests, then I need to know and be able to do at least a slight bit more than the others. But not everyone is enthused over that prospect, since some are not up to it.

The situation is compounded by the fact that the retarding factors in the management system receive indirect support from the position of certain executives of local Party bodies. During the years of predominantly administrative methods they developed forms of management that no longer work today. In particular, they spent a great deal of time and energy on monitoring levels of plan fulfillment and then on seeing that plan targets were met at all costs. What's more, they were able to order construction organizations, for instance, to build facilities that were not in the plan, although that could cause even production capacity that was highly important to the national economy to miss its deadline for commissioning. The shift to economic methods, the development of self-management, and the creation of elective management positions sometimes strike Party functionaries as all but a deathblow to their former skills and experience.

I am not even talking about the "Old Believers" of sorts, who take a stand against restructuring on "theoretical" grounds. Though they do not malign material incentives outright, they attempt to replace them with social interest, a notion that smacks of romanticism. They carry on about dangers, they issue warnings, and they admonish against overdoing things. Essentially, what they are defending is not even centralism, but centralism's vehicle—the bureaucratic administrative apparatus.

But nonetheless, I feel that the aforementioned groups are not the principal retarding factors. Their resistance could easily be swept aside by a mass movement of the working people based on the will of the Party leadership. But that is precisely the problem: A movement of that kind in support of the new management system has yet to acquire the requisite scope.

It has not acquired scope because, over the decades that we planned from the achieved level, we taught even our best workers, our best brigades, and entire factories, collective farms, districts and provinces that you must not surge ahead too strongly—otherwise the next year's plan will be even greater.

But the most alarming thing is the caution being shown by "ordinary" employees—workers, engineers and executives alike. In my opinion, their stand is explained by the fact that nonlabor income accounts for a part of their earnings. Usually nonlabor income is understood as a bribe, or speculation. But in my opinion, the main flow of nonlabor income is more often than not always from the paid wages of average workers.

The fact of the matter is that average workers, collective farmers, executives, scientists, physicians, and engineers receive part of their earnings (and not infrequently a significant part) not for the end results of their work but for a certain percentage of plan fulfillment, for time worked, for the positions they hold or for their academic degrees. Here, they abolish certain certain NI, in which all of their social organizations spent their Sundays clearing newspaper billboards. But, this was not an important nor realistic return on their output. and although the employees considered themselves honest laborers, who truly broke no law, they still dealt a blow to the country directly, by wasting money, and obliquely, in not supporting technical progress. Perhaps the damage was even greater than that inflicted by salespeople, or by speculants, who accept bribes.

And that is a blatant example.

How much non-labor income there is in the form of excess staff at various institutions, as well as pay and bonuses for meeting unduly easy plan targets!

It is sometimes said that there are no such non-labor earnings, since most people do not earn much. But much or little is of no importance here. I can receive very little, but I will get the same for a high standard of finished labor. Consequently, I live, wholly or in part, on non-labor income. Fears for that guaranteed income—be it ever so small—that is not tied to work, fears for that "bonus", are what make employees passive during the transition to the new system.

The result is that there are workers and employees who, in their hearts, still do not want restructuring—who prefer today's small bird in the hand to tomorrow's large bird in the bush. Certain enterprise executives are entirely satisfied with the present system, which exempts them from accountability and risk-taking. And passivity in the basic production unit is the base that allows even management personnel who outright regard restructuring to hold onto their jobs.

Who does want changes? It's the far-sighted political leaders and management personnel and the outstanding people in science and the cultural sphere. They understand that in the 21st Century the present variant of development will be dangerous for the country. Further, it's the leading contingent of the working class and of collective farmers, engineers and technicians who are striving to improve their lives and who want to earn more, but to earn it by their own labor, without any finagling. And it's the segment of the intelligentsia that is interested in scientific and technical progress.

At present, restructuring is proceeding slowly. To speed it up, we need to find a suitable mechanism. The decisions of the Party congress tell what remains to be done. We need to make maximum use of material incentives in order to activate the human factor. And to do that, we need to put enterprises on full economic accountability, give them independence in day-to-day management decisions and, where necessary, in the area of expanded reproduction as well.

Concurrently, we need to identify the tasks that the enterprises are either entirely unable to accomplish by themselves or would be slower and less efficient at accomplishing than are the central bodies. In other words, the center, freed of routine concerns and day-to-day management would focus its efforts on solving fundamental problems of scientific and technical progress. In some respects, that would be reminiscent of the stratagem devised during NEP [New Economic Policy instituted by Lenin in 1921, and destroyed by Stalin by 1927.] expanding independence at the lowest level and concentrating all efforts at the upper level on the future—on industrialization.

And now, as concerns the **methods of acceleration**. Sometimes one hears the following idea put forward: Let's not touch a thing, let's just pay more for labor-productivity growth and quality of output. Outwardly, this makes sense, but it would be difficult to carry off in practice. First of all, there is a lag of sorts between the growth in productivity and the ability to provide goods to cover the increased purchasing power. As a result, the money supply would grow still further, which would simply serve to discredit acceleration. The method in question could become a basic one in the future.

But for the present, a different scheme makes better sense. At the initial stage, in my opinion, we should do away with wage levelling as a means of distributing the benefits of our existing consumption fund. In other words, we should **increase** the pay of the best employees by **decreasing** the pay of the worst. As the reader knows, it is not our custom to cut people's pay. and that's too bad. The basic job of overcoming wage levelling and redistributing earnings must be put in the hands of the employees themselves. This approach will seem unfair to those who want to live tension-free lives. But without aggravating relations among co-workers, we will scarcely be able to generate a truly mass movement for restructuring and acceleration.

In the first part of the article several absolutely unsuitable methods have already been discussed. It is very important that the instructions worked out after the release of the decisions of the directorate fully correlate with the [latter], and do not complicate, but aid their realization.

And finally, as **concerns procedural arrangements for acceleration**. Restructuring presupposes a radical change in the functions and authority of the central economic bodies. And that being the case, these bodies will very likely prove unable to become true creators of the new economic mechanism without a radical restructuring of their own.

Specialists at the USSR State Planning Committee, for example, are in a position to make any sorts of proposals except those that require fundamental changes in their functions and, consequently, a "purge" of their staff. The Ministry of Instruments, Automation Equipment and Control Systems will propose restructuring virtually anything in the work of other ministries and departments, but will not, for example, recommend cutting its own staff to a third of its size in order to recruit personnel able to utilize economic methods. Particularly important, in the words of V.I. **Lenin**, is "in order for the better elements which exist in our social order, and particularly progressive workers first and foremost, and secondly, the truly enlightened elements, for whom one can vouch, that they will take nothing on faith, will say nothing against their conscience, will not be afraid to assume any hardships or be afraid of any struggle for the attainment of goals, seriously proposed for oneself."

We must encourage those who honestly want change, and leave no escape for those who hope to wait it out and sit it out. We must remove from office those who have chosen to actively hamper restructuring or who are attempting to put in its place an administrative fake in the guise of an economic mechanism. Today we have just politics and a clearly defined goal. All our strength must be put toward its attainment.

G. Popov, "Problemy i suzhdeniia. Perestroike v ekonomike," *Pravda* (20 and 21 Jan); a condensed translation is in CDSP, 39:3 (1987), 1-5. Popov is a professor economics, Moscow University.

In the USSR Council of Ministers. "On the Procedure Governing the Creation on USSR Territory and the Activities of Joint Enterprises with the Participation of Soviet Organizations and Firms of Capitalist and Developing Countries" (27 Jan 87)·
On 13 January 1987 the USSR Council of Ministers adopted a resolution "On the Procedure Governing the Creation, on USSR Territory, and the Activities of Joint Enterprises With the Participation of Soviet Organizations and Firms of Capitalist and Developing Countries."

The resolution is aimed at further developing trade, economic, scientific and technical cooperation with the capitalist and developing countries on a stable and mutually advantageous basis.

It is established that joint enterprises, with the participation of Soviet organizations and firms of capitalist and developing countries, are created on USSR territory with the authorization of the USSR Council of Ministers on the basis of contracts concluded by the participants in such enterprises.

Joint enterprises are guided in their operation by the decree of 13 January 1987 of the Presidium of the USSR Supreme Soviet "On Questions Having to Do With the Creation, on USSR Territory, and the Activities of Joint Enterprises, International Associations and Organizations With the Participation of Soviet and Foreign Organizations, Firms and Management Bodies," the present resolution and other acts of USSR and Union-republic legislation, with the exceptions established by the USSR's interstate and intergovernmental treaties.

Proposals for the creation of joint enterprises, together with technical and economic substantiating documents and draft articles of incorporation, are submitted by the concerned Soviet organizations to the ministries and departments to which they belong. Republic ministries and departments submit such proposals to the corresponding Union-Republic Councils of Ministers.

The aforementioned USSR ministries and departments and Union-republic Councils of Ministers clear the proposals with the USSR State Planning Committee, the USSR Ministry of Finance and other concerned ministries and departments.

Once cleared, these proposals for the creation of joint enterprises are submitted to the USSR Council of Ministers.

In creating such enterprises, the ministries and departments that have jurisdiction over the Soviet participants in joint enterprises pursue the objective of more fully meeting the country's needs for specific types of industrial output, raw materials and food products, making advanced foreign equipment and technology, managerial experience and additional material and financial resources available to the USSR economy, developing the country's export base and reducing irrational imports.

The Participants, Property and Rights of Joint Enterprises

The participants in joint enterprises can be one or several Soviet enterprises (associations and other organisations) that constitute legal entities, and one or several foreign firms (companies, corporations or other organizations) that constitute legal entities.

The Soviet side must have at least a 51 percent share in the initial capitalization.

Joint enterprises are legal entities under Soviet legislation. On their own behalf, they can conclude contracts, acquire property and personal nonproperty rights, incur obligations and be plaintiffs and defendants in a court and in an arbitration court. Joint enterprises are financially independent and operate on the basis of full economic accountability, self- support and self-financing.

A joint enterprise must have a charter, and such charter is subject to confirmation by its participants. The charter defines the object and objectives of the enterprise's operation, its location, the composition of its participants, the amount of the initial capitalization, the size of the participants' shares, the procedure governing the way initial capitalization is to be formed (including foreign currency), the structure, composition and competence of the enterprise's management bodies, the procedure governing the adoption of decisions and the range of questions whose resolution requires unanimity, as well as the procedure governing liquidation of the enterprise. The charter can also include other provisions that are not in conflict with Soviet legislation and relate to specific aspects of the joint enterprise's operation.

The term of operation of the joint enterprise is agreed upon by the parties to the agreement to create the enterprise or in its charter (articles of incorporation).

After their articles of incorporation have taken effect, joint enterprises created on USSR territory register with the USSR Ministry of Finance and acquire the rights of legal entities as of that moment. An announcement of the creation joint enterprises is published in the press.

The initial capitalization of the joint enterprise is comprised of contributions from its participants. It can be augmented with profits from the enterprise's economic activity and, when necessary, with additional contributions from its participants as well.

Contributions to the joint enterprise's initial capitalization can take the form of buildings, structures, equipment and other material valuables and rights to use land, water, other natural resources, buildings, structures and equipment, as well as other property rights (including the use of inventions and know-how) and money in the currencies of the countries participating in the joint enterprise and also in freely convertible currencies.

The Soviet participant's contribution to the initial capitalization of the joint enterprise is stated in rubles, on the basis of contractual prices and with due regard for prices on the world market. The contribution of the foreign participant or participants stated in the same manner, with the value of the contribution recalculated in terms of rubles, based on the USSR State Bank's official exchange rate on the day that the contract is signed creating the joint enterprise, or on some other date agreed upon by the participants. In the event that world market prices are lacking, the value of the property being contributed is determined by agreement between the participants.

The equipment, materials and other property imported into the USSR by the foreign participants in a joint enterprise as their contribution to the enterprise's initial capitalization are exempt from customs duty.

The property of a joint enterprise is subject to mandatory insurance through USSR insurance agencies.

In accordance with Soviet legislation, the joint enterprise has the right to possess, use and dispose of its property in accordance with the objectives of its activity and the intended purpose of the property. Its property is not subject to requisition or confiscation by administrative procedure.

The property rights of a joint enterprise enjoy protection in accordance with the provisions of Soviet legislation established for Soviet state organizations. Claims can be assessed against the property of joint enterprises only by decision of the agencies that, in accordance with USSR legislation, can hear disputes involving joint enterprises.

The participants in a joint enterprise have the right, by mutual agreement, to transfer all or part of their shares in the joint enterprise to third parties. In each individual instance, the transfer of such shares is carried out with the permission of the USSR Council of Ministers' State Foreign Economic Relations Commission. The Soviet participants have priority in acquiring foreign participants' shares.

In the event of reorganization of a joint enterprise, its rights and obligations are transferred to its successors.

The rights to industrial property belonging to joint enterprises are protected in accordance with Soviet legislation, including protection in the form of patents. The procedure by which rights to industrial property are transferred to a joint enterprise by participants in that enterprise, and by which a joint enterprise transfers such rights to its participants, as well as the procedure for the commercial use of such rights and their protection abroad, is specified in the articles of incorporation.

A joint enterprise answers for its obligations with all the property belonging to it.

The Soviet state and Soviet participants in a joint enterprise are not liable for the joint enterprise's obligations, and the joint enterprise is not liable for the obligations of the Soviet state and its participants.

Joint enterprises' branches that are set up on USSR territory and that constitute legal entities are not liable for the obligations of the joint enterprises, and the joint enterprises are not liable for the obligations of such branches.

Joint enterprises created on USSR territory can open branches and offices, provided that their articles of incorporation grant them that right.

Joint enterprises created with the participation of Soviet organizations on the territory of other countries may open branches on USSR territory by following the procedure established for the creation of joint enterprises.

In accordance with USSR legislation, disputes between joint enterprises and Soviet state, cooperative and other public organizations and disputes among themselves, as well as disputes between the participants in a joint enterprise over questions concerning its operation, are heard by USSR courts or, with the sides' consent, by an arbitration court.

The Procedure Governing the Operation of Joint Enterprises.
The ruling body of a joint enterprise is a board consisting of persons appointed by its participants. The procedure governing the adoption of decisions by the board are specified in the articles of incorporation.

Management of the joint enterprise's day-to-day operation is exercized by management, which consists of Soviet and foreign citizens.

The chairman of the board and the general director of the enterprise are USSR citizens.

A joint enterprise deals with central bodies of USSR and Union-republic state administration through the agencies with jurisdiction over the Soviet participant in the enterprise, and it deals directly with local administrative bodies.

A joint enterprise independently drafts and adopts programs for its business activities. USSR state agencies do not set mandatory plan assignments for the joint enterprise or guarantee the sale of its output.

A joint enterprise is granted the right to independently conduct export and import operations necessary to its economic activity, including operations on the markets of CMEA member-countries.

The aforementioned export and import operations can also be conducted through Soviet foreign-trade organizations or through the foreign participants' marketing operations, on the basis of appropriate contracts.

A joint enterprise's importation into the USSR and exportation from the USSR of goods and other property are conducted on the basis of permits issued in accordance with the procedure established by USSR legislation.

A joint enterprise has the right to carry on correspondence and telegraph, teletype and telephone communications with organizations of other countries.

All foreign-exchange outlays of a joint enterprise, including the payment of profits and other sums owed to foreign participants and specialists, must be paid by the joint enterprise with receipts from the sale of its output on the external market.

Sales of a joint enterprise's output on the Soviet market and deliveries to the joint enterprise from this market of equipment, raw and other materials, components, fuel, energy and other output are paid for in rubles through the appropriate Soviet foreign-trade organizations, at contractual prices, with due regard for prices on the world market.

If necessary, a joint enterprise can use credits obtained under commercial terms:

—in foreign exchange, from the USSR Foreign Trade Bank or, with the USSR Foreign Trade Bank's consent, from foreign banks and firms;

—in rubles, from the USSR State Bank or the USSR Foreign Trade Bank.

The USSR State Bank and the USSR Foreign Trade Bank have the right to monitor whether credits issued to a joint enterprise are used for their intended purpose, adequately secured and promptly repaid.

The funds of a joint enterprise are deposited in its ruble or foreign- exchange accounts in the USSR State Bank and in the USSR Foreign Trade Bank, respectively, and are expended for purposes related to the enterprise's activity. The joint enterprise is paid interest on the sums credited to its accounts:

—in foreign exchange, on the basis of interest rates on world money markets;

—in rubles, under the terms and in accordance with the procedure determined by the USSR State Bank.

Differences in exchange rates that affect joint enterprises' foreign- exchange accounts or their operations in foreign exchange are reflected in their profit and loss statements.

The joint enterprise sets up a reserve fund and other funds essential to its operation and to the social development of its collective.

Deductions from profits are deposited in the reserve fund until the fund reaches 25% of the enterprise's initial capitalization. The amounts of annual deductions are determined in accordance with the procedure established by the articles of incorporation.

A list of other funds and the procedure governing their formation and expenditure are specified in the articles of incorporation.

The profits of a joint enterprise, minus amounts deducted to cover dealings with the USSR State Budget and amounts used for creating and building up funds, are distributed among its participants in proportion to their pro rata participation in the enterprise's initial capitalization.

Foreign participants in a joint enterprise are guaranteed the transfer abroad, in foreign exchange, of the amounts due to them as a result of the distribution of profits from the enterprise's activity.

Joint enterprises recognize depreciation in accordance with the directives in effect for Soviet state organizations, unless otherwise specified in the articles of incorporation. The sums recognized as depreciation remain at the joint enterprises' disposal.

The design and capital construction of joint enterprises' facilities, including social facilities, are carried out under contract and paid for with the enterprises' own or with borrowed funds. Prior to final approval, project designs are subject to clearance under the procedure established by the USSR State Construction Committee. Construction-and-installation work by Soviet organizations, and the material resources needed for construction, are allocated to joint enterprises on a priority basis, based on orders placed by them.

Joint enterprises' freight is shipped in accordance with the procedures established for Soviet organizations.

Taxation of Joint Enterprises

Joint enterprises pay a tax in the amount of 30% of the portion of profits remaining after payment to the reserve fund, as well as to other funds of the joint enterprise earmarked for the development of production and for research and technology. The tax constitutes revenue for the Union budget.

Joint enterprises are exempted from payment of the tax on profits for the first two years of their operations.

The USSR Ministry of Finance has the right to reduce the amount of the tax.

Computation of the tax on profits is done by the joint enterprise.

An advance payment of taxes for the current year is determined by the enterprise with due regard for its financial plan for the current year.

Financial agencies have the right to verify the correctness of a joint enterprise's computation of its tax.

Overpayment of a tax amount for a past year can be credited to current tax payments or returned to the payer at his request.

A joint enterprise has the right to protest actions by financial agencies to recover taxes due. An appeal is filed with the financial agency that verified the tax computation. A decision on the appeal is reached within one month of the date on which it was filed.

A decision on an appeal can itself be appealed to a higher financial agency within a month's time.

The filing of an appeal does not stay payment of the tax.

Unless otherwise specified by an agreement between the USSR and the foreign participant in question, the portion of profits due the foreign participant in a joint enterprise is assessed a tax in the amount of 20% upon transfer abroad.

The aforementioned procedure governing taxation applies to income received by joint enterprises created on USSR territory and by branches located in the USSR of joint enterprises created with the participation of Soviet organizations in other countries, whether the income is from their activity on USSR territory, on the USSR continental shelf, in the USSR economic zone or on the territory of other countries.

Directives on the taxation of joint enterprises are issued by the USSR Ministry of Finance.

Oversight Over Joint Enterprises' Operations

In accordance with the procedure specified in their articles of incorporation, the participants in a joint enterprise are provided, for purposes of exercising their rights of oversight, data relating to the operation of the enterprise and the state of its property, profits and losses.

A joint enterprise may have an audit commission, formed in accordance with the procedure specified in the articles of incorporation.

Joint enterprises maintain operating, accounting and statistical records in accordance with the procedure in effect in the USSR for Soviet state enterprises. The forms of this record-keeping and reporting are established by the USSR Ministry of Finance, in conjunction with the USSR Central Statistical Administration.

Joint enterprises may not provide any reports or information to state or other agencies of foreign states.

The audit of a joint enterprise's financial, economic and commercial operations is done for a fee by a Soviet auditing organization operating on a profit-and-loss basis.

Personnel of Joint Enterprises.
Joint enterprises are staffed primarily by Soviet citizens. The management of a joint enterprise is obliged to conclude collective contracts with the trade-union organization created at the enterprise. The content of these contracts, including provisions regarding the social development of the collective, is determined by Soviet legislation and the articles of incorporation.

The terms of labor remuneration and work and rest schedules of Soviet citizens employed at joint enterprises and their social security and social insurance are regulated by Soviet legislative norms. These norms extend to foreign citizens employed at joint enterprises, with the exception of questions concerning remuneration, paid vacation and pension entitlements, which are to be resolved in contracts with each foreign citizen.

The USSR State Committee on Labor and Social Questions and the All-Union Central Council of Trade Unions have the right to determine the specifics as to how Soviet legislation on social insurance applies to foreign citizens employed at joint enterprises.

The joint enterprise remits to the USSR State Budget, payments for Soviet and foreign employees' state social-insurance coverage and contributions to Soviet employees' pensions, at the rates established for Soviet state organizations. Contributions to the pensions of joint enterprises' foreign employees are transferred to the appropriate funds of the countries of which they are permanent residents (in the currency of those countries).

The wages earned by foreign employees of a joint enterprise are assessed an income tax according to the procedure and in the amounts specified in the 12 May 1978, decree of the Presidium of the USSR Supreme Soviet "On Income Tax From Foreign Legal Entities and Individuals." The unexpended portion of these wages can be transferred abroad in foreign currency.

Liquidation of Joint Enterprises.
A joint enterprise can be liquidated under the circumstances and according to the procedure specified in the articles of incorporation, as well as by decision of the USSR Council of Ministers, provided its activities are in conflict with the objectives and tasks set forth in these documents. An announcement of the liquidation of the joint enterprise is published in the press.

Upon liquidation of a joint enterprise or withdrawal from such an enterprise, a foreign participant receives the right to a return of its contribution in the form of cash or goods, on the basis of the residual value of its contribution at the time of the enterprise's liquidation, after repayment of its obligations to Soviet participants and third parties.

The liquidation of a joint enterprise is registered with the USSR Ministry of Finance.

"V Sovete Ministrov SSSR. 'O poriadke sozdaniia na territorii SSSR i deiatel'nosti sovmestnykh predpriiatii s uchatiei sovetskikh organizatsii i firm kapitalisticheskikh i razvivaiushchikhsia stran," *Pravda* (27 Jan); a translation is also in CDSP, 39:6 (1987), 15-16, 23.

Economic Reform. Finance and Economic Accountability. Should the Ruble Control Production? (12 Dec 87)·
Financial and credit reform was named as one of the most important tasks in the fundamental restructuring of the management of the economy at the June (1987) Plenum of the CPSU CC. The CPSU CC and the USSR Council of Ministers have adopted resolutions specifying fundamental changes in the financial and credit mechanism. It is proposing a transition to the formation of a 5-year financial plan, to shift to a bridgeway relationship with enterprises [operating] on the basis of norms, (and) to support financial accountability in the local banking institutions. Reorganization of the banking system has begun; apart from the nation's principle bank, the USSR Gosbank, the changes will effect the branches—Vneshtorgbank [Bank for Foreign Trade], Promstroibank [Industrial Construction Bank], Agroprombank [Agricultural Construction Bank], Zhilsotsbank [Housing Bank], and the Sberegatel'nyi bank [Savings Bank].

What sort of problems need to be resolved in the process of this reform? What sorts of issues should be addressed by a program for putting the national economy on a sound financial footing?

V. **Belkin**, Doctor of Economics and member of the USSR Ministry of Finance's Scientific Methodology Council, and A. **Kazmin**, Candidate of Economics, answer questions from an *Izvestiia* correspondent.

Q The present time is a time when a new economic mechanism is being created. What role, in your opinion, do finances and credit play in this mechanism?

V.B The reason for the creation of a new mechanism is the transition from administrative methods of management to economic (ones). Management by economic methods—this is, in the final analysis, financial management by using money. Financing, credit, price tax, in a word, are valuable instruments; they are the most sensitive of all management tools. Forming a system of naturally-located planning and funded material-technical supplies have provided (these monetary devices) a secondary role which cannot be completely ignored. In the new economic mechanism, money flows should anticipate and determine the functioning of material and manpower resources. This sort of management is most in keeping with the principle of democratic centralism. It is free from narrow local and departmental interests. It strengthens the principle of centralization, but it does not weaken production units' independence where economic accountability is concerned.

But in order to use monetary instruments in the management process, we need to reinstate the meaning of money as a universal equivalent. In order to do this we need to enhance and maintain the balance between available goods and the money supply. At present this balance has been seriously upset. A gap has formed between effective demand and the goods available to meet it. The causes of the trade-finance imbalance is multiple.

Q How can this be? There exists strict rules for the credit-financing system. Every kopeck is accounted for, if not in the enterprise, then by a bank.

V.B The problem is not with accounting, but with the fact that the credit-financing system in the natiuonal economy regularly produces surplus money. The fact of the matter is that excess money regularly enters the national economy from the credit and finance system. And this not only does not contradict existing regulations and instructions, it is actually in complete accordance with them.

Q And where does this "excess" money come from?

V.B This is a paradox, but the "excess" money goes into the budget. The turnover tax, which accounts for approximately one-fourth of the state's revenues, is paid into the budget regardless of whether a product has been sold to the end user or whether it stayed in the warehouse. What's more, enterprises make payments based on their planned profits, not on their actual profits. The due dates for budget payments are not coordinated with the lengths of production cycles either. So what happens is that a product has not been sold yet, but money has already been paid into the budget.

Q So where does this money come from ultimately?

A.K In all these cases the budget revenues come from loans from the State Bank, which has been assigned the role of providing cash for the state budget. According to available estimates, approximately every fourth ruble that goes into the budget is loaned. The system whereby the State Bank guarantees financial agencies prompt receipt of budget payments, and enterprises prompt disbursement of these payments, gives rise to all-around irresponsibility on the part of both financial agencies and enterprises.

Q But what is behind finance and credit relations of this sort?

A.K In my opinion, the formation of a significant share of budget revenues using short-term loans from the State Bank was intended to ensure the deficit-free functioning of the state budget.

This system made sense as a temporary measure to be used in exceptional circumstances—such as covering the budget deficit during the NEP years or the economic and financial blockade. This was a serious accomplishment of the young Soviet state. However, the deficit-free operations that were achieved in this manner subsequently came to be interpreted as an inherent feature of the socialist method of production, as a kind of advantage of the socialist budgetary system over the capitalist system.

Widespread dissemination and assertion of this point of view undoubtedly had an effect on the formation of the present budget system. Its end—a deficit-free budget—came to justify any means. As a result, the budget no longer reflected the true state of affairs in the national economy. For example, in 1981 the smallest grain harvest in the last 20 years was brought in—156.2 million tons. For the first time since the war there was no increase in the real per capita income. At the same time, the margin by which stage budget revenues exceeded expenditures was a record 10.8 billion rubles! Outwardly favorable budget figures can conceal a deficit. This kind of focusing on the formal budget 'indicators' relieves the financial system of any need to act to improve the national economy's effectiveness in order to provide real, not borrowed, budget revenues.

The blurring of the line between finances and credit, thereby creating the appearance of financial well-being, has a negative effect on credit relations and the circulation of money. As was noted at the 27th CPSU Congress, credit has lost its original purpose. And as long as the State Bank continues to cover for shortcomings in the financial system, it will be impossible to make any substantial progress in improving credit relations.

Q What needs to be done to make things right?

A.K In my opinion, one of the primary tasks of the credit and financial reform that is taking shape is to define clearly the boundaries of finances and credit.

V.B Economic and legal independence for banks is one of the prerequisites for a normalization of credit. Another very important condition is to replace the central allocation of materials and supplies with a system of wholesale trade—otherwise there is no way of ensuring that credit is repaid. Under the system of central allocations, suppliers do not choose their customers, and if the customers do not have the money, then, in essence, the bank pays for them by extending credit without any guarantee that it will be paid back. Restricting the extension of credit in this case would lead to a situation in which the enterprises that provide goods to customers who cannot pay would themselves be left without any money. As long as material and technical supply is unreliable, you also can't cut off the extension of credit for production stocks either. That would threaten to shut down production. With a transition to wholesale trade in producer goods and industrial supplies, it would be possible to restrict (or reduce) the amount of money invested in excessive inventories, in order to establish a better balance between the turnover of goods and money.

Q But there are enterprises that are operating at a loss. A clearer distinction between finances and credit, as you say, would mean financial collapse for them: After all, no real bank is going to support a losing operation.

A.K Indeed, our bank is the most humane in the world! It not only pays all debts after it has extended a loan, but it also asks that the loan be paid off only after everyone else has been paid: after wages have been paid, after payments into the budget have been made, and after suppliers have been paid off.

It's true, this "unselfishness" on the part of the bank is certainly not a good thing: It undermines the very basis of credit. In place of this sort of unselfishness we need to introduce equivalent, economic-accountability relations between bank and enterprise. For this purpose, a system of regular periodic payments will be introduced as of 1 January 1988, a system whereby debts to the bank will be just as important to enterprises as are their obligations to pay wages, make budget payments, and so on. In order that the tightening of the credit system not lead to a "chain of nonpayment" for want of enterprise funds and access to credit, suppliers will be paid on behalf of the enterprises out of the funds of higher organizations, on condition that those organizations be repaid. This measure is designed to tighten payment discipline and increase ministries' accountability for the performance of enterprises under their jurisdiction.

Economic accountability for banks is also not possible without a solution to the critical problem of allocating enterprises their own working capital at the beginning of the financial and credit reform. If this is not done, credit will inevitably be used, as in the past, to cover enterprises' financial failures. Accordingly, banks should also be allocated their own working capital in amounts sufficient for providing normal credit support for the economy, and they should have the right to increase their own funds in proportion to increases in the volume of credit extended.

Furthermore, a law needs to be passed establishing a norm for the ratio between banks' own funds and the volume of credit they have extended. A one- sided orientation toward maximizing profits will make banks even less discriminating in extending loans, thereby leading to a new burst of credit expansion, an increase in the excess of payment instruments in circulation, and a decline in the purchasing power of the ruble.

Q Under those conditions the role of the banks increases immeasurably. Even certain of the industrial ministries' functions are to be shifted to them. Is this practical?

A.K It is no coincidence that banks now have the right to declare an enterprise insolvent that has regularly failed to pay its debts.

Once the banks are given the exclusive right to declare an economically independent enterprise insolvent, then a law is needed to also give banks the exclusive right to decide the question of whether and under what conditions a given enterprise can be shifted to operating on a self-supporting and self- financing basis. In order to have the "moral right" to declare an enterprise bankrupt, a bank should first provide evidence of the extent to which a given enterprise is prepared to operate on a self-supporting basis.

Such a procedure is not yet in place. As a rule, enterprises are being converted to self-supporting operations not on an individual basis, but as entire branches of industry—branches that include many enterprises that are operating on low profit margins or are losing money. Banks are not being asked for their recommendations on a change in operations of that sort but are simply being confronted with the accomplished fact. Organizational steps of this sort that lack a reliable economic basis can be left hanging in the air, as they say. "Self-supporting" enterprises that have not handled old debts acquire new ones. The present "financial crisis" of State Bearing Plant No. 1 and the Milling Machine Production Association, for example, was caused primarily by the fact that industrial ministries did not prepare their enterprises for the transition to self-supporting operations and took a perfunctory approach to this work, as if it were just one more campaign that one simply had to be among the first to join. This is the only way to explain the decision to launch self-supporting operations at enterprises that had been having serious financial problems for a long time. We need to learn a lesson from the mistakes that have already been made.

Q What is your opinion on whether it makes sense to revive the extension of credit among enterprises?

V.B When we extend broad rights to enterprises in managing their own affairs, we cannot restrict their rights in maneuvering their own monetary resources. Where necessary and possible an enterprise should have the right to send its products to a customer on a deferred-payment basis, that is, on credit—a practice that was done away with in 1930. The shift to central allocation of resources was the reason why that form of credit was eliminated at the time, and the time has now come for central allocation to be replaced by wholesale trade.

One has to wonder what sort of objections there could be to commercial credit under these conditions. There are objections, though, especially among bank personnel. Commercial credit is perceived as practically an attribute of capitalism. But these people are forgetting that state socialist enterprises are the creditors and borrowers in this relationship. They will be extending credit and using credit only from their own funds. The introduction of commercial credit will enable enterprises to put such debts—money owed for deliveries of goods—on a contractual basis. These debts now total 100 billion rubles.

Legalization of commercial credit will also help cut down excessive inventories and put the goods in question into production; it will put enterprises' settlement of accounts on an orderly basis and will teach them to meet their obligations. If commercial credit is not "rehabilitated", it will be impossible to truly expand enterprises' economic independence.

In conclusion, I would like to stress once again that credit and financial reform must be carried out in coordination and simultaneously with the other components of radical economic reform: converting enterprises to true economic accountability, replacing central allocation of supplies with wholesale trade, and price reform.

"Reforma ekonomiki: finansy i khozraschet. Rubliu upravliat' proisvodstvom?" *Izvestiia* (12 Dec); a condensed translation is in CDSP, 39:50 (1987), 17-18.

AGRICULTURE

M.S. Gorbachev had his first experiences in agriculture policy fulfillment while he served as first secretary in the Stavropol oblast, 1971-78. According to David Dyker (1987), he was successful at a time when overall Soviet agricultural productivity fell into serious decline. In 1977 Gorbachev helped organize a renovated harvesting program in one of his districts (Ipatovo) where large fleets of tractors and combines were centralized and utilized on a grand scale reminiscent of the 1930s.

The apparent success of this project resulted in Gorbachev's appointment to Moscow to replace F.D. Kulakov as secretary responsible for agriculture in the CPSU CC. An excellent harvest in 1978-79 saw him elevated again, to a position as candidate member of Politburo (November 1979).

But success in agriculture has always been a fleeting phenomenon in the USSR. Shortages of fodder for growing livestock herds, very bad transportation systems, including abyssmal roads, poor storage facilities, low productivity of both collective and state farm labor, and so on, all continued to undermine Party/government efforts to upgrade the agriculture sector. Thus, 1979 was followed by poor harvests and food shortages. Gorbachev felt compelled to introduce more and more autonomy to farming operations, to expand the collective contract system, and to provide increasing incentives to the private agricultural sphere.

Re-organization was essential. The service organizations responsible for such matters as equipment repair, fertilizer utilization, and land improvements had caused much duplication of effort and waste. These were replaced first with District Agro-Industrial Associations (RAPSs), the purpose of which was to unify agriculture and appropriate local industrial enterprises; for example, canning factories, slaughter houses, and mills. Shortly after he became Secretary General, Gorbachev introduced a new "Superministry", the USSR State Agro-Industrial Committee, or Gosagroprom (See *Ekonomicheskaia gazeta*, No. 48 (1985), 17-18). Its purpose was to combine the efforts of the existing ministries for agriculture, fruit and vegetable production, the meat and dairy industry, the food industry, and rural construction.

Gosagroprom was instructed to re-organize the RAPOs, asure quality control, coordinate matters associated with irrigation, fertilizers, and equipment building for agriculture. Agricultural management was placed on a detailed incentive system. Pricing, research, the collective contract, and management of private plots also were to be re-organized.

In 1987, two years after Gosagroprom started its work, it was clear that much still had to be done. Private agricultural contracting was given high priority as a means for improving production. Gorbachev also proposed that that large farms be broken up into small autonomous groups, which would be self-financing and reimbursed according to their output. Even smaller family contracts were given official status in August 1987 and such groups were allowed to lease land for periods of 12 to 15 years.

The documents included in this section demonstrate an impatience with the lack of progress shown in the field of agriculture. For further general information, see Karl-Eugen Wädekin, "Agriculture," in Martin McCauley, ed, *The Soviet Union under Gorbachev* (1987), 113-34.

In the CPSU Central Committee. "On the Work of Party, Soviet and Economic Organs of the Tadzhik Republic to Complete the 1986 Cotton Harvest" (24 Feb 87)
The CPSU CC has discussed the question, "On the Work of Party, Soviet, and Economic Organs of the Tadzhik Republic to Complete the 1986 Cotton Harvest without Enlisting the

Students of Technicums or Vocational-Technical Schools or Interrupting Schoolchildren's Studies." The resolution notes that in 1986, Party, Soviet and economic organs, collective farms, and state farms in the Tadzhik SSR did a considerable amount of work growing and harvesting cotton. Collective contract forms of labor organization became widespread. Equipment was marshalled into harvesting and transport complexes and used in two shifts.

Around 900 temporary Party and Party-Komsomol groups were established to strengthen Party influence on all elements of the cotton-harvesting complex. Competition was launched among the crews of the cotton harvesting combines and among the gleaners for a daily overfulfilment of the output norms, and publicity for competition was ensured. A great deal of attention was devoted to improving labor and recreation conditions for cotton growers and medical, trade, cultural, and consumer services for them.

(According to the adopted resolution), the republic's collective farms and state farms have fulfilled their assignments and socialist obligations and sold 22,000 tons of cotton over and above the plan. A total of 920,000 tons of raw cotton was sold to the state, including 308,000 metric tons of the fiber cotton, more than 84 percent is first or second grade.

In contrast to the practice in past years. when students were called upon to pick cotton for two or three months during the school year, last year the cotton crop was harvested without the participation of students from technicums or vocational-technical schools, and without interfering with the studies of schoolchildren. The academic program has been completed in all educational institutions. (This is) a source of great satisfaction for the working people of the republic. The economic advantages of increasing the amount of machine-harvested cotton, as well as avoiding the use of students for harvesting, amounted to approximately 8 million rubles.

Nevertheless, the resolution notes that last year there was still not enough attention paid to the introduction of machine harvesting of cotton in the Tadzhik Republic. One-third of the combines were not used during the busiest period of the harvest. The same type of attitude toward machine-harvesting can be seen in all the other cotton-growing republics. In this connection emphasis is placed upon the need to further intensify the work of the republics' Party, Soviet and economic organs on the comprehensive mechanization of cotton growing, and better utilization of the equipment at the disposal of collective and state farms.

The CPSU CC has recommended that the Uzbek, Turkmen, Kazakh, Kirgiz, and Azerbaidzhan Communist Party CCs adopt measures before the year is out to disseminate widely the experience of the Tadzhik Republic's cotton growers in organizing the harvest without calling on students in technicums or interrupting the studies of schoolchildren. The achievement of this task should be regarded as an important social and economic enterprise.

The Tadzhik Communist Party CC has been advised to accomplish the necessary organizational and political measures to increase further the level of full mechanization in cotton growing, and to make widescale use of the mechanized method for raw cotton harvesting. The USSR Gosplan [Gosplan is USSR State Planning Committee] the USSR Agro-Industrial Committee, the State Committee for Science and Technology, and the USSR Ministry of Tractor and Agricultural Machine-Building were instructed to adopt additional measures to create improved and reliable cotton harvesting machinery and pickup attachments of a high technological standard with which to supply state and collective farms with them. The USSR Ministry for Mineral Fertilizer Production and the USSR Ministry of the Chemical Industry must ensure production of highly effective defoliants for the fine-fibre strains of cotton.

The CPSU CC demanded that the Party Committees of the above-mentioned ministries and departments strictly supervize the work of Communist and all *apparat* personnel in carrying out the instructions.

"V Tsentral'nom komitete KPSS. 'O rabote partiinykh, sovetskikh i khoziaistvennykh organov Tadzhikskoi SSR po yborke khlopka yrozhaia 1986 goda'..." *Pravda* (24 Feb 87); a translation can also be found in FBIS (2 Mar 87), R1-2; translated excerpts are in CDSP, 39:8 (1987), 18.

The Family Contract (16 Jun 87)

The team brothers **Konopliannikov**, from the collective farm "Kochkovskii", have set a good example for the farmers of Novosibirsk province with their mechanized team. The three of them cultivated 1200 hectares of arable land, which grew wheat and corn. From their first day out in the fields until the first appearance of grain, the brothers worked full force. The family team mastered technology intensively. They developed each of their products 5-6 times more than their counterparts from other collectives.

This is only one example of the good consequences of the comparatively new form of organized work—the family contract. In the resolution of the CPSU CC, "About Urgent Measures for Raising the Productivity of Labor in Agriculture on the Basis of the Introduction of a Rational Form of Organization and Self-Financing", the necessity for a widespread development of family contracts was noted. As one of a variety of collective contracts, they are increasingly found on the land, and show themselves to have high economic effectiveness. In the family collectives, it is true, there is little chance of a conflict situation and it is generally not necessary to set up some manner of control over the distribution of funds for salaries. In a family group there is less chance of awkwardness and waste.

More than 1 million rural families have now concluded agreements with state farms and collective farms of the production of the most diverse products from field and livestock units. The family contract is playing an increasing role in the production of milk and meat on small livestock units in Estonia, in sheep rearing in Kazakhstan, Kirgiziia, and Turkmenia, and in the domestic cultivation of silkworms in Uzbekistan. Families have been doing a great deal to develop hop growing in the Chuvash ASSR and tobacco growing in Armenia.

The conditions for the wider dissemination of the family form of labor organization have arisen everywhere. But one's attention is drawn by the fact that the deep-seated opportunites offered by the family contract are as yet being insufficiently revealed. Many farms are in no hurry to employ it. Certain leaders and specialists fear the complexities arising during the assimilation of the new methods. Working conscientiously in family collectives brings high earnings, which trouble certain people. The question of, as it were, not overpaying families prevents them seeing the indisputable advantages of the family form of labor organization for social production.

The editorial mailbag shows that in many places due attention is not being paid to disseminating the family contract system. Here is a collective letter for the "Voskhod" collective farm in the Mari ASSR's Sernurskii District. Its authors are delighted by the way in which the family contract has been implemented on one of the farms in a neighboring autonomous republic and ask the question: Why don't we do the same ? Indeed, why isn't there a single family collective under contract in Sernurskii, Yurinskii, or Gornomariyskii Districts? And in fact the entire Mari ASSR still numbers scarcely more than 20 families working under contract. Great scope is opening up here for the organizational activity of the agro-industrial complex' management organs and state farms and collective farm leaders and specialists.

It also happens like this: All the conditions have emerged on a farm for transferring to the family contract, and there are also people wishing to do this, but the leaders and specialists hold back, awaiting orders from above. This is just what is happening on the "Sokolovskii" state farm in Tiumin Province. Everyone there agrees that in individual sectors the livestock fattening is best contracted out to family links. The **Maksimov** family is offering its services. But the state farm economic service is waiting for recommendations on labor remuneration and is afraid of displaying any initiative.

Still quite often a family contract is handled only formally. After concluding an agreement with a family, the farm leadership then forgets the need to fulfill the terms of it. Look—the family has repudiated the contract.

The times insistently demand that when forms of labor organization have justified themselves they should be practiced more widely. Party, Soviet, and economic organs must erect a solid barrier against formalism, stereotyped behavior, and attempts to repackage old content. The enterprizing leaders and specialists who are boldly pursuing the experiment and revealing new facets and potential in family labor organization must be given every support.

The use of the family contract in conjunction with economic accountability and the checkbook form of expenditure control produces the greatest effect. A good example of this is provided by the economic service of the "Zavet Ilicha" collective farm in Moscow Province's Krasnogorskii District, where a cattle-fattening livestock unit contracted out to the **Piataev** family forms part of the general economic mechanism whereby payment for labor comes out of gross revenue. Both the conscientiously working family and the entire collective farm benefits from this.

It is the urgent task of collective farm and state farm economic services and of rayon agro-industrial association specialists to ensure that the family contract system is organically incorporated in the system of economic accountability relationships within the collective farms and state farms.

The new forms of labor organizations needs more peristent propaganda. Here much could be done by the local organs of the press, television, and radio. However, at the moment this theme is receiving extremely poor coverage in the republic, province, and district mass media. Meanwhile, opponents of the family contract who doubt its usefulness and unjustly accuse conscientious workers of self-seeking tendencies frequently come to light. The psychological brakes impeding the introduction of the family contract must be released as soon as possible.

Skillful organizers of agriculture production have shown how the internal strength of the family contract, in all of his mutlifaceted aspects, prompts initiative coupled with an intense sense of responsibility for its results. The Party, trade unions and Komsomol organizations have shown great concern about the breakup of family units. One of the answers to this concern is the family contract, which can raise the level of the general fulfillment of the country's production plan.

"Semeinyi podriad," *Sel'skaia zhizn'* (16 Jun 87). Translated excerpts appear in FBIS (24 Jun 87), T2-T3.

In the CPSU Central Committee. "On the Unsatisfactory Use of the Natural and Economic Potential of the Agro-Industrial Complex in the Uzbek, Tadzhik, and Turkmen Republics" (20 Jun 87)

The CPSU CC has discussed the question, "On the Unsatisfactory Use of the Natural and Economic Potential of the Agro-Industrial Complex in the Uzbek, Tadzhik, and Turkmen Republics. The resolution points out that the Agro-Industrial Complex of the Uzbek SSR, the Tadzhik SSR, and the Turkmen SSR occupies an especially important place in the All-Union division of labor. The state and collective farms of those republics are the main producers of cotton, and supply other agricultural products which are in increased demand. A strong material and technical base of the agrarian sector has been created in that region. Over the past ten years state and collective funds, to the amount of 43 billion rubles, have been directed towards these ends—which is twice as much as all investments during the previous analogous period. Provision of production capital has increased 110 percent in Uzbekistan and 90 percent in Tadzhikistan and Turkmenia. The area of irrigated land in Central Asia has reached 6.9 million hectares.

The tremendous production and economic potential of the region, its water resources, and also its favourable natural conditions, are being used in an unsatisfactory manner. The growth rate of total agricultural production in the republics has diminished sharply in recent years, plans for purchases of raw cotton have not been fulfilled, and fiber quality has declined. Vegetable, grape, fruit, and berry growing remain at a low and stagnant level, and there are shortfalls in deliveries of many sorts of this product to the All-Union stocks.

A disdainful attitude toward the introduction of scientifically proven systems of farming and of intensive animal breeding—an attitude that has taken root throughout many farm, district, province and republic officials—has seriously depleted agricultural production. The continuing process of introducing crop rotation has resulteds in soil loss and massive contamination of soils with insects and diseases. The poor state of farm management has had an unfavourable impact on attempts to supply the public with food products produced locally, and food deliveries from state stocks are not growing less. These conditions in the Agro-Industrial Complex have been affected to a great extent by unfavorable phenomena which involve report-padding and the practice of fraud and deception against the state, which means that great moral and economic harm has been done.

All-Union agricultural, water-resource. and planning bodies have made major errors in the development of irrigated farming. A large part of all the irrigated land needs capital repair and reconstruction because of poor quality land reclamation work, careless construction and mismanagement. The operating service for irrigation systems is badly organized and is run in an uncoordinated way and on a limited scale. Organizations of the USSR Ministry of Land Reclamation and Water resources fail to carry out repair and operating work on a schedule and to a high quality. To the disadvantage of everyone, water resource organizations continue to direct their work mainly towards bringing new land under cultivation.

The Central Asian republics still must overcome an incorrect attitude toward organizing the production of fodder, which is the main cause of the continued lag in animal breeding. No effective measures have been taken to build facilities for storing and processing fodder. Livestock productivity in the republics is among the lowest, while fodder consumption per unit of output is almost twice the consumption in the country as a whole.

It is emphasized in the resolution that Party, Soviet and agricultural bodies have failed to take full steps to train agricultural officials and specialists in economics in the new conditions. Vocational training for machinery operators and for other personnel to take up the most common occupations in irrigated farming and animal breeding has fallen seriously behind. No measures are being taken to sponsor economic management methods, to achieve a sharp rise in labor productivity or to improve labor organization. The introduction of economic accountability and of collective, family, and rental contracts has yet to move beyond individual farms. Formalism permeates these efforts, and as a result the cost-containment mechanism practically does not exist in the rural economy. Labor productivity has not risen in the Uzbek Republic in the past 10 years and has actually declined in the Tadzhik and Turkmen Republics, even though wages have risen 30 percent to 40 percent.

It is the opinion of the CPSU CC that the level of organizational and political work being done by the Uzbek Communist Party CC, the Tadzhik Communist Party CC, and the Turkmen Communist Party CC, and of the Councils of Ministers of those Republics, does not meet the requirements of the 27th Party Congress and the January (1987) Plenum of the CPSU CC in regard to speeding up social and economic development and [in the matter of] Party personnel policy. Bureaucratic administration, petty supervision, and regimentation remain characteristics of the party organization's activity—which adversely affects the education, initiative, and independence of farm leaders, specialists and middle link workers. Many of the executive personnel of the republics are inclined to dependent attitudes, and there is a highly developed practice of trying to obtain as much material and cash resources from the state as possible, without showing proper concern for their efficient use. Many Party committees and Soviet and agro-industrial organs underestimate the entire acuteness of the social problem. While the rural population is poorly provided with housing and with health care, trade and cultural projects, the funds allocated for these purposes are not being assimilated. Consumer cooperatives display inertia and lack of acumen in resolving social tasks in the countryside. In the republics as a whole, the produce processing and storage base is being developed inadmissably slowly.

The Uzbek Communist Party CC and Uzbek Republic Council of Ministers (Comrades **Usmankhodzhayev** and **Kadyrov**), the Tadzhik Communist Party CC and Tadzhik Republic Council of Ministers (Comrades **Makhkamov** and **Khayoyev**), and the Turkmen Communist Paryt CC and Turkmen Republic Council of Ministers (Comrades **Niyazov** and **Khodzhamu-radov**) are ordered to devise and implement a concrete program of action to eliminate the above mentioned serious deficiencies and failings in the development of agricultural production, to switch the sector to an intensive path of development and of complete self-sufficiency in terms of livestock products in the next few years, and to make highly efficient use of the natural economic potential of the entire agro-industrial complex. The satisfaction of the requirement of the national economy for high-quality cotton fiber and the unconditional fulfillment of the food program are to be ensured.

This is the chief task in the coming period, and its speediest realization must be the core of organizational work at all levels of the agro-industrial production in the republics.

The resolution observes that the Collegium of the USSR Ministry of Land Reclamation and Water Resources and the Minister, Comrade **Vasilev**, personally have been slow to restructure the work of water-management organizations and to concentrate their efforts, as a top-priority basis, on guaranteeing the effective use of existing irrigated land. The ministry has been advised to take urgent and full measures to put the situation in order.

It is noted in the resolution that the USSR State Agro-Industrial Committee (Comrades **Ievlev** and **Romanenko**) and the USSR State Planning Committee (Comrade **Paskar**) failed to judge the growing situation in the development of agriculture in the Central Asian Republics in time, and [failed] both to map out a clear course investment policy and to improve the structure of agro-industrial production. (They also failed) to channel capital investment, material resources and equipment into rebuilding irrigated land and improving its effectiveness. Questions in relation to the manufacture of highly productive equipment for the comprehensive mechnization of cotton growing are being solved at a slow pace, and proper steps are not being taken to accelerate the development of facilities for processing and storing products.

The USSR State Planning Committee, the USSR State Agro-Industrial Committee, and the USSR Ministry of Land Reclamation and Water Resources, together with the Uzbek Republic Council of Ministers, the Kirgiz Republic Council of Ministers, the Tadzhik Republic Council of Ministers, and the Turkmen Republic Council of Ministers, are ordered to formulate and implement a program to fundamentally improve the effectiveness with which irrigated land is utilized, with a view to concentrating no less than 70 percent of all capital investments allocated for reclamation during th Five-Year Plan on measures to reconstruct such land, to improve its quality and to make economical use of water resources.

"V tsentral'nom komitete KPSS," *Pravda* (20 Jun 87); a translation appears in FBIS (29 Jun 87), R22-R25; a condensed version is in CDSP, 39:25 (1987), 22.

Normatives are not Curbs. How to Eliminate Distortions in Planning Agricultural Production. An Interview (22 Sept 87)

The "Morskoi" State Farm today is one of the front-ranking farms in Novosibirsk Province. It became thus largely thanks to experimenting with the introduction of the collective contract. Over the past 3 years output and labor productivity have exceeded the growth rates planned for the 5-Year Plan by a factor of three or four. Whereas in 1980 the state farm owed the Gosbank 735,000 rubles, in 1986 it earned 1.8 million rubles in profit. The level of profitability has reached 48 percent. Having paid off its debts, "Morskoi" has been operating for 2 years now essentially on a self-financing basis.

Bekker. The essence of fundamental restructuring of economic management, as defined by the CPSU CC June (1987) Plenum, is a transition to management of and through interests. This is linked with encouraging people's activeness. To what extent does the experiment at "Morskoi"—where you are the scientific leader—confirm this idea?

Stolbunov. The "Morskoi" experience convinces us yet again that interest is a great force and that contracts based on economic accountability can do everything in terms of specifics and nothing in terms of generalities.

Bekker. That is? Please explain.

Stolbunov. Given the combination of the necessary conditions, with the help of economic accountability individual links, shops, or enterprises can, of course, work wonders. But it is not possible to achieve a fundamental improvement in affairs in the agro-industrial sector as a whole through this alone. To do so we need to change the existing economic mechanism. For instance, I am convinced that in 2 or 3 years' time the economy at "Morskoi" will again be undermined by the practice of planning "on the basis of what has been achieved."

Bekker. But surely so-called normative planning has now been introduced?

Stolbunov. Yes, since this January. But you should have seen how this year's plans compared.

Strictly speaking, under the methods adopted by the USSR State Agro-Industrial Committee, the Gosplan, the State Committee for Labor and Social Problems, and the V.I.Lenin All-Union Academy of Agricultural Sciences farms can only have imposed on them from above purchases of agricultural products, wages funds, ands the volumes of material and technical resources and capital investment calculated according to normatives. But provincial agro-industrial committees still take liberties, "correct" sowing figures, take us to task about cattle numbers, and alter output delivery figures.

But the main point is that normatives are just for show. Take the handbook and open the section on purchase calculation options—table three. Have a look at option three, for instance. According to the handbook, a district which has utilized its potential to the tune of 80.6 percent will have its plan set at 83.1 percent of the normative—that is, 2.5 percent more than what was "achieved." But another district that has made an effort and utilized its resources to the tune of 102.9 percent will receive a target of 111.1 percent of the normative—or just 1.8 percent below what was "achieved." You see what sort of calculation that is: Poor performers only have to add a trivial amount, while strong performers have their achievements virtually turned into the plan. Those who succeed are burdened and punished for their industriousness.

This is not emotion. After all, according to the handbook wage funds are established by taking an average of the actual level over the last 3 years. That is, those who have produced little but "consumed" a lot again get the benefit. Whereas the industrious lose out.

After comparing may state farms in Novosibirsk Province, I chose two: "Maiak" and "Chanovskii", which indeed operate under equal conditions. What has happened ? The former produced more than 3 million rubles in profit in the 10th Five-Year Plan while the latter turned in a loss of around 3 million. But the average earnings of workers on the two state farms turned out to be identical. Out of each 100 million rubles of gross output wages accounted for 37.9 million on the front-ranking state farm and 49.6 million on the loss-maker. This trend has continued in the 11th Five-Year Plan. What is the point of working in a shock fashion? Everyone has long since realized this. Now, I hope, it is clear to you why there are few "Maiaks" and many "Chanovskiis."

It was thought that normative planning would eradicate this distortion. Everyone would be paid on the fair basis of what they had earned. But, as we can see, there is not so much as a trace of a normative approach in the normatives that were adopted. Pseudoscientific calculations provide a screen for hiding the notorious planning system based in "what has been achieved"—the system which led us to stagnation.

Bekker. Has fear not played its part? At the Novosibirsk Province Agro-Industrial Committee I saw the district economists defending their annual industrial finance plans. I remember their confusion. Calculating normative purchases of agricultural produce (on the basis of the new methods, of course) produced, in their view, incredible distortions: Strong farms had to be set plans lower than what they had achieved, while the reverse was true for weak farms—their plans had to be increased on the basis of the resource potential actually at their disposal. A.**Borodina**, an economist at the Iskitimskii District Agro-Industrial Association, said: "Our 'Svetlyi' State Farm is a perennial loss-maker. But what are we supposed to say to the Director, 'Fulfill this honest and fair increased plan with your available capacity.' He cannot cope with the current plan." Poor farms cannot be turned around in 1 or 2 years. What about those dragging a burden, should we now lighten their load?

Stolbunov. Things are not that bad. Why not change the procedure for concluding output delivery contracts? Suppose you are currently only able to fulfill 75 percent of the purchase normative. Go ahead and conclude a contract for that amount. But be aware that your wages fund will be cut back correspondingly. If you are able to produce output at 120 percent of the normative, please obtain a wages fund for the same amount. In the future, those farms that provide high-quality output at lower prices—and at times they may have to offer reductions—will receive most-favored status when concluding contracts. Let there be real economic competition. Everyone will conclude feasible "contracts." A leader of an enterprise able to exceed the normative will not refuse to do so. He currently conceals reserves and holds back growth rates merely because he knows that he will have imposed on him a plan based on "what has been achieved" while wage funds remain static. He will be publicly upbraided for producing only a small amount of growth. Yet "weak" enterprises are recognized as competition winners, even though they have not even reached the normative. One cannot imagine a worse incentive for hard work.

Bekker. I want to return to where we started. The methods that have been adopted are crude and inaccurate, you say. Clearly the problem is that in developing these methods the experience of, say, Lithuania or Estonia, where normative planning has been used successfully for many years, has gone by the board.

Stolbunov. I am convinced that even if we now had good methods and used them properly that alone would not be enough to ensure the normal working of the economic mechanism. It is supposed rather than actual production conditions that are taken into account during planning. But real people work under specific conditions. If these do not coincide with the plan conditions, then the principle of "from each according to his ability, to each according to his labor" does not apply. Consequently, the human factor fails to operate. For it to work, we must separate those things that depend on human abilities from those that people are unable to change. We have so far been unable to do this because economically accountable contracts are not working and the economic mechanism is not working as it should.

Bekker. I would like you to dwell on the proposed system of contracts. As is clear from the decision of the June (1987) Plenum, particular importance is attached to them. But what are farms that are still unable to meet normative targets supposed to do? Workers who lose wages will go elsewhere.

Stolbunov. We are tackling a major job, and it requires definite firmness. I recall that **Lenin** wrote: "...manage without the slightest hesitation, manage more firmly than the capitalists managed before you. Otherwise you will not succeed." But this firmness must not consist of defending one's own arbitrary decisions, in administration by decree, or in exercising one's vocal chords. Firmness means normative planning and incentives, with no deviations—people must be paid strictly according to their work. That is fundamental. The second thing is that weak state farms must be given access to commercial credit for a period in order to get back on their feet. The third point: Collectives must choose leaders capable of boosting their business. I am sure that the country has not run out of people with bright ideas. There are more than enough examples of intelligent leaders turning farms into front-rankers in the space of 2-3 years.

In my view, since we are unable to foresee all production conditions and factors—particularly weather conditions in crop farming at the planning state—we obviously cannot do without normative regulation of the set plan on the basis of actual conditions. It is from actual conditions that assessments must be made and incentives provided for workers and collectives on the basis of actual results.

Bekker. What does all this look like in practice?

Stolbunov. Suppose that a grain team collective has been set a normative yield of 23 quintals per hectare. It is allocated a certain amount of mineral fertilizer and certain types of equipment. During the cultivation process the team finds itself short of several tons of fertilizer, or it is delivered after the sowing. A quintal of fertilizer—and this has been quite clearly established—ensures a definite amount of extra yield. Surely it would be fair to reduce the plan figure correspondingly? And vice versa. Thus, things should be done strictly according to the normative on the basis of how much certain factors produce yields. In this instance a resourceful economic manager will know that if additional fertilizer and equipment is allocated he will have his plan increased too. What about droughts? Under our conditions just a single day of hot dry winds can cost 108 kg of yield per hectare. That is why I believe that the normative regulation of plan indicators on the basis of actual production conditions must be an obligatory element in the economic accountability mechanism. This also, as you can see, does not contradict normative planning, but strengthens it, making it more concrete and trustworthy.

Bekker. That is putting yourself on the firing line. You will be accused of pushing the principle of "downgrading" plans.

Stolbunov. Some economists will be horrified, of course. For "regulation" they read "downgrading," which is rightly assailed in the press.

But the proposed normative regulation of set plans on the basis of objective production conditions has nothing to do with the notorious idea of of downgrading. On the basis of "realistic" downgrading a "captain" of a sector, for instance, can with a stroke of a pen turn a friend who is a mediocre enterprise leader into a front-ranker. That will not work under normative regulation—then we will clearly see who is who.

Finally, in order to make the principle of "payment according to work" a reality, normative incentives must be provided to labor collectives for their end results. To this end it will be enough to compare the results obtained with the regulated normative volume of production, expenditure, and profit and to assess the collectives and allocate the relevant material rewards on the basis of that comparison.

Bekker. You have not dispelled all doubts. In regulating plans at the year's end—on the basis of prevailing conditions—will we not disrupt output deliveries to the state? Things are not the same as the Kuban everywhere, where not a year goes by without a drought or some other disaster. Add to that the cost of material and technical supply. Plans will have to be reduced all the time. Agricultural workers, I grant you, will earn their wages, but the country has to look out for its own interests.

Stolbunov. There is never "bad weather" everywhere. Some places are better or worse than others. This means that some people's normative purchasing plans will be higher and others will be lower. But this will make everyone work more intensively and obtain more output, if, of course, they want to earn more rather than win a lottery.

This sort of economic mechanism makes for flexibility and adaptability in changing capital investment and funds. The transfer of resources will not influence the assessment of enterprises' activity and incentives nor, I think, harm the interests of people engaged in production. At any rate it will not reduce their activeness. An unfulfillable plan is so disorganizing that collectives do not even do what they are able to do. A reduced plan is no less harmful since it dampens people's enthusiasm and corrupts them with easy earnings.

On three occasions over the last 30 years I have checked the elements of the proposed mechanism in the field, as they say. I introduced a nonregulated link system in machine operator links at an experimental station at the end of the fifties and subsequently at the "Kiialinskii" State Farm. In the mid-sixties a whole district—Bishkulskii District, also in Kazakhstan—was working on the basis of economic accountability. You already know about the "Morskoi" State Farm. So, even though it has been only partially tested as a result of various bans and limitations, the mechanism has produced considerable increases in labor productivity and wage rates, reduced price costs, and boosted profitability.

Bekker. But perhaps all we need is flexibility in price formation and then corrections' to plans on the basis of actual production conditions would be unnecessary.

Stolbunov. In our economy prices are also a plan normative. Since this is the case, prices too must change and be flexible. For instance, for many years economic managers in Novosibirsk Province claimed that the price of vegetables was low and production was unprofitable. But over the past two years, having organized its work, "Morskoi" State Farm has ensured a 90 percent profitability level for vegetable farming. Should such prices last forever, one wonders? If not they must be changed. On what basis? On the basis of yield normatives according to conditions, expenditure, and so forth.

In short, I see no contradictions in this area which would prevent the normative method of planning involving the regulation of plans on the basis of specific production conditions and factors from being established in economic management practice. The point of this work is to harmoniously combine the interests of people, collectives, and society and make full use of the potential of the socialist method of production.

"Normativ ne uzdechka. Kak ustranit' perekosy v planirovanii sel'skokhiaistvennogo proizvodstva," *Izvestiia* (22 Sep 87). A partial translation is in FBIS (28 Sep 87), 50-54. Correspondent A. Bekker interviews Ye. Stolbunov, Scientific Associate at the West Siberian Branch of the Scientific Research Institute of Labor.

In the CPSU Central Committee (25 Sept 87)

The CPSU CC and the USSR Council of Ministers have adopted resolutions "On Additional Measures for the Development of Citizens' Personal Plots and of Collective Horticulture and Truck Gardening" and "On The Further Development of Subsidiary Farms of Enterprises, Organizations, and Institutions."

For the purpose of creating more favorable conditions for the development of citizen's personal plots and of collective horticulture and truck gardening and eliminating the major shortcomings existing in this work, the CPSU CC and the USSR Council of Ministers have made it incumbent upon union republic Communist Party CCs and Councils of Ministers, the USSR Agro-Industrial Committee, territorial Party Committees, regional Party Committees, city Party Committees, and regional Party Committees, autonomous republic Councils of Ministers, and Executive Committees of Soviets of regions, provinces, cities and territories to implement effective measures to encourage the production of meat, milk, potatoes, vegetables, fruit, berries and other agricultural products on citizens' personal plots and in collective gardens and truck gardens. Special attention is to be given to the development of cooperatives of citizens' personal plots and social production on contractual terms applying the principles of collective and family contracts.

It is laid down that the size of plots and the norms for livestock and poultry to be kept on citizens' personal plots are to be determined by rural and village soviets of people's deputies, collective farms, and state farms with due consideration given to the participation of state collective farm members, state farm workers and employees, and other rural residents in social production.

Collective farms are instructed, and state farms and other agricultural enterprises are authorized, to make broader use of rental contracts for the long-term leasing of additional plots of land to collective farm members, state farm workers, and other citizens living in the countryside who have expressed the desire to rear livestock and poultry or to grow potatoes, vegetables, berries, greens, feed, and other crops for sale under contracts with farms and consumer cooperative organizations.

The USSR State Agro-Industrial Committee, Union and Autonomous Republic Councils of Ministers, and local Executive Committees have been set the task of elaborating and implementing specific measures to significantly expand the sales of young livestock and poultry to the population's personal plots.

State farms and other state enterprises are authorized, and collective farms are instructed, to sell horses and other draft animals to citizens with the right to keep them and use them for work on personal plots or to perform work under contract with the farms.

It is deemed expedient to organize beekeeping societies in rural districts, supply them with the necessary stock and mobile platforms, and improve the work of beekeepers with a view to fully satisfying the citizens' needs for bee colonies.

Party Committees and Soviet and economic organs are instructed to show greater concern for the provisions of housing to collective farm members and to workers and employees of collective farms and other agro-industrial complex enterprises.

State farms and other agro-industrial complex enterprises and organizations located in the countryside are authorized, and collective farms and consumer cooperative organizations are instructed, to sell to their workers farmstead-type houses and outbuildings constructed using either state capital investments or the own resources of farms, enterprises, and organizations, with these workers having to repay 40 percent of the cost of the farmstead-type house and outbuildings in equal monthly installments over a period of 50 years from the day of the sale.

In order to generate more interest in the development of individual housing construction in the countryside and the running of personal plots, provision is made to give citizens living in the countryside credit: to build individual houses and outbuildings up to a total amount of 20,000 rubles with repayments over 50 years starting in the 3rd year following receipt of the credit; to build outbuildings to keep livestock and poultry up to a total amount of 4000 rubles with repayments over 10 years starting in the 3rd year following receipt of the credit; to acquire small-scale mechanization equipment for work on the personal plot up to a total amount of 1000 rubles with repayment over 3 years.

It has been decided to increase the amount of credit available to citizens to purchase cows and calves to l000 and 500 rubles respectively, each credit to be repaid on the terms laid down in the current legislation.

It has been deemed expedient to add to the total work service of women with small children, and therefore not employed in social production, any time spent by them on rearing livestock and poulty or growing potatoes, vegetables, greens, and other crops on personal plots under contract with collective farms, state farms, and consumer cooperative organizations.

It has been decided to speed up in every province, territory, and Autonomous or Union Republic not subdivided into provinces, the completion of the elaboration of plans for the siting of collective gardens and truck gardens, with due provision for proper amenities, power and water supply, and provision of telephone communications by district. The land allocated to collective gardens and truck gardens should come from the state land stock including, whenever necessary, land belonging to collective farms, state farms, and other agricultural enterprises. It is also necessary to bear in mind the possibility of organizing horticultural associations of collective farm members and workers of state farms and other agricultural enterprises living in multistory housing blocks.

It is laid down that the allocation of land plots for collective gardens and truck gardens in line with approved siting plans is to take place on the basis of executive committee of district and city soviet resolutions within 1 month from the date of the application.

Enterprises and organizations under the USSR Ministry of Land Reclamation and Water Resources, the USSR Ministry of Power and Electrification, and other USSR and Union Republic Ministries and departments are instructed to speed up work on the provision of water and power supply and construction of amenities for collective gardens and truck gardens with a view to completing the bulk of this work within the current Five-Year Plan period. This work must be done under direct contracts with horticultural associations and must be included in the plans for contractual work and volume of services performed.

Members of horticultural associations are authorized to construct on the land plots allocated to them heated summer houses with a construction area of up to 50 square meters excluding balcony area and loft space, as well as utility buildings (standing on their own or on blocks) to keep domestic poultry and rabbits, to store farm tools, and to meet other needs. Hothouses and other heated ground facilities can be erected on the plot to cultivate agricultural crops. The siting of cellars beneath the house or utility building is allowed. All former restrictioons on the fitting out of garden plots are lifted.

The resolution authorizes the granting of credits to members of horticultural associations to build summer houses and amenities for garden plots up to an amount of 5000 rubles with repayment over 10 years starting in the 3rd year following receipt of the credit.

Union Republic Councils of Ministers, the USSR Ministry of Trade, the USSR Ministry of Health, the USSR Tsentrosoiuz [Tsentrosoiuz is Central Union of Consumers Cooperatives. See *Sobranie postanovlenii pravitel'stva USSR*, 10 (1987), No. 42 (5 Feb 87), 209-213], and Soviet and economic organs are instructed to improve trade and medical services for horticultural and truck garden workers, ensure full satisfaction of their demand for horticultural and garden stock and other goods, and develop the network of reception centers to purchase any excess of agricultural products grown by them. Particular attention is to be given to satisfying the population's needs for summer houses, construction materials, and transportation, construction, repair, and other services.

Union Republic Councils of Ministers, Gosagroprom, the USSR Tsentrosoiuz, and USSR ministries and departments, are instructed to significantly expand the volume and range of paid services for citizens running personal plots and for horticultural and truck garden workers, and to encourage the development of cooperative and individual activity in this work. Special attention is to be given to the provision of services like cultivation of land plots, sale and application of fertilizers, application of plant protection agencies, construction and repair of houses and utility buildings, rental of small-scale mechanization equipment and horticultural and truck gardening implements, dressing of domestic animal and rabbit pelts, processing of output on contract, and veterinary and agronomical services.

Instructions are given for every collective farm and state farm and other agricultural enterprises, on the basis of accumulated experience, to organize links for the provision of services to the population in running personal plots and collective horticultural and truck gardening.

The USSR Ministry of the Production of Mineral Fertilizers and the USSR Ministry of the Chemical Industry are instructed to adopt additional measures to increase the output of mineral fertilizers and pesticides packed in quantities and range to fully satisfy the population's demands.

The resolution instructs autonomous republic councils of ministers and local executive committees, jointly with trade union organizations and agro-industrial committees and associations, to make broader use of the practice of holding reviews and competitions for the best personal plot, garden, or truck garden and to organize appropriate fairs and exhibitions publicizing advanced experience. It has been deemed expedient to hold union-wide reviews of the work of citizens' personal plots, gardens, and truck gardens with the results being summed up at the USSR Exhibitions of National Economic Achievements and republic, territory, and provincial exhibitions, with incentives for the winners.

Attaching great importance to the further development of subsidiary farms of enterprises, organizations, and institutions in order to improve food supplies for labor collectives, the CPSU CC and the USSR Council of Ministers have made it incumbent upon USSR ministries and departments, union republic Communist Party CCs and Councils of Ministers, territorial, provincial, city, and district Party Committees, autonomous republic Councils of Ministers, and executive committees of territory, province, city, and district Soviets to implement the specific practical measures to boost food production on subsidiary farms of enterprises, organizations, and institutions stemming from the CPSU CC June (1987) Plenum demands. Orders are given to analyze the production and economic activity of each such farm, to take exhaustive measures to ensure the fullest possible utilization of potential to boost the output of meat, dairy, and other products so as to improve supplies for labor collectives, to impose proper order in the utilization of material, technical, and financial resources, to assimilate economic accountability as quickly as possible, and to ensure profitable operations by subsidiary farms of the country's enterprises, organizations, and institutions.

Councils of Ministers of Union Republics (not divided into provinces), Councils of Ministers of Autonomous Republics, and territory and province executive committees are ordered to seek out plots of land for the subsidiary farms of enterprises and organizations. If necessary they are authorized to hand over loss-making and low-profit state farms or sections of them to enterprises and organizations in order to set up subsidiary farms, and to attach to them economically weak state farms.

In order to increase fish production it is recommended that more extensive use be made of the potential of inland bodies of water and that they be attached on a long-term basis to enterprises, organizations, and institutions. To that end an inventory of existing ponds, lakes, and reservoirs is to be made before the end of the year, and questions pertaining to organized subsidiary farms on the basis of them are to be solved.

When organizing subsidiary farms it is necessary to make more extensive use of the cooperative principle, set up joint fattening enterprises, livestock units, and hothouse combines by combining the resources of enterprises in different sectors, make maximum use of other organizational forms, and develop production links with collective and state farms and interfarm enterprises more extensively on a contract basis.

Union Republic Communist Party CCs, territory and province Party Committees, Union and Autonomous Republic Councils of Ministers, territory and province Soviet executive committees, and leaders of ministries and departments are instructed to elaborate and approve in 1987 plans for the development of hothouse farms for the production of early vegetables with a view to having 0.6-0.8 sq.m. of covered ground per city inhabitant by 1990.

The USSR State Agro-Industrial Committee, Union Republic agro-industrial committees and agro-industrial committees and associations are instructed, on the basis of apllications from enterprises, organizations, and institutions with subsidiary farms, to ensure the allocation and sale of tractors and agricultural machinery, mineral fertilizers, and other material and technical resources (on the USSR Gosagroprom schedule) to them in accordance with the normatives laid down for collective and state farms in the particular region, and to organize supplies of pedigree livestock and poultry, quality seeds and plants, veterinary and agro-chemical services, and services for the repair of tractors and agricultural and other machinery.

The USSR Gossnab [Gossnab is State Committee for Material and Technical Supply] and USSR Gosagroprom are instructed to provide for the allocation, in line with ministries' and departments' requests, of the requisite technology, for the construction of meat processing and dairy shops, canning units, refrigerators, storehouses, and other production facilities on subsidiary farms.

When planning and constructing new power stations, gas compressor stations, and other enterprises with resources in the form of waste heat and remodeling and expanding existing ones the USSR Ministries of the Gas Industry, of Power and Electrification, of the Petroleum Industry, of Mineral Fertilizer Production, of the Chemical Industry, other USSR ministries and departments, and union republic Councils of Ministers are ordered to make provision for the obligatory creation of hothouse, fish, and other subsidiary farms and shops at them. In 1988-1989 all bodies of water at existing TETS's are to be brought into use for the production of fish.

The credit terms for expenditures on the organization and expansion of the material and technical base applicable to state farms are to be extended to the subsidiary farms of enterprises, organizations and institutions.

It is laid down that as of 1988 land reclamation work on the land of subsidiary farms is to be carried out in accordance with the procedures and on the terms established for agricultural enterprises.

If necessary, leaders of enterprises, organizations, and institutions are authorized, by agreement with executive committees of province and territory Soviets, Autonomous Republic Councils of Ministers, and the Councils of Ministers of Union Republics not divided into provinces, to increase in newly organized subsidiary farms for the first 2-3 years the salaries of leading workers, specialists, and chief accountants by 1-2 grades above [the grade appropriate to] the planned volume of sales of products for the given year.

The USSR Gosagroprom, in accordance with USSR ministries' and departments' requests, is called upon to train and improve the skills of leaders and specialists of enterprises', organizations', and institutions' subsidiary farms and pay more attention to generalizing leading experience of the work of these farms.

"V tsentral'nom komitete KPSS," *Pravda* (25 Sep 87); translation in FBIS, No. 188 (29 Sep 87), 51-53. See also A. Tenson, "Easing of Restrictions on Private Plots," RFE/RL RL369/87 (18 Sep 87).

In the CPSU Central Committee. On Urgent Measures to Accelerate the Solution of the Food Question in Accordance with the CPSU CC June (1987) Plenum Guidelines (25 Sept 87)

The resolution notes that the work being done in accordance with the decisions of the 27th CPSU Congress and the CPSU CC May (1982) and April (1985) Plenums on assimilating the new economic management mechanism and intensive techniques in the agro-industrial complex are having a positive effect on increasing labor collectives' interest in end results and helping to increase the return on investments. In the past year the increase in agricultural gross output was 5 percent, which corresponds to the growth rate envisioned for the current 5-Year Plan. The number of loss-making collective and state farms has been reduced, their profitability has increased, and for the first time in recent years costs per unit of output have fallen.

At the same time, as the CPSU CC June (1987) Plenum noted, the great potential that exists for rapidly increasing the food supply is far from fully utilized. The rate of growth of agricultural growth output in Tadzhikistan, Armenia, and Novgorod, Chelyabinsk, and Amur provinces is 2-3 times below the sector's average. The stagnation in Uzbekistan's agrarian economy has not been eliminated.

Many provinces of the RSFSR and the Ukraine are lagging considerably behind the Food Program's targets in grain production, as is Moldavia in the production of oleaginous plants, and Kazakhstan and Lithuania in meat production.

Substantial shortcomings in the social development of the countryside are having an adverse effect on the solution of food problems. Despite a 40% increase in capital investments for these purposes in the past 4 years the amount of housing commissioned per resident in the countryside is considerably lower than in the cities. There is a serious lag in the provision of amenities, the development of the medical, cultural, and consumer services network, and hard-surfaced road building.

Factors continue to operate which are slowing down the development of the economic activeness and independence of labor collectives and cramping the population's initiative. Insufficient use is being made of economic levers for regulating production, normative methods of planning are being assimilated too slowly, and contractual relations are not being developed properly. Supplements added to purchase prices for produce sold by collective and state farms making either a low profit or a loss are often used primarily as labor remuneration. Excessive administration and the rigid regulation of the activity of farms, enterprises, and organizations have still not been eliminated.

Union and local planning and economic organs have been underrating the importance of accelerating the development of the processing base for resolving the food problem.

The CPSU CC instructs Union Republic Communist Party CCs and Councils of Ministers, territory, province, city, and district Party committees, ASSR Councils of Ministers, soviet executive committees, economic organs, and trade unions, Komsomol, and other social organizations to formulate and implement in accordance with the demands of the CPSU CC June (1987) Plenum urgent measures to ensure a further considerable improvement in the food supply in each district, city, province, territory, and autonomous and union republic.

It is proposed to comprehensively expand and deepen the processes of democratization, to develop the initiative of the labor collectives of the agro-industrial complex and the enterprises and organizations of other ministries and departments, the rural population, and all citizens, and to boost their interest in increasing food resources. Guided by **Lenin**'s ideas on cooperation, they are to embark more boldly on new forms and methods of economic management and with those aims in mind resolutely to eliminate all the obstacles and restrictions preventing an increase in production of agricultural output on collective and state farms, and on the subsidiary plots of industrial enterprises and in the individual sector. The work experience of those organizations which under the new economic management conditions have rapidly achieved a considerable increase in the production of agricultural output, fulfilled the plan targets for supplies to centralized funds, and secured a noticeable improvement in local supplies should be consistently supported and disseminated. At the same time it is necessary to resolutely eliminate parasitism, the desire of some leaders to work below full capacity, and the attempt to make up for food shortages resulting from ommission in their own work at the state's expense.

It is deemed necessary to sharply increase the return on the resources invested in land reclamation and thereby to achieve a quick and significant increase in the food supply. The USSR State Agro-Industrial Committee, the USSR Ministry of Land Reclamation and Water Resources, and union republic Councils of Ministers are instructed to establish the proper order in this important work, to prevent the inefficient investment of resources, and to use them in the light of the paramount needs of collective and state farms in the interests of producing extra output and strengthening their economics.

The earliest possible attainment of a significant increase in the food supply growth rate by the comprehensive use of all food sources is regarded by the CPSU CC as the most important and central task of the party's policy. It is necessary here to proceed from the premise that the accelerated development of social production in the agrarian sector of the economy is a reliable foundation for resolving the food question in the country and is also a good basis for making the fullest possible use of the potential of the subsidiary plots belonging to enterprises and citizens and other sources of obtaining additional output.

To intensify the influence of economic management methods on the agricultural production growth rate and to prompt labor collectives to make the most efficient use of their production potential, the CPSU CC instructs the USSR State Agro-Industrial Committee and ministries and departments belonging to the agro-industrial complex to complete the transfer of all subordinate collective and state farms and other enterprises and organizations to full economic accountability and self-financing in 1988-1989.

Planning and financial organs and agro-industrial committees and associations are instructed to provide methods for regulating economic relationships within the agro-industrial complex which ensure expanded reproduction on farms, enterprises, and organizations chiefly by means of their own resources. Special attention is to be paid here to fixing purchase prices which cover socially necessary costs and provide an incentive for improving output quality, increasing labor productivity, and reducing costs. Work to improve planning, finance, labor organization and remuneration, and the democratization of management is to continue.

Every enterprise and organization should transfer to the new conditions of economic management in the light of the actual situation that is taking shape and the demands of economic accountability, and expenditure should be in strict accord with their own money revenue and the deadline for loan repayment. The consumerist approach to the use of credits for labor remuneration not backed up by real output must end. It is proposed that a program for improving the financial state of collective and state farms, and other agro-industrial complex enterprises and associations be drawn up within 3 months.

The CPSU CC demands that Party Committees and Soviet and economic organs complete the transfer of all production subunits to contractual forms of labor organization in 1988. In so doing, the maximum account is to be taken of the full diversity of conditions when selecting the forms and methods of the contract, and formalism, inertia, and stereotyped working in this important matter are to be resolutely eradicated. Comprehensive support must be given to production collectives which take out a long-term (10-15 year) lease on means of production and work as true stewards of the land.

The attention of Party, Soviet, and economic leaders is drawn to existing cases of an incorrect attitude and prejudice toward the family and individual contract and the failure to appreciate the great potential that they contain. Effective measures are to be taken to ensure the broad application of these organizational forms. Labor remuneration for all participants in production, including leaders and specialists, is to be made directly dependent on gross income and other forms of production incentives are to be used as well. The proportion of remuneration in kind for agricultural workers is to be increased according to a scale linked strictly to end results.

The CPSU CC believes that the complete assimilation of economic accountability and contractual forms of labor organization in conjunction with the intensification of crop farming, stockraising, and the processing industry and the attainment on this basis of a considerable improvement in the population's food supply are the most important criteria for assessing the restructuring that is being carried out in the agro-industrial complex.

The resolution notes that it is necessary to continue to widely utilize the potential of industrial, construction, transport, and other enterprises in cities to overcome the lag in the economic and social development of the countryside. City enterprises and organizations are called upon to take part actively in consolidating the material base of collective and state farms, especially those located in remote areas, in helping to build housing, schools, preschool and medical establishments, cultural and consumer facilities, and roads in the countryside, and to provide rural population centers with public utilities and amenities. This work is to be carried out on a contract basis and to involve the workforce and means of both enterprises and the farms themselves.

The CPSU CC instructs Party, Soviet and economic organs in the center and at local level to focus efforts on the speediest possible solution of a task of statewide importance—the accelerated development and retooling of the processing industry—in order to obtain the biggest possible real increase in the production of quality food products through better processing and improved storage of agricultural produce. In their practical work planning, financial, agro-industrial, and other economic organs must proceed from the fact that at present and in the near future the development of the processing sphere is the most economical and swift way of obtaining additional food and thus ensuring an increase in the country's national income.

In view of the importance of accelerating the solution of this problem, the CPSU CC has instructed the USSR Council of Ministers to draw up and submit within 2 months proposals for the additional production in 1988-1995 of equipment for agricultural produce processing and storage enterprises. It is deemed necessary to involve enterprises of all the national economic sectors in the solution of this task.

The resolution makes provision for radically improving the work of the Tsentrosoiuz and its organs at local level in procuring agricultural product surpluses from the population and from collective and state farms, organizing the processing of these surpluses at its enterprises for its own purposes and also as a service to consumers, and improving its supply and marketing activities. In order to improve the organization of the procurement, processing, and marketing of livestock, milk, fruit, vegetables, and wild berries and mushrooms and to expand the services for the inhabitants of villages and workers' settlements, it is deemed necessary to follow up proposals from local level to create an extensive network of trade, procurement, and processing enterprises on a cooperatie basis.

With a view to developing economic initiative, enhancing openness in management, and eliminating administration by decree in the leadership of collective and state farms, and processing, construction, and other subdivisions, it is deemed expedient to further improve the activity of agro-industrial organs, especially at district level. Here it is necessary to make extensive use of the positive experience whereby the district agro-industrial association should be headed by a council elected at a meeting of representatives of collective and state farms, and other enterprises and chaired by one of the most authoritative farm leaders. The association's working apparatus must be accountable to the council.

Party Committees and Soviet and economic organs are instructed to suuport and disseminate in every way the new, promising formations in the agro-industrial complex such as the agro-industrial combines and associations, agrifirms, and production systems which make it possible to accelerate the introduction of the achievements of scientific and technical progress, achieve closer integration of production, processing, storage, and marketing of products, reduce losses, and get the products to the consumer more quickly.

Union republic Communist Party CCs and territory, province, city, and district committees are instructed, guided by the decisions of the CPSU CC January (1987) Plenum, to resolutely improve work in selecting, placing, and training cadres and staffing collective and state farms, and other agro-industrial complex enterprises with ideologically mature and competent leaders and specialists. Constant care must be taken to enhance the standing of state farm chairmen and enterprise directors, to form a stable detachment of farm and enterprise leaders, and to protect them against outside interference in affairs within their sphere of competence and against unjustified fines and other sanctions. Paramount importance must be attached to the training of cadres at all levels which must be continuous and ensure a profound assimilation of modern methods of management.

Attention is drawn to the need to enhance moral incentives for agro-industrial complex workers for the successful solution of tasks in ensuring the country's food supply. It has been decided that it would be expedient for the USSR Supreme Soviet Presidium to draw up conditions and a procedure for nominating workers from agricultural and allied sectors for state prizes for the achievement of targets, set for each zone, in agro-industrial production and specific contributions to the development of the social sphere.

The CPSU CC has instructed the USSR State Agro-Industrial Committee and the USSR Ministry of Higher and Secondary Specialized Education to ensure a quality improvement in the training of specialists in higher and secondary specialized agricultural educational establishments, close linkage between the educational and training process and modern methods of practical production techniques, the latest achievements of scientific and technical progress, and management skills in conditions of expanded rights and independence of farms and enterprises and their switch to full economic accountability and self-financing.

The resolution instructs the Komsomol CC and the USSR State Agro-Industrial Committee, jointly with party, Soviet and economic organs, to carry out work to ensure the extensive enlistment of young people in the main sectors of the agro-industrial complex and to take proper care to ensure the necessary production, housing, cultural, and living conditions for them. Special attention must be paid to the formation of stable labor collectives at economically weak collective and state farms at the RSFSR Non-Black Earth Zone, Siberia, and the far East. Groups of Young People made up of specialists in agriculture, public education, culture, medical, trade, and consumer services and the mass professions are to be sent to these farms.

The Komsomol CC, the USSR State Agro-Industrial Committee, and the Soviet Army and Navy Main Political Directorate are instructed to carry out the necessary explanatory work among servicemen who are being released into the reserve. Those who express a desire to work in agriculture should be dispatched to collective and state farms, or other enterprises.

"V tsentral'nom komitete KPSS. "O neotlozhnykh merakh po uskorenniu resheniia prodovol'stvennogo voprosa v sootvetstvii s ustanovkami iiun'skogo (1987) Plenum Ts KPSS'," *Pravda* and *Izvestiia* (25 Sep); a translation is also in FBIS, No. 189 (25 Sep), 61-63; a condensed translation is in CDSP, 39:40 (1987), 15-17. On this, see also Karl-Eugen Wädekin, "Two Agricultural Decrees of September 1987," RFE/RL RL408/87 (16 Oct 87).

Chapter 5

GLASNOST AND THE MEDIA

Glasnost—openness or publicity—is the part of Gorbachev's reform campaign which has attracted the greatest attention in the Western media. It is the mechanism by which he hopes to maintain the momentum of perestroika. By means of glasnost, with its emphasis upon self-criticism and accountability, the sponsors of reform can use the threat of exposure to compel reluctant bureaucrats and workers to get their own jobs done properly. Glasnost also gives the enthusiast a means and motivation for participation in the new society the General Secretary hopes to create.

Above all, glasnost is an appeal to the artistic and scientific intelligentsia who want freedom of expression. It has taken on multiple forms: an opening up of the media to serious debate; a new and vibrant cultural world, with the appearance of films, plays, and television programs that would have been unthinkable only a few years ago; open attacks on officialdom and even Party members; a dramatic review and revision of previously inviolable historical themes; the rehabilitation of individuals who were victims of stalinist terror, or long since 'unpersoned', or both.

Previously forbidden subject matter like drug abuse, AIDS, prostitution, the moral degeneration of youth, corruption scandals, nepotism; economic and management issues like harvest failures, bureaucratism (formalism); the reporting of natural and human disasters; all have become common issues in the media.

Public opinion is now important in the USSR and is being catered to by Gorbachev. See, for example, V.S.Korobeinikov, *Pressa i obshchestvennoe mnenie.* Moscow: Nauka, 1986; M.A.Fedotov, *Sovety i pressa,* Moscow: Iuridicheskaia literatura, 1987. Most importantly for the Soviet leader, is the fact that glasnost has revitalized the Soviet creative intelligentsia—which now leads the struggle against the entrenched bureaucracy in the economic and educational sectors. The following section show the variety of ways in which glasnost has revealed an attitudinal change—or an area where the CPSU hopes that attitudes will change. It is also here that "backfire" is possible, for Gorbachev himself could well be the target of criticism from the "pandora's box" he has helped to open.

Aside from the items in the Bibliography below, see the following 1987 RFE/RL essays: Viktor Yasmann, "Drafting a Press Law: *Glasnost'* as an Alternative to the Free Flow of Information," RL14/87 (8 Jan); Julia Wishnevsky, "A. Yakovlev and the Cultural 'Thaw'," RL51/87 (5 Feb); V.Tolz, "*Moscow News*—The Cutting Edge of *Glasnost'*," RL54/87 (4 Feb); Tolz, "A Chronological Overview of Gorbachev's Campaign for *Glasnost'*," RL66/87 (23 Feb)

Aleksandr Mar'iamov. **Together in Front of the Television. Straight Talk** (17 Jan 87)
I don't know about you, but I have been feeling somewhat intellectually uncomfortable lately. All of a sudden, what used to be, what we had plenty of, what we fed each other for many years, has begun to disappear. Rumors have stopped. There is less gossip.

And it is not that we believed those rumors—most likely we did not believe them—it is just that over a period of years they managed to flatten us, to entangle us in their nets, and to swaddle us. A certain set behavior, normal to most people, made its appearance. We all became terrified when faced with a movie camera, went silent in front of a microphone, and grasped at salvation in the form of a text on paper, as if clutching at a straw. What people said off-the-record was one thing, but what one said on-the-record was another thing.

The sweetness of forbidden fruit is well-known. The tree of half-truths, which we had so lovingly nurtured, under whose branches we so outwardly thrived, was completely studded with such ripe fruit. Now we must pay for our unregulated indulgence in the sweet fare, and get used to the new taste sensation of reality. To doctor a diabetic soul has fairly sapped our creative and social energy. And this (situation), you know, does not happen all at once. You do not immediately realize where you will put the fig which you have slipped from your pocket. To whom can you show it ? To you, yourself?

Our present-day complete turn-around toward renewal and openness presupposes a mutuality of strength. Above all it depends upon reconstruction occurring within ourselves, that we will finally be able to do that of which we are capable, and say what we are thinking.

Almost 20 years ago, we might have been able to listen to **Lenin**'s words on this subject from the (TV and movie) screen. (And learn) how any bitter truth was more useful than lies. We were able, but did not hear them! The series of films by **M.Shatrov** and **I.Pokelnik**, "Sketches for a Portrait of V.I.**Lenin**" existed all those years outside our field of vision. I am sure that had it not been for this, our inner need for change, and our preparation for it would have been heightened today.

Tensely following the extraordinary movement of ideas, hearing the limpid clarity of the Leninist message, no doubt all of it being useful, we are struck by the fact that it is very much for our time, (it) very closely corresponds with what is happening now, and with what we are thinking. Perhaps that is why the fate of these film chronicles was so exceedingly hard. Was this why our ignorance of their existence remained so persistently and voicelessly prolonged?

Recently we learned about the events in Alma-Ata [Kazakhstan]. Once again, rumors started to fly. Why whisper, you might ask? The news did not come by means of the grapevine—a Central Television announcer reported it to the entire country the day it happened. Yesterday we would not have believed our ears.—something like that, and on TV no less? But today? Today, also, you know, not everyone could believe his ears. The unexpectedness and unlikelihood of the event had an effect, as did the force of habit. The fact that reports from on-the-spot correspondents did not immediately follow the reports also had an effect. And suddenly, there were rumors. Tall tales, each more harsh than the next. And frankly, no one was able to lay them to rest right away. Thus there is still something we do not know how to do, something that we still have not got the hang of. There is still something we were not able to do. And that is true for more than television. It applies just as well to the press.

Nonetheless, we do have experience in overcoming rumors. That is what helped us to survive and master the tragedy of Chernobyl. It opened our hearts to human grief when we heard about the disaster of the *Admiral Nakhimov*. We knew everything and because of that we stood united.

There is no scale with which to measure the level of openness they say. This is the range of the permissible, but for the moment that is off limits. Once you have said, "A," be so kind as to continue—speak on.

We are fairly well aware that unfinished statements and incompleteness of information breeds distrust. Openness can only be called openness if it is absolutely unlimited, if it is accessible to everyone and if it means an exchange of views about all the problems which life sets before us.

In general, the "cardboard people" prophesying paper truths are beginning to disappear, and thankfully so. The main characters, the central heroes of the broadcasts are becoming living people, (for example), the young announcers of the local Moscow Balashikhi from the show, "Allow me a Word," the debaters of the "12th Floor", the state arbitration workers, or the academics confidentially talking things over with us.

It is heartening to hear such straight and intelligent talk.

Television today is entering upon a new level of discourse. Its fans are very wide, but before all else these forms mean truth. There is (now) a clear understanding that the viewer wants to and should know everything.

Mar'iamov, "Vmeste y televisora: Priamaia rech'," *Izvestiia* (17 Jan); a condensed translation can be found in CDSP, 39:3 (1987), 19-20.

Z.Tazhurizina, **Just How is Religion "Useful"?**(10 April 1987)

This is not the first year I have taught scientific atheism. In my business, just as in any other, there is much that is difficult. One needs to understand the spiritual question of youth. One needs to understand why a young person will suddenly say, "I am an unbeliever and I have never read religious books, but I think that religion is useful for the individual and society." Where does this idea of religion's usefulness come from?

It is very important that there existed a world view which united philosophy and artistic culture. You know that the wide masses perceive ideological principles not so much by means of books and pamphlets as by artistic productions. Thus, a world point of view based on Marxist theory exists: Soviet culture for a long time has taken on for itself the function of explaining the realistic and materialistic relationships of reality, of the propagandization of Communist ideals.

Beginning in the 1960s, several problems arose: a tendency has gradually been making headway which Party documents have deemed to be confusion in world outlook, eclecticism, God-seeking motifs and an omnivorous world outlook. For a long time, in certain circles of the intelligentsia, a conciliatory and sometimes even apologetic attitude towards religion and idealistic philosophy has been seen as "a broad view" and "civic courage." The religious orientation of culture came to be regarded in these circles as a means of humanizing society and increasing its spiritual potential. In the past 10 to 15 years, various spheres of culture have gradually become saturated with an ever-increasing number of religious subjects, images and ideas, which are presented positively.

Idyllic assumptions about religion are mainly a result of insufficient theoretical literacy. In reading certain works of belles lettres and publicist writings, it is possible to detect that their authors do not have a scientific notion about religion, that they are interpreting it very broadly, without perceiving its specifics and, consequently, its essence. Elementary mistakes are made. Thus, religion is confused with other forms of social consciousness: with morality, art, philosophy, politics. But as is known, religion is not morality and not politics.

But there exists also deeper reasons why certain cultural figures turn to religion. The unfavorable social atmosphere of the 1970s and the early 1980s played a significant role here. The violation of the principle of social justice, the growth of private ownership and dependent sentiments, the division between words and deeds, and the strengthened influence of a consumption-minded stratum on public and spiritual life. Some people began to blame the "official doctrine"—that is, Marxism—for this. Religion, then, in the opinion of those people, is an ideology "undefiled" by negative phenomena. In search of ways of overcoming negative phenomena, of ways to enhance morality, certain cultural figures have turned to religion.

Paradoxically, the formation of antisocialist morality has been understood not as a result of deviations from socialism but as a result of the loss of religiosity and the spread of materialism and atheism among working people in the post-October period.

This does not exclude, however, the possibility that some of the cultural figures who, in searching for the ideal have turned to religion, reflect the sentiments and interests of people with private ownership mentality. We have still inefficiently explained the connection between religion and the needs of people who lead an anti-socialist way of life. Meanwhile, observations show that this connection exists. If a certain segment of our people is drawn to religious illusions while suffering from a shortage of social justice (by this, unfortunately, deviations from socialist principles are taken for socialism as such), another part of the population, commonly called moneygrubbers, is drawn to religion out of fear of the consequences of their actions.

The presence of such strata has been observed by several Soviet writers for some time. A.**Ananev,** a penetrating and brave writer who opposes the soulless alternatives to authentic socialist culture in his novel, *Years Without Wars*, (in which he) describes our society at the end of the 1960s, with concern portrays the strengthened position of that stratum for which the higher ideals seem to be the code of the inviolablity of ownership.

Previously, said A.**Ananev**, this stratum was considered depressed, effaced, destroyed at its very base; but, as the times have shown, disguising their clothes for self-defence, they waited until it was possible for them to reappear on the historical scene. Obviously, socialism for such people is an alien force, just as is Marxist scholarship about social equality and social justice; this means that by their very existence the principle of equality is trampled. It is no accident that a tendency has appeared for the idealization of the way of life and the values of the ruling, propertied strata of prerevolutionary Russia. The social nostalgia could not avoid being reflected in a desire to restore the spiritual "values" of the ruling classes of prerevolutionary Russia, first of all religion and the ideas of the Russian religious philosophers.

There is still another important circumstance in my opinion. Since during the last 15 t0 20 years those who entered the higher schools most easily were the children of people who have a privileged social or property status, there has gradually formed a certain dilettantish element that arrogantly ignores the principles of social equality, Communist morality and, therefore, atheism.

It seems to me that a tendency to reorient ideals from revolutionary, Communist ones to religious ones **is becoming noticeable**. It is not surprising that this has become part of the attempts to reexamine the class approach to the past. In speaking of the so-called "moral quests" of certain intellectuals, A. **Ananev** very accurately notes that history has been revised. Attempts have been made "to make it appear as if in the past there had been neither rich nor poor, neither serfs nor gentry, but all that had existed was national unity and national fraternity, thanks to which the people's culture and character were created."

In the 1970s there began a revision of the attitude towards revolutionary democrats and in general toward the progressive tradition in our culture, and there were more frequent attempts to find flaws both in the position and in the moral makeup of fighters against serfdom, the autocracy and the church. In a number of books, **Belinskii, Dobroliubov, Pisarev, Chernyshevskii** and **Saltykov-Shchedrin** were mocked. It is hardly coincidental that the school program in literature that was worked out several years ago gave very little space to revolutionary-democratic literature in the higher grades. It removed **Belinskii**'s *Letter to Gogol* and all of **Herzen**, and **Shchedrin** was reduced to two stories.

To counter-balance the revolutionary-democratic ideology, the religious aspect of the works of the great Russian writers **Gogol** and **Dostoevskii** was overemphasized. This aspect was made out to be the most fruitful component of their world outlook.

There is often talk to the effect that atheism has created a moral vacuum in people's souls. Atheism is blamed not only for amoralism but also for destroying artistic monuments. Individual literators, with Olympian indifference, have ignored a great many extremely interesting studies and popular works in the field of scientific atheism and have begun to accuse it of narrow-mindedness and "iron" dogmatism and even of replacing enlightenment with administrative fiat.

Interestingly, the past few decades have seen almost no artistic works embodying images of the freethinkers and atheists of the past. On the contrary, more often than not personages from the Bible and the Koran, or clergymen, as well as monks, are put forth as moral examples.

Frequently, religious holidays and ceremonies have been propagandized in the press, movies, and television. In a strange way, during the current period of the revolutionary restructuring of society, some writers are beginning to compete with one another, as it were. Who will go the farthest in advocating religious or abstract-humanist views? It has become fashionable to switch from the idea of social transformation to the idea of "transformation of the soul", to shift the center of gravity to individual self-perfection.

The ideas of general sinfulness and a universal sense of guilt, which are supposedly felt by the truly moral person, and of Christian all-forgiving, humility and submissiveness have been fermenting, as it were, in our cultural life for 15 to 20 years now. During this period, a desire has been observed to present religious norms of morality and religious ideals as common to all mankind and to impart a religious nature to simple norms of morality that are common to all mankind. They say even that we contemporary Soviet people are still living under the Ten Commandments. In doing so, "they forget" to add that the first four Commandments carry a purely religious character, and the next six are simple norms of morality which have concrete historical content.

What is the effect of all these tendencies on the spiritual and social life of our youth?

In the first place they erode the scientific-materialistic world view on which Communist upbringing is based. For approximately a decade, the idea that there is a need for philosophical, world-view pluralism in spiritual life has been spreading in a certain segment of the intelligentsia. As a philologist told me, "We must make it possible for all philosophical trends to exist." "And let Marxism be one of them," he added generously.

However, pluralism can only be a relatively brief transitional stage, followed by the predominance of a single world outlook. The predominance of a religious-idealistic orientation would bring nothing but harm to society. The entire experience of historical development indicates this. God-seeking tendencies of various kinds prepare the soil for the spread of bourgeois ideology and facilitate ideological disarmament.

(To one with) writing talent, it is not difficult to skirt around evangelical subjects and personages, often relying upon ancient legends. But it is much more difficult, it seems, in our many-sided, contradictory life to portray the really positive tendencies, drawing on what is probable and to form images based on the surrounding world and on one's ownself.

The attempts to attract people to religious-moral sentiments is dangerous utopia, which distracts attention from the really formative internal and external life of mankind. The attempt to raise the moral level of society by turning to religion is too oversimplified and too superficial, or, more to the point, too faulty an approach to the solution of the very serious problems facing us. We must not forget that God-seeking motifs in culture are also linked with nationalistic sentiments.

There is still another consideration. The publication of works that contain idyllic ideas about religion in one form or another brings far greater harm than the output of purely religious literature. Our country's population sees Soviet publications as authoritative, unlike theological publications, which are valued only by believers.

It is time to remove the halo of civic courage from attempts to propagandize religious ideas in Sovet culture.

Tazhurizina, "Tak chem zhe 'polezna' religiia?" *Komsomol'skaia pravda* (10 April); a condensed translation can be found in CDSP, 39:19 (1987), 10-11. The author is a teacher at Moscow State University.

Stanislav Kondrashov, **Together in Front of the Television. Every Cloud Has a Silver Lining** (11 Apr 87)
Of the international televisions programs in recent months, I cannot remember a single one that attracted such a wide and powerful response as the interview with Margaret **Thatcher** by three Soviet journalists. More than a week has passed since that program was shown almost

at midnight, but on all sides one still hears: Well? What do you say? There is malice in that question, and a stone is thrown into our garden—the garden of us international journalists—and in the bed that political commentators cultivate.

One is astonished by how wide the television audience is—practically the entire nation—and by how great the interest is in international politics, especially in the live showing of its principal actors and figures.

The magnifying glass of television raises the effect of the presence, passion, and heat of the spectators. One on one with an event that takes place before his eyes, the television viewer draws his own opinion.

A professional journalist like me sees the dominance of emotion in this opinion. Indignation: how could they attack her like that? A woman?!...Delight: and she gave it to them!!! And a criticial generalization, once again on the level of feelings and sarcasm: commentators! This means me as well ...

Thus, the spectators, demonstrating their objectivity, agree that the match did not end to our advantage. In the sentence they pass, if one thinks about it, there is even a certain secret satisfaction. It betrays dissatisfaction with the state of affairs in our international journalism, which, in no hurry to part with its accustomed stereotypes, lags behind the pace of restructuring in the minds of viewers and readers. As often happens, a phenomenon that is hidden for a certain time awaits an opportunity to surface. The television interview with the British Prime Minister was just such an opportunity.

I wish to look at the situation through the eyes of a professional, from which one would expect not emotion, but cold-blooded and careful analysis. In doing so, I will not throw stones in someone else's garden—that caused me no harm. I will put myself in the place of my three colleagues who behaved honorably, but showed some discomfort. The interests of the field, as well as professional and public interests, demand that I reflect on this and draw some lessons.

The first lesson, which concerns all of us international reporters, is that we must not simplify or make caricatures of our Western partners or adversaries. The new time of openness, by opening up the outside world in a more complex and extensive fashion, is now calling in some debts.

In the eight years in which Margaret **Thatcher** has held the position of Prime Minister of Britain, we have tried very hard to create a stereotype of an "iron lady," in which the unacceptable political views of a British Conservative seemed to be automatically linked to unattractiveness as a human being. A simplification. It did not stand the test of experience, or, more to the point, of our television screen. Moreover, since it was present in the minds of viewers, the old simplification, according to the law of contrast and compensation, helped the new image of Margaret **Thatcher**, for we saw an English lady in a high government post who is intelligent, very experienced, attractive, and has an appealing sense of dignity. A Conservative? Yes. That judgement did not change one iota. But who said that you must not feel respect for a confirmed conservative with whom you are carrying on a dialogue in search of peace? No one said it. However, neither was it acceptable to say something the opposite: that without such respect, without a certain trust, there can be no peaceful coexistence, no productive contacts between state leaders.

A second lesson must be learned by both journalists and the audience. No matter how high the passions of the spectators may run, an interview, by the very nature of the genre, cannot be a sporting event in which there are inevitable winners and losers. Those who see an interview as a means to "press" the other side "to the wall" are mistaken. With rare exceptions, that is a task beyond the powers of journalists, especially when dealing with experienced and tried political figures. A simple truth must be understood—they do not agree to interviews so as to be "pressed", but so as to set out their positions and views (or to mask them). If one considers the purely propagandistic effect of an interview, the person giving the answers has many more chances to achieve it than the person asking the questions. What the latter can hope to achieve is to obtain information, old or new. In fact, that is the law of the genre—getting information, not a confrontation that offers the prospect of victory or defeat.

Margaret **Thatcher** succeeded in exploiting the opportunity given her. The journalists had many fewer opportunities. The level of their success or failure is defined only by how fully they took advantage of them. As an example, we heard no answer to the question of plans to increase Great Britain's nuclear potential, because such a question was not asked. We did not learn what grounds there might be for compromise or mutual advantage, what grounds the British doctrine of nuclear restraint and the Soviet plans for attaining a nuclear-free world might meet on. There was no question of that kind either.

But was anyone hurt by this? And is anyone surprised—on the level of analysis, not emotion—that each side has its own logic which draws from the vitality of the other? Not from any philological tournament can we find a victor, any more than we can from one interview. Openness, along with everything else, assumes the television viewers' and readers' right to draw their own conclusions.

The third lesson is a lesson of tact and tactics. In regard to tact, the reaction of the public was quite strong, while tactics seemed to remain outside the scope of its attention. However, it was the tactics in conducting the interview that were, in my opinion, not worked out properly. Fifty minutes is a very long time on the screen. That is perhaps enough to answer 20 questions. They never made their appearance. Far too many minutes were spent on "pressing", on an unproductive twisting of the theme of nuclear restraint. That aggravated the emotions of the viewers.

To be sure, it is possible to extract other lessons. And important extractions. Every cloud has a silver lining. The practice of openness promises new interviews, meetings, experiments—and new tests. One way or another, international journalists must restructure, learn and re-learn.

Kondrashov, "Vmeste u televizor: Net khuda bez dobra," *Izvestiia* (11 April); a condensed translation can be found in CDSP, 39:15 (1987), 16-17.

N.Kudriavtsev, **Speech on Glasnost'** (2 Jul 87)

Comrade Deputies! Discussion of proposed changes in the laws and their implementation—is the aspect and form of the emergence of glasnost, which has subsequently and fully entered all aspects of our social life.

Sociological and legal research shows that our citizens highly value this process. As many as 69 percent of the respondents in a survey undertaken by the Institute of Sociological Research at the USSR Academy of Sciences notice that the level of information held by the population recently has risen quite dramatically when it comes to questions of the domestic and foreign policy of our government. The extent of participation by citizens in decision-making also has grown (this was indicated by 59 percent of the respondents).

These are positive facts. At the same time, however, another matter is attracting attention. In response to the question, "Are you satisfied with the level of openness in questions affecting the life of your city and borough?," only 40 percent answered in the affirmative, and 42 percent gave a negative response. Only 27 percent of the respondents were satisfied with the level of openness at the places where they lived. They also judge the level of their influence on local problems to be quite low. A strange and, I must say, very paradoxical image emerges. Working people know more about the problems of the life of the country as a whole and, generally often have a stronger impact on those problems than they have on the solution of issues within their own regions.

I think that the new law will help to settle this situation and to accelerate restructuring and democratization at the local level. In this regard, I would like to touch upon two questions.

The first is the degree to which there is legal regulation of various spheres of public life. It is very imbalanced in our country. On the other hand, the amount of regulation, especially regulation through department resolutions and in the field of national economy, must be sharply reduced. Some perfectly accurate things were said about this at the CPSU CC Plenum Committee. I think that three things are needed here. First, an 'inventory', so to speak, must be taken of all departmental resolutions and normative acts, in order to discern and repeal everything that slows down restructuring. However, this work must not be entrusted solely to the departments themselves, as it has been in the past; rather it must be conducted under the supervision of the government, with the participation of the Ministry of Justice and the USSR Procurator's Office. Absolute deadlines should be set for conducting this work.

Secondly, judicial agencies must be given the right, and not just the procurator's agencies, at least to suspend (if not repeal) the operation of departmental acts that do not coincide with the law, when this is revealed while specific case are being considered. There are quite a few such cases. Thirdly, a legal act must be adopted on the procedure and grounds for and the limits of so-called "departmental law-making" and on its supervision.

This is one side of the matter. There is, however, another side as well. Democracy does not mean spontaneous activity and ambiguity. Certain sides of life should be more clearly regulated by legal means. In regard to restructuring, this applies to an entire series of new laws—for example, on cooperation, on invention, on procedures for government services, on openness and the role of the mass news media, on voluntary societies and creative unions, on procedures and legal guarantees for the implementation of various rights and legal interests of citizens, on responsibility in the field of environmental protection and urban planning, and others.

One task of research institutions is preparing the conceptions underlying these acts and, I must say, elaborating a tactic for the legal development of our state. The tactic should be elaborated in stages—for the near future and for the distant future. It must be recognized that many recent political decisions have been considerably advanced over what social scientists might have suggested.

Finally, about legal standards. Legal nihilism, the idea that we can do without laws, does not merely exist; these opinions still are rather widespread, especially among personnel at the lower level of the state *apparat*. The implementation of recently adopted laws is often managed unsatisfactorily. About a year might pass until an adopted law begins to be applied at the local level. Some personnel still wait for all sorts of explanations and instructions. And there are not enough texts of the laws.

Respect for the law is the one indisputable aspect of democracy. At the same time, democracy itself cannot successfully thrive without firm adherence to the law. It is not coincidental that today's Supreme Soviet session is discussing the drafting of new laws, whose principles of democracy and socialist legality will subsequently be introduced into all spheres of life in our society.

"Rech' V.N. Kudriavtseva," *Izvestiia* (2 Jul); a condensed translation can be found in CDSP, 39:28 (1987), 12-13. Kudriavtsev is Director of the USSR Academy of Sciences' Institute of State and Law. The speech was delivered at the Congress of the Supreme Soviet.

Fyodor Burlatskii, **Learn Democracy. Notes of a Publicist** (18 Jul 87)
The country has begun to move and act. Openness and democracy have given each individual the opportunity to speak out about every painful item. In terms of the pitch at which life is being lived, the last two years have been more action-packed than certain entire decades because so many problems have been raised at political forums, at labor collectives, in the press, in literature, in the theatre and on television. Public opinion is becoming an increasingly important factor in acceleration. But even in ancient times it was known that the Word must be followed by the Deed. Otherwise the Word is merely a source of irritation to the soul. Need it be said that unconstructive criticism is merely the level at which social consciousness begins. Everyone rightly rejects the complacent daydreaming of **Gogol**'s character Manilov—a practice which for so long had fed the people with promises of a land flowing with milk and honey. But no less harmful were the impudent escapades—typical of **Gogol**'s Nozdrev [Manilov and Nozdrev are characters from Gogol's *Dead Souls* (1842).]—which were as vacuous as soap-bubbles. What is needed most of all is business-like work to accelerate the country's development and to heal our economic and social ills.

As M.S.**Gorbachev** said at a meeting with leaders of the mass media and of the creative unions, we are once again, as it were, passing through a school of democracy. Everyone, leaders and the masses alike, is learning to work under new conditions, cultivating in social awareness the seeds of a genuine political culture which serves restructuring. Our political culture has quite a long and, to put it bluntly, a rather contradictory tradition. And, as **Pushkin** said, tradition is the soul of the state.

We have behind us Kievan Rus' and the Novgorod *veche*, [city council] which few people recollect, the 300 years of the Eastern yoke [Tatars], **Ivan** the Terrible, **Peter** the Great, gloomy **Nicholas I**, pitiful **Nicholas II**—**Pushkin**'s "the people keep silent" reflected the political tradition of authoritarianism. And not long before that, Jean-Jacques **Rousseau** had passed the terrifying judgement: In Russia there will never be a democracy because it is a country of slaves; the people have the government they deserve. **Chaadaev**, that unfortunate Russian genius, threw out to those who came after a cry wrenched from his sick consciousness: Russia—a land without a future.

Fortunately, he was mistaken, just as the thinker from Geneva [**Rousseau**] was mistaken.

In October 1917, under the leadership of the Bolsheviks, the people, who had been oppressed for centuries but not crushed, made a tremendous leap towards democracy. We are not slaves, we are indeed not slaves! But the path to power for the people was strewn with thorns and soaked with blood.

In **Lenin**'s time, workers, sailors, soldiers, and peasants began learning how to govern the state, But the deficiencies in their overall and political culture, were a significant factor that led to a situation in which, instead of a government by the working people, what emerged was government for the working people.

The trend towards the bureaucratization of government, against which **Lenin** resolutely fought, intensified after his death. History has still to tell the story of that epoch. It has still to tell of what was created for the first time on our soil (something in which we will always take pride) through the selfless, furious struggle of the Party and of all our people for technical and social progress. It will tell how in the Patriotic War our great and courageous people were able to stand their ground and triumph at such a terrible cost. It will tell how we cannot and have no right to forgive or excuse the brutal repressions against cadres in the Party, in the Army, and among the intelligentsia, and of the human tragedies.

Incidentally, allow me to point out that the personality cult itself was not merely imposed from above. Unfortunately, it reflected the nature of that particular stage in the political culture of the masses.

Light and shadow were also strangely mixed in the period that began after the 20th CPSU Congress [1956]. Guarantees were set up against the restoration of the personalty cult and repression. But a radical transformation of our society could not be undertaken at that time. In the 1970s, negative processes, unsolved problems and phenomena of stagnation and conservatism began to accumulate.

And then came April 1985. How much, indeed, we have experienced in so short a time! Openness, democratization, economic reforms—all this has stirred the soul of every individual.

To a great extent, a new Soviet political culture has begun to take shape before our very eyes. And, along with that, (there is also taking shape) a political person who is an active participant in the social process. Now something has been discovered that might have been predicted. We have opinions that do not fully coincide, even though all of us believe in socialism, Soviet rule, and the Party's leadership of the country.

Where does the resistance to restructuring come from? Who are the vehicles of the resistance? Many people are sure that it is only the bureacrats who are resisting.

But resistance is by no means a monopoly of the administrative *apparat*. The part of the masses that is indifferent to the changes should also be taken as a factor which inhibits restructuring, although, with few exceptions people are taking a very responsible attitude towards what is going on.

Let us begin with the bureaucrat, because for the time being he has far greater influence and more depends upon him. The fact is, each executive, even in the most modest official position, is faced with the problem of making a choice. What should he serve by his personal work: bold structural changes in the conditions of labor and in the provision of incentives for such work, and the promotion of the development of people's initiative, or should it be cautious little steps and minor organizational and cadre changes?

It would seem to be obvious that the most ineffectual of all would be micro-reforms—a kind of dinosaur, so to speak, a monster, half horse or half bird, which can neither gallop nor fly. But the former overcautious individual as before still bides his time and even tries on the sly, casting glances over his shoulder, to put the brakes on the Party decision ascribed to him— on the introduction of the team contract, on the development of the cooperative movement, on the family contract, on individual labor, and on the effective struggle against corruption and unearned income.

After all, a decision does not directly establish a norm of law, that is, the obligation to carry out some particular action under threat of sanction—be it financial, administraive, or even criminal sanction. For some time the old laws and a multitude of instruction have continued to operate which to this day can be used as a refuge by those "cautious" local representatives of authority and management.

The CPSU CC June Plenum took into account the whole significance of the juridical form of social relations and the humanitarian and ethical impact of socialist law. The Plenum discussed a whole package of documents which were adopted at the USSR Supreme Soviet session. A firm legal foundation is thereby beng laid beneath the edifice of economic reforms which is being erected. Let us hope that juridical backup for all decisions will become an obligatory means for their implementation.

Apart from the "old bureaucrat" and cautious advocate of "playing safe", the resourceful phrase-monger of restructuring, who flourished in the past and who is very eager to consolidate his position in the new period, is once again trying to emerge on the surface. However, what is needed now is not cleverness, not the sharp-witted ability to jump on the restructuring bandwagon, but devotion to the cause, professionalism, and indeed straightforward decency and sincerity.

And so we come to yet another kind of impersonator. A person has been elected to a post— at a plant, in a scientific establishment, in a creative organization. In which direction does he channel his energy: toward the common cause or serving himself first and foremost? As soon as a new leader gets caught up, so to speak, in an activity which was customarily in the past— acquiring titles, bonuses, awards and official positions, and taking trips to Europe—it is clear that what we have is a "self-seeking re-structurer."

Alongside the fervent advocates of restructuring, who have brought it into being literally through the sufferings of their own experiences, people are turning up who used to hold their tongues but now, rushing to make up for lost time, are not shrinking from the most extreme opinions. Of course, any opinion which is dictated by a desire to serve the cause of renewal merits attention. But the right to criticize presupposes also the right to criticize the criticism, as **Marx** said.

For example, we hear superficial views about the inevitability and even usefulness of unemployment as a pressure mechanism conducive to growth in labor productivity.

It is hardly necessary to recall that guaranteed labor and social security make up the chief gains of the socialist system. No one in our country will agree to renounce these gains, which were achieved at high price. But let us also look at this issue form a practical viewpoint.

More than once I have heard many enterprise managers say that they are prepared to reduce their complement of employees by one-fourth or even by one-third on condition that they be allowed to use the remaining wage fund to pay their remaining workers. On a national scale, one-fourth means tens of millions of people. What would be done with them?

The state is not able to pay them pensions. Throwing them out on the street—that is impossible to even contemplate. Thus we must look for other ways—the redistributing and retraining of the work force. That means that we must give serious thought as to which agency will take on the problem on a national scale, a problem that will become increasingly acute as new equipment and production processes are mastered and labor becomes more intensive.

Moreover, will it be fair to assign to the working people the burden of the transitional period to the new system of economic management?

The following dilemma that has been posed does not appear to be all that naive either: the "free market" of the planned economy. Of course, today we face the task of developing commodity-money relations. But posing the above-mentioned dilemma can lead to further fruitless debate, instead of a search for ways of carrying out structural reforms.

We are aware of how acute the problems of overcoming excessive centralization and departmentalization are in our country. Eighteen million people in the administrative *apparat*—that is too high a price to pay for the excessively developed principle of centralization. It is obvious that in conditions of the reform, in which the enterprise and the association are becoming the main unit of planning and management, the central *apparat* of departments and ministries could profitably be cut by half or even by two-thirds. But do we have to return to the idea of the economic councils—that is, to an attempt that failed in the 1960s? Experience is now being accumulated with elections held in accordance with the multi-seat system in the Soviets and the labor collectives. During the first experiments real problems came to light in the matter of improving the procedure for nominating candidates, conducting election campaigns, and developing the political structure of the masses. It is self-management which must ensure that not everyone is nominated for leadership posts, but rather the most capable, talented organizers and genuine "doers."

The "grassroots" are also not free of the influence of social conditions. Restructuring is being opposed too by those who up to now have preferred to take more and work less, and who enrich themselves at the expense of this "deficit."

The CPSU CC June Plenum convincingly showed that solutions must be sought by relying on contemporary experience and taking a long look into the future. Only profound revolutionary reforms can create a highly effective economic system which absorbs scientific and technical progress like a sponge and which is capable of sustaining competition with the leading industrial powers of the modern world.

There is also another kind of impersonator. Among the mass of people who are making honest and conscientious use of their new rights, including the right to elect managers, some individuals are also appearing who are taking advantage of openness to compromise exacting and principled managers and more gifted specialists, to settle personal scores and to capture places they do not deserve, because the level of their professional training is too low.

I remember a person who, during a meeting, demanded unlimited "freedom to demonstrate." This is typical ochlocracy (ochlocracy, according to **Aristotle**, is mob rule). Such people, who fanatically believe in only one idea, are unable to even hear an opponent out. They take to the streets to make an often undeserved protest and to inveigh against those who disagree with them.

Who in our country is for an unlimited "right to demonstrate"? Local nationalists, extremists from *Pamiat* [The *Pamiat'* (Memory) group is made up in part of extreme anti-semitic Russian nationalists.] and certain other groups of similar orientation, people pursuing selfish interests, so called "refuseniks" ["Refuseniks" are Soviet citizens, usually Jewish, who apply to emigrate and are refused the right to do so.] who want to emigrate, and so forth. Each of these groups opposes the other and if they are given a free rein you will see if they do not start engaging in fisticuffs.

We have enough experience to understand that local nationalism and Great Power chauvinism, anti-semitism and Zionism nurture one another and, in so doing, drink from the same dipper—anarchy, disorder, and a wretched, uncivilized political culture.

How quickly the mingling of democracy and ochlocracy takes place! Only yesterday, for example, representatives of *Pamiat* insisted on the proper idea of preserving Russian national culture—monuments of days gone by, architecture, the names of cities, streets and districts. In a word, they used to defend our national property and the widespread utilization of the values of the past. And that was a good thing. But people who operate from nationalistic and chauvinistic positions attached themselves to this movement.

Our society is the most educated in the world, but need one have to try to prove how much still has to be done in order to nurture the political culture and true civilization to which **Lenin** attached such tremendous significance? Much time will elapse before we all really master the art of conducting honest and conscientious polemics, hearing out one's opponents and even adversaries, and overcoming in oneself the atavistic urge to "crush" or "liquidate" at any cost an opinion which does not coincide with our own opinion.

It is now necessasry to solve pressing problems step by step, passing from the elementary ones—instilling order, overcoming corruption and the crudest forms of bureaucratism and uncivilized behavior—to the more complex ones—the introduction of cooperatives, the family contract, and individual labor in the structure of socialist production—and then finally, to the most revolutionary problems—the transformation of the system of management of the national economy in accordance with the principles of the Plan, full economic accountability, and the use of the achievements of the technical revolution. Now the problem of the responsibility of each Soviet person for the destiny of socialism, and for the destiny of the Motherland has appeared more acutely than ever before. It is toward this end that the CPSU CC June Plenum orients the Party and the country.

Burlatskii, "Uchit'sia demokratsiia. Zametki publitsista," *Pravda* (18 July); condensed translations are in FBIS, No. 141 (23 Jul 87), R21-R25; and in CDSP, 39:29 (1987), 8, 13.

M.S Gorbachev, **To Deepen Restructuring by Practical Deeds** (14 Jul 87)
So we meet again: a praiseworthy tradition. We highly appreciate the contribution made by our media on behalf of the restructuring. Our journals and magazines, including literary magazines, with their topical journalism, are prominent in the effort. I would even go as far as to say that the Party might never have achieved the present level of debate on all aspects of the restructuring process, with the many and diverse problems involved, if the media had not actively and seriously taken up the reforms immediately after the April 1985 Plenary Meeting of the CPSU CC.

Things have started changing. Maybe they are not changing as completely and fast as we would like. Opinions differ on that point. Some think we are too slow about restructuring; others say we are in too much of a hurry. In my view the task of reforming society requires a great sense of responsibility and careful consideration, and this is what must decide our pace. Ours is a vast country with an enormous population, which has made great sacrifices to consolidate and enhance the gains of the October Revolution, to turn our country into a mighty socialist power. Every step we take therefore requires of us that we show a great sense of responsibility to the nation and to the world, so great is the part the Soviet Union plays on the present-day international scene.

Changes are here for all to see. The situation is quite different from what it was prior to the January Plenary Meeting of the CPSU CC. As we prepared for the Plenary Meeting in June, we saw that we would have to discuss the restructuring as a whole if we were to put radical reforms in economic management on our agenda. That was quite understandable. Whatever the importance of our basic economic structure, the processes of remodelling the economy will not continue if not linked to changes in all other spheres of our society—above all, the cultural, spiritual and political spheres, democratization and many other matters. All those processes thoroughly changed after the January Plenary Meeting. The debates got livelier and more acute. The substance of the decisions made was different, too. Let us be quite frank: everything came to a head—which means that we posed the question correctly at the January Plenary Meeting, and the restructuring process had begun to spread to all spheres of society, to all sectors of the population. Millions of people joined the effort, and the participation of millions is the starting-point for important and responsible politics.

That was why we decided to include a political section in the report to the June Plenary Meeting: an analysis of the overall restructuring process, summing up what we had accomplished and our present position. It was evident that the restructuring process was just starting, yet it was clearly a new period in our development. We had arrived at a new stage in the reform effort, and had set new targets for the future.

As we gain momentum, it is especially important for the Party and the media to coordinate their efforts. This is still more essential after the June meeting, with the key issues of the reforms in our system of economic management it dealt with. I am sure you all know the Plenary Meeting materials to the letter, and have your own opinions on the matter. I think you agree with the main point: everything we have been doing since the April Plenary Meeting is dictated by the development of our society, by the great number of problems and urgent tasks we face.

I keep referring to the whole of society because the CPSU CC and its Political Buro determine their policies taking into consideration the interest of the society's development, the trends existing in it, and the issues that arouse public concern and debate. Society is, of course, not something impersonal. It consists of specific forces—the working class, farmers and the intelligentsia. Each of these forces contains different strata, with their special features and interests. Each social class and stratum has its own viewpoint on restructuring, depending on its experience and conditions of life.

We must realize that our society has many unsolved problems, the economic situation, in particular, is under a strain. Realization of the current state of society should be our point of departure when we seek to find our bearings. We must understand that the choice we have made is the right one. These past two years have shown growing public awareness of the necessity of restructuring. Many are even afraid that the restructuring process will miscarry.

I want to stress—and this point was also made at the June Plenary Meeting of the CC— that the restructuring process is not a negation, or if it is a negation, then only a dialectical one. In pursuing the course of acceleration and restructuring we are standing on the firm ground, rather than on a quicksand, the ground that was formed through the efforts of many generations of Soviet people as a result of the struggle of our pioneers. We have experienced everything—impressive achievements and losses as well. We have had to endure difficult trials. The reason I am saying this is that even in your midst I see concern lest this new stage might be a negation of all our past, lest we might forget our history, lest underestimation of what the preceding generations have done might creep into current policies. It would be a mistake to think like that, comrades.

I am asking you to rise above emotions and comfortable stereotype thinking. Look up and think about the people, about society. Otherwise we will be unable to carry through what we have begun. I have already said—and I feel we all are in agreement about this idea—that we have always been and will continue to be in the same boat, we have always been and will continue to be on the same side of the barricades, we have marched along the same road and will continue to do so. Therefore, when passions ran high at a session of the Board of the Union of Writers of the Russian Federation, I asked that it be conveyed to the assembly that we would have been very much concerned if, instead of the consolidation of our creative and artistic intelligentsia, a kind of squabble was taking place, and its participants tried in the context of openness and democratization to seek revenge for any criticism. This, comrades, is inadmissible; this would be toying with the people, with the country, with socialism. We will not agree to this under any circumstances!

We must discuss the thorniest issues with respect for one another. Even the most extreme viewpoint contains something valuable and rational, since a person who defends it honestly shows concern for the common cause. You remember **Lenin**'s idea that one should be able to analyze the position of one's opponent, even one's class enemy, because no one poses questions as profoundly and acutely, no one searches out the weaknesses in your position so persistently as does your enemy. But today we are not talking about a class or an antagonistic struggle; we are searching for and debating ways of finding the road that leads to successful restructuring, how to progress more rapidly and firmly and make our progress irreversible. For this reason I see no cause for alarm in debating different points of view. This is perfectly normal.

Today we are in a way relearning democracy. We still lack political culture, we lack the culture to conduct debate and respect the viewpoint even of a friend, a comrade. We are an emotional people. We will certainly get over all of this. We will mature. I have asked that it be conveyed to the assembly that we set great store by everything that has been done since April 1985 by our artistic intelligentsia, and we hope that this contribution will grow.

So, we must constantly synchronize our efforts. I have no grounds for any substantial political criticism. Even if there were excesses—incidentally, there were, and we saw them—

this happened, after all, within the framework of the effort to improve socialism, an effort which is in the interests of the people.

But if some people begin searching for and offering us values and discoveries beyond the bounds of the interests of the people and beyond the bounds of socialism, the CC will publicly assess and criticize this and—within the framework of democracy and openness—voice its views in a principled manner. This is, I think the right thing to do.

I am being extremely frank with you, and you must sense this. I am talking to you about my deep convictions. I can be mistaken on some points—I make no claim to absolute truth. We must search for the truth together. We must search for the truth as a concept, in practical policies, in methodology, and on the basis of our common ground. This involves really stimulating individuals and utilising their rich political, cultural and scientific potential which has been accumulated in our society over the years of Soviet government.

For this reason we proposed at the January Plenary Meeting of the CC an entire constructive program that focuses on launching the process of democratization in order to utilize individuals' activity and interest in all the processes taking place in Soviet society. This, comrades, is the main point of what we are doing.

The economy is no exception here either. Our approach to it is to make the individual an active part of the production process. Socialism offers tremendous opportunities for this. After all, it is based not on private property, but on our common property. This point of departure makes it possible to explore entirely new ways to make the individual a co-manager of production, of the economy as a whole, not just in word but in deed. To realize this idea was the task that faced the June Plenary Meeting of the CC.

In his article "On Cooperation", **Lenin** wrote that the degree of combination of private, that is personal, interest with public aims, the degree of state supervision and control of this interest, and the degree of its subordination to the common interest had been a stumbling-block for very many socialists. And he also regarded cooperative societies as one of the methods of combining socialism with people's interests. We have been guided by this general methodological principle, aware that there would be no progress unless we ensured a combination of public ownership with people's interests, both their material and individual interests. It is impossible to make society dynamic and vigorous without taking all interests into account, without these interests in their turn influencing politics and society. That is why the question of interests was raised at the June CC Plenary Meeting. Taking people's interests into consideration in the overall economic system will assure them an independent role, and induce them to actively participate in every process of the life of our society.

And we began, as you know, with the Law on the State Enterprise (Association), and with defining the ways to implement it. Following a nationwide discussion we included everything that could be included in the law, and made appropriate amendments. True, some people also suggested things that went beyond our system, in particular abandonment of the planned economy. This we did not accept and never will accept because we intend to strengthen socialism, and not replace it with another system. This is absolutely clear, and consequently much of what was suggested to us from another economic system is unacceptable to us. Moreover, we believe that socialism, if its basic principles are made to work, is well capable genuinely to utilise people's interests while benefiting from the advantages of our planned economy. And, in view of the state of our present-day society, this will enable us to make our economy more dynamic.

Everything that contradicts this Law on the State Enterprise (Association) must be reviewed, each provision relating to any economic body: the State Planning Committee, the other economic departments of the country, the management bodies in each industry. Their functions from now on must conform to this law. This is the direction in which we are working now. This is, in fact, the implication of the June Plenary Meeting's decisions. They basically continue the policy of the January Plenary Meeting: to involve the individual in all processes—both economic and productive—and make him in effect his own master, by combining state interests with those of the individual and of the work collective.

Events will most likely correct and alter this process, but we are confident that we are on the right path, because in this case too we have relied on actual experience.

Now, with a favorable spiritual and moral atmosphere in society, an atmosphere of openness, and with the processes of democratization developing in the country, we have yet to provide an appropriate legal basis. We still have a lot of a "mass meeting-type" democracy, though we should let the existing legal framework do its work and fully use what is already available. We are giving thought to this and will prepare appropriate proposals in time for the 19th All-Union Party Conference. By adopting a program for the radical reform of economic management, we have prepared, as it were, a front for full-scale offensive in every area of democratization of society, for acceleration and for further development of the restructuring process.

These are some of my reflections on our plans and on the importance of the work done by the June Plenary Meeting of the Party CC. I would say that the main strategic problems have now been solved, that we have created the conditions for the restructuring process to evolve on a new basis: political, ideological, moral, economic, and legal. However, everything still lies ahead; these are only the basic conditions, and practical work is in its initial stage.

The question, naturally, arises: where do we stand right now? A new situation has developed; it must also be thoroughly analyzed. If we are agreed that we have created the preconditions I have mentioned, then perhaps the most crucial moment has now come. Now we must put everything into practice. This means that millions, indeed tens of millions of people, will be engaged in a gigantic effort. This amounts to a real revolution, including people's minds, their thinking, and their attitude to this cause. But, as we all know, **Lenin** warned that revolutions are not to be trifled with, that you can't play with a revolution. Once we have set things going, we must handle them properly, with a great sense of responsibility and awareness of the fact that a delay in implementing the decisions already made and defined in our restructuring programme would be fatal.

So, in my view, we have now come to the stage of constructive work. Some comrades are probably ready to say that this means "enough of criticism". No, I don't think it's right to say that. I believe that without maintaining the atmosphere of openness, publicity and criticism, without wide and serious discussions inspired by concern for the needs of the people, for the destiny of the state and society, there will be no constructive work, and no constructive phase will set in.

The most important task for us now is therefore to act vigorously and purposefully; to look for alternatives, criticise blunders and shortcomings and at the same time back up what is new and constructive; to promote activeness and initiative and extend democracy and openness, for that is what will reinforce the spirit of the restructuring and help accelerate our social and economic growth; to search for new forms of work which would encourage still wider participation of the people, of the working millions. This is the socio-political essence of the present stage of the restructuring.

It is important now that we see in time everything, even the smallest thing, that could help us advance our cause. At the June Plenary Meeting of the CC I cited many facts in order to show that a positive process has started and that we must be able to see clearly all the signs of the new trend. Here we must learn from **Lenin**. Recall the *subbotnik* at the Moskva-Sortirovochnaia depot. This event led **Lenin** to ideas which have been used for many decades, ideas which are being put into practice even today and this will continue for many years to come.

At the present stage of our constructive work it is very important that we see every change for the better. Comparisons are particularly important here. Take, for example, two neighboring districts, two enterprises, two regions, or two republics. In one of them there is movement forward, progress, tangible results, while in the other inertia, adherence to the old way of doing things and conservatism are discouraging people and dampening their enthusiasm. this is now the main topic of discussion in newspapers and magazines and, for that matter, in literature as well.

You will probably agree with me—I'm sure that you have also reached this decision—that today we must be especially efficient, responsible and practical. I think that you have understood, you should have understood, at least two of the main ideas we wanted to get across in the report at the June Plenary Meeting of the CC besides what was said at the Plenary Meeting in presenting the program for economic development.

First, the Party must not fall behind the processes taking place in society. Whenever it fails to keep up with these processes, even in the smallest way, distortions and excesses are inevitable. But when the Party is on top of things, it is able to use all its potential, authority and all the opportunities open to it and thus take the vanguard positions in this process, rather than hand out orders prohibiting or banning one thing or another. This is not a position. The Party is supposed to be able to lead the people. And it is capable of doing this because it has the necessary potential—human, theoretical, political and moral potential. It is the moral potential that I want to emphasize here. Having shown in the first part of the report at the June Plenary Meeting the contradictory features of the current process of restructuring, having spelled out the immediate and long- term goals and having formulated the concept of a radical reform, the Party once again demonstrated that it is performing its mission as the guiding force of society. The Party is the genuine organizer of society and its political vanguard.

I don't think that anyone today would support the view that we can get by without the Party. We have 70 years behind us and we can draw definite conclusions on this issue, especially now when our vast country is at a point of dramatic change, when we have begun the processes of democratization, discussion, searching, and, as we move ahead along this path, we must promote the restructuring.

This can't be achieved without a party capable of formulating a scientifically sound policy and a strategy for carrying out the practical tasks and without the cadres it has reared over the decades. If someone thinks otherwise, he is at the very least mistaken. A socialist society needs an active and strong party and the Party itself must be active if it is to perform its organizing and guiding role. At the All-Union Party Conference next year we shall discuss many questions in detail, including those pertaining to the activities of the Party itself.

This is the first idea. Secondly, the people are extremely worried about the future of the restructuring. I have already told you about my trip to Baikonur where I had a look at our space technology and met with the people there. After one such meeting someone asked me: "When will the restructuring policy start affecting us?" I replied: "Ask your leaders. Let them think about this carefully and then give you an answer." You know, there is something very good about our people: they can never be deceived.

When we were painting life in rosy colors, the people saw through it all and began losing interest in the press and public activities. They were simply humiliated and insulted when they were told untruths, for they knew what the truth was. **Lenin** used to say that an illiterate person is outside politics. Our people are now well educated but our actions in the past few years have kept people away from politics. It was a kind of elitism, of disrespect for the people. We must now put everything in its proper place through further democratization. There is one decisive force—the people. It is the people who produce the cadres, the leaders, the writers... Everything comes from the people and everything goes back to the people.

People have learned from experience to see the contradictions between words and deeds. This means that something is wrong, that there are braking mechanisms and that there are things seriously worrying the people. People realize that there are aspects of the restructuring that will take five, ten or even fifteen years to solve. These are fundamental problems of great importance and their solution will change the face of our country. But there are also matters such as the work of the trade network, city transportation, order on the streets and the services. How is the person treated in these spheres? Is he treated with respect or is he abused? Is any progress being made in housing, have there been any improvements, any changes in the way housing is being built? So this is the real life which confronts a person as soon as he leaves work: how to take care of the kids, how to support the family, what to do about this or that problem. And then one day a person gets fed up with all of this and says: "The leaders might be talking differently, but life is just the same as it ever was..."

That is why there was a section in the report at the Plenary Meeting about the priority tasks which cannot be put off and which we have to tackle in real earnest. The press must be constantly aware of these tasks and the needs of the people and show the different approaches to these tasks and needs. And a person's approach to them indicates that person's attitude towards the people.

And in general, no matter what office a person holds, if he loses this ability—to understand the needs of the people, their troubles, to be aware of how they live—this person who happens to hold that office must be replaced. We don't need him. I spoke about this at the Plenary Meeting. Such an approach does not at all imply disrespect for the cadres. Indeed, our cadres, our intelligentsia, our talented people must be well taken care of. If everyone in society is treated in one and the same way, there will be no talented and honest workers left. That is not socialism or social justice; such an approach is demagogy and levelling. But, incidentally, some social demagogues have got onto editorial boards of newspapers and magazines. They are attacking the cadres with a vengeance. But we must be well aware that the cadres bear a heavy burden of the restructuring. Of course, you can also find among them some people who have made districts or farms their own private domain. Such people must, so to say, be brought to light. But the cadres in general should not be treated with disrespect.

And at the same time there must be no callous and uncaring individuals in positions of responsibility, those who cannot see the people's needs, don't feel for them, and don't take their problems to heart. We talked about this at the CC's Plenary Meeting in June, and I ask you to take note of all that and proceed accordingly. You must work to ensure that all those who care about the individual, about people, about the simplest things, whether in faraway regions or in the centre of the country, make the headlines in our press, while those indifferent people you can't get through to no matter what should also be making the headlines.

At a recent meeting of the Political Buro of the CC we recalled that in the last two or perhaps three years we have adopted a whole series of decisions on the issues of providing people with garden plots, country cottages, building materials, repair services and so on. Moreover, we said that no matter what the demand of our construction organizations for these materials, some of them have to be set aside for the people and put on sale. When we started checking the compliance with these decisions, we found that department after department systematically ignored them. So we decided that if we saw this happening again, if we saw that the decisions were being ignored, we would remove the guilty persons from their positions, and we would do this openly, for the whole nation to see.

You know that there are plants, factories, districts and collective farms that have already decided to resolve their housing problems in 7 to 10 years, instead of by the year 2000. They are using all their reserves. And people have got down to business. In the Volgograd Region, the rate of housing construction has gone up 1.4 times. All the reserves must be used. People want to invest their own resources in this. People have started a good thing, so let them proceed.

Or take the food issue. In fact, many regions are coping well with it. Republics and regions have been granted the right to keep whatever is left after they have met their national procurement targets and to use it for meeting their own local needs. And they got down to business and have been doing well. Many of you know about this. In Saratov, there are 17 types of vegetable on sale all year round, and as for other foodstuffs, things look good too. Volgograd has changed in this respect and so have Tselinograd, Stavropol, Krasnodar, Omsk, Barnaul, Belgorod and other major towns. They are doing a big job there and already have something to show for it. I can name many such regions and cities. It's nice to see that this kind of process is under way in Tula and Kaluga as well. This means that it is possible to find a good solution to these issues even in the country's most difficult regions. This also holds true for the non-black-soil zone which is truly a source of pain for us. In fact, we've got to get things moving there: to build homes and roads, and to make it a liveable place in every respect. People are moving to that region; there are many people who want to live there. We will be consistent in carrying out everything we have planned for the development of the non-black-soil zone. Everything will go well in even the most difficult regions if we let our people apply their intellect and talent.

As you understand, I am emphasizing these top-priority tasks because the whole policy of restructuring will fail unless everyone feels that things really are changing in the resolution of pressing, paramount issues. So it is these two issues—that of the Party and that of our priority objectives—that I wanted to draw your attention to, so that we could get a clearer view of our priorities and the sustained effort we have to make to promote the restructuring.

There is yet another important subject—the 70th anniversary of the Great October Socialist Revolution. This major event for us must get better coverage. We are all products of the October Revolution, and our society today is the result of our development over the 70 years that have passed since then. This is our common asset, a turning point in the history of humanity and the way to a new world.

How much has changed since our Revolution—not only in our country, but throughout the entire world as well, and what processes it has launched! We must take a broad look at all of this and never succumb to one-sided impressions and sentiments. We can't use such impressions and sentiments in determining our positions on everything that has taken place since the October Revolution. For then we might lose our bearings altogether, comrades. I think we cannot and must never forgive or justify what happened in 1937 and 1938. Never. It is those who were in power at that time who are responsible for all of that. But that does not detract from everything that we have today, from everything the Party and the people have done after having lived through that ordeal. The losses were serious and great. We know what 1937 and 1938 cost us and how the Party cadres, the intelligentsia and our servicemen suffered. Yet we must be able to see the immense force that lies in socialism and in our system which stood that test and at the same time fought Nazism and won too. Therefore, we should speak of our 70th anniversary with a sense of pride for our great people, their history, and their victories.

We tell the truth and nothing but the truth. We take pride in every day we have lived. And we cherish every day, no matter how difficult it might have been, because this is all part of our history and our lessons from history. We have lived through all of this together. We cannot therefore tolerate disrespect for our people, for those generations that went through all of that and made the country what it is today. Let's speak out loud and clear about the October Revolution and socialism, about who we are and where we have come from, and about what we have as a result of the Revolution and socialist development.

We have already begun talking about these things without sensationalism, and with a serious and responsible attitude, because such things cannot be spoken of derisively or with malice. All this is, after all, the fate of the people.

We must also speak this way about the present and about the restructuring in particular. New forms should be found to cover developments. It's great when an author tells us his position, but it's even more interesting to read publications that contain talks with workers, secretaries of district Party Committees, collective farm chairmen, scientists and cultural personalities. They give you food for thought. Or take letters from readers. They, too, don't leave you indifferent.

And one more thing. I have already told you that it's undemocratic when dailies and periodicals are usurped by Moscow authors, for magazines and newspapers are circulated nationwide. However, when I read newspapers, I often wonder what people think in other places, in the localities, throughout the country.

I am asking you, comrades, to think what you can do to portray our great Revolution more vividly, to recall the heroes of the Revolution, the workers, professional revolutionaries, poets and those people who have been forgotten. We must do this with a sense of responsibility, trying to be thorough, and in the spirit of democracy and openness.

We have said more than once, and I think this is our common view, that openness and democracy do not mean that we can do anything we feel like doing. Openness is supposed to strengthen socialism, the spirit of the individual and public morality. Openness also presupposes criticism of our shortcomings. However, it is not intended to undermine socialism and our socialist values.

We have things to affirm and uphold. I mean the historic achievements of our society which is socially protected better than any other. Only those people whose ambitions, which have nothing in common with the interests of the nation, are impeded by our socialist democracy and our demands for responsibility can have any doubts here. We have fought such things and will continue to do so. We are open to all and we don't need to prettify our policies and values. However, democracy presupposes a fight to uphold these values. I would put it this way: the restructuring processes are gaining both scope and depth. A difficult transitional period has set in and what we are in particular need of today are competence and responsibility.

If we are to achieve the results society needs, we must work to strengthen public morale, to overcome all the difficulties, and change our ways. That's why you need to draw many more competent people into your work. Economic matters are getting a great deal of coverage in the mass media. Unfortunately, the coverage is often inadequate, shallow, sometimes even clamorous and absolutely incompetent. As we get further into the restructuring, our demands on you will grow. Therefore, your contributors should be highly reliable experts—managers, engineers, economists and scientists—and you must make full use of the nation's intellectual potentialities.

You still have a tendency to limit the number of your permanent contributors to three or five persons. This smacks of cliquism. Let's have a greater variety of people contributing to the media so that all of society would take part, so that socialist pluralism would be evident in every publication. This is what we need.

In conclusion I would like to say that the CPSU highly appreciates the contribution of the media to the restructuring. Why? Because the restructuring is all about people. The people are ahead in this process and therefore their attitudes will be decisive for its success. We must explain this to people every day, using the tremendous capabilities of the mass media. There is still only one criterion, comrades—more socialism and more democracy. We must search for the answers to all the new question within the framework of socialism. The people chose socialism. The Party serves the people. The most important duty of the mass media is also to serve the people.

I hope that I have told you frankly and in a spirit of Party comradeship all I wanted to say here after the June Plenary Meeting of the CC.

M. Gorbachev, "Prakticheskimi delami uglubliat' perestroiku," *Pravda* (15 July); *Izvestiia* (16 July); a condensed translation is in FBIS, No. 136 (16 Jul 87), R18; translated excerpts are in CDSP, 39:28 (1987), 6-7. This speech was delivered at a meeting of the CPSU CC to leading representatives of the "mass media and unions of cultural and art workers, 14 July 1987."

Conference in the CPSU CC (with "mass news and propaganda media") (17 Sept 87)
A conference has been held of the CPSU CC with executives of the mass news and propaganda media, at which some questions connected with the fulfillment of the CPSU CC's resolution on preparations for the 70th anniversary of the Great October Socialist Revolution were examined.

Ye.K.**Ligachev,** member of the Politburo of the CPSU CC and Secretary of the CPSU CC, spoke at the conference.

He noted that the Soviet press is actively facilitating the process of restructuring, democratization and openness, is energetically combating everything that is outmoded and unsuitable, and is affirming the positive elements in our life. The CPSU CC is providing all-out assistance and support to the press and the literary community. The CPSU CC has adopted resolutions on a number of publications. All attempts, centrally as well as locally, to hush up businesslike criticism will continue to be resolutely rejected.

In documents adopted early this year in connection with the 70th anniversary of Great October, the CPSU CC emphasized that it is necessary, in political work among the working people, to convincingly disclose the organic connection between the achievements of the October Revolution and the current, essentially revolutionary transformations of all aspects of the life of Soviet society and to show, in a well-reasoned way, the achievements of socialism and its fundamental advantages over capitalism. Newspapers, magazines, television, radio and other news and propaganda media are doing extensive work in this respect. People's interest in television and in the printed word has grown.

However, some publications, the public notes, have been unable to properly find their bearings and to organically combine the truthful treatment of our history with coverage of the present-day problems of restructuring. Moreover, certain periods of history are sometimes given one- sided treatment.

At the meeting with executives of mass news and propaganda media and creative unions that was held after the June (1987) plenary session of the CPSU CC, it was noted that we cannot permit a disrespectful attitude toward our people, toward the generations that built socialism and defended it in a battle to the death with fascism. Therefore, we must speak at the top of our voices about October, about socialism, about what we are, where we came from and what we have as a result of the Revolution and the victory and development of socialism.

The materials of the 27th Congress and the plenary sessions of the CPSU CC, the speeches of M.S.**Gorbachev** and other leaders of the Party and the government, and the CPSU CC's Address to the Soviet People in connection With the 70th Anniversary of Great October are helpful in obtaining a correct understanding of our history and its complex periods. Editorial collectives and journalists should constantly turn to these documents.

Since the April (1985) plenary session of the CPSU CC, the Soviet press has been increasingly active in publishing materials that reflect various opinions, which is a manifestation of democracy and openness. However, it has been noted that some editors readily publish what agrees with their viewpoint, but what does not agree with it either is not published or is accompanied by editorial commentary that rejects the publication out of hand. The upshot is one-way democracy, which must be overcome. and it goes quite beyond the bounds of democratic practice when materials are published according to the editor's one-man decision, without being considered by the editorial board of the newspaper or magazine.

Raising standards of debates and polemics is an important task. Everyone must take a respectful attitude toward their opponents' opinion, not unthinkingly reject them. After all, the matter at hand is the search for truth in order to strengthen the Soviet way.

Attention was called to the following. In ideological work, it is necessary to take into account the fact that our adversaries abroad are thoroughly changing their tactics and restructuring their ranks. Realizing that the Soviet Union will emerge from restructuring still stronger and that the attractiveness of socialism in the world is growing, our adversaries have begun to gather together all reactionary forces in a united front to impede and, if possible, thwart our policy of acceleration, restructuring and democratization. Special emphasis is being put on the revival of nationalistic sentiments.

Ye.K.**Ligachev** devoted part of his speech to the accomplishment of the tasks in the field of economics that confront the country this year. He emphasized that one of the most important results of restructuring should be providing the population with adequate quantities of high-quality food in the next few years.

Day after day, the mass news and propaganda media must keep progress in fulfilling the plans of social and economic development at the center of public attention and struggle for a better material and spiritual life for Soviet people. It is necessary to show interest in how things are going with the changeover of enterprises and branches to full economic accountability and self-financing. What is retarding the actual, mass-scale involvement of the working people in the management of state affairs? What is obstructing the moral improvement of society, the overcoming of bureaucratism and wage- leveling and the affirmation of a sober way of life? How are the various elements of the Party and the state restructuring themselves? What is new in the activity of the mass public organizations? What processes are taking place in science, culture, literature and the arts? These and many other questions should be dealt with by newspaper, magazine, television and radio editors.

It is very important to display perseverance in disseminating the valuable experience of restructuring everywhere and to improve the productivity of socialist competition for a fitting greeting to the glorious anniversary of our socialist homeland.

"Soveshchanie v TsK KPSS," *Pravda* (17 Sept); *Izvestiia* (18 Sept); full translations are in FBIS, No. 181 (18 Sept), 33-34; and CDSP, 39:37 (1987), 1-2.

Chapter 6

EDUCATION

The resolution, "Guidelines for Reform of General and Vocational Schools," was approved by the CPSU CC and the USSR Supreme Soviet in April 1984, and went into effect that Fall. Thus, an overhaul of Soviet general schools was well underway before Gorbachev became General Secretary. Among the main curriculum features of that reform were the lowering of the age for school beginners to six from seven (thereby adding a year to the standard 10 class program), an increase in class hours for Russian (or native) language and literature, further civics courses (on patriotism, Communist ideals, and socialist internationalism), and an added hour per week of basic military training for boys. Teachers wages were raised, and the syllabus was oriented more toward vocational training than it had been. A two-year course on computer studies was supposed to have been introduced. This was the most sweeping reform of schools since Nikita Khrushchev tried to change the system in 1958. If one includes the two preparatory years, the new proposals were expected to take up to 13 years to implement. Bearing in mind that a traditional characteristic of Soviet schools has been the great attention given to the development of a model Soviet citizen, or character-building (*vospitanie* -upbringing), the following documents suggest that not much progress has been made since the Fall term, 1984.

The hope that all children would be taught a trade so that they could then move right into the work force to perform socially useful labor has not been fulfilled. Gorbachev voiced his displeasure at the slowness of educational progress during his address to the 20th All-Union Komsomol conference in April, and schemes are now in place to alter the original reform (see, e.g., *Uchitel'skaia gazeta*, 22 August 1987). Very few of the promised programs for computer training actually have been instituted, and enterprises have been reluctant to take on general school students—many of whom, of course, are under-age for employment—in cooperative education/industry projects and be responsible for both their training and their salaries.

Reform did not begin for higher education until after Gorbachev and his supporters realized that his new economic mechanisms, self-sufficiency, democratization, and *perestroika* generally, could not succeed until young experts were taught what they meant. Small steps have been taken to institute student self-government and co-operative courses have been organized with industrial and agricultural projects. Calls have been made to bring "democratization" to the university classroom. It has been announced that there will be a major CPSU CC Plenum in 1988 expressly for the purpose of discussing restructuring and its implications for schools.

On this generally, see S.Voronitsyn, "Educational Reform on the Eve of the Central Committee Plenum," RFE/RL. RL 513/87 (23 Dec 87).

New Rules for Admission to Higher and Secondary Specialized Education (VUZ) (21 Feb 87)

The USSR Ministry of Higher and Secondary Specialized Education has confirmed the 1987 VUZ admission rules. G.A.**Yagodin**, USSR Minister of Higher and Secondary Specialized Education [since 1985, ed.], reported on the rule changes at a news conference held on 20 February. The new rules, the minister stressed, stem from the basic guidelines for restructuring the country's education outlined by the CPSU CC. They are aimed at selecting the foremost young people who are best prepared for VUZ education.

This year, the awarding of additional credits based on the results of vocational discussion has been rescinded. The experiment showed that it did not always have a valid influence on the results of the competitive selection. Admission committees have been authorized to conduct all written examinations. This will increase the reliability of teacher assessment and exclude oversubjectivity in testing knowledge.

School-leavers will take three examinations. One examination in Russian (or native) language and literature in essay form and two examinations in the educational institution's discipline. Competition based on examination results for the day section among school-leavers with more than 2 years of work experience and those deemed comparable and among those without it will be held separately.

Preference has been given to school medal winners; excellent-rated pupils of secondary specialized, vocational, and technical educational institutions; and school-leavers whose discipline or labor activity matches the specialty chosen in the VUZ.

Additional requirements, reflecting the specific nature of the training of specialists in specific disciplines, have been set for applicants to medical, teacher training, agricultural, and some other VUZ's. Thus, people who have an inclination for or experience in working with children and also have the recommendation of pedagogical councils of schools, secondary specialized educational institutions, vocational and technical colleges, public education bodies, labor collectives, and city and district Komsomol committees will be admitted to teaching training specialties.

Medical VUZ's will begin switching over to enrolling students from among young men and women who have worked as junior or intermediate-grade medical personnel for at least 2 years and those discharged into the military reserve.

The experiment in the VUZ's of Moscow, Moscow Province, and Leningrad, which envisions conducting student admissions in July, will be continued. VUZ's in other cities will hold entrance examinations in August.

"Novye pravila priema v VUZ," *Izvestiia* (21 Feb); *Sovetskaia Rossiia* (21 Feb); a translation of the latter is in FBIS (2 Mar 87), R3-R4; a condensed translation of the former is in CDSP, 39:8 (1987), 20.

Evgeniia Albats, **Reconstruction at the USSR Academy of Science** (22 Mar 87)
Two hundred and sixty Academicians and 500-odd Correspondent Members attending the annual meeting of the USSR Academy of Sciences listened attentively to the report delivered by President G.I.**Marchuk**. [Formerly Chairman of the USSR State Committee for Science and Technology.] The keyword to the report was "reconstruction:"

The changes, so urgently needed, seemed to be more than enough: the extension of rights of the Academy's specialized branches, the reorganization of the Far Eastern and the Ural centers, the setting up of a system for foreseeing the most promising trends in science, amendments in the Rules. However, the meeting was waiting for what in the official language of the report was called "the lowering of the average age limits for scientific section heads."

"An order has been set up," said the President, "under which the Academy members— heads of research institutes, departments, laboratories and sectors—give up their burdensome responsibilites of organizers at the age of 70. As for those who are not Academicians or Corresponding Members, their age limit is even lower: they resign at 65."

What is the significance of this decision? Does it concern many people? Suffice it to say that at present the average age of Full Members of the Academy, according to statistics, is 69.9 years. By itself this would be of no special importance (because the word Academician always brings to mind such notions as wisdom and experience), if it were not for the fact that many of those who have already passed even this, let me repeat average age, are still occupying leading positions. Even a cursory glance at the USSR Academy of Sciences' directory shows that, out of every 25 heads of institutes, 20 belong to the demographic group of seniors and elderlies. It is no wonder that we are used to the fact that today a Candidate of Science's average age is 37, a Doctor's is 48.

A 50 year-old Corresponding Member is simply a miracle.

To think that at the age of 36 Albert **Einstein** had formulated his general theory of relativity; Niels **Bohr** put forward his theory of the structure of the atom at 28; **Sobolev** became a Member of the Academy at 31 .... An improper comparison, you may think? Right. But would it be proper if today's young scientists, brimming with ideas and initiative, became independent just before retiring on pension, having wasted in the meantime initiative and ideas, and not seldom, some moral principles?

However, it is not a question of the young and their fates, but of science itself. As has already been said more than once, those lagging behind in scientific research lose in everything—in technology, new machinery, and labor productivity. They lose in perspective. At the same time, it is quite obvious that everything gets fatigued—even metal. The same is true of people— even those with outstanding creative potential. They get fatigued from many years of conflict situations and concerns, from the burden of constant responsibility that does not give them a moment's rest.

Science calls for a versatile mind and new ideas. It does not tolerate stagnation. Authoritarianism in science is equal to death!

As I see it, the essence of the innovation consists precisely in that it recognizes that one must not hold a position all his life, and it is inadvisable to make one single person's (even a great one's) point of view absolute. Paradoxical as it may seem, it turns out that a scientist, who only yesterday fought against authoritarianism and proved the fallaciousness of monopolism (in science included), today professes the same methods of argumentation, the same principle of power pressure, patronage and other kind of influence. As a result, research work gives way to the struggle for power; there is no search for truths, but a loss of priority in quite a number of branches of science; and no life-breathing scientific debate, but a loss of skilled cadres.

One more important point. The decision envisages the setting up of an institution of counsellors, that is to say the Academy is being set the task of preserving the vast life, scientific and ethic experience of its members. The title of "honorary director", "counsellor to director", "counsellor to the Presidium of the USSR Academy of Sciences" guarantees Academicians and Corresponding Members their former salaries.

Moscow News, No. 12 (22 Mar 87), 11.

Iurii Riurikov, **What the Cradle of the Future Holds. School Through a Sociologist's Eyes** (22 May 87)
The school reform has been underway for 3 years, but every day something becomes clearer: the reform is hindered by a braking mechanism. Two of them are: bureaucratic management of schools, and a disregard of innovative experiments. The third brake, in my opinion, is the absence of enlightened guidelines for strategy in schools—how should schools be reformed— what should the minimum programs be?

There are three main spheres for mankind—family, labor, and public life; and three main roles—as parent, worker, and citizen. The first responsibility of schools is to prepare children for all these roles. But they prepare children for citizenship weakly, as workers poorly, and provide almost nothing for the family.

What does the public say about this? Two years ago a sociologist explained that about one-third of workers actively achieved what they put their spirit into; the rest did not achieve the needed norm, and a fifth worked very poorly.

What strategic changes are needed, in my opinion, in the system of public education? Above all, the school obviously must show what life will be like in 10-20-30 years and prepare children for it: as tommorrow's professionals, family people, and public leaders.

From this model, it must be decided what to instill in children, what types of personality and what kinds of knowledge.

Today the school overwhelms the pupil with masses of information, most of which is useless in life. And does not provide the most important mainline knowledge—human, psychological, labor, family and citizenship.

At the same time the schools have, in their teaching methods, access to experiments done already by people on the multifaceted formation of youngsters for physical and mental work, labor and management of society. In the last quarter century, there have been many educational discoveries of great sociological significance.

In preschool education, there have been various developments introduced by the famous family, **Nikitin**. They discovered, first, the best impetus to "launch" human characteristics in young children when they are the most impressionistic. Secondly, the best methods to nurture these characteristics—in a multi-sided manner when their different traits (physical, mental, moral) can acutely deepen and strengthen each other.

Among the school innovators there are others, like M.**Shchetinin**. In his *School of the Year 2000*, there are five primary schools—regular, sport, choreographic, artistic, musical—and brigades of agriculturists, florists, biologists, and clubs of young technicians and naturalists.

The merits of **Shchetinin's** accomplishments for schools are noteworthy. He won the N.K.Krupskaia medal. Although his talent was clear, for a half-year Minpros [Ministry of Education] and the Academy of Pedagogy could not give him a school to continue his experiments. Thus we lost his creative energy in education, like quicksand.

For the normal development of a person one needs gradual undertaking of ideas, which effect the spirit and body, brain and muscles, health and council. In the family and in the school of life one must find one of the most humane ideals of labor—the need "to work not with the head alone, but also with the hands." (**Marx**). Manual labor is useful for one's development in other skills; it must begin very early in life. But it has been a long time since we have practiced this.

To make renewal work,we need to act wisely in our schools. Rather than passive learning, which decreases the mental agility of the mind and of creativity, we must be actively creative, interesting, and clear.

The old school method is the main hindrance in schools. The innovators, especially **Shatelev, Shchetinin, Amonashvili, Ilin, Lysenkova, Paltyshev**—have created new methods with which to connect the laws of the brain and children's nature. Their methods include training in logic, utilizes their senses, and draws from their reserve potential. Their methods are 2-3 times more effective than the old ones. This means that the present-day objects of learning can be gained in 10 years—or sooner. New methods (and new content of learning) can allow school time for work, physical activity, art, and social work.

In order to pass for a good student today, one does not have to be a good person at all—helping comrades or dear ones, and participating in public life makes no difference.

The current instructional process is dominated by the "individual piecework system." A comrade's failure is not regarded as partly your fault, and his success is not seen as partly your success. The circumstance where every pupil is on his own is one of the main mechanisms of contemporary schools, and it spawns the characteristic of self-seeking individualism in tens of millions of children. The influence that this subsequently has on our work, families, and public life is understandable.

Fundamentally revolutionary experiments in educational collectivism were conducted decades ago—first by **Dyachenko** and **Ivanov**, later by **Shchetinin, Shatalov** and **Kurbakov**. Unfortunately, their experiments were not followed up. In order to structure new schools, evidently, it is not necessary to rework the entire system. Much of the research has already been done; we have the innovations, discovered by many years of testing. This speech is not about deciding whose tests are better, not about the objects of innovation or their main principles; rather they are about the main principles on which they should be based.

What are these principles? The democratic rather than authoritarian relations between teacher and pupil that cooperative teaching provides; new teaching methods, which included intensive and game-oriented methods; multi-sided lessons for children and the application of creativeness to all of their tasks, a characteristic that would in turn inculcate creative abilities in the children themselves; and collectivism in study, plus production labor—the fundamental premises of an enlightened moral and social viewpoint.

These principles were treated differently by the innovative educators. Their accomplishments lay in opening new vistas of "spiritual education." They demonstrated in practice how to raise the new type of worker, citizen, and family-oriented person capable of accomplishing the strategic tasks of restructuring. But their discoveries so far have been nearly unused in general practice.

What is the reason for this situation? It can be blamed on the education administration.

Towering over the school today is a five-story administrative pyramid: the district public education department, the city public education department, the republic Ministry of Education, and the USSR Ministry of Education. Most of the ministries have been using a three-level system for a long time and are starting to make the transition to a two-level system. Unfortunately, education officials will not eliminate the multi-tiered barrier between themselves and the schools willingly.

What is the first step which can be taken toward a complete democratization that will help education get rid of its current authoritarianism? Clearly, the cornerstone of such a democratization would be the practice of widespread elections at all the levels—from school principles and directors of studies, to officials of all the public education departments and Ministries of Education. And, in my view, they should be elected at all levels—from the individual school to the All-Union hierarchy—by the teachers themselves at their conferences and congresses.

The congress of teachers scheduled for July could mark a turning point in the manner in which schools operate. It could. But preparations for the congress are being undertaken in the same old administrative-bureaucratic spirit.

There is no a single innovative educator on the organizing committee of the congress—not a single teacher and no representative whatsoever of industry, science or culture. It is made up entirely of educational administrators. The selection of delegates is proceeding in a similar fashion. In many of the provinces and cities teachers are not being added to the list. The pedagogical innovators have not been selected as delegates: **Nikitin, Lysenkova, Karmanov, Guzik, Ilin, Tkachenko,** and others.

It seems to me that the congress of teachers is being prepared in secret, like the congress of some agency instead of a congress of the entire society. In these circumstances, it will hardly succeed in breaking up the mechanism that slows down reform or in creating a mechanism to accelerate it. In my opinion, preparations for the congress must be sharply democratized and discussion must center upon the must urgent strategic problems of the schools.

Generally restructuring has not yet altered the school day. It must be started with a new interest in pedagogical innovation, and a change in relations of many thousands of teachers with their pupils. Thus there needs to be a change in training teachers for higher and specialized schools. Minpros of Estonia is an example where this has begun to take place. Thus in the renewal of public education much has been done there. This gives us hope that the decisive change is just around the corner.

Riurikov, "Chto v kolybeli budushchego: Shkola glazami sotsiologa," *Pravda* (22 May); translated excerpts are in CDSP, 39:21 (1987), 27.

N.Anisin, **According to the Old Schedule. USSR Ministry of Education and the School Reform** (25 Aug 87)

The Power of Directives

It is an old private residence on Shabolov Street, [with] an unpretentious name. It has three stories. People fill them up at nine in the morning, and they tap away at their typewriters, make telephone calls, receive visitors, and hold meetings until six in the evening.

But at the same time the unassuming Shabolov Street building has an enormous influence. Six million people are subordinated to it; and they command an army of 16 million. Every decision and recommendation made in the old house—the USSR Ministry of Education—has nearly the effect of an order on all those millions. Our children, all mothers, fathers, grandmothers and grandfathers, all depend on those decisions.

We depend on them because for parents and for all the public is associated with schools. Life is regulated as in a monastery, by rules which are established by Minpros.

The Ministry of Education and the ministry alone decides what is to be taught and how it is to be taught; it evaluates educational methodologies, gives the go ahead to one experiment and puts a stop to another. One would assume that this is the way it should be. But is it right that society, in the form of labor collectives, research organizations, and creative unions, should be absolutely excluded from forming educational policy? The USSR Ministry of Education can simply declare any viewpoint of these organizations to be incompetent or untested, it can reject any suggestion by calling it immature or out-of-date. So who works in the Ministry of Education?

There are 320 employees in the USSR Ministry of Education. Some have higher degrees, but none are acknowledged as outstanding in our country, or even distinguished educators of today. It would be useless to search among Minpros's cabinets and pedagogs for those who are well-known in the republics, provinces and regions. For the last 10 years, the Ministry served all three levels. Only for Muscovites does Minpros serve some kind of value. Let us open the proceedings of the meeting of Party Committee of the Ministry on 26 December 1986, and read 3 statements:

Iu.**Rogovskii**, Director of Chief Inspectorate of Public Education: "Our cadres watch over the different management operations of work—that is, they prepare documents to guide brigades for verification, and contact with Soviet and Party organs."

G.**Bogomolov**, Director of Training for Labor Education and Professional Preparation: "New cadres oversee our preparation of rules, different documents for use by the collegium."

V.**Rozov,** Director of Educational Institutions Administration: "Scholars with higher degrees find it hard to master the clerical nature of our work, so we appoint our own people, from the administration, to management positions."

Why does Minpros not staff itself with people who have the most contemporary ideas, pedagogs and the best practical experience?

The All-Union education ministry was created in the early 1960s. At that time, the achievements of our schools were beyond question. The year 1966 saw the final triumph within the ministry of the assumption that nothing in the public education system need be changed, and that the task of the USSR Ministry of Education is to keep working smoothly, regularly "cleaning and oiling" the educational machinery with orders and directives. Scientific and technical progress advanced quickly, children entered school with a different perception of the world than their predecessors, and many of the new teachers were people who had failed the entrance examinations to other higher schools. The need for a radical modernization of the curricula and teaching methods, for a large increase in the school facilities and equipment, and for measures to draw talented people into the ranks of teaching became more and more acute with each passing year. But the Ministry of Education failed to sound the alarm; on the contrary it even covered up the problems. The leadership of the Ministry, from the highest tribunal, believes that it provides the country with "all the conditions for upbringing and education of the young generation necessary for our epoch."

The ministry bureaucracy refused to pay attention to the idea that the public education system was not perfect, and any truly innovative search was regarded as something seditious. Educational periodicals subject to the Ministry of Education were allowed to mention V.**Shatalov**'s name only in articles in which he was criticized, and teachers could utilize his methods only behind the backs of the authorities. The current methods of collective upbringing developed by Leningrad Professor I.**Ivanov** were not disseminated either. The latest experience in labor education, based on the principles of A.S.**Makarenko** which had been forgotten at our pedagogical Olympus, was foiled by the spread of educational production combines by mass administrative decree. Schools could be run only in the way that a group of clerks on Shabolov Street in Moscow thought was necessary. Consequently, the educational system was preserved under glass for many years. School reform seriously needs a change in Minpros and its way of functioning.

In the last three years the 320 Minpros workers have prepared 1,200 long documents which, for the most part, end with the words: "For information about the above work, write to ...." In response, B.**Kubulina**, Firest Secretary of the Ministry of Education of Latvia, gives out such information from Riga almost 3 times a month. The life of schools, as before, is subordinated to chancellory fiat: the office writes it, the matter is done. The education machine for the most part remains where it was before the reform.

Applying the Brakes

At the All-Union Congress of Teachers in 1978, the sounds of celebration completely drowned out the teachers' expressions of dissatisfaction and their desire to improve and correct matters. Thus when the CPSU CC Plenum in the Summer of 1983 pointed to the need for reform and national discussion began on the draft school reform, the myth of well-being was literally smashed. At the same time, a number of radically new ideas for updating the schools appeared. But practical implementation of the ideas for reform and the preparation of documents for it was handed over to the same people whose leadership had led the schools to their situation of stagnation.

So instead of a full re-working of public education, only "first-level" measures began to be implemented: pay raises for teachers, a shift to 11 years of schooling, more hours dedicated to vocational training, and a partial review of curricula and textbooks. The basic principles of the educational system were left untouched. The reform did not disturb the unwieldy, many-stage administrative structure under which the schools were subject to five "masters"—the district, city and province public education departments, the republic Ministry of Education, and the USSR Ministry of Education—and did not eliminate the administrative paperwork, red tape and formalism. The public school teacher still had no rights in relation to the school inspector and the student had none in relation to the teacher; the obstacles which separated the family from the school had not been taken down. Measures to overcome the gap between pedagogical research and practice were not developed. Recommendations to introduce different instructional approaches at an early age and to put more emphasis upon the humanities were rejected.

The restructuring of the schools began earlier than the radical restructuring of society, and we can regret that only a plan for superficial alterations became a reality in our life. But how can we accept the fact that since April 1985 the ministry's leadership has not organized the tasks of the schools with changes in society and has not been able to coordinate the reform to coincide with the restructuring that is going on in our country?

"The actions and methods of our workers," said G.**Makushkin**, secretary to the Minpros Party committee, "continue to be guided by the old customs and views, which have been formed over many years."

The restructuring of schools have fallen victim to the pits and bumps carried over from the past. Minpros was and remains guided by the same chancellory methods. After the speech of M.S.**Gorbachev** at the 20th Congress of Komsomol, where he said that stagnant, empty-minded thinking, was holding back the reform attempts in Minpros called for by the Party *aktiv*, it was assumed that more progress would be made.

Solution to the Impasse

On 14 July 1987 the USSR Ministry of Education published treatises in *Uchitel'skaia gazeta* [Teachers' Gazette] for the upcoming All-Union Congress of Teachers. They were prepared by a labor group headed by First Deputy Minister A.**Korobeinikov**, who had been appointed to the post a few months earlier. The treatises show some sore spots in the educational system—the first time the Ministry of Education has done so—and developes guidelines for its re-working. One would like very much to shout, "the ice is broken!". But the treatises still will not usher in the arrival of an icebreaker. They point out problems the solutions of which will be long and hard in coming.

The treatises argue that the operation of schools is characterized by bureaucratism, formalism and arbitrariness. Consequently, a new system for managing education is necessary. But even its outlines are still vague.

The treatises acknowledge that dogmatism rules in the curriculum and in teaching methods, and they present the problem of fundamentally up-dating teaching plans and curricula. Therefore a new concept of general secondary education is needed. But it does not yet exist, and it is unclear as to how it will be discovered. The USSR Academy of Pedagogy lost its role as a wellspring for new ideas long ago. The average age of its full members is over 65, the efforts of members go into scholarly works for which there is practically no demand in the schools, and to assume that they will get a new breath is naive. The academy's research institutes produced 1,084 dissertations over the past five-year period, but not a single one out of this huge mass of authentic ideas was of interest to ordinary educators.

The educational potential of productive labor remains untouched by the schools. The process of combining academic instruction with labor in current circumstances is not based in theory and is not being realized in practice. Fourteen and fifteen-year olds at A.S.**Makarenko**'s factories made cameras which met with world standards. The majority of today's teenagers, on the other hand, are either not engaged in productive work at all or are slapping together mailboxes or making rough bolts. It is again unclear as to who will create conditions for them to do real productive work, or where the funds will come from.

From the elementary to the senior grades, the Ministry of Education's treatises continue, the number of students with vision problems, diseases of the digestive organs or psychological-neurological defects is increasing. The health of more than half of the children in school (53%) is deteriorating. This is not only due to an excessive amount of homework and badly planned daily routine; it is also due to poor diet in the schools, insufficient medical care, crowded school gymnasiums, and the lack of outdoor athletic fields, and limited opportunities for youngsters to swim, ski, and hike. We must begin to strengthen children's health right away. But how? Here we also need a clear-cut program.

The percentage of the state budget that goes to finance general education schools of all kinds has declined 1.5% over the last 25 years. We are already reaping the fruits of the principle of financing something out of what remains. By continuing to apply this principle, we actually undermine the national economic and spiritual potential.

Hauling the public education up out of the mud means solving a whole set of problems: organizational, scientific and pedagogical, and sociological. The Ministry of Education, even if it becomes a research and methodological center instead of an office of administrative clerks, is the only one able to deal with some of these problems. Thus perhaps we should listen to the many voices from those people who suggest that we immediately call and hold an All-Union public conference on the problems of instruction and upbringing, where the flower of our science, culture and literature, the best minds in economics, and our production innovators would be represented.

On the one hand, the proposals of the All-Union public conference, and on the other, those of the upcoming congress of teachers would assist in bringing the basic guidelines for school reform into line with the guidelines of restructuring and would give the reform a long-awaited impetus. Only by a wide democratic sweep will the schools be able to turn their energy to the solution of the major questions of our time.

"Po staromu raspisaniuu...Minpros SSSR i shkol'naia reforma," *Pravda* (25 Aug); a condensed translation is in CDSP, 39:34 (1987), 11-12.

[Ye.K.Ligachev] Deepen Reform of General Education and Professional Schools (26 Aug 87)

The city of Elektrostal near Moscow is a city of metallurgists and machine builders. It is also famous for its experience in the general education and vocational training of young people. Its 17 schools, 4 vocational and technical schools, and 4 technical colleges have more than 20,000 students and over 1000 teachers. A conference was held here today for personnel from the educational and vocational-technical educational systems, with the participation of executives of the Party, Soviet, and economic organs of the city and of Moscow Province and representatives of the public.

Problems of ensuring the necessary depth in implementing the reform of general education and vocational schools and related tasks of the city's Party organizations and the teaching collectives of its educational institutions were discussed in detail and with self-criticism, in light of the decisions of the 27th Party Congress and the subsequent Plenums of the CPSU CC. In their speeches, Ye.**Shabunik**, First Secretary of the Gorkom, M.N.**Rubanova**, Chief of the city Public Education Department, G.M.**Sosin**, Director of the no.18 School, M.V.**Nedopeka**, Director of the no.33 Rural Vocational and Technical School, History Teacher V.V.**Kostriukova**, B.F.**Borin**, Director of the "Elektrostal" Electrometallurgy Plant, named for I.F.**Tevosian**,

Russian Language and Literature Teacher, V.I.**Shishova**, and others analyzed in detail the accumulated experience and difficulties in implementing the school reform and suggested ways and means for its acceleration.

Ye. K.**Ligachev**, member of Politburo of the CPSU CC, spoke at the conference.

It has become a sound tradition in our country, he said, to discuss school affairs at the end of each summer and to hold a kind of all-union conference of teachers, with the public taking part, and a broad review of the preparedness of Soviet general educational and vocational schools for the new academic year. The work of this year's pedagogical conferences is strongly influenced by the entire political and spiritual atmosphere of restructuring in which soviet society is living today.

The CPSU CC Plenum in June this year emphasized that restructuring has won an ideological and moral victory. It has spread both widely and deeply. Moreover, the process of the democratization of social life in the interests of strengthening socialism is linked with the restructuring of the economy. This guarantees the success of the strategy of acceleration. A political and legal basis is being created now for the improvement of self-management in the sphere of material production and for bringing state and public principles closer together in management. Great importance in this work attaches to the recently adopted USSR Law on the State Enterprise.

The speech noted the significant changes that have taken place in the composition of the leadership cadres of the Party and the state. Those who, because of their health, can no longer work at a top level of efficiency have stepped down. Those who misused their authority and sullied the honor of the title Communist-executive with dishonorable acts have been relieved of their duties. Guarantees are being created in society that will eliminate the possibility of violations of socialist legality, and an obstacle has been set up against irresponsibility and the embezzlement of public property, which were common phenomena recently.

The specific social and economic plans contained in the current 5-Year Plan, in contrast to the past several 5-Year Plans, are being fulfilled without adjustments. At the same time, and the current year has demonstrated this, the economy does not yet have the proper stability and moderate pace. There are a good many obstacles and barriers in the way of full-fledged changes. The main obstacles are bureaucratism and wage-leveling. They are the opposite to socialism and socialist democracy. They are created and sustained by those who are mired in bureaucratism, who thrive in the swamp of wage-leveling, and who cannot stand fundamental changes to their way of life. Realizing that they cannot stand up to the pressures of restructuring, such people are prepared to reduce everything to partial changes. Such a position does not coincide with the Party strategy or with the interests of the Soviet people. Only profound changes in productive forces and production relations, and resolute and consistent actions within the framework of developed socialism, are capable of leading our country to the forefront of the world economy.

Are there any guarantees that the planned reforms will be implemented in full, without distortions and deviations? Of course there are. The primary guarantee is the Communist Party's leading role in restructuring and the improvement in the style and methods of its activity. Reliable guarantees are also provided by the real involvement of the broad masses in the process of acceleration through the deepening of democracy and self-management in society. The people led by the Party—this is the decisive force of acceleration.

Another guarantee of success is the fact that the process of renewal is all-embracing and that the fundamental transformations extend to both base and superstructure and affect the economy, the political system, the social sphere, science, and culture.

As an inalienable part of the entire program of the renewal of Soviet society, Ye.K.**Ligachev** went on to say, the school reform should be carried out at priority speed and should predetermine positive changes in other spheres of social life. More than 50 million pupils and students are now attending schools, vocational and technical schools, technical colleges, and VUZ's. Almost one half of them will join the country's labor collectives in the current and the 13th Five-Year Plan. Schools must prepare the future generation of patriots intellectually, morally, and psychologically for work in the new conditions for the sake of the triumph of communism—in conditions of spreading scientific and technical progress, global economic accountability, democratization, and broad self-management.

What is the state of affairs in this very important sector? How is the reform of public education progressing today? We can all see that the measures outlined by a whole series of CPSU CC and government resolutions are yielding real results. There has been a marked increase in annual appropriations for public and vocational-technical education have grown considerably. The material base of [general education] schools, vocational-technical schools and children's preschool institutions is getting stronger. About 1.3 million pupil places for productive labor by schoolchildren have been created in our country. The wages of teaching personnel and stipends for (high-school) students have been raised substantially.

The stronger pull exercized by the leading profession is a good sign. A great many teachers who for one reason or another had been working in branches of the national economy have returned to the schools, the competition among those who apply to higher teacher training schools has increased, and the number of young people admitted to institutions has increased by one-third. Schools and vocational and technical schools are addressing the needs of modern production and the achievements of scientific and technical progress.

At the same time, the past several years have also revealed significant shortcomings in the implementation of reform. For many schools and vocational schools, the restructuring of work remains only a slogan. The main thing is that as yet there are no tangible results to suggest that the quality of teaching and the upbringing of students has improved. Questions of universal computer education are being resolved slowly. Liberalism in evaluating schoolchildren's knowledge has not been eliminated. Some graduates of vocational-technical schools do not confirm in practice the categories of skill that have been awarded to them.

The re-writing of textbooks and study guides has been dragged out for an unjustifiable period. There is no excuse for this. Naturally there are certain difficulties here in matters involving the social disciplines. It has now been recognized that we need new textbooks in the social sciences. But the preparation of them will take much time. Where then will the teacher look for answers to questions asked today by life? He must look to the Party documents. Many aspects of the development of the Communist Party, the Soviet state, and the world situation in the 1970s and the 1980s were covered by the materials for the 27th Party Congress and June (1987) Plenum of the CC.

For example, a good deal is being said now about the personality cult. It is very important to sort out the reasons for this phenomenon in a rational way, but the main things is to create circumstances in which such a thing would now be impossible. This is our sacred duty, our obligation. The Party and the people are now engaged in this work, the essence of which is the process of democratization of the life of society.

But something else must not be passed over. Some people overseas—and in our country also, for that matter—are attempting to undermine the entire process of the construction of socialism in the USSR, to present it as an unrelieved chain of errors, and to use the facts of unjustified repression to push into the background the deeds of the people that have shaped a powerful socialist power.

However, the historical truth is that the Party, at its 20th Congress [1956] and on the basis of decisions adopted there, performed work of particular importance, condemned the personality cult, removed the brand of enemy from many thousands of honest Soviet people, and restored socialist legality. As far as the 1930s are concerned, in those years the country took second place in the world in industrial volume, undertook the collectivization of agriculture, and reached unprecedented heights in the development of culture, education, literature and the arts. This is an undisputed fact. And another point. The overwhelming majority of the Communists who were subjected to repressions remained true to **Lenin**'s wishes and to the cause of socialism to the end of their lives.

Comrade M.S.**Gorbachev** has noted that we value every day of our history and that those who were in power during the 1930s should answer for the illegalities perpetrated at that time. We must proceed from this and tell young people about the heroic history of the Party and the country in a reasonable and capable way; that is to say, we must honor the truth. It is absolutely forbidden to talk about the tragic errors of those years with gloating, in a philistine manner, without pain and emotion. After all, everything that takes place in our home concerns every citizen and entire generations.

Pedagogical science has been assigned an important role in the school reform's implementation. We have a broad network of academic institutes. The certainly make a specific contribution in providing teachers with teaching and methodological support. Today the schools need new productive ideas and methods of teaching and upbringing. Such ideas and methods are precisely what is missing in the activity of the Academy of Pedagogy. There is a desparate need for a thorough restructuring there.

Ye.K.**Ligachev**'s speech devoted a great deal of attention to issues of the training of teaching personnel. It was emphasized that the teacher's vocation requires of a person total exertion of spiritual energy, constant creativity, generosity of spirit, love for children, and boundless loyalty to his duty. Through their selfless labor, Soviet teachers have earned the recognition of the whole people. Today 197 Soviet teachers bear the lofty title of Hero of Socialist Labor, 74 bear the honorary title of People's Teacher of the USSR, and more than 20,000 are Honored Schoolteachers. In short, the country has a great many talented educators in fact, and they fully warrant society's trust and are making an actual contribution to the implementation of the school reforms.

At the same time, many disturbing things can be noticed in teaching. A lower level in the professional training of teachers and the absence in some of them of authentic culture, which, we must say, always has been among the qualities of a teacher, have often been noticed. An indifferent attitude towards school life on the educator's part has appeared sometimes. Naturally, students react sensitively to this and do not enter into open, confidential contacts with the teacher. There can be no learning in such cases; there is no no upbringing without trust, without faith in the teacher.

These processes, it was said in the speech, must be of concern to the Ministry of Education, the Academy of Pedagogical Sciences, the entire teaching public, and our press. There is probably nothing more important here than to enhance teacher's personal authority and professional rsponsibility and supplement the teaching staff with young people capable of working innovatively in conditions of the democratization of schools and their self-management.

To bring order into all school affairs, one must enhance the prestige of the principle of the general and vocational school, strengthen his status. In recent years an obvious distortion has become evident. The principle is given added duties each year, but the means for fulfilling them are insufficient. It is necessary to review all the many types of official instructions that have entangled our schools and to free schools from excessive regulation. The agencies that administer the general and vocational schools and the financial agencies must tackle the job and put things in proper order.

Ye.K.**Ligachev** stressed that the Party attaches special importance to a fundamental improvement in the training of the younger generation for productive labor. This problem has been posed sharply in the school reform. Currently, about 80,000 base enterprises have been allocated to schools, and 3,000 inter-school production-training combines are in operation.

However, on the whole what has been done is clearly insufficient. We must carry it further. Unfortunately, not all executives of ministries and base enterprises have a clear idea of the necessity for this. Contrasts can be seen in Elektrostal too. There are enterprises whose leaders display a state approach towards school needs. The collective of School no. 4 has nothing but praise for the Elektrostal Boiler Combine. The enterprise is sincerely concerned for the affairs of the school. I had an opportunity to see that for myself when I visited the complex. At the same time, powerful enterprises such as the "Elektrostal" Plant and the "Elektrostaltiazhmash" Production Association could do much more for schools and the city's vocational colleges. After all, it is not a chore for these enterprises to take an interest in the pupils who will join their production collective tomorrow.

In our country there are also whole ministries which do little to create the technical base for the labor education of the young generation.

It was said in this connection that no one should sidestep problems now. It is necessary to clarify the procedure for allocating material resources to base enterprises for general and vocational schools and the procedures for resolving financial, staff and personnel enterprises questions. The regulations on base enterprises need to be amended. Obviously, certain directives of the USSR State Committee on Labor and Social Questions [Goskomtrud] are getting in the way of progress.

The speech gave a positive appraisal of the system of vocational guidance for students that is in force in the city of Elektrostal. A vocational center has been established here on the principle of self-financing, and the position of specialist in vocational guidance has been instituted in the schools. This makes it possible to hope that good experience will be gained that will be useful [as a model] for other regions as well. Vocational guidance is a passport to life.

Ye.K.**Ligachev** went on to say that the absence of proper dedication and purpose in the activity of the USSR Ministry of Education is one of the main reasons for the present day deficiencies in public education. The ministry does not play the role of genuine organizer of the school reform; it displays sluggishness and lack of indecisiveness in overcoming current difficulties and shortcomings. The system of advanced training which now exists in general and vocational-technical education operates at low efficiency. Neither the Ministry of Education nor the USSR State Committee for Vocational and Technical Education has created an united system of work with teachers, from the methods rooms in educational institutions to the USSR Academy of Pedagogy. These are all major gaps in the system of public education itself. Given sufficiently active work on the part of the Ministry of Education itself, its organs at the local level, and educational establishments' teaching collectives, they might not exist today.

At the same time, schools are a special concern of local Party organs and Soviets. The center is responsible above all for defining the trends of school development, the content of education and upbringing, the elaboration of syllabi, textbooks and pedagogical science. Locals organs exercize direct control over teaching and education, the formation of teaching collectives, teacher training, contacts between labor collectives and schools, the consolidation of the material base of schools and vocational and technical schools, and the creation of the necessary living and working conditions for teachers.

True reform has not yet moved into the school, or into the classroom. Achieving such a move is now the most important thing. The efforts and attention of local Party, Soviet, and economic organs and social organizations must be focused on this. Teaching collectives and their internal reserves and potential must be mobilized to this end. They must not endlessly point the finger at the Ministry but struggle by action rather than words to establish everything new and progressive in the school itself and combat all stagnation and conservatism.

The school reform in the new conditions badly needs teachers' councils, parents' committees, Komsomol, and Pioneer organizations to act with initiative, to take into their own hands the fundamental questions of the life of schools and vocational and technical schools, and at the same time to refrain from petty tutelage of pupils and to involve them more extensively in school self-management.

Naturally, that does not mean that teachers can remain indifferent to everything that happens in the classroom. Is the schools' indifference toward the craze for primitive music that has swept up children really permissible? We should actively take on the task of improving musical standards and introducing pupils to the best works of our country's composers and to folk music, and we must orient the organization of choral and instrumental collectives and musical ensembles in schools for this purpose. Is indifference to the fact that there are many physically soft youngsters in the schools, pupils who do not take part in sports, really permissible either? It is perfectly obvious that the system of physical education in general and vocational schools needs fundamental improvement.

At the same time, many concerns must be entrusted to the youngsters themselves, while helping the schoolchildren with good advice and homework requirements. Attempts by the teacher to watch over his pupils all the time, to supervise each step, are the problems of our schools. From this point of view, the situation in the schools does not fall in line with the process of democratization of all life. What is necessary here is a serious change in relations between teacher and pupil, a broad openness in the work of schools, and the development of criticism and self-criticism.

The speech noted deficiencies in the development of the material base of education, especially in rural areas. Twenty schools in Moscow Province are still in dilapidated premises and 45 schools and 26 vocational and technical schools need capital repairs. The vocational and technical school construction plan was only 65% fulfilled in terms of the assimilation of capital investments in the 11th Five-Year Plan, 59% fulfilled in 1986, and only 56% fulfilled in the first 7 months of this year. The oblispolkom, the city and territory Soviets and economic leaders must take responsibility for this.

Addressing the leaders of enterprises, organizations, and institutions, and soviet trade union and Komsomol workers attending the conference, Ye.K.**Ligachev** said: All of you are not merely connected with education, you must not simply be school helpers, but you must be actively involved in educational matters, active participants in the molding of new generations of Soviet people.

In conclusion, he emphasized the great interest in our country and overseas in the policy of restructuring and openness and in everything which is taking place in the USSR. The processes that are developing in the USSR have great international importance and are strengthening the attractive force of socialism in the world.

At the same time, among our class adversaries there are those who commend us for restructuring, investing it with a distorted content that suits them, and who entertain hopes that the Soviet Union will turn away from socialism and towards a market economy, ideological pluralism, and Western democracy. Vain hopes. We will never leave the Leninist path; we will never surrender the gains of socialism. The glorious 70-year history of Soviet rule and its supreme achievements are evidence of this.

Our country has made mistakes, but they have always been combined with real successes. Take the 1960s and 1970s. In the central committee's Political report to the 27th Party Congress. M.S.**Gorbachev** spoke about the necessity for an all-encompassing approach to judging the results of the country's development during that period. They were impressive. The fixed production assets of the national economy increased seven times. National income grew by almost 300%. People's lives became richer materially and spiritually. Military-strategic parity between the USSR and the USA was achieved.

At that time, Ye.K.**Ligachev** continued in this regard: I lived in Siberia: I worked in Tomsk and Novosibirsk Provinces. If you were to ask me what my attitude was toward that time, it was a truly great life. There were many difficult days, but not one of them was burdensome. A mighty center of Soviet science was established during that period in the expanses of West Siberia through the efforts of the entire country and under the Party's leadership and an oil and gas complex of world dimensions was formed. It was there, in difficult conditions, that true Communist were forged, people of strong character and high moral purity. I am infinitely grateful to fate for throwing me together with them But this is only one side of the coin.

The other side is that, along with the positive changes, negative phenomena were growing in the country, the pace of extensive economic development was slowing, abuses of power were becoming widespread, discipline was falling off, and the USSR's international prestige was declining. All that time, the country's former leadership was being praised in an unrestrained manner. The Party was in danger. "All the revolutionary parties that have perished before now," V.I.**Lenin** taught, "perished because they became conceited, were unable to see where their strengths lay, and were afraid to talk about their weaknesses." Following **Lenin**'s bidding, the Party was not afraid to uncover errors, to talk about them openly and undertake to eliminate them.

All this taken together makes up the real truth and a dialectical comprehension of the core of that time. In short, we should cultivate in young people, including schoolchildren, more respect for the achievements of all generations of Soviet people and for our historical experience, assessing the pluses and minuses of our progress and drawing lessons. This is an important area of the education and Communist upbringing of student youth.

V.K.**Mesiats**, First Secretary of the Moscow Province Party Committee, and G.S.**Strizhov**, head of the CPSU CC's Department of Research and Educational Institutions, participated in the work of the conference.

While in the city of Elektrostal, Ye.K.**Ligachev** visited the Elektrostal Boiler combine, and saw for himself the work of the coordinating center for the vocational guidance of school pupils, set up as an experiment by the USSR State Committee for Labor and Social Problems.

Ye.K.**Ligachev** met the city's residents in the streets.

"Uglubliat' reformu obshcheobrazovatel'noi i professional'noi shkoly," *Pravda* (27 Aug); *Izvestiia* (28 Aug); a translation can also be found in FBIS, No. 171 (3 Sep 87), 23-27; a condensed translation can be found in CDSP, 39:34 (1987), 13-14.

Place the School's Concerns at the Center of Attention (15 Dec 87)

In connection with the upcoming discussion of urgent public education questions at the CPSU CC Plenum, a number of meetings were held in the Party CC with people employed in secondary and higher education, science, culture, the press, the USSR Academy of Sciences, and in Party, state, trade union, and Komsomol bodies.

Taking part were G.M.**Sosin**, Director of no.18 Middle School in Elektrostal, Moscow Province; V.A.**Karakovskii**, Director of Middle School no. 825, Volgograd Region, Moscow; A.A.**Katolikov**, Director of School-Internship, no.1, Syktyvkar, Komi ASSR; V.Kh.**Khadaev**, Director of Experimental Middle School no.315, APN SSSR, Moscow; I.P.**Volkov**, teacher of Middle School no.2, Reutov, Moscow Province; C.D.**Korobov**, Director of the Moscow Radio-Training Technicum; M.F.**Bazhin**, instructor at SPTU no 1, Perm; A.V.**Levchenko**, Chief of Day Care Center, no 1, Prokhladno, Kabardino-Balkarskii ASSR; I.A.**Ziaziun**, Rector of Poltava State Pedagogical Institute; S.P.**Merkurev**, Rector of Leningrad State University; Iu.L.**Ershov**, Rector of Novosibirsk State University; V.E.**Shukshunov**, Rector of Novocherkasskii Polytechnical Institute; Iu.A.**Ryzhov**, Rector of Moscow Aviation Institute; O.P.**Tabakov**, Rector of School-Studies under MKhAT SSSR; M.K.**Rodionov**, Secretary of the Party Committee of the Kiev Polytechic Institute; B.S.**Gershunskii**, Chief of the Laboratory NII General Pedagogy of the USSR Academy of Pedagogical Sciences; V.I.**Martsinkevich**, Chief specialist of the Institute of World Economy and International Affairs, AN SSSR; Academician A.P.**Epshov**, Head of Section of the Statistical Center of the Siberian Branch of the AN SSSR; writer A.A.**Likhanov**, Chief editor of the journal *Smena*, representative of the management of the V.I.Lenin Soviet Children's Fund; Iu.S.**Brodskii**, Head of the Division of popular education of the Sverdlovsk Party executive committee; N.N.**Masal**, delegate form the Council of Ministers of the Belorussian SSR; P.A.**Papilov**, delegate from the CC of the union of creative workers; N.V.**Bagrov**, 2nd Secretary of the Crimean obkom of the Ukrainian CP; A.Ia.**Degtiarev**, Secretary of the Leningrad CPSU obkom; A.A.**Shtaiberga**, First Secretary of the Tsesisskii raikom of the Latvian CP; and other comrades. They discussed the most important issues and the most effective form and methods of teaching upbringing in schools, raising the quality of the preparation of specialists, the qualifications of workers cadres, and the regeneration of the process of democratization of life in schools.

General opinions on a wide circle of questions connected with the completion of the formation and education of the young, the leading reforms of both general and professional schools, the restructuring of higher and middle specialized education in the country were broadly discussed. It was emphasized that the realization of existing resolutions of the 27th CPSU Congress were fundamental concerns for all spheres of our public life and had an especially profound meaning for the life of Soviet schools.

It was noted that restructuring of the work of secondary and higher education is still moving slowly. Serious deficiencies in the organization of the teaching and upbringing process have not been completely overcome. A poor job is being done of disseminating pedagogical expertise. A discussion about the need to speed up the process of freeing the initiative of educators and heads of educational institutions, and of the need to remove excessive restrictions on the use of funds that are allocated to schools, took place. There is a serious shortage of modern methods, texts, and teaching guides—especially computers.

In this regard, criticism was directed against the Ministry of Education, the State Education Employees Trade Union, and the Ministry of Higher and Specialized Secondary Education [VUZ], which have been slow to get rid of excessively close supervision of educational institutions and which often focus attention on specific questions which are not important, while at the same time ignoring basic problems. It was proposed that some of the function of the ministries be shifted to the local level, that the authority of local bodies and educational institution staffs be expanded, and that firm measures be taken to overcome narrow departmental approaches to the administration of public education.

At a meeting held at the USSR Academy of Pedagogy, it was noted that there is a desperate need for fundamentally restructuring this leading center of Soviet pedagogy, for bringing fresh blood into the organization, and for increasing the academy's role in providing scientific-pedagogical support at all levels of public education.

At the meetings it was stressed that one of the main tasks of schools and preschool institutions is to identify and develop abilities in children at an early age. Currently, educational institutions are not coping with this task to the fullest extent. In this regard, there was an exchange of ideas about improving vocational-guidance work in the schools, and about creating a state system of vocational guidance and shifting to a system of intensive training for students in the upper grades based on their abilities and interests, especially scientific disciplines.

Questions of the upbringing of youth took up a large part of the exchange of ideas. In discussing the implications of a parasitic and superficial attitude about life and the deviations from our moral norms that exist among young people, the delegates to the meeting noted that schools bear a large responsibility for such things. Many Komsomol and Young Pioneer organizations do very ineffective work. Social science teachers are not influential enough in inculcating a scientific viewpoint in youth . At the same time, there was sharp discussion about the fact that it is time that families and parents take more responsibility for children's upbringing. There is a need for a deeper study of the changes and the social, psychological, and moral processes that are taking place in the family.

Directors of general and vocational-technical schools spoke of how, with enterprises shifting to economic accountability and self-financing, a tendency to limit assistance to educational institutions has been noticed in several places. In this regard, the question was raised of reviewing or amending the regulations which govern secondary and vocational-technical schools' base enterprises. There also were recommendations for developing elements of economic accountability relationships in the activities of the education institutions themselves—especially in vocational-technical schools, specialized secondary schools, and higher educational institutions. The need to work out a reliable mechanism for unifying higher education, production and scientific research was noted, as was the need for more measures to strengthen the ties of schools with production. The chore of re-equipping educational institutions and expanding the production of equipment and instruments for their use was deemed to be a most urgent one, which needs immediate solution. Attention was drawn to the inadmissability of a situation in which plans for the construction of educational facilities regularly are unfulfilled in many of the republics, territories, and provinces, and not everything is done to improve the living and working conditions of educators.

Participants in the discussions said that the Party's policy of restructuring and the task of creating an integrated system of lifelong education—a task set by the 27th CPSU Congress—pose a need for corrections in the Basic Guidelines [September 1984] for the school reform. Now, when in the activities of the Party the aim is to move restructuring into a new stage, it is extremely important to strengthen attention of all Party organizations to the problem of education, to complete Party leadership in the affairs of schools, to raise the responsibility of Soviet organs and public organizations, and finally the participation of collectives in education, learning, and the professional preparation of youth.

Ye.K.**Ligachev**, member of Politburo of the CPSU CC and Secretary of the CPSU CC, spoke at the meetings.

USSR Ministers S.G.**Shcherbakov** and G.A.**Yagodin**, Chairman of the USSR State Education Employees' Trade Union A.P.**Dumachev**, and officials of the State Planning

Committee, State Supply Committee, State Committee on Labor and Wages, and the USSR Ministry of Finance took part in the discussions.

"Zaboty shkoly—v tsentr vnimaniia," *Pravda* (15 Dec); a condensed translation is in CDSP, 39:50 (1987), 30-31.

Chapter 7

NATIONALITY ISSUES

In his 1981 address to the CPSU Congress Leonid Brezhnev asserted that the "nationality question" in the Soviet Union had been "solved." He had said that already in 1973, but two years later had been compelled to create a council on nationality affairs—attached to the USSR Academy of Sciences. The 1985 CPSU Program also asserts that the "nationalities question has been successfully solved." But at the 27th CPSU Congress (1986). Gorbachev hedged, saying that although "national oppression and inequality of all types have been done away with," there could still be problems in the "national process." He warned against "national narrow-mindedness, arrogance, nationalism and chauvinism."

But by "problems", Gorbachev could not have foreseen thousands of Kazakhs taking to the streets of Alma Ata in December of that year shouting nationalistic slogans ("Kazakhstan for the Kazakhs"). Nor could he have foreseen the extent of peaceful national demonstrations throughout 1987—by Crimean Tatars, Jews, Baltic peoples, and even by Russian nationalists. The process began to turn toward further violence in October when hundreds of Armenians demonstrated in Erevan for the "return" of the Nagorno-Karabakh AO and the Nakhichevan ASSR from Azerbaidzhan. These demands were later to provide the USSR with a setting for the most violent clashes between non-Russian nationalities in the Soviet Union since the 1920s.

After the outbreak in Alma Ata, and the subsequent trials of participants, Gorbachev continued to write that the "nationality question" had been solved "in principle" (*Perestroika* (1987), 118), but he acknowledged that the "national processes are (not) problem free." The Alma Ata outbreaks against the appointment of a Russian (Kolbin) as First Secretary of the Kazakh CP caused the first serious re-examination of the issue in many years. In March, the Scientific Council for National Problems of the Presidium of the USSR Academy of Sciences co-sponsored a conference on this issue with the Academy's Institute of the History of the USSR (See *Istoriia SSSR*, no. 6 (1987), 50-120).

The conference was co-chaired by Iu.V.Bromlei, Chairman of the Scientific Council and Director of the Academy's Institute of Ethnography, and Eduard V. Bagramov of the Institute of Marxism Leninism. Bromlei's introductory address to the conference is included here as the first document in this chapter.

CPSU assumptions about the nationalities "drawing together" has long irritated the non-Russians in the USSR. Indeed, the conference saw some forthright objections to the assimilation process and clear support for ethnic pluralism. Nevertheless, Party theory continues to support the idea that a merger of nations into a single Soviet community is inevitable, though well into the future.

Meanwhile, Gorbachev remains cautious. In his speech—2 November—at the official celebration of the 70th anniversary of the October revolution he again insisted that the "national question" had been solved and that the revolution had ushered in a new age of equal rights to all nations of the USSR. But he was clearly aware that his new renewal mechanisms of glasnost' and democratization might lead to an unstable situation on the "nationalities" front. Therefore, he said, the CPSU must be particularly attentive and "tactful" on matters of national feeling.

For a recent chronology and analysis of the "nationality" issue in the USSR during 1987, see Allan Kagedan, *Gorbachev and the Nationalities. Soviet Ethnic Protest, December 1986 to December 1987*. ORAE Extra-Mural Paper, No.47 (April 1988). Aside from items in the Bibliography see Vera Tolz, "The "Russian Theme" in the Soviet Media," RFE/RL, RL33/87 (26 Jan 87); and Ann Sheehy, "Round Table on National Processes in the USSR," RFE/RL, RL505/87 (14 Dec 87);

The following documents indicate the scale of Gorbachev's "nationality" dilemma.

Academician Iu. Bromlei, **The National Processes In the USSR. Achievements and Problems. Questions of Theory** (13 Feb 87)

The USSR's solution of the nationalities question in the form we inherited it from the past is one of the most evident achievements of socialism. At the same time, as M.S.Gorbachev noted, "our achievements should not create the impression that the national processes are problem free."

Consistency and continuity in the Party's implementation of the Leninist nationalities policy do not rule out careful consideration of the changes occurring in this sphere, rather they presuppose it. Under the conditions of restructuring, this acquires particular importance because, as the CPSU CC January (1987) Plenum pointed out, "the negative phenomena and deformaties against which we have launched a struggle are also present in the sphere of national relations."

From its very first years, Soviet power proclaimed the legal equality of peoples. That did not mean that they had achieved actual equality, especially in the economy. A struggle to eliminate the heaviest burden inherited from the tsarist monarchy—the gigantic differences in the economic development of the peoples- was launched immediately after October. Enormous assistance had to be rendered, primarily by Russia's working class, to enable the former national backwaters to overcome their poverty and backwardness.

All the necessary prerequisites now exist to enable us to approach economic questions primarily from the viewpoint of the interests of the state as a whole. This is why it is particularly important to ensure that each republic's contribution to the development of the unified national economic complex corresponds with the potential it has acquired.

In the implementation of this task it is necessary to bear in mind the negative tendencies in the economy that showed up in the 1970s and early 1980s, which were noted at the 27th CPSU Congress They could not help but influence national processes. This applies above all to the low growth rates of industrial labor productivity in certain republics. Inter-republic differences in the structure of industry, special features in the vocational training of personnel and shortcomings in management, as well as the slow introduction of scientific and technical achievements, also made themselves felt.

One must also take into account the specific features of agriculture in individual regions, particularly in connection with the difference in indices of soil productivity. These differences between southern and northern regions give an appreciable advantage to the southerners (Transcaucasia, Central Asia). As a result, in many instances personal household plots enable people to have rather high incomes. This impedes migration from labour-surplus rural areas, reduces labor activeness in the communal sector of agriculture, deforms the income structure of certain urban residents, and so on. Phenomena of this kind, in which personal interests are made the only rule of life, are accompanied by the revival of vestigial norms of daily behavior, which in some places are given national significance.

The solution of modern economic problems is impossible without taking into account both the interests of the country as a whole and the interests of each republic. Consequently, the Basic Guidelines for the Economic and Social Development of the USSR in 1986-1990 and in the Period Through the Year 2000 presupposes profound qualitative advances in the structure of republican economic complexes. A special system of measures for efficient utilization of production potential will be implemented in each one of them.

Demographic factors, including population migration, also have an effect on national processes. As a result, the republics are becoming increasingly multinational. At present, roughly 20% of the country's population is being made up of people who do not belong to the indigenous nationalities of the republics in which they live.

In conditions of socialism, any changes in the nature of national relations are determined primarily by transformations in the social and class sphere. The creation of a uniform social structure for the socialist nations is extremely important. An enormous role in the process is played by the formation of a national working class. Its percentage in the population of the republics has gradually increased.

However, this increase has taken place mainly in rural localities, particularly as a result of the transformation of collective farms into state farms. As a consequence, differences remain between republics in the percentage of the republics' basic nationalities that is accounted for by the working class, especially the industrial working class and its skilled groups.

All republics have also developed a national intelligentsia; where initially this was mainly an intelligentsia of workers in the creative fields, administrative and managerial personnel and people in the most common professions (physicians, teachers, etc.), during the post-war years intensive growth began in the numbers of the scientific and technical intelligentsia. One must take into account the fact that among previously backward peoples this segment of the intelligentsia was essentially created fom scratch. To this end, special measures were taken: Instruction in national languages was introduced, individuals of the indigenous nationality were given preference in admissions to higher schools, and so on. As a result, in the late 1970s, there was a change in the disparity, among the nationalitites of the various Union republics, between the highest and the lowest percentages of skilled personnel engaged in mental labor. Whereas the disparity used to be measured by a factor of 10 or more, that factor is now only two. At the same time, the increase in the number of (higher school) students in the republics has been accompanied by substantial changes in their national makeup. Thus, in 1979 the representation of young people of the indigenous nationalities among students in a number of republics (Georgia, Kazakhstan, Azerbaidzhan, Armenia, Lithuania, Estonia and others) exceeded those nationalities' shares of the total population. At Yakutsk State University, for example, in the 1985-86 school year Yakuts made up 79.5% of the students in the day division, while at the same time their share of the Yakut Autonomous Republic's population was only 31.1%.

The universal growth of educational standards was highly significant in harmonizing the social structure of nations. A particularly substantial role is played in this by the further economic advance of republics and primarily their industrialization and urbanization.

A very important achievement of the CPSU's Leninist nationalities policy is the formation and development of a culture of the Soviet people that is uniform in terms of docialist content, diverse in terms of national forms and internationalist in spirit on the basis of the best models and distinctive progressive traditions of the peoples of the USSR. The process of cultural interaction has encompassed all spheres of spiritual life. It would, of course, be an oversim-plification to believe the culture of all people's must be completely uniform. the multitude of hues of national cultures constitutes an asset of ours.

The traditions of peoples, their customary norms of behavior and their value orientations are factors making for the acceleration of the social, economic and spiritual development of the republics and the overcoming of negative phenomena in the moral life of society.

At the same time, it would be wrong to reduce everything to the development of national cultures, forgetting about the importance of their convergence. "... It is important," the 27th Congress noted, "to ensure that healthy interest in everything valuable that exists in each national culture does not degenerate into attempts at isolation from the objective process of interaction and alignment of national cultures." Meanwhile, unfortunately, in some works of belles lettres and art and in some scientific works one encounters attempts, in the guise of national distinctiveness, to idealize reactionary-nationalistic and religious vestiges and to embellish the history of one people while belittling the role of others.

The free development of national languages, with the simultaneous dissemination of the Russian language as the language of communication between nationalities, is an achievement of the Party's Leninist nationalities policy. In the 1970s, a tendency developed for an increase in the percentage of individuals of non-Russian nationalities who are fluent in Russian. At the same time, it was discovered that, in the first place, one-third of all persons of non-Russian nationalities are not fluent in Russian, and in the second place, the dissemination of the Russian language among the Union republics' indigenous nationalities was proceeding unevenly. Therefore, the qualitative improvements of knowledge of the Russian language, especially in rural areas of Central Asia, Transcaucasia and the Baltic republics, remains an urgent task.

At the same time, the mastering of languages of the republics' indigenous inhabitants by Russians and individuals of other nationalities is a matter of great importance. This improves interpersonal relations and facilitates adaption to a different ethnic environment.

The improvement of socialism depends largely on the extent to which we succeed in mobilizing the spiritual energy and boosting the labor and social activeness of people. In must be borne in mind in this work that the problems of the human factor have their national and ethnic aspect. It is, after all, specific people who are the direct vehicle of the national element.

The works of our social scientists have focused primary attention on studying the ratio between the national and the international at the republic and interrepublic levels, while the specifically national traits of individuals have remained in the shadows. As a result, there has been an underestimation of the problem of the dialectical combination of the national and international in people's awareness and behavior.

It must be said that the process of the internationalization of most spheres of the life of our society is accompanied by an increase in national self-awareness. The primary basis for this is the economic, social and cultural progress of Soviet nations, which gives rise to legitimate national pride among their representatives. At the same time, as is known, the growth of national self-awareness among representatives of all nations is combined with feelings of all-Soviet pride and all-Soviet self-awareness. But, of course, one must not forget that social awareness and social psychology sometimes may not accurately reflect objective social processes. In certain conditions, some people evince various manifestations of nationalism, which, from the standpoint of social psychology, is a form of egoism- the desire to secure privileges for one's own nationality at the expense of others.

What are the causes of such phenomena? References are usually made first of all to vestiges of the past in people's consciousness and to the influence of bourgeois propaganda. These factors certainly play a role. However, that is not all there is to it. The causes of the indicated manifestations can frequently be found in a discrepancy between words and deeds, in contradictions in the development of present-day society and, to a considerable extent, in matters relating to the sphere of social consciousness.

In a number of instances, feelings of unrealized expectations in specific situations of life that, more often than not, are connected with production activity can be shifted to a national footing. In particular, in conditions of the higher level of educational attainment of the republics' population, including people of the indigenous nationalities, the appearance of disproportions between the supply of skilled jobs and the demand for them is not ruled out. For example, in 1981-1985 about 19% of all higher-school graduates in Georgia were not assigned jobs according to plan. One must also consider the fact that, with the rise in their level of education, people's social expectations also grow. In these conditions, an international personnel policy assumes a special role. National affiliation in itself cannot be a privilege or a reason for limitation. It is for this reason that, from the very first years of Soviet power, the personnel problem at all levels has often been resolved in the republics at the expense of all-Union potential.

The improvement of Soviet democracy and the consistent implementation of the principles of socialist self-government-in particular, the active participation of representatives of all nationalities in the work of bodies of power and administration- are called upon to facilitate the overcoming of negative phenomena in the sphere of communication between nationalities. This applies to representation not only on a republic scale but also in all-Union bodies, as well as in public organizations.

At the same time, some other trends emerged. It was noted at the 27th CPSU Congress that sentiments of parochialism and preference by geographic origin have gained the upper hand in many places. They have hampered interregional exchanges of personnel and exchanges of experienced employees between the republics and the center and between different districts and cities in the country. In a number of instances, this has led to self-isolation, stagnation and other negative phenomena. Vestigial forms of local-clan ties have made themselves felt in the approach to personnel questions. It is also necessary to take into account the fact that nationalistic vestiges are closely interwoven with private-ownership tendencies and careerism.

It must also be borne in mind that various dissatisfactions that people feel in the sphere of everyday life can be projected into the field of national relations. That is why the Party's line aimed at intensifying production with a view to increasing the well-being of Soviet people (expanding housing construction, improving consumer services, and so on) is of cardinal importance for the sphere of national relations as well.

The problems that exist here find a strong response among young people. At first glance, this seems odd -after all, young people are the most receptive group to the internationalization of culture, are better educated, and are socially mobile. But young people are also especially sensitive to any social distortions and often react to them emotionally rather than rationally. Moreover, young people, as a rule, have no experience in positive labor contacts with other nationalities.

The legitimate process of the internationalization of culture and the interethnic mingling of the population can sometimes be perceived in an unhealthy way. When this process is especially intensive, some representatives of certain nationalities regard it as a threat that their national distinctiveness, culture, language, and so on, will be lost. This leads to sentiments of traditionalism, the underestimation of the Russian language as the means of communication among nationalities, the temptation to shut oneself up within the narrow confines of national culture, and the dulling of internationalist conscience. Nationalistic elements take advantage of these sentiments- and sometimes not without success.

Multinational cities and construction sites play a great role in regulating relations between nationalities. Joint labor and prolonged association give rise to friendly contacts between nationalities. At the same time, it is in multinational collectives that people most often notice specific features of others' culture and everyday behavor and compare the occupations and ways of life of representatives of their nation and others. Here both a sensitive personnel policy and concern for the satisfaction of the cultural needs of people of all nationalities are needed.

All this requires thoughtful work by the Party and Soviet agencies. As the new version of the CPSU Program notes, there must be a persistent effort to give every Soviet person an inherent "intolerance towards manifestations of nationalism, chauvism, national narrow-mindedness and national egoism." At the same time, it must be consistently explained that traditionalism and a desire to remain shut up inside one's own national culture inevitably engender provincialism and a lag behind the flow of history. Active propaganda for the successes of republics and peoples, especially those that have been backward in the past, should be combined with slowing their practical stake in close utility, a desire for the common good and the instilling of lofty feelings of love for their homeland -the Union of Soviet Socialist Republics. A thoroughgoing analysis of the real content of national processes in all their complexity and contradictoriness is assuming a special role. This is especially important because until recently, as was noted at the January (1987) Plenum of the CC, "the mistakes committed in the field of national relations and their manifestations remained in the shadows, and it was not accepted practice to talk about them." Comprehensive, varied (using television, literature, museums, etc.) and truthful propaganda of knowledge about progressive historical traditions and the characteristic features of the cultures of various peoples, especially neighbouring peoples, is also necessary. Here as nowhere else, high-flown bragging, prejudiced opinions, superficially and haste are intolerable.

The development of socialist nations and the new conditions of their interaction, when they are equal not only in their rights but also in their actual socioeconomic position, persistently demand that ideological work should pay due attention to national aspects. An important role in the acceleration of our society's socioeconomic development and in the attainment of a qualitatively new position by them is played by the strengthening of fraternal friendship between peoples and the education of working people in the spirit of Soviet patriotism and socialist internationalism.

Bromlei, "Natsional'nye protessy v SSSR. Dostizheniia i problemy. Voprosy teorii," *Pravda* (13 Feb). A translation is also in FBIS, No. 34 (20 Feb 87), R29-34; a condensed version is in CDSP, 39:7 (1987), 1-2, 10.

G. Dildiaev and T. Esilbaev, **Staring Truth in the Face. From the Plenum of the Central Committee of the Communist Party of Kazakhstan** (16 Mar 87)

The work of this Plenum began long before the meeting opened; one could even say that it began back in mid-December last year with the changes in the Kazakh Communist Party CC leadership. Those three intervening months showed just to what extent stagnation had taken hold of life in Kazakhstan. In the space of just 90 days changes were made which were truly revolutionary. Ideas and authorities that once seemed so entrenched were shaken and finally toppled. Old links began to be broken; the web of favoritism and nepotism was swept away. Democratic principles are now being firmly established, to enthusiastic acclaim by the people of Kazakhstan.

The run-up to these changes was prepared by the new political situation in the country following the 27th CPSU Congress. However, in Kazakhstan the implementation of the Congress decisions was delayed if not actually sabotaged- by the chosen few who prospered during the decades of the "golden age".

The Turning Point. Letters to *Pravda* suggest that the present interest in Kazakhstan stems not so much from the nationalistic outburst manifested in the Alma Ata demonstrations of last December—and indeed though their significance should not be underestimated, it would be an injustice to the people of Kazakhstan to exaggerate their importance—as from the way in which the crisis was tackled by the Republic's new Party CC and other governing bodies.

The plenary meeting which discussed how the republic Party organization should implement the decisions taken in January 1987 at the CPSU CC Plenum "On the Reorganization and the Party's Personnel Policy" was the logical outcome of the changes occurring in the republic—the consolidation of healthy forces, and the introduction of new organizational forms and approaches. The plenary meeting was a brainstorming session in which answers had to be found and the truth needed to be faced.

A detailed and principled response to a number of recent criticisms has been published in *Pravda*, with the names of those who personify the negative processes. It would serve no useful purpose to repeat them; the emphasis here will be placed on the meeting's conclusions.

Describing the situation, Gennadi **Kolbin**, First Secretary of the CC of the Communist Party of Kazakhstan, quoted **Lenin** with regard to leaders who have lost a sense of reality: "The machine refused to obey the hand that guided it. It was like a car, which, while having a man at the wheel, is not going in the direction the driver desires... the car is not going quite in the direction the man at the wheel imagines, it is going often in a different direction altogether."

And what is the result of this? There was a great deal of speech-making about the achievements in fostering a sense of internationalism, speeches which culminated in the disturbances provoked by nationalist-minded elements; speeches were made about a flourishing economy while production growth rates were falling rapidly and the republic was constantly receiving subsidies from the state fund; public assertions that the republican bodies were vigilantly ensuring observance of the principles of social justice, while the reality was that people were confronted by blatant injustice.

A select circle of leaders throughout the republic built themselves veritable stately homes— palatial residences and hunting lodges with saunas, greenhouses, billiard rooms, cinemas, and swimming pools. These were luxuriously furnished with all the trappings of a princely lifestyle. All these mansions stood empty for most of the time, awaiting the arrival of distinguished guests. How many people were paid to look after these places, which were all concealed from the eyes of the public?

Was it perhaps that there was nothing else to spend money on? No, the republic faces many problems.

"At our factory, urgent problems such as housing, catering and leisure dragged on for years," declared V. **Dukhovnykh**, senior foundry worker of the Ust-Kamenogorsk Titanium-Magnesium Combine, at the plenum.

Over the past 10 years, only 68% of the funds earmarked to develop health care in Kazakhstan were used for this purpose. Patients, especially those suffering from oncological diseases and tuberculosis, have not had adequate treatment. The republic has inadequate maternity facilities; the waiting list for housing has continued to grow from year to year; the cultural and sporting facilities are insufficient; pre-school establishments are in very short supply, and in many schools classes have had to be held in three shifts.

The plenum also analyzed the causes of these economic failures. Some leaders, still clinging to their parochial ambitions, claimed in the face of all evidence to the contrary that Kazakhstan's agriculture was so good that it was supplying almost half the country with bread and meat. The meeting cut through the rhetoric on this question too, noting how the desire to deliver fine-sounding reports about yet another billions poods of grain,no matter what the cost, had badly hit the rural economy. In the zeal to "earn distinction", fodder grain and seed had been delivered to the state, thereby lowering the output of livestock products and reducing the supply of foodstuffs to the local population.

A Policy of Readjustment. Having taken over the wheel of the "runaway machine", the new CC leadership is now seeking to steer it towards realistic goals and targets, towards bringing about the democratization of social life, towards establishing openness as a norm, and stimulating the creativity of the population.

The plenum noted that the CC of the Communist Party of Kazakhstan had of late redoubled its efforts, generating ideas and proposing concrete ways and means by which all republican Party organizations could carry them out. The Presidium of the Republican Supreme Soviet, the Republican Council of Ministers and the Kazakhstan Trade Union Council have begun to function with markedly greater efficiency.

"We need to motivate people to get involved in the reorganization," **Kolbin** stresses, "in order to make them believe that it is possible to resolve even the most difficult of problems, to give them confidence in their own strength and in ours, and to make them feel that our efforts are yielding result."

Those attending the meeting saw this bridging of the gap between words and deeds as the main indication of the changes taking place in the CC's activity. The people of Kazakhstan have welcomed the fair distributions of products and the transformation of palatial residences and "small hotels" into kindergartens and holiday homes, and into homes for large families. Measures designed to improve the study of both the Kazakh and Russian languages in the republic and to improve contacts between the nationalities and also meeting with approval.

Changes area being introduced in the criteria for assessing success in dealing with the housing problem, the basis now being the rate at which people move up the waiting list rather than the impersonal yardstick of how many square metres are available per family. Reserves have been tapped which make it possible to achieve a 30% increase in the annual rate of housing construction. It is now normal practice for leaders to report on progress in this area.

Karaganda is a regional centre where the housing problem is perhaps most acute, with over 37,000 on the waiting list. Mikhail **Ustinovskii**, First Secretary of the City Party Committee, said: "Even if we had reached the planned housing construction targets, it wouldn't have shortened the waiting list. However, the CC's Housing-91 Program has completely overturned our views as regards our possibilities in this area. It has stimulated initiative. Thus, this year, we will provide flats or houses for 6000 families.

Scotching the Rumors. Until recently no sooner than the business part of a meeting would end than the person in whose office it was held would lower his voice conspiratorially: What's the news? Whose man got the post? Which clan is he from?

The universal enthusiasm for the manipulation of personnel appointments is now coming to an end. There are no longer areas closed to criticism. The press, radio and television keep the population constantly informed about the CC's measures to put things in order and to enforce discipline. For the first time in many years, reality has been presented in its true colours, with no fuss or frills.

A lot of the material in the local press indicates that glasnost in the republic is taking on an increasingly vigorous and uncompromising character. With no fear of naming names, the newspapers speak out openly and honestly about those who abused their high positions to favour their numerous relatives. "Poisoning Through All-Out Permissiveness" was the caption given to a *Kazakhstanskaia Pravda* article on A. **Askarov**, former First Secretary of the Chimkent Party Regional Committee.

Such truthful and timely information knocks all kind of gossip and rumor firmly on the head. The press regularly publishes character references of those occupying top administrative posts, as well as the results of the performance evaluation of Party functionaries and employees in government and economic bodies. The republican newspapers carry weekly reviews of public opinion.

Last January and February, the republic's Communist Party CC received almost as many letters as they had during the whole of 1986—and indication of the sharply increased social awareness of the people of Kazakhstan, who are now denouncing the unacceptable methods used by the republic's former leaders. These letters tend to reflect the belief that lack of control and all-out permissiveness were the main causes of the problems.

The plenum unanimously condemned favoritism and nepotism in terms of the appointment of personnel, and advocated that work collectives should have the first and final say regarding personnel decisions. Today, when someone wins a contest for an important post, it is not only his personal victory but also a victory for democracy, [and] for collective opinion.

Nowadays, when a purge is under way and the names of the officials who violated basic moral principles and Soviet laws are being published, many ask the question: "Why do they include people who reported directly to **Kunaev**?"

This is certainly no idle question. As the head of Kazakhstan's Party organization over many years, **Kunaev** did much to develop the republic. However, over a period of time, his services and his authority became a smokescreen behind which were concealed major shortcomings in his management of the economy, as well as gross violations of the principles of social justice, and distortions in personnel policy. Specific examples of this were given by Slamat **Mukashev**, Chairman of the Presidium of the KSSR Supreme Soviet; Yuri **Trofimov**, First Secretary of the Aktiubinsk Regional Party Committee; Erskin **Auelbekov**, First Secretary of the Kzyl Orda Regional Party Committee; and Nursultan **Nazarbaev**, Chairman of the republic's Council of Ministers.

"Undeserving and immature people, often infected with patriarchalism and parochialism, were promoted to leadership posts," said M. **Mendybaev**, First Secretary of the Alma Ata Regional Party Committee at the plenary meeting. "Individual instances of favoritism developed into a trend. All this was done with the tacit agreement and at times even direct support of the leadership of the Kazakhstan Communist Party Central Committee. It was extremely difficult to get rid of these employees who had compromised themselves, since this was impeded by **Kunaev**'s retinue and often by **Kunaev** himself."

The plenum concluded that the Party should call former First Secretary **Kunaev** to account for gross violations of the norms of Party life, for creating of a cult of his own personality, for distorting personnel policy, and for all-out permissiveness—all of which led to the development of favoritism, abuse of posts, bribery, corruption, and nationalist and other negative manifestations. The Bureau of the Kazakhstan Communist Party Central Committee was instructed to inform the CPSU CC, of which **Kunaev** is a member, of this opinion.

The plenum instructed the Commission of Party Control under CPK CC to investigate the reasons for the subjective approach of writer Olzhas **Suleimenov**, CPK CC member, to the defence of the criminal **Lovinko**, former Director of the Alma-Ata meat-packing plant, and also the circumstances under which the full-length film on **Kunaev**'s 70th birthday was released.

Many of the Central Committee members took the floor to make wider allegations. The roots of the present apolitical attitude manifested in a section of the population they said, must also be sought in their ignorance of the true history of the republic and its Party organization. In time those people would discard that was alien to them. The present difficult and critical period in the history of the republic and its Party organization would not be allowed to be distorted by half-truths, silence or embellishment; it should, and would, they said, become a solid launching pad for rapid progress.

Dildiaev and Esilbaev, "Pravde v glaza. C Plenuma TsK Kompartii Kazakhstana," *Pravda* (16 Mar). A partial translation is in FBIS, No. 53 (19 Mar 87), R11-R15.

Ye. Losoto, **In Forgetfulness** (22 May 87)

Perhaps the reader already knows that a certain so-called informal association named "Memory" [Pamiat] exists in our country. It calls itself a "patriotic association." At "Memory" meetings speakers are introduced as the follows:

"Architect and patriot so-and-so has the floor."

If not architect, then something else, but the second part is always "patriot". "Patriotism" is the moving spirit of these meetings. But then let's take a look at the content that is invested in this word. Generally it is good word among many others. Freedom, equality, brotherhood, wisdom, patriotism, love ... Only by looking at their content and what is invested in them, can one then see if they are good words.

Several anarchists, for example, in their time used the word "freedom" as a slogan, as have bandits, parasites, hooligans and prostitutes. It depends upon what one understands as freedom and what it is one wants to be free to do. No one gathers people under a name or slogan with bad words. Everyone gathers under an attractive one. However, one needs to separate substance from form.

Thus, there is patriotism. In this idea there is also invested different meanings. **Lenin** defined the new Soviet patriotism in this way: socialism as the fatherland. With those words, **Lenin** defined the position of the class-conscious proletariat, which, needless to say, was his own position as well. We will remember this, as we read further; for some among us refer to am abbreviated "Leninism"—which has no relationship to the authentic Leninist idea.

Dragging behind us from out of the past is a patriarchial patriotism—the dusty tail of a country that has moved ahead rapidly and was quite recently populated by vast, benighted masses of almost totally illiterate peasants who had believed for centuries in God and tsar and had for centuries ascribed all evil to devil and infidel. The patriotism of the small-scale property owner (petit bourgeois patriotism) is quite different from the patriotism of the class-conscious proletariat. The first kind of patriotism has on its banner not socialism as the fatherland but its own farmstead and landholdings as the fatherland, Orthodoxy as the fatherland, and national traits as the fatherland. That kind of patriotism turns into nationalism in the twinkling of an eye. Touch the lighted match of anti-Semitism to it, and you will see "Memory".

The archaic can be crude and obvious to everyone. Or it can be "cultivated."

An interest in history, in the past, is natural. To not know the past is not to know the present, and then one is not able to look into the future. Everyone should study it! But one does not have to drag everything behind oneself, declaring both the progressive and the reactionary equally to be the single Russian culture that we need. Lenin always separated progressive culture from reactionary culture (including Black Hundreds culture, clerical culture, etc.). We should take for ourselves all the best, not everything in general

Let's keep this in mind, since we are going to come up against the unscrupulous (or ignorant) association of "Leninism" with the ideological platform and "Memory"'s leaders. An unscrupulous mixture of clericalism and mysticism with "Leninism" is a characterisitc feature of their statements. And not only theirs! There are even "theoretical" works appearing in our periodicals whose authors shamelessly claim **Lenin** as an ally, in the process expressing thoughts that are directly antithetical to both the spirit and the letter of Leninism. One of the most vivid examples is V. **Kozhinov's** article in the magazine *Moskva*, (it's not for nothing that it is glorified by some speakers at "Memory" meetings). Every phenomenon has its organizers, its agitators, its ideologists, and its artists—you and I are going to become acquainted with organizers and agitators of "mass meetings."

I get out of the Kropotkin Street subway station, not in the direction of the Moscow Swimming Pool, which "Memory" hates and calls "the round ablution puddle" at its meetings, but in the opposite direction, toward Moscow City's Lenin Borough Party Committee. For certain reasons, the borough Party committee was forced to give space to "Memory". Strange speeches, of which a brief summary is offered for the reader's attention, can be heard from the conference hall. There are quite a few young people in the hall, as there are at other evening gatherings held by "Memory".

As we go into the "Memory" meeting we are given extracts so as to help readers separate the important matters from nonsense, and the nonsense from mystical nonsense, in order that the reader could see where there were drops of truth, where there is a sea of speculation on these drops of truth.

K. **Andreev**, the chairman of "Memory"'s council, says that the provision of space, "is to the credit of the borough Party committee."

"The news of this will travel across all of great Rus, to the glory of socialism and communism."

In the speaker's firm opinion, we must improve people's attitude toward labor, and to do this we have to give the people's history back to them, but the history must be "rehabilitated." What does this mean?

"I will work for the rehabilitation of our history. The people have had their history knocked out from under them. If you look at a calendar, there was an ice age or virgin soil in our land before 1917."

Certainly, the people should know their history and their heroes. Representatives of all trends of thoughts in our society agree on this. To know it, yes. But to know doesn't mean exalt. That is, to take everything without analysis, to include in turn workers' information, the requirements of logical developments, the work of propagandists and artististic writers. But now people are exalting various things. Every trend of thought exalts its own heroes, its own monuments, its own historical events and segments of history.

One trend exalts the Bolsheviks and Democrats.

Another, in contrast, exalts that which has no relation to the revolutionary struggle: abstract humanism and pluralism.

A third lives in the 1930s.

A fourth digs up and restores the olden times of Orthodoxy. Not just what is artistically beautiful (about which there are no arguments; it's necessary) but everything that is Orthodox and "holy." To what point to we read: 1917. It was an active turning point for "Holy" as well; He actively emphasizes "holy." And if the Orthodox consider our history, then that history from most matters did stop as if night time came, and rightfully so.

A. **Gladkov,** who has spent many volunteer workdays restoring churches and "cleaning up desecrated graves on the grounds of the Dynamo Plant," is given the floor.

For the reader's information: We recently wrote that the plant, needless to say, was not engaged in the deliberate "desecration of graves." Heroes of the Battle of Kulikovo are buried in a church building on the plant's grounds. The people who installed the compressors in that spot didn't know that the heroes were buried there. This is not a justification, merely an explanation. That spot has now been placed under the protection of the state, and the plant has been instructed to remove the compressor station; to date, however, it has not removed it. Yes, the Dynamo Plant did throw gasoline on the fire.

A.**Gladkov** says that after **Lenin**'s death the Leninist concept of national culture (**Lenin** had no such concept at all, but a concept of two cultures) was distorted. He reads some lines of Proletkult verse form the 1920s about how **Minin** and **Pozharskii** should be pulled down from their pedestal because they were "shopkeepers." In this instance, Proletkult, which vulgarized the Party's policy in the field of culture and which (despite **Lenin**'s Party position) rejected the cultural heritage, is passed off as the Party policy.

Then the speaker moved on to a description of the Moscow Swimming Pool, which the audience hates (the Church of Christ the Savior once stood there).

"Year-round, steam pours from the swimming pool, steam that has a disastrous effect on the masterpieces in the Alexander III Museum (now the Pushkin Museum)."

For the reader's information: The swimming pool's disastrous effect on the museum has not been confirmed. Too much is being ascribed to the swimming pool. It's too bad about the church, and it's too bad, moreover, that its destruction was caused not by the demands of the revolutionary situation but by thoughtlessness and a lack of understanding of the beautiful. More Precisely: we narrowly recognize only new things as beautiful. But waving one's fists after the fight is over is futile. Although, of course, it will do for exciting an audience.

The following speaker is a member of the council, O.**Zhurin**. In his words, "some individuals have ignored **Lenin** by saying that culture is class-based." But Lenin, in his opinion, said that culture was based on class only before October; after October he started to say other things:

"There are patriotic forces, and there are pogrom forces." The "progrom forces", in the words of the orator, were the ones who destroyed the monuments. "All this was accompanied with nasty little rhymes. Proletkult and the Union of Militant Godless were at its head. There is no longer a single building from **Pushkin**'s epoch in Pushkin Square. **Pushkin** has turned his back on Russia—symbolically!"

(The speaker has in mind the Rossiia cinema theatre, which has a monument to **Pushkin** in front of it.)

Two people are named specifically as being the villains responsible for the severe reduction in the number of churches in Moscow: "Lazar Moiseevich **Kaganovich**, who handled the reconstruction of Moscow. He said, "All old cities were built haphazardly. When you walk around Moscow, you get the feeling that it was built by a drunken builder...." Also **Iaroslavskii** (i.e., Gubelman), the director of the Union of Militant Godless...."

Member of council, V.**Vinogradov**, speaks: Again, the speaker starts with **Lenin**'s ideas. Then he goes on to Moscow as the "Third Rome, the heavenly city." In light of the fact Moscow is the Third Rome, it is the "leading shrine of the world."

"Old Russian city planning was not understood by those who rebuilt Moscow. The architect **Ginsburg** said in the 1930s: "It is simply not necessary to invest any money but deterioration will to the job for us." Now is the moment when it is necessary to save the fatherland. The destruction of national shrines is being continued by accomplices of **Kaganovich**'s crimes...."

D.**Vasil'ev** says: "Agitprop [Agitprop is USSR State Committee for Agitation and Propaganda] is sewing political labels on us. If this does not cease, we will have to turn to the criminal code's article on slander. A stream of cosmopolitanism has swept up the mass news media. Rock groups are Satanism; they give their oath to Satan!"

For the information of the reader, here and throughout keep in mind what the term Satan means to the "Memory" society. Satan means the Devil, the opposition to God.

V.**Shumskii** runs onto the stage from the assembly. he talks enthusiastically about V.**Kozhinov**'s article and proclaims: "We are for Leninism! What was destroyed was destroyed by the hands of Satan!

For the information of the reader: This is not a misprint. It is written exactly as it was said by three people in official circumstances. Namely that they were for Leninism and against Satan.

"I was surprised by the fact that many of the designs for the monument on Poklonnaia Hill contained (he had in mind the concourse which originated in the Central Exhibition Hall) masonic and zionist symbols and even fascist ones! This is how the werewolves of culture act. Since New Year, the Order of Lenin has disappeared from the cover of the magazine *Ogoniok*." [A weekly magazine edited by Vitalii Korotich which has been a leading forum for glasnot, and has attacked Pamiat sharply].

For the reader's information: what he says about *Ogoniok* is true.

"Certain people are coming to us in Moscow from overseas by the thousands! Away with them! We do not need them here!"

Everyone claps and shouts: :"Away with them!" "Hail to the Russian People!"

In conclusion, D.**Vasilev** proposes that K.**Andreev** be nominated for the borough Soviet. A furor arises once again when the audience recalls the name of the hated key official with the patronym "Moiseevich." A tape of an interview with a Dr. **Iosifovich** had been played. The audience's reaction to such patronymics can be expressed in one simple sentence: "Ah, then everything is clear."

It is interesting that the audience is not embarrassed by the public playing of a secretly made tape recording. In my view this is indecent. To make notes is accepted by all members of the meeting. In contrasting case, the decent people do not make notes.

As some journalists say, "there are facts, and then there are facts." "Memory" meets in one of Moscow's Palaces of Culture. The themes is, "Your Civic Position." D.**Vasilev** says:

"Good evening dear colleagues and friends! Here are gathered people who are not indifferent to the fate of the Fatherland, who struggle for the success of restructuring...."

As one might have guessed he often refers to "Leninism", connecting it with current realities and then constructs a place for his favorite theme. This is how everything starts. Here is his type of logic:

"**Lenin** warned: only truth can solve all problems. For decades we have been taught that the bureaucrat is merely an official who pushes paper. No, the bureaucrat is an insidiously conspiring enemy of our Fatherland and our people. One American said to a correspondent: bureaucracy is a powerful international movement."

I will give as brief a resumé of the speech as possible: Imperialism and Zionism are planting agents who breed bureaucrats. This enemy has ensconced itself everywhere and has driven us into a corner. Among those of us who are sitting here in this hall, every third one is a genius, but the enemy has not allowed us to show our true value. Those who ruin the economy and science are given send-offs into retirement, but they ought to be put against the wall. They are the enemy.

Then follows the names of " enemies with Party membership cards," while the "experience of P.A.**Stolypin**," who gave the go ahead to the kulaks and whose name justly symbolizes the reactionary period of the early 20th century, is called an example of genuine patriotism.

Examples of masonic-zionist intrigues follow. Babies' jackets bearing a picture of the moon are being sold in stores. "The moon is a symbol of protection of the Jews." "You see? They are swaddling you and me in these swaddling clothes!"

Zionism and Masons have spread their nets everywhere in order to destroy Orthodoxy. Examples: the article in *Komsomolka* titled, "Flirting with God," and an editorial in *Pravda* dealing with the atheistic upbringing of the working people, which repeated **Lenin**'s words "flirting with God" in the "spirit of the 1930s", and an official statement by a major Party worker (named) who expressed "harmful thoughts" at a conference dealing with the social sciences.

The speaker curses those who dare to criticize the mistaken patriarchal views of "our Russian writers."

On the whole, "a caste of thinkers has been created who insult us, yet live on the people's money." These thinkers themselves "do not know up from down"—all they can do is "desecrate our historical past." But what must be done now is not to desecrate the past but "open the churches with the chiming of bells."

Again, it is the non-Orthodox, the non-Russians, the Masons, who have "destroyed the Orthodox monuments."

Hold the newspapers up to the light! They write about the purity of the Dnieper water, while showing through the other side of the page—if you hold it up to the light—is a skull! "This is what our press amuses itself with!"

The headlines: "Lessons of Chernoby!"—but when it is held up to the light one can see "It must become a tradition." "This is material for the KGB!"

The audience applauds.

Everywhere in the newspapers are "coded menorahs" and "6-pointed stars", and this "signifies their (Jews) presence." Set squares and compasses are masonic symbols. So are rectangles and squares. The number 33 is the sign of a "special masonic initiation."

Now I will outline the concluding call. We must "form ranks to carry out the new political course" and wage a "final, decisive battle against bureaucratism—that hydra of world masonry, Zionism and imperialism." "Brothers and sisters! We must unsheathe our weapons" and give battle to purify the country "of the black forces of evil. It has gone far enough!"

I purposely set to the side the personality and life styles of members of the "Memory" council. I have no desire to lower myself to the level of name-calling and categorizing in the company of this especially alien way of life. It is assumed that any idea has figures. But when they "clothe" the figures, they still do not know what they mean.

Let us now undertake a first hand analysis of "Memory" as a fact of public life.

It is a manifestation of the multi-sided attitudes of the petty bourgeois. The bourgeois is cosmopolitan, the small-scale property owner is nationalized, and the proletariat is internationalist.

The ideology of the small-scale owner is tenacious, and from time to time there are great upsurges of it.

In place of heroes, we are offered "Saints."

They refuse to see the class struggle; in place of it, it is proposed that we detect the odor of a "single national spirit" so strong that in one novel a Chekist kills himself because he is unable to bear the death of White bandits **who are of his own nationality**, although he has risked his life every minute to do away with them.

The clerical idea of "orthodoxy as the fatherland" is rejected by the proletariat formulation "socialism as the fatherland." The object of their pride of the country is not October, owing to which we have the first. before anyone else, social policy; rather it is Orthodoxy which once named us the Third Rome. Moscow is changed from the largest center of world socialism to the "head of the moral Holy world," for they see it as the Third Rome.

Thus there is established an especially narrow view from which our sober, responsbile contemporaries judge world activities. Under such a point of view it is impossible to see that the opponents of socialism are capitalism and bourgeois propaganda—and not Satan.

If the class evaluation of events is lost, its place can be taken to the advantage of the religious-mystical standpoint. If tsarism is considered idyllic, then that suggests that it is not class struggle, not social contradictions which define one or the other phenomena—it is something else. If it is not found in actuality, then it is found in mysticism. If not in a social storm, then the mass movement which swept away the landowners and the signs and symbols of the tsars and God must have been led by something else. Satan. Zion, masons.

If in losing not only class interpretation, but also historical reasons for events, it is clearly demonstrated that the so-called historical tactlessness, then certainly it is completely impossible for them to understand what the memorials really mean. Indeed, they were not just monuments, but represented the yoke of clerical reaction.

It is understood that it is possible to make mistakes, and even distortions in any matter; but in such inexperienced and unprecedented affair like the creation of a new society, then distortions are more likely. They were, and naturally must be.

How does Satan come into this?

Now about bureaucracy.

Bureaucratism, according to **Lenin**, is "... the subordination of the interests of business tro the interests of one's cushy job, to turn one's attention on his position and to ignore work...." That is personal, selfish interests, so as to maintain his personal perquisites; and not the interest of international zionism.

All in all, it is true to say that "Memory" shgould gladden the hearts of Zionists, since it only plays into their hands. They have a reason to shout loudly about anti-Zionism in the USSR.

We have talked to you about the petty bourgeois ideology of the small-scale property owner. Now let me say a few words about the petty bourgeois mentality.

The small-scale property owner would not be himself if he did not suffer from strong jealousy for everyone who rises above his level and stick in his throat. Thus, the narrow attempts to scorn anything noteworthy by man, to show: he is no better than I. Thus, the mean spirited view of officials. Remember the report of D.**Vasil'ev**: "Every third one of us is a genius," but someone has kept us from realizing our potential. Against the background of nationalism, this "someone" is very often a person of a different nationality or a different faith. In this version, it is the Jew. Add mysticism and the "culprit" is a mason.

And now if you have the chance, look in on a group of these "geniuses", this time in the company of the Jewish nationality. You will be regaled until morning with stories about how those who prevented them from realizing their potential are anti-semites!

There is only one way out of this closed circle—internationalism. Proletarian internationalism. No nation and no fatherland is better or worse than another. Good things, honors and status come strictly in accordance with work for the good of the people.

It is understood tha mafia, clans, elites can be organized not only from society of their membership to a specific natiuonality, but also around national symbols and on the basis of any printed archaic clan-tribe relationship. But their nature—bourgeois and petty bourgeois, is a question of class contradiction and not a question of nationality "enemies", or the "aggression" of Judaism against Orthodoxy.

As one of my acquaintances said to me: "You again are printing words of mourning for the masons...."

"What?"

"In a funereal masonic context.... That means that the masons have condemned you and will warn each other about this."

Mind you! My acquaintance is a fully decent man. He by no means intends to shatter my nerves or cause a provocation. This is his sincere opinion and he simply wants to warn me of the danger.

He opened the newspaper to that article. There are strong double sides, in which concentrated gathered serious publicists: the theory of Marxism, information about delegates to congresses, reviews of political literature, and so on.

But what about the mysticism of the middle ages? With their mystical "presence"? And should I go and (with him I have a good relationship) and beg as to why he has once again put me in the framework of "those condemned as masons"! And in the meantime, I will make arrangements to write something about, for instance, "Tragedy at Sunrise" or "An Unfortunate Incident." Unfortunately, the interval will not come about. On other pages, there are other sentinels, and thanks to my whims none of these will ever put an unseemly headlines over their articles.

A newspaper is fashioned in metal. If someone has an inclination to take time out to stand an article, connected to these metal frameworks, on its end; firstly, nothing will be seen, and secondly, the metal will dissolve into metal lines. There will be cute scandal and a fine. Tomorrow a reprimand. They will suspect an intoxicated condition....

But I am all talked out. I will be briefer. Mysticism is mysticism, and must one bother to refute it?

Ye. Losoto, "V bespamiatstve," *Komsomol'skaia pravda* (22 May); a condensed translation is in CDSP, 39:21 (1987), 1-4.

E.Bagramov, **The National Problem and Social Science** (14 Aug 87)

Socialist transformation of national relations, the confirmation of the friendship and fraternity of nations is the special achievement of socialism, about which the people have spoken with special pride since the beginning of the seventies. Together with these characteristic signs of our times is a sharpness of the reaction of society to still unfulfilled, negative manifestations in the sphere of nationalities' relations, and active discussion of urgent problems and unsolved questions. Refuting the premise of an absence of problems in the national process, showing itself progressive here in cutting a swath through the contradictions, the 27th CPSU Congress has unchained the thinking of social scientists, and created the conditions for a theoretical breakthrough in this scientific area, which hardly more than the others has suffered from dogmatism.

In the conditions of renewed socialism, there are a sequence of tasks, founded on scientific analysis, and reactions to current demands of the national policy of the CPSU. In the resolution of the CPSU CC, "About the Work of the Kazakh Republic Party Organizations on the Internationalist and Patriotic Education of the Working People", it was said, "Today, when the revolutionary process is being renewed by all sides of society, a variety of decisions which emerge from problems in the sphere of national relations have become extremely important." And this suggests a deep struggle for the Leninist position to evaluate the dynamic national relationships, which in his view must be free from sterotype formulas. The just criticism at the January (1987) Plenum of the CC demands that the loss of contact between scientific research and reality must be overcome.

In the area of theory, this was reflected in the rejection of a realistic analysis of emerging problems, the substitution of mechanical selection of facts and figures on the Soviet republics for the study of the realities of life, the limitation of scientific thought only to certain principles and notions (the definition of a nation, abstract concepts about the future of languages, and so on), the eternal rehashing of general truths, and the obviously insufficient study of questions about nationality policy that would be in keeping with the country's present stage of development. Proceeding from an oversimplified understanding of the thesis concerning the national question in our country, some social scientists have portrayed the state of national relations only in a very rosy light, in a static, metaphysical manner.

Evidently some social scientists lacked philosophical culture when faced with characteristics, according to an observation from M.S.**Gorbachev**, for these essentially very complex and contradictory socio-economic and spiritual processes.

The relations between nationalities and minorities is a living process of complex interdependence of the national and the international, where the new is confirmed in continual conflict with the old, which is not wholly discarded, but is re-worked, retaining all that is valuable and positive.

It is important to comprehend properly the core of the national problem itself, a problem that never has existed anywhere in its pure form, so to speak, but always has included the sum total of economic, social-class and spiritual relations that determine mutual connections among peoples. The restructuring of these relations is leading to deep changes in national relations as well, but, because of the relative independence of the national factor, which is founded in history, in this sphere the inertia of outmoded traditons will have to be confronted for a long time to come.

The class approach is the true path to comprehending the specific content of national problems. It rules out any emasculation of their essence and any exaggeration of the national element. Attempts to present the national factor in the form of some kind of foundation or as an obstacle in the path of social development are also incorrect.

Internationalization has been discussed often as if it meant the standardization of everything, without exception. As a consequence of this, the many-sided and highly beneficial process has been portrayed as an inert abstraction. By means of this approach, if the equality of peoples was examined, it was understood rigidly as if there were no differences between regions. Gradually, the unfounded idea was established to the effect that society is moving toward a greater fraternity of peoples voluntarily and practically automatically, up to and including the fusion of nations. It goes without saying that it is not right to fall into extremism, to forget what was both a courageous performance by scholars, writers, publicists, and serious labor, which was indicated by the recommendations for improving matters.

In practice, the sphere of national relations was out of bounds for criticism and treated as a topic of universal harmony, and anything which did not fit into this harmony was merely dismissed and stigmatized as a manifestation of bourgeois nationalism. Many of the real needs and requirements of both state and national development were in fact ignored, and scholars often did not dare raise these questions.

Therefore, the logical shift in the 1950s and the 1960s from excessive centralization to expansion of the rights of the Union Republics was not granted appropriate study in social science works. There was no clear and concise notion of the correlation of forces between All-Union and local, or between that of internationalist and national. Means for overcoming unhealthy tendencies were not reflected in scientific literature. The June 1987 Plenum paid attention to the necessity of accounting for an entire complex of issues—those of the individual, the collective, class, nationalities, minorities,social and professional groups. The harmonization of nationalities, republics, inter-national and inter-governmental interests has shown itself to be the most important aspect of restructuring. The Party is developing a new path, a form of action in the interests of the people, nurturing and directing them through a new mechanism of stewardship, through democratic institutions, and through politics, ideology and culture.

Rather than conduct abstract discussions about internationalism, the mechanism of implementing nationalities policy should be examined. For example the issue of the actual economic equality of peoples should be more closely tied to social justice. The diversity of regional and national conditions does not rule out the formulation of a single measure of labor and consumption, so that appropriation can be carried out everywhere on the basis of common criteria in evaluating work and its results.

In overcoming departmentalism and localism, the Party creates opportunities for the concentration of resources in important areas of scientific and technical progress, something that benefits the whole country and every republic individually. It is important to give full attention to specific national features and to support healthy areas of the development of local initiative, while preventing it from becoming controlled by bureaucratic centralism.

Nationality policy must not be interpreted narrowly, stressing at one time the flourishing of nations and at other times the convergence of nations. Restructuring means general agreement with the CPSU's Leninist course—attention to the special features of nationalities and their needs in the name of international unity, with no setting of one group of cadres off against another.

In an atmosphere of the growth of democratic principles in all spheres of life, processes of the spiritual life of peoples and nationalties, especially linguistic processes, are being discussed in a creative way. Concern for one's native language and for its development in relationship with the Russian language is quite natural. But here one can meet both legitimate requirements and a deliberate, especially among writers, dramatization of linguistic processes. The most important thing is that a legitimate love for the native language does not turn into linguistic chauvinism, which would be a barrier in the way towards internationalization.

A lack of consideration for the language of people with whom one lives will lead to a justified protest. Naturally, those who believe that the voluntary principle in choosing a language of instruction relieves them or their children of the duty to show respect for the traditions and culture of the people are in error. It is a question of tact, of culture in intra-national communication, which exists according to our upbringing as Soviet people in the spirit of internationalism. However, practice shows that in a number of cases deterioration in instruction in the national language is explained usually by the poor training of teachers and a shortage of them. Some authors (for example in Estonia) put their native language up against the language of communication between nationalities. The proper practice of operating schools with parallel classes (in the native and Russian language), which was instituted widely in Latvia at one time, deserves general support.

National-Russian bilingualism is the main area of language development in the USSR. This does not change the legal status of languages. But their equality does not mean that their social purposes are the same. Thus, the Russian language is the language of communication between nationalities and is the universally recognized means for giving the masses access to the culture of the peoples of the USSR and of the entire world. Any demand that the use of the Russian language be limited administratively has nothing to do with the real concern for the growth of a native language and national culture. It is also hard to agree with the proposal that ministries rather than parents should decide the question of which school, in terms of language of instruction, children are to attend—particularly in the conditions of democratization of our life.

Thus, Marxists are for equality and the free development of languages and are opposed to national privileges. Soviet citizens treat national sentiments with respect. At the same time, they are opposed to attempts to take advantage of those feelings.

Theoretical and methodological clarity in the ideas of "national" and "nationalistic" is necessary. The time when social scientists avoided a profound analysis of the category "national" (afraid, not unreasonably, that they would gain a reputation of having nationalistic flavor) is long over. Nonetheless, philosophers still have not completely decided under what conditions the national, as a phenomenon basic to socialism, develops into its antipode, the nationalistic.

Here is a typical circumstance. Misunderstandings and sometimes even rivalries arise from time to time in relations between neighboring regions or provinces of the various republics. People argue with one another in unofficial settings. Meanwhile, Party and Soviet *apparat* remain silent and avoid making fundamental decisions. They do not anticipate or stop passions.

Perhaps the questions at issue are too sensitive, too complicated. But why not use such a democratic medium as a survey of public opinion to find out how the two sides feel a a particular question?

Manifestations of nationalism have traditionally been explained as "awareness lagging behind reality." In doing this, have we not turned this formula into a sort of push button with which analysis has been turned off at the point where it should begin? It is important to study the sum total of objective and subjective factors that influence the resilience of unhealthy sentiments. These factors include economic disorders, violations of Soviet laws and the Leninist principles of cadres policy, and a conciliatory attitude toward such sentiments.

Naturally, national interests, national self-consciousness and a sense of national dignity are real charateristics of our existence. If class consciousness is not utilized to correct these phenomena of spiritual life and no internationalist obligation is shown, it is easy to slip into an exaggeration of national elements and even to raising their status to that of absolutes. From the perspective of social psychology, this ethnocentrism is the view of other peoples through the prism of the value of one's own ethnic commonality. Nationalism leading up to exclusivity is a conception of one's own nation and its mission.

There does exist a loyal element which never falls into nationalism or chauvinism—which stands on the class principle of equality for workers of all nations, thinking not only of one's own nation, but putting the interests of class above it. For this, one should study Leninism: national interests must not be defended from a position in isolation from other nations, rather [they should be defended] in the interests of the international fraternity of workers.

This principle is proclaimed in part in the creation of a committee to review the problem of the Crimean Tatars. Soviet people have taken this as a hint from Soviet organs everywhere as being in the interests of all peoples to study the question and make a decision according to the traditions of friendship of nations of the USSR.

Socialism has disproved the myth of the immutability of international antagonisms. The national factor has already ceased to divide peoples. No less important is the receptivity to nationality problems by a certain portion of the population on the strength of historical factors, as the multi-national character of the country is still noticeable. Incidentally, bourgeois ideology, where influential forces are whipping up and exaggerating nationalist sentiments and the contradiction between national and international values, counts on this.

The confirmation of internationalism requires persistent efforts—that is what the lessons of the Alma-Ata incident and the struggle now under way against negative phenomena in Kazakhstan and other republics teach us. It must be said frankly that theoretical analyses on the social consciousness of the population of the Central Asian republics and Kazakhstan obviously lacked realism and featured idealization. The jump from feudalism to socialism was a major achievement of the Soviet system, but in the conditions which existed at the time there were also some drawbacks—the insufficient number of national working class cadres, the continuation of vestiges of tribal relations, and so on. The rapid growth of national self-consciousness, given the absence of concern for internationalist upbringing, is filled with the danger of a one-sided tendency towards national features.

In the popular book, *A Trip to Zher-Uyuk*, published in in the 1970s, the following assessments of national characteristics were put into the mouth of an old folk poet: the Ukrainian is noted for his cheerful disposition, the Georgian by his hospitality, the Armenian by his hard work, the Russian by his love of native land and courage, the Estonian by his industriousness, the Tadzhik by his quest for knowledge, and the Kazakh by all these qualities put together. Imagine, how great is the desire to magnify the national vanity! And how this contradicts the traditions of the people who gave the world Chokan **Valikhanov** and Abai **Kunanbaiev**! [Kazakh intellectuals who opposed religion and praised Russian culture in the 19th century. See K. Beisembiev, *Iz istorii obshchestvennoi mysli Kazakhstana vtoroi poloviny XIX v.* (Alma-Ata, 1957)].

It is no secret that an understanding of national character is built to a great extent on subjective assessments. Stereotyped opinions about peoples, opinions that in a great many cases are offensive, circulate widely. To a large extent they are the basis of resilient and insulting evaluations of people's national dignity, manifested as everyday nationalism or chauvinistic arrogance, against which, in a great many cases no effective struggle is waged. How are these judgements separated from the real distinction in national character? It is essential to study the history, culture, traditions, and everyday life of a nation in detail, since the genuine virtues of the national spirit are rooted in these spheres. Socialism improves national feelings, and eradicates their former features of isolation, egoism, and intolerance.

In our time, interest is growing in the historical past, monuments of national culture, folklore, and so on. But why do those who want to set peoples against one another on the basis of nationality worm their way into this affair, which is sacred to the Soviet people? If they proclaim themselves to be "patriots", this means that we are doing a poor job of propagandizing Soviet patriotism as an ideology that is incompatible with the concept of national exclusiveness—be it chauvinism, Zionism, or other manifestations of national conceit. It is impossible to lose sight of the fact that underlying all nations is the commonality of the historical fate of the peoples of the USSR, and the international traditions of their battles for socialism.

In nations who live under the same conditions for socio-economic development, it is difficult to discover such characteristic virtues which would absolutely differentiate them from each each other. The specifics of national character obviously must be found in in the unique coincidence of mutual values, in the special expression of one or more features—and not be exaggerated as signs of exclusivity. Thus, the problem for scholars and artists is not to emphasize one-sided psychological differences, but to discover various manifestations of the universally human, something new which is borne by socialism, by the evolution of social and international commonality—the Soviet nation.

The fear of dissolving nationality problems in psychology (as if Marxism-Leninism never cultivated a scientific-methodological investigation into national psychology and nationalities' relations), has led to a situation where social scientists have not studied these phenomena for a long time. In recent times research has turned to [a study of] actual national processes.

I note: what is particularly needed now is not uncoordinated research results of historians, philosophers, and so on, but complex interdisciplinary work.

The interests of proletarian solidarity, speaking the words of **Lenin**, demand that "we never formally address ourselves to nationalities' problems...." (Vol.45, p.360). This must be understood in the sense of finality, that is, that a single eternal given solution for one of the most complex human problems does not exist, nor can it ever exist. Each new stage presents new problems. Probably this will continue to be true for as long as nations exist.

Eduard Bagramov, "Natsional'naia problema i obshchestvoznanie," *Pravda* (14 Aug); a condensed translation is in CDSP, 39:34 (1987), 9-10. Bagramov is a professor of philosophy.

Chapter 8

FOREIGN POLICY

It has been said in a number of places that Gorbachev's perestroika has had the least impact on Soviet foreign policy. To a great extent this is true, because the geo-political interests of the USSR remain the same no matter what new economic or political theory is being espoused in Moscow. Nevertheless, the "New Way of Thinking" has seen some very specific results: a wide cross-section of policy proposals—mainly focusing on arms control—; active summitry with the USA; multiple initiatives about arms limitation; and offers of mutual solutions to regional crises—among them Afghanistan.

Although relations with the USA remain the crucial determinant of Soviet foreign policy, Japan and Western Europe have taken on greater significance for the USSR in the 1980s. Gorbachev pushes co-operation between between the Council for Mutual Economic Assistance (CMEA) and the European Economic Community (EEC), and organizational contact between NATO and Warsaw Pact. He has signed trade, culture, and research agreements with Japan. Initiatives have been sent out from Moscow to China—though with little in the way of concrete results.

A major change in foreign policy administration began shortly after Gorbachev became General Secretary. The removal of long-time Minister of Foreign Affairs, Andrei Gromyko, in July 1985 was symbolic of changes that saw replacements of the top staff in the ministry and in the Central Committee departments most concerned with foreign policy. Eduard Shevard-nadze, who had no experience in foreign affairs, replaced Gromyko. At the 27th Congress of the CPSU, in 1986, A.Dobrynin, former ambassador to the United States, took over foreign policy matters in the Central Committee, and V.Medvedev became the secretary for Liaison with Communist Parties of Socialist States. The chief propaganda post went to A.N.Yakovlev, former ambassador to Canada and director of the prestigious Institute of World Economics and International Relations [IMEMO]. The Institute of the USA and Canada, the Institute of Oriental Studies, and IMEMO were assigned large-scale research tasks as the Party and government officials sought information for their own use and personnel to help persuade foreign states of the merits of change in the USSR.

Gorbachev himself has been unusually active in foreign policy. Aside from highly publicized meetings with Ronald Reagan, he met with Margaret Thatcher, Francois Mitterand, and Rajiv Gandhi. He and Shevarnadze also visited with the leaders of Warsaw Pact and CMEA countries, and with a wide cross-section of representatives of the Third World. They offered mediating services or proposals to help solve almost every regional conflict. In short, Gorbachev's statement in *Perestroika* (1987) to the effect that the USSR "is striving to handle foreign affairs in a new way" seems to be a fair representation of his activities in 1987. He stressed that dialogue is the essence of his new approach, and claimed to have met with no less than 150 delegations from foreign countries during his first two years in office. Gorbachev expressed resentment of the fact that many of his foreign policy initiatives were met with charges from abroad that they were merely acts of propaganda.

A number of domestic reforms are linked closely to the sucess—or failure—of his foreign policy. Foreign trade is a sphere in which the success of his program on joint ventures and on many domestic economic innovations depend. The degree to which glasnost and democ-ratization become part of Soviet domestic practice will help shape contacts with foreign governments and enterprises, for Western firms and officials remain reluctant to deal with the

USSR in many matters as long as the human rights issue hangs as an albatross over their relations. Western business operations need to know how independently their Soviet counterparts really can act.

Soviet publications make much of the intimate relationship between domestic and foreign policy as a Leninist concept. See, for example, O.Selyaninov, "Lenin on the Connection between Domestic and Foreign Policy," *International Affairs* (Moscow), 10 (1987), 57-64, and N.Kapchenko, "The CPSU Foreign Policy Strategy and Today's World," *ibid.*, 65-74. Nevertheless, foreign policy statements by the USSR are much less ideological in content and tone than they were just a few years ago. Even economic integration with socialist countries, which has been granted a renewed priority, is being urged on practical—not ideological—grounds; and the USSR has expressed a readiness to extend aid in the Third World to emerging capitalist countries along with socialist ones.

The following documents emphasize the "New Way of Thinking" and do not dwell on the specifics of Soviet foreign policy as, for example, the ongoing Soviet intervention in Afghanistan or the USA/USSR arms control talks—both subjects which are dealt with at great length elsewhere.

Evgeni Primakov, **A Major Step Forward. Some Thoughts on M.S.Gorbachev's Visit to India** (5 Jan 87)

The Soviet-Indian Aspect

The ties between the Soviet Union and India are strong and go back over many years. Both countries have shown a sense of continuity and consistency in their desire to expand and deepen their mutual relations.

After India won its independence, this line was resolutely followed by Jawaharlai **Nehru** and later by Indira **Gandhi**. Even when the Indian National Congress Party was replaced for awhile by the opposition, Prime Minister Morarji **Desai** let it be known by his visit to Moscow that the policy of maintaining and expanding relations with the Soviet Union cut across party lines and ideologies.

The continuous development of Soviet-Indian relations has a stable objective basis-a unity of similarity in terms of their national interests and no incompatibility between them in the geopolitical sense. For all this, the ten hours of talks between M.S. **Gorbachev** and Prime Minister Rajiv **Gandhi** will almost certainly give fresh impetus to the further all-around strengthening of Soviet-Indian relations. Several things indicate this.

First, India has embarked upon the arduous undertaking of securing economic progress—a task complicated by the remnants of the colonial past and, indeed, by continuous population pressures. This present stage makes economic, scientific and technical assistance from outside vitally important. In recent times, however, the obstacles to obtaining such assistance from the United States have made themselves felt more keenly than ever before. Not, of course, that all forms of cooperation have been blocked by the USA or, for that matter, by all the other advancecd capitalist countries; contacts do exist. Foreign capital and transnational corporations are active in India, and various channels through which India obtains technology remain open and are functioning. But all this comes in doses that suit the neoglobalist philosophy of the United States, which does not want India to be economically, scientifically or technologically independent, let alone capable of enhancing its defence capabilities. This is particularly evident given America's all-out political and military backing for Pakistan, to which the Indian leadership cannot turn a blind eye.

Secondly, the Soviet Union has proved itself a reliable partner. Furthermore, the ongoing acceleration, renewal and reorganization of the Soviet economy, which promises a technological breakthrough within the next few years, promises new levels of cooperation, of which India is well aware.

Thirdly, judging by the public pronouncements of Rajiv **Gandhi** and the nature of the documents he has signed, the Indian leadership favors, and India's interests are well served by, the Soviet Union's foreign policy—notably, its constructive bid to have nuclear weapons eliminated worldwide before the end of the century. This policy appeals to India as an acknowledged and influential power in the non-aligned movement, as one of the chief organizers of the influential Delhi Six, and also as a state that has a considerable stake in international stability.

Fourthly, the Soviet Union, too, is aware of the place and role of India in the modern world. On the political plans, it is not merely a great power in Asiatic terms but also in terms of the world as a whole. Its influence on world affairs continues to mount and further extension of relations with India is seen in the Soviet Union as a strategic objective in terms of securing peace.

Then again, on the economic place, despite incontestable disproportions and other painful legacies of the colonial feudal period, India is rapidly advancing into the modern age, and this, among other things, through the development of scientific methods in industry. This, too, especially given the Soviet Union's economic objectives, stimulates Soviet interest in cooperating with India.

Cumulatively, the above factors are working to encourage closer Soviet-Indian relations. the socio-economic and political distinctions between the two countries are recognized, and there is no question of any convergence in these fields. The times are long gone since it was held that India was developing on something like socialist lines, when this was taken as an important argument in favor of Soviet-Indian cooperation. No one expects either side to forego its national interests; but, despite the differing social systems, the range of coinciding interests is appreciated ever more clearly as is the similarity of perspective and of approaches to the cardinal problems of our time.

Asian Security

Among the key results of the Delhi negotiations is Prime Minister Rajiv **Gandhi**'s support for the idea of an all-embracing system of international security. It is, indeed, only natural that Asian security be seen as an organic part of this concept, though it is certainly the most difficult to achieve. In Europe, in the military field, for example, the issue consists essentially in reducing the confrontation between the two opposing alliances-the Warsaw Treaty Organization and NATO. In political terms it amounts to working out a variety of measures to promote detente and peaceful multilateral cooperation between states belonging to two differing systems— socialist and capitalist.

There is no denying that in Europe, too, these objectives are far from easy to attain; but as I see it, the tasks in Asia are far harder. In Asia, the military problems are not confined to the confrontation between the Soviet Union and the United States. The region of Asia and the Pacific involves the USSR, the USA, and People's Republic of China, India and Japan. In other words, there is more polycentrism here than anywhere else in the world. Asia is also the site of several armed conflicts-that of the Middle East, the Iran-Iraq war, the troubles around Kampuchea and around Afghanistan, and so forth. Furthermore, a number of Asian countries have outstanding territorial claims against one another.

How can we achieve Asian security under these circumstances? Prior to M.S. **Gorbachev**'s visit to India, Western and certain Indian newspapers produced incomplete or incorrect accounts of the Societ position on this score. There were those who suggested that the Soviet Unon wanted mechanically to apply the "European model" to Asia and start the process of convening a conference that would create an Asian security system without further delay. Yet, in his Vladivostok speech [1986], M.S. **Gorbachev** had called for measures that bore no resemblance whatsoever to such a process. Speaking in India, he gave additional explanations outlining the Soviet position as consisting of the following:

(1) without mechanically applying the European experience to Asia, to use all the valuable elements that are likely to take root on Asian soil and thus further the security of the Asian countries;

(2) to advance to this goal in every sphere including bilateral and subregional accords, and, finally (where realistic), to conclude a regional agreement on security;

(3) to consolidate politico-military stability by reducing the strength and limiting the activity of Soviet and US naval forces in the region; to negotiate military confidence-building measures with the United States and interested Asian countries with respect to Asia and the adjoining Indian and Pacific oceans;

(4) to negotiate multilateral accords guaranteeing the security of sea lanes and the sovereignty of littoral states over their natural resources;

(5) to encourage and support movements promoting peace zones, in particular the movement for making the Indian Ocean into a peace zone;

(6) to draw up an international convention aimed at combating terrorism at sea and in the air, and to act upon it.

It is true that other measures could certainly be added, but at the present stage the above are the most important, and there is reason to believe that India is of the same opinion.

One of the most acute regional security problems for India is its relations with Pakistan. Delhi is legitimately disturbed by the vigorous flow of US arms to Pakistan. The Soviet Union is therefore aware of the necessity of buttressing the defence capability of peace-loving India. At the same time, as M.S.**Gorbachev** said at the press conference in Delhi, the Soviet Union favors a peaceful political settlement of the the contentious problems that exist between India and Pakistan. An important element of the new way of things that the Soviet Union is promoting in international affairs is the categorical renunciation of playing on contradictions between countries, of setting one against another, of fishing in troubled waters.

In general, the Soviet Union does not want its relations with any country to be damaging to any other country. All the evidence indicates that India understands and accepts this position. Such, for example, is the Soviet approach to the aim of normalizing and building up relations with China. The same principle applies to Soviet policy regarding India.

A Document of Global Significance

M.S.**Gorbachev**'s visit to India culminated in the signing of the Delhi Declaration, which proclaimed the principles of a nuclear-weapon-free and non-violent world. The document is one of the most important ever signed, and not only because it was signed by the leaders of two countries whose population add up to one billion or one-fifth of the human race. The Delhi Declaration has significance for the whole world.

The 27th Congress of the CPSU declared that we need new political thinking in our time, because, as distinct from the past, the ever-growing sophistication of the weapons of mass destruction calls into question the survival of the human race. The Delhi Declaration may be described as a model of this new political thinking.

Time and time again, the West has advanced variants of "crisis diplomacy" and "rules of conduct" when conflict situations developed into crises threatening to involve the USA and the Soviet Union. As such, they may have made sense. But how much more vital and important it is to work out rules of conduct designed to prevent crises from developing, to settle conflicts, and to halt the slide towards the nuclear abyss. The Delhi Declaration is just such a document.

Its ten principles represent a recipe for peaceful coexistence in our time.

The Declaration states that peaceful coexistence should become the universal standard in international relations, and stresses that this is not simply a universal renunciation of war as a means of resolving controversies, but a vigorous activity aimed at political rather than military solutions to all conflict situations.

For peaceful coexistence to be stable and lasting, each member of the world community must have confidence in its own security. No "balance of terror"—the system that, in effect, currently underlies global security—can yield such confidence. The Delhi Declaration calls for the creation of an all-embracing system of international security to replace that ill-fated "balance".

Peaceful coexistance can be made irreversible provided we can arrive at a nuclear-weapon-free and non-violent world, and this is attainable through a system of immediate, concrete measures aimed at further disarmament. Measures of this kind are suggested in the Delhi Declaration.

Peaceful coexistence is not simply security, however important that may be. The Delhi Declaration calls attention to the need to marshal the material and intellectual resources of all mankind in order to resolve global problems related to food, population, illiteracy, environmental protection, health, and the peaceful use of the world's oceans, sea beds, and outer space.

Alongside the signature of the Soviet Union on the Delhi Declaration stands the no less significant one of India. In due course, other countries will put their signatures to the principles of that historic document. We are quite justified in saying that the Delhi Declaration has its eyes firmly fixed on the future.

Primakov, "Krupnyi shag vpered. Razmyshleniia posle vizita M.S. Gorbacheva v Indiiu," *Pravda* (5 Jan); a partial translation can also be found in FBIS, No. 094 (10 Jan 87), R1-R2. Primakov is A. Yakovlev's successor as director of the Institute for World Economy and International Relations.

M.S. Gorbachev, **For a "Common European Home", for a New Way of Thinking** Speech at Czechoslovakia-Soviet Friendship Meeting (10 Apr 87)
Dear comrades and friends!
I want first of all to thank you wholeheartedly for your cordiality and hospitality, which we have felt since stepping on Czechoslovak soil. And I must tell you of the deep impressions I have received from meetings, and from frank and friendly conversations with residents of Prague, with workers at the CKD shops, and with Party leaders and statesmen. My sincere thanks for this display of friendship for our Party and the Soviet people, for our country.

I am very grateful for this opportunity to address you, Party and state leaders, the representatives of all strata of the Czech and Slovak populations.

Our gathering is a kind of meeting with your country's public at large. I would like to use this occasion to express the Soviet people's strong feelings of friendship for their Czechoslovak brothers.

The character of our relations, the strength of the ties between Czechoslovak and Soviet Communists and between the peoples of the two countries, and the importance of our cooperation were well described by Comrade **Husak**. I fully support his statements. Thank you for the high appraisal of our Party's policy and of the line of the 27th CPSU Congress.

There is every reason to believe that the ties between our Parties and countries will widen and deepend in the near future. The ensurance of just such a development—that was the basic objective of the talks we held yesterday and today here in Prague.

A joint document on the results of the talks will be published, but I can say even now that we have a common approach both to domestic and international affairs. There is a mutual desire to continue the efforts to deepen and enrich all areas of Soviet-Czechoslovak cooperation.

As always, an exchange of information on the course of socialist development and on future plans figured prominently in our conversations. Our Czechoslovak comrades described the implementation of the program outlined by the 17th Congress of the Communist Party of Czechoslovakia.

Each of your successes truly makes us happy. You really have something to be proud of. Present-day Czechoslovakia has won a world-wide reputation as an advanced and economically and socially developed state. Its national economy is distinguished by enviable stability and is free of the burden of foreign debt. Your country possesses a sizeable industrial, scientific and technological potential and has an intensive agriculture. The population's living conditions, the system of education and health services, and the care of children and labor veterans are up to the highest world standards.

All these are the visible gains of socialism, the result of the purposeful work of the working masses led by the Communist Party, and first and foremost, of the efforts of the working class which has proved with its entire history that is is the motive force of social progress in Czechoslovakia and in other socialist countries as well.

In their conversations with us the Czechoslovak comrades did not avoid discussing the problems and difficulties that have still not been resolved. We had a frank talk about this too, as Communists always do. With whom else, if not with friends, can we share our thoughts, joys and concerns, and think together about what else must be done to ensure better working and living conditions.

I do not doubt that all those present in this hall, like most of the working people in your country, are well informed about the processes now going on in our country. The Czechoslovak mass media carry quite extensive and detailed reports on the essence of the restructuring under way in USSR. And still we would like to share our plans and concerns with you.

How are things in our country today?

The idea of restructuring did not emerge all by itself, but was put on the agenda by the entire objective course of society's development and by the country's pressing needs. A person might live in a basically good house with a strong foundation and a reliable framework, but nevertheless be dissatisfied with many aspects of this house, for they no longer meet his increased requirements and needs. Minor repairs are not enough here: a major overhaul is in order.

That is why we have begun on the reliable foundation of socialism the restructuring of the economy and politics, the intellectual and cultural sphere, and the style and methods of Party work.

In the seven decades that have passed since the October Revolution, our people, led by the Communist Party as they traverse a path never crossed before, have honorably endured many ordeals—the imperialist invasion and the most destructive war in history-and have brought their Motherland to the heights of social and scientific progress.

The Soviet Union's achievements in the various spheres of social activity are well known. But it is exactly against the background of these achievements that the serious problems and stagnation phenomena which emerged in the 1970s have become especially intolerable. Quite frankly, sharp contrasts have emerged in our country. For example, the large-scale production of steel, raw-material, fuel and energy resources-the sphere in which we have long been the leaders-versus the shortage of them due to their wasteful and inefficient utilization. Holding one of the first places in the world output of grain versus needing to buy millions of tons of fodder grain annually. The generally recognized achievements of Soviet science, especially in the field of fundamental research, and the largest number of physicians and hospital beds per thousand inhabitants versus the substantial shortcomings in the quality of medical aid.

Our rockets find Halley's Comet with astonishing accurary and fly to rendezvous with Venus, and yet, in contrast to this triumph of engineering and research, there is an obvious lag in the practical application of scientific achievements for economic needs and annoying imperfections in simple household appliances.

Of course, socialism is not to blame for this, as our ideological opponents assert, but rather the blunders in leadership, in governing the country, about which we have frankly told the Party and the people. We have also spoken out openly about the weakening in discipline and the lack of incentives for efficient, creative work.

It is often asked, even by friends, if such scathing criticism of our shortcomings is totally justified and if this doesn't hurt the prestige of the USSR and socialism in general.

We know not only from books, but from our own past experience as well that without criticism and self-criticism socialism cannot devleop successfully or make any progress. Unfortunately, this wise rule was not always followed in practice. The evaluations of the real situation that alleged that all was well did us a disservice: a credibility gap appeared, engendering social passiveness and disbelief in the slogans proclaimed. As for the attraction of socialism, in the end it is created not by words, but by real deeds. The honest admission of our omissions and errors and the resolve to correct them only strengthen socialism's prestige.

Our efforts are not being aimed at reorganizing the entire social mechanism. In the economy, this means a shift from extensive to intensive methods and rapid economic and social growth based on the latest achievements of science and technology.

In the political sphere, this means the promotion of broad democracy and the people's self-government, the eradication of bureaucracy and the abuse of power and the strengthening of socialist law.

In ideology and the spiritual sphere, this means the creative development of Marxist-Leninist theory as a counterweight to dogmatism, and the affirmation of the principles of high morality and socialist values.

In a word, we are in need of radical changes in the organization of all our activities, in social consciousness, in the psychology of people and in their attitude towards work. And these changes must be revolutionary in character.

Is it appropriate to speak of revolutionary changes in a country that has gone through the most profound social revolution in human history, a country where socialism has been built? I think that this is correct, for it accurately reflects the essence of what is taking place.

I will let myself dwell on this question, which is not only of theoretical value, but also of great political importance.

The October Revolution marked a major upheaval in the political realm, in the entire system of social relations. It removed some classes from power—the bourgeoisie and the landowners—and gave the levers of government to others—the proletariat and the poorest peasants. It took away the means of production from private owners and handed them over to the people. The new social and political base of society, created as a result of these radical transformations, was and remains the firm foundation of scialist development.

But in practice there can and does arise within this process the need for periodic renovation of the forms of social relations. Or, as the famous law discovery by Karl **Marx** and the Friedrich **Engels** stipulates, the need to bring these forms into conformity with the develoment level of the productive forces. This task under socialism must in principle be solved constantly, by perfecting particular aspects of social relations. But if the time is ripe for transformations and they are not, meanwhile, carried out, if these transformations are put off and problems accumulate, then radical means must be resorted to, and action must be taken using revolutionary methods.

Lenin used to say that there will be many times when we will have to complete or even remake something (all over again) in our system. This is the task we have set for ourselves today. Accomplishing this task means precisely a fuller unfolding of the creative potential of socialism and the strengthening of our social system. It is fundamentally important that the Communist Party acts as the initiator of the revolutionary process now under way in our country and that all the Soviet people, all classes and all social groups participate in it.

The ultimate aim of the restructuring is to provide a better life for Soviet people and to establish higher models of social organization and social justice. Is this feasible? Our confident reply is yes, it is. The restructuring is not a utopia or a fantasy, but a workable plan based on realistic estimates and a well-considered forecast. Our potentialities are truly enormous. Ths job is to get these social mechanisms that have been working below capacity or have even worked irregularly working at full capacity, to discard that which is impeding our development and to introduce that which leads to acceleration.

So where is the engine that will ensure the success of the restructuring and give us the desired acceleration? We see this engine in the further broadening of our socialist democracy. The direct involvement in the governing of the country of the vast working masses, including that of each and every honest Soviet worker-this is essentially the main idea behind the decisions of the January Plenum Meeting of the CPSU CC. Only a people that possesses full state power and is aware of its being the master responsible for the state of affairs in the country, in every region, in every city, and at every enterprise can solve the complex and diverse tasks of the restructuring and can take Soviet society to new frontiers of social, economic, scientific and technological progress.

The main paths for progress in this direction have also been established. They are the development of all the forms of representative and direct democracy, the universal broadening of self-government, the enhancement of the role of work collectives, the Soviets, and public organizations, and the strengthening of the legal and economic guarantees of personal rights, legality, openness and public control.

Life sometimes outstrips our plans. Thus, changes in the electoral system are still only being worked out, while many Party and public organizations, enterprises, groups of scientific and art workers are already electing leaders in the new way. This was the decision of the working people. We welcome this.

The drive to broaden democracy has opened up a wide range of possibilities for promoting the people's initiative and creativity. Under democracy, everyone is able to reveal his talents.

Meanwhile, the money-grubbers, idlers, demagogues and bureaucrats don't feel very well in this democratic atmosphere and the struggle is being stepped up against such dangerous social ills as alcoholism, drug-addiction and crime. Broader democracy also means an ethical cleansing of society and the restoration of its moral health.

I would like to tell you about our plans for boosting economic efficiency. The key task here is to reach as soon as possible the highest levels of scientific and technological progress— in the fields of informatics and computers, industrial electronics and robots, rotary and rotary— conveyer lines, biotechnology and in other key areas.

As for our investment and structural policy, we are shifting the emphasis from increasing the output of raw materials and fuel to saving resources, from launching new construction projects to modernizing and retooling existing enterprises. Resources are being allocated primarily for the priority line of research and technology. We are even halting the construction and modernization of enterprises that do not promise the best performance possible in terms of technology and the economy.

The projected technological updating of the economy is backed by an unprecedentedly large program for modernizing and developing mechanical engineering. By the 1990s the renovation of engineering products is to have been basically completed and the mass production of the new machinery is to begin for all sectors of the economy.

These are strategic reserves that will begin to be used by the end of this Five-Year Plan period and later. Until then we are emphasizing the organizational, economic, moral and political factors such as tightening discipline and introducing progressive ways of organizing labor and paying wages, including such effective ways as team contracts. You probably already know that we now have a government acceptance inspectorate at enterprises to combat slipshod work and violations of technological standards.

We highly appreciate the active support that the working class and all the working people of our country are giving to these major measures taken in the interests of millions.

We have pinned high hopes on the new system of economic management and incentives based on profit-and-loss accounting. This system is to help harmoniously combine the interests of individual, work collectives and society, those of producers and consumers, and those of the Plan and the market.

The economic autonomy of enterprises and workers' self-management will foster initiative and socialist enterprise and will help the worker feel that he is in charge.

Major changes are also needed in the upper echelons of management. Central agencies must concentrate on strategy and change over to normative planning and performance-based management methods. The authorities in the center must overhaul their relations with the lower echelons. Ministries and government departments must be aware of their responsibility for the scientific and technological progress made in individual sectors and for meeting society's needs.

We have decided to make major changes in the management, planning and administration systems. The difficult process of introducing new methods and refining them after they have been introduced has begun. We are increasingly aware of the need to organize the measures we have taken into a system and create a new structure of management. The forthcoming plenum of the CPSU CC will deal with these matters.

We realize that these are the first steps and that the bulk of the work still lies ahead. We do not think that we have found the absolutely best answers to all the questions life itself has posed for us. And we are not at all urging others to follow indiscriminately our practices. Every socialist country is unique and the fraternal parties shape their policies according to the conditions in the given country. Also, some of the most important issues for the USSR have been or are being handled in other socialist countries in ways different than in the USSR.

However, we are confident that the restructuring process currently under way in the Soviet Union is in conformity with the basic principles of socialism and meets the urgent demands of social progress. Our resolve to reach the targets advanced by the 27th Party Congress and the January Plenum of the CPSU CC is increased many times over by the support our friends and allies give our policy. We greatly appreciate this support.

Communists, friends of socialism, democrats and progressives everywhere applaud the USSR's major restructuring effort, seeing it as a guarantee for the future. Is is only diehard reactionaries and militarists who are seething with malice, for they realize that our plans will make socialism better and increase its appeal.

Western politicians like to speculate about our restructuring process and argue about what kind of a Soviet Union would be best for them: weak or strong, fully democratic—by their yardstick—or not very democratic. Some want to sow seeds of doubt regarding the feasibility of our plans or, resorting to speculation, to provoke discord among the socialist countries. All kinds of opportunists are misinterpreting the objectives of the restructuring and trying to get on its bandwagon.

We must be aware of all this. But we cannot, of course, abandon the perfection of socialist society because of the scheming of our ideological adversaries! We have chosen our road and we shall not depart from it.

And now let me dwell on the issues involved in the cooperation among the socialist countries.

At the working meeting of the leaders of the Communist and Workers' parties of the member countries of CMEA, held last November in Moscow, the unanimous conclusion was made that our cooperation needs greater dynamism and the mechanism of cooperation needs to be restructured.

This is a good basis from which to start. Socialism has become a powerful international entity in the past-war period. A unified network has been established for relations among the fraternal nations along Party, state and public lines. A solid foundation has been laid for the international socialist division of labor. A wealth of experience has been accumulated in the running of the socialist counties' multilateral organizations. Exchanges of scientific and cultural values have expanded considerably.

Today, however, many of the forms and methods of cooperation which were developed in the past no longer meet today's possibilities and demands. One could say that the period of the formation of socialism as a world system is over. A new phase has begun which demands that the entire system of cooperation among our countries be raised to a qualitatively new level.

What is the most important here, what are the major principles of our cooperation?

First and foremost we proceed from the premise that the entire system of the socialist countries' political relations can and must be built on the basis of equality and mutual responsibility. No one has the right to claim special status in the socialist world. We consider the independence of every party, its responsibilty to the people of its own country, and its right to decide the questions of the country's development to be unconditional principles. At the same time, we are of the firm conviction that the community of socialist nations will be successful only if every Party and country is concerned not only about its own interests, but also about the common interests, and only if every Party and country treats its friends and allies with respect and is sure to take their interests into account.

The consensus is that what we need in the sphere of economic relations is consistent observance of the principles of mutual advantage and mutual aid. The fair exchange of nationally produced goods is in full keeping with the nature of socialism and forms the natural basis of integration. At the same time, the very internationalist nature of our social system presupposes assistance to less developed countries so that they could have a fuller part in the socialist division of labor which, eventually, will lead to the evening out of the economic development levels.

And now, finally, about our cooperation in the international arena. This is geared to resolving such issues of vital importance to us as security, the prevention of a nuclear catastrophe and the ensurance of normal external conditions necessary for people's peaceful work. Experience has shown that the more actively and resourcefully each of the socialist states functions, the more successful they are in attaining the common objectives.

We think that one of the major qualitative characteristics of the present stage of cooperation among socialist countries is that the importance of exchanges of experience in socialist development has greatly increased, along with the general conclusions to be drawn therefrom.

Lenin's words that complete socialism can be created only by a series of attempts, each of which, taken by itself, will be one-sided, are well known. History so willed it that the Soviet

Union would be the only country with experience in socialist development at the initial stage of the world socialist system's formation. This experience was naturally perceived as a standard. In our time, a number of fraternal countries have garnered rich experience in socialist development and singular forms and unusual approaches have been employed. No one Party can have a monopoly on truth. And it goes without saying that all of them are vitally interested in using, keeping in mind the specifics of their respective countries, everything valuable in the socialist world.

One can say that a reliable criterion of the seriousness of the ruling Communist Party today is its attitude to its own experience as well as to the experience of its friends. As regards the value of this experience we have one criterion: socio-political practice, the results of socio-economic development, the actual strengthening of socialism.

The assessment and conclusions made at the working meeting of General Secretaries of the CCs of fraternal parties open up a new stage in the expansion of socialist economic integration, including the economic integration between the USSR and Czechoslovakia.

The cooperation between our two countries in the economic sphere is today large-scale. Mutual trade turnover between them will reach 14,000 million rubles this year. But the reserves of integration inherent in the production, scientific and technological potentials of our countries are far from exhausted. And they cannot be used in the old way, on the basis of an extensive increase in the exchange of goods. Economic relations are in need of a major restructuring and qualitative improvement.

It will be possible to make major improvements in the structure of the mutual division of labor as early as the next Five-Year Plan period. We agree with our Czechoslovak comrades that the emphasis here could be put on the development of such forms of integration as specialization and coproduction, especially in machine-building. All indications are that we need greater cooperation in the manufaturing of metallurgical, chemical and power equipment, as well as in the manufacturing of robots, automobile engines, videos, personal comupters and other high-tech products.

Direct industrial, scientific and technological links are being promoted and joint establishments and organizations are being set up in order to resolve these tasks. The first steps have already been taken. I have in mind the "Robot" research and engineering association and the biotechnology laboratory in the city of Nitra. Other agreements have also been signed. And the important thing is to ensure that bureaucratic obstacles, of which unfortunately there are still many, do not impede their implementation.

Of course, promoting direct links, not to mention setting up joint enterprises, is not a simple task by far. Quite a few economic, managerial and legal issues, such as pricing, pay, management organization and the distribution of profits, have still not been settled. Today it is important for all of us to take a constructive approach to these issues, fostering in every way possible the new forms of socialist cooperation. This will be repaid a hundredfold.

Active cooperation between many Soviet and Czechoslovak industrial, research and development establishments should also be promoted within the framework of the Comprehensive Programme for Scientific and Technological Progress of CMEA Member Countries up to the Year 2000.

I'm sure, dear comrades, that, given our close cooperation, our two countries will successfully resolve the tasks now before them, and make the proper contribution to the effort to revitalize and upgrade socialism and consolidate its position.

Dear comrades!

We live in a time in which we are confronted with difficult and, perhaps, even puzzling questions concerning the destiny of the world, the future of the human race.

Today world nations are interdependent, like mountain climbers attached to one rope. They can either climb together to the summit or all fall into the abyss. To prevent this from happening, political leaders must rise above the narrow-minded considerations and realize now dramatic the contemporary situation is. This underscores the vital need for a new way of political thinking in the nuclear age. This kind of thinking alone will lead to all nations taking urgent measures to prevent a nuclear disaster, a disaster that would wipe out the human race.

Not that there is no response to the idea of a new way of thinking. On the contrary, there is a growing acceptance of it in the world. Increasingly, scientists, doctors, people in the arts and in many other professions realize the need to think in a new way; witness the international forum "For a Nuclear-Free World, for the Survival Humanity" recently held in Moscow.

A number of leading Western politicians and statesmen are also showing a new approach to some international issues. But this is just a beginning. Old stereotypes are still strong in the West, and they affect foreign policy. We cannot really speak of the new political thinking as an actual force until the disarmament process finally gets under way.

Can we hope for that? What prospects do we face today?

I can say right off that there is hope for a lessening of the military danger. I base this view partly on the growing understanding around the world that a nuclear conflict would be suicidal, and partly on the opportunities that surfaced at the Reykyavik summit to achieve agreement on the drastic reduction and elimination of the most destructive types of nuclear weapons.

The Soviet Union has stated with full responsibility its desire to look for mutually acceptable solutions to the entire range of nuclear disarmament issues. Deep cuts in offensive strategic weapons remain a pivotal problem. It is well known that we are prepared for the most drastic steps in that direction, including both a 50% cut to be effected over a five-year term and complete elimination in the course of ten years, but under the indispenable condition that the ABM Treaty be strickly honored and that there is no arms race in space.

Hoping to make the first and therefore crucial step towards disarmament, we have offered to achieve an agreement on medium-range missiles. We have duly taken into account views voiced by the world public on this matter, as well as the commitment of our Western counterparts to ridding Europe of such missiles. Paradoxically, however, certain politicans and even governments are dropping their earlier-proposed "zero option" like a hot potato and are trying to attach all sorts of reservations and linkages to an accord on medium-range missiles.

Much is being written and said in the West about shorter-range missiles. We are prepared to resolve the issue in a constructive manner, but not in such a way as to impede an accord on the key issue—that of medium-range missiles.

To promote an urgent accord on medium-range weapons in Europe we offer to begin discussing prospective cuts in missiles deployed in Europe with a range of 500 to 1,000 kilometres and their subsequent elimination, avoiding linkage of the issue either to progress in the discussions on medium-range missiles or their outcome.

The sides could pledge not to increase the number of shorter-range missiles as long as the talks continue. I want to emphasize: we are for deep cuts in shorter-range missiles in Europe and their ultimate elimination, we think we must leave no loopholes in pending accords so as to rule out any chance of their future build-up and improvement.

Upon the signing of an agreement on medium-range missiles, irrespective of the progress on shorter-range weapons, the Soviet Union will, after consultations with the governments of Czechoslovakia and the German Democratic Republic, withdraw from these countries the missiles which were deployed there in reply to the deployment of the Pershing-2s and Cruise missiles in Western Europe.

The implementation of a accord on shorter range missiles should be subject to effective verification, of course, as should agreements on medium-range and strategic nuclear weapons.

In the context of reductions, even more so of elimination of whole classes of nuclear weapons in Europe, verification of future agreements takes on a new meaning. Under such conditions verification becomes one of the most crucial means for achieving security. We will therefore insist on stringent verification measures, not to make verification an end in itself, but to make sure that the sides are honoring their commitments at all stages of nuclear disarmament.

Appropriate verification measures, including on-site inspections, must encompass the missiles and launchers remaining after the reductions, including those on combat duty and at other facilities, i.e. , testing grounds, manufacturing plants, training centres, and so on. Inspectors must also be guaranteed access to the other side's military bases on the territory of third countries. This is necessary to ensure absolute certainty that the agreement is really being fully observed.

Another pressing issue bearing directly on European security is the region's huge troop concentration and tremendous stockpile of conventional arms.

For Europe, of course, just as for the world in general, the elimination of nuclear weapons—strategic, medium-range and shorter-range—is a priority task. This point is hardly arguable. But let us put the question this way: is that vast concentration of tactical nuclear and non-nuclear weapons and of the opposed armed forces on the continent really consistent with the notion of a safe world? The answer, I think, is obvious.

Unfortunately, nothing has been done as yet to amend this highly unsatisfactory situation. We must radically change it by adopting measures for the reduction and subsequent elimination of tactical nuclear weapons and for drastic troop and conventional arms reductions in order to rule out the possibility of a surprise attack.

The Budapest Program of the Warsaw Treaty countries, which provides for the settlement of the issues of troop and conventional arms reductions in one package with tactical missiles, attack aviation, atomic artillery and other tactical muclear forces, could be a major step in that direction. The majority of tactical nuclear systems being "dual-purpose" weapons, meaning that they can carry both conventional and nuclear warheads, dictates the need for this kind of comprehensive approach.

Reducing troops and armaments in Europe requires the joint efforts of all European states, the United States and Canada. Consultations are going on at the moment in Vienna between the Warsaw Treaty and NATO countries. But is it not high time that the foreign ministers of all the states participants in the Conference on Security and Cooperation in Europe got together and decided to begin large-scale negotiations on radically reducing tactical nuclear weapons, troops and conventional arms?

At such negotiations a number of priority measures could be discussed aimed at lowering the level of military confrontation and averting the threat of a surprise attack, and also those involving a mutual withdrawal of the more dangerous, offensive weapons systems from the zone of direct contact between the two military alliances.

The ultimate objective of such talks would be major troop and arms reductions with international verification and on-site inspections. Last year's conference in Stockholm has provided the necessary experience in working out appropriate measures.

Naturally, exchange of relevant data on the armed forces and armaments of the USSR , the United States and the region's other countries would also be necessary.

The West often complains about inequalities and imbalances. Of course, there is a certain asymmetry in the armed forces of both sides in Europe, due to historical, geographic and other factors. We are for redressing the imbalances that exist in some of the elements—not through a build-up by the party trailing behind, but through a build-down by the one that is ahead.

As we see it, the process of lowering the level of military confrontation in Europe should proceed stage by atage, maintaining the balance at each stage at a level of reasonable sufficiency. Such measures could help get the job of reducing the mountain of troops and armaments in Europe under way at last. A truly unique chance for doing that now exists, and it would be unpardonable to miss it.

The goals of stronger European security could also be furthered by such measurers as the establishment of nuclear-free zones and zones free of chemical weapons. I want to say that wo cupport tho proposal addressed to the government of West Germany by the governments of the GDR and Czechoslovakia to establish a nuclear-free corridor in Central Europe. As we all know, the Social-Democratic Party of Germany has contributed to the formulation of that idea.

Subject to withdrawal from such a zone would be all nuclear munitions, including nuclear mines, shorter-range and tactical missiles, atomic artillery, nuclear-capable aircraft of the tactical strike aviation and also nuclear-capable anti-aircraft rocket systems. A considerable share of these weapon systems are "dual-purpose".

For our part, we are prepared to withdraw all Soviet nuclear forces from such a corridor. We are prepared to safeguard and respect its non-nuclear status. Of course, any agreement on such a corridor must provide for the removal of nuclear weapons on the NATO side of the corridor proposed by the GDR and Czechoslovakia.

We think it would be important to implement the proposals of Bulgaria, Romania and Greece on establishing in the Balkans a zone free of nuclear and chemical weapons. Poland's active approach to building confidence on the European continent deserves attention and support, as does the proposal by Finland and other North European countries to set up a nuclear-free zone in that region.

And another burning issue—that of banning chemical weapons. We have consistently spoken for a appropriate international convention to be worked out at an early date, already this year. We are actively negotiating towards this end. I can tell you that the Soviet Union has stopped manufacturing chemical weapons, while other Warsaw Treaty countries have never produced such weaponry, nor maintained them on their territories. The Soviet Union has no chemical weapons beyond its frontiers. As to the stockpiled weapons, I can tell you that we have already started constructing a special facility for their destruction. Its becoming operational will speed chemical disarmament once an appropriate international convention is concluded.

Let us return to the issues of nuclear disarmament. The problem of medium-range missiles in Europe is now the closest to a possible solution. Throughout the world the appeals to the United States to make that first and essential step towards disarmament, thereby helping to create a thoroughly new climate of mutual understanding between the East and West, are growing ever more insistent.

We think it is a crucial political factor that Greece, the Netherlands, Spain, Italy, Finland and many other European countries have spoken in favor of the Euromissile settlement.

We invite Paris, London and Bonn to help, in their turn, to clean Europe of medium-range nuclear missiles and finally move to nuclear disarmament.

Europe is just the place to initiate a new way of political thinking.

In this connection, let me say a few words regarding Europe's role in today's world. It is very appropriate to speak of this here, in Czechoslovakia, the heart of Europe, where stands the stone marking Europe's geographical centre.

We attach primary importance to the European direction of our foreign policy. We do so because our people live on this continent and are, together with others, the lawful heirs to Europe's civilization, and make their important contribution to European progress.

Socialism marked a turning-point in the centuries-long history of this part of the world. Wars were its landmarks for ages. The rout of fascism and the victorious socialist revolutions in Eastern Europe changed the European situation. A mighty force has arisen to break the endless chain of armed conflicts. Our continent has lived in peace for over forty years. We owe that to socialism.

Our continent is divided into opposing military blocs, with stockpiles of weaponry. We are just as resolutely against such a state of affairs as before. We oppose everything that generates a threat of war.

New political thinking has led us to propose the idea of a "common European home". This isn't simply a beautiful fantasy, but a result of a careful analysis of the situation in Europe. The concept of such a "common European home" assumes a degree of integrity, even if its states belong to different social systems and opposing military-political blocs. The concept takes due account of burning problems and the possibility of settling them.

Densely populated and highly urbanized, Europe bristles with weaponry. Armies three million strong oppose each other here. Even a "conventional" war would be fatal. This is not only because conventional weapons are many times more destructive than they were during the Second World War, but also because Europe has about 200 nuclear power units and a ramified network of major chemical works whose destruction would make the continent uninhabitable.

Or take the problem of environmental pollution. Industry and traffic have reached a point in their development where the danger to the environment on our continent is close to critical. This problem has crossed far beyond national borders. It is shared by all of Europe.

It is time we considered the further development of integrative processes in both parts of Europe. The world economy is governed by objective laws. Progress in science and technology compels us to seek mutually beneficial cooperation in one form or another.

The CMEA has invited Europe to build bridges for the sake of all European nations. Hopefuly, the latest economic processes in the socialist community will help to accelerate economic cooperation between both parts of Europe, and enrich it with new content.

From the Atlantic to the Urals, Europe is a cultural-historical entity of rich spiritual significance. It has contributed much to world civilization: the ideas of the Renaissance and the Enlightenment, the humanist tradition and the theory of socialism to which it gave a powerful impetus, and treasures in all fields of science and the arts created by the people of genius from every European nation.

In other words, we are proposing the peaceful progress of European culture, integral and multifaceted, instead of a nuclear holocaust.

Our idea of a "common European home" does not mean that we want to shut anyone out. On the contrary, European progress would mean the continent's even greater contribution to the world's advancement. Europe should not hesitate to help in the battle against hunger, backwardness and foreign debts, or to help in settling armed conflicts.

All European nations without exception undoubtedly want their continent to enjoy a good neighbourly atmosphere of confidence, coexistence and cooperation, which would be a triumph of the new political thinking.

It is not only ethical considerations that demand progress towards that goal. Such progress is in the basic interest of every European nation. For this is an age of interdependence, and increasingly, problems can only be settled through European and world cooperation. For instance, the problems of terrorism, crime, drug addiction and other threats to civilization-we must unite in order to defeat them. AIDS is another disaster threatening the world, and if we don't pool our efforts to combat it today, tomorrow it may be too late.

And the list continues. There are dozens of formidable problems of global proportions that take the entire world community to save. Europe can offer an example to emulate in this. Our countries are fully determined to make a worthy contribution to such a cause.

We regard Czechoslovakia's proposed economic forum in that context. Certainly, such a forum would be instrumental in strengthening the economic security of nations and promotion mutually beneficial cooperation.

Our proposal to hold in Moscow a meeting of the European Conference participants on developing humanitarian cooperation was guided by the same aspirations.

As we see it, any idea that helps to ease confrontation in the slightest is worth proposing and debating. Joint efforts have yielded enough fruit to strengthen the concept of a common European home. Europe's postwar arrangement is universally recognized, and the Helsinki process has gradually allowed confidence among all European states to strengthen.

Working in this direction, finding common interests, reducing the level of military confrontation, and working for a nuclear-free world-this is how we should like to see European affairs conducted.

Dear comrades,

Towards the end of this year we shall celebrate the 70th anniversary of the Great October Revolution. Early next year comes the 40th Anniversary of Czechoslovakia's February Revolution. The two events are closely connected, since they reveal the historical regularities of the transition to socialism, and the rich variety of its forms.

We have done and achieved much together. History poses formidable tasks before the socialist countries. But we are confident that we can accomplish them. The will of our Parties guarantees that, as do the inexhaustible potentials of the socialist system, and the friendship between our nations.

Long live our unity!

Let the fraternal friendship of the Soviet and Czechoslovak peoples grow from year to year!

Our nations have made their choice in favor of socialism. They closely cooperate with each other. Let them enjoy the ever new and rich benefits of that choice and cooperation!

Let there be peace on earth!

M. Gorbachev, "Za 'obshche evropeiskii dom', za novoe myshlenie." *Pravda* and *Izvestiia* (11 Apr); a translation is available in FBIS, No. 069 (10 Apr 87), F4-F7; a condensed translation is in CDSP, 39:15 (1987), 8-11.

M.S. Gorbachev Meets with M. Thatcher (30 Mar 87)

M.S. **Gorbachev** met the British Prime Minister Margaret **Thatcher** in the Kremlin on 30 March1987. Their discussions lasted several hours, during which they touched upon the major issues of our time, including the most important topic, disarmament.

The conversation proceeded on a friendly note, though there were heated moments when each side tried to elucidate the other's different political standpoints and intentions.

The British Prime Minister's visit was important and useful. For no matter how much the two views differ, the Soviet Union and Great Britain are partners in a drive to reduce the danger of war.

The idea behind the dialogue at the highest level is to find a way to achieving a better world.

Mikhail **Gorbachev** made it patently clear that he disagreed with the view that security is based only on a position of strength. He regards this concept as obsolete and as one which has caused enough disasters in the postwar period.

Mrs. **Thatcher's** standpoint favored retaining nuclear weapons, indeed increasing Britain's nuclear stockpile, as she is convinced that the Soviet Union's intentions are to export communism all over the world. She also believed that the threat of a Soviet attack on Western Europe is real.

M.S. **Gorbachev** expounded to Margaret **Thatcher** the philosophical concept of the world today as formulated by the 27th Congress of the CPSU. He thought her fears entirely groundless, and pointed to the objective link between the aims of the restructuring of Soviet socialist society and Soviet foreign policy. Politics in a world in acute danger of war must be based on the coexistence between states with differing social systems and on the right of all countries to choose their own path of development. This is especially important in relation to the developing world.

The Soviet Union recognizes certain historical ties between countries and regions in the contemporary world, both East-West and North-South. But it is possible to balance security, and political and economic interests and it should be our aim to make it so. M.S. **Gorbachev** went on to say that it is a good sign that discussions, sometimes sharp, are taking place, concerning relations between states with differing social systems. Only such discussions can clear away some of the misunderstandings of Soviet intentions.

Though differing over the origins of regional conflicts, **Gorbachev** and **Thatcher** agreed that they should be settled by political means.

Mrs. **Thatcher** spoke at length about the virtues of Western, and especially British democracy. M.S. **Gorbachev** presented strong counter-arguments. The fact that an outspoken exchange of opinions had taken place can only be welcomed.

The uppermost topic in the talks was the curbing of the arms race. The USSR has no intention of going to war against the United States or Britain or anyone else, **Gorbachev** said. This is the spirit behind all the Soviet initiatives and actions. But the Soviet Union is not getting the right response. For two years we have seen the same situation: as soon as the possibility of a positive solution is flickering on the horizon, wheels begin to turn in Washington, London, Paris, and Bonn for finding new objections.

As to the latest Soviet initiative, spanners are being thrown into the works to wreck the medium-range missiles negotiations. When the Soviet Union singled out medium-range missiles from the rest of the package, it had counted on the support of Britain and France. But where is it?

The Soviet Union has gone more than halfway to meet the West. It set aside the issue of the British and French nuclear potentials, although they are still being upgraded. This was quickly forgotten, too, and more concessions are called for.

M.S. **Gorbachev** firmly rejected the view that scrapping nuclear weapons in Europe would give the Soviet Union an edge in conventional arms, thus creating a political threat to Western Europe. He reaffirmed Soviet readiness to start on far-reaching and comprehensive talks on the reduction of conventional arms and armed forces of the two military blocs.

He emphasized that the latest Soviet proposals take account of the apprehensions of Western Europe, and especially Great Britain, including those concerning conventional arms and chemical weapons. For this reason alone the USSR is set in its determination to dispel Western mistrust. This is no bluff. This is the Soviet Union's policy, worked out after long deliberations and endorsed by the country's highest organ of government.

Confidence cannot grow in a vacuum. More talks are necesssary to clear the air. Let's have Stockholm-2 and discuss conventional arms, too. Let's have a comprehensive look at the arms question, leaving nothing aside, **Gorbachev** said.

The Soviet leader informed Margaret **Thatcher** in detail on how the talks in Reykjavik had really proceeded and stressed his view that a unique opportunity for effecting a historic step had been forfeited.

The two sides also discussed in great detail the problem of preserving the ABM Treaty. **Gorbachev** reiterated the Soviet standpoint that the link between reducing strategic offensive arms and the non-militarization of outer space was a strategic solution. That is a package the Soviet Union would never untie, he said. The USSR has worked out ways for depreciating SDI without spending the insane sums of money that America will have to spend on it. But who wants this, except the people who expect billion-dollar profits? M.S. **Gorbachev** called on Mrs **Thatcher** to agree that it is intolerable to let the world, and Europe first of all, be made hostage of the military-industrial complex, which has set its sights on SDI.

At Mrs. **Thatcher's** request, M.S. **Gorbachev** gave a detailed account of the substance, character and progress of the ongoing reorganization in the Soviet Union, dwelling on problems and difficulties that have to be resolved, and on the outloook for Soviet society. The country has come to grips with a paradox that surfaced in the Soviet Union's development when what is probably the world's most educated society could not for a long time properly benefit from its enormous intellectual resources. And we will cope with the problem by broadening democracy and setting in motion the entire potential of the socialist system.

Mrs. **Thatcher** revealed a deep interest in what was happening in the Soviet Union, and said she hoped the undertaking would lead to success. She declared that she, and the West in general, wanted the processes going on in the Soviet Union to yield fruit.

As for the humanitarian issues, **Gorbachev** said, much of what is being said is spurious and deliberately aimed at distorting the image of the Soviet Union. We must resolve all problems by meeting each other halfway, while remaining different, he said. This is an advantage rather than a flaw. The Soviet Union is willing to take a broad approach in politics, for it is aware that interdependence applies not only to Europe, but also to the entire world. Western Europe should waste no more time shaking off its fears of the Soviet Union. It must contribute more to world politics, to the international process. It has every opportunity.

So far, we have the impression that Great Britain and its Prime Minister are not playing the role they could play at the present crucial juncture, when the most urgent thing to do is take the first steps towards reducing nuclear arms.

M.S. **Gorbachev** and Margaret **Thatcher** noted that their frank exchange of opinions yielded mutual understanding and helped close some gaps in the position on scrapping medium-range missiles in Europe. They said they were prepared to take the negotiations on the scrapping of chemical arms to their logical conclusion, and favored solving all problems related to the need for reducing conventional arms and armed forces in Europe.

The talks were open and far-ranging, and highlighted a constructive approach and search for solutions to make the world a safer place to live in.

The two sides said they wanted the political dialogue to expand and deepen, and closer relations to develop between their two countries.

They took note of the need for advancing the Helsinki Agreement in order to build a European home and secure economic, scientific, and cultural progress on the humanitarian side; reuniting families and the opening up of travel was discussed—all that would build confidence and work for better international relations in general.

The Soviet Union is in favor of cooperation with Great Britain, M.S. **Gorbachev** said, adding that he wanted this to expand and deepen, in order to develop mutual trust. He said he hoped that this would, indeed, happen in the long run, benefitting Great Britain, the Soviet Union, Europe, and the rest of the world.

"Vstrecha M.S. Gorbacheva s M. Tetcher," *Pravda* (31 Mar); *Izvestiia* (1 Apr); a translation is also in FBIS, No. 061 (31 Mar 87), G3-G6; a condensed translation is in CDSP, 39:13 (1987), 11-12.

Mikhail Gorbachev Speaks with the Delegation from the House of Representatives of the US Congress (15 Apr 87)

On April 15 M.S. **Gorbachev** received in the Kremlin a US Congressional delegation led by Jim **Wright**, Speaker of the House of Representatives. The delegation of 20 congressmen, which includes leading figures in the House of both the Democratic and Republican Parties, has already had a number of meetings with Soviet representatives in Kiev and Moscow and has begun a discussion on a broad range of issues with a delegation of the USSR Supreme Soviet.

Before the full-fledged meeting, M.S. **Gorbachev** held a brief exchange of opinion with Jim **Wright**, Thomas **Foley**, House Democratic majority leader, and Dick **Cheney**, who represents the Republicans in the delegation.

All the participants in the meeting, many of whom were accompanied by their wives, were then introduced to Mikhail **Gorbachev**.

Mikhail **Gorbachev** welcomed the visit to the Soviet Union of such an authoritative delegation, and congratulated its leader on his recent election to the high post of Speaker of the House. He noted with approval that although the dialogue between the US Congress and the USSR Supreme Soviet is a difficult one, this dialogue is picking up momentum. This assumes greater significance in light of the growing inluence of the US Congress on the policy of the United States and the role played by the USSR Supreme Soviet in the implementation of the restructuring.

You may rest assured, M.S. **Gorbachev** said, addressing the guests, that the reforms launched in our country do not in any way pose a threat to the United States or to anybody else. We welcome your visit, all the more so because we would especially like to be understood now by both the US Administration and the American people. There has been some progress here recently and we have noticed that. But this has so far had little impact on actual cooperation, the level of which does not at all correspond to either the potentialites or the duties of both our countries. The role of the USSR and the USA that history itself predetermined obliges them to know each other better. This is the only way the possibility of surprises in politics can be eliminated as well as the possibility of decisions that could have extremely bad consequences for both countries and for all of mankind. If each of our countries is to be confident in its future, we need mutual understanding and cooperation. Therefore, no matter how difficult it may be, no matter how complicated relations may become at times due to foreign and domestic factors, we must never lose sight of this goal.

M.S. **Gorbachev** voiced the hope that with the election of a new leadership to Congress, the process of the Soviet-American dialogue would become more regular, more intensive and more productive.

M.S. **Gorbachev** briefed the congressmen in detail on the contents of the talks with George **Shultz**. He suggested that both countries are close to an agreement on the issue of medium-range missiles in linkage with shorter-range missiles. He emphasized the Soviet union's willingness to scrap, on a unilateral basis, this type of nuclear weapon in the course of several months, or roughly a year. In connection with this he once again expressed his perplexity at the "upside-down logic" in the attempts to respond to the Soviet Union's new major initiative with an arms buildup.

This initiative provides yet another chance for making a radical change in international relations. The true intentions and capabilities of making real steps towards international security will have to be judged by whether or not the chance is used. Our steps, our initiatives, M.S. **Gorbachev** said, are motivated by our country's deep, fundamental interests and are closely linked to the period which it is going through now. They are the result of a new thinking which involves understanding the responsibility the current state of the world situation has placed on the great powers.

M.S. **Gorbachev** dwelt upon the problem of reducing the triad of the strategic offensive weapons. He reaffirmed the immutable connection between the resolution of that issue and observance of the ABM Treaty. He briefed the Congressmen on the proposal made to George **Shultz** in regard to ABM research and stressed that our specified compromise proposal on this issue is also motivated by the desire to find a way out.

M.S. **Gorbachev** refuted the conjectures about the Soviet Union's alleged violations of the SALT-2 agreements, which come in waves in the United States and at times heavily influence the US Congress. He pointed out that the Soviet Union had considerably reduced its strategic weapon systems in order to be within the limits set by these agreements.

M.S. **Gorbachev** listened attentively to the ideas put forth by the US Congressmen, in particular to Jim **Wright**'s statement that the Soviet Union's year-and-a-half-long moratorium on nuclear explosions might yield tangible, practical results in the near future, even though the US government never joined it. In response to the call the Speaker of the House made to the Soviet leadership to continue observing the restrictions imposed by the SALT-2 Treaty, M.S.**Gorbachev** said that he welcomes his words. But in all fairness, the Congress ought to address the US Administration with the same call, for it openly violated the treaty in 1986.

M.S.**Gorbachev** supported all the kinds of cooperation proposed by Jim **Wright**: cooperation along parliamentary lines, exhanges among citizens and students, television link-ups, cultural ties, and so on. He found interesting the idea of conducting joint studies of Soviet and American regions of the North which are adjacent to one another, and of launching a joint project for fighting famine and disease in Africa, although all this, naturally, requires concrete studies by experts.

We are sincere in our proposal to exchange experience in the solution of various problems, including national ones. But if this is to be useful, speculation and attempts to interfere in the internal affairs of others must come to an end and policing and preaching ways must be eliminated. The "enemy image" must be abandoned. All these belong to the past and cannot be allowed in the present situation. Every people and every country must be given attention; we must all practice self-criticism as regards ouselves and the problems of our countries. We must treat each other with a sense of responsibility, whether we like each other or not.

Humanitarian issues and matters of emigration were touched upon. The congressmen basically said that the changes taking place in the Soviet Union are helping to strengthen the atmosphere of confidence and this, in turn, will help find a solution to many problems, both bilateral and international.

But it must be noted that thus far methods that can only impede positive processes are still being used in the handling of human rights issues. We witness actions about which, as M.S.**Gorbachev** put it, it is awkward even to speak, as, for instance, when dissatisfied persons are specially sought out among the Soviet people and are used to present a distorted image of Soviet society.

In conclusion, M.S.**Gorbachev** noted that there are no issues that are taboo in the dialogue with the US Congress and with the West in general. And personal contacts are very important, for policy is not something abstract. It always has its messengers, specific persons who enjoy confidence or are even invested with power. And when they know each other, they can predict what will be the response to a certain action, to a certain political move. This helps to make a correct appraisal of the conditions under which decisions are made and the consequences of these decisions. So, in this respect, too, the visit of such an important delegation from the USA is clearly a positive event.

The detailed conversation with the congressmen was marked by mutual awareness of the importance of normalizing Soviet-American relations and by a desire to search for ways of solving urgent international problems.

Anatoli **Dobrynin**, Lev **Tolkunov**, Yuri **Dubinin** and Georgi **Arbatov** participated in the meeting.

"Beseda M.S. Gorbacheva s delegatsiei palaty predstavitelei kongressa SShA," *Pravda* (16 Apr); a translation also is in FBIS, No. 072 (15 Apr 87), A1-A6.

Evgenii Primakov, **A New Philosophy of Foreign Policy** (10 Jul 87)

I

Often it is possible to hear: From the first days of Soviet power, our country has been struggling for peace among peoples—what kind of new approaches, and, especially, what kind of new foreign-policy philosophy can one talk about, when peace remains the main goal of the USSR's foreign policy?

Certainly, the continuity of the Soviet state's foreign-policy line is indisputable. But all the same, at present qualitatively new conditions, as M.S. **Gorbachev**, General Secretary of the CPSU CC, has repeatedly emphasized, make it necessary—perhaps more insistently necessary than at any earlier time in our history—to treat a whole series of key problems of international life in an innovative way.

As the world approached the 1980s, it was rapidly losing faith in the incontrovertibility of its long-held perspective. The problem of survival, which had existed before this as well, was now posed acutely as the problem of preserving human civilization from inevitable destruction in the event of a thermonuclear war.

Relatively recently, we still said—and not only said but were certain of it—that if the imperialist forces committed aggression against us, they would be consumed in the flames of the war they had kindled. In the past, this conclusion had every right to existence. Its function in giving warning to a potential aggressor was obvious, but perhaps the main thing consisted in the mobilizing power of such a statement: It pointed to the need for increasing fighting efficiency as virtually the only means of maintaining the country's security at the proper level.

Comparatively recently, we considered peaceful coexistence a respite that would be cut short by those who again would try to strangle the first country of victorious socialism. This situation also insistently dictated the requirement for an increase in fighting efficiency, once again as virtually the only means of ensuring the country's security.

Today such assessments and interpretations are clearly insufficient and inaccurate. While maintaining the great importance of improving its defense capability, the Soviet Union is bringing to the forefront political means of ensuring its security. We are operating in a fundamentally new situation: With the accumulation of weapons of mass destruction in such quantities and of such high quality, there can be no victors in a thermonuclear war. Thus, peaceful coexistence is becoming a vital requirement for the survival of mankind. Isn't it natural for such a situation to insistently demand not only new methods of carrying out foreign policy, especially for the great powers, but also a fundamentally new philosophy of approaching international problems?

But why did this indisputable, true idea begin to materialize intensively in our country only after the April (1985) Plenum of the CPSU CC? It must be admitted that the experience of preceding development, when we sometimes used the epithet "historic" in vain, is by no means conducive to the setting of new "historic landmarks." However, in this case the matter at hand is not an artificially designated but a real Rubicon, from which a radical qualitative change began in the USSR's domestic and foreign practice alike.

Perhaps the organic link between our country's domestic policy and its foreign policy has never before been so obvious as it is today. After the April plenum, a course was set aimed at the acceleration of the economic, social and political development of the Soviet Union. The vital need for this course is indicated by, for one thing, the dynamics of such a largely synthesizing index as the growth rate of national income. Over the decade preceding the April plenum (1976-1985), the growth rate of the USSR's national income was only 30% higher than the corresponding index for the US. Consequently, the gap in national income between the USSR and the US not only did not decrease, it increased.

The 27th CPSU Congress and the subsequent plenums of the CC have defined that main instrument of accelerating development as the democratization of all spheres of the vital activity of Soviet society. Openness, criticism, self-criticism, emancipation, the abandonment of the "presumption of infallibility"—all this, initially directed inward, has also been reflected in the practice of working out and implementing our state's foreign-policy course.

There is also another side to the unity of domestic and foreign policy, one that has been manifest in an especially clear way since the April plenary session of the CPSU CC: Given the emphasis on a sharp speedup in the economic and social development of the Soviet Union, the need for optimizing the ratio between productive expenditures and military expenditures necessary for the country's reliable security has been manifest as never before.

II

The new foreign-policy philosophy of the Soviet Union, as I have already said, was not born in a vacuum, but current conditions have not allowed it to become a new edition of reformulated or even better formulated old principles. The 27th Party Congress placed the emphasis on the dialectics of the unity and struggle of opposites in today's world. The CC's Political Report corrected the distortion under which the confrontation of two world systems—the socialist and capitalist—was regarded apart from their interdependence. It is important to note that the growing interrelationship of today's world is expressed not only in the problem of survival, which is common to all parts of the world, but also in the existence and development of a world economy and in the presence and intensification of common human interests related to the preservation of the environment, the overcoming of the backwardness of the so-called Third World, victory over disease, the discovery of new sources of energy, the use of space and the oceans for the progress of mankind, and so on.

An understanding of all this is the basis of the new foreign-policy philosophy.

Of course, one of the main questions that cannot be ignored is the extent to which this philosophy takes into account the social changes that are objectively occurring in the world and what the relationship is between ideology and foreign policy. The social renewal of the world is an objective requirement for mankind. But the mechanism of this renewal—both revolutionary and evolutionary—is put in motion by the internal contradictions in each country. Back at the dawn of Soviet power, V.I. **Lenin** spoke out resolutely against the transformation of the first state of victorious socialism into an exporter of revolution to other countries, limiting its international influence to the framework of setting an example. Excluding the export of revolution is an imperative of the nuclear age.

At the same time, the stabilization of the international situation not only should not but also cannot take place through the artificial maintenance of the social status quo, or, in other words, through the export of counterrevolution.

Interstate relations in general cannot be the sphere in which the fate of the confrontation between world socialism and world capitalism is decided. However, the US administration still does not understand this. During the **Reagan** Presidency, the ideological coloring of USA foreign policy has become even more striking. For example, the deliberate orientation of USA foreign policy toward a struggle against socialist principles and the socialist social order in a number of states is well known.

The new philosophy of foreign policy should be realized above all in new conceptual approaches to the problem of security.

First, political measures are coming to the fore in the matter of ensuring the security of states. The functional goal of these measures is to work out accords and agreements between the USSR and the USA and between the Warsaw Treaty and NATO on arms reduction, confidence-building measures, and the elaboration and introduction of a system of comprehensive international security.

There is no reliable alternative to political measures in the field of security. At present, strategic parity exerts a deterrent effect, but even now military measures of deterrence—a balance of terror—are not only immoral but unreliable. But if the level of parity continues to rise with the bringing into "deterrence" of new spheres—space, for example—and new means—"exotic weapons," for example—the risk of war in general will increase. The adoption of major military decisions will become the prerogative of technology, and that will push the world to the brink of catastrophe.

Second, certain changes should involve the military component, which in present conditions still retains its significance in ensuring the security of the two opposing sides. The recent conference of the Political Consultative Committee in Berlin adopted a document on the Warsaw Treaty countries' military doctrine. Its defensive nature is not just declared but is realized: in refusing to be the first to use nuclear weapons or to begin military operations at all, and in introducing the principle of the reasonable sufficiency of military means into military planning and construction. The military doctrine is aimed at preventing an all-destroying war. At the same time, its function should be to rebuff an aggressor if one encroaches on the sovereignty of the countries of the socialist commonwealth. The dialectical interconnection of these two aims is obvious. Readiness to rebuff an aggressor is a very important means of deterrence.

At a time when there are still nuclear weapons in the world, the strategic parity between the USSR and the US, despite all its minuses, will continue to retain its stabilizing significance. At the same time, in this period sufficiency will be realized while lowering the level of parity. This should be the main trend. The Soviet proposals of 15 January 1986, which provide for the **step-by-step** elimination of nuclear weapons and other means of mass destruction, serve this end.

When we talk about reasonable sufficiency in this period, what comes to the fore, despite the great importance of the quantitative aspect of strategic parity, is its qualitative aspect: the inability of either side to avoid a devastating retaliatory strike. Western experts estimate "unacceptable" damage to be the loss of 60% of all industry and about 30% of the population.

After the elimination of nuclear weapons, stability in the world will be maintained primarily with the help of political and legal means, international means included, while military means will be based on reasonable sufficiency to repel an attack.

One should, obviously, talk about yet another aspect of the problem of sufficiency: In the past, in a number of cases we agreed to the "rules of the game" that were imposed on us, which consisted in symmetrical responses to American steps in the arms race. In this way, the US, one can assume, deliberately wanted to wear us out economically. Now, with the introduction of the principle of reasonable sufficiency, the US will find such attempts very difficult.

However, the accumulated sufficiency for defense is not of such magnitude that it gives us safety once and for all, and it by no means predisposes us to put our minds at ease and sit with hands folded. It is known that the USSR maintained a unilateral moratorium on nuclear tests for 18 months, while tirelessly suggesting to the US that it follow our example—something that won very broad support among the public of various countries—but we were forced to give up the moratorium when a limit appeared beyond which continued nuclear tests by the United States could have damaged the Soviet Union's security.

As sufficiency increases, a countertrend also develops—the improvement of destabilizing systems, such high-precision and powerful systems as the MX, Trident-2 and cruise missiles. For this reason, the sufficiency gained for defense does not in the least reduce the urgency of the need to halt and curtail the arms race.

Third, the security of some cannot be ensured at the expense of the security of others. Searches for military superiority will inevitably backfire against those who make them—after all, the other side will inevitably search for and find countermeasures, and, in critical situations, it may even not want to be "driven into a corner." The new foreign-policy philosophy takes into account the need to recognize the objective nature of the national interests of various countries and not to oppose them but to conduct a painstaking search for areas of combining these interests.

The universalization of security and the rejection of one-sided security are also expressed in the idea of its comprehensive nature. On the one hand, a security system should encompass all geographic regions: in other words, the entire globe. On the other, it should extend to various spheres: not only the military but the economic, the political and the humanitarian.

Fourth, the new foreign-policy philosophy should include a rejection of the horizontal spread of confrontation between the USSR and the USA and between the Warsaw Treaty and NATO. In this connection, giving up the examination of regional conflicts through the prism of Soviet-American rivalry, which obstructs their settlement, is assuming special importance. However, the US is sticking to this line. Suffice it to cite two examples: Washington is not supporting but, in point of fact, is undermining the efforts of the Contadora group—a number of Latin American states that are advancing realistic proposals the adoption of which would eliminate the conflict around Nicaragua and stabilize the situation in Central America. Instead, the USA is whipping up tension around that country, supporting the Samosista bandits, from whom the so-called contras have been recruited, supplying them with up-to-date weapons, and urging on neighboring Honduras against Nicaragua by giving the former military assistance.

The USA position with respect to a settlement of the "Afghan problem" is also indicative. At the very time when the leadership of Afghanistan has adopted a course aimed at national reconciliation and has opened the doors of the government to all forces that are prepared to uphold the country's national interests, American deliveries of arms to the Afghan rebels have reached a peak.

III

Has the USSR's new philosophical approach to questions of foreign policy been productive?

Of course, the situation is still a long way from one in which these new approaches and the new political thinking are adopted by the American leadership. More than that, the US is putting up a fierce resistance to the Soviet course. Militarism doesn't surrender so easily, and it isn't going to its positions.

All the same, the situation today is far from what it was two or three years ago. It is becoming more and more difficult for the anti-Sovieteers in the West to maintain their artificially created image of the USSR as a bellicose undemocratic state that threatens the world and thinks about nothing but expansion. Public opinion polls in the US and West European countries indicate that this myth is not holding up when it collides with restructuring and openness in the USSR and the Soviet Union's constructive foreign policy. The popularity of the Soviet state and our leadership abroad—among the masses and among intellectuals—is unprecedented.

Of course, a change in public opinion in the West still does not create, in and of itself, a decisive swing in the international situation, but important preconditions are forming for such a swing. The flexibility and constructiveness of the Soviet Union's foreign-policy measures are certainly conducive to the development of this trend.

Sometimes these measures are perceived as concessions on the part of the USSR. In fact, one must say in no uncertain terms that in a number of cases concessions are made and are designed to reduce things to a common denominator whre the problem of arms reduction is concerned. But these are concessions to common sense, not a retreat under US pressure. When we agree to the "zero option" for operational-tactical missiles in Europe as well.

Events have shown that stagnation is by no means a synonym for firmness; the flexible and dynamic Soviet proposals, which are being constantly developed and clarified, keep the militaristic forces that felt much more comfortable without this flexibility and this dynamism on our part in a state of constant tension and give them no respite.

We proceed from the premise that the new approaches to international affairs that are guiding Soviet policy are not just the only approaches possible in today's conditions but also are perfectly realistic.

Primakov, "Novaia filosofiia vneshnei politiki," *Pravda* (10 July); a complete translation can also be found in CDSP, 39:28 (1987), 1-4. On this editorial see Viktor Yasmann, "The 'New Political Thinking' and the 'Civilized' Class Struggle," RFE/RL, 292/87 (29 Jul 87)

M.S.Gorbachev, **The Reality and Guarantees of a Seoure World** (17 Sept 87)

The 42nd Session of the United Nations General Assembly opened a few days ago. It is this fact that suggested the idea of this article. Objective processes are making our complex and diverse world increasingly interrelated and interdependent. And it increasingly needs a mechanism which is capable of discussing its common problems in a responsible fashion and at a representative level and being a place for the mutual search for a balance of differing, contradictory, yet real, interests of the contemporary community of States and Nations. The United Nations Organization is called upon to be such a mechanism by its underlying idea and its origin. We are confident that it is capable of fulfilling that role. This is why in the first autumn days, when the period of holidays is over and the international political life is rapidly gathering momentum, when an opportunity for important decisions in the disarmament field can be discerned, we, in the Soviet leadership, deemed it useful to share our ideas on the basic issues of world politics at the end of the 20th century. It seems all the more appropriate since the current session of the United Nations General Assembly is devoted to major aspects of such politics.

It is natural that what we would like to do first of all in this connection is to try and see for ourselves what the idea of the establishment of a comprehensive system of international security—the idea advanced at the 27th CPSU Congress—looks like now that 1.5 years have passed since the Congress. This idea has won backing from many states. Our friends—the socialist countries and members of the Non-aligned Movement—are our active co-authors.

The article offered to you deals primarily with our approach to the formation of such a system. At the same time it is an invitation for the United Nations member-countries and the world public to exchange views.

I

The last quarter of the 20th Century has been marked by changes in the material aspect of being—changes revolutionary in their content and significance. For the first time in its history mankind became capable of resolving many problems that were hindering its progress over centuries. From the standpoint of the existing and newly-created resources and technologies there are no impediments to feeding the population of many billion, from giving it education, providing it with housing and keeping it healthy. Given obvious differences and potentialities of some or other peoples and countries, there has taken shape a prospect for ensuring befitting conditions of life for the inhabitants of the earth.

At the same time dangers have emerged which put into question the very immortality of the human race. This is why new rules of coexistence on our unique planet are badly needed and they should conform to the new requirements and the changed conditions.

Alas, many influential forces continue adhering to outdated conceptions concerning ways for ensuring national security. As a result the world is in an absurd situation whereby persistent efforts are being made to convince it that the road to an abyss is the most correct one.

It would be difficult to appraise in any other way the point of view that nuclear weapons allegedly make it possible to avert a world war. It is not simple to refute it precisely because it is totally unfounded. For one has to dispute something which is being passed off as an axiom—since no world war has broken out after the emergence of nuclear weapons, hence, it is these weapons which have averted it. It seems that it is more correct to say that a world war has been averted despite the existence of nuclear weapons.

Some time ago the sides had several scores of atomic bombs apiece, then each came to possess a hundred nuclear missiles, and finally, the arsenals grew to include several thousands of nuclear warheads. Not so long ago Soviet and American scientists specially studied the issue of the relationship between the strategic stability and the size of the nuclear arsenals. They arrived at the unanimous conclusion that 95% of all nuclear arms of the USA and the USSR can be eliminated without stability being disrupted. This is a killing argument against the "nuclear deterrence" strategy that gives birth to a mad logic. We believe that the 5% should not be retained either. And then the stability will be qualitatively different.

Not laying claims to instructing anyone and having come to realize that mere statements about the dangerous situation in the world are unproductive, we began seeking an answer to the question if it was possible to have a model for ensuring national security which would not be fraught with the threat of a worldwide catastrophe.

Such an approach was in the mainstream of the conceptions that had taken shape during the process of evolving the new political thinking permeated with a realistic view of what is surrounding us and what is happening around ourselves—the view characterized by an unbiassed attitude to others and the awareness of our own responsibility and security.

The new thinking is the bridging of the gap between the Word and the Deed. And we embarked on practical deeds. Being confident that nuclear weapons are the greatest evil and the most horrible threat we announced a unilateral moratorium on nuclear tests which we observed, let me put it straight, longer than we could have done. Then came the January 15, 1986 statement putting forth a concrete program for a stage-by-stage elimination of nuclear weapons. At the meeting with President **Reagan** in Reykjavik we came close to the realization of the desirability and possibility of complete nuclear disarmament. And then we made steps which made it easier to approach an agreement on the elimination of two classes of nuclear arms—medium—and shorter-range missiles.

We believe that it is possible and realistic. in this connection I would like to note that the government of the FRG assumed the stand which is conducive to it to a certain extent. The Soviet Union is proceeding from the premise that a relevant treaty could be worked out before the end of the current year. Much has been said about its potential advantages. I will not repeat them. I would only like to note that it would deal a tangible blow at concepts of limited use of nuclear weapons and the so-called "controllable escalation" of a nuclear conflict. There are no illusory intermediate options. The situation is becoming more stable.

This treaty on medium -and shorter-range missiles would be a fine prelude to a break-through at the talks on large-scale-50%-reductions in strategic offensive arms in conditions of the strict observance of the ABM Treaty. I believe that, given the mutual striving, an accord on that matter could become a reality as early as in the first half of the next year.

While thinking of advancing toward a nuclear weapon-free world it is essential to see to it even now that security be ensured in the process of disarmament, at each of its stages, and to think not only about that, but also to agree on mechanisms for maintaining peace at drastically reduced levels of non-nuclear armaments.

All these questions were included into proposals set forth jointly by the USSR and other socialist countries at the United Nations—the proposals for the establishment of a comprehensive system of international peace and security.

What should it be like, as we see it?

The security plan proposed by us provides, above all, for continuity and concord with the existing institutions for the maintenance of peace. The system could function on the basis of the U.N. Charter and within the framework of the United Nations. In our view, its ability to function will be ensured by the strict observance of the Charter's demands, additional unilateral obligations of states as well as confidence measures and international cooperation in all spheres-politico-military, economic, ecological, humanitarian and others.

I do not venture to foretell how the system of all-embracing security would appear in its final form. It is only clear that it could become a reality only if all means of mass annihilation were destroyed. We propose that all this be pondered by an independent commission of experts and specialists which would submit its conclusions to the United Nations Organization.

Personally, I have no doubt about the capability of sovereign states to assume obligations in the field of international security already now. Many states are already doing this. As is known, the Soviet Union and the People's Republic of China have stated that they will not be the first to use nuclear arms. The Soviet-American agreements on nuclear armaments are another example. They contain a conscious choice of restraint and self-limitation in the most sensitive sphere of relations between the USSR and the United States. Or take the Nuclear Nonproliferation Treaty. What is it? It is a unique example of a high sense of responsibility of states.

In the present-day reality there already exist "bricks" from which one can start building the future system of security.

The sphere of the reasonable, responsible and rational organization of international affairs is expanding before our very eyes, though admittedly timidly. Previously unknown standards of openness, of the scope and depth of mutual monitoring and verification of compliance with adopted obligations are being established. An American inspection team visits an area where exercises of Soviet troops are held, a group of United States congressmen inspects the Krasnoiarsk Radar Station, American scientists install and adjust their instruments in the area of the Soviet nuclear testing range. Soviet and American observers are present at each other's military exercieses. Annual plans of military activity are published in accordance with accords within the framework of the Helsinki process.

I do not know a weightier and more impressive argument in support of the fact that the situation is changing than the stated readiness of a nuclear power voluntarily to renounce nuclear weapons. References to a striving to replace them with conventional armaments in which there supposedly exists a disbalance between NATO and the Warsaw Treaty in the latter's favor are unjustified. If an imbalance or disproportion exists, let us remove them. We do not tire saying this all the time and we have proposed concrete ways of solving this problem.

In all these issues the Soviet Union is a pioneer and shows that its words are matched by its deeds.

What about the question of the comparability of defence spending? Here we will have to put in more work. I think that given proper effort already within the next two or three years we will be able to compare the figures that are of interest to us and our partners and which would symmetrically reflect the expenditures of the sides.

The Soviet-American talks on nuclear and space arms, the convention on the prohibition of chemical weapons which is close to being concluded will intensify, I am sure, the advance to détente and disarmament.

An accord on "defence strategy" and "military sufficiency" could impart a powerful impulse in this direction. These notions presuppose such a structure of the armed forces of a state that they would be sufficient to repulse a possible aggression but would not be sufficient for the conduct of offensive actions. The first step to this could be a controlled withdrawal of nuclear and other offensive weapons from the borders with a subsequent creation along borders of strips of rarefied armaments and demilitarized zones between potential, let us put it this way, adversaries. While in principle we should work for the dissolution of military blocs and the liquidation of bases on foreign territories and the return home of all troops stationed abroad.

The question of a possible mechanism to prevent the outbreak of a nuclear conflict is more complex. Here I approach the most sensitive point of the idea of all-embracing security: Much will have to be additionally thought out, re-thought and worked out. In any case, the international community should work out agreed upon measures for the event of a violation of the all-embracing agreement on non-use and elimination of nuclear arms or an attempt to violate this agreement. As to potential nuclear piracy, it appears possible and necessary to consider in advance and prepare collective measures to prevent it.

If the system is sufficiently effective then the more it will provide effective guarantees of averting and curbing a non-nuclear aggression.

The system proposed by us precisely presupposes a definiteness of measures which would enable the United Nations Organization, the main universal security body, to ensure its maintenance at a level of reliability.

II

The division of the world's countries into those possessing nuclear weapons and those not possessing them has split also the very concept of security. But for human life security is indivisible. In this sense it is not only a political, military, juridical but also a moral category. And contentions that there has been no war for already half a century do not withstand any test on the touchstone of ethics. How come there is no war? There are dozens of regional wars flaring in the world.

It is immoral to treat this as something second rate. The matter, however, is not only in the impermissible nuclear haughtiness. The elimination of nuclear weapons would also be a major step towards a genuine democratization of relations between states, their equality and equal responsibility.

Unconditional observance of the United Nations Charter and the right of peoples' sovereignly to choose the roads and forms of their development, revolutionary or evolutionary, is an imperative condition of universal security. This applies also to the right to social status quo. This, too, is exclusively an internal matter. Any attempts, direct or indirect, to influence the development of "not one of our own" countries, to interfere in this development should be ruled out. Just as impermissible are attempts to destabilize existing governments from outside.

At the same time the world community cannot stay away from inter-state conflicts. Here it could be possible to begin by fulfilling the proposal made by the United Nations Secretary General to set up under the United Nations Organization a multilateral center for lessening the danger of war. Obviously, it would be feasible to consider the expediency of setting up a direct communication line between the United Nations headquarters and the capitals of the countries that are permanent members of the Security Council and the location of the chairman of the Non-aligned Movement.

It appears to us that with the aim of strengthening trust and mutual undrstanding it could be possible to set up under the aegis of the United Nations Organization a mechanism for extensive international verfication of compliance with agreements to lessen international tension, limit armaments and for monitoring the military situation in conflict areas. The mechanism would function using various forms and methods of monitoring to collect information and promptly submit it to the United Nations. This would make it possible to have an objective picture of the events taking place, to detect preparations for hostilities early on, to prevent a sneak attack, to take measures to avert an armed conflict, or prevent one from expanding and becoming worse.

We are reaching the conclusion that wider use should be made of the institute of United Nations military observers and United Nations peace-keeping forces in disengaging the troops of warring sides, observing ceasefire and armistice agreements.

And of course at all stages of a conflict extensive use should be made of all means of a peaceful settlement of disputes and differences between states and one should offer one's good offices, for mediation with the aim of achieving an armistice. The ideas and initiatives concerning nongovernmental commissions and groups which would analyze the causes, circumstances and methods of resolving various concrete conflict situations appear to be fruitful.

The Security Council permanent members could become guarantors of regional security. They could, on their part, assume the obligation not to use force or the threat of force, and to renounce demonstrative military presence. This is so because such a practice is one of the factors which exacerbate regional conflicts.

A drastic intensification and expansion of the cooperation of states in uprooting international terrorism is extremely important. It would be expedient to concentrate this cooperation within the framework of the United Nations Organization. In our opinion, it would be useful to create under the UNO's aegis a tribunal to investigate acts of international terrorism.

More coordination in the struggle against apartheid as a destabilizing factor of international magnitude would also be justified.

As we see it, all the above-stated measures could be organically built into an all-embracing system of peace and security.

III

The events and tendencies of the past decades have expanded this concept, imparting new features and specificities to it. One of them is the problem of economic security. A world in which a whole continent can find itself on the brink of death from starvation and in which huge masses of people are suffering from almost permanent malnutrition is not a safe world. Neither is a world safe in which a multitude of countries and peoples are stifling in a noose of debt.

The economic interests of individual countries or their groups are indeed so different and contradictory that consensus with regards to the concept of the new world economic order will be hard to achieve. We do hope, however, that the instinct of self-preservation should snap into action here as well. It is sure to manifest itself if it becomes possible to look into the chain of priorities and see that there are menacing circumstances, and that it is high time that the inert political mentality inherited from past views of the outside world be abandoned. This world has ceased to be a sphere divided by the big and strong into domains and spheres of interest.

The imperatives of the times compel us to institutionalize many common-sense notions. It is not philanthropy which prompted our proposal to agree on the reduction of interest payments under bank credits and the elaboration of extra benefits for the least developed nations. This proposal should provide everyone a secure future. If the debt burden of the developing world is alleviated, the chances for such a future will grow. It is also possible to limit debt payments by each developing country to the share of its annual export earning without detriment to development, accept export commodities in payment for the debt, remove protectionist barriers on the borders of creditor-nations and stop adding extra interest when deferring payments under debts.

There may be different attitudes to these proposals. There is no doubt, however, that the majority of international community members realize the need for immediate actions to alleviate the developing world's debt burden. If that is so, it is possible to start working out the program through concerted effort.

These words, "through concerted effort" are very important for today's world. The relationship between disarmament and development, confirmed at the recent international conference in New York, can be implemented if none of the strong and rich keep themselves aloof. I already expressed the view that Security Council member states, represented by their top officials, could jointly discuss this problem and work out a coordinated approach. I confirm this proposal.

Ecological security. It is not secure in the direct meaning of the word when currents of poison flow along river channels, when poisonous rains pour down from the sky, when the atmosphere polluted with industrial and transport waste chokes cities and whole regions, when the development of atomic engineering is justified by unacceptable risks.

Many people suddenly have begun to perceive all that not as something abstract, but as quite a real part of their own experience. The confidence that this won't affect us, characteristic of the past outlook, has disappeared. They say that one thorn of experience is worth more than a whole wood of instructions. For us, Chernobyl became such a thorn.

The relationship between man and the environment has become menacing. Problems of ecological security affect everyone—the rich and the poor. What is required is the global strategy of environmental protection and the rational use of resources. We suggest starting its elaboration within the framework of the UN special program.

States already exchange appropriate information and notify international organizations of developments. We believe that this order should be legitimatized by introducing the principle of governments' annual report about their conservationist activity and about ecological accidents, both those that occurred and those that were prevented on the territory of their countries.

Realizing the need for opening a common front of economic and ecological security and starting its formation mean defusing a delay-action bomb planted deep inside mankind's existence by history, by people themselves.

IV

Human rights. One can name all the top statesmen of our times who have threatened to use nuclear weapons. Some may object: It is one thing to threaten and another to use. Indeed, they haven't used them. But campaigning for human rights is in no way compatible with the threat to use weapons of mass destruction. We hold it is unacceptable to talk about human rights and liberties while intending to hang in outer space overhead the "chandeliers" of exotic weapons. The only down-to-earth element in that "exoticism" is the potentiality of mankind's annnihilation. The rest is in dazzling wrapping.

I agree: The world cannot be considered secure if human rights are violated in it. I will only add: If a large apart of this world has no elementary conditions for a life worthy of man, if millions of people have the full "right" to go hungry, to have no roof over their head and to be jobless and sick indefinitely when treatment is something they cannot afford, if, finally, the basic human right, the right to life is disregarded.

First of all, it is necessary that national legislation and administrative rules in the humanitarian sphere everywhere be brought in accordance with international obligations and standards.

Simultaneously it would be possible to turn to coordinating a broad selection of practical steps, for instance, to working out a world information programme under the UN auspices to familiarize peoples with one another's life, the life as it is, not as someone would like to present it. That is precisely why such a project should envisage ridding the flow of information of the "enemy image" stereotypes, of bias, prejudices and absurd concoctions, of the deliberate distortion and unscrupulous violation of the truth.

There is much promise in the task of coordinating unified international legal criteria for handling in the humanitarian spirit issues of family reunification, marriages, contacts between people and organizations, visa regulations and so on. What has been achieved on this account within the framework of the all-European process should be accepted as a starting point.

We favor the establishment of a special fund of humanitarian cooperation of the United Nations formed from voluntary state and private contributions on the basis of the reduction of military spending.

It is advisable that all states join the UNESCO conventions in the sphere of culture, including the conventions on protection of the world cultural heritage, on the means of prohibition and preventing the illicit import, export and transfer of ownership of cultural property.

The alarming signals of the recent times have pushed to the top of the agenda the idea of creating a world-wide netweork of medical cooperation in treating most dangerous diseases, including AIDS, and combating drug addiction and alcoholism. The existing structures of the World Health Organization make it possible to establish such a network at relatively short notice. The leaders of the world movement of physicians have big ideas on this account.

Dialogue on humanitarian problems could be conducted on a bilateral basis, within the forms of negotiation that have already been established. Besides, we propose holding it also within the framework of a international conference in Moscow: We made the proposal at the Vienna meeting in November last year.

Pooling efforts in the sphere of culture, medicine and humanitarian rights is yet another integral part of the system of comprehensive security.

V

The suggested system of comprehensive security will be effective to the extent in which the United Nations, its Security Council and other international institutes and mechanisms will effectively function. It will be required to enchance resolutely the authority and role of the UN, the International Atomic Energy Agency. The need for establishing a world space organization is clearly felt. It could work in the future in close contact with the UN as an autonomous part of its system. UN specialized agencies should also become regulators of international processes. The Geneva Conference on Disarmament should become a forum that would internationalize the efforts on transition to a nuclear-free, non-violent world.

One should not forget the capacities of the International Court either. The General Assembly and the Security Council could approach it more often for consultative conclusions on international disputes. Its mandatory jurisdiction should be recognized by all on mutually agreed upon conditions. The permanent members of the Security Council, taking into account special responsibility, are to make the first step in that direction.

We are convinced that a comprehensive system of security is at the same time a system of universal law and order ensuring the primacy of international law in politics.

The UNO Charter gives extensive powers to the Security Council. Joint efforts are required to ensure that it could use them effectively. For this purpose, there would be sense in holding meetings of the Security Council at Foreign Ministers' level when opening a regular session of the General Assembly to review the international situation and jointly look for effective ways for its improvement.

It would be useful to hold meetings of the Security Council not only at the headquarters of the UN in New York, but also in regions of friction and tension and alternate them among the capitals of the permanent member states.

Special missions of the Council to regions of actual and potential conflicts would also help consolidate its authority and enhance the effectiveness of decisions adopted.

We are convinced that cooperation between the UN and regional organizations could be considerably expanded. Its aim is the search for a political settlement of crisis situations.

In our view, it is important to hold special sessions of the General Assembly on the more urgent political problems and individual disarmament issues more often if the efficiency of latter's work is to be improved.

We emphatically stress the need for making the status of important political documents passed at the United Nations by consensus more binding morally and politically. Let me recall that they include, among others, the Final Document of the 1st Special Session of the United Nations General Assembly devoted to disarmament, the Charter of Economic Rights and Obligations of States, and others.

In our opinion, we whould have set up long ago a world consultative council under the UN auspices uniting the world's intellectual elite. Prominent scientists, political and public figures, representatives of international public organizations, cultural workers, people in literature and the arts, including laureates of the Nobel Prize and other international prizes of world-wide significance, eminent representatives of the churches could seriously enrich the spritual and ethical potential of contemporary world politics.

To ensure that the United Nations and its specialized agencies operate at full capacity one should come to realize that it is impermissible to use financial levers for bringing pressure to bear on it. The Soviet Union will continue to cooperate actively in overcoming budget difficulties arising at the United Nations.

And finally, about the United Nations Secretary-General. The international community elects an authoritative figure enjoying everybody's trust to that high post. Since the Secretary-General is functioning as a representive of every member-country of the Organiztion all states should give him the maximum of support and help him in fulfilling his responsible mission. The international community should encourage the United Nations Secretary-General in his missions of good offices, mediation and reconciliation.

Why are we so persistent in raising the question of a comprehensive system of international peace and security?

Simply because it is impossible to put up with the situation in which the world has found itself on the threshold of the third millenium—in the face of a threat of annihilation, in a state of constant tension, in an atmosphere of suspicion and strife, spending huge funds and quantities of work and talent of millions of people only to increase mutual mistrust and fears.

One can speak as much as he pleases about the need for terminating the arms race, uprooting militarism, or about cooperation. Nothing will change unless we start acting.

The political and moral core of the problem is the trust of the states and peoples in one another, respect for international agreements and institutions. And we are prepared to switch from confidence measures in individual spheres to a large-scale policy of trust which would gradually shape a system of comprehensive security. But such a policy should be based on the community of political statements and real positions.

The idea of a comprehensive system of security is the first plan for a possible new organization of life in our common planetary home. In other words, it is a pass into the future where security of all is a token of the security for everyone. We hope that the current session of the United Nations General Assembly will jointly develop and concretize this idea.

M. Gorbachev, "Real'nosti i garantii bezopasnogo mira," *Pravda* (17 Sep); *Izvestiia* (18 Sep); a full translation can also be found in FBIS, No. 180 (17 Sep 87), 23-27.

M. Titarenko, **The USSR and China. For the Further Development of Cooperation** (26 Sept 87)

The past few years have been marked by a substantial improvement of relations between the USSR and the CPR. The outlines of bilateral cooperation are becoming ever wider and are being filled with new content. The level of contacts between the two countries' statesmen is rising.

There have been regular exchanges of visits by the two countries' deputy heads of government since December 1984. The Ministers of Foreign Affairs of the USSR and the CPR have had a number of meetings during sessions of the UN General Assembly. Political consultations on bilateral and highly important international questions are being held on a regular basis, border talks have resumed, and the Soviet-Chinese Commission on Economic, Scientific and Technical Cooperation has been holding meetings.

Among the significance events in the normalization of relations between the USSR and China was the renewal, after more than 20 years of the interuuption, of contacts between legislative bodies. At present these contacts have taken on an annual character. Thus, in July 1987, a delegation from the USSR Legislative Commission and the Nationalities Soviet of the USSR Supreme Soviet, headed by G.P.**Razumovskii**, met with Chinese parliamentarians in the CPR. In Augusat of this year, delegates of the All-China Peoples' Assembly, led by director U.**Venem**, sat in on our Commission for Nationality Affairs.

A new consular treaty went into effect in 1987, in accordance with which a USSR Consulate General in Shanghai and a CPR Consulate General in Leningrad have been opened. A two-year (1986-1987) plan of cultural cooperation is being successfully implemented, and ties are being organized between trade union, women's and young people's organizations and friendship societies.

The volume of reciprocal trade is growing at a rapid pace. Between 1981 and 1986 it increased tenfold in value terms, reaching 1.822 billion rubles. The facts of widening and deepening Soviet-Chinese cooperation cannot help but bring deep satisfaction to our country.

It is obvious that the improvement of relations between the two largest socialist powers is of great importance for the fate of world peace and the cause of socialism. History has placed a special responsibility on the Soviet and Chinese peoples, above all for preserving the atmosphere of peace in Asia.

The development of Soviet-Chinese relations during the implementation in both countries of large-scale economic reforms aimed at improving the socialist system and disclosing its advantages presupposes a broad exchange of experience in construction in all fields and is a powerful stimulating factor making for the accelerated realization of the goals and tasks of restructuring and modernization in the area of achieving a fundamental upswing in the well-being of the Soviet and Chinese peoples. In the coming 21st Century, the outcome of the historic peaceful competition between the two social and political systems will depend in large part on the successes of restructuring in the Soviet Union and of reforms in the CPR and other socialist countries. We do not consider it useful to divide the spheres of political relations and the concrete connection in different fields and, as M.S.**Gorbachev** emphasized in his answers to the Indonesian newspaper *Merdeka*, he does not intend to hold back from political dialogue.

Set forth by M. S. **Gorbachev** in Vladivostok, the idea of a comprehensive approach to ensuring peace and security in the Asian-Pacific region has a very direct bearing on Soviet-Chinese relations. In the final analysis, the part of the Vladivostok proposals having to do with the CPR not only envisages the complete elimination of the negative incrustations that formed in Soviet-Chinese relations in the previous period but also, based on the experience and lessons of the past, makes it possible to fully set in motion the enormous potential of cooperation and good-neighbourliness.

The operation of such objective factors as the common nature of social and economic systems, geopgraphic proximity, the identical nature of priorities in strategic tasks aimed at the acceleration of social and economic development and the self-improvement of socialism and historically evolved mutually complementary nature of the Soviet and Chinese economies creates clear and very promising prospects in this area.

The most important task of the present stage in the development of Soviet-Chinese relations is ensuring the uninterrupted nature and dynamism of this process and creating the most favorable conditions possible for its qualitative development.

In the **political field,** the Soviet Union's efforts are directed toward the further expansion of mutual understanding with China, raising the level of political contacts, and strengthening the contractual-legal foundations of mutual relations. In our opinion, the necessary precon-ditions exist for changes for the better in the field of political relations between the two countries and for narrowing the sphere of disagreements. The most important condition for the realization of these changes is strict observance of the principles of equality, independence, respect for each other's sovereignty, mutual trust, and consideration for the national interests of each side.

The Soviet Union is fully cognizant of the role of the CPR as a great power that pursues and independent foreign policy aimed at strengthening peeace throughout the world. Our country has invariably supported and continues to support China's efforts to protect and defend its state sovereignty, including its rightful position with respect to Taiwan as an inalienable part of the CPR.

While welcoming the enhancement of China's constructive role in international affairs, the Soviet Union sees it as a key factor of international and regional security. Without China—a great socialist power that was present at the birth of the five principles of peaceful coexistence and possesses a far-flung system of international ties and interests—at present a just and lasting solution of international problems, on both an Asian and a global scale, is essentially impossible.

The sphere of coincident approaches by the USSR and the CPR to cardinal theoretical problems of the construction of socialism and interntional development is gradually expanding. It will be no exaggeration to say that, on a number of these problems, the degree of proximity that has now been reached is the greatest in the past 25 or even 30 years.

There is a growing similarity in our two countries' approaches to the most important question of our time—the problem of war and peace. Both countries regard the need for a peaceful international situation, an active struggle for peace and peaceful coexistence, as the only alternative for the survival of mankind, as decisive factos and conditions for national and worldwide development.

The USSR and the CPR—the two socialist nuclear powers—have unilaterally decided not to be the first to use nuclear weapons. Soon after the Soviet Union proclaimed a moratorium on nuclear tests, the CPR government announced that it would refrain from nuclear weapons tests in the atmosphere.

The Soviet Union and China actively support the process of creating regional zones free of nuclear weapons. Similar principles of international relations were formulated and introduced in the political practices of socialist countries, and therefore such socialist states as the USSR and the CPR are fully capable of setting an example for the entire world by their further development.

There is a similarity in the two countries' positions with respect to the impermissibility of the militarization of outer space, as well as concerning the settlement of such acute regional conflicts and problems as the Middle East problem, the situation in southern Africa and that in Central America. With respect to the situation in the Asian-Pacific region, our countries hold similar positions as far as their negative attitude toward the processes of militarizing the region and attempts to achieve some kind of monopoly there in determining the fate of the region and the prospects for its development are concerned. At the same time, one can note a difference in the approaches of the USSR and the CPR to such an important question as the causes of the arms race and the tension in the world. China adheres to the viewpoint that "the two superpowers" bear the responsibility for this. On this question, new, more realistic and more differentiated evaluations of the foreign-policy strategy of the Soviet Union and the other world powers have recently appeared in the CPR.

In the field of **confidence-building**, the Soviet Union, as is known, proceeding from the idea of providing a comprehensive system of international security, has proposed and is carrying out a whole complex of interrelated bilateral and multilateral measures.

They are aimed at achieving a fundamental improvement of the military-political situation in the Asian-Pacific region, ending the arms race there, and setting up multilateral, mutually advantageous cooperation....

The USSR's readiness to eliminate 100 warheads on medium-range missiles in Asia, provided that the US takes a similar action, creates a real prospect for a substantial change in the military-political situation in the Asian-Pacific region and for a significant rise in the leevel of security for the states there, including China. On the whole, the Chinese leadership has reacted positively to the new Soviet initiative.

As far as confidence-building measures in the field of bilateral Soviet-Chinese relations are directly concerned, the Soviet Union, attaching great importance to a radical reduction of armed forces and conventional arms in Asia, has proposed that concrete steps aimed at a proportionate lowering in the level of the two countries' ground forces be discussed with the CPR. The reaching of an accord between the two powers in this area would not only be a substantial contribution to the cause of detente in the region and the world over but also would set an excellent example for other countries, and it would facilitate an easing of tension in China's relations with India and Indochinese countries.

In his Vladivostok speech, M.S. **Gorbachev** formulated a proposal concerning drawing the boundary line along the main navigation channel (or in midstream, for nonnavigable rivers) of border rivers. The border talks between the USSR and the CPR, which resumed in February 1987, are proceeding in a businesslike atmosphere. They are of great importance for both countries and are facilitating an improvement in the overall atmosphere of bilateral ties.

Seeking to make a concrete contribution to the improvement of the situation in Asia and to the creation of an otmosphere of confidence in this vast region, the Soviet government decided, after pertinent consultations with the governments of the Mongolian People's Republic and the Democratic Republic of Afghanistan, to withdraw from Afghanistan six regiments of the limited contingent of Soviet troops temporarily stationed in that country, and also announced a significant reduction in Soviet military personnel in Mongolia and carried out that reduction.

China considers the so-called "Kampuchean problem" to be one of the main obstacles on the path to the complete normalization of political relations between the USSR and the CPR. Our countries' approaches to this problem differ substantially, but the main thing is that both of them are in favor of a political settlement of the problem. We believe that the course of national reconciliation advanced by the government of the People's Republic of Kampuchea and the withdrawal, agreed upon with Kampuchea, of Vietnamese troops by 1990 can serve as a real path to such a settlement. In our view, such a course in no way damages the interests of China and corresponds to the long-term goals of creating a favorable, peaceful and stable situation on the CPR's southern borders.

Vast possibilities and potentials are included in the **growth of economic relations between our countries.**

The Soviet Union respects the strategic goal, advanced by the CPR's leadership, of modernizing the country and eventually building a socialist society worthy of a great people. The wide-ranging exchange of experience in socialist construction that is projected during the implementation of large-scale economic reforms in both countries is capable of becoming an important factor in accelerating our development and in saving time and economizing on human and material resources. Also, the CPR is watching the progress of restructuring in our country with great interest.

The current volume and depth of Soviet-Chinese economic relations are far from commensurate with their potential. In conditions of the operation of such a favorable factor as the historically evolved mutually complementary nature of the Soviet and Chinese economies, the USSR's share of China's foreign trade in 1985 was only 3.2%, while other shares were 28% for Japan, 11.7% for the countries of the European Economic Community and 10.8% for the US.

An important reserve for ensuring a breakthrough in this area of cooperation is the wide-ranging technical reconstruction of industry, including the participation of Soviet organizations in the modernization of industrial enterprises in the CPR built during the 1950s with the Soviet Union's assistance. Under a July 1985 agreement, the USSR will provide assistance in building seven new and reconstructing 17 existing enterprises in the fields of power engineering, ferrous and nonferrous metallurgy, machine buiding and the coal and chemical industries, including such major enterprises as the Anshan, Baotou and Wuhan Metallurgical Combines, the Luoyang Tractor Plant, and others. In turn, the Soviet Union is interest in China's experience in the technical reconstruction of a wide range of light- and food-industry enterpreises. This oommitmont impoœes a groat rosponsibility on the relevant Soviet departments and enterprises, since our participation in the modernization of Chinese industrial facilities will take place in conditions—greatly different from the situation in the 1950s—of competition not only from Western firms but also from organizations of other socialist countries and of China itself.

Border trade, which is developing rapidly, is a promising new element in the system of trade and economic ties between the USSR and the CPR.

The active search for new forms of trade, economic, scientific and technical ties, including such forms as joint societies and enterprises, the collective development of the natural resources of vast border areas and the development of transportation and the infrastructure, is opening up great potential for further stepping up the pace of trade and economic cooperation. The restructuring of foreign economic acitivity now under way in the USSR, combined with the advantages of the policy of expanding foreign economic ties that is being pursued by China, can give a new impetus to cooperation in these fields. In this connection, the signing of an agreement on cooperation between the top planning agencies of the USSR and the CPR, signed during the September 1986 visit to the CPR of N.V.**Talyzin**, Vice-Chairman of the USSR Council of Ministers, is very important.

A problem of enormous national-economic and social importance for both countries, a problem that can be tackled on a broad scale only in conditions of the closest interaction, is the comprehensive development and rational utilization of the water resources of the Amur, the Irtysh, the Ili and other border rivers. According to calculations by Chinese specialists, five large and medium-sized hydroelectric stations could be built in the Amur Basin alone. This also could eventually create conditions for joint economic activity in developing the natual resouces of adjacent areas of the USSR and the CPR.

The commissioning of a section of railway that will link the CPR's Xinjiang-Uygur Autonomous Region with Soviet Central Asia will open up broad prospects for the development of cooperation. Chinese specialists note that in the future this route may become a "new Great Silk Road" and the shortest transport artery linking China with the countries of Europe and the Middle East.

Needless to say, the development of economic ties between the USSR and China is encountering certain difficulties along the way. In essence, it could not be otherwise, in view of the incrustations accumulated between the two countries in the past. The insufficiently developed nature of the contractual-legal foundations of long-term mutual relations, the uncoordinated nature of the two countries' economic planning, a certain constriction in export opportunities, and so on, are making themselves felt. However, for the most part these difficulties are growing pains. They are fully surmountable, and they put no fundamental barriers in the way of a substantial development of economic ties between the USSR and the CPR. Contacts in the fields of science, culture and sports and ties between public organizations are now an important component of Soviet-Chinese relations. Ties between the two countries' creative unions, exchanges of trade union delegations and delegations of social scientists and specialists in the field of the natural sciences, ties between friendship societies, exchanges of students and instructors between the Soviet Union and China and other kinds of contacts have received significant development.

The Soviet Union welcomes the development of the CPR's relations with the countries of the socialist commonwealth and calls for the earliest possible normalization of relations with the Indochinese countries.

We respect the path of socialist modernization that the CPR has chosen, a path that envisages broad participation in international economic exchanges and the development of contacts with Western countries. The Soviet Union does not link prospects for improved Soviet-Chinese relations with any country or group of countries. However, we expect the same approach from our Chinese partners. We are convinced that this model of building relations corresponds to the realities of today's world and the principles of new political thinking.

The Soviet Union is not inclined to idealize the picture of Soviet-Chinese relations. It is often rather motley. We do not close our eyes to the differing approaches and divergences that exist between our countries, but the Soviet side does not regard them as something that is fatally inevitable. Our path is a constant search for way of overcoming existing contradictions. The Soviet leadership has repeatedly emphasized its readiness "at any time and at any level, to discuss with China in the most serious way questions of additional measures to create an atmosphere of good-neighborliness."

We have taken the first large steps on the road to cooperation and good neighbourliness, on which [relations] of our countries and people's began. This is only the beginning of a great step. As M.S.**Gorbachev** notes, "Thinking about the future, it is possible to say that the potential of cooperation between the USSR and China is vast. They are great because such cooperation serves the interests of both countries, because the common road for both of our peoples are socialism and peace.

Titarenko, "SSSR—Kitai. Za dal'neishee rasvitie sotrudnichestva," *Izvestiia* (26 Sep); a condensed translation can be found in CDSP, 39:39 (1987), 8-9. Titarenko, a Doctor of Philosophical Science, is director of the USSR Academy of Sciences' Institute of the Far East.

M.S.Gorbachev's Statement on Soviet Television (14 Dec 87)

Good evening, dear Comrades!

The visit to the United States is over. The way to it was far from simple: there was Geneva and Reykjavik, an intensive dialogue between the leaders of the Soviet Union and the United States, and intensive diplomatic negotiations.

We constantly cooperated with our allies and had an active exchange of views with the leaders of other states. We lent a particularly attentive ear to the sentiments of people internationally, workers in science and culture, and representatives of the different political trends advocating peace. All that enriched our idea of the processes taking place in the world and infused us with confidence that we are acting in the right direction.

Thus we went to Washington with the mandate of our people and our allies. We also took into consideration the sentiments and aspirations of millions of people of goodwill the world over.

Our visit to the United States was preceded by thorough preparations and numerous comprehensive discussions at the Politburo of the principles which would guide us when we got there. We once again calculated everything fromthe military-technical viewpoint. Philo-sophically and politically, these preparations were based on the decisions of our Party's 27th Congress and the program for a nuclear-free world proclaimed on 15 January 1986.

The content and results of our visit are known. The President of the United States and I have signed a Treaty on the elimination of intermediate-range and shorter-range missiles. The agreement reached on that issue is a major international event, a victory for the new political thinking.

The intensive talks, which took up most of the time, centered on the issues of the reduction of strategic offensive weapons. We have reaffirmed our preparedness for a 50 percent cut in the strategic offensive weapons on condition the ABM Treaty be preserved in the form it was adopted in 1972, which is reflected in the joint statement on the results of the Summit. We again brought into sharp focus the issue of the need for an early conclusion of a treaty to end nuclear tests. We discussed thoroughly the questions of the elimination of chemical weapons and the reduction of conventional arms and armed forces in Europe.

In general, our aspiration was that the issues of disarmament, the elimination of the nuclear threat, lessening of tensions and confrontation in the world, and strengthening of the new approaches in building international relations would be brought to the fore. These things actually happened in the course of the talks.

The main outcome of the Washington visit is, certainly, the signing of the Treaty on the elimination of two classes of nuclear missiles. This is the first step toward a real destruction of the nuclear arsenal. Only yesterday that seemed utopian to many people. Today it is becoming fact.

They say that just a modest step has been made—humanity will get rid of only 4 percent of nuclear weapons. Yet, it should not be forgotten that scientists have estimated that it would take only 5 percent to destroy every living thing on earth.

But this is not all. The Treaty has shown for all to see the possibility of a turn from the arms race to disarmament. Now the point is to preserve the atmosphere which made it possible to conclude the Treaty, and to continue to act constructively and consistently. To this end it is necessary, in the first place, to give the Treaty its legitimate force by ratifying it.

As far as the USSR Supreme Soviet is concerned, I hope that it will support the Treaty, since this is the will of our people. It is also important that many deputies to the USSR Supreme Soviet, its commissions, in the first place foreign affairs commissions, took an active part in examining issues connected with the drafting of the Treaty.

We know that struggle around ratification is under way in the United States. But we also know that the American people support the Treaty. We felt this most acutely once again when staying in America.

This is a very important period. And I wish to tell you that awareness of the importance and pivotal character of this moment was manifest in full measure at the meeting in Berlin of leaders of the Warsaw Treaty countries. Having unanimously endorsed the results of the visit in the adopted communiqué, they resolutely declared that at the new stage they will continue acting in concord in the interests of disarmament and international cooperation.

It can be said that there was a very positive response to the results of the Washington meeting in most countries of the world.

But when old views are being changed, the resistance of those who link their political and material well-being with them invariably increases. Scarcely three days have passed since our return home, but already certain circles in the United States and in other Western countries are rallying to prevent change for the better. Voices calling on the leadership of the United States not to go too far, to halt the process of disarmament, sound ever louder. Demands are being made for urgent measures to "compensate" for the elimination of intermediate-range and shorter-range missiles by bringing new nuclear forces closer to Europe and into Europe and by modernizing the nuclear and other armaments remaining in Europe. Certain persons even try to assert that the talks in Washington have removed differences on such a problem as SDI and under that pretext make calls for speeding up work on that program.

I must say outright that these are dangerous tendencies and that they should not be underestimated. They may undermine the nascent turn in the process of demilitarization of international relations.

We hope that the world community, above all the peoples of the United States and the Soviet Union, and the sound forces in all countries will redouble their efforts to save the first sprout of nuclear disarmament which has pushed its wasy through concrete walls of prejudice and stereotypes of hostility. It is now important for all to work together to promote the deepening of positive tendencies and the strengthening of mutual understanding and cooperation. The agreements reached offer a historic chance for all humanity to start getting rid of a heavy burden of militarism and war which has taken a horrible toll in human life and rolled back economic development and material culture, shackled freedom and the spiritual and social creativity of peoples.

At the discussion of each question during the visit, the issue of the role and responsibility of the United States and the Soviet Union as to how they should interact and build their relations, came up one way or another. This is important for both our countries and the whole world. Awareness of this is growing not only in the Soviet Union, but also in the United States. We noticed this when meeting and talking with political leaders and public figures, with representatives of science and culture.

During our talks with the President and other American politicians, we emphasized more than once that the new realities must be grasped and that our two countries must act in accordance with them, coexist, and show respect for the choice of each nation.

We said outright that we came to Washington not to engage in altercations and mutual recriminations, as is often the inclination of the US side, but to engage in real politics.

I think that all of you, Comrades, would be interested in learning how the USA Administration responded, what its positions and its view of our relations were, whether there were any changes in this respect. Our delegation more than once exchanged views related to this question, a question that was not easy to comprehend. I should tell you: if we firmly adhere to the hard facts and do not indulge in exaggerations, it is too early today to speak about a drastic turn in our relations. It is still too early.

Nevertheless, I want to point out that the dialogue with the President and other political figures of the United States was different than before—it was more constructive. After talking with representatives of intellectual and business circles and the mass media, I formed the impression that changes do take place. What riveted our attention most was the mounting wave of goodwill on the part of ordinary Americans—as they learned through television and the press our objectives, our true views, what we want and how Soviet people really regard America and Americans.

I said to the President: the Soviet leadership is ready to transfer our relations into a channel of mutual understanding, into a channel of constructive interaction in the interests of our countries and the entire world. It is precisely within this context that we raised other issues, inviting the USA Administration to join us in the search for solutions to the most acute problems of present-day politics.

We persistently raised before our counterparts the issue of our two countries' possibilities in promoting the political settlement of regional conflicts.

Although we did not move far ahead in this area, the discussion of these issues has clarified the situation and gives us grounds to believe that the dialogue can be continued.

The Joint Soviet-US Summit Statement, as you noticed, gives much place to the development of bilateral relations between the USSR and the United States. Specific agreements were reached on a number of issues—in the sphere of scientific cooperation, cultural exchanges and individual contacts. In the talks and especially during the meeting with businessmen we had an interesting discussion of issues relating to expanding economic cooperation and trade. Positive changes in that sphere would be of major importance for an improvement in the entire atmosphere of Soviet-American relations and the situation in the world, for that matter. However, as I have already said, enormous efforts will be required here from both sides, primarily, from the American side, through whose fault there appeared a large number of artificial barriers in the way of normal and mutually beneficial economic ties.

I would like, dear Comrades, to make one more point. The visit to the United States has demonstrated very plainly the extent of attention with which the entire world is watching our restructuring drive. Numerous questions of a most diverse character are asked. What is restructuring? Is there resistance to it? How determined are we to carry restructuring through? Won't we stop half-way? Is the nation willing to accept such a profound renewal of Soviet society?

This interest in what is happening in Soviet society along the lines of restructuring is genuine and sincere. It attests to the recognition of our country's role in the world today. And for all of us it is a further reminder that the more successful we are in furthering the revolutionary cause of restructuring, the better the state of international affairs will be.

Such is the situation today, such is the dialectics of the world development—one more proof of the interconnection and integrity of the present-day world despite its inherent diversity and contradictory nature. We should understand this well and bear this in mind as we tackle specific practical tasks in every town and village, in every work collective and countrywide.

Let me say words of gratitude to the Soviet people for their growing contribution to the restructuring drive, for their practical deeds in response to the Party's call for a revolutionary renewal of society, for their active participation in the transformations that have begun, for their support of the efforts of the CC and the government in the work for peace. Without all this there would have been no success in the recent talks, and those talks could have hardly taken place at all.

Thank you, Comrades!

Let us congratulate ourselves on this success and let us keep working.

Good night.

"Vystuplenie M.S. Gorbacheva po sovetskomu televideniiu," *Pravda* (15 Dec). This was the final statement to the Soviet public after the week of summit meetings with President Reagan in Washington, 7–14 December 1987. Documents of this meeting can be found in both English and Russian in, *USSR-US Summit. Washington, December 7–10 , 1987. Documents and Materials*, Moscow: Novosti, 1987; *Vstrecha v verkakh. Vashington, 7–10 dekabria 1987 goda. Dokumenty i materialy*. Moscow: Novosti, 1987; a translation is also in FBIS, No. 240 (15 Dec 87), 14–16.

Chapter 9

ENVIRONMENTAL AND HEALTH ISSUES

The protection of the environment against the ravages of uncontrolled and resource development has been a sphere for increasingly vitriolic debate in the USSR during the 1980s. The Chernobyl disaster was only the most spectacular of recent ecological crises in the Soviet Union, and the new policy of glasnost has brought the real dimensions of pollution to the attention of the Soviet population.

The salinification and drying up of the Aral Sea may be a greater tragedy than Chernobyl in the long run. A new desert in that area will effect dramatically the production of cotton, the weather, health conditions, drinking water and irrigation from tributary rivers (e.g., the Amu Darya). On this see, for example, James Critchlow, "Desertification of the Aral Region. Economic and Human Damagers" in RFE/RL RL392/87 (26 August 1987).

There have been public demonstrations against environmental pollution in Armenia—against toxic emissions from chemical and industrial plants around Erevan, and for new safety regulations at the Medzamov nuclear power station. The first trials of individuals deemed responsible for the Chernobyl accident, which were held in secret, prompted considerable public discussion; and the entire issue of nuclear energy in the USSR has come under review by the intelligentsia if not yet by policy-makers.

In March the USSR Ministry of Health banned the production and use of Butifos, a highly toxic defoliant which has been used for decades in the cotton industry. The decree acknowledged that Butifos had polluted water, some food products and the atmosphere, and had made workers ill. It remains to be seen, however, how effective the law will be.

These specific actions are symbolic of a wide array of pressing environmental issues, and they mark the culmination of a process toward ecological enlightenment which began as early as the 1960s with a campaign to clean up Lake Baikal. An environmental lobby of sorts grew out of that campaign, and various resolutions and laws on environmental protection were passed in the 1970s. Only in 1979 was there formed a State Committee on Hydrometeorology and the Environment, and in 1981 a Committee on Environmental Protection and Rational Utilization of Natural Resources was attached to the presidium of the Supreme Soviet.

But ecological issues continued to have low priority for enterprises which were expected to fulfill quotas and at the same time cut costs. Glasnost has played a vital role in changing Soviet attitudes towards environmental protection. Now that disasters of all sorts, including ecological crises, receive detailed attention in the press, the Soviet public has learned of the extent of current and potential damage. Moreover, glasnost make it possible to pillory perpetrators of environmental crimes. An emphasis upon resource protection—a major part of perestroika—also has had valuable spin-offs for environmentalists, whose influence is said to have been important in the shelving of the huge river diversion projects which were outlined in the 1985 Five-Year Plan.

The following documents reveal both the scope and the interest in environmental issues in the USSR. For further reading, aside from items in the bibliography below, see Joan De-Bardeleben, *The Environment and Marxism-Leninism. The Soviet and East German Experiment.* (Boulder, 1985).

In the field of medicine, the most important development in 1987 was the publication in August of a draft guideline for a complete restructuring of health care services in the USSR. The draft guideline has been included here in its entirety. The proposal for a full renovation of health care services in the Soviet Union has come after wide discussion on almost every aspect of medical care. The most important consequence of this has been a public debunking of many widely touted myths about the high quality of "free" health care in the USSR.

As early as 20 January, *Izvestiia* carried a piece in which Prof. Iu Shteingardt, director of the Tomsk Medical Institute, sharply criticized both the training and the examination of prospective doctors; in April the USSR Minister of Public Health, Y.Chazov, criticized the underfunding of medical research and the imbalance of quality in medical faciltiies throughout the USSR in *Literaturnaia gazeta* (29 April); obstetrical institutes came under severe criticism for poor sanitation and hygiene, for example in *Pravda* (7 Feb); and debates over whether medical aid really should be free appeared in the press, for example in *Izvestiia* (24, 29 Sept) and *Moscow News* (30 Aug).

The fact that the issue of AIDS finally became a subject for public discussion in the USSR was a sign that sensitive medical (and social) matters could no longer be regarded as taboo, or passed off as products of bourgeois influences. *Literaturnaia gazeta* (25 Feb) drew the subject to public attention with an article, "AIDS-The Plague of the 20th Century," and a decree passed in August made its transmission a criminal offence *Izvestiia* (26 Aug). The article by Nikolai Filippov, "The Mystery of Skull Valley (The Pentagon and AIDS)," *International Affairs*, 6(1987), at least did not represent the norm in 1987!

Responsibility to Nature. Intensify Attention to Ecological Problems (10 Jan 1987)
According to the dry academic definition, the term "ecological" today covers problems relating not only to our well being and to the quality of life, but to legal ones as well. Why do we live and toil on our earth? Only for warmth, a roof over our heads? We are thinking of those who constitute one of our greatest joys, our children and our grandchildren, of their future, and of future generations. They will have to live on this earth. They will not understand if we do not leave them the nightingale's song, the sweet coolness of springs, the bubbling waters of a river and the blue of a clear sky.

Creativity and artistry are laid into the very being of man. The materialize to actualize these qualities are natural resources, the workshop—nature itself. Man will cease to be man if he submits to the principle that nothing in nature must be touched. But he loses his proud name, "rational man", if he does not think of a wide range of problematical ecological consequences brought about by his creative activities. They are far from being innocuous.

"Socialism, with its planned production and humanistic world outlook is capable of contributing to the symbiosis between man and nature," the 27th Congress noted in a political document.

One example of how such harmony can be served is the closed resource conservation system of industrial waterworks and scrap recycling of the May First International Complex, in the Ukraine. Its efforts have been commemorated in past years by the receipt of the State Prize of the USSR. Today already many of the nation's factories have ceased to pollute water supplies with dirty effluence, although only in the past Five Year Plan has their sewage into rivers and lakes been cut by a third. In the drainage system of the water supply approximately 250 cubic kms of water circulates—as much as the Volga carries into the Caspian each year. In our country the release of pollutants into the atmosphere is being limited. Work on the reclamation of waste and worked out mines is being increased. Care is heightened over the question of felling young forests.

The Party and the government pay unremitting attention to the problems of nature protection. Resolutions on strengthening nature protection and improving the use of natural resources everywhere in the country, as well as at specific sites and in certain regions, are widely known and remain an indispensable guide to action. Concrete decisions on Yasnaya Polyana and Lake Baikal have been made. The resolution on halting operations to divert part of the flow of northern and Siberian rivers has evoked the broadest support and public satisfaction.

In our country, nature conservation is an inalienable part of state policy. A number of the decisions of the Party and the government are essentially aimed at correcting mistakes caused by ignorance of ecology on the part of executives of certain departments and planners who only know how to think in departmental terms. Such mistakes cannot be permitted in the future. Greater accountability should also be an issue-accountability not only to nature, but to the people. The decline and disappearance of fish stocks in the Aral Sea is a tragedy for many inhabitants of the coastal areas. In this specific instance it may be difficult to determine who is guilty of mistakes in organizing water management on the rivers flowing to the sea. But there are more obvious culprits. *Pravda* readers ask, for example, what sort of accountability was required of the executives who decided to build a solid embankment, one that did not permit the release of water into the gulf if necessary, at the entrance to the Kara-Bogaz-Gol Gulf. As we know, it took money and effort to correct the mistakes and time was lost. In the letters several not insignificant facts of regional and local importance are reported. In one instance, a big irrigation system which came with a pump, which in several years of not paying for itself by raising crop production to the promised level, was not produced any longer.

Production units of the USSR Ministry of Land Reclamation and Water Resources and the ministry as a whole are a constant target of the criticism expressed in readers' letters. Many readers think that its subordinate organizations are most often guided in their activities not by the interests of genuine land reclamation, or land improvement, but by the attainment of high incomes for gross output and the volume of capital investments they have "used." The ministry's executives and its Party organization must pay the closest attention to the critical remarks found in the press and in letters discussing their performance and draw the proper conclusions from them.

Among other things, the Volga-Chograi Canal and other large-scale water-management projects to the river's lower reaches, which were designed to supplement the Volga with water from northern rivers, require immediate reassessment and additional ecological feasibility studies. All major projects of regional importance should be submitted beforehand for a broad and thorough discussion by the scientific community. The failure of many ministries to pay sufficient attention to the problems of nature protection gives rise to criticism. There is no question that the USSR Ministry of the Timber, Pulp-and-Paper and Lumber Industry, whose enterprises are among the most inveterate polluters of the country's water, should draw profound and practical conclusions from the fact that sanitation agencies have shut down operations at the Priozersk Pulp and Paper Plant on Lake Ladoga. The large-scale exploitation of mineral riches that is just beginning in the Caspian Lowlands requires a stepping up of nature-protection efforts by the Ministries of the Petroleum, Gas and Petroleum-Refining and Petrochemical Industries, whose enterprises have made many mistakes in this respect while mining the riches of the Tiumen North. Local Party and Soviet organs are responsible for activating attention to ecological problems.

Our responsibility is to rationally, carefully, and variously exploit our natural resources. We have no other earth except our own. The duty of each is to conserve and to increase its wealth. The Soviet land is huge, its landscape multifaceted, and it is simply essential that her fertile diversity, which has given and will give not only bread, fuel and iron, be preserved. Nature provides inspiration. Let it be preserved in all of her strength, beauty and majesty.

"Otvetstvennost' pered prirodoi: usilit' vnimanie k ekologicheskim preblemam," *Pravda* (10 Jan); excerpts are translated in CDSP, 39:2 (1987), 18-19.

Valeri Legasov. **For Safe Nuclear Energy.** An Interview (13 Jan 87)
Trud correspondent converses with the first director of the Institute of Atomic Energy in the Name of I.V.**Kurchatov**, the Leninist Laureate and State Award winner Academician V.A. **Legasov**, on the problem of the further development of nuclear energy and improving its safety,

Q Readers are asking, Valerii Alekseevich, in letters to editors whether we should stop using nuclear energy altogether, or at least for a time, and revert to the use of electroenergy. What is your opinion?

A This is a timely question, one that even experts are raising. And they are answering it by looking at the many factors in cold blood.

Today, nuclear power provides the world with 15 percent of electric power, this percentage being considerably higher in some countries. For example, 70 percent in France, 60 percent in Belgium, 43 percent in Sweden, 40 percent in Switzerland and Finland, and 31 percent in the FGR. Although the Soviet Union was the first country in the world to construct a nuclear power plant, subsequent development of this energy source was rather slow so that today it accounts for less than 11 percent. Is it possible to stop using nuclear energy completely and return to coal, gas, oil and water power? Yes, but raw material reserves would run out within a rather short time, and it would lead to higher production costs. However, that could be dealt with. The question is: would the world's ecology benefit from such a replacement program? Would accidents, environmental destruction and loss of life be prevented? Estimates indicate: no.

Present technology cannot prevent the emissions of toxic, including carcinogenic, substances when organic fuels are used at thermoelectric power stations. Nor are these toxic products the result of an accident; they are by-products. Moreover, concentrating power generation at electric power stations, transporting huge quantities of fuel by rail or pipeline and storing it carry the risk of fire or even explosion. Loses from such accidents are significant even now.

Q What have scientists done to guarantee the complete safety of nuclear power stations?

A We live in a very complex world of science and technology. This is something all of us would do well to remember. The accidents at Chernobyl and the US power station, Three Mile Island, as well as other tragic occurrences, such as the loss of the Challenger space shuttle, the explosion in Bhopal, India, and also sea and railway disasters, have shown us that the man-machine interrelationship still presents problems and requires our constant attention. The enemy is not technology itself but rather our incompetent, irresponsible approach to it.

Q Are you proposing any safeguards to prevent this?

A Yes, for example, there is a proposal to organise a multi-hierarchical system for taking especially important decisions so that, in addition to the operator, someone else with higher engineering qualifications would hold the key to operation control. And there is a need for better information. The operator must identify the most salient aspects through information and must know their implications. At present visual information signals are relied upon for the most part, audio only in the case of emergency. But we should consider combining the two more effectively or introducing alternative methods.

Looking even farther ahead, experts are considering systems which would have built-in safeguards. Any deviation from programmed instructions would cause the system to slow down all physical and chemical processes inside the potentially dangerous units.

Our goal is to be able to receive not only information about the state of each individual piece of equipment affecting safety but also to be informed if, for example, a crack or other defect is likely to occur in a particular part. The physical principles for such diagnostic techniques already exists, now they must be engineered into the equipment.

Q What do you think about proposals to build nuclear power stations in the taiga, tundra or desert?

A This possibility has been considered. Again, we will not speak about economic feasibility: the power stations would be located thousands of kilometers from the consumers. In the end, this is not what is important. Let us take the problem of safety. It would be illogical to build a small station in an uninhabited area, and if we construct a large one, a city will spring up around it. Why should these people be subjected to danger? And who knows what will happen to an uninhabited region decades from now? It is important to solve the problem in principle: to do everything to make nuclear energy, as well as all industrial enterprises, as safe as possible. Even so it would hardly make sense to site powerful energy generation too close to densely inhabited towns.

Q Has the construction of the Chernobyl reactor been re-examined and has the technological process been changes in any way?

A Basically, the construction has not been altered, but individually improvements are being introduced. These involve, primarily, lowering the equipment's sensitivity to deviations from normal operation and also preventing even the possibility of an accident similar to Chernobyl. These changes have been introduced in most stations.

Q There have been rumours that reactors at several nuclear power stations, specifically the Armenian plant, were shut down due to faulty operation. Is this true?

A There were in fact some shut-downs, but they had been planned previously. These nuclear power stations, including the Armenian plant, were built a long time ago. Over the last 25-30 years not only has technology advanced but safety procedures and operating regulations are also no longer the same as those used at the dawn of nuclear energy. In 1982, after the unfortunate incident at Three Mile Island, stricter operating regulations were introduced. Projects for new nuclear power plants were re-examined, and modifications were to be introduced gradually in all previously constructed plants over a period of several years. But events compelled us to act quickly, and reactors at older plants were either shut down or the period for their scheduled maintenance prolonged and the necessary modifications, which I have already mentioned, introduced.

Q Chernobyl's fourth reactor has been encased in a sarcophagus. Is it safe?

A The reactor has been encased in such a way as to prevent the emission of radioactive particles no matter what might happen inside. Careful studies are being made to determine what is occurring inside the sarcophagus. Some observation systems are recording temperatures and radiation and checking to ensure that no radioactive particles escape through the filters. Others are helping scientists discover what happens to radioactive residue and how equipment and materials are affected by radiation, information that was previously unavailable. The results of these studies may prove invaluable.

Q Recently Chernobyl's first and second reactors were put back into operation. How are they working and why are they still being tested?

A They are working as they should be, reliably. The tests runs are considered necessary because general conditions at the station must be closely monitored due to the fact that radiation particles were emitted, and work was still going on to protect and operate the two other reactors.

Q You mentioned that the accident revealed the urgent need to adopt measures for technological control and the prevention of human error. Is any fundamentally new research being conducted at the moment? Are there any new proposals for application?

A Certain new concepts concerning the construction of reactors had been developed in laboratories in this country and abroad even before Chernobyl, but their introduction did not appear to be a matter of urgency... We know now that we cannot be satisfied with state-of-the-art technology; new ideas for improving safety must be carefully considered, and there are quite a number of them.

Q In a television broadcast in May, 1986, M.S. **Gorbachev** proposed the creation of an international control system for the safe development of nuclear energy. This idea was later proposed for discussion at a session of the International Atomic Energy Agency. What are the main proposals and what has been the reaction of other countries to them?

A The Soviet Union has proposed, for example, the immediate release of information on nuclear power plant accidents, the creation of an information centre to provide data about radiation levels in different geographical areas, the adoption of international standards for acceptable concentration levels of radiation and levels of radioactive contamination, the provision of international assistance should an emergency situation arise, joint research and the pooling of expertise in the development of a new generation of reactors, etc. Inasmuch as these Soviet proposals have taken into account the actual state of affairs in the world—after all, the development of nuclear energy in one country affects the interests of neighbouring states and the world at large—they have been met with complete understanding by the representatives of other countries. One practical step already taken has been the conclusion of two international conventions. One on the early notification of a nuclear accident or radiation emergency. Both these documents have already been ratified by the Soviet Union.

V. Legasov, "K bezopasnoi asdernoi energetike," *Trud* (13 Jan). V.A. Legasov is First Deputy Director of the Kurchatov Institute of Atomic Energy. He is interviewed by A. Pankov.

It's Still Not Too Late (29 Mar 87)

Naturally, we are in favor of our industrial growth, in order to have more mills and factories in our country, so that year after year our Fatherland is economically strengthened and enriched. One could say that this concern is our general concern. But we also are in favor of our national wealth finally being responsibly and wisely husbanded, in the spirit of not only today's but of future needs.

Entering into present social problems is not only the question of economics, actual as that is. No less important is the preservation of nature and of our environment, in the final analysis, preservation of the physical and moral health of the individual. Still, until recently, every time a choice was presented it stood between a new factory or a pine forest, the preference without an exception would be given to the factory: the pine forest would go under the axe. In the opinions of their defenders, the forests, rivers, and the clarity of the heavenly zephrys are more often than not ignored. These supporters of the environment are irritatingly sneered at as spokesmen of the sclerotic, torn from the demands of transient points of view, having been accused of almost a complete lack of patriotism. Of nature, it is said, we have enough to push aside in favour of progress. Progress is viewed through new factory pipes. What has emerged from the recent unrepentant attitude towards nature, too many ecological disasters which we have, and those abroad: the "problem of Baikal", the "problem of river diversion", and alas, "the problem of Chernobyl."

And so with all the burgeoning anxieties, we came to discover that although we have nature enough, yet we seem unable to prevent that living nature from dying before our eyes. What will be left for us tommorrow, and to our future generations the day after? It seems that today we have an increasingly clear understanding of the malevolent nature of negligence and irresponsibility toward the environment, and we are happy that these things are really being combatted now. Here is what such irresponsibility has done. It has contrived to site chemical-industry enterprises that are hazardous to people, water, trees, and even stones in the historical part of ancient, inimitable and invaluable Novgorod and of equally unique Pereslavl-Zalessky. It has placed equally hazardous chemical plants in immediate proximity to **Tolstoy**'s Yasnaya Poliana and **Nekrasov**'s Karabikha. Of all places !

And now a new historical victim has been found. Twenty years ago, someone came up with the idea of building yet another large enterprise—a second production line for the Zavolzhsk Chemical Plant—in immediate proximity to Shchelykovo, where the A.N. Ostrovskii Museum and Nature Reserve is located, eight kilometers away from the great writer's grave; now it's been decided to implement the plan.

In environmental terms, the site chosen for the new chemical plant is the most unspoiled place in the trans-Volga area—a place that marks the beginning of one of the last regions of pine forests, birch groves and pristine forest rivers and lakes in the European part of the country that has not been disfigured by the hand of man. As scientists have proven, this virgin area has now been suffering ecological damage for many years now from its neighbor, the veteran Zavolzhsk Chemical Plant, and the area's coniferous forests are especially suffering. What's going to happen when the buildings of the new, much larger chemical plant go up—a plant that falls into the most hazardous classification? A plant that, moreover, will be in immediate proximity to the nature reserve and, from the standpoint of the prevailing winds, in a location that is highly unfavorable for the greenbelt? One thing is clear: The natural, cultural and historical wealth not only on the Shchelykovo Reserve itself but also of the entire trans-Volga area will be doomed to gradual destruction. Eventually the Volga too will be endangered.

And yet, as we know, at this very time, the Kostroma province authorities- in response to a proposal by the public at large-have launched an initiative to create a Bolshoe Shchelykovo National Park and to turn a sizeable part of the trans-Volga wooded area into a mass recreation and tourism zone in the near future, where the museum preserve of A.N.Ostrovskii is located, eight kms. from the grave of the great dramatist. This timely initiative requires broad support. Our traditional resort areas of the Black Sea, the Baltic area and the Carpathian foothills, where already the growth in numbers of vacationers cannot be coped with.

In informal conversations, the defenders of the idea of constructing a plant at the chosen site tried to persuade us that the new enterprise would pose absolutely no danger for the reserve. They even gave us guarantees and assurances. But we do not believe those guarantees. Guarantees were also given when the Shchekino plant was being built, but the "guarantors" have long since left their official posts, while their thoughtless assurances have led to a situation in which irreparable damage has been done to the Yasnaya Poliana and the state has suffered immense losses: revamping the production process will take millions of rubles. It is well known that even the most dependable chemical technology cannot be insured against sudden accidents. It is necessary to account for other, not unimportant circumstances—such as the volume of regional growth And how is it possible to have such an increase in a given region? A factory will begin to encroach upon a nature reserve meter by meter, and soon it ceases to be a reserve, and it is transferred into a mere approach to a gigantic enterprise; into its landscape are etched factory chimneys and through its pine forests wend industrial mains for eliminating factory wastes.

Yet another alarming situation is taking shape before our very eyes, a situation that is very similar to the one at Lake Baikal and Yesnaia Poliana. Construction has not yet gotten way outside Zavolzhsk. So far, there are only blueprints, and it's not too late to properly and carefully think everything through and double-check whether the project is warranted.

In sending this letter to *Pravda*, we are convinced that we are expressing the sentiments of the general public. We therefore request that the USSR Council of Ministers heed our arguments. -[signed] S.**Zalygin**, writer and USSR State Prize winner; Hero of Socialist Labor and Academician D.**Likhachev**; Hero of Socialist Labor and Academician I. **Petrianov-Sokolov**; Hero of Socialist Labor M. **Ulianov**, Chairman of the Russian Republic Theater Workers' Union; and Academician B. **Laskorin**, Lenin and USSR State Prize winner and Chairman of the Environmental-Protection Committee of the All-Union Council of Scientific and Technical Societies.

"Eshche ne pozdno!" *Pravda* (29 March); translated excerpts are in CDSP, 39:23 (1987), 21.

In the CPSU Central Committee (16 May 1987)

The CPSU Central Committee has examined the question of the responsibility of the individuals guilty of failing to fulfill previously adopted decision with respect to the implementation of conservation measures in the Lake Baikal basin.

In a resolution adopted on this question, the CPSU Central Committee notes that the executives of the USSR Ministry of the Timber, Pulp-and-Paper and Lumber Industry, the USSR State Forestry Committee, the USSR Ministry of Power and Electrification, the USSR Ministry of Construction in Eastern Regions, the USSR Ministry of Machinery for Construction, Road Building and Municipalities, the Russian Republic Ministry of Forestry, the Russian Republic State Agro-Industrial Committee, the Siberian Division of the USSR Academy of Sciences and the ministries and departments have displayed indiscipline, failing to ensure the fulfillment, in their entirety and by the appointed deadlines, of the assignments set by the USSR Council of Ministers' resolution , "On Measures for the Conservation of the Lake Baikal Basin and the Rational Utilization of Its Natural Complexes," dated 21 January 1969, by the resolutions of the Central CPSU Central Committee and the USSR Council of Ministers "On Additional Measures to Ensure the Rational Utilization and Conservation of the Natural Resources of the Lake Baikal Basin," dated 16 June 1971, and "On Measures for Further Ensuring the Protection and the Rational Utilization of the Natural Resources of the Lake Baikal Basin," dated 21 July 1977, and by other decisions, as a result of which the pollution of this unique body of water and its natural environment with industrial and agricultural wastes and gaseous emissions is continuing, the irrational utilization of timber resources is taking place, reforestation and the protection of forests from fires is organized in an extremely unsatisfactory way, and the water and wind erosion of land is developing.

The CPSU CC believes it advisable to remove Comrade G.F. **Pronin**, USSR Deputy Minister of the Timber, Pulp-and-Paper and Lumber Industry, from his post for his irresponsible attitude towards the fulfillment of the CPSU CC and the USSR Council of Ministers' resolutions of 21 July 1977, with respect to the creation of a water-recycling system at the Selenga Pulp and Cardboard Combine, for low efficiency in the work of this enterprise, for pollution of the environment with industrial sewage and gaseous discharges from the Baikalsk Pulp and Paper Combine, and also for the profound lag that has been permitted in the development and technical reequipment of the pulp and paper industry.

Comrade R.V. **Bobrov**, Russian Republic Deputy Minister of Forestry and a CPSU member, has been given a sharp reprimand for lax supervision over the observance of established rules for forest use in the Lake Baikal basin, for failing to take measures to improve the conditions of forests and intensify their water protection functions, for shortcomings in reforestation work and for the extensive destruction of forests by fire that has been permitted. The Russian Republic Council of Ministers will resolve the question of whether it is possible to retain Comrade R.V. **Bobrov** in his post as Russian Republic Deputy Minister of Forestry.

The application of Comrade L. Ye. **Mikhailov**, First Vice-Chairman of the USSR State Forestry Committee, for retirement on pension will be taken under advisement.

The attention of Comrade A.I. **Zverev**, Chairman of the USSR State Forestry Committee, and Comrade N.M. **Prilepo**, Russia Republic Minister of Forestry, has been called to the irresponsibility they have displayed in organizing the fulfillment of Party and government resolutions on questions of protecting the Lake Baikal basin. They have been warned that if they do not take comprehensive measures to improve the ecological situation in the forests of the Lake Baikal area they will be held strictly accountable.

The Presidium of the USSR Academy of Sciences (Comrade **Marchuk**) is to consider the question of raising the level of responsibility of scientific organizations for working out recommendations on questions concerning the protection and utilization of natural resources.

Proceeding from the requirements of the decisions by the CPSU CC and the USSR Council of Ministers of 13 April 1987, the Presidium of the Siberia Department of the USSR Academy of Sciences and Irkutsk Oblast CPSU Committee are instructed to strengthen the management and carry out the restructuring of the scientific activity of the Limnology Institute, and raise the effectiveness and quality of research.

Comrade V.I. **Gorin**, member of the CPSU, member of the collegium of the USSR Ministry of Power and Electrification, and Director of the ministry's Chief Scientific and Technical Administration for Power and Electrification, has been given a severe reprimand, and CPSU members Comrade A.N. **Makhukin**, USSR First Deputy Minister of Power and Electrification, and Comrade I.P. **Peresypkin**, Russian Republic Minister of the Fish Industry, have been warned for sluggishness and red tape in implementing the assignments established by the Party and government resolutions on protecting the natural environment of Lake Baikal.

The attention of Comrade A.S. **Systov**, USSR Minister of the Aviation Industry; Comrade A.A. **Babenko**, USSR Minister of Construction in the Eastern Regions; Comrade A.I **Maiorets**, USSR Minister of Power and Electrification; and Comrade N.I. **Kotliar,** USSR Minister of the Fish Industry, has been called to the impermissibility of failing to meet deadlines for the construction of facilities connected with the protection of the Lake Baikal basin, and they have been required to rectify the state of affairs.

The Buryat and Irkutsk Province Party Committees, the Buryat Autonomous Republic Council of Ministers, the Irkutsk Province Soviet Executive Committee and the Party committees of the USSR Ministry of Timber, Pulp-and-Paper and Lumber Industry, the USSR Ministry of the Fish Industry, the USSR Ministry of Construction in the Eastern Regions, the USSR Ministry of Power and Electrification, the USSR Ministry of Machinery for Construction, Road Building and Municipalities, the USSR Ministry of the Aviation Industry, the USSR Academy of Sciences, the USSR State Forestry Committee, the Russian Republic Ministry of Forestry and the Russian Republic State Agro-Industrial Committee are to examine the question of personal responsibility of officials of central and local agencies who are guilty of failing to fulfill Party and governments assignments for protecting the environment.

It has been noted that the Russian Republic Council of Ministers (Comrades **Tabeev** and **Yermin**) is doing a poor job of monitoring the fulfillment of the resolutions of the CPSU Central Committee and the USSR Council of Ministers pertaining to the protection of the Lake Baikal basin and the rational utilization of its natural resources.

"V tsentral'nom komitete KPSS," *Pravda* (16 May); a translation is also in FBIS, No. 096 (19 May 87); a condensed translation is in CDSP, 39:19 (1987), 5–6.

Vladimir Sokolov, **The Fate of the Aral Sea** (18 Nov 87)
A big trunk with articulated wings, the AN-2 buzzed over a multi-colored ravine, across a wasteland which radiated the sun's outpourings above cotton washes, canals, and swamps, and now and then—the green ribbon of the still not quite exhausted Amu Darya. The trunk carried a writer's brigade to Muinak, just as before this it more than once transported ministers, academic, representatives of powerful committees. In the past few years, prestigious people wanting to see for themselves the spectacle of an ecological catastrophe, have become constant visitors to the Aral Sea.

The gray-haired secretary of the district Party committee led us writers along the former sea floor to a former harbor, where on the sand, side by side like beached whales, lay the rusting mummies of a fishing fleet. A strong, steady wind blew from the north, bringing a salty taste to our lips- far off in that direction, every sunny day the mass of strong salt solution, lifeless, but still called the Aral Sea, continued to shrink and recede. In a matter-of-fact way (how many times had he done this before ?), the secretary talked about the productive past of these fishing ships, about the crews that had all departed and the engines that had been removed, about the poverty that had come to the families of those fishermen who had nowhere to go or did not want to leave, and about the fact that the salt content in the breast milk of the women in Muinak is now several times higher then the norm.

For some reason, it was only when I heard about this salty milk that I finally understood that there is a catastrophe here.

From old newspaper clippings: "If the volume of fish with a high market value is increased in the Aral Sea to 1.5 million centners, and such a possibility has been demonstrated by specialists, then it will mean the same as breeding a herd of more than one million sheep. The sea is a centuries-old barrier asgainst arid winds, without which the Central Asian oases will perish. Only those who do not love their native region could injure the Aral Sea."—from a letter in the newspaper, 1965.

"The inevitability of the drying up of the Aral Sea is obvious to everyone."—from a response sent to the newspaper by the All-Union Design, Surveying and Research Institute, 1968.

So much has been written and said about the dying Aral Sea in the past 20 years, so many commissions, created with great fanfare, have quietly disbanded, but the imperturbable institute still seems to be right in its prophecy. But it has not been right about everything. Here is another one of its prophecies:

"The bringing of new areas of the Aral Basin into agricultural cultivation will not stop in the future. The total area under cultivation will double. Over 70 cubic kilometers of water will be spread over these fields, instead of the current 40 cu. km. The increase of irrigated land promises not only to double the cotton and rice harvests but also to quadruple the production of meat and increase the harvests of vegetables, fruits, and grapes" -September, 1962.

It is now the second half of the 1980s, time to tally the results. The total area of land under irrigation in the Aral Basin has not doubled, it has increased by a half, and the hypothetical harvests of cotton and rice have not doubled either. As far as food is concerned, the very rich land of Central Asia is now producing the following amounts per capita: meat is 26 percent below the medical norm, milk is 42 percent below, and fruit and grapes are 53 percent below. What has increased? The use of chemicals. There are not many other places in the country where such high dosages of mineral fertilizer are applied, and the amount of pesticides used on the cotton fields is dozens of times (!) greater then the average for either the Soviet Union or the US. What else has grown? The consumption of water for irrigation. Not the 70 cu. km. of water needed for the doubled land area but a whole 90 cu. km. is now applied "to the fields"! Isn't that absurd ?

If the problem were only the promises made by the institute-well, the country heard quite a few promises during the 1960s! But the development strategy for an entire region was built on these promises. This mistaken strategy has now resulted in some serious troubles, and it is simply inhumane and incompatible with the principles of socialism today for those in the upper echelons of the planned management of the economy to continue to take no notice of them, to regard Central Asia as a subtropical paradise where rich Uzbeks (Tadzhiks, Turkmenians, Kirgiz) eat pilaf and melons and get rich on "white gold".

Today we must admit that, despite all the undoubted achievements (mainly in a quantitative nature), the billions of rubles in capital investments put primarily into increasing cotton production have not brought this land prosperity. Instead, that money aggravated the land's problems in the extreme. The fertility of irrigated plowland was undermined by decades of sowing cotton followed by cotton, and the total area of that land has been decreasing recently, despite the putting into cultivation of more and more new land. Whereas at the beginning of the 1980s we had only 0.2 hectares of irrigated land per capita (the size of a garden plot !), by the end of the century even this scrap will have diminished to 0.13 hectares ! The rural resident is getting poorer—his total income per capita, including receipts from private farming, is only two-thirds of the all-Union figure. Together with what we know about the "cotton case" [The minister of agriculture in Uzbekistan was arrested for corruption and suspicion of murder in 1983. He committed suicide.] the State farm directors and representatives of factory interests have manipulated funds allocated for the peasantry, have pushed their limits to the utmost and have exalted their leadership. But this wealth brought nothing, as we now know, except for a round of thousands of trials.

Even the climate has worsened appreciably, because the stands of timber that used to occupy up to 15 percent of the irrigated land have nearly disappeared, and now hot dry winds and dust storms race across Central Asia. The Kyzyl-Kum and Kara-Kum Deserts have come together on the bare bottom of the Aral Sea, salty sand covers the once-fertile Amu Darya delta, and man has already lost more than 1 million hectares. The winds, which used to bring rain from the glassy sea, now come with trains of millions of tons of salt, poisoning the land and the air even farther to the south, in the oases of Kara-Kalpakia, Khorezm and eastern Turkmenia.

It is not enough to see the damage, we must nip the sources of the problem in the bud. Many think, for example, that all of these obviously tragic situations today are the necessary return for our agricultural needs in cotton textile production. But is this really so?

"From 1950-1960 they increased the irrigated land in Amidar' by 400,000 hectares. Because of this the decade's standard rose by 0.8 m. In the period from 1965-1970 the units of irrigated land in the Ural Basin rose more than 7 percent, although the overall level fell by 2.1 m. The reason for this phenomenon appearing already by 1966 was revealed by the Uzbek Academy of Sciences Lapkin Institute—a wastage of water on arable land in those republics which have already obtained 14 cu. km/year. Today it is considerably more."—V.**Kovalev**, candidate of geo-mineralogical science.

Not all, I am sure, know that in order to maintain the sea's level merely at its present mark, the rivers must bring to it at least 45 cu. km. of water al year- two-fifths of the Basin's entire water resources. It doesn't seem like all that much does it ? But even this figure seems unrealizable if one knows that the Syr Darya stopped emptying into the Aral Sea a long time ago, while the once turbulent Amu Darya now barely carries the "sanitary minimum" to the sea-3 to 4 cu. km. per year. In dry years -and they have followed one after another over who knows how many five-year plans—virtually the entire flow of the basin, about 90 cu. km., is used for irrigation. It seems that it's all over, that the Aral Sea is doomed. But what sort of irrigation is this. If even the guideline watering norms, already generously overstated, are exceeded by 60 percent in Uzbekistan, 70 percent in Turkmenia and 100 percent in Kazakhstan! The water is free, so why not let it pour forth?

So, we see that if the farms were made to take only as much water as they need, it least one-third of what now goes into "irrigation"- about 30 cu. km.-would be freed up. About 10 cu. km. can be saved through the reconstruction of the existing irrigation systems, which are as full of holes as a sieve, and the same amount can come from a scientifically substantiated lowering of watering norms for old arable land. All this means one thing: Even now it would be possible for us not to give the farms 40 to 50 cu. km. a year of water that the Aral Sea needs so badly- what we are doing is sheer mismanagement!

In recent years, some serious attacks have been launched against mismanagement. In Uzbekistan, for instance, the construction of water collectors, which will be able to return recycled water to the Aral Sea, has begun. A great deal of money has been allocated to line irrigation canals with concrete and to save the moisture that now seeps into the ground where is does no good. But, as in the past, many people would like to put every cubic kilometre of water that is conserved into new irrigation, into the development of virgin land. What about the Aral? Remember, young one, that your Aral is finished just the same.... Even these devices to redirect the flow of water to the Aral will not help it: 27.1 cu. kms of water, promised from Siberian waters, would have been "wasted" along the way to irrigation.

Those "many" do not see in the Aral the dilemma posed by its fate, the voice of environmental protection for all of Central Asia. How can we revive agriculture under such catastrophic conditions?

Just as there has not been one single reason for drought in the Aral region, there is not one single radical measure which could be directed especially towards its renewal. But if we cure agriculture from the sickness of neglect in Central Asia; if we truly observe the goals of future regional development; if we put first and foremost the welfare of the citizen, then one of the results of such policies will be to avert the destruction of the Sea, and subsequently restore it.

The *aktiv* of the most active members of the USSR Ministry of Waterworks in Central Asia is necessary to guarantee the main result, the independence of the national cotton industry" —from a letter by specialists from the "Sredazgizgiprovodkhlopka" factory to writer S.**Zalygin**.

At certain stages of our country's history, independence in cotton was just as important as independence in grain or in technology, for instance. This is still important today. But is it right to regard it in the same way now, in the changing world of the 1980s, as we did in the 1940s? Have we not fallen into paralyzing dependence on narrow and linear military definitions of "independence"? We must not forget that cotton growing in our country, in an area farther north than any other cotton zone in the world, necessarily involves sizable outlays and risk. Countries that lie closer to the equator and that do not experience our eternal thirst can grow cotton with nothing like the costs we incur. Isn't it time to take a new look at the thesis of independence in cotton?

It has now been established that even in the most favorable year so far, 1980, Uzbekistan harvested only 5.5 million tons of raw cotton (the reports said 6.2 million!), and in recent "stagnant" years, when the reports showed figures of 6 million tons or more, the actual harvest was not even 5 million. But after all, money was allocated for the production, and then for the purchase, of 6 million tons—wasn't it that excess money, in part, that provoked an outbreak of report-padding, outright thefts and bribery ? Fertilizer and pesticides were also allocated on the basis of 6 million tons—could those extra chemicals have been put to better use? Uzbekistan was also supplied with water for 6 million tons of cotton—where is that extra water now, in what swamps?

The reluctance to account for actual possibilities is, in our circumstances, not simply an agricultural oversight. In thousands of similar "cotton cases" it has turned to human tragedy, on a million hectares ancient environmental systems, dense woods, wetlands, the virgin expanse of the steppe, and the most fertile oases on earth, the fish-laden Aral, have been destroyed. More necessary than money in Central Asia today is precise knowledge of its condition, clear recommendations from science, and the humanity of those who will make the decisions.

The Alternative of Academician Aganbegyan: "The water deficit in the context of Central Asia must be met by passing the most regulatory and limiting factor in the growth and development against those industries which demand large volumes of water, essentially polluting natural reservoirs."

There is a great deal here that needs restructuring. That includes the view of Central Asia as primarily an agrarian region of the country, which God has ordained to produce industrial and water-loving crops. But industrial crops have to be grown at the expense of food crops, and the cultivation of water-loving crops means the consumption of water that is already in short supply.

Economists' Alternative: "In the remote future (15 to 20 years from now), the republic will be able to provide its growing population with milk, meat, potatoes, vegetables, fruits and grapes (taking into account deliveries to all-Union stocks) and to produce 2 billion to 2.3 billion rubles more in gross agricultural output then can be produced by any other option, but in doing so it will be able to produce only about 1 million tons of raw cotton."

Given the current understanding of "cotton independence," this proposal looks so seditious that the authors themselves, specialists working at the Central Asian Agricultural Economics Research Institute, are not insisting on it. Another option seems much more realistic, of course- to limit cotton production to the level that has already been achieved, approximately 5 million tons, and put the freed resources into improving Uzbekistan's land, water and farms. This sensible step has already been taken, and the appropriate government decisions have been made.

But other problems remain that must be reckoned with. How do we intend to use Central Asia's only surplus (and constantly growing !) resources- free manpower? Today every fifth able-bodied person here is not participating in social production, and what these people are living on is a real question. Even vegetable growing done totally by hand, not to mention highly mechanized cotton framing, is basically unable to provide work for these growing legions, even if rivers from all over the country are diverted here. They can be fed, but work can never be found for all of them!

What will happen when the program for increasing labor productivity in agriculture that is getting under way in the republic gains momentum? Economic accountability and up-to-date machinery will inevitably force additional millions of workers out of the cotton fields—where will they go?

There is just one way out—to develop industry in Central Asia, and not just any kind of industry but something in keeping with the region's special features. First, industry that requires a large number of diligent workers. Second, industry that is ecologically clean and does not use large quantities of water. Third, industry equipped with the most up-to-date technology, so that its output will have a demand in other parts of the country and even abroad. There are any numbers of examples of this sort of industry—the garment, electrical equipment, footwear and electronics industries, among others.

Not only the country's Cotton Plantation but its Workshop—that is a fitting future for Uzbekistan. If one considers that industry and municipal services combined consume only one-tenth as much water as irrigated farming does, then a Workshop orientation alone can save the Aral Sea, as well as the entire natural environment of this wonderful part of the planet. Only a Workshop orientation can raise the standard of living and the levels of education and vocational training for millions of people who are now residents of villages; will be able to condense them into a qualitatively new guard of the soviet working class and by this solve urgent complex social problems arising in the shadow of difficulties in the cotton industry. Not only persistent, as has been the tradition here, but qualified and highly productive labor of the people living in Central Asia will give the national economy a powerful boost, and bring in more hard currency by virtue of observing quality, than trade in cotton textiles. Developed industry, and only it, will finally allow a transition to a qualitatively new system of irrigation—by pipe, dew collection, rainfall, increasing the efficiency of every irrigated hectare, in order to free every new cu. km. of water for the Aral Sea.

It would not be desireable, as a rule, to fall into "reconstruction" pathetics, but already too often have I come into the same thing. To preserve the depths of a sea for future generations, to restore the unique environment of Central Asia is possible only by a deep restructuring of the petrified system of management and moss-covered conceptions of the possibilities and needs of the future.

Sokolov, "Sud'ba Arala," *Literaturnaia gazeta*, No. 47 (18 Nov), 12; a condensed translation is in CDSP, 39:51 (1987), 11–12. See also James Critchlow, "Desertification of the Aral Region. Economic and Human Damage," RFE/RL. RL392/87 (27 Aug 87).

CPSU CC and USSR Council of Ministers. Draft Law, "Basic Guidelines for the Development of Health Services for the Population and the Restructuring of Public Health in the USSR During the 12th Five Year Plan and in the Period to the Year 2000" (15 Aug 87)

The course of accelerating the country's socioeconomic development mapped out by the 27th CPSU Congress envisages the implementation of major social programs. The party and the state deem it a matter of paramount importance to protect and strengthen Soviet people's health, to extend their life expectancy and creative activeness, and to fundamentally improve the quality of medical services.

Health is an asset and a boon for everyone and a necessary condition for the growth of labor productivity, the country's economic might, and the people's prosperity. The concern of the Communist Party and the Soviet state for each citizen's health is in line with the principles of humanitarianism and social justice, serves the goals of socialist society's flourishing, and lays the foundations of its economic and social prosperity in the future.

The Great October Socialist Revolution marked the beginning of the implementation of fundamental political, economic, and social transformations to meet the Soviet people's most urgent and innermost aspirations. For the first time in history the state shouldered responsibility for the population's health and guaranteed the legislative, organizational and material backing of all economic, social, and medical measures to protect the people's health.

The USSR has created a truly nationwide health service system based on the Leninist principles of free and universally available medical help and preventive medicine, the unity of science and practice, and the public's active participation in health improvement measures. At all stages of our society's development this system has reliably guaranteed the protection of the population's health and the country's sanitary welfare.

A fundamental improvement has been achieved in the state of the population's health during the 70 years of Soviet power as a result of the consistent implementation of plans for socialist building, the introduction of large-scale state measures to prevent diseases, the improvement of working and living conditions, and the development of health services and medical science. The general mortality rate has been reduced by a factor of 3 and the infant mortality rate has been reduced by a factor of 11, average life expectancy has doubled, and many dangerous infectious diseases have been eliminated. The incidence of industrial injuries, occupational diseases, and disability among working people is steadily declining. The steady trend toward the social homogeneity of public health must be listed as one of the undisputable gains of socialism. Improved physical development indicators, reduced mortality rate, and increased creative life expectancy are typical of various population groups and all nations and ethnic groups in the Soviet Union. Many people, doomed to extinction before the Great October Socialist Revolution, have now achieved high indicators of health standards.

Soviet public health has become a major sector of the social sphere. Tens of thousands of polyclinics, hospitals, first aid, and emergency medical service stations, children's institutions and hundreds of scientific research institutes and teaching establishments have been built and equipped. A mother-and-child protection system, a sanitary and epidemiology service, and a widespread network of sanatoriums and rest homes has been created. The sector employs 1.3 million physicians and 3.3 million middle-level medical workers. There have been radical changes in the standards and nature of medical services. The growth of the scientific, cadre, material, and technical potential makes it possible to supply the population not only with general medical services but also with specialized types of medical services.

The impressive achievements by Soviet public health are universally recognized. Its principles and the system of organizing primary medical and sanitary services have been recommended by the WHO as a model for the creation of national services.

The successes scored testify to socialist society's enormous advantages and potential in solving the problems of protecting the population's health. But, as an objective analysis would show, this potential is far from fully utilized. Negative trends began to emerge and develop in the activity of health service organs and institutions during the seventies and early eighties. The slowing of economic growth rates in the country and the slackening of attention to questions of health protection resulted in a reduction in the proportion of public health expenditure in the state budget and a deceleration in the processes of renewing public health's material and technical base and the assimilation of new medications and methods of treatment. Organizational shortcomings and slack monitoring of the work of medical institutions, reduced demandingness, and errors in health services caused serious mistakes in determining the basic guidelines for the sector's activity and the priorities for the development of various services. The prevailing procedure for evaluating the activity of health service institutions was not oriented toward improving the quality of medical services for the population.

Phenomena such as bureaucratism, bribery, callousness, indifference, rudeness, and an irresponsible approach to the performance of professional duties have become widespread among health service workers. Moral and ethical distortions have spread to the admission to higher medical education establishments, the assessment of training and work results, and service promotions. The existing labor compensation system has failed to stimulate any desire to master knowledge and work habits, improve qualifications, or raise work standards.

Less attention is given to preventive work—the main avenue in protecting the health of the USSR population. Ministries and departments and local soviets of people's deputies do not implement the proper volume of measures to prevent water reservoir, air, and soil pollution and to create safe working conditions in production. The population in a number of the country's regions is not supplied with good-quality drinking water, while the concentration of pollutants in the air above several cities is several times higher than the set normatives. The sanitary and epidemiology service displays inactivity and passiveness in the solution of ecological problems and is failing to utilize the broad powers vested in it for this purpose. The sanitary supervision of the observance of sanitary and hygiene norms and regulations at enterprises, institutions, and organizations is insufficiently effective.

For many years new proper attention has not been given to work on cultivating a healthy way of life. Over two-thirds of the population are not involved in systematic physical culture and sport, up to 30% are overweight, and there are about 70 million smokers. Drunkenness and alcoholism are widespread, and there are growing numbers of drug addicts. A resolute and implacable struggle has been launched in the country against these phenomena alien to socialist morals. But this struggle is not being waged everywhere with due persistence and consistency.

The standards and quality of medical services fail to fully meet Soviet people's increased requirements. Advanced experience and new and more effective methods for the detection and treatment of diseases are being introduced into practice only slowly. There is no continuity in the work of inpatient and outpatient institutions. Many polyclinics have not organized their reception hours at times convenient for the population, and there are instances of unjustified refusals to accept hospital patients, delays in taking patients in need of emergency services to institutions for treatment, the inefficient use of the available beds and treatment and diagnostic equipment, and overly protracted hospital examinations.

The state of work on protecting the health of mothers and infants is a cause of particular alarm. Maternity homes, children's polyclinics and hospitals, and prenatal clinics fail to provide modern standards of prevention, diagnosis, and treatment owing to their unsatisfactory material and technical base and the inadequate theoretical and practical training of cadres.

Many maternity homes and departments and units for the delivery of premature babies and the treatment of newborn infants fail to meet sanitary and hygiene standards.

The material and technical base of public health is in serious need of strengthening. Many hospitals, maternity homes, polyclinics, and outpatient departments are located in converted and even dilapidated premises in need of capital repair or reconstruction, and they lack central heating, main water supply, sewerage, and hot water. The standard-design treatment and preventive medicine institution premises now in use make no provision for the full use of modern medical techniques. From year to year the funds appropriated for the construction of public health projects are not assimilated.

The requirements of treatment and preventive medicine institutions and the population for medical equipment, medication, dressings and disinfectants, and patient care equipment are not being full satisfied. In terms of performance most of the equipment and apparatus manufactured by Soviet industry is inferior to the best foreign models.

The major potential of Soviet medical science is not being fully utilized. The existing research planning and coordination system fails to take into account the social requirements and priority avenues of practical work, and results in the duplication and dissipation of efforts and resources. The efficiency of fundamental and applied research is poor, with only 5% of the product capable of being patented. The methodological, scientific, and technical standards of many institutes' work are below the achievements of world science, with one-third of Soviet developments duplicating work abroad. The introduction of scientific achievements is intolerably slow. The problem of training young scientific replacements is acute.

The USSR Academy of Medical Sciences does not unite scientific forces. It provides feeble leadership for them, and does not display proper rigor as regards the quality and importance of research work. VUZ science, which employs almost one-half of the best trained cadres in medical science, owes a large debt to practice.

These and other shortcomings have had a negative effect on the state of the population's health. The dynamic of the demographic processes in the country has deteriorated, infant mortality and mortality among men of working age are high, average life expectancy has not increased for a long time, and there has been virtually no decline in the incidence of cardiovascular and oncological diseases. The national economy suffers major losses through the disability of workers, employees, and kolkhoz members resulting from diseases and injuries, and also through leave of absence to look after sick children. About 4 million persons daily fail to report to work for one of these reasons, while the sum of annual benefit payments in respect of temporary disability is in excess of 7 billion rubles.

The state of the protection and strengthening of the people's health causes justified complaints by working people and is a matter of serious concern for the CPSU CC and the Soviet Government. Shortcomings in the activity of public health organs and institutions cause considerable damage to the implementation of the party's social policy, the consolidation of the socialist way of life, and the acceleration of the development of society as a whole.

The CPSU CC and the USSR Council of Ministers are setting the task of fundamentally restructuring public health, eliminating shortcomings, ensuring efficient utilization of the existing potential, and sharply improving the quality of medical services. It is necessary to reach a stage at which the activity of all links in the sector and of each medical worker meets modern demands. The population's needs for medicinal compounds and patient care equipment must be satisfied in full and everywhere.

For this purpose, and in line with the Basic Guidelines for the Economic and Social Development of the USSR in 1986-1990 and Through the Year 2000, a package of measures must be implemented to step up the prevention of diseases, gradually introduce medical checkups for the entire population, improve the professional skills of medical cadres, and raise the quality and standard of work by treatment and preventive medicine institutions.

Union Republic Communist Party CCs, kraikoms and obkoms, union and autonomous republic Councils of Ministers, local soviets of people's deputies, leaders of ministries, departments and enterprises, and public organizations must give more attention to public health needs, the solution of environmental protection issues, and the improvement of the population's working and living conditions; must ensure the unconditional fulfillment of plans for the strengthening of medical institutions' material and technical base; and must play an active part in inculcating a healthy way of life among citizens and in the supply, retention, and ideological and moral education of medical cadres.

Support must be given to the working people's initiative to set up a Soviet Health Foundation, funded by voluntary contributions from labor collectives, public organizations, creative unions, and individual citizens, so as to involve the broad public in work on health services for the population, the active propaganda of a healthy way of life, the management and restructuring of public health, and broadening information on the USSR's achievements in this sphere.

The boosting of Soviet public health to a qualitatively new level is a matter for the whole people and the state. The solution of the set tasks will demand a creative approach to the improvement of the protection and strengthening of the population's health by all medical workers and party, soviet, and trade union organs and Komsomol organizations.

1 Enhancing the Efficiency of Preventive Medicine—the General Line of Soviet Public Health Care

At all stages of Soviet public health's development, preventive medicine has been and remains its fundamental principle, the ideology of the protection of the people's health. By its nature preventive medicine is not a narrow departmental sector of the activity of public health organs and institutions but comprises a package of measures aimed at raising the material and cultural standards of the people's life, protecting the environment, improving the conditions for Soviet people's labor, life, and rest, boosting the human organism's resistance to the effects of factors adverse to health, and eliminating the causes and conditions conducive to the emergence of these factors.

There can be no doubts about preventive medicine's role in the successes of Soviet public health. At the same time, the USSR Ministry of Health, the AUCCTU, ministries and departments and local soviets of people's deputies still make insufficient use of preventive medicine's potential. Preventive medicine is largely of a declaratory nature and makes no provision for the implementation of large-scale health improvement measures.

Perceiving the implementation of large-scale environmental protection measures as a mandatory condition of mass preventive medicine work, it is necessary to ensure priority for measures involving the relocation away from residential districts of enterprises which are sources of environmental pollution, the introduction of waste-free and low-waste technologies, and the improvement of technological processes which exclude harmful discharges. Enterprises must not be allowed to operate unless sanitary protective zones have been established. The population everywhere must be assured of supplies of good-quality drinking water, and immediate measures must be taken to return to normal atmospheric conditions in regions where the atmosphere has been polluted. Stricter economic sanctions must be imposed on enterprises inflicting damage to man's health and the environment.

The role played by the USSR Ministry of Health in the implementation of environmental protection measures must be substantially enhanced. It is incumbent upon the ministry to head the struggle against environmental pollution and disruptions of the ecological balance, and this work must be perceived as one of the paramount avenues of preventive medicine activities. The organs of state sanitary supervision must make more decisive use of the existing legal levers in the interest of strict observance of legislation regarding the sanitary protection of the soil, water reservoirs, and the atmosphere.

There must be more effective sanitary supervision as regards the observance of sanitary and hygiene and antiepidemic regulations and norms in enterprises, institutions, and organizations. For this purpose there must be stricter monitoring of the fulfillment of the sectorial and territorial "Health" programs aimed at reducing the incidence of industrial injury and occupational disease, reducing the proportion of manual labor and workplaces involving production factors, which are adverse to health, releasing women from work at sectors involving hard physical labor, and improving safety techniques and the conditions for working people's relaxation.

It is deemed necessary to codify in a single act the rules and regulations governing the observance of sanitary and hygiene norms in force throughout the country's territory and mandatory for all enterprises, institutions, organizations, officials, and citizens of the USSR.

Prosecutor's office and sanitary supervision organs must adopt exhaustive measures to bring to light instances of breaches of sanitary and hygiene and antiepidemic rules and norms, and must more actively apply legal means for the purpose of reliably protecting Soviet people's health and life by instituting material, disciplinary, administrative, or criminal proceedings against offenders according to established procedures.

There must be stricter supervision and exactingness at all stages of the manufacture of foodstuffs, and there must be particularly thorough monitoring of the application of mineral fertilizers, pesticides, and other chemicals so as to rule out the possibility of adverse effects on people's health.

There must be increased monitoring of the processing, storage, transportation, and marketing of foodstuffs. No foodstuff production processes can be in breach of technological demands or contravene sanitary and hygiene normatives. USSR state standards for food industry and agricultural output must be brought into line with scientifically substantiated hygiene requirements. Particular attention must be given to the observance of sanitary and hygiene rules at public catering enterprises so as to rule out any likelihood of mass infection caused by the use of substandard products in catering.

Bearing in mind the importance of balanced and wholesome nutrition for the population's health, measures must be gradually implemented to improve the quality and rational utilization of foodstuffs. Provision must be made to include among USSR state standards indicators describing the nutritional and biological value of foodstuffs. There must be increased output of products with enhanced biological value and a lower content of animal fat, sugar, and common salt, as well as more vegetable fat and dietary, vitamin-enriched, and protein products. The need of infants for semisolid dairy products, canned children's food, and powdered formula milk products must be fully satisfied by 1991.

At the same time, active sanitary education work must be done to raise dietary standards with a view to ensuring that the quantity and calorific content of nutritional intake meet the organism's energy-consumption and physiological requirements.

The cultivation of a healthy way of life for everyone and for society as a whole must underlie all preventive medicine work. A conscientious and responsible attitude toward health as an asset belonging to the whole people must become a norm of all Soviet people's life and behavior. This presupposes the eradication of harmful habits, the inculcation of standards of human contacts, behavior, and diet, the observance of a work and relaxation regime, systematic physical culture and sports exercises, the enhancement of general sanitary standards and knowledge of hygiene, and the harmonious development of the personality.

Purposeful work along this avenue must begin in childhood. It is necessary to enhance the family's role and responsibility for protecting and strengthening children's health, and to improve the parents' education as regards rules governing the hygiene education and care of children. Measures must be taken for the broad practical implementation in the work of preschool institutions of modern methods to build up children and ensure their all-around development.

The USSR Ministry of Education and the USSR State Committee for Vocational and Technical Education, jointly with the USSR Ministry of Health, must elaborate a program for the hygiene education of the rising generation and must actively aim to create conditions for the cultivation of a healthy way of life among young people. There must be mandatory implementation of health improvement measures in schools, vocational and technical schools, young pioneer camps, and preventive medicine sanatoriums for parents and children. Special sanatorium-type preschool institutions must be organized for weaker and frequently ill children.

Concern for the health of the present and future generations demands the resolute intensification of the struggle against drunkenness and alcoholism, drug addiction, and smoking, and the development of effective medicines for this purpose. It is necessary to intensify the assertive nature of sanitary propaganda, and to convincingly and intelligibly explain to the population the harm caused by using alcoholic beverages and drugs. A program to eradicate smoking must be developed in 1988, envisaging an extensive package of medical, legal, organizational, and educational measures.

A standard program for the population's physical education must be elaborated and introduced in 1989, laying down scientifically substantiated norms and demands for the physical training and physical activeness of various social and demographic groups.

Additional physical education periods must be introduced in general education schools, vocational and technical schools, and higher and secondary specialized education establishments during the 12th and 13th Five-Year Plan periods so that, taking extramural activities into account, the physical- activeness load of school pupils and students is not less than 6-8 hours weekly. The network of sports sections under enterprises, institutions, and organizations must be expanded, and economically accountable 'Physical Culture and Health' Associations must be established at places of residence. Sports and health promotion facilities must be more efficiently used. Health centers must be set up and funded by trade union and labor collective resources (subject to their consent), including centers operating on an economic accountability basis, making extensive use of physical training methods, psychological corrective treatment, reflex therapy, and other methods of recuperative treatment.

There must be a fundamental restructuring of the work by public health and physical culture organs, and there must be better collaboration between them as regards improving the population's physical development.

A most important task of preventive medicine work in today's conditions is the active propaganda of sanitary and hygiene knowledge. The mass media, jointly with public health organs, must increase the number of television and radio programs and newspaper and journal publications on questions of the population's hygiene education and sanitary knowledge, paying particular attention to the intelligibility and cogency of the published materials. There must be broader coverage of the experience gained in work to implement preventive medicine and health improvement measures.

The USSR Ministry of Health and union republic councils of ministers must implement measures to considerably reduce the incidence of infectious diseases, primarily influenza and other respiratory diseases, which account for about one-half of all temporary disability cases and cause economic damage totaling about 3.5 billion rubles annually. For this purpose it is necessary to develop effective means for prevention and treatment, make broad use of general hygiene and resistance-buildup procedures, especially among children, and improve the organization of vaccination work. The incidence of intestinal infections and viral hepatitis must be reduced by preventing the bacterial and viral pollution of drinking water and foodstuffs.

An important place in the modern strategy of preventive medicine work is occupied by annual medical checkups of the entire population. The implementation of this program, which is highly ambitious in terms of its scale and social importance, will represent a qualitatively new stage in the development of Soviet public health, whereby the state will undertake care for each citizen's health in the supreme form of this care-active and dynamic monitoring throughout citizens' lives.

The main objective of medical checkups is to create a unified system ensuring assessment and dynamic monitoring of the state of health of Soviet men and women and of society as a whole. Relying on the achievements of scientific and technical progress, the medical checkups system must adopt an active stance ensuring the delivery of a "preemptive strike" against everything that could cause the emergence and development of diseases.

The introduction of medical checkups is to be implemented in two stages: In addition to the chronically ill, medical checkups and monitoring must extend to children and adolescents, students, pregnant women, war veterans, and workers and employees in certain sectors of industry and agriculture everywhere by 1991, and must embrace the country's entire population by 1995.

The USSR Ministry of Health, union republic councils of ministers, the AUCCTU, and local public health organs must ensure extensive explanatory work among the population as regards the objectives and tasks of universal medical checkups and must step up the medical community's participation in this work on a broad scale.

It is to be deemed the duty of every USSR citizen to undergo medical checkups and participate actively in the preventive medicine and health improvement measures being implemented.

2 Improvement of the Quality of Medical Services for the Population—the Main Task of Public Health Care

The main task of public health organs and institutions is to promptly and fully satisfy the population's needs for high-quality medical services everywhere. For this purpose it is necessary to implement a radical restructuring and intensification of the activity of public health organs and institutions, making active use of advanced forms of work organizations, new technologies, and modern methods and means of preventive medicine, diagnosis, and treatment. In this process it is necessary to ensure a decisive turn away from the extensive approach to the development of public health toward a qualitative appraisal of its activity.

Provision must be made for the accelerated development of the network—and the substantial consolidation of the material and technical base—of outpatient and polyclinic institutions, which constitute the basic element of the public health system, the element effecting constant and dynamic monitoring of the healthy and the sick alike and ensuring the implementation of an extensive package of preventive medicine, diagnosis, treatment, and health improvement measures.

In order to ensure complete and prompt diagnostic work among adults and children at the prehospitalization stage, a network of diagnostic centers must be organized in each republic, oblast, and krai, concentrating within this network complex and highly efficient modern equipment and medical apparatus—computerized tomography equipment, apparatus for ultrasonic, radio isotope, X-ray contrast, and other methods of investigation, and cadres comprising the best-trained specialists. Broader use must be made of the potential of educational establishments, scientific research institutes, and general hospitals to ensure the further development and improvement of polyclinic consultation and diagnosis services.

The number of persons undergoing treatment in polyclinics or at home must be increased through effective diagnosis methods using modern medical equipment and medication. The work of dispensaries must be restructured, and continuity must be ensured in their work with outpatient and polyclinic institutions. The practice of organizing polyclinic-based teams to provide therapy and treatment for long-term patients at home, including the free supply of medication, must be continued.

Polyclinics must considerably step up their work to improve the population's health and prevent diseases, and their role in patients' medical and social rehabilitation must be enhanced, with the organization of departments for preventive and recuperative treatment in all polyclinics being completed by 1990. Medical services must be made available to working people in their free time from work, taking into account the working hours of enterprises and organizations in production sectors.

It is necessary to boost the role and prestige of the district physician—the basic specialist who implements the package of treatment, prevention, and health improvement measures and systematically monitors the state of the population's health. The system for training district physicians must be changed by orienting it toward the training of general-practice physicians. All the necessary conditions for district physicians' fruitful activity must be created.

Leaders of outpatient and polyclinic institutions must take into account the suggestions of the population they serve when defining quotas for physicians' territorial districts. There must be gradual transition to the provision of medical services on the "family physician" principle.

With a view to expanding the opportunities to satisfy the population's needs for different types of medical services, economically accountable polyclinics, including stomatology, physiotherapy, and cosmetic surgery clinics and health improvement complexes, must be organized in every oblast, krai, and republic center during the 12th and 13th Five Year Plans.

The main avenue for improving inpatient services for the population must be via the development of a network of modern general hospitals and specialized centers. It is necessary to intensify the treatment and diagnosis process in hospitals, making the maximum possible use of highly skilled cadres, complex medical equipment, and effective medication. The principle of the phased organization of inpatient care must be actively introduced, the network of anesthesiology, resuscitation, and intensive care departments must be developed, the number of hospitals and departments for recuperative treatment must be increased, and the network of hospitals providing day-care services for patients and economically accountable boarding houses for persons needing full-time care must be expanded.

The rehabilitation side of sanatorium and resort services must be developed, and sanatoriums and departments must be established in all regions to provide aftercare for patients who have suffered acute myocardial infarction or cerebral thrombosis, undergone heart and main blood vessel surgery, suffered serious injuries, and so on. The efficiency of sanatorium and resort treatment and rest must be enhanced. In parallel with the further expansion of the network of clinics, it is necessary to develop a network of specialized sanatoriums for patients suffering from diseases of the circulatory, digestive, respiratory, and nervous systems, and sanatorium facilities must be made available as near as possible to the places of the population's permanent residence through the development of local resorts, primarily in regions of intensive economic development.

Patient care must be improved through the broad application of team forms for the organization and remuneration of medical personnel's labor, the expansion of the zone of services, the holding of more than one job, and the introduction of small-scale mechanization. Medical institute students, students attending secondary medical education establishments and general educational schools, and members of the Red Cross and Red Crescent Societies' aktiv must be involved in this work. Use must also be made of the opportunities provided by the USSR Law on Individual Labor activity to ensure patient care. Broader use must be made of the practice of concluding contracts with municipal and consumer service enterprises for the cleaning and maintenance of premises and for the provision of other types of services. Strict observance of sanitary and hygiene regulations must be ensured in all treatment and preventive medicine institutions.

With a view to the prompt provision of flawless emergency services the organization of the first-aid and urgent medical services system must be completed, taking into account the prehospitalization and hospital treatment stages. This system must be supplied with specialized transportation and communications facilities and modern equipment, as well as the necessary reagents and medication, and the organization of specialized first-aid teams must continue.

Republic, krai, and oblast centers and cities with over 1 million inhabitants must establish "Emergency Medical Services" Associations incorporating first-aid and emergency service units, hospital aircraft, and hospitals providing emergency services for adults and children.

The improvement of mother and child protection by all possible means is a priority avenue in the development of Soviet public health. It is necessary to fundamentally restructure the work of outpatient and polyclinic institutions for women and children and of maternity homes and children's hospitals, to raise the standards of their preventive medicine work, and to step up the propaganda of a healthy way of life. In order to ensure the prevention of diseases and raise the health standards of the younger generation it is necessary to improve the system of medical services for women and children by setting up unified obstetrics-therapy-pediatrics departments.

Various types of sanatorium and resort treatment facilities must be made available by 1995 for all children who need them, the network of young pioneer sanatorium camps must be expanded, and broader use must be made of the sanatorium and dispensary facilities of industrial and agricultural enterprises to improve the health of pregnant workers and children.

In order to prevent premature births and reduce disease and mortality among newborn babies specialized departments for pregnant women with a previous history of heart, lung, kidney, and endocrinological disorders must be set up under general hospitals in union republic capitals and in krai and oblast centers and cities. The development of specialized maternity homes and departments for women with pregnancy problems must continue. Broader use must be made of children's hospitals for the diagnosis and treatment of diseases among mothers staying in hospital to care for sick children.

The work of gynecological consultations to prevent miscarriages must be restructured, bearing in mind the modern methods of contraception. Provisions must be made in union republic capitals and in krai and oblast centers to establish units for the prenatal diagnosis of fetal diseases and for "Marriage and Family" consultations, as well as medical-genetic units and centers for children's recuperative treatment. Conditions must continue to be created in maternity homes and children's hospitals to facilitate the joint hospitalization of mothers and children.

Mobile facilities for providing emergency services for women and children must be developed. Major general hospitals and first-aid and emergency medical service units must organize specialized teams for the intensive care and resuscitation of newborn or premature babies, infants, and women with a history of delivery and postnatal problems. Provisions must be made to create a network of day-care hospitals for children.

The provision of medical and sanitary services to industrial sector workers must be improved. The network of medical and sanitary units, sanatoriums and dispensaries, health improvement complexes, and specialized shops and sections for medical, sanitary, occupational, and labor rehabilitation must be expanded. City territorial polyclinics must develop a shop service for workers in industrial enterprises employing fewer than 1,000 persons. Shop medical sections must be broken down into smaller units, bringing the number of persons served to them as 1,600.

The standards of medical services in the countryside must be improved. Bearing in mind that central raion hospitals are the basic institutions providing skilled medical services for the rural population, their material and technical base must be significantly consolidated through the construction of new hospitals and the reconstruction of existing ones, making extensive use of the pooled resources of kolkhozes, sovkhozes, and other enterprises. The number of interraion specialized hospitals, clinics, and departments must be increased to satisfy the rural population's needs for specialized services.

The district hospital system must be further strengthened, their material and technical base must be improved, and broader use must be made of them as departments of central raion hospitals and for the provision of social assistance to elderly residents and to those living alone. Paramedic and midwifery stations must play a greater role in the implementation of preventive medicine measures in the countryside.

Mobile types of medical services must be developed: mobile outpatient treatment units, clinical and diagnostic laboratories, and fluorographic, stomatological, and other units. The organization of first-aid and emergency medical service stations in every raion and their staffing with medical cadres must be completed before 1990.

The role of oblast hospitals as consultation, diagnosis, and treatment centers must be enhanced, and broader use must be made of major specialized and general hospitals and diagnosis centers in cities to provide highly skilled medical services for the rural population.

It is necessary to aim for a steady decline of diseases resulting in workers' temporary or long-term disability on the basis of improved labor safety practices, health improvement measures, and better-quality medical services and medical examinations.

The development and strengthening of specialized services is an absolute condition for further raising the quality of medical services and reducing the incidence of disease and mortality among the population. For this purpose it is necessary to establish a network of republic and interoblast (regional) centers with departments and branches for microsurgery, electrocardiac stimulation, joint replacement, organ and tissue transplants, cardiovascular surgery, treatment of patients with chronic renal insufficiency, and other types of specialized services.

The establishment of cardiology clinics in all republic, krai, and oblast centers and the increase in the number of cardiology units and departments in polyclinics and hospitals respectively, as well as the number of specialized first-aid teams, must be completed within the 12th Five Year Plan.

The effective treatment of patients suffering from oncological diseases must be ensured, with special attention given to the early detection of malignant neoplasms using modern diagnostic methods. When planning oncological services for the population the specific regional features of the spread and prognosis of individual types of oncological diseases must be taken into account. Oncological centers must be set up in all union republics, and the construction of oncological clinics and radiology units must be expanded. Institutions of this type must be equipped with modern diagnostic and treatment apparatus and supplied with radioisotope preparations and medication, and the incidence of disease and mortality among the population resulting from individual types of malignant neoplasms must be reduced.

The standards of surgical services must be raised. Cardiovascular surgery, orthopedics, traumatology, neurosurgery, urology, proctology, burns units, and other specialized departments must be developed and strengthened. It is necessary to ensure more effective treatment of patients suffering from acute diseases and injuries requiring surgery, to make considerably broader use of microsurgery and dialysis, and to more actively introduce organ and tissue transplants and new methods of surgical intervention.

There must be fundamental improvement in the provision of stomatological services to the population and primarily to children, and the total satisfaction of the need for all types of such services must be ensured during the 13th Five Year Plan period. The network of stomatological polyclinics, departments, and units must be expanded. With a view to preventing oral cavity diseases work must be organized everywhere to inculcate hygienic habits and to ensure the uninterrupted operation of fluoridation installations at water supply stations. Provisions must be made for production of fluoridated common salt and the increased output of fluoridated and other preventive toothpastes. Modern dental prosthesis methods must be introduced.

There must be improved prevention of eye diseases, especially shortsightedness and eye injuries, and new methods and organizational forms for the early diagnosis and treatment of cataracts and glaucoma must be implemented. Interraion opthalmology departments must be developed. Active use must be made of the experience accumulated by leading scientific research and treatment institutions in further improving medical services for patients suffering from eye diseases. Broader practical use must be made of microsurgery methods and laser equipment.

Modern microanalysis methods must be assimilated for the early diagnosis of allergy and immunodeficiency diseases, and allergological units and immunology laboratories must be organized in every republic, krai, and oblast.

Measures must be implemented to prevent the most common diseases of the nervous system and mental disorders. The organization and improvement of the work of departments for patients with acute cerebral circulatory disorders must continue. Major cities must establish recuperative treatment centers for the labor and social rehabilitation of persons suffering from cerebrovascular diseases and diseases of the peripheral nervous system. The network of psychoneurological clinics and hospitals and their rural departments and of boarding houses with occupational therapy workshops must be expanded. Industrial and agricultural enterprises must organize the necessary quantity of special sections for the social and labor rehabilitation of patients with mental disorders.

There must be a fundamental improvement in work on the early diagnosis and effective cure of persons suffering from alcoholism and drug addiction. The development of a network of addiction clinics and units and of sections under enterprises in industry, construction, and agriculture must be completed before 1990 and they must be staffed with skilled cadres. Economically accountable outpatient addiction clinics and anonymous treatment units must be established.

It is necessary to strengthen and develop specialized types of services in the therapeutic sphere: pulmonology, gastroenterology, endocrinology, hematology, and others.

It is necessary to substantially raise the standards of medical services for the aging and the old, and a comprehensive system of geriatric services must be organized in the country.

3 The Training and Education of Medical Cadres and the Organization of Their Labor in Line with Modern Demands

The successful solution of the tasks facing public health care is largely dependent on the competence of medical and pharmaceutical workers, on their professionalism, ideological, and moral character, and commitment to all that is advanced and progressive, and on their desire to restructure their activity for the achievement of high end results.

Physicians are entrusted with something that is most precious—Soviet people's life and health. Humaneness and nobility, selflessness and compassion, the ability to be totally dedicated to the patient's interests, the constant improvement of knowledge—for a physician these are not simply personal features meriting respect but qualities which determine his professional and civic maturity. Soviet physicians are the bearers of the most advanced communist world outlook. They must be distinguished by lofty ideological beliefs, a sense of duty to socialist society, and awareness of their profession's social importance.

The physicians' labor is highly valued by the people of our country and enjoys deserved prestige and trust, and the overwhelming majority of physicians honorably and conscientiously perform their civic and professional duty. The prestige of medical workers must be further enhanced, conditions for their high-quality and creative work must be created, and a feeling of profound respect for their labor must be cultivated among the population.

The restructuring of public health and the enhancement of its role in the life of Soviet society make new demands as regards the training and education of medical cadres and the organization of their work.

The high quality of health care specialists' training and of the upgrading of their qualifications and technical progress and the accelerated introduction of the latest methods for the prevention, diagnosis, and treatment of diseases, and the inculcation of loyalty to the oath of physicians of the Soviet Union constitute the paramount task of medical education.

For this purpose it will be necessary to improve the system for the selection of vocationally oriented young people for higher medical education establishments. VUZ vacancies must be filled with those who have had some work experience in medical and preventive medicine institutions and servicemen from the reserve who have demonstrated a calling for the profession of physician. The instruction of school pupils in medicine-oriented interschool training-and-production combines must be extended, and their labor must be utilized in medical and preventive medicine institutions to care for the sick. The conditions for VUZ admission applying to persons with practical experience in public health work must be extended to them and also to teaching and auxiliary personnel in medical and pharmaceutical VUZ's and scientific research institutes (laboratory technicians, laboratory assistants, and others). The organization of training departments under all medical and pharmaceutical institutes must be completed during the 12th Five Year Plan period, targeted forms of training for public health workers must be expanded, and the numbers of those admitted to higher and secondary education establishments must be brought in line with scientifically substantiated cadre requirements.

In order to improve the training of physicians it is necessary to revise the curricula, the tuition content of medicobiological and clinical disciplines, the organization of production practice, and the system of monitoring students' knowledge so as to bring instruction as close as possible to the requirements of practical public health care. Provision must be made to increase the volume of future physicians' vocational training and ensure the earlier study of clinical disciplines according to uniform programs; to change the proportional balance of different types of study in favor of students' independent work and their acquisition of practical skills, including the study of modern and future medical equipment; to reduce the number of subjects by combining and extending related study courses; to intensify vocational orientation in the tuition of social sciences in medical VUZ's; and to introduce transferable state examination credits coupled with student certification in the second and fifth years of study.

Demands on the quality of students' knowledge must be stepped up. An atmosphere of creative activeness and competitiveness in the acquisition of knowledge must be created within student collectives. The stage-by-stage certification of students' practical skills must be introduced from the 1988-1989 academic year. Students adopting irresponsible attitudes toward their studies must be firmly discarded in the junior grades.

The final stage of the training of physicians and pharmacists must take place in modern institutions supplied with the latest medical equipment. The efficiency of traineeship must be enhanced by guiding young specialists toward the acquisition of detailed knowledge and skills in their chosen specialized field.

The organizational conditions must be created to further the integration of higher medical and pharmaceutical education, public health practice, and science. Associations comprising medical science institutes and VUZ's and major hospitals must be organized, with specialized departments sited on the base of scientific research institutions.

Standard regulations must be elaborated and introduced from the 1988-1989 academic year for treatment, preventive medicine, and other institutions used to train specialists or to provide facilities for students' practical training and for graduates' internship and probation.

It is necessary to enhance the importance and improve the organization of state examinations. Uniform demands must be ensured as regards the theoretical and practical training of VUZ graduates. It is necessary to introduce comprehensive certification of students' readiness for independent professional work as a condition for admission to state examinations. Representatives from public health practice must be included in the membership of state examination commissions. These commissions must be given the right to decide the question of conferring the title of intermediate medical worker to VUZ graduates who have failed their state examination. Provision must be made for them to acquire a physician's diploma following one year's work at the location where they have been posted and after they have retaken the state examination.

An important role in the fundamental improvement of medical services to the population has to be played by intermediate and junior medical workers. Paramedics, nurses, pharmacists, and orderlies are not just a physician's direct assistants, they are also the link on which public health depends. The vocation of intermediate medical worker demands accurate execution of physicians' instructions, powers of observation, resourcefulness under difficult circumstances, and a sense of sympathy, responsiveness, and compassion.

The complexity of modern diagnostic and treatment methods demands better standards of training of specialists with secondary medical and pharmaceutical education. In this context it is necessary to review school curricula and programs and increase the time allocated to working practice and to training in the forms and methods of operating modern equipment and small-scale mechanization means. It is necessary to eliminate existing imbalances in the training of specialists with secondary and higher medical education.

The standard of young specialists' knowledge is primarily determined by the skills of professional and tutorial staff. It is a most important task to improve work on the selection of teaching cadres and the utilization and organization of their labor. Practical training in the country's leading scientific centers and clinics must be introduced in order to raise their professional standards. Leading scientists, specialists, and public health organizers must be more broadly involved in students' training.

Tho certification of medical and pharmaceutical institutes is to be carried out in 1988-1990 during which the question of category changes, cutbacks in the admission to some faoultioc, and the closure of some VUZ's is to be resolved.

Competition must be introduced in the writing of new textbooks for students and school pupils, and print runs must be increased in order to fully satisfy demand. The systematic publication of reference and encyclopedic literature in sufficient quantities must be ensured. Specialized encyclopedias for physicians in the outpatient and polyclinic link and for intermediate medical personnel must be published during the 12th 5-Year Plan period. A new edition of the *Great Medical Encyclopedia* is to be published in 1993-2000.

The system for the retraining and further training of medical cadres must be restructured. Effective measures must be implemented for the further development of institutes and faculties for physicians' further training. The attention of professorial and tutorial staff must be concentrated on introducing active methods of training, the advanced work experience of public health organs and institutions, and new scientific developments. There must be an increase in the number of specialists with higher and secondary medical education assigned to further training, primarily from among workers in the primary link of public health and in children's and obstetrics institutions.

Specialists must be encouraged to show more interest in constantly augmenting and refreshing their knowledge by making their career prospects and salaries directly dependent on the results of improved qualifications and professional competence. Broader use must be made for this purpose of the periodical certification of medical workers based on assessments of their professional training, the results of their work, the observance of labor and executive discipline, and their moral and ethical qualities and ideological and political maturity. A competitive system must be introduced for the conferment of qualification degrees involving broad discussion of the candidates by labor collectives. Leaders and chief specialists in public health organs and institutions must be made more responsible for the quality of certification, formalism in the course of certification must be eradicated, and certification commissions must operate under conditions of broad glasnost.

An implacable struggle must be launched against all negative phenomena in public health and against persons committing irresponsible actions, abusing their official position, or sullying the lofty name of medical workers. It is necessary to resolve issues of a legal nature making it possible to deprive such persons of their physician's diploma.

It is necessary to eliminate imbalances in the supply of cadres for various regions in the country and to ensure that cadres are available for the most important public health sectors: children's and maternity institutions, polyclinics, first aid and emergency medical service units and departments, and rural hospitals and outpatient units. In order to retain medical workers it is necessary to provide them with the necessary working and housing conditions and to ensure that they fully enjoy the privileges and benefits established by law. Broader use must be made of moral and material incentives for high work indicators and the active introduction of the achievements of science and technology.

Work must continue on further improving the training of leadership cadres for all public health links. Their business qualifications must be systematically enhanced, and the aim must be to ensure that they become profoundly familiar with the elements of public health management and economics, create within labor collectives an atmosphere of high demandingness and favorable conditions for the performance of professional duty, and develop initiative, mentorship, and socialist competition. It is necessary to ensure the training of an effective reserve of leadership cadres.

The frequency of *Meditsinskaia Gazeta's* [Medical Gazette] publication must be increased in order to raise the standards of ideological education work among medical workers, disseminate advanced experience, and introduce new methods of preventive medicine, diagnosis, and treatment in public health practice.

The conditions for medical workers' labor, daily life, and relaxation must be improved; general sanitary premises, dining rooms, cafeterias, and service desks must be set up in medical treatment and preventive medicine institutions; and the network of housing construction cooperatives, sanatorium-dispensaries, rest bases, and young pioneer camps must be expanded. More travel vouchers must be issued for sanatorium and resort treatment and relaxation.

Public health workers are called upon to establish in every labor collective an atmosphere of creative activeness, of a quest for new ways to improve health services for Soviet people, and of the pooling of the efforts of physicians from all countries in the struggle against the threat of thermonuclear war.

4 To Develop Medical Science More Actively, To Make Broader Use of Its Achievements in Public Health Practice

Medical science plays a leading role in the strengthening of the people's health, and the development of fundamentally new means and methods of providing medical services, and the formulation and affirmation of Soviet people's healthy way of life.

Soviet medical science has gained solid prestige in the world. Its achievements are weighty and universally recognized. But the crucial revolutionary period through which our society is living makes greater demands of it. The potential of Soviet medical science is still not being fully used to solve the most important task—strengthening people's health and extending their active life expectancy. There is hardly any major comprehensive research on fundamental public health problems. The quality of much scientific research work remains poor. A lag has developed in the sphere of fundamental research in immunology, genetics, biotechnology, transplant surgery, hematology, stomatology, and pharmacology. The achievements of modern science are only slowly being implemented in medical practice.

The laggardness of medical science has also been conditioned by formalism in planning and financing scientific work, the absence of a social imperative for the research being carried out, and insufficient demands on the quality of the end results of scientific development. The methodological, scientific, and technical standards of the work of many collectives are not up to the achievements of world medical science. The network and structure of scientific research institutes fail to ensure the conducting of full-scale scientific research up to modern standards.

The achievements in world medicine and the experience of intensively developing sectors of the country's national economy indicate that the prompt and large-scale introduction of new methods and means of preventive medicine, diagnosis, and treatment in public health practice can be ensured only via the establishment of specialized subdivisions with highly skilled cadres and material incentives for the introduction process.

All this demands a fundamental restructuring of the management of medical science and of the planning and organization of scientific activity, and the imparting of a specific, target, and assertive nature to these processes. It is necessary to conduct research work in line with the social requirements of public health. Scientists' efforts must be concentrated along the main fundamental avenues of medicobiological, clinical, and biological research whose results must bring about a radical solution to the problems of practical public health and, primarily, the detection of the causes of diseases with a view to their prevention, early diagnosis, and treatment. The paramount tasks of science must be to study medicosocial problems and to analyze the state and dynamics of the population's health consequential upon demographic changes, changing conditions of production and environment, and migration processes. Particular attention must be given to the protection of the health of mothers and children and the prevention of cardiovascular, oncological, neuropsychic, endocrinal, infectious, hematological, allergic, and stomatological diseases.

Efforts must be concentrated on scientific research in the sphere of genetic engineering and biotechnology and the development of modern instruments and automated systems of methods for remote and automated environmental monitoring. It is necessary to step up the development of new principles for the organization and management of scientific institutions, the implementation of the achievements of scientific and technical progress, and the creation of modern data retrieval systems. The efforts not only of medical specialists but also of sociologists, demographers, mathematicians, and representatives of other branches of science and technology must be concentrated along all these most important avenues.

The USSR Academy of Medical Sciences must become a real headquarters for the leadership and planning of all medical science in the country and must organize its activity in the closest contact with the USSR Academy of Sciences and with scientific research institutes in other sectors of the national economy. One of the most important tasks of the USSR Academy of Medical Sciences must be to considerably boost the efficiency of the work of every scientific collective and associate and to enhance their responsibility for the theoretical and practical value of scientific developments.

The USSR Ministry of Health and the union republic ministries of health must ensure the formulation of the social demands to be made of science, the intensified use of the scientific potential, and the efficient organization of the large-scale practical introduction of the results of scientific research and advanced experience. It is necessary to considerably expand the volume and improve the quality of scientific research conducted in VUZ's and institutes for physicians' further training, and measures must be taken to intensify the connection between sectorial and VUZ science and practical public health.

The USSR Ministry of Health and the USSR Academy of Medical Sciences must enhance the role played by expert medical opinion in the assessment of planned and completed scientific developments and must improve the sector's information and patent and licensing services.

In order to intensify the fruitfulness of scientific research work, the USSR Ministry of Health, jointly with the USSR Academy of Medical Sciences, must review in 1987-1988 the network of scientific research institutions and abolish any scientifically sterile institutes, using the staff and material and financial resources thus released in the most topical scientific areas.

Scientific workers must be made more interested in the acceleration of scientific research developments and their implementation via the introduction of differentials in a worker's labor compensation depending on his specific contribution to the achievement of end results. When expanding the volume of the work performed scientific institution leaders must be given the right to approve additional salary payments for engineering and technical staff, laboratory assistants, and service personnel.

The intensification of scientific institutions' work must be used to expand the practice of concluding contracts to perform additional research of great practical importance on the basis of economic accountability. The funds received from clients must be channeled toward strengthening the material base of these institutions, additional labor incentives, and the improvement of workers' social and general living conditions.

Leaders of parent scientific research institutions must be given broader rights in the leadership of subordinate institutions and departments, the planning of scientific research, the training and certification of scientific cadres, and the rational use and allocation of financial and material resources. It would be expedient to set up prototype and experimental production units under scientific centers and parent scientific research institutes.

The USSR Academy of Medical Sciences, together with the USSR Academy of Sciences, the USSR Ministry of the Chemical Industry, and other ministries and departments, must create intersectorial science and technology complexes, primarily for the development and industrial production of high-quality chemical and biological reagents and efficient medications.

Broader use must be made of the organization of scientific centers, science-and-practice (production) associations, intersectorial science and technology complexes (laboratories), and temporary scientific collectives for the comprehensive elaboration of topical problems and the intensified introduction of research results.

The USSR Gossnab, the USSR State Committee for Science and Technology, and the machine building ministries must supply scientific institutions in the public health arena with Soviet-made instruments and apparatus meeting the standards of the best world models.

Research in the social hygiene and public health organization spheres must become more fruitful, trends in the state of the population's health must be more profoundly analyzed, and the level of disease incidence ought to be forecast.

Measures must be implemented to further improve the training of scientific and science-teaching cadres, and ideological education and methodological work must be tirelessly improved with paramount attention being given to the nurturing of scientists' lofty professional and moral qualities.

The development of the system of medical and medical-technical information must be ensured. It is necessary to restructure the propaganda of the achievements of Soviet medical science and public health by the mass media, making it active and assertive.

The USSR Ministry of Health and the USSR Academy of Medical Sciences must develop international cooperation in the sphere of medical science, primarily with socialist countries; there must be broader exchanges of scientific information, and the most valuable developments must be introduced more promptly. International scientific and scientific-practical associations must be created.

5 The Necessary Material and Technical Backup for Public Health

The new tasks set by the party and the government in the sphere of protecting Soviet people's health demand a substantial consolidation of the material and technical base of public health institutions, and that they be supplied with modern technical equipment and the necessary medications. This work must become an organic part of the implementation of the 27th CPSU Congress stipulations aimed at developing and strengthening the material and technical base of the social and cultural sphere.

At present, medical services to the population are provided by 23,000 hospitals and 39,000 outpatient and polyclinic institutions.

At the same time, almost one-third of hospital beds are located in converted premises in breach of established sanitary and hygiene norms. Many treatment and preventive medicine institutions are inadequately supplied with medical equipment, medication, appliances, and patient care supplies.

In order to fundamentally improve the material base of public health institutions, capital investment funds allocated for the construction of such institutions must be substantially increased during the 12th-14th Five Year Plan periods. Specific capital investment funds for the construction of hospitals and polyclinics must be increased 2-2.5 times, at the same time increasing to 40 percent the proportion of funds channeled toward the supply of modern medical equipment to newly commissioned installations. The structure of the allocated capital investments must be decisively changed, channeling them primarily toward the reconstruction, technical renovation, and upgrading of treatment and preventive medicine institutions sited in converted premises to meet established sanitary and hygiene norms. Finance from all sources must be used to commission hospitals with 1.3-1.4 million beds and polyclinics with a capacity of 2.9-3.2 million visits per shift. Public health projects must be built exclusively according to new standard and individual designs elaborated with due consideration for the achievements and future prospects of scientific and technical progress and providing the best possible conditions for patient treatment and efficient work by the personnel.

The construction of maternity homes, gynecological consultation units, and children's hospitals and polyclinics must be effected at preferential rates, channeling at least 40 percent of the allocated capital investment funds to this purpose. The population's needs for maternity homes and children's treatment and preventive medicine institutions must be fully satisfied by 1995, and for inpatient, outpatient, and polyclinic institutions by the year 2000. Conditions for their high-quality work must be ensured.

The potential and resources of enterprises and organizations in industry, transportation, and agriculture must be more broadly used for the construction and technical reequipment of treatment and preventive medicine institutions, as must be the voluntary contributions made by labor collectives and citizens to the Soviet Health Foundation.

Boarding houses for the temporary accommodation of patients and persons accompanying them must be set up on an economically accountable basis under republic, krai, and oblast treatment and preventive medicine institutions, and primarily under consultation and diagnosis centers.

With a view to substantially improving health care work among urban and rural working people the labor collectives of enterprises and farms must be instructed to set up medical-sanitary units and sanatoriums-dispensaries during the 12th and 13th Five Year Plan periods, and to develop the network of recuperation complexes and special shops and sections for the medicosocial, vocational, and labor rehabilitation of workers.

During construction wider use should be made of the practice of pooling the resources of several enterprises and organizations.

According to labor collectives' requests, the medical-sanitary units built are to be transferred to the budget of the enterprises and organizations and their financing and maintenance authorized.

There must be a substantial improvement in the provision of medical services for the rural population. The practice of building doctors' outpatient clinics within complexes containing pharmacies and apartments for medical and pharmaceutical workers must be continued. More than 14,000 such complexes must be built during the 12th-14th Five Year Plan period.

The material and technical base of clinics, sanitary-epidemiology stations, and other public health institutions must be radically strengthened, as must that of scientific research institutes, higher and secondary medical education establishments, and physicians' further training institutes.

The questions of creating a proper material base for economically accountable polyclinics must be solved everywhere during the 13th Five Year Plan period through new construction and the allocation of additional premises by local ispolkoms. The volume of paid medical services to the population must increase fivefold by the end of the year 2000.

Union republic councils of ministers and USSR ministries and departments must ensure the high quality of construction work and the unconditional assimilation of appropriated funds. When planning public health projects provision must be made for the construction of housing to enable at least 25 percent of employees to be allocated departmental housing.

In order to ensure the prompt and proper maintenance of public health institutions, specialized maintenance and construction organizations subordinate to local public health organs must be set up during the 12th-14th Five Year Plan periods in union and autonomous republic capitals and krai and oblast centers.

In order to fully and promptly satisfy the needs of the population and of treatment and preventive medicine institutions for medications and medicinal articles it is necessary to increase the output of modern medications with a view to ensuring that all needs are fully satisfied with Soviet-made medications by 1993. The volume of sales of medications and medicinal articles must double by 1995.

The medicines product list must be revised, the manufacture of ineffective medicines must be steadily reduced, and the capacities and resources thus released must be used for the production of new medications. It is necessary to ensure their distribution in various regions of the country with due consideration of population numbers and actual requirements.

The network of pharmacies must be expanded and their material base must be strengthened. The number of pharmacies must increase to reach the set normatives by the year 2000.

During the 12th and 13th Five Year Plan periods monetary norms for expenditure on the acquisition of medications must increased 1.8-2.2 times in hospitals and 2-3 times in polyclinics, with monetary norms for expenditure on patient food in hospitals increasing 1.5-2.5 times. Provision must be made to further expand the list of diseases whose treatment involves the free supply of medication.

Public health institutions must be reequipped with modern medical equipment, appliances, and instruments, primarily X-ray units, computerized tomography equipment, ultrasonic, electronic, and endoscopic equipment, laboratory analysis equipment, continuous patient monitoring systems, computers, and small-scale mechanization means. Particular attention must be given to equipping the consultation and diagnosis centers being created, as well as maternity homes and children's treatment and preventive medicine institutions.

The production and deliveries of medical equipment must increase 2.5 times during the 13th Five Year Plan period and 3.5 times during the 14th Five Year Plan period. Enterprises in the defense sectors of industry must be more broadly involved in its manufacture. The manufacture of disposable medical supplies and patient care items in the required quantities must be ensured by 1992.

Leaders of public health institutions, including scientific research institutes, must be made more responsible for the rational and efficient use of technical resources and equipment. The material base of organizations within the USSR Ministry of Health system ensuring the supply of medical equipment and its installation and maintenance must be strengthened, and they must be fully staffed with skilled engineering and technical personnel.

Manufacturer's maintenance and the prompt repair of complex medical apparatus by manufacturing plants must be organized on a contractual basis.

Maximum use must be made of the production-sharing potential of CEMA countries as regards the technical reequipping of public health institutions and the supply of medications to them. Joint enterprises for the manufacture of medical equipment and medications must be created with foreign firms.

The requirements of public health institutions for ambulances must be fully satisfied during the 14th Five Year Plan period. It is necessary to develop qualitatively new specialized means for motor vehicle, aviation, and river transportation to provide first aid and emergency medical services and comfortable transportation for patients. The pool of all-terrain motor vehicles and of mobile units to provide specialized diagnosis, treatment, and medical services to the rural population must be expanded.

District physicians in territorial polyclinics must be given the right to acquire small cars for their personal use on preferential terms, with a view to these cars being used to call on patients at their homes.

The supplies of soft furnishings and furniture to treatment and preventive medicine institutions must be improved. Appropriations for the acquisition of such articles must double in 1995 compared with 1986, and must increase 2.8 times by the year 2000.

The requirements of public health services for disinfectants, bandages, and other articles for medicinal purposes must be fully satisfied during the 12th and 13th Five Year Plan periods.

The implementation of the measures planned to strengthen the material and technical base will require considerably larger financial and material resources. For this purpose state plans for the country's economic and social development must make provision for a substantial growth in funds channeled into the development of public health care and ensuring the solution of the set tasks.

USSR ministries and departments and party, soviet, trade union, and Komsomol organizations must perceive as a matter of paramount political importance the fulfillment of the set tasks for commissioning and strengthening the material base of public health institutions.

6 To Improve the Management of Public Health Services
The intensive development of public health and the provision of highly skilled medical services for the population persistently demand a radical improvement in the management, planning, and financing of this sector on the basis of broader democratic principles, the development of self-management, and the fuller use of economic accountability.

Under present-day conditions particular attention must be given to:

—the elaboration and implementation of targeted and multitargeted medicosocial programs, which are the most rational form of long-term planning in public health;

—the implementation of special sectorial and regional "Health" programs aimed at accelerating the medicosocial development of both labor collectives and individual regions of the country;

—the concentration of financial, material, scientific, and labor resources in priority areas for the development of public health;

—ensuring the high-quality transformation of the work of public health institutions and the fundamental renewal of their material and technical base;

—the transition to planning and evaluating the activity of public health organs and institutions not in terms of "bed numbers" or "polyclinic visits" but in terms of indicators reflecting the state of the population's health—including the incidence level of general and infectious diseases, temporary incapacity, disability, mortality, sanitary-epidemiological welfare, and other qualitative indicators.

The financing of public health (excluding capital investment limits) in individual republics, krais, and oblasts must be implemented on the basis of normatives taking into account population numbers and with due consideration for a region's specific demographic, social, economic, and ecological features.

With a view to improving the organization of management in the protection of the population's health, the role of the USSR Ministry of Health, republic ministries of health, and krai, oblast, and city public health departments must be enhanced, and they must be given broader rights as regards the solution of financial, organizational, and staffing questions within the limit of funds allocated to the sector. The possibility of maneuvering material, financial, and cadre resources must be made available at all levels of management.

The organization of and technical supplies for management labor must be improved and the number of instruction and accounting and reporting materials must be reduced. Duplication, formalism, and bureaucratism in the work of the sector's organs and institutions must be decisively eradicated.

The paramount task of management organs in public health must be to investigate as soon as possible the state of affairs in every medical institution, to competently and objectively evaluate its potential, place, and role in the overall structure of the region's economic and social development, and to outline specific measures stemming from the restructuring of the entire public health system.

The center of gravity of all work on providing medical services for the population must shift to the outpatient and polyclinic link and prehospital diagnosis. A large-scale experiment is to be conducted in several regions of the country in 1988-1991 to work out new forms for the management, planning, and financing of public health institutions.

In order to raise the standard of management and improve methodological work, public health departments under kraiispolkoms, oblispolkoms, and gorispolkoms must be consolidated via the abolition of raion departments in cities with a population of less than 500,000. The organizing role of central raion hospitals and the interraion specialized centers being created must be strengthened in rural areas. Republic, krai, and oblast hospitals and clinics and the chief specialists in public health organs must be held more responsible for the development of specialized types of medical services and the improved quality of medical services.

It is necessary to ensure the scientific substantiation of long-term forecasts and of long-term and current planning for the development of different types of medical services and the requirements for medications and medical equipment on the basis of the specific features of demographic processes and the social and economic development of the country's regions, and their ecological and other features.

Each region must elaborate normatives for the provision of medical services for the population and rational plans for the development and location of the network of public health institutions.

The planning and assessment of the activity of organizations ensuring the supplies of medications and medical equipment to the population and to public health institutions must be done in terms of indicators reflecting how promptly and fully the requirements for these products are satisfied.

With a view to ensuring high standards of mass diagnostic tests of the population (computerized tomography, ultrasonic and endoscopic investigations, and so on) 25 diagnosis centers are to be set up by the end of the 12th Five Year Plan period, and such centers must be set up in every republic, krai, and oblast center during the 13th Five Year Plan period.

A network of intersectorial medical-technical complexes must be created in order to ensure the swiftest possible introduction of the latest medical techniques, the assimilation of the production and application of unique treatment and diagnosis equipment, and the training of highly skilled cadres for the development and operation of such equipment.

The sector's economic mechanism must be improved, and it must play a greater role in providing incentives for the intensification of the work of public health organs and institutions and for the improved quality of medical services to the population. Leaders of public health institutions must be given broader rights in questions of planning and utilizing financial and material resources.

Further differentiation must be ensured as regards salaries and labor incentives for medical personnel, and compensation must be made more dependent on the complexity, intensity, and quality of work and the achievement of the best end results. Team forms of labor organization and compensation must be introduced for technical staff and intermediate and junior medical personnel.

To enable flexible maneuvering and the implementation of immediate measures, public health organs must be allowed to form monetary reserve funds of up to 5 percent of the funds allocated for the maintenance of medical institutions.

"Health passports" must be introduced for every USSR citizen in order to improve health protection and ensure continuity in the provision of medical services to patients and the standardization of medical documentation and reporting. Physicians must be relieved of extraneous functions and their efforts must be concentrated only on work directly linked with the provision of medical services to the population.

In order to enhance responsibility for improved working and living conditions and for the implementation of preventive medicine and health improvement measures it is to be prescribed that, in the event of workers suffering temporary disability as a result of adverse production conditions, enterprises, organizations, or kolkhozes will partly reimburse public health organs for the cost of their treatment. In the event of the disability resulting from industrial injury or poisoning, road traffic accidents caused by transport organizations or private individuals, or food poisoning or acute intestinal infections caused by breaches of antiepidemic regulations at catering facilities, public health organs and institutions and trade union committees must be given the right to file claims for reimbursement of patient treatment costs against enterprises, institutions, organizations, or private individuals.

Associations, enterprises, organizations, and kolkhozes are to be authorized to conclude contracts with public health institutions for the provision of additional medical services for their workers and their families. Such medical services are to be provided, subject to consent by the medical institutions' workers and trade union committee, over and above the physician's established work norm, with payment according to established procedures. Part of the funds earned under such contracts are to be channeled into the public health institutions' incentives funds.

It should be possible for medical institutions to organize on a contractual basis supplementary catering in response to individual orders—taking medical recommendations into account—to be paid for by the patients, their relatives, or labor collectives.

The AUCCTU is to be instructed to adopt measures for the more rational use of social security funds and to increase the proportion of such funds spent on measures to prevent diseases and improve medical services for the population.

Ispolkoms must implement measures to centralize technical and maintenance services for public health institutions (heat and water supplies, elevator equipment, and others).

In order to enhance the efficiency of state sanitary supervision, the management of the sanitary-epidemiological service is to be restructured, and the normative and legal foundations of its activity are to be improved. Sanitary-epidemiological stations within the medical services system of the USSR Ministry of Civil Aviation and the USSR Ministry of Railways are to be abolished, and their functions, staff, and resources transferred to republic, krai, and oblast sanitary-epidemiological stations within the system of the USSR Ministry of Health. City sanitary-epidemiological stations in cities with populations of less than 500,000 are to be consolidated through the abolition of raion stations.

Republic, krai, and oblast "Medtekhnika" [medical equipment] administrations ensuring the supply, installation, and repair of medical apparatus are to be reorganized into production and trade associations.

The development of automated control systems for public health services in republics, krais, oblasts, major hospitals, polyclinics, medicosanitary units, and clinics and of sectorial automated control systems for mother and child care, universal medical checkups for the population, cardiology, oncology, medical supplies, sanitary-epidemiological services, and cadre records must be completed by 1990, and the introduction of these systems must take effect by 1995. The organization of computer centers and sections in the sector's organs and institutions must be accelerated, and technical supplies for them must be ensured. A unified system of scientific-medical information must be created in the country.

The improvement of work to protect and strengthen Soviet people's health and the satisfaction of their needs for highly skilled medical services everywhere constitute one of the key questions of the party's and the Soviet state's social policy, and an urgent requirement of the time.

The restructuring of public health is a large-scale state measure, an important event in the life of Soviet society. The restructuring process must bring about the development of all the best achievements of Soviet medicine, the elimination of barriers to further improvements in the protection of the population's health, the increased contribution of public health to the development of socialist society and its economy, and the strengthening of the country's defense capability.

Every union and autonomous republic, krai, oblast, city and raion must, with due consideration for specific local features, elaborate specific plans to improve the system for protecting the population's health.

The basic measures for restructuring public health must be implemented gradually during the 12th, 13th, and 14th Five Year Plan periods (1987-2000).

The Union Republic Communist Party central committees and kraikoms, obkoms, okruzhkoms, gorkoms, and raikoms must step up party leadership of the work to protect the population's health, and must enhance the role and responsibility of primary party organizations in public health organs and institutions for ensuring highly skilled medical services for the population everywhere, for the selection and placement of cadres, the development of democratic principles, and the creation in the collectives of an atmosphere of principledness, creative activeness, implacability toward shortcomings in work, and an interest in high end results. The activity of ministries and departments, soviet organs and economic leaders, and trade union, Komsomol, and other public organization must be oriented toward the urgent solution of questions involving the protection and strengthening of people's health.

The improvement of every Soviet citizen's health is a matter of paramount importance, a humanitarian and noble goal of our society's economic and social development.

"Proekt TsK KPSS i Soveta Ministrov SSSR, 'Osnovnye napravleniia razvitiia okhrany zdrov'ia naseleniia i perestroiki zdravookhraneniia SSSR v dvenadtsatoi piatiletke i na period do 2000 goda'," *Pravda* (15 Aug); a condensed translation is in FBIS, No. 174 (9 Sep 87), 36-51.

GLOSSARY

Agitprop	Propaganda and agitation
Aktiv	The most active members of the Party
Apparat	Top officials of the CPSU or Soviet government
ASEAN	Association of Southeast Asian Nations
AUCCTU	All-Union Central Committee of Trade Unions. See also CCTU
CC	Central Committee of the CPSU
Chernozem	Black earth
CDSP	Current Digest of the Soviet Press
CIIPS	Canadian Institute for International Peace & Security
CMEA	Council for Mutual Economic Assistance; Comecon
COCOM	Coordinating Committee [NATO]
CPSU	Communist Party of the Soviet Union
CPSU CC	CPSU Central Committee.
CCTU	Central Council of Trade Unions. See also AUCCTU
Edinonachalie	One-man management
FBIS	Foreign Broadcast Information Service
FTA	Foreign Trade Association
GKES	State Committee for Foreign Economic Relations
glasnost	Publicity; often translated as "openness"
Gorispolkom	Executive Committee of a city (town) Soviet
Gorkom	City Party Committee
Gosagroprom	State Agro-Industrial Committee
Gosbank	State Bank
Goskomizdat	State Committee for Publishing Houses, Printing Plants and the Printing Trade
Goskomtrud	State Committee on Labor and Social Questions
Goskomtsen	State Committee for Prices
Gosleskhoz	State Committee for Forestry
Gosplan	State Planning Committee
Gossnab	State Committee for Material and State Supply
Gosstandart	State Committee for Standards
Gosstroi	State Committee for Construction Affairs
Gostelradio	State Committee for Radio and Television Broadcasting
Ispolkom	Executive Committee
KGB	Committee for State Security
Kholkhoz	Collective Farm
Khozraschet	Economic accounting; cost accounting
Komsomol	YCL. Young Communist League (All-Union Communist League of Youth).
Krai	Territory
Kulak	"Fist" —word used to describe peasants whom the state deemed to be profiting from NEP in the 1920s
Kraikom	Territory Party Committee
MINVUZ	Ministry of Higher and Secondary Specialized Education
MINTORG	Ministry of Trade
Nomenklatura	Party appointment, or patronage, list
Oblast	Province, region
Oblispolkom	Executive Committee of Provincial Soviet
Obkom	Region or Province Party Committee
Perestroika	Restructuring; reconstruction; re-building
Plenum	Assembly of members, e.g., of the CPSU CC
PPO	Primary Party Organization
Raion	District
Raiispolkom	Executive Committee of District Soviet
RSFSR	Russian Soviet Federative Socialist Republic
Sovkhoz	State Farm
Subbotnik	Voluntary Workday
TASS	Telegraph Agency of the Soviet Union
Tsentrosoiuz	Central Union of Consumers Cooperatives
TsK VLKSM	Central Committee of Komsomol
Uskorenie	Acceleration; speeding up
VTs SPS	Presidium of the Supreme Soviet
WTO	Warsaw Treaty Organization; "Warsaw Pact"
YCL	See Komsomol

BIBLIOGRAPHY OF RELATED WORKS IN ENGLISH

GENERAL

Battle, John M. & Thomas D. Sherlock, comps., *Gorbachev's Reforms. An Annotated Bibliography of Soviet Writings,* Pt. 1 (1985-June 1987). Gulf Breeze, 1988 (Institute of Soviet and East European Studies, Bibliographic Series No. 6)

Bialer, Seweryn & Joan Afferica, "The Genesis of Gorbachev's World," *Foreign Affairs*, 64:3 (1986), 605-645.

Brown, Archie, "Change in the Soviet Union," *Foreign Affairs*, 64:5 (Summer 1986), 1048-1065.

Brown, Archie, "Gorbachev: New Man in the Kremlin," *Problems of Communism*, 34:3 (May-June 1985), 1-23.

Brown, Archie, "Can Gorbachev Make a Difference?", *Detente*, 3 (May 1985).

Brown, Archie & Michael Kaser, eds., *Soviet Policy for the 1980s*. London, 1980.

Byrnes, Robert F., ed., *After Brezhnev. Sources of Soviet Conduct in the 1980s*. Bloomington, 1983.

D'Agostino, Anthony, *Soviet Succession Struggles. Kremlinology and the Russian Question from Lenin to Gorbachev*. Winchester. Mass., 1987.

Dallin, Alexander & Condoleezza Rice, eds., *The Gorbachev Era*. Stanford, 1986.

Dibb, Paul, *The Soviet Union. The Incomplete Superpower*. Chicago, 1986.

Frank, Peter, "Gorbachev's Agenda. Opportunities and Obstacles," *The Journal of Communist Studies*, 1:1 (March 1985).

Friedgut, Theodore H., *Gorbachev and Party Reform*, Research Paper No. 62 (The Soviet and East European Research Centre). The Hebrew University of Jerusalem (January 1986), 33 pp.

Gustafson, Thane & Dawn Mann, "Gorbachev's First Year. Building Power and Authority," *Problems of Communism*, 35:6 (May-June 1986), 1-19.

Hough, Jerry F., "Gorbachev's Strategy," *Foreign Affairs*, 64:1 (Fall 1985), 33-55.

Lukacs, John, "The Soviet State at 65," *Foreign Affairs*, 65:1 (Fall 1986), 21-37.

Lyne, Roderic, "Making Waves. Mr. Gorbachev's Public Diplomacy, 1985-86," *International Affairs*, 63:2 (1987), 205-224.

Niiseki, Kinya, ed., *The Soviet Union in Transition*. Boulder, Colo., 1987.

Schmidt-Hauer, Christian, *Gorbachev. The Path to Power*. London, 1986.

FOREIGN POLICY

Bialer, Seweryn & Michael Mandelbaum, eds., *Gorbachev's Russia and American Foreign Policy*. Boulder, Colo., 1988.

Dawisha, Karen, "Gorbachev and Eastern Europe. The Case for Detente," *World Policy Journal*, 3:2 (Spring 1986).

Gelman, Harry, "Gorbachev's Dilemmas and His Conflicting Foreign Policy Goals," *Orbis*, 30:2 (1986), 231-247.

Horelick, Arnold J., *U.S. Soviet Relations. The Next Phase*. Ithaca, 1987.

Kanet, Roger, ed., *Soviet Foreign Policy in the 1980's*. New York, 1982.

Keeble, Curtis, ed., *The Soviet State. The Domestic Roots of Soviet Foreign Policy*. Boulder, Colo., 1985.

Simes, Dimitri, "Gorbachev. A New Foreign Policy," *Foreign Affairs*, 65:4 (1986), 477-501.

Veen, Hans-Joachim, *From Brezhnev to Gorbachev. Domestic Affairs and Soviet Foreign Policy*. New York, 1987.

IDEOLOGY: Domestic and Foreign Policy

Agursky, Mikhail, *The Third Rome. National Bolshevism in the USSR*. Boulder, Colo., 1987.

Evans, Alfred B. Jr., "The Decline of Developed Socialism? Some Trends in Recent Soviet Ideology," *Soviet Studies*, 38:1 (January 1986), 1-23.

Frei, Daniel, *Perceived Images. U.S. and Soviet Assumptions and Perceptions in Disarmament*. Totowa, N.J., 1986.

Gordon, Joseph S., ed., *Psychological Operation. The Soviet Challenge*. Boulder, Colo., 1988.

Hammer, Darrell P., *Russian Nationalism and Soviet Politics*. Boulder, Colo., 1988.

Herrmann, Richard K., *Perception and Behaviour in Soviet Foreign Policy*. Pittsburgh, 1985.

Light, M., *Soviet Theory of International Relations*. New York, 1988.

Mitchell, R. Judson, *Ideology of a Superpower. Contemporary Soviet Doctrine on International Relations*. Stanford, Calif., 1982.

THE ECONOMY

Bergson, A. & H. Levine, eds., *The Soviet Economy. Toward the Year 2000*. London, 1983.

Communist Party of the Soviet Union, *Guidelines for the Economic and Social Development of the USSR for the Period 1986-1990, and for the Period Ending in 2000*. Moscow, 1986. Current Five Year Plan.

Csaba, Laszlo, "CMEA and the Challenge of the 1980s," *Soviet Studies*, 40:2 (April 1988), 266-289.

Desai, Padma, *The Soviet Economy. Problems and Prospects*. Oxford, 1987.

Goldman, Marshall I., "Gorbachev and Economic Reform," *Foreign Affairs*, 64:1 (Fall 1985), 56-73.

Hewett, Ed A., "Gorbachev at Two Years. Perspectives on Economic Reforms," *Soviet Economy*, 2:4 (1986), 283-326.

Hewett, Ed A., *Reforming the Soviet Economy. Equality Versus Efficiency*. Washington, 1988.

Kiss, K., *Domestic Integration of the Soviet Economy. The Case of the Central Asian Republics*. Issue no. 56. Trends in World Economy. Hungarian Scientific Council for World Economy, 1987.

Lane, David, *Soviet Economy and Society*. London, 1985.

Linz, Susan J., "Managerial Autonomy in Soviet Firms," *Soviet Studies*, 40:2 (April 1988), 175-195.

Moses, Joel C., "Consensus and Conflict in Soviet Labor Policy. The Reformist Alternative," *Soviet Union/Union soviétique*, 13:3 (1986), 301-348.

Nove, Alec, *The Soviet Economic System*. 3rd edition. Boston, 1986.

Medvedev, Zhores, *Soviet Agriculture*. New York, 1988.

Rumer, Boris, "Realities of Gorbachev's Economic Programme," *Problems of Communism*, 35:3 (May-June 1986), 20-31.

Wädekin, Karl-Eugin, *Soviet Agriculture. Reform and Prospects*. London, 1987.

Weichhardt, R., ed., *The Soviet Economy. A New Course?* Brussels, 1987.

POLITICS

Amann, Ronald, "Searching for an Appropriate Concept of Soviet Politics. The Politics of Hesitant Modernization," *British Journal of Political Science*, 16:4 (October 1986), 475-494

Bialer, S., *Stalin's Successors. Leadership, Stability and Change in the Soviet Union.* Cambridge, 1980.

Blough, Roger A. & Philip D. Stewart, "Political Obstacles to Reform and Innovation in Soviet Economic Policy. Brezhnev's Political Legacy," *Comparative Political Studies*, 20:1 (1987), 72-97.

Brown, Archie, "Soviet Political Developments and Prospects," *World Policy Journal*, 4:1 (Winter 1986/87).

Colton, Timothy J., *The Dilemma of Reform in the Soviet Union.* New York, Council on Foreign Relations, 1984. 2nd revised edition, 1986.

Communist Party of the Soviet Union, *The Programme of the CPSU (A New Edition).* Moscow, 1985.

Communist Party of the Soviet Union, *Rules of the Communist Party of the Soviet Union.* (Approved by 27th Congress of CPSU, 1 March 1986) Moscow, 1986.

Doder, Dusko, *Shadows and Whispers. Power Politics Inside the Kremlin from Brezhnev to Gorbachev.* New York, 1987.

Gill, Graeme, "The Future of the General Secretary," *Political Studies*, 34:2 (June 1986), 223-235.

Goudoever, Albert P. van, *The Limits of Destalinization in the Soviet Union.* London, 1986.

Hill, Ronald J. & Peter Frank, "Gorbachev's Cabinet Building," *Journal of Communist Studies*, 2:2 (June 1986).

Hough, Jerry, *Soviet Leadership in Transition.* Washington, 1980.

Hough, Jerry & Merle Fainsod, *How the Soviet Union is Governed.* Cambridge, Mass., 1979.

Lane, David, *State and Politics in the Soviet Union.* London. 1985.

Narkiewicz, Olga A., *Soviet Leaders: From the Cult of Personality to Collective Rule.* Brighton, England, 1986.

Nogee, Joseph L., ed., *Soviet Politics. Russia After Brezhnev.* New York, 1985.

Pravda, Alex, *How Ruling Communist Parties are Governed.* London, 1987.

Slider, Darrell, "More Power to the Soviets? Reform and Local Government in the Soviet Union," *British Journal of Political Science*, 16:4 (October 1986), 495-512.

Smith, Gordon B., *Soviet Politics. Continuity and Contradiction.* New York, 1987.

Tucker, Robert C., *Political Culture and Leadership in Soviet Russia From Lenin to Gorbachev.* New York, 1988.

Urban, Michael E., "From Chernenko to Gorbachev. A Repolitization of Official Soviet Discourse?" *Soviet Union/Union soviétique*, 13:2 (1986), 131-162.

White, Stephen, "Soviet Politics Since Brezhnev. A Survey of Political Developments, 1982-1985," *The Journal of Communist Studies*, 1:2(1985), 115-131.

White, Stephen, "The New Programme and Rules of the CPSU," *The Journal of Communist Studies*, 2:2 (June 1986).

DISSENT, NATIONALITIES, RELIGION

Akiner, Shirin, *Islamic Peoples of the Soviet Union.* London, 1986.

Alexeeva, Ludmilla, *Soviet Dissent. Contemporary Movements for National Religious and Human Rights.* Middletown, Conn., 1985.

Bissinger, Mark & L. Hajda, eds., *The Nationalities Factor in Soviet Society and Politics. Current Trends and Future Prospects.* Boulder, Colo., 1988.

Bilocerkowycz, J., *Soviet Ukrainian Dissent.* Boulder, Colo., 1987.

Conquest, Robert, ed., *The Last Empire. Nationality and the Soviet Future.* Stanford, Calif., 1986.

Karklins, Rasma, *Ethnic Relations in the USSR. The Perspectives from Below*. Boston, 1986.

Motyl, A.J., *Will the Non-Russians Rebel? State, Ethnicity, and Stability*. Ithaca, 1987.

Olcott, Martha B. & L. Hajda, eds., *The Soviet Multinational State*. New York, 1987.

Ramet, Pedro, ed., *Cross and Commissar. The Politics of Religion in Eastern Europe and the USSR*. Bloomington, 1987.

SOCIETY AND DEMOGRAPHY
Herlemann, Horst G., ed., *The Quality of Life in the Soviet Union*. Boulder, Colo., 1987.

Lane, David, ed., *Labour and Employment in the USSR*. New York, 1986.

Millar, James R., ed., *Politics, Work, and Daily Life in the USSR. A Survey of Former Soviet Citizens*. New York, 1987.

Reid, Carl V., *Soviet Reform in the 1980s. The Anti-Alcohol Campaign as Antidote for a Flagging Economy*, DND-ORAE Report, no. 41 (July 1986). Ottawa.

Sacks, M.P. & J.G. Pankhurst, eds., *Understanding Soviet Society*. Winchester, Mass., 1988.

Shlapentokh, V.E., *The Politics of Sociology in the Soviet Union*. Boulder, Colo., 1987.

EDUCATION, PRESS, SCIENCE
Avis, George, ed., *The Making of the Soviet Citizen*. London, 1987.

Bassow, Whitman, *The Moscow Correspondents. Reporting on Russia from the Revolution to Glasnost*. New York, 1988.

Dizard, William P. & S. Blake Swensrud, *Gorbachev's Information Revolution. Controlling Glasnost in a New Electronic Era*. Boulder, Colo., 1987.

Dunstan, J., ed., *Soviet Education Under Scrutiny*. Birmingham, 1987.

Fortescue, Stephen, *The Communist Party and Soviet Science*. London, 1987.

Lubrano, L. & S. Solomon, eds., *The Social Context of Soviet Science*. Boulder, Colo., 1980.

McLeish, J., *Soviet Psychology*. London, 1985.

Shurtman, Dora, *The Soviet Secondary School*. London, 1987.

Strickland, L.H., V.P. Trusov & E. Lockwood, eds., *Research in Soviet Social Psychology*. Berlin, 1986.

Tomiak, J.J., ed., *Soviet Education in the 1980s*. London, 1980.

Tomiak, J.J., ed., *Western Perspectives on Soviet Education in the 1980s*. London, 1986.

GORBACHEV REFORMS, 1987/88 BOOKS
Aganbegyan, Abel, *The Economic Challenge of Perestroika*. Bloomington, 1988.

Bialer, Seweryn, ed., *Politics, Society, and Nationality in Gorbachev's Soviet Union*. Boulder, Colo., 1988.

Daniels, Robert J., *Is Russia Reformable? Change and Resistance from Stalin to Gorbachev*. Boulder, Colo., 1988.

Dawisha, Karen, *Eastern Europe, Gorbachev and Reform. The Great Challenge*. New York, 1988.

Dyker, David, ed., *The Soviet Union Under Gorbachev. Prospects for Reform*. London, 1987.

Frankland, Mark, *The Sixth Continent. Russia and the Making of Mikhail Gorbachev*. London, 1987.

Friedberg, M. & H. Isham, eds., *Soviet Society Under Gorbachev. Current Trends and Prospects for Change*. New York, 1988.

Glasnost: How Open? Lanham, Md., 1987.

Gorbachev, Mikhail, *Political Report of the CPSU Central Committee to the 27th Party Congress*. Moscow, 1986.

Gorbachev, Mikhail, *On the Tasks of the Party in the Radical Restructuring of Economic Management. CPSU Plenary Meeting (25-26 June 1987)*. Moscow, 1987.

Gorbachev, Mikhail, *Socialism, Peace and Democracy. Writings, Speeches and Reports by Mikhail Gorbachev*. London, 1987.

Gorbachev, Mikhail S., *Mandate for Peace*. New York 1987. Speeches 1984-1986.

Gorbachev, Mikhail, *Perestroika*. New York, 1987.

Goldman. Marshall, *Gorbachev's Challenge. Economic Reform in the Age of High Technology*. New York, 1987.

Hazen, Baruch A., *From Brezhnev to Gorbachev. Infighting in the Kremlin*. Boulder, Colo., 1987.

Laird, Roy D., *The Politburo. Democratic Trends, Gorbachev, and the Future*. Boulder, Colo., 1986.

Legvold, Robert, *The New Thinking and Gorbachev's Foreign Policy*. New York Institute for East-West Security Studies, July 1987.

Lewin, Moshe, *The Gorbachev Phenomenon*. Berkeley, Calif., 1988.

MccGwire, Michael, *Perestroika and Soviet National Security*. Washington, 1988.

McCauley, Martin, ed., *The Soviet Union Under Gorbachev*. London, 1987. Essays by McCauley, Ronald J.Hill, W.E.Butler, Bohdan Nahaylo, Philip Hanson, Karl-Eugen Wädekin, Alan H.Smith, David Lane, Michael Shafir, Condoleezza Rice, Margot Light.

Marantz, Paul, *From Lenin to Gorbachev. Changing Soviet Perspectives on East-West Relations*. CIIPS Occasional Papers, No.4. Ottawa, 1988.

Miller, R.F., J.H. Miller & T.H. Rigby, eds., *Gorbachev at the Helm. A New Era in Soviet Politics?* London, 1987.

Naylor, Thomas H., *The Gorbachev Strategy. Opening the Closed Society*. Lexington, Mass., 1987.

Owen, Richard, *Comrade Chairman. Soviet Succession and the Rise of Gorbachev*. New York, 1987.

Thompson, Terry L., *Soviet Ideology and Policy from Khrushchev to Gorbachev*. Boulder, Colo., 1988.

Treadgold, Donald W. & Lawrence W. Lerner, eds., *Gorbachev and the Soviet Future*. Boulder, Colo., 1987.

Walker, Martin, *The Waking Giant. Gorbachev's Russia*. New York, 1986.

GORBACHEV'S REFORMS, 1987/88 ARTICLES

Baranov, Alexander & Gennady Seleznev, "That New Word 'Glasnost': Expanding not Only Language but Horizons," *World Press Review* (April 1987), 16-17. Two Soviet editors discuss with US editor.

Bechtold, Heinrich, "Parallels and Differentiations of Reforms in Peking and Moscow," *Aussenpolitik*, 11 (1988), 125-137.

Bernstein, Mikhail S., "Anatomy of the Soviet Reform," *Global Affairs*, 3 (Spring 1988), 663-88.

Besancon, Alain & George Urban, "Language and Power in Soviet Society. Can Gorbachev Change the System? A Conversation," *Encounter*, 68:5 (1987), 3-13; 69:1 (1987), 13-22.

Bialer, Seweryn, "Inside Glasnost," *The Atlantic Monthly* (February 1988), 65-72.

Black, J.L., "Can Gorbachev Do What Khrushchev Couldn't?" *International Perspectives*, 16:1 (1988), 26-27. Review essay of Gorbachev, *Perestroika* (1987) and K. Niiseki, *The Soviet Union in Transition* (1987).

Brabant, J. van, "The CMEA Summit and Socialist Economic Integration. A Perspective," *Jahrbuch der Wirtschaft Osteuropas*, 122:1 (pt.1, 1987), 129-160.

Brancaccio, David A.,"Disarming the Press," *Psychology Today* (June 1988), 40-41. On the "Gorbachev fever" among journalists at the December summitt of 1987.

Brown, Archie, "Change and Challenge," *Times Literary Supplement* (27 March 1987). Review of T.J. Colton, *The Dilemma of Reform in the Soviet Union*; Jerry Hough, *The Struggle for the Third World*; Ion Ratiu, *Moscow Challenges the World.*

Brown, Archie, "Gorbachev and Reform of the Soviet System," *The Political Quarterly*, 58:2 (1987), 139-151.

Brown, Archie, "The Soviet Leadership and the Struggle for Reform," *The Harriman Institute Forum*, 1:4 (1988).

Colton, Timothy J., "Taking Gorbachev's Measure. The New Soviet Regime has Caught a Generation of Kremlin-Watchers Off-Guard," *Peace and Security*, 2:2 (1987), 8-9.

Colton, Timothy J., "Moscow Politics and the El'tsin Affair," *The Harriman Institute Forum*, 1:6 (June 1988).

"Entrenching Perestroika. A Soviet Debate," *Detente*, No.12 (1988), 3-8.

Ericson, Richard E., "The New Enterprise Law," *The Harriman Institute Forum*, 1:2 (February 1988).

Ford, Daniel, "Rebirth of a Nation (Perestroika)," *The New Yorker* (28 March 1988), 61-80.

Gagnon, V.P., "Gorbachev and the Collective Contract Brigade," *Soviet Studies*, 39:1 (1987), 10-23.

Galbraith, John Kenneth, "Letter from Moscow. The Soviet Economy's Prospects for Change," *Harper's* (June 1987), 52-56.

Gati, Charles, "Gorbachev and Eastern Europe," *Foreign Affairs* (Summer 1987), 958-975.

Gill, Graeme, "A Gorbachev Revolution? 'Openness' in Action," *Current Affairs,* 64:1 (June 1987), 4-16.

"Glasnost'," *Encounter* Special Series (May, June 1987).

Golan, Galia, "Gorbachev's Middle East Strategy," *Foreign Affairs,* 66:1 (Fall 1987), 41-58.

"Gorbachev: Testing Time," *World Press Review* (June 1988), 9-18.

Griffiths, Franklyn, "'New Thinking' in the Kremlin," *Bulletin of the Atomic Scientists*, 43:3 (1987), 20-24.

Gross, Natalie, "Glasnost'. Roots and Practice," *Problems of Communism* (November/ December, 1987), 69-80.

Gustafson, Thane & Dawn Mann, "Gorbachev's Next Gamble," *Problems of Communism*, 36:4 (July-August 1987), 1-20.

Hallick, Stephen P. Jr., "Caveat Emptor: Gorbachev's Glasnost," *The Ukrainian Quarterly*, 43:1/2 (Summer 1987), 100-113.

Harasymiw, Bohdan, "The CPSU in Transition from Brezhnev to Gorbachev," *Canadian Journal of Political Science,* 21:2 (June 1988), 249-67.

Hauslohner, Peter, "Gorbachev's Social Contract," *Soviet Economy,* 3:1 (January-March 1987).

Hertzberg, Arthur, "Glasnost and the Jews," *The New York Review of Books,* 34:16 (22 October 1987), 20-23.

Hilborn, Kenneth H.W., "The Communist Threat in the Age of Glasnost," *Mackenzie Paper No. 7* (Toronto, 1988), 9-38.

Hill, Ronald J., "Gorbachev's Reforms. Prospects of Success," *Esprit,* 5 (1987), 21-36.

Hofheinz, Paul, "Gorbachev's Double Burden. Economic Reform and Growth Acceleration," *Millennium. Journal of International Studies,* 16:1 (Spring 1987), 21-55.

Hough, Jerry F., "Gorbachev Consolidating Power," *Problems of Communism,* 36:4 (July-August 1987), 21-43.

Hyland, William G., "Reagan-Gorbachev III," *Foreign Affairs,* 66:1 (Fall 1987), 7-22.

Jones, David R., "Gorbachev, the Military and Perestroika," *International Perspectives* (May/June 1988), 10-13.

Kaiser, Robert G., "The Soviet Pretense," *Foreign Affairs,* 66:2 (Winter 1986/87), 236-251.

Kempton, Murray, "In Gorbachev's Russia," *The New York Review of Books,* 35:12 (21 July 1988), 29.

Laird, Roy D., "Perestroyka and Soviet Agricultutre," *Problems of Communism* (November/December, 1987), 81-86.

Lapidus, Gail W., "Gorbachev and the Reform of the Soviet System," *Daedalus,* 116:2 (1987), 1-30.

Laptev, Ivan, "Glasnost, a Reliable Instrument of Perestroika," *International Affairs* (Moscow), 6 (1988), 20-26.

Lebahn, Axel, "Political and Economic Effects of Perestroika on the Soviet Union and its Relations to Eastern Europe and the West," *Aussenpolitik,* 11 (1988), 107-124.

Legvold, Robert, "Gorbachev's New Approach to Conventional Arms Control," *The Harriman Institute Forum,* 1:1 (January 1988).

Legvold, Robert, "Gorbachev's Foreign Policy. How Should the U.S.Respond?" *Headline Series,* No.284. Foreign Policy Association (April 1988).

MacFarlane, Neil, "The USSR and the Third World. Continuity and Change under Gorbachev," *The Harriman Institute Forum,* 1:3 (1988).

Martiny, Albrecht E., "Whither Gorbachev ?" *Problems of Communism,* 36:1 (January/February 1987),65-70. Review of Gorbachev, *A Time for Peace* (1985); T.G. Butson, *Gorbachev. A Biography* (1985); C. Schmidt-Hauer, *Michail Gorbatschow. Moskau im Aufbruch* (1986); N. Poljanski, *Gorbatschjow. Der Neue Mann* (1986); Zhores Medvedev, *Gorbachev* (1986).

Michnik, Adam, "Gorbachev. The Great Counter-Reformer," *Harper's Magazine* (November 1987), 19-20.

Nove, Alec, "The Credibility of Soviet Statistics," *Soviet News,* 3:5 (27 April 1987).

Nixon, Richard, "Dealing with Gorbachev," *The New York Times Magazine* (13 March 1988), 26-30, 66-68, 78-80.

O'Dell, Peter R., "Gorbachev's New Economic Strategy. The Role of Gas Exports to Western Europe," *The World Today,* 43:7 (1987), 123-125.

Odom, William E., "How Far Can Soviet Reform Go?" *Problems of Communism* (November/December, 1987), 18-33.

Pearson, Geoffrey, "So Gorbachev is Serious.... Now What?" *Peace and Security,* 3:2 (Summer 1988), 4-5.

"Perestroyka" [Special Section], *Problems of Communism* 36:4 (July/August 1987), 76-107. Includes Russell Bova, "The Role of Workplace Management;" Valentin Litvin, "Reforming Economic Management;" John E. Tedstrom, "Analyzing the 'Basic' Provisions;" Dale R. Herspring, "Gorbachev, Yazov, and the Military."

Peterson, Peter G., "Gorbachev's Bottom Line," *New York Review of Books,* 34:11 (25 June 1987), 29 ff.

Reddaway, Peter, "Gorbachev the Bold," *New York Review of Books,* 34:9 (28 May 1987), 21-25. Review of Dusko Doder, *Shadows and Whispers. Power Politics Inside the Kremlin from Brezhnev to Gorbachev* (1987).

Sanders, Jonathan, "Glasnost' Means Never Having to Say You're Sorry. Glasnost' on Soviet Television," *World Monitor,* 1:1 (1987).

Sestanovich, Stephen, "Gorbachev's Foreign Policy. A Diplomacy of Decline?" *Problems of Communism,* 37:1(Jan/Feb 1988), 1-15.

Simes, D., "Gorbachev. A New Foreign Policy?" *Foreign Affairs,* 65:3 (1987), 477-500.

Slider, Darrell, "The Brigade System in Soviet Industry. An Effort to Restructure the Labour Force," *Soviet Studies,* 39:3 (1987), 388-405.

Smith, Hedrick, "On the Road with Gorbachev's Guru" [Aganbegyan], *The New York Times Magazine* (10 April 1988), 36-19.

Snyder, Jack, "The Gorbachev Revolution. The Waning of Soviet Expansionism?" International al *Security,* 12 (Winter 1987/88), 93-131.

Stewart, Philip D., "Gorbachev and Obstacles Towards Detente," *Political Science Quarterly,* 101:1 (1987), 1-22.

Tökes, Rudolf L., "Gorbachev's Reforms and the 'Hungarian Model'," *International Review* (November 1987), 22-23, 44.

Tucker, Robert, "Gorbachev and the Fight for Soviet Reform," *World Policy Journal,* 4:2 (Spring 1987), 179-206.

"The USSR under Gorbachev—*Glasnost* and its Implications. A Seminar". Radio Free Europe/ Radio Liberty. Munich, 19 May 1987. 19 pp. Participants: Peter Reddaway, Robert Conquest, Vladimir Bukovsky, Michel Tatu, Henrich Vogel, Leonard Marks, and Gene Peli.

Volgyes, Ivan, "Gorbachev and Eastern Europe," *International Review* (November 1987), 6-9.

Yanaev, G.I., "Soviet Restructuring. The Position and Role of the Trade Unions," *International Labour Review,* 126:6 (Nov/Dec. 1987), 703-713.

INDEXES

The indexes contain page references only to material found in the documents themselves, and do not cover the introductions. A number of the references in the Subject Index are to items which appear on almost every page of the collection, in one form or another, e.g., perestroika (restructuring). For that reason, references to many of the terms in the index are only to those which are highlighted in a document, or provide some form of definition.

Index of Names

Shchetinin, M., 280
Shcherbakov, S.G., 291
Shevardnadze, E.A., 120, 122, 123, 126, 127, 130,134,135, 137, 141, 143, 153, 155, 157, 158, 159
Shishova, V.I., 285
Shitov, S.K., 70
Shostakovskii, V.N., 203
Shtaiberga, A.A., 290
Shukshunov, V.E., 290
Shultz, George, 130
Shumskii, V., 302
Silaev, I.S., 42,
Silkova, N.P., 203
Sinitskii, I.G., 47
Skitev, V.V., 215
Skliarov, Yu.A., 205
Slyunkov, N.N., 125
Smirnov, George, 198
Soares, M., 156
Sobolev, 278
Sokolov, S.L., 138
Sokolov, V., 354,
Solomentsev, M.S., 128, 137
Solovov, S.I., 149
Sorsa, Kalevi, 83,119,
Sosin, G.M., 284, 290
Stalin, J.V., 92, 95, 97, 231

Stolbunov, Ye., 246-49
Suleimenov, O., 299
Systov, A.S., 353
Tabakov, O.P., 290
Tabeev, 354
Talyzin, N.A., 41,130, 342
Tarasov, Iu.I, 203
Tazhurizhina, Z., 259
Tereshchenko, V.D., 26
Tevozian, I.F., 284
Thatcher, M., 127, 128, 261-3, 324-6
Titarenko, M., 338
Tkachenko, 281
Tolkunov, Lev, 327
Tolstoy, Leo, 351
Travkin, N.I., 26, 226
Trotskii, Leon, 92
Trofimov, Yu., 299

Ulianov, M., 352
Urbany, R. 133
Usmankhodzhayev, 245
Ustinovskii, M., 298

Vagin, M.G., 26,
Valikhanov, S., 308
Vasiliev, D., 302, 04
Vasiliev, V.A., 217
Vasilevskii, A., 97
Velichko, V.M., 49

Venem, U., 339
Vinogradov, V., 219, 302
Volkov, I.P., 290
Volochenskii, A.A., 46
Voronin, Lev, 41,
Vorobov, N.N., 46
Voyenushkin, S.D., 48,
Vranitzky, F. 143

Welzsaecker, R. von, 143
Wright, J., 130, 326

Yagodin, G.A., 277, 291
Yakovlev, A.N., 120,125, 143
Yanovskii, R.G., 203
Yaroslavskii, E.M., 302
Yasov, D.I., 159
Yeliseev, A.S., 218
Yermin, 354

Zaikov, L.N., 150, 158, 202
Zalygin, S., 352
Zaslavskaia, T., 198
Zatvornitskii, V.A., 222
Zemskov, A.I., 212
Zharov, V.A., 211
Zhivkov, T., 135
Zhukov, 97
Zhukova, R.V., 214
Zinov'ev. Grigorii, 92
Ziaziun, I.A., 290
Zverev, A.I., 353

Index of Subjects

ABM Treaty, 83,157, 320, 325, 327, 333, 343
Acceleration (iskorenie), 7, 12, 14, 28, 30, 35, 36, 197, 222, 227, 231-2, 269
Admiral Nakhimov, 15, 168
Afghanistan War, 341
Agriculture, 10, 43-7, 104, 124, 148, 159, 241-47, 293, 298, 356-7;
  Agro-Industrial Complexes, 9, 14, 124, 241, 244-6;
  food supply, 11, 45, 72, 76, 121,147, 227, 243-57, 250f, 273, 298, 315, 354, 362;
  (See also Collective Farms, State Farms, Industries, Private Plots).
AIDS, 323, 337
Alcoholism, 7, 9,10, 136, 199, 317, 337, 359, 362, 367;
  alcohol industry, 53, 72;
All-Union Socialist Competition, 120, 148
All-Union Teachers' Conference (1987), 119, 281, 283, 284;

(1978), 283, 285
Alma-Ata Incident, 308
Anti-Semitism, 21, 82, 300, 302, 304, 331
Apartheid, 335
"Appeasement," 96
Architecture, 146-7, 155
Arctic (See Index of Places)
Armed Forces, 34, 43,137-8, 159, 257, 320-1, 328;
  history of, 88-9
Armenians, 306
Arms Race, 81, 82, 83-4, 143, 146,153-4, 157, 320-2, 324, 326, 328, 329-39, 331-4, 343-5, 337-8, 340;
  "Nuclear Deterrence," 329, 332;
  "Reasonable Sufficiency," 330-334;
  (See also Chemical Weapons, Strategic Defence Initiative; ABM Treaty; INF Treaty)
Astrakhan Gas Complex, 32
Automobiles, 224

Index of Institutions, Ministries, Committees and Councils

Index of Geography and Places

FROM ACADEMIC INTERNATIONAL PRESS